Psychological Anthropology

Psychological Anthropology

Edited by PHILIP K. BOCK

Westport, Connecticut
London

The Library of Congress has cataloged the hardcover edition as follows:

Handbook of psychological anthropology / edited by Philip K. Bock.
p. cm.
Includes bibliographical references and index.
ISBN 0–313–28433–4 (alk. paper)
1. Ethnopsychology. I. Bock, Philip K.
GN502.H363 1994
155.8—dc20 93–43434

British Library Cataloguing in Publication Data is available.

A hardcover edition of *Handbook of Psychological Anthropology* is available from Greenwood Press, an imprint of Greenwood Publishing Group, Inc. (ISBN 0–313–28433–4).

Library of Congress Catalog Card Number: 93–43434
ISBN: 0–275–94956–7 (pbk.)

First published in 1994

Praeger Publishers, 88 Post Road West, Westport, CT 06881
An imprint of Greenwood Publishing Group, Inc.

Printed in the United States of America

The paper used in this book complies with the Permanent Paper Standard issued by the National Information Standards Organization (Z39.48–1984).

10 9 8 7 6 5 4 3 2 1

Copyright Acknowledgments

The author and publisher gratefully acknowledge permission to reprint material from the following copyrighted sources.

From C. Grob and M. Dobkin de Rios. 1992. Adolescent Drug Use in Cross-Cultural Perspective. *Journal of Drug Issues* 22: 121–138.

From B. Rogoff and G. Morelli. 1989. Perspectives on Children's Development from Cultural Psychology. *American Psychologist* 44: 343–348. Copyright 1989 by the American Psychological Association. Reprinted by permission.

Adapted from Barry S. Hewlett. 1991. Pp. 53–57. *Intimate Fathers*. Ann Arbor: The University of Michigan Press.

CONTENTS

PREFACE

In preparing this reference work for publication I have had several goals. The renewal of interest in psychological anthropology seemed to call for a critical appraisal of past schools and approaches as well as an up-to-date review of the literature and evidence from contemporary research. The handbook is therefore organized in two parts.

Part I presents an overview of the research traditions that have contributed to the field, from the classical culture and personality studies of the 1930s to the cultural psychology that is just taking form in the 1990s. Between the chapters on these two ways of conceptualizing the relationship of individuals to society, other authors present basic information on approaches that stress, respectively, cross-cultural (correlational) studies, variables of social structure, cognitive-linguistic analysis, emotional expression, and neo-Darwinian theory. Readers who are interested in the history of psychological anthropology will find in these chapters a useful summary and guide to the literature together with a critical appraisal of concepts and major figures.

Each chapter in part II discusses a different line of evidence that has been explored by researchers in order to increase our understanding of human thought and behavior. Here, topics that have fascinated members of different schools—from myth, dreams, and trance to initiation rites and the construction of the self—are treated in some detail. The emphasis in part II is on contemporary research and, especially in the chapters on discourse, development, and behavioral observation, on methodology.

I want to acknowledge the help of Richard Shweder, Raymond Fogelson, Jack Bilmes, William Hanks, Howard F. Stein, Patricia Draper, Douglass Price-Williams, Mark Erickson, and Roy D'Andrade, who were not able to contribute to this work but who provided valuable advice. The contributors were thoughtful and prompt and responded to editorial comments in a generous manner. My wife, Barbara, provided encouragement and love. Special thanks go to Mary Kay Day, who processed the manuscripts with great efficiency and helped me to keep track of wayward documents. Copy editor Charles Eberline did a superb job, clarifying and correcting many passages and references. My part in this project is dedicated to the memory of Bruno Bettelheim, teacher and friend.

Philip K. Bock

INTRODUCTION

UNIVERSAL AND PARTICULAR

Philip K. Bock

Our topic is *humanity*, and these are the central questions that guide our inquiry: What characteristics of our species are found in all times and places? What features are limited to specific groups of humans? How can we best take account of individual uniqueness?

These questions outline an ambitious program for psychological anthropology, which I have elsewhere defined as "anthropological investigations that make systematic use of psychological concepts and methods" (Bock 1988:1). An anthropology that takes account of individuals must make use of ideas from neighboring disciplines; and the history of psychological anthropology (surveyed in part I of this handbook) shows successive waves of influence from psychophysical, Gestalt, Freudian, behaviorist, Piagetian, and many other psychologies. The use by psychologists of anthropological concepts and data is generally known as "cross-cultural psychology" and tends to be a separate enterprise (Edgerton 1974; Segall et al. 1990).

Questions relating to universals ("human nature") and particulars ("personal uniqueness") tend to be debated polemically. It is mainly in the intermediate zone of group differences that specific relationships between individuals and sociocultural variables have been proposed and tested. The various types of evidence used in these studies are surveyed in part II of the handbook. But whether they are focusing more on the general or the specific ends of the continuum, psychological anthropologists are obliged to recognize the constant interaction between culture and biology as codeterminants of behavior (figure I.1). For example, the genetic uniqueness of each human being is realized in a specific sociocultural environment that affects the developing organism even before birth (e.g., through maternal nutrition and activity levels, environmental pollutants, and obstetric technology). (See the chapter by Susan Oyama in this volume.)

Figure I.1
The Interaction of Culture and Nature from the Universal to the Particular

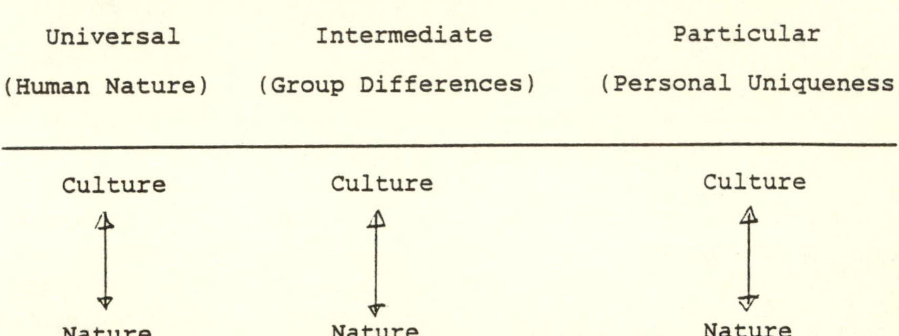

At the universal pole, we recognize that our species has long been dependent on cultural means to complement and perhaps to stimulate the biological evolution of body and brain. Thus any claims about a universal human nature must be tested against the ethnographic record, not because a single "negative instance" destroys empirical generalizations, but because documented cultural differences in, for example, parenting, gender roles, or leadership exemplify the variability within our abstract categories of behavior and lead us to question the applicability of such categories across social boundaries. For example, anthropologists are very suspicious of extending terms such as "grief," "aggression," or "rape" to other societies (see Bock 1983).

At the risk of overstating the case, I would assert that anthropology has played a mainly critical role in its relationship to psychology. Sometimes this has taken the annoying form of challenging generalizations about human nature ("Yes, but the Trobrianders do not appear to experience Oedipal hostility") or clinical judgments of individuals ("She's not hysterical; that's the way Italian widows are expected to behave following a husband's death"). The tendency of psychological anthropology, then, is to draw all polar statements into the intermediate zone, demonstrating the influence of local "conventional understandings" on human experience and behavior (see the chapter by Alice Schlegel in part I). Certain fundamental features of the human condition, of our being-in-this-world as members of a specific ethnos with its own history, language, and status, enter into our every thought and action. Without slighting the organic "givens" of our species, psychological anthropology attempts to explore the existential situation of people everywhere on the planet. At their best, these studies reveal the dynamic interplay between genetic, historical, and situational factors in all human experience.

Western psychology currently divides human experience into three major categories: perception, motivation, and cognition (though the ready acceptance of this tripartite schema should make us cautious about its general validity). Let us treat these divisions as offering useful headings for the further consideration of our general questions.

PERCEPTION

A naive psychology of perception that assumes direct, mechanical transfer of the ''external'' world into human experience will not do. Psychology, physiology, and neurology continue to unravel the complex process by which stimuli are transformed into perceptions: how a relatively stable, colorful, meaningful world is constructed out of the hints given by spurts of energy passing through our nervous system. Our sense organs have evolved to sample only certain ranges of stimuli. Our nervous system then interprets this information as the experience of color, shape, distance, sound, pressure, pain, odor, taste, and so forth. But these interpretations are always influenced by the physical and social context in which they occur. They can also be altered by suggestion, disease, psychoactive drugs, or simple fatigue, while deprivation of external stimuli can enable the nervous system to supply its own material for interpretation.

Culture enters into every step of the perceptual process, initially by providing patterned material for perception (from the form of dwellings, the smells of cooking, or the sounds of music) and later, through verbal and nonverbal means, by suggesting (or insisting on) the proper labeling of and responses to perceived patterns. Socialization, both in childhood and adulthood, involves learning to perceive the world (or at least to respond to it) in the same way as one's group.

The use of standardized optical illusions to study group differences in visual perception goes back nearly a century. (For a good summary of early work, see Segall, Campbell, and Herskovits [1966].) Hypotheses attributing differential susceptibility to biological/racial differences soon gave way to cultural/environmental explanations, including the perceptual learning that takes place when people live in a ''carpentered world'' or in a forested region with few opportunities to use the horizon as a reference line. Recent studies recognize different classes of illusions to which groups may be differently susceptible, due to the interaction of biographical and cultural factors.

When we consider less controlled stimuli, however, the exact role of culture in shaping interpretation becomes difficult to specify. A. I. Hallowell pioneered in the exploration of this topic, both in his use of the Rorschach test with Native Americans (see Spindler and Spindler 1991) and his emphasis on the cultural construction of a ''behavioral environment'' (Hallowell 1955).

Most anthropologists of the Culture and Personality school held similar views. Edward Sapir, like his student, Benjamin Whorf, wrote of the ways that language affected worldview (see Bock 1992), while Ruth Benedict emphasized selectivity as the essence of culture, implying a ''filtering'' model of perception. Many anthropologists were attracted to the ''New Look'' theories of perception during the 1950s and 1960s, because they emphasized both the social situation and the state of the perceiver (Bruner 1973). Contemporary views utilize these ideas supplemented by computer analogies and more or less coherent borrowings from artificial intelligence (especially studies of "pattern recognition"). However, few psychological anthropologists are directly involved in perceptual studies today. A recent text mentions the term only once, and then in the context of "self-perception" (Erchak 1992:9).

MOTIVATION

The question of what motivates human behavior is an old one, debated—no doubt—around the campfires of the Paleolithic. "Why did they do that?" "How can we get them to do this?" From such questions arise lists of "basic needs" and theories of action, conflict, and redemption: "The Devil made me do it."

Freud's basic theory of human motivation was set forth in a few brief paragraphs in *Civilization and Its Discontents* (1961:23–24):

(1) Humans seek "happiness" (i.e., sustained pleasure and avoidance of pain); however,
(2) The world is not arranged to permit this; therefore,
(3) all human life is, necessarily, a compromise between individual striving for instinctual satisfaction and the renunciations that culture requires.

For Freud, the instincts fall into two great categories—erotic and aggressive—that, sometimes opposed and sometimes intertwined, motivate all behavior. Culture constitutes the mechanisms by which instinctive needs are controlled, transformed, and indirectly satisfied. It follows that different cultures have constructed alternative means to the same ends.

Standing against this and other, similar, reductionist theories are a number of views that posit contrasting motivations as the "mainsprings" of human action in different cultures. For Ruth Benedict and her associates, the key to understanding a society was discovering the unique configuration of motives that drive its members to pursue culturally defined goals such as glory in battle, accumulation of property, cooperative self-denial, or paranoid self-defense (Benedict 1934). This approach strove for a poetic evocation of cultural differences by focusing on the ideal person as conceived in various societies (see the chapter by Steven Piker in part I). It demonstrated that culture gave meaning to life by selecting and emphasizing specific motives and goals from "the great arc" of human potential, and building these choices into satisfying ways of life. Part of this process involves learning to satisfy generalized needs in specific ways, so that, for example, hunger is best relieved by a bowl of rice, or toasted manioc cakes, or a Big Mac with fries. Such "canalization" of desire is an essential part of socialization in all human groups and helps to account for resistance to change.

Contemporary anthropological studies take quite a different approach to motivation, linking it to concepts of self and emotion and inferring cultural differences in these concepts from extended samples of discourse. These studies are as relativistic as those of the older Culture and Personality school, but they rely more on explicit analysis of texts and less on intuitive grasping of patterns. For example, the title of Michelle Rosaldo's (1980) study of the Ilongot of Luzon, *Knowledge and Passion*, refers to native conceptions in which mature knowledge (*beya*) is expected to balance youthful passion (*liget*), and an ethnopsychology of motives is derived from observations of interaction and analysis of discourse (see the chapter by Janis Jenkins in part I).

COGNITION

An overview of anthropological studies of cognition, from early speculations about "primitive thought" to contemporary investigation of concept attainment and mental representations, is beyond the scope of this introduction (see the chapter by Ronald Casson in part I). A few remarks will have to suffice as an orientation to this vast area of research (cf. Dougherty 1985).

The opposition of universal to particular may again be used to sort out various approaches to cognition. In regard to content, while a few anthropologists have investigated alleged universal symbols, there has been great interest in the notion that basic color terms (and perhaps some other semantic sets) follow a general, evolutionary pattern, although their lexical representations are highly variable (Berlin and Kay 1969; C. H. Brown 1986). Studies of individuals and their idiosyncratic knowledge (Wallace's "mazeway"; Spiro's "cultural heredity") have also been neglected, though outstanding examples from Radin (1926) to Keesing (1983) and Dwyer (1987) show how much such biographical works can reveal about variability in the knowledge and beliefs of group members (cf. Runyan 1984).

Much of the research in ethnosemantics has been concerned with distinctive cultural contents in the intermediate zone, documenting the organization of cultural knowledge in particular groups or societies (Tyler 1969; Casson 1981). Whether they focus on kin terminology, the classification of plants and animals, diagnostic categories of disease, color terms, or more general "cultural models," these studies have demonstrated the complexity of societal modes of thinking (at least as revealed by language) and have suggested hypotheses about the processes by which concepts are attained, shared, and modified.

Cognitive processes are more difficult to study, but there are plenty of relevant hypotheses (including the incredible variety of "learning theories" found in academic psychology). Anthropologists have explored a number of general ideas concerning natural logic, rationality, developmental stages, and categorization, as well as the "mythical thought" and "science of the concrete" proposed by Lévi-Strauss (1966), but with no generally accepted conclusions. The more practice-oriented approach advocated by Jean Lave (1988) reveals group and individual differences in the cognitive processes related to everyday tasks (such as shopping); this approach suggests modification in more formalized accounts of cognition, but has yet to be integrated with psychological anthropology. Also at this particular pole belong studies of highly creative individuals (Roe 1967; John-Steiner 1985) whose distinctive patterns of thought transform the arts and the sciences, and of clearly pathological cases (Sacks 1985) that upset our assumption about "intelligence" or "rationality" by showing the fragility of normal functioning when a person is subjected to trauma or disease. Many of these topics will recur in the remainder of this handbook. (For a recent attempt to integrate cognitive and motivational structures, see D'Andrade and Strauss [1992]).

PERSONALITY

As understood by most anthropologists, personality involves the relative *integration* of an individual's perceptions, motives, cognitions, and behavior within a sociocultural matrix. (The subjective view of this unity is more often referred to as the *self.*) The importance of consistent social feedback to individual functioning has been demonstrated by a number of studies that (experimentally) remove normal supports of selfhood. Personality is thus revealed as part of a dynamic interactive system between a human organism and its physical-social environment such that any item of behavior takes on meaning only in this wider context (Erikson 1963; Bateson 1972). In this view, "personality disorder" or "mental illness" is an integral part of a family system, an ethnic community, a national identity, and even a planetary ecology.

As I will argue in part I, personality must also be understood as a function of the individual's position in the social structure, including his or her social class, gender, occupational role, and even birth order. These quasi-universal structural constraints cut across conventional divisions into "cultures" and even nations so that one may, for example, investigate "peasant personality" in diverse social and cultural settings. Nearer to the particular pole would be studies, say, of eminent scientists or of charismatic leaders of revitalization movements.

Not too long ago, the concept of "personality" seemed about to be discarded as an illusion in favor of less unified assessments of behavioral variables, just as "intelligence" was being dissolved into independent faculties and as "culture" is being deconstructed in postmodern writings. Some contributors to this handbook may sympathize with such radical efforts, but most of us, I believe, recommend a careful straining of the "bathwater" to ensure recovery of what is most valuable from the past century of psychological anthropology. The notion of personality (or self, if you prefer) is one of those concepts that will inevitably return if "repressed."

Still, it must be admitted that we are unsure of how to relate individual personality to culture. Over forty years ago, Melford Spiro suggested that this was a dilemma of our own making: that the distinction between culture and personality was a "false dichotomy," and that its proper resolution required the recognition that culture was not external to the individual (as Durkheim had maintained), but that "the development of personality and the acquisition of culture . . . are one and the same learning process" (1951:42). Spiro has since moved to a more psychoanalytic stance and barely mentioned this conflation of concepts in his anthology of theoretical papers, where he argued for a "pan-culture human nature" (1987:30).

A somewhat simplistic resolution of the dilemma would maintain that "culture" and "personality" are alternative kinds of inferences from behavior, the former referring to patterns observed in the interactions among members of some groups, the latter referring to patterns observed in the actions of a specific individual over a variety of settings and relationships. The fact that an observer's sampling of behavior is often inadequate for valid inferences does not alter the general principle; and since both culture and personality are inferred from behavior, the difference between them is based entirely on the different operations used by the analyst to arrive at his or her descriptions (cf. LeVine 1973).

From the "native's" point of view, however, all is one. Cultural patterns that strike an outsider as distinctive may, to the native, simply be "the way things are done." When he or she becomes aware of a rule, it is most often to negotiate its application in specific circumstances. In this view, culture is (largely) created by people in the discourse justifying their behavior as rational and moral. As Jack Bilmes (1986:191) has written, "Instead of focusing on the relationship between behavior and internal states of the actor, our interest is in the relationship between behavior and discourse." The implications of this shift in focus are far-reaching and will be discussed in several of the contributions in part II (see the chapters by Niko Besnier and by Barbara Tedlock).

UNIVERSALS OF NATURE AND CULTURE

Returning to the problem of universals, we must recognize that—beyond the general statements of Spiro (1987) and LaBarre (1954)—the most significant and recent contributions to this topic have come from sociobiology and its successors. These materialist and reductive approaches have proposed and tested a large number of specific hypotheses concerning (human) reproductive and subsistence behavior that clearly reveal the continuities between human behavioral strategies and those of other animals. The further assumption that whatever exists must have evolved to maximize the inclusive fitness of individuals gives a coherence to these theories that is sadly lacking in other approaches (see the chapter by Jerome Barkow in part I). Even extensive variability in response to changing environmental circumstance can be traced to an evolved capacity for flexibility.

The kinds of generalizations about human nature put forward by these evolutionary theorists, including numerous quantitative predictions, need to be carefully considered by psychological anthropologists; for example, articles in Betzig, Borgerhoff Mulder, and Turke (1988) suggested explanations for polygamy, child care, and other phenomena. Attacks on evolutionary explanations by ethnologists such as Harris (1979) and Sahlins (1976) often seem more political than scientific, intent on preserving "culture" as an adaptive or symbolic system relatively free from genetic constraints. Yet caution is advisable in evaluating biological explanations for alleged universals, or for more particular phenomena.

In a lucid discussion entitled *Human Universals*, Donald E. Brown (1991) has considered a wide range of alleged universals from a position sympathetic to evolutionary explanations. He recognized that some universals are "cultural conventions that have come to have universal distribution," but he maintained that "evolutionary psychology is a key to understanding many of the universals that are of greatest interest to anthropology" (1991:6).

Brown examined six studies that suggest universal/biological explanations for phenomena that had previously been considered by relativistic anthropologists to be culture-specific. The selected cases were the following:

1. Derek Freeman's (1983) critique of Margaret Mead on Samoan adolescence
2. Deborah Gewertz's (1981) reconsideration of Mead's Tchambuli case
3. M. Spiro's (1982) reanalysis of Malinowski's Trobriand material
4. E. Malotki's (1983) refutation of Benjamin Whorf's views of Hopi grammar
5. P. Ekman's (1973) studies of universals in facial expressions
6. B. Berlin and P. Kay's (1969) demonstration of universals in color terminology

Each of these studies was presented as a "refutation of cultural relativism" (D. E. Brown 1991:10), but this is actually the least convincing part of the book. I have discussed Freeman's intemperate attack on Mead elsewhere (Bock 1983). Mead's representation of female assertiveness among the Tchambuli [Chambri] was quite likely overdrawn, but Gewertz answered a study of "temperament" with arguments about history, politics, and economics, which Brown further linked to the issue of universal male dominance. Spiro was committed to the universality of the Oedipus complex, but his refutation of Malinowski's matrilineal exception would not, even if generally accepted, constitute final proof of a universal.

The three other cases, while presenting stronger arguments for universals, also need to be considered carefully regarding what they do and do not prove. Malotki's demonstration that the Hopi language does indeed have grammatical tense and spatial metaphors for time (the absence of which Whorf claimed to affect Hopi worldview) is convincing, but it mainly proves that Whorf's work was often superficial and biased, not that any particular concepts of "time" are universal. Ekman's studies of facial expressions do show that certain expressions appear to be universal and have presumably developed in the course of hominid evolution. However, Brown's discussion slighted the role of what Ekman has called "display rules," that is, the culture-specific norms that specify when emotional expression should be masked, allowed, or amplified. Brown also neglected the interaction of biology with gender (cf. Lutz 1988).

The case of basic color terms is more complex. I believe that most anthropologists would accept the findings that color perception is rooted in evolved physiological and neurological processes, and that these processes favor the perception of certain frequencies (''focal colors''). The evidence of ''colorblind'' persons furnishes exceptions that prove the rule. But Berlin and Kay went beyond this to assert *semantic universals* in the naming of color categories and demonstrated, for example, regularities in the *salience* of color terms and in the *sequence* in which ''basic terms'' are added to vocabulary. While I accept some of these findings and have even added a confirming case study (Bock 1984:123–33), I join with others in critiquing the notion of ''basic color term'' and in questioning the degree to which the methods used in these studies may produce artificial results that accord with the theory. Specifically, the use of a standardized but decontextualized display of color chips to elicit color categories and focal colors together with a restrictive definition of what can count as a ''basic term'' eliminates alternative modes of dealing with color before the investigation begins.

While I greatly admire the work of Berlin and Kay, I think that it is essential to recognize the limitations of their approach to universals because these limitations apply to other less well supported claims. The central dilemma, I feel, is how to define a universal. Too narrow a definition, for example, of ''marriage'' will lead to the conclusion that it is not universal (e.g., the Nayar case, duolocal residence, and many societies where cohabitation is not ritualized). But definitions that are too broad, for example, of ''magic,'' lead to the inclusion of such diverse phenomena that the proposal universal becomes vacuous. Somewhere between the ''extreme relativism'' rightly decried by Brown and the too-ready acceptance of universals or vague concepts that disguise diversity is an area where psychological anthropology can contribute to our understanding of human similarities and differences.

THE INTERMEDIATE ZONE

Most of the research discussed in this handbook deals with the relationship between cultural and individual phenomena in specific communities or small-scale societies. Like its parent discipline, ethnology, psychological anthropology arose in the context of late colonialism, and it has struggled to free itself from the assumptions and biases inherent in that situation. Sometimes naively and sometimes cynically, we have tried to analyze cultural stability and change with reference to the psychological characteristics of subordinate populations. But increased sensitivity to past and present political relationships has not relieved us of the need to collect reliable data on individuals—data that are absolutely essential for testing hypotheses about human social life. The other social sciences deal with behavior at second hand, through economic indices or survey responses. Only anthropologists continue to work for extended periods, in local languages and through personal relationships, with people who do not share the tacit assumptions of Western industrial civilization; and only psychological anthropology makes use of methods and concepts that both record the behavior and tap the private experience of our subjects.

Those who know my critical history of the field (Bock 1988) will realize that I am quite aware of the flaws in past and present approaches to these topics. Yet I insist on the importance of this enterprise. Located in the intermediate zone, we can consider plausible propositions about human universals and test them in the natural settings where we have been personally accepted, drawing on the experience of individuals with known backgrounds to enrich our understanding of abstract notions such as "stress," "bonding," or "maternal neglect" (Scheper-Hughes 1992). For only a genuine psychological anthropology is positioned to have access to this kind of material. Context is the key. (See the chapter by Barbara Tedlock in this volume.)

Experimental psychology attempts to control as many variables as possible in order to isolate those that are relevant to its hypotheses. Psychological anthropology should strive to enrich the context of its gathered material—to present "thicker descriptions"—so that individual thoughts and actions can be appreciated as the outcomes of a complex interplay of forces.

Most of the contributions to this handbook adopt this point of view. Whether they are describing the historical development of concepts and models in part I or examining specific types of evidence and methods in part II, the authors show the interplay between universals of human existence and particular human lives as realized under local sociocultural conditions. This is a difficult undertaking, and serious errors of fact and interpretation have been made; but I believe that it is important that we try, with humility, to relate the universal and the particular in human experience to one another and to the constantly changing circumstances of our world. I hope that this handbook will be useful as psychological anthropology moves into its second century.

REFERENCES

Bateson, G. 1972. *Steps to an Ecology of Mind.* New York: Ballantine Books.

Benedict, R. 1934. *Patterns of Culture.* Boston: Houghton Mifflin.

Berlin, B., and P. Kay. 1969. *Basic Color Terms: Their Universality and Evolution.* Berkeley: University of California Press.

Betzig, L., M. Borgerhoff Mulder, and P. Turke, eds. 1988. *Human Reproductive Behaviour.* New York: Cambridge University Press.

Bilmes, J. 1986. *Discourse and Behavior.* New York: Plenum Press.

Bock, P. K. 1983. The Samoan Puberty Blues. *Journal of Anthropological Research* 39:336–40.

———. 1984. *Shakespeare and Elizabethan Culture.* New York: Schocken Books.

———. 1988. *Rethinking Psychological Anthropology: Continuity and Change in the Study of Human Action.* New York: W. M. Freeman.

———. 1992. World View and Language. Pp. 248–51 in W. Bright, ed., *International Encyclopedia of Linguistics*, vol. 4. New York: Oxford University Press.

Brown, C. H. 1986. *The Growth of Ethnobiological Nomenclature. Current Anthropology* 27:1–19.

Brown, D. E. 1991. *Human Universals.* New York: McGraw-Hill.

Bruner, J. S. 1973. *Beyond the Information Given*. New York: Norton.

Casson, R. W., ed. 1981. *Language, Culture, and Cognition: Anthropological Perspectives*. New York: Macmillan.

D'Andrade, R. G., and C. Strauss, eds. 1992. *Human Motives and Cultural Models*. Cambridge, Eng.: Cambridge University Press.

Dougherty, J.W.D., ed. 1985. *Directions in Cognitive Anthropology*. Urbana: University of Illinois Press.

Dwyer, K. 1987. *Moroccan Dialogues*. Prospect Heights, IL; Waveland Press.

Edgerton, R. B. 1974. Cross-Cultural Psychology and Psychological Anthropology: One Paradigm or Two? *Reviews in Anthropology* 1:52–65.

Ekman, P., ed. 1973. *Darwin and Facial Expression*. New York: Academic Press.

Erchak, G. M. 1992. *The Anthropology of Self and Behavior*. New Brunswick, NJ: Rutgers University Press.

Erikson, E. H. 1963. *Childhood and Society*. Rev. ed. New York: Norton.

Freeman, D. 1983. *Margaret Mead and Samoa*. Cambridge, MA: Harvard University Press.

Freud, S. 1961. *Civilization and Its Discontents*. New York: Norton.

Gewertz, D. 1981. A Historical Reconsideration of Female Dominance among the Chambri of Papua New Guinea. *American Ethnologist* 8:94–106.

Hallowell, A. I. 1955. *Culture and Experience*. Philadelphia: University of Pennsylvania Press.

Harris, M. 1980. *Cultural Materialism*. New York: Vintage Books.

John-Steiner, V. 1985. *Notebooks of the Mind*. Albuquerque: University of New Mexico Press.

Keesing, R. 1983. *'Elota's Story*. New York: Holt, Rinehart and Winston.

LaBarre, W. 1954. *The Human Animal*. Chicago: University of Chicago Press.

Lave, J. 1988. *Cognition in Practice: Mind, Mathematics, and Culture in Everyday Life*. New York: Cambridge University Press.

LeVine, R. A. 1973. *Culture, Behavior, and Personality*. Chicago: Aldine.

Lévi-Strauss, C. 1966. *The Savage Mind*. Chicago: University of Chicago Press.

Lutz, C. 1988. *Unnatural Emotions: Everyday Sentiments on a Micronesian Atoll and Their Challenge to Western Theory*. Chicago: University of Chicago Press.

Malotki, E. 1983. *Hopi Time*. Berlin: Mouton.

Radin, P., ed. 1926. *Crashing Thunder*. New York: Appleton.

Roe, A. 1967. *Personalities of Eminent Scientists*. Pp. 368–82 in R. Endleman, ed., *Personality and Social Life*. New York: Random House.

Rosaldo, M. 1980. *Knowledge and Passion: Ilongot Notions of Self and Social Life*. New York: Cambridge University Press.

Runyan, W. McK. 1984. *Life Histories and Psychobiography*. New York: Oxford University Press.

Sacks, O. 1985. *The Man Who Mistook His Wife for a Hat*. New York: Summit Books.

Sahlins, M. D. 1976. *The Use and Abuse of Biology*. Ann Arbor: University of Michigan Press.

Scheper-Hughes, N. 1992. *Death without Weeping*. Berkeley: University of California Press.

Segall, M., D. Campbell, and M. Herskovits. 1966. *The Influence of Culture on Visual Perception*. Indianapolis: Bobbs-Merrill.

Segall, M., P. Dansen, J. Berry, and Y. Poortinga. 1990. *Human Behavior in Global Perspective*. New York: Pergamon Press.

Spindler, G., and L. Spindler. 1991. Rorschaching in North America in the Shadow of Hallowell. *Psychoanalytic Study of Society* 16:155–82.

Spiro, M. E. 1951. Culture and Personality: The Natural History of a False Dichotomy. *Psychiatry* 14:19–46.

———. 1982. *Oedipus in the Trobriands*. Chicago: University of Chicago Press.

———. 1987. *Culture and Human Nature: Theoretical Papers of Melford E. Spiro*. B. Kilbourne and L. L. Langness, eds. Chicago: University of Chicago Press.

Tyler, S. A., ed. 1969. *Cognitive Anthropology*. New York: Holt, Rinehart and Winston.

Wallace, A.F.C. 1970. Culture and Personality, Second Edition. New York: Random House.

Psychological Anthropology

PART 1
SCHOOLS AND APPROACHES

CHAPTER ONE

CLASSICAL CULTURE AND PERSONALITY

Steven Piker

Anthropology has always been importantly, if erratically, psychological. Earlier cultural formulations, from Herodotus through medieval Renaissance times to the Enlightenment, have relied upon concepts of an essentially psychological order. From its beginning in nineteenth-century Europe and America, the discipline has turned frequently to psychological formulations, whether drawn from the emerging discipline of psychology or created ad hoc by imaginative anthropologists. Indeed, even the stridently antireductionist classical British structural functionalism, inspired by Radcliffe-Brown, is replete with bootleg psychology. This circumstance is perhaps not surprising in light of the influence of Durkheim's *Elementary Forms of the Religious Life* on this school. Marvin Harris, one of the most adamant and persistent critics of psychological interpretation in anthropology, wrote of the "pervasiveness of emic and psychological categories" in nineteenth- and early twentieth-century cultural anthropology (1968: 395). Certainly, the distinctively American anthropology of the early twentieth century was in significant part psychological in orientation, in the work of Boas and many of his students and followers.

These several pedigrees of psychological anthropology are germane to this chapter, but not part of its focus. Rather, my intention is to depict the emergence of a school of psychological anthropology that is properly called Culture and Personality and to outline some important early developments associated with this school. The suggestion is that Culture and Personality developed between about 1920 and 1945, largely as the result of important intellectual exchanges between psychoanalysis and psychologically oriented American anthropology. We begin with an appreciation of Freud, as his findings and theories are a major starting point for the exchanges just mentioned. We will also discuss the psychiatrists and anthropologists who began the critical exchange of ideas.

Emphasis will be placed on the work of Bronislaw Malinowski, Margaret

Mead, Ruth Benedict, and Edward Sapir, and on that of Abram Kardiner and his associates at Columbia University in the late 1930s and early 1940s. Finally, we will examine the national character and modal personality approaches, several variants of classical Culture and Personality, and the theoretical and methodological legacies of this school. At the outset, a disclaimer: intellectual history, of which this chapter is an exercise, often paints too orderly a picture of developments in a field. When we examine some of the variants of classical Culture and Personality and its legacies, we will see that it has not been entirely as orderly as this introductory overview may suggest.

FREUD

No one was more important to the development of classical Culture and Personality than Sigmund Freud. But of what has this importance consisted? Freud's published work in psychoanalysis appeared over almost half a century (1894–1938) and comprised more than twenty volumes. The topics he treated in depth include clinical cases of psychopathology, cultural institutions and practices, dreams, mental symbolism, ontogenesis of personality, and theories of human psychology. His theoretical position changed strikingly throughout his career, and he never produced a final, integrated theory of human psychology. Freud's followers are legion and populate numerous disciplines and professions, but among practitioners of classical Culture and Personality, there has been little agreement over just which parts of the Freudian oeuvre are vital to the field: they selectively adopted and significantly adapted certain Freudian theories, concepts, and methods.

Freud's most anthropological work, which applied psychoanalysis to the understanding of cultural institutions and usages, includes a number of books and papers, the first of which—*Totem and Taboo*—appeared in 1913. I suggest, however, that his most important contributions to Culture and Personality came not from his forays into anthropology, but rather from his theory of mental symbolism, parts of which were developed in his early work on hysteria, and which received full presentation in *The Interpretation of Dreams* (1900). Key elements of the theory include the following:

1. A dynamic conception of the personality consisting of an unconscious as well as a conscious mind, the two separated by the barrier of repression
2. The identification of psychosymbolic mechanisms by which unconscious materials (e.g., images, wishes, drives, memories, fantasies) are transformed and thereby enabled to appear in conscious thought
3. An ontogenetic account of how the unconscious mind comes to be constituted, emphasizing the lifelong importance of the psychic residues of the experiences of infancy and childhood
4. An empirical method, free association, for investigating the content of the unconscious mind and its influence on the conscious mind

5. Several implied research agendas, including devising psychoanalytically relevant ways to study childhood empirically

Parts of Freud's late work relevant to classical Culture and Personality may be organized as follows:

1. Development of a structural mode of the personality featuring id, ego, and superego, and exploration of the psychosymbolic processes by which the unconscious/conscious transformations occur. (The concept of defense mechanisms is central to this and received its most influential phrasing by Anna Freud.)
2. Elucidation of the ontogenesis of the personality with reference to structure (e.g., *The Ego and the Id*) and content (e.g., *Three Essays on the Theory of Sexuality*). The psychoanalytically relevant empirical study of childhood, with major implications for Culture and Personality, was initiated by Freud's followers, for example, M. Klein, E. Erikson, and G. Róheim.
3. Applications of psychoanalysis to cultural analysis. This is a tangled jungle populated by wild metaphors and discredited theories, but it is also a treasure trove for those who seek understanding of personality/culture relationships.

In making our way through this maze, we may be guided by Bock's gloss: "In the Freudian view, *culture is to society as neurosis is to the individual*" (1988:28). For Freud, the psychodynamics of symptomatology are the starting point for psychocultural analysis. This is at once a brilliant insight and a shackle. The brilliant insight was to recognize that much of what we do and think and, especially, feel in our everyday lives (whether culturally constructed or idiosyncratic) stands in the same psychosymbolic relationship to the unconscious mind as do, for example, the manifest content of dreams and neurotic symptoms. This insight was the basis for Kardiner's concept of projective institution, to which we will return shortly.

The shackle is the tendency to conflate cultural institutions and symptoms, as Freud sometimes did with religion and primitive culture generally. The brilliant insight is the main mooring in Freud of the bridge that links psychoanalysis to classical Culture and Personality. In developing and extending the insight anthropologically, Culture and Personality rebutted the conflation of culture and neurosis and has enabled a richer, more dynamic and accurate understanding of the culture/personality relationship than Freud attained.

FORERUNNERS

Anthropological interest in Freud and psychoanalysis, which was considerable, had two main foci. Some looked at specific Freudian cultural or evolutionary formulations and on anthropological grounds found them to be wanting. The resultant negative critiques contributed little to later Culture and Personality formulations.

Others, while not uncritical of Freud, looked upon the (still-emerging) Freudian oeuvre as a fertile source of inspiration for the production of anthropological knowledge. Malinowski and Mead, through attention paid to Freudian ideas of their fieldwork, helped anthropologists to see the widespread applicability of psychoanalysis to cultural anthropology, but they contributed little of a definite sort to later theories. Sapir and Benedict, on the other hand, raised theoretical issues that figured prominently in the birth of Culture and Personality, although neither did so mainly with reference to his or her fieldwork.

Bronislaw Malinowski

Perhaps no twentieth-century cultural anthropologist traversed more of the field's terrain than did Malinowski. We need to abstract his contributions to Culture and Personality from the broad scope of his anthropological endeavors. Malinowski's (1944) enduring theoretical orientation, psychobiological functionalism, at once embraced central postulates of psychoanalysis and presaged emphases of Culture and Personality: biological and psychological needs are the starting point in exploring the individual's relationship to culture; correlatively, the major function of any culture is its fulfillment of individual psychological and biological needs. Specifically, the expressive component of culture (e.g., religion, magic, art, play) is instrumental to the fulfillment of these needs (1948).

The vicissitudes of human sexuality are seen as vital to the integration of individual and culture (1959). For Malinowski, the child is the parent of the culture-bearing adult. The psychological consequences of socialization populate the adult's involvement in his or her culture.

Malinowski is widely known for his test of Freud's Oedipus complex formulation against Trobriand case materials. Here, perhaps more clearly than anywhere else in his work, we see Malinowski actually practicing Culture and Personality. As Spiro (1982) has argued, Malinowski's critique of Freud suffered on both conceptual grounds (his grasp of Freud's formulation was flawed) and methodological grounds (his empirical indices for the presence or absence of the Oedipus complex were inadequate). However, in attempting the test, Malinowski raised questions that later became of major importance to Culture and Personality:

1. How are universal psychodynamic processes, as posited by psychoanalysis, affected by cross-cultural variability in socialization practices?
2. How do the experiences of infants and young children become transformed into enduring culture orientations of adults?

Malinowski took his intellectual preoccupations, including his concerns for expressive culture, childhood, and sexuality, into the field. His psychobiological functionalism attempted an integration of individual and culture. As an explanatory system, it failed in part for the same reasons that all ''basic needs'' approaches to cultural and behavioral diversity fail: you cannot explain variability by reference to a constant. Functional explanations proved to be sometimes plausible, but always untested, just-so stories. Regrettably, functional analyses in anthropology, sociology, and biology all too often exhibit this last failing. That an anthropologist of Malinowski's stature even attempted to establish a theory of psychologically mediated culture/individual relationships legitimated the agenda, despite the flaws contained in this particular theory.

Margaret Mead

Mead contributed vitally to the emergence of Culture and Personality, yet she remained apart from its most salient interpretive approaches (with, perhaps, the exception of her involvement in the National Character school). Her prolific career predated the emergence of Culture and Personality and outlasted the classical period of the school. She has been one of the most psychological of American anthropologists throughout her career and arguably the most attended to, both within the profession and without. As she wrote, ''Our materials were organized in the 1920's [to document] the fact that human nature is not rigid and unyielding'' (1939:x).

Franz Boas dispatched the young Margaret Mead to Polynesia to test the psychological assumption that puberty and adolescence are invariably periods of *Sturm und Drang* on the rocky maturational road to adulthood. The results of the ''test,'' published in *Coming of Age in Samoa*, supported the Boasian postulate of plasticity of human nature and catapulted Mead to prominence. Like Malinowski's ''tests'' of the Oedipus complex, Mead's results at once refuted an article of psychoanalytic orthodoxy and drew attention to psychoanalysis as a source of inspiration for the investigation of personality/culture relationships. The negative results of the two famous ''tests'' did not so much discredit psychoanalysis as they recast it. Instead of seeing psychoanalysis as a body of universal truths the applicability of which could (or should) be discoverable anywhere and everywhere, some anthropologists came to see it as a set of concepts to be adopted selectively and adapted to purposes that its founder and orthodox custodians did not envision and perhaps would not have approved of.

Complementary heterodoxies were developing at about the same time within psychoanalysis in the work of, for example, A. Freud, Horney, Klein, Erikson, Hartmann, Kris, and Loewenstein and Fenichel. These figures by and large accepted psychoanalytic postulates concerning the ontogenetic development of unconscious symbolic structures and looked to the vicissitudes of early life experiences for the sources of variable adult personality outcomes. Many of these figures devoted themselves to the direct empirical study of childhood. With the major exception of Erikson and Róheim, however, the heterodox analysts did not systematically investigate adult culture and, therefore, did not empirically explore the complexities of the adult personality/culture relationship.

Mead's preoccupations with gender and culture and the relevance of cross-cultural materials to the understanding of our culture led to canons of investigation that became central to Culture and Personality. First, there was her abiding conviction that the foundations of the individual/culture relationship are laid down in the process of growing up; and, correlatively, her career-long preoccupation with the study of childhood, both ethnographically and, later in her career, at a distance (1928, 1939, 1950). Second, Mead devised ways to evoke the psychological aspects of culture. In pursuit of these, she probed the expression of cultural character in everyday lives and fashioned qualitative research procedures, including biography, film, and heavy reliance on native accounts of feeling and context. Mead's reportage featured evocative narrative in which native accounts mingled with her own empathetic grasp of the texture of native lives.

Mead helped to define a range of often vexing methodological issues that have been central to Culture and Personality, namely, what empirical field procedures enable inference of the psychological processes that concern us, and, correlatively, how we can best report what we learn in the field about the psychologies of ''our'' natives. One view has held that this is more an art than a science: the artful fieldworker will rely on the qualitative methods, and results are best reported in narrative fashion. This view received an early and highly influential formulation in the work and career of Margaret Mead (1942, 1949, 1953).

Ruth Benedict

As a doctoral student of Boas, Benedict's dissertation (1923) partook of two of the major legacies of her teacher's prolific career—the use of culture-trait distribution patterns to refute unilineal evolutionism, and seeing cultures as patterned, integrated wholes. As Benedict developed this last idea, it brought her into the psychological stream of anthropology and, specifically, into the currents that soon would coalesce in classical Culture and Personality. Her close colleagueship with Mead and Sapir figured importantly here.

To be sure, Benedict (1923) documented the distribution of guardian-spirit traits in their variable association with other traits, thereby fulfilling her task. But Benedict used the same data to argue that a specific trait, that is, the guardian spirit, must vary in significance according to the cultural context in which it was embedded. She came to see cultures as integrated amalgams of parts on the model of the individual personality: ''A culture, like an individual, is a more or less consistent pattern of thought and action'' (1934:42); however, as with individual personalities, lack of integration seems to be as characteristic of certain culture as extreme integration is of others (1934:196). From this it was but a short step to portray the configuration of a culture in terms of integrating psychological themata ''as a clinical psychologist might describe the personality structure of a patient'' (Bock 1988:49). Ruth Benedict's *Patterns of Culture* was probably the most widely read of all anthropology books. Its central ideas contributed vitally to the emergence of classical Culture and Personality and its development—witness the Apollonian Pueblos, the Dionysian Plains cultures, the paranoid Dobuans, and the megalomaniac Kwakiutl. In arriving at these formulations, Benedict was indebted to Gestalt psychology; she was also influenced by the historical idealism of Wilhelm Dilthey and by Nietzsche's *Birth of Tragedy*, from which she drew the idea of the Dionysian/Apollonian contrast. Indeed, Benedict's work, perhaps more than that of any other figure, reflects the multiple and disparate pedigrees of psychology in anthropology.

There is much in Benedict's configurationalism that contributed to the emergence of classical Culture and Personality. First, Benedict (1932) construed "cultural configuration" as isomorphic with personality pattern, thereby suggesting exploration of the culture/personality relationship. Second, she likened the historical development of a cultural pattern to the biographical development of a personality. As Bock noted, the cultural pattern "integrates the diverse elements provided by history, giving each a new significance, just as each individual integrates diverse life experiences into a coherent personality" (1988: 47–48). This emphasis anticipated recent theoretical developments that attempt to align personality with social history and evolutionary theory, endeavors virtually unknown to classical Culture and Personality (e.g., Scheper-Hughes 1992; the chapter by Jerome Barkow in this volume).

Benedict envisaged a personality/culture fit on the order of that later posited by the basic personality model, according to which most individuals can live comfortably with the dominant culture configuration of their group. But Benedict also recognized the inevitability of the "abnormal," the deviant for whom conformity and comfort are problematical or impossible, thereby anticipating the culture and mental health concerns of a number of the practitioners of Culture and Personality (e.g., Hallowell 1955; Spiro 1965; Caudill and Li 1969). Benedict's best-known work was thus devoted to understanding culture on the model of personality, rather than to developing ways to explore the relationship between culture and personality. This last endeavor has been the main charter of classical Culture and Personality, one to which Edward Sapir devoted a series of seminal papers.

Edward Sapir

Although Sapir's anthropological fame rests mainly on his accomplishments as a historical linguist, he had a career-long interest in many of the core issues of Culture and Personality. This expressed itself in the collegial encouragement he provided for pioneer workers in the area (e.g., Benedict, Mead, Linton), as well as in a series of theoretical papers that helped to chart the early course of the school.

As early as 1917, Sapir attacked the superorganic concept of culture. To be sure, he objected to it on its own terms. But Sapir found fault with its restrictions, which ruled out of bounds for anthropology virtually all exploration of the relationship between psychology and culture. Finding merit in the traditional anthropological aim to discover "the generalized forms of action, thought and feeling which . . . constitute the culture of a community" (1956:140), Sapir insisted that we attend to the individual's relationship to the generalized culture.

For Sapir, "The true locus of culture is in the interactions of specific individuals and, on the subjective side, in the world of meanings which each one of these individuals may unconsciously abstract [from] participation in these interactions" (1956:147). Further Sapir anticipated the important conclusion that different individuals (or groups) make disparate psychological uses of the shared culture. In his exploration of these insights, Sapir broached the question of the individual's psychological adjustment to his or her culture, as well as the question of the relationship between culture and mental health.

ABRAM KARDINER AND BASIC PERSONALITY THEORY

The period 1930–45 was a time of growth and consolidation for the study of psychology and culture. Freud's work in this area had developed and diversified over two decades; a number of psychoanalysts (e.g., Róheim, Erikson, Devereux) had begun careers that would prominently merge ethnography and psychoanalysis; and Róheim in particular, agreeing with Freud in assigning to cultural institutions the ego-defensive functions of neurosis, proposed a culture/personality relationship suggestive of what Kardiner and his associates were soon to develop. Yet other analysts (e.g., A. Freud, Horney, Klein) were pioneering methods that pointed toward the psychoanalytically relevant ethnographic study of childhood. The (in part) psychoanalytically inspired work and writing of anthropologists of great stature—Malinowski, Mead, Benedict, Sapir—were widely attended to; and the carers of other, younger anthropologists, who were trained in psychoanalysis and bound to become leaders within Culture and Personality (e.g., Caudill, LeVine, Gorer), were getting under way. At Yale, in part inspired by Sapir, a multidisciplinary group led by John Dollard had begun explorations that would eventuate in the merging of a statistical, hypothesis-testing methodology with, especially, the Cross-Cultural school of psychological anthropology. Meanwhile, at the University of Pennsylvania, the brilliant and eclectic Hallowell was pioneering approaches to psychology and culture that were to bear rich fruit all over the field of anthropology.

But it was at Columbia University during this period that the first organized school of thought emerged within the general area of psychological anthropology. From the 1890s, Franz Boas's work was in important part psychological in orientation (e.g., *The Mind of Primitive Man*). His leading students included Mead and Benedict, whose pioneering work in psychological anthropology has already been discussed. Although Boas's stewardship as chair ended in 1937, he was replaced by Ralph Linton, whose interest in psychology and culture was on the rise, even though he had yet to do major work of his own in this area.

Early in his chairmanship, Linton helped to sponsor a series of seminars during which he and other anthropologists presented their own ethnographic materials and Abram Kardiner, along with other psychologists, attempted psychodynamic interpretation of the cultures. Kardiner's own work had been under way at the New York Psychoanalytic Institute for a few years. By 1940, these seminars were established within the anthropology department at Columbia. In addition to Linton and Kardiner, the seminars prominently included Cora Du Bois, Ruth Bunzel, and James West. Cultures from which materials were analyzed included Marquesan, Tanala, Comanche, Alor, Zuni, and "Plainville." The seminars also analyzed a number of cultures in which its participants had not worked, relying upon published ethnographies. (Kardiner and Linton 1939)

The seminars were guided by Kardiner's convictions that the joining of selected aspects of psychoanalysis and ethnography was a likely way to advance Freud's cultural agenda and that no one person could master both fields. Accordingly, he fostered a division of labor in which anthropologists (interested, but untrained, in psychoanalyis) presented cultural materials from their own ethnographic research, and he, a trained analyst with only a smattering of anthropology and no fieldwork, provided psychodynamic interpretations grounded in his clinical experience. From this procedure came a theory of culture and personality and a method for testing its validity (see Manson 1988).

The core of Kardiner's theory can be summarized in the following diagram:

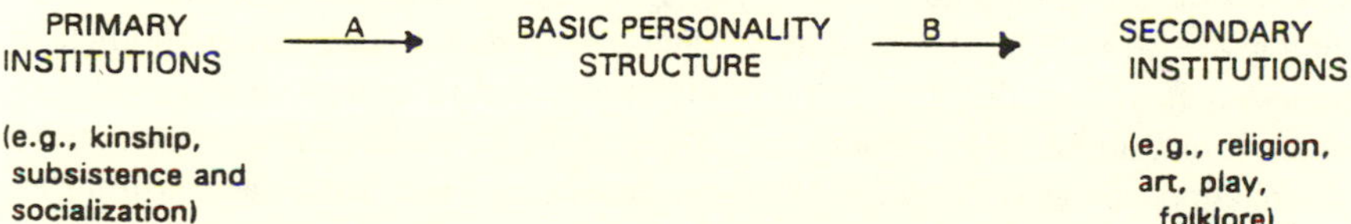

That is, primary institutions gave rise to (*A*) basic personality, which, in turn, creates or maintains (*B*) secondary (or "projective") institutions.

Notwithstanding frequent use by Kardiner of such terms as "origin," "develop," and "give rise to," this schema does not treat historical issues. Analysis begins with primary institutions. Their cross-cultural variability is of vital importance, but the theory makes no real attempt to account for it beyond the unexplored suggestion that its source is to be found in the adaptation of subsistence practices to the environment. This idea was later developed by the Cross-Cultural school.

Arrow *A* denotes personality development. Of particular concern to Kardiner were "nuclear traumatic experiences" of youngsters, the psychological residues of which are repressed and appear in the projective subsystem of the personality. These repressed materials and the ego-defensive system that arises to accommodate them are the basis for the individual's involvement with the secondary institutions of his or her culture. The adult personality also contains a reality system that houses consciously assimilated meanings and knowledge and is vital for the individual's participation in practical everyday activities. Kardiner and his associates were not much interested in this system.

The personality-development relationship may fairly be seen as cause and effect; not so for the relationship denoted by arrow *B*, notwithstanding that Kardiner asserted that basic personality "maintains" secondary institutions. The heart of the matter is *projection*, by which Kardiner meant not the specific ego defense featured, for example, in paranoia, but rather the general psychosymbolic processes by which unconscious materials are transformed and admitted into consciousness. This makes possible a reciprocal relationship between the projective subsystem of the personality and secondary institutions. The projective subsystem of the personality provides, via this unconscious mechanism, much of the motivation for the individual's adherence to and participation in the secondary institutions of his or her culture. Reciprocally, because of the psychosymbolic nature of this relationship, religiousness, for example, serves for the religious psychological functions on the order of those served by, for example, dreams or neurotic symptoms.

The referent of basic personality structure is the individual: "A group can no more have a common character than it can have a common . . . pair of lungs" (Kardiner et al. 1945:24). When basic personality structure was applied by Kardiner to a culture, it was a statistical summary justified by establishing that as a result of similar socialization experiences, "similar projective systems operate in all (or most) individuals in a given society" (Kardiner et al. 1945:20). A specific socialization pattern (e.g., prolonged and close mother-son relationship) may give rise to common personality elements (e.g., strong Oedipal conflicts in males) that in turn find psychosymbolic expression in specific features of secondary institutions (e.g., belief in a judgmental and punitive male deity). Such personality-mediated relationships between primary and secondary institutions are called integrational series. Identification of integrational series was the main explanatory task for Kardiner.

How can this Culture and Personality model be tested? Three theoretically independent procedures are involved: for the culture under study, ethnographic materials on socialization were clinically analyzed by Kardiner to infer the content of the projective subsystem of the personality; ethnographic materials on projective institutions were similarly analyzed, also to infer the content of the projective subsystem of the personality; finally, projective test protocols (typically, Rorschach), collected by the ethnographer, were interpreted blind by an expert, this also to infer the content of personalities. If the results of the three independent inferences agree, and if, moreover, the content of projective institutions and tests can be seen as the end products of integrational series, then, for the culture under study, the concept of basic personality has been validated. This must be done one culture at a time.

Among the principal legacies of the Kardiner seminars were the formulation of a theory of culture and personality in which explanation depends mainly upon a variant of psychoanalysis, and the establishment of an empirical agenda for the application of the theory. Central to the agenda was the ethnographic study of infancy and childhood. To the structural/functional and configurational models, the Kardiner school added the personality integration model, according to which primary and secondary cultural institutions are integrated by mediating personality processes. In this approach, individual conformity to social/requirements and the solidarity of the society are understood by reference to the psychological functions of culture.

MODAL PERSONALITY AND NATIONAL CHARACTER

One finds national character formulations all the way from the writings of Herodotus to the speeches of Ronald Reagan; thus the problem is to identify those parts of this sprawling domain to be treated in this chapter. Briefly, we are looking for studies that attempt to understand national characteristics in terms of culture and personality relationships. As Bock (1988:67–95) recognized, many of the issues embedded in Kardiner's theory of basic personality are also involved here. Several landmark studies in Culture and Personality may help us to see the links between "modal personality" and national character, as well as to identify problems in the national character approach.

Cora Du Bois was a charter member of the Kardiner seminars, and her work on the island of Alor (1944) presents at once a founding example of the basic personality approach and the wherewithal to criticize some of its central postulates. On the one hand, her book (in which Kardiner's psychodynamic interpretations form a vital part) embraces the basic personality model. On the other hand, Du Bois was the first member of the Kardiner group to bring from the field extensive psychological data on individuals, including biographies, projective test protocols, and rich accounts of socialization. Kardiner had called for just such materials, and Du Bois was unusually well equipped by training to provide them. But, upon inspection, these data revealed significant personality variability within Alorese culture. This led Du Bois to the concept of modal personality and also led her, in the 1961 edition of her classic, to suggest that she and Kardiner had overstated the congruities between Alorese culture and personality (see Singer 1961).

Anthony Wallace, a doctoral student of Hallowell in the 1940s, used the Rorschach test in his work with the Tuscarora and seconded Du Bois's reservations concerning culture and personality congruence. Most earlier users of the Rorschach test often had either arbitrarily glossed over interpersonal variability or had adopted averaging procedures that artifactually masked it. Wallace (1952) attended scrupulously to individual variability, while his representative sample of 70 out of 350 Tuscarora adults further lent validity to his study. Using the statistical concept of *mode*, Wallace was able both to establish central tendency and to chart variability in Tuscarora personalities. He showed that notwithstanding significant commonalities, even homogeneous societies can and do accommodate a great deal of personality variability. Wallace developed the theoretical implications of this circumstance later in his career (1970:chap 4).

World War II and the Cold War produced many national character studies of our enemies and allies. Arguably, the most attended to and the most insightful of these studies has been Ruth Benedict's book on Japan, *The Chrysanthemum and the Sword* (1946). A major part of the work interprets contradictory features of restraint and fanaticism of adult Japanese character in terms of Japanese social codes pertaining to obligation, which in turn are grounded in socialization practices that induce shame in children. Although Benedict eschewed specifically psychoanalytic or clinical usage, her work is conceptually akin to the basic personality model: she discriminated between cultural variables and personality variables, departing from the conflation of culture and personality that is characteristic of *Patterns of Culture*. Having never done fieldwork in Japan, Benedict helped pioneer the "study of culture at a distance" (relying, e.g., on literature, history, travelers' tales, movies, art, and expatriate interviews), which became standard in national character work during the 1940s (see Mead 1953). For example, Gorer and Rickman (1949) presented the famous "swaddling hypothesis," according to which pervasive features of Russian emotional life (which allegedly explain much in Russian history and culture) are consequences of the practice of swaddling of infants (see Bock 1988:84–87).

Another question dealt with by national character studies was: Why did Germany increasingly embrace Hitler's Nazi movement and participate in its historic atrocities? One answer was that an authoritarian personality is widespread among Germans and that people with this personality type insist on unquestioning obedience to authority and enjoy demeaning inferiors. A people among whom this personality type is prevalent will welcome the opportunities to "escape from freedom" offered by a totalitarian movement and will also welcome its organized scapegoating (Fromm 1941). Moreover, the rigid discipline and organization that go along with the authoritarian personality ensure that its bearers will be devoted and efficient servants of a totalitarian regime. Adorno et al. (1950) generalized the concept of authoritarian personality, sought its socialization antecedents, related it to the political process, and considered the problem of how to prevent its recurrence among our defeated enemies (and its occurrence in the Western democracies). (See also Erikson 1950.)

The modal personality approach recognizes that congruity between culture and personality must be an empirical question, not an assumption. This finding has had important theoretical implications, some of which will be considered shortly. In the interests of studying the psychological aspects of culture more reliably, proponents of the modal personality approach refined empirical methods, including new procedures for projective testing, the ethnographic study of childhood, and psychobiography.

National character studies are a mixed bag in terms of results. The most successful part of this work is the depictions of nuances of the cultures, for example, Ireland (Arensberg 1940); America, China, and India compared (Hsu 1961, 1970); Bali (Bateson and Mead 1942); England (Gorer 1955); the United States (Gorer 1964; Riesman, Glazer, and Denney 1961); and France (Métraux and Mead 1954). Attempts to interpret cultures in terms of the personalities of their members often fall short for a number of reasons: the failure empirically to establish the presence of the ostensible personality traits; the untested assumption that posited personality traits are widespread or universal in the national cultures under study; or lack of reliable, direct information on socialization practices.

THE LEGACY OF CULTURE AND PERSONALITY

Although classical Culture and Personality can be said to have ended in the 1950s, its continuing legacy may still be detected in the Cross-Cultural school and in the work of several leading figures whose ideas were formed under its influence, even if they later departed from its premises and methods. In the ongoing work of John and Beatrice Whiting and their many students one can find Freudian hypotheses being tested by statistical methods using cross-cultural data from standard ethnographies and original studies (see the chapter by Alice Schlegel in this volume; also that by Ruth Munroe and Robert Munroe in part II).

The founding work of the Cross-Cultural school (Whiting and Child 1953) at once embraced Kardiner's theory of personality and culture and strenuously criticized his empirical methodology. An outgrowth of this approach was a fundamental recasting of the mode of inquiry, such that personality terms become theoretical constructs from which hypotheses positing covariation between primary and secondary (projective) institutions are deduced (e.g., Whiting, Kluckhohn, and Anthony 1958). Along with this came an elaborate conceptual and empirical methodology for the implementation of this research agenda. The Cross-Cultural school has systematically pursued the idea that cross-cultural variability in socialization practices was determined by environmental and subsistence variables (Barry, Bacon, and Child 1959).

The work of the Whitings and of many other still-active anthropologists is well summarized in the anthology edited by G. Spindler (1978). A few examples will help connect the research of these pioneers with the more recent developments described in succeeding chapters.

Anthony Wallace's early work on modal personality has already been discussed. The modal personality approach showed that shared culture does not presuppose uniformity of personalities, against the view of the basic personality and national character schools. Wallace (1970) later argued that cultures accommodate and organize psychological diversity, rather than replicate psychological uniformity. This suggests that diverse psychological resources that may be critical for adaptive response to change exist even in small-scale societies. Wallace's acculturation studies placed culture and personality in history and launched a collaborative exploration of common borderlands of anthropology, psychiatry, human biology, and neuroscience. The result has not been a unified theory but rather a multidisciplinary research agenda. (See Wallace [1980] for a fine narrative account of the first two decades of this remarkable enterprise.)

It is difficult if not impossible to draw a line between Culture and Personality and what has been called psychoanalytic anthropology (Bock 1988: chaps. 2 and 7; LeVine 1982; Paul 1989). As Mead noted, the core theory of Culture and Personality has always been psychoanalytic. This is illustrated in the careers of two still-active anthropologists whose work has a profoundly clinical character, as it was in the writings of the late George Devereux (1978, 1980).

Weston LaBarre has studied an enormous range of topics, from human evolution to Japanese national character, and from the Bible to the ghost dance of the American Indians. His book on the latter topic (LaBarre 1972) is ultimately concerned with the origins of religion (as was Freud's *Totem and Taboo*). He argued that magic and religion have great "emotional plausibility" because the "locus of the supernatural world is the subconscious mind" (1978:291–92). His autobiographical chapter in the Spindler anthropology is aptly titled "The Clinic and the Field," suggesting the interplay of individual and ethnographic analysis of his work (cf. Devereux 1980).

The long and fruitful career of Melford Spiro also illustrates the ability of anthropology, grounded in fieldwork, to address some of the most fundamental and timeless questions of human nature. Spiro incisively treated a number of the key issues of Culture and Personality. For example, like Kardiner, Spiro (1952) saw religion as a projective institution; however, he further developed an analysis of religion as a "culturally constituted defense mechanism" (1965), thereby extending the Culture and Personality framework to the domain of mental health, developing new functional perspectives on social integration, and amplifying Hallowell's (1955) classic statement on culture and experience. Spiro (1958) also conducted a study of socialization and personality development in an Israeli kibbutz. It is remarkable for its careful development of methodology for the study of personality development and for its use of the kibbutz case to probe fundamental human nature and culture issues (specifically, the universality of psychoanalytically posited development stages). This anticipated his later major work on the Oedipus complex (1982) and biological constraints on gender (1979).

Finally, although many of the practitioners of classical Culture and Personality attended to theory, Spiro does so self-consciously and systematically. He had relied heavily upon psychoanalysis and social learning theories; but he is also usually fluent in social systems theory and the philosophy of science, including the logic of functional analysis. The result has been the production of a body of theory (1987) that treats the interaction of personality, social system, and culture and identifies the personality elements that render social systems problematical as well as the cultural resources that make solutions possible.

RETROSPECT

My first anthropology course (taught by Melford Spiro in 1959) was entitled "Culture and Personality." For a long time, what I learned from this course and the field it depicted was my bread and butter. The basic ideas are with me still. In retrospect, then, what can we say of this school?

I believe that the main accomplishments of Culture and Personality were the development of the personality-integration-of-culture model and commitment to empirical exploration of the relationships suggested by this model. In these respects, Culture and Personality was far ahead of earlier psychological formulations in anthropology. Careful attention to socialization helped to remedy anthropology's previous neglect of the transgenerational transmission of culture.

There was an amateurism to the field, born in part of the enthusiasm of early practitioners to work across all of its ramifying domains, often without requisite professional training. Notwithstanding the unusual (for American anthropology in the first half of this century) attention to theory, the relationship between fact and interpretation was often treated with insufficient rigor.

During the heyday of Culture and Personality, a new cohort of psychological anthropologists came of age. It included, to name only some, John and Beatrice Whiting, Anthony Wallace, Melford Spiro, Weston LaBarre, George Devereux, Francis Hsu, John Honigmann, George and Louise Spindler, and Erika Bourguignon. All attended closely to the classical Culture and Personality school, and all were highly qualified to follow the several roads they took away from it. Where they went with psychological anthropology is the subject matter of the rest of this volume.

REFERENCES

Adorno, T., E. Frenkel-Brunswick, Daniel J. Levinson, and R. Nevitt Sanford. 1950. *The Authoritarian Personality*. New York: Harper and Brothers.

Arensberg, C. M. 1940. *Family and Community in Ireland.* Cambridge, MA: Harvard University Press.

Barry, H., III, I. L. Child, and M. K. Bacon. 1959. Relation of Child Training to Subsistence Economy. *American Anthropologist* 61:51–63.

Bateson, G., and M. Mead. 1942. *Balinese Character: A Photographic Analysis.* New York: New York Academy of Sciences.

Benedict, R. 1923. *The Concept of the Guardian Spirit in North America.* Memoirs of the American Anthropological Association 29:1–97.

———. 1932. Configurations of Culture in North America. *American Anthropologist* 34:1–27.

———. 1950. *Patterns of Culture*. New York: Mentor.

———. 1946. *The Chrysanthemum and the Sword.* Boston: Houghton Mifflin.

Boas, F. 1939. *The Mind of Primitive Man*. New York: Macmillan.

Bock, P. 1988. *Rethinking Psychological Anthropology: Continuity and Change in the Study of Human Action*. New York: W. H. Freeman.

Caudill, S., and Li, Tsung-Yi, eds. 1969. *Mental Health Research in Asia and the Pacific.* Hawaii: East-West Center Press.

Devereux, G. 1978. The Works of George Devereux. In G. D. Spindler, ed., *The Making of Psychological Anthropology*. Berkeley: University of California Press. Pp. 361–406.

———. 1980. *Basic Problems of Ethnopsychiatry*. Chicago: University of Chicago Press.

Du Bois, C. 1961. *The People of Alor*. 2 vols. New York: Harper and Row. (Original work, published 1944).

Durkheim, E. 1965. *The Elementary Forms of the Religious Life*. New York: Free Press.

Erikson, E. H. 1950. *Childhood and Society*. New York: W. W. Norton.

Freud, A. 1936. *The Ego and the Mechanisms of Defense*. New York: International Universities Press.

Freud, S. 1900. *The Interpretation of Dreams*. London and New York: Hogarth. *Standard Edition* vols. 4, 5 (1955).

———. 1905. *Three Essays on the Theory of Sexuality*. London and New York: Hogarth. *Standard Edition*, vol. 7 (1949).

———. 1913. *Totem and Taboo*. London and New York: Hogarth. *Standard Edition*, vol. 13.

———. 1923. *The Ego and the Id*. London and New York: Hogarth. *Standard Edition*, vol. 19 (1962).

Fromm, E. 1941. *Escape from Freedom*. New York: Farrar and Rinehart.

Gorer, G. 1955. *Exploring English Character*. New York: Criterion Books.

———. 1964. *The American People*. New York: Norton.

Gorer, G., and J. Rickman. 1962. *The People of Great Russia*. New York: Norton.

Hallowell, A. I. 1955. *Culture and Experience*. Philadelphia: University of Pennsylvania Press.

Harris, M. 1968. *The Rise of Anthropological Theory*. New York: Crowell.

Honigmann, J. J. 1954. *Culture and Personality*. New York: Harper and Row.

Hsu, F.L.K. 1961. *Clan, Caste, and Club: A Comparative Study of Chinese, Hindu, and American Ways of Life*. Princeton: Van Nostrand.

———. 1970. *Americans and Chinese: Two Ways of Life*. New York: Doubleday and Natural History Press.

Kardiner, A., with R. Linton. 1939. *The Individual and His Society*. New York: Columbia University Press.

Kardiner, A., with R. Linton, C. Du Bois, and J. West. 1945. *The Psychological Frontiers of Society*. New York: Columbia University Press.

LeBarre, W. 1972. *The Ghost Dance*. New York: Delta.

———. 1980. The Clinic and the Field. In G. D. Spindler, ed., *The Making of Psychological Anthropology*. Berkeley: University of California Press.

LeVine, R. 1982. *Culture, Behavior, and Personality*. 2nd ed. Chicago: Aldine.

Malinowski, B. 1944. *A Scientific Theory of Culture, and Other Essays*. Chapel Hill: University of North Carolina Press.

———. 1948. *Magic, Science and Religion, and Other Essays*. Ed. R. Redfield. New York: Free Press.

———. 1959. *Sex and Repression in Savage Society*. New York: Meridan Books.

Manson, W. 1988. *The Psychodynamics of Culture*. Connecticut: Greenwood Press.

Mead, M. 1928. *Coming of Age in Samoa*. New York: Morrow.

———. 1939. *From the South Seas*. New York: Morrow.

———. 1942. *And Keep Your Powder Dry*. New York: Morrow.

———. 1949. *Male and Female: A Study of the Sexes in a Changing World*. New York: Morrow.

———. 1950. *Sex and Temperament in Three Primitive Societies*. New York: New American Library, Mentor Books.

———. 1953. National Character. Pp. 642–67 in A. L. Kroeber, ed., *Anthropology Today*. Chicago: University of Chicago Press.

Métraux, R., and M. Mead. 1954. *Themes in French Culture*. Stanford, CA: Stanford University Press.

Paul, R. A. 1989. Psychoanalytic Anthropology. *Annual Review of Anthropology* 18:177–244.

Riesman, D., with N. Glazer and R. Denney. 1961. *The Lonely Crowd*. New Haven: Yale University Press. (Original work published 1950.)

Sapir, E. 1917. Do We Need a Superorganic? *American Anthropologist* 19:441–47.

———. 1956. *Culture, Language, and Personality: Selected Essays*. Ed. D. Mandelbaum. Berkeley: University of California Press.

Scheper-Hughes, N. 1992. *Death without Weeping*. Berkeley: University of California Press.

Singer, M. 1961. A Survey of Culture and Personality Theory and Research. Pp. 9–90 in B. Kaplan, ed., *Studying Personality Cross-Culturally*. New York: Harper and Row.

Spindler, G. D., ed. 1980. *The Making of Psychological Anthropology*. Berkeley: University of California Press.

Spiro, M. E. 1952. Ghosts, Ifaluk, and Teleological Functionalism. *American Anthropologist* 54: 497–503.

———. 1958. *Children of the Kibbutz*. Cambridge, MA: Harvard University Press.

———. 1965. Religious Systems as Culturally Constituted Defense Mechanisms. Pp. 100–113 in M. E. Spiro, ed., *Context and Meaning in Cultural Anthropology*. New York: Free Press.

———. 1979. *Gender and Culture: Kibbutz Women Revisited*. Durham, NC: Duke University Press.

———. 1982. *Oedipus in the Trobriands*. Chicago: University of Chicago Press.

———. 1987. *Culture and Human Nature: Theoretical Papers of Melford E. Spiro*. Ed. B.Kilbourne and L. L. Langness. Chicago: University of Chicago Press.

Wallace, A.F.C. 1952. *The Modal Personality Structure of the Tuscarora Indians as Revealed by the Rorschach Test*. Bureau of American Ethnology Bulletin 150. Washington, DC: Smithsonian Institution.

———. 1970. *Culture and Personality*. 2nd ed. New York: Random House.

———. 1980. Basic Studies, Applied Projects, and Eventual Implementation. Pp. 203–16 in G. D. Spindler, ed., *The Making of Psychological Anthropology*. Berkeley: University of California Press.

Whiting, J.W.M., and I. L. Child. 1953. *Child Training and Personality: A Cross-Cultural Study*. New Haven: Yale University Press.

Whiting, J.W.M., R. Kluckhohn, and A. Anthony. 1958. The Function of Male Initiation Ceremonies at Puberty. Pp. 359–70 in E. Maccoby, T. Newcomb, and E. Hartley, eds., *Readings in Social Psychology*. 3rd ed. New York: Holt.

CHAPTER TWO

CROSS-CULTURAL COMPARISONS IN PSYCHOLOGICAL ANTHROPOLOGY

Alice Schlegel

The dialogue between psychology and anthropology was a lively one in earlier years of this century. Anthropologists back from the field, where they had come to know not only ''cultures'' but also the persons who lived them, were eager for theories and methods that would help to explain the variations between and within cultures. Some psychologists were quick to pick up on the vast expansion of the human laboratory that anthropology offered. This exchange resulted in the subdisciplinary orientations of psychological anthropology and cross-cultural psychology. The early results of this dialogue were based on the premise that features of culture mold personality. Appropriately, the writings in this genre have come to be known as the Culture and Personality school (see the chapter by Steven Piker in this volume). One long-lasting contribution of this approach was to challenge and refine the deterministic hypotheses of both the biological and the psychoanalytical movements in psychology.[1]

Child-training practices and the other ways in which messages about cultural expectations were conveyed from adults to children soon came to be seen as the link between culture and personality. Psychoanalyst Abram Kardiner and anthropologist Ralph Linton (Kardiner 1939, 1945) devised a model of personality development that connected the environment, at one pole, to secondary institutions such as symbols and beliefs, at the other. The intervening stages were the primary cultural institutions, those necessary for survival, and the child-rearing practices affected by them—the ways in which infants and young children were disciplined, gratified, and inhibited.

Few anthropologists were willing to accept an unmodified version of psychoanalytic psychology, but no anthropologist concerned with personality could overlook its impact. With its premise that the child is the father of the man,

Freudian psychology provided the theory that allowed observers to explain the interpersonal and expressive behavior of their subjects. From being a peripheral category, barely noticed by students of culture, children became an object of study. Child training was assumed to be the cause of adult behavior, and culturally established methods of treatment and training were believed to account for similarities or at least common understandings among members of a culture. Emphasis was put on the areas that Freud had established as critical points in early human development: feeding and weaning (the oral stage), toilet training (the anal stage), sexual socialization (the genital stage), and parent-child relations (the Oedipus complex). General neglect of child training beyond puberty is probably due to the fact that earlier analytic psychology assumed that by puberty the child had reached the psychologically mature "genital" stage.

Most of the early Culture and Personality research was centered at Columbia University, where Margaret Mead, Ruth Benedict, and Abram Kardiner were major figures in the 1920s and 1930s. In the years following World War II, psychology was taking a new direction, and anthropologists responded to its lead. Behavioral psychology was the new wave, although analytic psychology still appeared in the theoretical tool kit of all but the most rigid behaviorists. Followers of this research strategy did not attempt to interpret the personalities or read the minds of their subjects; rather, they measured observable behavior and used these measures as quantitative data for testing their hypotheses.

Two major interdisciplinary efforts at that time brought together behavioral psychologists, anthropologists, and sociologists to work on theories of human behavior. It was at the Department of Social Relations at Harvard and the Institute of Human Relations at Yale that some of the most important work in psychological anthropology of the 1940s and 1950s was done. An important link between these institutions is John Whiting, who was trained at Yale in the 1940s and took a faculty position at Harvard in the following decade. He has remained at Harvard since that time, working in collaboration with his wife Beatrice B. Whiting. They and some of their students have been leaders in comparative studies of child rearing and behavior.

The year 1953 saw the publication of a landmark study combining the psychoanalytic and behavioral approaches to socialization, *Child Training and Personality*. In the introduction, John Whiting and his coauthor, the psychologist Irvin Child, acknowledged their debt to Clark Hull, a leader in learning and behavior theory, as well as to other psychologists of this persuasion. From their analysts, John Dollard and Earl Zinn, they learned about the dynamics of personality development through the lens of psychoanalysis. They stated the following position (Whiting and Child 1953:2–3):

> We will deal with personality processes as mediating between certain aspects of culture which lead to them and others to which they in turn lead. Specifically we have taken child training practices and customary responses to illness as the two aspects of culture which are mediated by principles of personality development.

Their independent variables, those they believed to be the causes, are behaviors related to oral, anal, sexual, dependence, and aggression socialization, while their dependent variables, those they believed to be the result of training practices, are beliefs about the causes of illness. They used data on socialization to test hypotheses, some of which were supported by the statistical correlations.

The method used by Whiting and Child had been developed at Yale by George Peter Murdock. It involved coding data from a large number of ethnographies and subjecting the coded data to statistical analysis. This method grew out of Murdock's interest in testing theories of society, his fascination with probability theory (G. P. Murdock, personal communication, 1978), and his understanding that a large assemblage of ethnographic accounts could be put to use to test theories in ways that single cases could not. The cross-cultural method that he pioneered in America and developed as a widely used research method will be discussed later.

COMPARATIVE METHODS

Theory testing was the goal of most psychological anthropology in the 1960s and 1970s. One negative result may be sufficient to disprove a theory that claims universality, but it is not enough to discredit a tendency, nor does one positive result constitute proof. It was clear that systematic multiple observations were necessary. There are several ways that these observations can be made. One way is to make systematic multiple observations within single society, thus ascertaining within-culture (or interindividual) variation. This method is commonplace for psychologists and sociologists, but many anthropologists generalize about a culture from unsystematic observations or informant statements. While such generalizations may be appropriate for discussions about "culture," that is, normative behaviors and expectations, they do not capture the range of actual behavior and expectations.

Several research techniques exist for overcoming this difficulty. Basically, they fall into two types: the closed observation, where the classification is built into the observations, and the open observation, where the researcher constructs a code for classifying the naturalistic observation. Closed observations include such techniques as the closed-end questionnaire, card sorting, and the various paper-and-pencil tests that informants may take. Open observations include time-allocation studies, spot observations, assessment of visual materials by either the researcher or the informant (e.g., the thematic apperception test [TAT] and Rorschach test), and open-ended questionnaires or interviews. Some of these techniques are described and discussed in Bernard (1988) and in the chapter by Ruth Munroe and Robert Munroe in this volume. Robert LeVine's (1966) study of achievement motivation among Nigerian youth exemplifies an early attempt by an anthropologist to systematize observations or personality features; Ralph Bolton's (1973) study of aggression ingeniously combined medical information with data on personality.

When systematic intracultural observation is combined with cross-cultural observation, that is, when several cultures are selected to provide a set of samples, the power of the study increases as the cultures themselves become variables. Two examples of such studies are relevant to psychological anthropology.

In 1961–62, a team of five anthropologists and one geographer conducted field research in four African tribes, the Pokot, Sebei, Kambe, and Hehe, as part of the Culture and Ecology in East Africa Project under the auspices of the University of California, Los Angeles (Edgerton 1971). Each of these tribes contained some communities that depended on horticulture and some that were pastoralist. A total of over five hundred men and women were interviewed and gave responses to visual material designed to elicit themes and values. Their responses were coded and analyzed according to content analysis categories that included such features as affection, depression, fatalism, hatred, hostility to opposite sex, self-control, and valuation of independence. Within-culture and across-culture comparisons showed both differences among the cultures and a contrast between all the farming and all the pastoral communities; however, women's and men's responses within cultures and subsistence types were strikingly similar.

Another major study of this general type is the Six Cultures Project, initiated by Irvin Child, William Lambert, and John Whiting. This project, begun in 1953, has had an impact on socialization studies up to the present. Teams of anthropologists and psychologists went to six different field sites, including one American town. These teams made detailed observations of child-rearing practices and behavior. The result was six ethnographies of child rearing, one by each team (compiled in B. Whiting 1963). A number of papers and doctoral dissertations also grew out of the project. The major works synthesizing the data have been *Mothers of Six Cultures* (Minturn and Lambert 1964) and *Children of Six Cultures* (Whiting and Whiting 1975).

A third way of providing systematic multiple observations is for each culture to be treated as a single case. This presupposes that there is uniformity within each case: X either has early or harsh weaning or it does not. Strictly speaking, this means that it is usual for X mothers to wean their infants before such and such an age or to combine weaning with practices that distress or discomfort the child. The small-scale comparative study that is appropriate for theory testing is the controlled comparison, in which two or more societies to be compared are very much alike in all but the variables under examination, so that there is a strong likelihood that it is the independent variables and not some other features that account for the cultural differences to be explained, the dependent variables.

This method was championed by A. R. Radcliffe-Brown, who introduced it into the United States when he taught at the University of Chicago (cf. Eggan 1961). One well-known study, written by a British social anthropologist, is S. F. Nadel's (1967) "Witchcraft in Four African Societies: An Essay in Comparison." Nadel compared two pairs of societies—the Nupe and Gwari of Nigeria and the Korongo and Mesakin of the central Sudan—on their witchcraft beliefs. He claimed to find the cause for the intense witchcraft beliefs of the Nupe and Mesakin in social tensions: within-marriage relations among the Nupe, and the relationship between mother's brother and sister's son among the Mesakin. True to the anti-Freudian bias of British social anthropology, he specifically disclaimed the idea that witchcraft beliefs arise from early experiences, locating them rather in the current situations of their adult carriers.

Let me play devil's advocate. While I tend to be more partial to situational than to psychogenic explanations, Nadel left himself open to alternative explanations of his data. In the case of the Mesakin, Nadel did not give us enough information to understand why older men should be so envious of the youth of their juniors, especially their sisters' sons, that they would want to bewitch them. The relationship between mother's brother and sister's son in this matrilineal society may account for the direction in which witchcraft accusations are channeled, but it is not a convincing explanation for the cause of the Mesakin's witchcraft-ridden ideology.

In the case of the Nupe, Nadel did provide enough information on early experience to allow us to challenge his situational explanation for their witchcraft belief, which is that an older woman victimizes a younger man, while men have the power to block women's witchery but may choose not to do so. Nadel found the model for this belief in Nupe family organization. Husbands resent the economic success in trading ventures of their wives, to whom they may be in debt, and project their resentment against women in this fashion. They see themselves as both the victims and the masters of women's witchcraft.

However, Nadel also told us that the mothers of very young children often leave them to go on trading expeditions. Fathers resent this "abandonment" but often depend economically on wives' trading. An alternative model for Nupe witchcraft is the powerful abandoning mother and the father who can either prevent her abandonment or stand helplessly by. Without more information than Nadel gave in his brief ethnographic sketch, it is impossible to decide between sociogenic and psychogenic explanations for this aspect of expressive culture.

The controlled comparison has been used relatively little by psychological anthropologists, yet it lends itself to fine-grained studies of cultural differences, for example, between neighboring ethnic groups or between a local group and its emigrants who have relocated. A variant of this method would be to assemble a group of disparate cultures that had one feature in common, say nonviolence, and to compare each with a similar, preferably neighboring, culture that exhibited a high degree of violence to detect and eliminate features that might account for the differing predilections.

A widely used method in psychological anthropology has been the cross-cultural method, developed by George Peter Murdock from antecedents in Great Britain and the Netherlands. This method is the opposite of the controlled comparison; whereas the latter selects similar cultures and looks for differences, the cross-cultural method assembles a sample of unlike cultures to find common causes and effects in spite of the differences among them. This deliberate ignoring of context has disturbed the many anthropologists who criticize this method, asserting that cultural features can only be understood within their cultural contexts. That may well be, but such an argument does not vitiate the method, for the purpose is not to "understand" the features of a culture, to determine how they are interpreted by its members, nor to trace their history; rather, the goal is to explain why these features came to be. By discovering the function of the cultural feature under examination, the investigator hopes to determine its cause.

THE CROSS-CULTURAL METHOD

The cross-cultural method tests theory by establishing statistically significant associations between and among variables such that one could be said to cause the other, or all could be the result of a common cause. The method is built on the premise that social facts are knowable and can be explained, that is, the social world follows "laws" as does the natural world. Over the years, users of the method have spoken less of social laws and more about tendencies, and students are warned from the beginning that correlations do not prove cause, so that the hopes of the early developers of the method to establish a science of society comparable to natural science have been somewhat modified. Nevertheless, comparison is the closest method anthropology has to experimentation in the natural sciences. This method allows for the large array of naturally occurring cases, individual cultures, to be utilized. There is a large literature on this method; basic instruction can be found in Naroll, Michik, and Naroll (1976). What follows is a few words on procedure.

The Problem

The problem to be studied has to be amenable to reduction into operationalized terms. The cultural variables that will be tested are measures of the social or psychological aspects of interest. For example, one might be interested in knowing whether poor maternal care is an antecedent of fear of female ghosts. "Poor maternal care" can be operationalized as harsh weaning practices, physical punishment by fear or by physical means, lack of attention to a child's needs, or any number of other measures. Of all possible measures, the ones chosen have to be those likely to be mentioned in ethnographies; otherwise, there will be too few cases of societies with information to allow for testing.

The Sample

There is no perfect sample of cultures, as the parameters of the universe from which the sample is drawn—all human cultures—are unknown and unknowable. Even if one were to take the universe of all human cultures at one point in time, say 1600, the cultures on which there was information would be incomplete and probably unrepresentative of the total universe. Even limiting the universe to preindustrial cultures on which there is adequate information presents a daunting task. The comparativist, therefore, must rely on a sample.

The purpose of a sample, of course, is to be representative of the universe to which the results of the study apply. Statistical purists insist that a sample be random, on the grounds that statistical tests of significance are not appropriate to other kinds of samples. However, cultures are not independent units; because of diffusion or common origin, neighboring cultures are in most cases more like one another than they are like cultures at great distances. The solution Murdock (1966) suggested, and the one he had applied in constructing the World Ethnographic Sample of 565 cultures, is to stratify the sample by geographic area. In this way, one avoids selecting close neighbors and also ensures that all world regions are equally represented. A later and more workable version of this, the Standard Cross-Cultural Sample of 186 cultures (Murdock and White 1980, first published in 1969), has been widely used in the preparation of codes and for testing hypotheses.

Coding

If the variables to be tested have been adequately operationalized, it would seem that coding from the ethnographic literature should be a fairly mechanical process. This is almost never the case. First, the operationalized variables themselves have to be carefully defined; thus the variable "harsh weaning practices" includes a range of behaviors like threats, punishment, unpleasant substances, ignoring by the mother, or anything else that frightens or discomfits the infant. Coders have to test the code; and if there is more than one coder, they have to work together to arrive at common understandings of the code. Codes that measure personality traits or dispositions through variables such as behaviors or socialization pressures are among the most complex and require the greatest degree of coder training (for an example, see Barry et al. 1980).

Testing

Statistical testing procedures depend on the type of the data, whether nominal, ordinal, or interval, and the quantity. Much of the analysis is bivariate; multivariate and linear regression analyses are often impossible because of the small number of societies with information on the selected variable. For example, one might be interested in the relationship among variables X, Y, and Z, but perhaps one-third of the sample has information on X and Y, one-third on Y and Z, and one-third on X and Z.

Interpreting the Results

The conscientious cross-cultural researcher understands that results, even those that support a hypothesis, can be interpreted in various ways, and that it is necessary to consider alternative explanations for positive (or negative) results. The analysis of deviant cases, those that do not conform to the pattern of association, is often illuminating and may allow the researcher to refine the hypothesis.

Triangulation

Social scientists often advocate triangulation, or the replication of the study by another method, as a means for checking results. The cross-cultural method is a useful method for testing hypotheses generated by or tested in single-case studies. Field-based studies, similarly, are useful for checking and developing further the investigations of cross-cultural research. John M. Roberts, whose work I shall discuss later, recommended that he called "subsystem validation," the within-culture test as a validation of the cross-cultural test. Triangulation often occurs spontaneously when people with different research methods, even scholars from different disciplines, work on similar or related problems.

Cross-cultural studies have been conducted on a number of topics that are directly psychological or have psychological aspects, such as adolescent initiation ceremonies (see the chapter by Simon Ottenberg in this volume), aggression, alcohol use, the couvade, father absence, sleeping arrangements, taboos concerned with reproduction (for example, menstrual, pregnancy, and postpartum taboos), taboos concerned with the ingestion of food or other substances, and other kinds of taboos (cf. Levinson and Malone 1980). I shall comment on three bodies of research to illustrate different approaches in psychological anthropology.

THE INCEST TABOO

It was received wisdom in nineteenth-century Western thought that all human societies tabooed all forms of incest, whereas animals bred indiscriminately. As it happens, both of these assumptions are false. Even if incest is minimally defined as sexual intercourse with a parent, child, or sibling, ethnographic evidence shows that incest is not limited to depraved or insane persons, as sibling marriage under specified conditions was practiced and culturally approved in a range of societies (see Goggin and Sturtevant 1964). Studies of animal behavior indicate that sexually reproducing animal species avoid close inbreeding by means of a number of mechanisms, from genetically determined repulsion of close kin to the practice of one sex or both leaving the natal group upon reaching reproductive age. Nevertheless, all human societies restrict unregulated mating between close kin, with rare exceptions, allowing incestuous marriage or extramarital sexual relations to certain categories such as royalty or chiefly families or cross-sex twins.

There are two phenomena to be explained here. One phenomenon is behavioral, the avoidance of sexual relations with close kin. This is extremely widespread and probably can be explained by the same argument that explains the existence of two sexes: increased fitness through genetic diversity. The other phenomenon is cultural: the incest taboo or set of beliefs that defines the prohibited kin, the consequences of violating the taboo, and the degree of evil attached to violating it, and that often gives some mythological reason for the taboo's existence. Most discussions of the incest taboo have conflated these phenomena. For clarity's sake I shall use "incest avoidance" to refer to this behavior and "incest taboo" to refer to the beliefs surrounding incest.

The two major theories that have informed subsequent discussions of the taboo originated with Freud (1950; originally published in 1913) and Westermarck (1902). Freud regarded the taboo as a defensive reaction against the Oedipus complex: fear of punishment by the same-sex parent for the child's desire for the opposite-sex parent and for the jealousy and hostility the child feels toward the same-sex parent cause desire to be repressed. The taboo is the reaction against the forbidden impulse. Westermarck (1894) believed that there was innate revulsion against sexual relations with close kin, that extreme familiarity since childhood reduced sexual interest. Malinowski (1927), who challenged the universality of the Oedipus complex, asserted that incest was tabooed because sexual competition within the family would cause jealousy and tension. This theory has not aroused much interest in later researchers. Fox (1962) attempted a synthesis of Freud's and Westermarck's theories.

The incest taboo was among the cultural facts of kinship and social organization surveyed by Murdock in his path-breaking *Social Structure* (1949). Among the 250 preindustrial societies surveyed, he found the taboo to be universally applied to the nuclear family, with some exceptions as noted previously, and to contain some extensions beyond the nuclear family. He found that extensions varied according to the type of descent system, whether patrilineal, matrilineal, double, or bilateal. While his data did not explain the origin of the taboo, they did allow him to generalize about the plasticity of human sexual behavior, amenable to cultural molding. Murdock believed that the taboo functioned to inhibit sexual relations within the family, which would otherwise occur, since "the approach responses which a child learns to make toward the parent or sibling of the opposite sex . . . will tend to be more and more specifically sexual and to be strengthened by generalization from other reinforced responses" (Murdock 1949:293). Without the repression of these responses by others indoctrinated with the taboo, the result would be familial incest. In other words, Murdock, like Freud, saw the incest taboo as the cause of incest avoidance. He did not, however, comment on the need for such avoidance except to remark that sexual relationships between parents and children would destroy the authority of the former. This says nothing about sibling incest; furthermore, it can be pointed out that sexual relationships with concubines or slaves do not destroy the authority of the master.

A major cross-cultural study focusing on the incest taboo was conducted by Yehudi Cohen (1964) on a sample of sixty-five preindustrial societies. He hypothesized that the incest taboo functions to preserve what he called "privacy," or the freedom from extreme emotional and physical stimulation (Cohen 1964: 161). Commenting on the effects of crowding and overstimulation in animal populations, and the tendency in most societies to provide some relief from constant interaction (menstrual huts, solitary hunting trips, or even ignoring others), he asserted that humans need to maintain some balance between stimulation and privacy. The taboo protects children and adult family members from the additional emotional load that sexuality would add to an already emotionally intense relationship. He implied that this psychological need is part of our biological makeup. It is noteworthy that neither Freud nor Westermarck are cited in Cohen's bibliography.

Like Murdock, Ember (1983) saw the incest taboo functioning to inhibit incest, which was necessary to avoid the genetically deleterious effects of close inbreeding. In a cross-cultural study, he found that the extension of the taboo to first cousins was more likely to occur in communities with lower population densities. He interpreted this as a mechanism for ensuring outbreeding. In populations with higher densities, first-cousin marriage could be permitted because a relatively smaller number of marriages would be of this type, given a larger marriage pool, and the general level of inbreeding would be lower. The incest taboo then becomes the proximal cause for incest avoidance, the final cause being the deleterious effects of inbreeding.

About the time that Ember's paper was first published, a great deal of research was being done on incest avoidance by ethologists and a few anthropologists. Interest in this subject was fueled by increasing publicity given to sexual abuse of children, especially by fathers or stepfathers. In this research, the Freudian hypothesis seems to have faded away, while Westermarck's gained new currency.

Seymour Parker (1976), an anthropologist, noted that a crucial factor inhibiting sexual behavior toward children by adults is not whether the adult is a parent or a stepparent but whether the adult was intimately involved in the child's rearing. In other words, early intimacy does discourage at least the expression of sexual interest in the child. Norbert Bischof (1975), an ethological psychologist, spoke of the "surfeit response" of the child to overly familiar stimuli. (This is much like Cohen's [1964] theory of privacy, discussed earlier). Such theories remove incest avoidance from the cultural realm and place them squarely within the psychological.

It would be difficult to categorize just where sexual separation within the family, as a mechanisms for inhibiting incest, belongs. Is the human family—involving at least one bonded (and usually mated) cross-sex pair along with sexually mature and immature children—cultural? Is is an inherited behavior pattern of our species and therefore within the biological realm? Or is it a response to human needs for attachment and therefore psychological? Such questions illustrate the futility of attempting to separate mind, body, and society where some of the major questions of human behavior are concerned.

However one categorizes sexual separation, it was noted as a widespread feature of adolescent life by Alice Schlegel and Herbert Barry (1991) in our cross-cultural study of adolescence. Even before adolescence, there is a tendency for children to associate more with other children of the same rather than the opposite sex. By adolescence, sexual separation is fairly marked and extends into the family, where both girls and boys associate more with family members of their own sex than those of the opposite sex. Schlegel and Barry hypothesized that whatever other functions this separation serves, it does create some distance between opposite-sex family members, which in turn reduces the opportunity for sexual relations.

We still have not answered the question of the origin of the incest taboo as a set of beliefs about proper behavior. One way of looking at it is as a cultural reinforcement of a ''natural'' tendency in humans. In this, it would be much like the horror felt at matricide and patricide. No one believes that most people want to kill their parents and are inhibited only by strong taboos against this act. The incest taboo, of course, is of another order, for it taboos what is pleasurable and in other circumstances is appropriate within intimate relationships, not what is violent and destructive. Nevertheless, we do not have to assume that taboos exist only to prevent people from doing what they would otherwise want to do.

For all the attention that the incest taboo has attracted, very little has been done to explain the culturally variable extensions of it. Ember (1983), noted earlier, hypothesized demographic reasons for its extension to first cousins. Goody (1983) argued that the extensions of the taboo–the interdiction of marriage—to more and more distant kin imposed by the Catholic church in pre-Reformation Europe was motivated by the church's desire to limit marriage. The purpose was to limit progency and assure that the church would be an heir. Whatever one might think of this hypothesis of greed as the motivation for extending restrictions, it does point out one fact generally overlooked, which is that taboos are created by people for reasons. In other words, the cultural variations of the incest taboo, to whom it is extended, might be understood if we knew what positions or institutions stood to benefit from particular prohibitions or permissions.

Still another problem has been the scope of the taboo, or how intensely it is felt. Murdock (1949) pointed out that sexual relations with close prohibited kin were interdicted more strongly than those with more distant prohibited kin. However, sexual relations are often considered to be worse with some categories of kin than with others. The only cross-cultural test of this form of cultural variability that I know of is one I conducted (Schlegel 1927) on a small sample of matrilineal societies. Controlling for descent type, I hypothesized that father-daughter incest is considered worse where husbands dominate wives, and brother-sister incest is worse where brothers dominate adult sisters.

Although the sample was small, twenty-seven cases, the findings were significant, $p = .005$ by Fisher's Exact Test. I gave two alternative explanations for this. The first was that the strength of the taboo serves to inhibit the dominant male from using his dominance to take advantage of the subordinate female, his sister in one case and his wife's (and his own) daughter in the other. The second was that the superordinate male is actually attractive to the subordinate female, who may unconsciously act seductively toward him as a way of ameliorating his dominance. The taboo, in this case, prevents a sexual response.

I have heard this notion referred to as the "blame the victim" theory of incest. This is a misinterpretation. In no sense do I imply that the seductiveness is conscious. Seductive behaviors such as deference, praise, and flattery are often characteristics of subordinates in relation to superordinates, whether in sexual courtship on the part of the one who wants the sexual favor or in nonerotic situations. Seductiveness toward powerful family members seems to me to be a normal feature of family life; the strong incest taboo warns the recipient against giving this a sexual interpretation or response. Taggart (1992) has found supportive evidence for the association between dominance and the direction of the incest taboo from a comparison of folktales in two Spanish-speaking communities.

In recent years, interest in incest has almost entirely switched from the taboo to the avoidance of incest. This neglect is unfortunate, for even if the taboo has some basis in material reality—as symbolic nd ritual behaviors often have—the taboo itself and its variants are not explained by incest avoidance. The subject is still an open field. For a comprehensive summary of recent work on incest avoidance, see Erickson (1989).

GAMES

The study of games languished in the backwaters of anthropology and psychology, neglected in comparison with other aspects of expressive culture like folktales, until it was rescued, individually and collaboratively, by John M. Roberts (anthropologist) and Brian Sutton-Smith (psychologist). Sutton-Smith (1989) told the story of their separate interests and how they came to coauthor cross-cultural and other studies of games.

Systematic cross-cultural research on games began with a paper by Roberts, Arth, and Bush (1959), "Games in Culture," published in the *American Anthropologist.* Limiting themselves to competitive games with winners and losers, they classified games into three major types—physical skill, chance, and strategy—and found that worldwide distribution is not random. Games of physical skill are the major type in societies that depend on physical skills such as hunting; games of chance are important where there is a high degree of unpredictability in subsistence level and "luck" or magic are relied on; and games of strategy appear in complex societies that emphasize obedience and achievement.

In this brief article, Roberts and his coauthors were not as explicit about their theoretical foundations as were Whiting and Child (1953) in their study of child training and beliefs, although the two studies arose out of the same background, a combination of depth psychology and social learning theory. Roberts, Arth, and Bush (1959:604) stated: "In general, this paper supports the psychoanalytic notion that games are exercises in mastery." They suggested that a preliminary investigation of child-training variables shows that games of physical skill are an attempt at mastery of the self and the environment, related to self-reliance; games of chance attempt mastery of the supernatural; and games of strategy attempt mastery of the social environment. (The concept of mastery originated in Freud's belief in children's play as an attempt to master areas in which there was conflict or anxiety.)

Out of this evolved the conflict-enculturation hypothesis (cf. Roberts and Sutton-Smith 1962). This holds that conflict engendered by child-training practices, in that one is both rewarded and punished for interest in certain behaviors, leads to an interest in expressive activities, such as games, that transfer this conflict to socially useful behavior (Sutton-Smith 1989). In a linear progression of causes reminiscent of that envisioned by Whiting and Child, Roberts and Sutton-Smith saw child-rearing practices as leading to conflicts, conflicts leading to an interest and involvement in activities that model the conflicts, and this involvement finally leading to mastery via a process that they called "buffered learning." Sutton-Smith (1989:10–11) noted that they relied on a "*post-Freudian, social-learning displacement* notion of conflict" influenced by "*Berlyne's conflict arousal and curiosity*" and "*Miller's displacement paradigm*" (italics in the original).

The enculturation aspect of this theoretical framework defines games as models of cultural power relationships, whereby success is achieved through force (physical skill), magical power (chance), or cleverness (strategy). Sutton-Smith (1989:5) stated: "We figured that children learned in games all those necessary arts of trickery, deception, and foul play that their teachers will not teach them, but that are most important in successful marriage, business, and war."

Roberts carried his interest in these three styles of games further, developing a triad of action-styles and decision making that he called the potent, the fortunist, and the strategist. He worked with several subsequent collaborators on studies of these varying styles of game play or other activities (for a review, see Chick 1984). I well remember his conversations about how one's airplane-piloting or car-driving style indicates whether one is a potent, a fortunist, or a strategist, and what kinds of combinations make for winning teams in car rallies, business, and marriage.

In their classic paper "Child Training and Game Involvement," Roberts and Sutton-Smith (1962) found that games of physical skill are associated with training that emphasizes achievement, while games of strategy are associated with obedience training. This paper also contained a subsystem replication, utilizing data on game preferences of 1,900 American schoolchildren. They found that along with many games that are played equally by both sexes (most of them games of strategy or strategy combined with physical skill), boys significantly prefer games of physical skill and a number of games of mixed strategy and physical skill, whereas girls prefer games of pure strategy or chance. They accounted for this by the greater obedience training that girls receive.

Another direct linkage between child-training practices and game types was found in a cross-cultural study by Barry and Roberts (1972). Focusing on games of chance, they found associations with social isolation of infants, who sleep apart from their mothers, are transported in rigid carrying devices, and are rarely held or fondled. However, their needs are met, and they are not abused or neglected. These practices engender conflicting feelings of both dependency and omnipotence and a belief in the world as beyond direct human control.

Critics of this approach have not been lacking (cf. Schwartzman 1978), and Sutton-Smith himself (1989) would now take a more symbolically oriented, textually sensitive approach. The model, however, was theoretically powerful, as indicated by the many studies by Roberts and other social scientists who used it. It cannot be neglected in any serious study of games, particularly studies that attempt to explain the nonrandom distribution of games worldwide.

CHILD SOCIALIZATION

Large-scale comparative studies of child socialization have been largely of two types, the multisite study and the cross-cultural study. The first type has been associated primarily with John and Beatrice Whiting and their students and collaborators. While John Whiting, along with Irvin Child, pioneered the use of cross-cultural research on child socialization in *Child Training and Personality* (1953), he moved on to the multisite comparative method. I have already mentioned the Six Cultures Project, the most ambitious of this type.

The underlying model for most comparative studies of child socialization has been one that assumes a linear causal chain from natural and social environment to adult personality and its expression in behavior or in expressive culture such as folktales and religious beliefs. This model was first enunciated by Kardiner (1939). "Primary institutions" are those that form the basic personality structure and include everything from family structure and subsistence patterns to child-rearing practices. The basic personality structure expresses itself in the "secondary institutions," projections of or defenses against needs created by the primary ones. Whiting and Child (1953) modified this: maintenance systems → child-training practices → personality variables → projective systems. A later version of this (J. Whiting 1977) altered the category of "child-training practices" to "child's learning environment," putting more emphasis on the total setting and less on specific socialization techniques.

An important contributor to cross-cultural research on child socialization has been the psychologist Herbert Barry. His early work with psychologists Irvin Child and Margaret Bacon included studies of child training; one of them, ''The Relation of Child Training to Subsistence Economy'' (Barry, Child, and Bacon 1959), was named a Citation Classic in 1986 as one of the most frequently cited papers in the social science literature. Working with coders at the Cumulative Cross-Cultural Coding Center, established in the Department of Anthropology at the University of Pittsburgh under the direction of G. P. Murdock and John M. Roberts, Barry oversaw the construction of three codes on child training that have been widely used. (These are collected in Barry and Schlegel [1980]).

It is clear from this discussion that in the comparative study of socialization, close collaboration and intellectual cross-fertilization between anthropology and social and developmental psychology have occurred. One such research team consists of Ruth Munroe (psychologist) and Robert L. Munroe (anthropologist), who have studied the behavior of children in a number of societies. For example, in one multisite study of child behavior in four cultures (Munroe, Munroe, and Shimmin 1984), they found that the amount of time children spend on productive labor is a consequence of the family's labor needs. As a consequence of child labor patterns, children who work are more responsible and ''businesslike,'' even when they are not working, than children who do not work.

In the preface to *Children of Six Cultures*, Whiting and Whiting (1975) related that they became disenchanted with the cross-cultural method when many of the hypotheses tested in Whiting and Child (1953) were not confirmed. They did not know whether lack of confirmation was due to false assumptions or to the unsystematic and often inadequate reporting on behavior in the ethnographies. To overcome this frustration, John Whiting joined with Irvin Child and William Lambert to develop the Six Cultures Project, noted earlier, with Beatrice Whiting as coordinator. *Children of Six Cultures* described this project and synthesized the data on children.

The method used was to make five-minute spot observations of target children's social interactions, no more than one a day per child. The total number of children in the six communities was 134. The behavior protocols were then coded by trained coders according to a set of acts, such as ''offers support'' and ''seeks assistance.'' The final analysis dealt with twelve acts, and the final data set consisted of 9,581 separate acts.

One kind of analysis was multidimensional scaling, which showed an association between behavior and cultural features. Children in simpler cultures were higher on the *nurturant-responsible* end of the dimension, while children in more complex cultures were higher on the *dominance-dependence* end. The Whitings attributed this to requirements that children in simpler cultures work more. (It would have been interesting to have included a foraging society, as children in these societies frequently contribute very little labor to the household.) Another association appeared between behavior and the household type. In cultures with nuclear-family households, children were higher on the *acts sociably* and *touches* end of the dimension, while in the patrilineal extended-family households, children were higher on the *assaults* and *reprimands* end. (There were no matrilocal or stem-family households in the sample. Stem-family households may produce a different kind of profile, as I shall discuss later.)

Behavior scores were sorted by sex and age of child for each culture. The consistent findings were that girls are somewhat more intimate-dependent and nurturant than boys, while boys tend to be more dominant-dependent and are significantly more aggressive. The Whitings explained this by the different learning environments of the two sexes: girls spend more time interacting with mothers and infants, while boys are less frequently at home and interact more with peers away from adult supervision. The Whitings did not indicate whether peer interaction unsupervised by adults stimulates aggressive behavior, or, conversely, aggressive behavior is checked by adult supervision. Either ''cause'' could explain the association.

Behavior is not fixed but is responsive to the social situation; it varies strongly according to the status of the person with whom the target child is interacting. Toward infants, children tend to be nurturant or aggressive; toward peers, they are most often sociable or aggressive; toward adults, they are most often intimate-dependent or sociable.

This inductive research has resulted in findings that are consistent with the findings of earlier cross-cultural studies (e.g., Barry, Bacon, and Child 1957) and a number of single-case studies. A theme running through the book is the authors' conviction that behavior is determined by setting more than by early experience. This was later stated succinctly by B. Whiting (1980:97), who asserted that parents' ''greatest effect is in the assignment of the child to settings that have important socializing influences.'' One could hardly find a stronger statement of the situational or sociogenic position.

A cross-cultural study on aspects of child rearing indicative of parental acceptance or rejection was conducted by Ronald Rohner (1975). Coders rated each of the societies in the Standard Cross-Cultural Sample for features of parental behavior, child personality, and adult personality. The targeted age was two to six, early childhood. Boys and girls were rated separately, but only composite scores were given in the code. This study tested the findings of psychologists concerning the effects of parental rejection among Western children. Rohner found that across cultures, rejected children are significantly more hostile, aggressive, and achievement oriented, while accepted children are more self-reliant. He also found that children are more often accepted when the father is around on a day-to-day basis. Generally, Rohner's findings support the conclusions drawn by psychologists working on related issues in Western societies.

Until recently, comparative studies of socialization, like other studies of child behavior in anthropology, have dealt with children below the age of puberty. The literature by psychologists and sociologists on adolescence was virtually ignored. The year 1991 saw the publication of a cross-cultural study intended to fill this lacuna. Herbert Barry and I began work on the Adolescent Socialization Project in 1976. Using the societies in the Standard Cross-Cultural Sample, we coded 341 variables separately for girls and boys. Several short reports were subsequently published, and the comprehensive report came out fifteen years later: *Adolescence: An Anthropological Inquiry* (Schlegel and Barry 1991).[2]

This study, like earlier studies of socialization, relied heavily on the theories and findings of psychologists. It also recognized the considerable work by sociologists on peer-group behavior. It diverged most strongly from earlier comparative studies of socialization by utilizing the theories and findings of primatologists and sociobiologists. Adolescence in humans is a social stage that finds its counterpart in a similar stage, one intervening between childhood and adulthood, among terrestrial primates. In other words, adolescence is part of the life plan of our species.

If adolescence is a constant in human social organization, among the many variants we found for this life stage is the expression of aggression and competitiveness. These features vary systematically with two other features of social organization, family structure and the amount of time spent with peers versus adults. Boys generally spend more time with peers and less with adults of the same sex than girls do. Boys also exhibit higher levels of competitiveness and aggressiveness, as well as more delinquency. To understand this sex difference, we looked at the effects of peer contact and family form separately for each sex.

For girls, there is insufficient variation in amount of peer contact to make much of a difference; but for boys, higher levels of peer contact correlate with higher levels of competitiveness. Lesser contact with adult men correlates with the expectation of adolescent antisocial behavior and with higher levels of competitiveness. The pattern for boys, then, appears to be that less time spent with adults and more time spent with peers stimulates competitiveness and sets the stage for delinquent behavior.

The structure of the household shows effects on both girls and boys. We divided household form into three types: the nuclear-family household (one central married couple plus their children); the stem-family household (the two-generational family of two married couples plus the unmarried children of both couples); and the extended-family household (several married couples of two or more generations plus unmarried children). We found that the stem-family household tended to dampen competitiveness for boys, while the nuclear-family household tended to raise it for both sexes. The stem-family household is associated with lower levels of aggressiveness for boys, and the nuclear-family household is associated with higher levels of aggressiveness for girls. The critical factor may be the ratio of adults to children: highest in stem-family households and lowest in nuclear-family households. (The extended-family household fails to show significant associations. This category includes several variant forms that differ in adult/child ratio.)

Putting together the findings on adult versus peer contact with those on household structure, we interpreted these results as indicating that adolescents are more compliant and less assertive (competitive, aggressive, and antisocial) when they have more contact with adults than with peers. These findings have implications for many societies undergoing changes that include taking adolescents out of the family or workplace and placing them in the classroom.

CONCLUSION

Comparative studies have been fundamental to the development of psychological anthropology. Single-case field studies had been effectively used to call assumed universals about human personality into question, as Margaret Mead's *Coming of Age in Samoa* (1928) was purported to do for a universal adolescent *Sturm and Drang*. More general psychological theories needed more broad-based tests, however. Ethnography—whether living societies for comparative field studies or the archives of existing reports—provided the laboratory, and comparisons substituted for experiments.

The avowed purpose of comparative research throughout most of this century has been to test theories. In psychological anthropology, these are usually theories arising from analytic or social psychology. Another type of study, however, is based on inductive research. The Six Cultures Project, for example, was informed by theories of behavior, particularly learning theory, and by the findings of previous cross-cultural research; however, the task seems to have been more a discovery of associations and their interpretation in light of existing knowledge than the testing of specific hypotheses (cf. Whiting and Whiting 1975: Introduction). In a similar fashion, the Adolescent Socialization Project was guided by the theories and findings of primatology and the social sciences, but we did not set out to test specific hypotheses. ''Guiding questions'' rather than hypotheses are the basis for these kinds of inductive research.

In my view, inductive research can be effectively utilized in psychological anthropology. Far from being a ''fishing expedition,'' the inductive study is one that aids the researcher to search for patterns of association among related variables. The explanation of phenomena is the goal of any scientific endeavor, and the finding of regularities is an important step toward this goal.

Comparative research had its heyday in the 1940s, 1950s, and 1960s, the decades of ''big'' social science. There was much interdisciplinary cooperation, and scientific foundations were willing to provide the substantial funds necessary to conduct large-scale field studies like the Six Cultures Project or to establish research centers like the Cumulative Cross-Cultural Coding Center. Enthusiasm for cross-disciplinary projects has waned, and research monies for large projects outside the United States are increasingly hard to find. Given present realities, the small-scale controlled comparison and the highly cost-effective cross-cultural method may turn out to be the methods of choice for comparative anthropology in the near future.

In recent years, psychological anthropology has witnessed a swing away from ''scientific'' studies, with their goal of explanation and their methods that require measurement and rigorous testing, toward ''humanistic'' studies, whose goal is the discover of meaning and whose methods involve the empathetic interpretation of emotions and self-image. But if the behaviorally oriented anthropologists have sometimes forgotten that behavior is the response to reality as the mind has constructed it, the interpretive anthropologists sometimes forget that regularities exist across cultures and cannot be explained by the meaning any particular culture gives to the way its members act. This is an old dialogue in anthropology, originating in the eighteenth- and nineteenth-century philosophical disagreements between positivists and romantics. It is likely to continue. Cross-cultural comparisons provide a testing ground for generations about human behavior and culture.

NOTES

1. The earlier ascendancy of Freudian psychology has been halted, and the fortunes of biopsychology have risen with studies that support inheritance of personality dispositions. Psychological anthropologists have not yet been influenced by these studies, which may be remote from anthropological concerns with group rather than individual similarities and differences.

2. During this time, Beatrice and John Whiting also established a project on adolescence in six cultures (not those in the Six Cultures Project). The result has been several ethnographies of adolescence in changing societies. Since these studies are not specifically comparative and no comprehensive summary has been published, I shall not discuss that project in this chapter.

REFERENCES

Barry, H., III, M. K. Bacon, and I. L. Child. 1957. A Cross-Cultural Survey of Some Sex Differences in Socialization. *Journal of Abnormal and Social Psychology* 55:327–32.

Barry, H., III, I. L. Child, and M. K. Bacon. 1959. Relation of Child Training to Subsistence Economy. *American Anthropologist* 61:51–63.

Barry, H., III, L. Josephson, E. Lauer, and C. Marchall. 1980 [1976]. Infancy and Early Childhood: Cross-Cultural Codes 2. Pp. 205–36 in A. Schlegel and H. Barry III, *Adolescence: An Anthropological Inquiry*. New York: Free Press.

Barry, H., III, and J. M. Roberts. 1972. Infant Socialization and Games of Chance. *Ethnology* 11: 296–308.

Barry, H., III, and A. Schlegel, eds. 1980. *Cross-Cultural Samples and Codes*. Pittsburgh: University of Pittsburgh Press.

Bernard, H. R. 1988. *Research Methods in Cultural Anthropology*. Newbury Park, CA: Sage.

Bischof, N. 1975. A Systems Approach toward the Functional Connections of Attachment and Fear. *Child Development* 46:801–17.

Bolton, R. 1973. Aggression and Hypoglycemia among the Qolla: A Study in Psychobiological Anthropology. *Ethnology* 12:227–58.

Chick, G. E. 1984. The Cross-Cultural Study of Games. *Exercise and Sport Sciences Reviews* 12: 307–37.

Cohen, Y. A. 1964. *The Transition from Childhood to Adolescence*. Chicago: Aldine.

Edgerton, R. B. 1971. *The Individual in Cultural Adaptation: A Study of Four East African Peoples*. Berkeley: University of California Press.

Eggan, F. 1961 [1954]. Social Anthropology and the Method of the Controlled Comparison.

Pp. 109–29 in F. W. Moore, ed., *Readings in Cross-Cultural Methodology*. New Haven: HRAF Press.

Ember, M. 1983. On the Origin and Extension of the Incest Taboo. Pp. 65–108 in M. Ember and C. R. Ember, eds., *Marriage, Family, and Kinship: Comparative Studies of Social Organization*. New Haven: HRAF Press.

Erickson, M. 1989. Incest Avoidance and Familial Bonding. *Journal of Anthropological Research* 45:267–291.

Fox, R. 1962. Sibling Incest. *British Journal of Sociology* 13:128–150.

Freud, S. 1950 [1913]. *Totem and Taboo*. London: Routledge and Kegan Paul.

Goggin, J. H., and W. C. Sturtevant. 1964. The Calusa: A Stratified Non-Agricultural Society. Pp. 179–219 in W. H. Goodenough, ed., *Explorations in Cultural Anthropology: Essays in Honor of George Peter Murdock*. New York: McGraw-Hill.

Goody, J. 1983. *The Development of the Family and Marriage in Europe*. Cambridge, Eng.: Cambridge University Press.

Kardiner, A. 1945. *Psychological Frontiers of Society*. New York: Columbia University Press.

Kardiner, A., with R. Linton, 1939. *The Individual and His Society*. New York: Columbia University Press.

LeVine, R. A. 1966. *Dreams and Deeds: Achievement Motivation in Nigeria*. Chicago: University of Chicago Press.

Levinson, D., and M. J. Malone. 1980. *Toward Explaining Human Culture: A Critical Review of the Findings of Worldwide Cross-Cultural Research*. New Haven: HRAF Press.

Malinowski, B. 1927. *Sex and Repression in Savage Society*. New York: E. P. Dutton.

Mead, M. 1928. *Coming of Age in Samoa*. New York: Morrow.

Minturn, L., and W. W. Lambert. 1964. *Mothers of Six Cultures: Antecedents of Child Rearing*. New York: John Wiley and Sons.

Munroe, R. H., R. L. Munroe, and H. S. Shimmin. 1984. Children's Work in Four Cultures: Determinants and Consequences. *American Anthropologist* 86:369–79.

Murdock, G. P. 1949. *Social Structure*. New York: Macmillan.

———. 1966. Cross-Cultural Sampling. *Ethnology* 5:96–114.

Murdock, G. P., and D. R. White. 1980 [1969]. Standard Cross-Cultural Sample. Pp. 3–42 in H. Barry III and A. Schlegel, eds., *Cross-Cultural Samples and Codes*. Pittsburgh: University of Pittsburgh Press.

Nadel, S. F. 1967. Witchcraft in Four African Societies: An Essay in Comparison. Pp. 907–20 in C. S. Ford, ed., *Cross-Cultural Approaches: Readings in Comparative Research*. New Haven: HRAF Press.

Naroll, R., G. L. Michik, and F. Naroll. 1976. *Worldwide Theory Testing*. New Haven: HRAF Press.

Parker, S. 1976. The Precultural Bases of the Incest Taboo: Toward a Biosocial Theory. *American Anthropologist* 78:285–305.

Roberts, J. M., M. J. Arth, and R. R. Bush. 1959. Games in Culture. *American Anthropologist* 61: 597–605.

Roberts, J. M., and B. Sutton-Smith. 1962. Child Training and Game Involvement. *Ethnology* 1: 166–85.

Rohner, R. P. 1975. *They Love Me, They Love Me Not: A Worldwide Study of the Effects of Parental Acceptance and Rejection*. New Haven: HRAF Press.

Schlegel A. 1972. *Male Dominance and Female Autonomy: Domestic Authority in Matrilineal Societies*. New Haven: HRAF Press.

Schlegel, A., and H. Barry III. 1991. *Adolescence: An Anthropological Inquiry*. New York: Free Press.

Schwartzman, H. B. 1978. *Transformations: The Anthropology of Children's Play*. New York: Plenum Press.

Sutton-Smith, B. 1989. Games as Models of Power. Pp. 3–18 in R. Bolton, ed., *The Content of Culture: Constants and Variants*. New Haven: HRAF Press.

Taggart, J. M. 1992. Gender Segregation and Cultural Construction of Sexuality in Two Hispanic Societies. *American Ethnologist* 19:75–96.

Westermarck, E., 1902 [1891]. *The History of Human Marriage.* 3 vols. London: Macmillan.

Whiting, B. B., ed. 1963. *Six Cultures: Studies of Child Rearing.* New York: John Wiley and Sons.

Whiting, B. B., and J.W.M. Whiting. 1975. *Children of Six Cultures: Psycho-Cultural Analysis.* Cambridge, MA: Harvard University Press,

Whiting, J.W.M. 1977. A Model for Psychocultural Research, Pp. 29–48 in P. H. Leiderman, S. R. Tulkin, and A. Rosenfeld, eds., *Culture and Infancy: Variations in the Human Experience.* New York: Academic Press.

Whiting, B. B. 1980. Culture and Social Behavior: A Model for the Development of Social Behavior. *Ethos* 8:95–116.

Whiting, J.W.M., and I. L. Child. 1953. *Child Training and Personality: A Cross-Cultural Study.* New Haven: Yale University Press.

CHAPTER THREE

SOCIAL STRUCTURE AND PERSONALITY

Philip K. Bock

It would be convenient to portray the approach described in this chapter as a reaction against Culture and Personality or cross-cultural studies; but though it received its name quite late (Cohen 1961), Social Structure and Personality has is roots in the nineteenth century and constitutes a parallel development with these other approaches, though it rarely interacts with them.

The central insight of Social Structure and Personality studies is that one's position in the social structure is a powerful determinant of behavior. This seemingly innocuous statement has been worked out in a variety of ways, as we shall see; but all of them contrast with the persistent assumption that it is possible to characterize any society by a single "dominant," "basic," or "modal" personality type. (Despite repeated disclaimers, this is what most studies in the Culture and Personality tradition actually do.) What I have termed the "uniformity assumption" (Bock 1988:98) is challenged by both the macroscopic and microscopic studies that reveal, on the one hand, psychological consistencies that cut across conventional social and cultural boundaries and, on the other, profound differences in perception, motivation, and cognition within even relatively small societies, but related to social position.

Much of the diversity within the Social Structure and Personality approach has to do with differing conceptions of social structure. Sociologists and political economists who have contributed to Social Structure and Personality have tended to work in large-scale, industrial societies with written histories; thus they have focused on macroscopic units (classes, institutions) and on change over time (e.g., Riesman, Glazer and Denney, 1961). Yehudi Cohen (1961:3–4) outlined the program of Social Structure and Personality as concerned with (1) institutional effects on the socialization of children and adults and (2) the "fit" of personalities with particular institutions. He further listed status, family, political change, and kinship as having "consequences for personality" and suggested that some of these consequences would be similar across national lines. Authors working in small-scale societies have given greater attention to specific interaction situations, gender roles, and local leadership phenomena, but there is considerable overlap among these studies.

In this chapter, a rather concrete notion of social structure will be employed (rather than, say, the Lévi-Straussian concept of "models built up after reality"). We will examine claims, hypotheses, and studies of institutional effect on socialization and on personality, starting with perhaps the most influential claim made about human functioning.

"ALL PSYCHOLOGY IS CLASS PSYCHOLOGY"

The Marxist approach to individual differences is at once global and powerful. It calls on us to ignore minor and unimportant particulars and to focus on the social cleavages in modern industrial society: to recognize the inherent conflict of interest between classes and the potential for revolutionary solidarity within classes, locally and internationally. The "workers of the world" should be able to unite precisely because they share the same (exploited) structural position relative to the bourgeoisie. When they do come together to overthrow their exploiters, "the proletariat will be the human race."

For one writing in the aftermath of the dissolution of the Soviet Union, it is difficult to recall the power of this utopian vision; but in the writings of Nikolai Bukharin we find a clear statement that still gives food for thought. Remember that Marxist analysis is primarily concerned with the "revolutionary potential" of different groupings (peasantry, underclass) and settled on the industrial proletariat as "most likely to rebel" for a number of reasons, including (1) shared material interests as economically exploited wage laborers separated from the means of production; (2) special conditions of work, with many members of this class brought together in factories, making communication and organization possible; and (3) lack of private property, meaning that the workers had "nothing to lose" by rebelling.

In Burkharin's *Historical Materialism* (1969, originally published in 1921), we find a clear exposition of the theory of class psychology, beginning with the premise that "the 'individual' always acts as a *social* individual, as a component part of a group, a class, a society" (p. 100). For example, the material conditions of the proletariat (some of which were listed earlier) are said to produce a class psychology characterized by "revolutionary spirit, the habit of organized action, a psychology of comradeship [and] a productive and constructive conception of things" (p. 289); whereas the peasantry, due to its dispersed conditions of work and attachment to private property, is characterized by opposition to change and by "individualism, exclusiveness [and] suspicion" (p. 290). Both of these exploited classes have psychologies that contrast with that of the bourgeoisie, which, particularly when it was coming to dominance by defeating the feudal nobility, was characterized by "*individualism*," "*rationalism*," and the "*liberal* psychology . . . of the entrepreneur" (p. 291). These rather vague statements can, in the hands of a clever Marxist, be made into plausible explanations of social stability and change. As Marx and Engels wrote in the *Communist Manifesto*, "The ruling ideas of each age have ever been the ideas of its ruling class" (1959:26). Thus the ruling class in any era imposes its ideas on the rest of society—a process known today as *hegemony*.

This approach recognizes that some psychological traits may be shared "in spite of class differences" (Bukharin 1969:210), and it takes account of subgroups, especially occupations, within each class. For example, the skilled worker who likes his work and looks down on unskilled workers "is ambitious, and assumes certain bourgeois inclinations," while the bureaucrat develops a "psychology of negative virtue: routine, red-tape delays, precedence of form over substance, etc." (p. 214; the bureaucratic personality will be discussed in more detail later). Furthermore, these class and group psychologies give rise to political programs and ideals that are based, however unconsciously, in their originators' material interests and conditions of work. For Bukharin, "*Ideologies are a coagulated social psychology*" (p. 215), and explanation must always begin from the material conditions in which a group finds itself, the economic structure of society.

Anthropological studies of peasant personality have departed from the Marxist interest in revolutionary potential to ask about reactions to technological change and economic development; however, they retain the interest in conditions of work and attachment to private property (land tenure) as well as in the internal differentiation of peasant communities. Probably the best-known of these studies are the works of George Foster and his critics, who during the 1960s and 1970s debated the nature and existence of typical peasant cognitive and/or emotional structure.

Foster's own research in Spain and Mexico led him to postulate a number of general concepts that he found supported in his readings and the work of his students. Prominent among these is the idea that all peasants—rural cultivators subject to state power—display a similar cognitive orientation that Foster labeled an *Image of Limited Good*. By this he meant that due to their subordinate positions in the larger society and their competitive relations in the local community, peasants see their total environment as one in which "land, wealth, and almost all desired things in life . . . *exist in absolute quantities insufficient to fill even minimal needs of villagers* [with no way] *to increase the available supplies*" (1967:123–24). Associated with this cognitive orientation are strong feelings of envy and suspicion generated by the rational anxiety that others are getting ahead at one's expense in the zero-sum game of life.

Foster argued that his concepts helped to explain a variety of attitudes and behaviors that he believed were common in peasant societies, including adherence to traditional methods of subsistence and reluctance to cooperate in ventures that might benefit the community as a whole. Even good health was thought to be viewed as available in a fixed quantity, so that a neighbor's healthy baby was a threat to one's own offspring, and beliefs about the evil eye or witchcraft practices were explained with reference to the "limited good."

This is not the place to review objections to Foster's ideas, which include insufficient attention to internal differences and to the external power structures that keep peasants in poverty. It was also argued that he mistook the psychological effects of a desperate economic situation for its cause and thus blamed the victims of oppression for their plight. But Foster's attempt to generalize psychological traits across cultures based on the social position of a class is typical of Social Structure and Personality studies.

POSITIONS IN THE SOCIAL STRUCTURE

The insights of orthodox Marxists into the economic determinants of group and individual psychology have been developed by others in ways that their originators would probably reject. But if subgroups such as "skilled workers" or "middle peasants" and occupations such as "bureaucrat" or "accountant" affect one's psychology, then what of other categories and positions? Scholars who are not concerned with revolutionary praxis have taken up these ideas and applied them to a wide range of "positions" (social statuses or roles). As in Marxist analyses, it is suggested that many of these personality determinants operate across national lines. For example, a Japanese and a Nigerian and a Canadian accountant might share certain psychological characteristics despite major differences in language and culture.

One of the most discussed topics in this area is bureaucratic personality. Bureaucracies in the sense of large, hierarchical institutions that administer various state and corporate functions have existed since the earliest civilizations, and it would not be surprising to discover an ancient Egyptian text that complained about bureaucratic delays or excessive papyruswork. Max Weber was the first social scientist to characterize the bureaucratic institution as an ideal type involving fixed areas of jurisdiction, graded authority, special managerial skills, general rules of procedure, and full-time official activities that are divorced from the employee's personal life (i.e., in principle, favoritism and profit are both excluded from decisions). Bureaucratic decision making contrasts with both autocratic and democratic forms by virtue of its "rationality" (impersonal application of rules).

It was the sociologist Robert K. Merton (1957), however, who drew the conclusion that red tape, formalism, and rigid rules were necessary consequences of bureaucratic organization. Merton went on to consider (1) the kind of person who would be attracted to bureaucratic work (with its rigid structure, job security, and seniority system) and (2) the personality characteristics that might be developed by individuals who continued for some time under comparable "conditions of work" anywhere in the world. His general conclusions were that bureaucracies (public or private) attracted quite timid, rigid, and often authoritarian individuals (who felt secure when going "by the book") and produced such traits in people who were socialized to the requirements of their jobs, in which staying out of trouble, mastering intricate regulations, and "overconformity" were required for success. Merton concluded his discussion with a call for "empirical studies" (1957:205) to increase understanding of the interaction between bureaucracy and personality, for his own influential essay was based mainly on social sources, with little or no data on individuals. (See Galvin 1992: 43, who suggested that shy, inhibited children are, later in life, likely "to take a job involving minimal uncertainty [e.g., bureaucratic].")

A contrasting study of successful (male) business executives (Henry 1949) suggested a shared psychodynamic pattern in which the following characteristics were present: strong desire for achievement and mobility; a positive attitude toward (and identification with) authority figures; decisiveness in decision making; strong self-identity; and an active, realistic approach to problems, coupled with strong feelings of frustration when blocked. Henry traced many of these traits to the ability of these men to break free of family ties, especially to the mother, for many executives retain a positive and admiring attitude to their fathers. There is also a price paid for success in the business world. Henry (1949: 291) wrote of the "uncertainty, constant activity, the . . . ever present fear of failure, and the artificial limitations put upon their emotionalized interpersonal relations [as] some of the costs of this role." He also maintained that a selection process operates so that individuals whose personalities are "most readily adaptable to this particular role tend to be selected, whereas those whose personality is not already partially akin are rejected" (1949:286). A number of studies summarized by Bronfenbrenner (1961:6–18) suggested that child socialization has quite different goals in American entrepreneurial families where boys especially are trained to "get ahead" than in bureaucratic families where both sexes are taught to "get along." Differential socialization by occupational group, region, and gender are important topics in this approach (see Endleman 1967).

CASTE AND CLASS

One of the more interesting empirical research projects in this tradition was designed as a follow-up to an influential study of the 1930s. In *Children of Bondage* (1964; originally published in 1940), a black anthropologist, Allison Davis, and a white psychologist, John Dollard, joined together to investigate the personalities of teenage black children in Natchez and New Orleans, with special attention to the aftereffects of generations of slavery and to the effects of race and class on child development.

Twenty years later, in *The Eighth Generation Grows Up* (1960), another interdisciplinary team headed by psychiatrist John Rohrer and anthropologist Munro Edmonson attempted to locate and study a sample of the New Orleans children first examined by Davis and Dollard. They were interested to see the extent to which traits identified in the children would still appear in the adult personalities. Using the files of the earlier study, they were able to show both continuities and changes. But perhaps the most interesting aspect of this longitudinal research was the development of the concept of *primary role identification* (PRI), which articulates elements of individual psychology with positions in the social structure.

Not all individuals in the study achieved a clear PRI, and these "marginal" personalities tended to be alienated from the conventional social world, some adopting a "bohemian" way of life. Most members of the sample, however, showed a remarkable stability of identity over a twenty-year period. The authors wrote that they "could isolate a primary role identification for most individuals, and that [it] was intimately related to the quality of integration of the individual's psychic functioning" (Rohrer and Edmonson 1960:299). Furthermore, there seemed to be a very limited number of PRIs available to these New Orleans "Negroes." The principal ones were the following:

1. For boys, identification with the middle class and its values
2. For girls, identification with "the maternal role in the matriarchal family"
3. For boys, identification with "age-graded peer groups—gangs"
4. For both sexes, identification with being a family member

The rich case studies (pp. 89–294) illustrate these four options as well as the marginality of people lacking a PRI. An interracial team administered the interviews and intelligence and projective tests on which the case studies were based, while additional research on language, folklore, and contents of black newspapers supplemented the clinical materials. To my knowledge, the concept of primary role identification has not been employed in other studies, but it illustrates one way in which psychological and social structural analysis can be creatively integrated.

The social positions represented by the terms *colonist* and *colonized* have also been studied to determine cross-cultural similarities in psychology under a colonial social structure. Thus whether we are considering the French in Algeria, the British in India, or Euro-Americans' relationship to Native Americans, certain psychological traits have been suggested for the dominant and subordinate groups in colonial societies. The colonists, due in part to their economic dominance based on military and technological superiority, view the native peoples as inferior: "stupid," "lazy," "treacherous," and "unreliable" are among the adjectives applied to colonized populations. But since these populations are generally much larger than those of the colonists, an element of fear is frequently attached to these views: "They might cut our throats some dark night."

For their part, the colonized view their colonial masters with a mixture of admiration and hatred: admiration for their wealth and power, but hatred for their oppression of native society and culture. The colonists' dress, housing, speech, and religious and social behavior may at first be sources of amusement or fear, but in time they come to be emulated by much of the native population, often with creative and adaptive modifications. Creole speech, syncretistic religions, and vital art styles arise in such contact situations, while "nativistic movements" often call for a return to traditional ways and rejection of the interlopers. Various degrees of identification with the colonists are possible, some leading to self-hatred on the part of the colonized. Where native populations have been decimated by disease and warfare, enslaved, or limited to inadequate territories, the tragic consequences have been similar throughout the world (Bodley 1990).

Here we are concerned with the psychological dimensions of the colonist/colonized relationship. Franz Fannon and Vine Deloria are among those who have written eloquently on this topic, but the Tunisian writer Albert Memmi best captured the "situation of the colonized." As he observed:

> If one chooses to understand the colonial system, he must admit that it is unstable and its equilibrium constantly threatened. One can be reconciled to every situation, [but] regardless of how soon or how violently the colonized rejected his situation, he will one day begin to overthrow his unlivable existence with the whole force of his oppressed personality.
>
> The two historically possible solutions are then tried in succession or simultaneously. He attempts either to [assimilate or to rebel]. The candidate for assimilation . . . discovers with alarm the full meaning of his attempt. It is a dramatic moment when he realizes that he has assumed all the accusations and condemnations of the colonizer, that he is becoming accustomed to looking at his own people through the eyes of their [oppressor].
>
> What is there left then for the colonized to do? Being unable to change his condition in harmony and communion with the colonizer, he tries to become free despite him. . . . We then witness a reversal of terms. Assimilation being abandoned, the colonized's liberation must be carried out through a recovery of self and of autonomous dignity. . . . After having been rejected for so long by the colonizer, the day has come when it is the colonized who must refuse the colonizer. (Memmi 1965:120–28)

Memmi's book (which should be read in its entirety) brilliantly explores the psychology of colonizer and colonized, starting from the material conditions of colonial life and continuing to a discussion of art, literature, and politics. His abstract analysis would seem to apply to any colonial situation, including "internal colonies" such as Native American reservations and African-American ghettos. But, surprisingly, an even more general statement is possible within the Social Structure and Personality tradition, though the relationship may not be immediately apparent.

SYMBOLIC INTERACTION

Stemming from the writings of social philosopher G. H. Mead, symbolic interactionalism calls for close attention to what "goes on" between individuals as they relate to one another in specific kinds of face-to-face situations. Symbolic interactionism often seems to focus on details of verbal and nonverbal exchanges, but its goals are quite general. Especially in the work of Erving Goffman, concepts have been developed that are of great importance to psychological anthropology (Bock 1988).

In one of his less known books, *Stigma*, Goffman developed a theoretical framework that embraces the situation of the colonized as well as that of racial and ethnic minorities, lower classes, women, the handicapped, and many other groups whose members suffer, in particular situations, from "impaired identity." Although presented as a sociological study, Goffman's exploration of the "moral career" of individuals with obvious or discoverable "defects" has profound psychological implications.

The prototype situation for his study was the encounter between a "normal" person and someone with a "stigma." Goffman called this one of the "primal scenes of sociology," and he analyzed the discomfort experienced and strategies used by both parties as the stigmatized person tests the limits of his or her acceptance (Goffman 1963:13). As in social life generally, information control is essential to successful interaction, but the situation of the stigmatized highlights the dilemmas of what to reveal, when, and to whom. In addition, people with unobtrusive stigmata are faced with the question of whether to "pass" as normal, in which case they betray their "own" (people who share their stigma) while being unsure of full acceptance. (The paradigm case would be German Jews who converted to Christianity long before the advent of the Nazis but who found that they were still candidates for extermination.)

The ex-convict, the addict, or the stutterer who usually speaks clearly are all in the same danger of having their claims to normality betrayed by a lapse in control, and this imparts a "furtiveness" to their existence. But, as Goffman showed, these dilemmas and their psychological counterparts are familiar to all people since there are some situations in which everyone departs from the normal ideal and thus faces the problems of acceptance and information control:

> [S]tigma involves not so much a set of concrete individuals who can be separated into two piles, the stigmatized and the normal, as a pervasive two-role social process in which every individual participates in both roles, at least in some connections and in some phases of life. The normal and the stigmatized are not persons but rather perspectives. These are generated in social situations during mixed contacts by virtue of the unrealized norms that are likely to play upon the encounter. . . . And since interaction roles are involved, not concrete individuals, it should come as no surprise that in many cases he who is stigmatized in one regard nicely exhibits all the normal prejudices held toward those who are stigmatized in another regard. (1963:137–38)

Elsewhere, Goffman considered a wide range of human interaction situations, from pedestrian traffic to academic lectures, showing in each case how constraints on human behavior and experience follow from the structure of interaction situations (see Drew and Wooton 1988). Together with other students of interaction and of conversation, Goffman argued for the moment-to-moment construction of the person in the very process of discourse. Above all, he revealed how very fragile is our presentation of self and sense of identity.

Among the anthropologists who have used symbolic interaction theory to understand aspects of behavior are Gerald Berreman (1962) and Thomas Gregor (1977). Gregor's ethnography, *Mehinaku*, described the daily life of this Brazilian people in terms of the interaction situations that occur within and outside the village, stressing the need for information control and self-dramatization in their small community. (See also Gregor [1985] for his more psychodynamic analysis of this society.)

Philip Bock (1986) has combined certain aspects of interactionism with cognitive anthropology to develop a "formal descriptive model of social structure." Defining an institution as an ordered set of recurrent situations, he showed how situations are structured by social concepts of Space (*S*), Time (*T*), and Role (*R*) so that the formula

$$S \mid T : R / R$$

represents a situation defined by the interaction of two social roles in a specific space-time setting. The interactional consequences of this model were given in a limited set of "fundamental role attributes" (1986:37), while a matrix notation displayed the complex constraints on persons who perform roles in various settings. One advantage of this descriptive model is that it can focus on interaction at any level of abstraction or specificity (1986:60–62). Thus Goffman's "primal scene" could be represented by the general formula

$$S \mid T : R \text{ ``normal''} / R \text{ ``stigmatized,''}$$

with the general attributes of each role specified; but the same concepts can be used to describe the structure of interaction between, say, hearing and deaf persons, or even between specific individuals in a particular setting (1986:31–35).

Another concept that helps to bridge the apparent gap between social structure and personality is that of the *personal role*, that is, "A category of persons consisting of a single individual together with his or her style of interacting; the label for such a role is the individual's personal name or alias" (Bock 1979: 335). The personal role is the public personality of an individual—the self that we present in a wide range of situations. If someone acts in an unusual manner, we may say that "he (or she) is not himself (herself)," referring to a deviation from the personal role, even if the same behavior would go unnoticed in another individual (1979:96). Refusal to use a name, or assignment of a number, often indicates "depersonalization," merging individuals into a category and leading to their treatment as "nonpersons," though in some societies this might be a sign of high respect, especially if the person is addressed by a title.

LEADERSHIP ROLES

One of the questions that the Social Structure and Personality approach raises has to do with the nature of leadership in different societies. It has been suggested that bureaucratic leaders who reach positions of authority by mastering complex rules and staying out of trouble as they gain promotions through seniority will share certain personal characteristics by virtue of selection and socialization (see the earlier section "Positions in the Social Structure"). Other types discussed in anthropology include hereditary, charismatic, and representative leaders as well as the "headman" type found in band-level societies (see Bock 1979:92–96).

An excellent discussion of this last type is found in *Force and Persuasion* by Waud H. Kracke (1978). The author combined a structural approach to authority among the Kagwahib of central Brazil with a detailed discussion of the differing styles of leadership in two neighboring villages. Kracke analyzed not only the leaders' actions and motivations but those of their followers as revealed in daily life, discourse, and dreams. Drawing on psychoanalytic theory, especially a classic paper by Fritz Redl (1942), he showed the varied reasons that people have for submitting to (or resisting) authority.

In traditional Kagwahib society, a headman gained authority by binding his sons-in-law to him during and after several years of bride-service, and by attracting other followers through the force of his personality and the prosperity of his village. Although the Kagwahib had been "pacified" and subjected to missionary influence and Brazilian law since 1923, the two leaders described by Kracke both adhered to traditional ideas of authority; however, their very different personalities and styles of leadership used these traditions in different ways.

"Homero," a man in his seventies, had been a warrior before pacification and exercised authority by giving orders and making demands. Although members of his village often complained that he did not join in the work, though his sons-in-law had left the group, and though the village had clearly declined from its former size and prosperity, Homero's forceful personality commanded respect, and he was grooming his son, Berto, to succeed him.

"Jovenil" was in his thirties when Kracke did his fieldwork. His style of leadership was quite different from that of Homero. He led more by example than command and was careful to sound out group members before making a request. Jovenil's elderly father had remained a member of the group after retiring as headman, and Jovenil avoided situations where authority might be divided, either with his father or with his brother (and probable successor).

Kracke skillfully analyzed the structural and ecological factors that contributed to differences between these two headmen so that he could relate their differing styles to personal characteristics. Jovenil was described as maintaining "a low profile within his group, leading by example and consensus, allowing his followers maximal autonomy . . . while insisting on his own autonomy as headman''; whereas ''Homero conducts his group with almost peremptory command [and] claims special prerogatives, such as not participating in work'' (1978:70).

Some of these differences were traced to the men's conceptions of leadership (all of which had ''traditional'' justifications) and to the age difference, including Homero's experience as a warrior, which probably influenced his more aggressive style. But as Kracke pointed out, there was much more to the story, and the dreams of both headmen and followers revealed conflicting motives, projections, and denials. ''Leaders . . . fill psychological needs in their followers' lives [and] continue to serve some parental functions; gratifying some emotional needs, helping develop self-control, and serving as a model for further maturation'' (1978:199).

In his conclusions, Kracke suggested that force and persuasion form an ''elementary polarity'' that will be found in styles of leadership in any society. Leaders help to mediate between the individual and the culture, though not all of them are equally skillful, and personal factors always enter into the outcome of any attempt to exercise authority.

> An examination of the interactions among . . . diverse personalities in leadership offers a fresh model for the relationship between individual and society, an alternative to the familiar culture-and-personality approach . . . and a model that gives each individual in a society a more active part in creating the social order in which he lives. (1978:252)

This, I think, is a central contribution of Social Structure and Personality to psychological anthropology.

GENDER ROLES

So much has been written about gender roles in the past two decades that it would be impossible to summarize this material here. (For an early anthology, see Rosaldo and Lamphere 1974.) In this section, I shall try to relate some of this work to the concepts of social structure that have already been presented.

As with many other aspects of human experience, such as race and ethnicity, we have increasingly come to realize the extent to which the supposedly eternal categories of gender are (1) socially constructed and (2) historically contingent. That is, the relations within and between the sexes are variable; even the number of genders is subject to cultural interpretation, and, despite the apparent universality of ''male dominance,'' the modalities of male-female interaction are situationally relative.

Variation is now recognized in every area of gender studies, starting with the late John Money's biological analysis of intersexual and transsexual individuals and the incredible complexities of gender identity. A memorable case is that of the ''male lesbian,'' an individual who was anatomically male but psychologically female, with a preference for women as sexual objects, but relating to them in a female-to-female manner. Such persons cannot be ''left aside'' in our studies, for it is exactly such exceptional cases that illuminate this topic. From the Social Structure and Personality perspective, "male" and "female" are positions in the social structure that affect one's behavior and experience in the same way as class, occupation, or leadership role. Furthermore, assignment to one or more of these positions turns out to be a negotiated matter, with some individuals occupying a marginal status (as with primary role identification).

Bruce Lincoln has convincingly argued that any taxonomy conceals a ranking of its categories, and that a division into male and female, with male as the marked, positive term, implies a ranking of male above female. But this scheme is "rendered unworkable by the anomaly of the androgyne" (1989:168), and the implicit hierarchy may be overthrown.

> The response of taxonomic systems—or more properly, of those who construct, maintain, and deploy such systems—to those things they cannot classify and thereby constrain are many and varied. Anomalies can be ignored, ridiculed, distorted, or suppressed, these all being means whereby they are relegated to the margins and interstices of both a given classificatory system and of lived experience. Alternately, the system under which they are judged anomalous can be modified or abandoned. (Lincoln 1989:165)

Symbolic interactionism would suggest that we examine the actual situations in which male and female (and other genders) interact. Goffman (1963:128) implied that the female is always the stigmatized member of this pair, subject to the uncertainties of all such roles, attempting to control harmful information (e.g., about her reproductive status, emotionality, and other conditions) and even, in some circumstances, being tempted to "pass" for male (e.g., in correspondence).

Social Structure and Personality approaches, then, examine the effects of changing social conditions on conceptions of "masculinity" and "femininity" (see Gewertz 1981). This is illustrated by changes in American appraisals of women's work during World War II, when many women labored in factories and in the military, and some even played professional baseball. But one can still hear arguments that women are too weak, too emotional, or too unaggressive to compete in a man's world. These attitudes go back to the beginnings of Western civilization:

> In the ancient world, Hippocrates, Aristotle, and Galen drew a picture of the nature of woman that provided a thoroughgoing justification of women's inferior social status. Aristotle argued that women are colder and weaker than men, and that women do have sufficient heat to cook the blood and thus purify the soul. Galen, following the Hippocratic doctrine of the four humors, believed that women are cold and moist while men are warm and dry; men are active, women are indolent. The medical assumptions of these ancients were incorporated into medieval thinking with few revisions and dominated much of Western medical literature until well into the seventeenth century. (Schiebinger 1986:46)

However, these prejudices may be set aside during periods of economic stress.

Above all, it is the anomalous individual or class that challenges the social hierarchy, "for in the very fact of their existence they reveal the shortcomings, inadequacies, contradictions, and arbitrary nature of such structures" (Lincoln 1989:166). By virtue of their marginal positions in the social structure, such people often gain deep insights into the working of the system, just as slaves who are treated as nonpersons become privy to the secret lives of their masters.

In her fascinating study of American female impersonators, *Mother Camp*, anthropologist Esther Newton made explicit the connection between sexism and the stigmatization of effeminate males, especially "drag queens." Their oppression is due to a world "driven by rapacious sexuality and competitiveness, which means the immorality of exploitation and degradation" (1979:126).

> To the impersonator, the world is a "jungle"; man in the jungle is a "savage"; this is wrong, but it is the actual state of affairs. Anyone who seems to be different is ignorant or unscrupulous. Exploitative sexuality is the root and framework of all human motivation. (1979:127)

Newton observed that the drag queens allot themselves a very low position in the moral order of society and that "the weight of depression in both an individual psychological sense and in a cultural sense . . . is heavy" (1979:129). As the ultimate outsiders, they regard themselves as losers in a brutal world, though this feeling of "victimization" offers a certain moral superiority, as does their cynical sense of humor (cf. Jenny Livingstone's extraordinary film, *Paris Is Burning*).

Viewing her research in retrospect, Newton noted that although she first disagreed with her informants' opinion that the "fundamental division" of the social world is into male and female, she came to agree with them and wondered why she was "blind where they could see."

> Middle class culture seems to me to have built-in social blindness, compounded by arrogance. I was prepared to find the views of deviants interesting, but never seriously considered that they could be correct. (1979:xvii)

In sum, one's position in society is in part defined by assignment to a standard or marginal gender role, and this affects perception, motivation, and cognition—including that of the anthropologist—in important ways.

LEAVING HOME AND STAYING BEHIND

In this final section, we will examine several phenomena from the Social Structure and Personality perspective, including how a change in social position can affect personality. The contemporary world is one in which millions of people are continually uprooted—willingly or not—and transported to unfamiliar surroundings where they must adapt in order to survive. Migrants, refugees, colonists, and anthropologists all face the shock and challenge of learning a new language and culture, often starting from a social position lower than that which they formerly occupied. It is not surprising, then, that migration is closely associated with psychological stress (Arthur 1971).

An excellent study of immigration, *The Sting of Change* by Constance Cronin, illustrates some of the mechanisms at work in this situation. Cronin studied Sicilian family life in a small, south Italian town and then interviewed Sicilian immigrants living in Sydney, Australia. The interviews covered topics such as reasons for migrating, work, residence, language preferences, food, education, and social life, revealing many attitudes toward kin, marriage, and mobility. Her fieldwork in Italy showed, for example, that parents dominate the lives of their children, but without much real intimacy or concern for them as individuals. Cronin noted that

> the Sicilian pattern is being perpetuated by most of the immigrant parents; only the educated as a group and a few individuals plus most of the second-generation adults have absorbed the Australian idea that children should be trained to independence and self-sufficiency while at the same time a much more personal interest is taken in the child as an individual. (1970:225)

Nevertheless, compared to those who remained in Sicily, immigrant families are more intent on providing for their children's futures and use various means to limit family size (1970:172).

Cronin's study reveals common patterns of attitudes in this immigrant group, as well as some differences correlated with age, education, and amount of time in Australia. Although she did not focus specifically on personality, she concluded from the interviews that "these differences are enormous and there can be no doubt that they play an extremely important part in change patterns" (1970:274).

Migrants have long been considered a high-risk group for mental illness, especially if their uprooting was involuntary. Arthur Kleinman (1988:56) noted that Southeast Asian "boat people" resettled in the United States and Canada "experience high rates of depression, anxiety, and psychophysiological disturbances." Certain "life events" such as loss of a spouse through death or divorce often precede the onset of mental problems, but at a more general level, "social class, the economy, historical forces . . . and social institutions are the chief determinants of health and mental well-being" (1988:57).

Under some circumstances, however, leaving may be a healthier choice than staying behind. *Saints, Scholars, and Schizophrenics* by Nancy Scheper-Hughes (1979) investigated the structural factors responsible for the high rate of mental illness in Western Ireland, an area from which generations of migrants have escaped. Those who remain are subject to a number of social conditions, including isolation, poverty, delayed marriage (or lifelong celibacy), and a repressive ideology that would create difficulties for the strongest person. But Scheper-Hughes showed that the greatest burden falls on those in a particular structural position. While many girls left for work in England and older sons often emigrated to America, it was the youngest son in a rural family who was designated to inherit the nearly worthless farm and to care for aging parents, giving up any chance of marriage or a family of his own, since Irish girls are now unwilling to marry a poor farmer.

The dilemma of these men is produced by a combination of "family values" that impose the obligations upon them and "differential socialization" that treats boys, and especially youngest sons, as dependent, helpless creatures, good for nothing but farm labor under their parents' autocratic rule and tied to their mothers by strong emotional bonds. If there are several sons, one of the older ones will often be treated quite differently, encouraged to develop his abilities and independence and to leave home to pursue opportunities. In one rural family, "Jimmy," the younger brother, was a quiet, fearful alcoholic, hospitalized for various phobias that made him unable to hold a job. "Robert" was the success in the family:

> According to Jimmy, Robert is his parents' pride and joy, a successful New York City construction worker, married to a Yankee woman, and the father of four children. Remittance money comes home faithfully each month from America, and the brother's enlarged photo is enshrined over the mantelpiece in the front kitchen— constant reminder to Jimmy of his own inadequacy. For while Robert's is a success story, Jimmy's is one of humiliation and repeated failure . . . .Yet, both Robert and Jimmy were born into the same household and parish, and both were reared by the same overbearing mother and absentee father. During adolescence each had to confront the same set of limited alternatives: whether to emigrate and try to "make good" elsewhere, or whether to stay behind and prove "loyal" to mother and motherland. (Scheper-Hughes 1979:165)

This case and many others like it demonstrate the effects that sex and birth order can have on "the quality of the child's socialization experience—especially during the critical period of . . . identity formation in late adolescence and early adulthood" (1979:166). Convinced by his overprotective mother that he was physically weak and incompetent with the opposite sex, Jimmy identified with the primary role of "leftover son"; as such, he was expected by the community to remain a bachelor and care for his parents.

Not all old Irish bachelors are this unhappy, but their unenviable social position clearly contributes to personality problems, often resulting in severe depression and schizophrenia. Scheper-Hughes also documented the extraordinary social isolation and harsh punishment of young children in her Irish village (1979:134–55), while in her recent book, *Death without Weeping* (1992), she examined child care and neglect in a Brazilian shantytown. Her work is classed here as Social Structure and Personality due to her focus on "the interplay of historical circumstances and economic determinants with the largely symbolic spheres of beliefs, values, and behavior'' (Scheper-Hughes 1979:4). Similar studies of the situations of poor migrants, sharecroppers, and children in the mountains of Appalachia will be found in the work of Robert Coles (1971), told with a simple honesty that will break your heart.

CONCLUSIONS

This chapter has illustrated what is distinctive about the Social Structure and Personality approach in psychological anthropology and related fields. In roughly historical order, we have considered analyses that break away from the ''uniformity assumption'' that whole societies can be characterized by a single personality type. By emphasizing position in the social structure as an important determinant of personality, most of these studies suggest structural features that may have similar effects in many different societies. (For example, Kracke's account of the leadership styles of Homero and Jovenil, despite the exotic details, seems all too familiar in light of the 1992 U.S. presidential campaign, with its leading candidates of contrasting social origins.)

Starting with the Marxist notion of class psychology, we saw that this was a part of revolutionary praxis, but that the central concepts of shared material interests and conditions of work could be used in other ways. Anthropological studies of peasant personality in the 1960s and 1970s debated the existence of shared ''cognitive orientations'' and the importance of internal differentiation of peasant communities, but all were willing to consider that similar material conditions would produce similar behavior despite ''cultural'' differences (Scott 1985).

Many aspects of peasant life can be explained by peasants' low position in the social hierarchy and their vulnerability to exploitation. Foster and his students were concerned with peasants' potential for capitalist development rather than socialist revolution; they saw the Image of Limited Good as an obstacle to innovation and cooperation in rural communities. But both visions ''cut across'' the preoccupation of Culture and Personality with particular societies.

The other key feature of Social Structure and Personality is its concern with differential socialization across the life cycle. This is illustrated in the discussions of alleged ''bureaucratic'' and ''entrepreneurial'' personalities and the attempts by Inkles, Bronfenbrenner, and others to tie them to distinctive modes of child training. The more empirical study of ''primary role identifications'' (Rohrer and Edmonson 1960) seemed to promise a better understanding of the consequences of differential socialization, especially since it was based on longitudinal data; but this lead has not, to my knowledge, been pursued by others.

Writings on the interaction between colonist and colonized have also tended to generalize across cultures, but with very little individual data beyond the author's introspections. (In many cases, the colonized were almost identical with the peasantry, causing some confusion.) Symbolic interactionism belongs in this tradition because even as it moves to more and more detailed studies of interaction situations, it, paradoxically, formulates behavioral generalizations (e.g., about "stigmatized persons" and "leaders") that may hold across cultures.

Bock's (1986) "structural descriptions" are likewise intended to identify interactional similarities and their psychological consequences across cultures. For example, the formula

$$S \mid T : R\,[i] \,/\, R[\$]$$

represents a space-time setting in which the expected interaction between roles is the exchange of information [*i*] for money [$]. This relationship could be construed as including various kinds of apprenticeships, tutorials, and informant relationships (police and anthropological). It leads us to ask about the psychological correlates of such situations for both participants.

Perhaps a more familiar example is Victor Turner's claim that groups of individuals undergoing similar transitions (e.g., during rites of passage, pilgrimages, or natural disasters) enter a "liminal state" in which their social status is ambiguous; this is accompanied by the experience of *communitas*:

> Liminal entities, such as neophytes in initiation or puberty rites, may be represented as possessing nothing. . . . they have no status, property, insignia, secular clothing indicating rank or role, position in a kinship system. . . . It is as though they are being reduced or ground down to a uniform condition to be fashioned anew and endowed with additional powers to enable them to cope with their new station in life. Among themselves, neophytes tend to develop an intense comradeship and egalitarianism. Secular distinctions of rank and status disappear or are homogenized. (Turner 1969:95)

Turner felt that this condition of *communitas* was necessarily temporary, but that it served an essential social and psychological function, providing the "ground," as it were, against which everyday structure could be defined. The experience of equality and/or status reversal enabled people to reflect on the nature of their society and its values.

Leaders are often put through a period of degradation before they are allowed to assume authority (Turner 1969:166–85; also most American election campaigns). As Kracke noted, leaders must often perform the psychological functions of parents, and they are likely to attract the ambivalent feelings of submission and rebellion that originate in the family. They may also be handy scapegoats for their followers' disappointments. Again, the processes involved in such relationships are surprisingly similar across cultures.

The last three studies discussed in this chapter are the richest in individual data. Newton's female impersonators, Cronin's Sicilian immigrants, and Scheper-Hughes's Irish bachelors all come alive as real people whose social positions have strongly influenced their behavior and given them a distinctive view of life. Migrants, marginals, and mama's boys are all subject to severe mental problems; yet some rise above adversity to take command of their lives and achieve happiness. Thus, while social position can help us to understand a great deal about human psychology, it is only part of the story, and the more we learn about particular lives, the greater our appreciation of the complexity of human existence. (For a recent examination of social relations and ''psychological models'' that attempts to simplify this complexity, see Fiske 1991.)

REFERENCES

Arthur, R. J. 1971. *An Introduction to Social Psychiatry*. Baltimore: Penguin.

Berreman, G. D. 1962. *Behind Many Masks*. Society for Applied Anthropology, Monograph no. 4. Ithaca, NY: Society for Applied Anthropology.

Bock, P. K. 1979. *Modern Cultural Anthropology*. 3rd ed. New York: Knopf.

———. 1986. *The Formal Content of Ethnography*. Dallas: International Museum of Cultures.

———. 1988. *Rethinking Psychological Anthropology: Continuity and Change in the Study of Human Action*. New York: W. H. Freeman.

———. 1992. Music in Mérida, Yucatan. *Latin American Music Review* 13:33–55.

Bodley, J. 1990. *Victims of Progress*. 3rd ed. Mountain View, CA: Mayfield.

Bronfenbrenner, U. 1961. The Changing American Child—A Speculative Analysis. *Journal of Social Issues* 17:6–18.

Bukharin, N. 1969. *Historical Materialism*. Ann Arbor: University of Michigan Press. (Original work published 1921.)

Cohen, Y., ed. 1961. *Social Structure and Personality*. New York: Holt, Rinehart and Winston.

———. 1964. *The Transition from Childhood to Adolescence*. Chicago: Aldine.

Coles, R. 1971. *Migrants, Sharecroppers, Mountaineers*. Boston: Little, Brown.

Cronin, C. 1970. *The Sting of Change*. Chicago: University of Chicago Press.

Davis, A., and J. Dollard. 1964. *Children of Bondage*. New York: Harper and Row. (Original work published 1940.)

Drew, P., and A. J. Wootton, eds. 1988. *Erving Goffman: Exploring the Interaction Order*. Cambridge, Eng.: Polity Press.

Endleman, R., ed. 1967. *Personality and Social Life*. New York: Random House.

Fiske, A. P. 1991. *Structures of Social Life: The Four Elementary Forms of Human Relations*. New York: Free Press.

Foster, G. 1967. *Tzintzuntzan*. Boston: Little, Brown.

Galvin, R. M. 1992. The Nature of Shyness. *Harvard Magazine* 94(4):41–45.

Gewertz, D. 1981. A Historical Reconsideration of Female Dominance among the Chambri of Papua New Guinea. *American Ethnologist* 8:94–106.

Goffman, E. 1963. *Stigma*. Englewood Cliffs, NJ: Prentice-Hall.

Gregor, T. 1977. *Mehinaku*. Chicago: University of Chicago Press.

———. 1985. *Anxious Pleasures*. Chicago: University of Chicago Press.

Henry, W. 1949. The Business Executive: The Psychodynamics of a Social Role. *American Journal of Sociology* 54:286–91.

Kleinman, A. 1988. *Rethinking Psychiatry: From Cultural Category to Personal Experience*. New York: Free Press.

Kracke, W. H. 1978. *Force and Persuasion: Leadership in an Amazonian Society*. Chicago: University of Chicago Press.

Lévi-Strauss. 1963. Social Structure. In *Structural Anthropology* pp. 277–323. New York: Basic Books.

Lincoln, B. 1989. *Discourse and the Construction of Society*. New York: Oxford University Press.

Marx, K. and F. Engels. 1959. [1848; Engl. Ed. 1888]. Manifesto of the Communist Party. In L. S. Fever, ed. *Marx and Engels: Basic Writings on Politics and Philosophy*, pp. 1–41. New York: Anchor.

Memmi, A. 1965. *The Colonizer and the Colonized.* Boston: Beacon Press.
Merton, R. K. 1957. *Social Theory and Social Structure.* Glencoe, IL: Free Press.
Newton, E. 1979. *Mother Camp.* Chicago: University of Chicago Press.
Redl, F. 1942. Group Emotions and Leadership. *Psychiatry* 5:573–96.
Riesman, D., with N. Glazer and R. Denney. 1961. *The Lonely Crowd.* New Haven: Yale University Press.
Rohrer, J., and M. Edmonson. 1960. *The Eighth Generation Grows Up.* New York: Harper and Row.
Rosaldo, M., and L. Lamphere, eds. 1974. *Woman, Culture, and Society.* Stanford, CA: Stanford University Press.
Scheper-Hughes, N. 1979. *Saints, Scholars, and Schizophrenics: Mental Illness in Rural Ireland.* Berkeley: University of California Press.
———. 1992. *Death without Weeping.* Berkeley: University of California Press.
Schiebinger, L. 1986. Skeletons in the Closet. *Representations* 14:42–82.
Scott, J. 1985. *Weapons of the Weak.* New Haven: Yale University Press.
Turner, V. 1977. *The Ritual Process: Structure and Anti-Structure.* Ithaca, NY: Cornell University Press.

CHAPTER FOUR

COGNITIVE ANTHROPOLOGY

Ronald W. Casson

Cognitive anthropology is a unified subfield of psychological and cultural anthropology. It is primarily concerned with the insider's view: the society member's perspective on what things mean and what is going on in his or her social world. The principal aim of cognitive anthropology is to understand and describe the world of people in other societies in their own terms, as they conceive and experience it. A further aim is to avoid the biases induced by ethnocentrism, that is, the distortions that result when an investigator imposes an outsider's view on life in another society and describes it from this external perspective. Cognitive anthropologists do not, for example, use the concepts and terminology of modern Western medicine in describing another people's beliefs and practices concerning illness and injury, because this would result in a warped picture of the indigenous medical concepts.

The desire to avoid ethnocentric distortions in describing other societies was a major factor motivating the development of cognitive anthropology. Much of the early work in the field during the late 1950s and early 1960s emphasized new methods and techniques for doing ethnography. One of the first names proposed for the new field was the New Ethnography; but the New Ethnography was not new in its insistence that the task of the ethnographer is to describe behavior and experience from the perspective of society members. This is one of the essential messages of cultural anthropology, established as a core component of the anthropological perspective in the early decades of this century.

The New Ethnography not only emphasized studying the cultures of other societies from the inside but also insisted that the object of study is a mental phenomenon. Cognitive anthropology originated in the middle 1950s as the result of a shift in the definition of culture, the single most important concept in cultural anthropology. Whereas previously culture had been regarded as including behavior and events in the physical world, it was redefined more narrowly at this time as a system of knowledge—as an internal conceptual system underlying and guiding actual behavior and observable events (cf. D'Andrade 1979:1). In 1957, Ward H. Goodenough published an article containing his highly influential definition of culture as cognition. As specified by Goodenough's definition, "A society's culture consists of whatever it is that one has to know or believe in order to operate in a manner acceptable to its members" (1957:167). This ideational conception of culture as a system of knowledge is basic to the content and scope of cognitive anthropology; it will be discussed in more detail later.

Cognitive anthropology did not, however, appear suddenly and fully developed on the anthropological scene in 1957. It had important connections with research in other areas of anthropology. This approach was, in fact, a development from work in two earlier anthropological research traditions. One of its sources was linguistic anthropology, particularly the research guided by the Sapir-Whorf or linguistic relativity hypothesis, which maintains that languages and cultures differ from society to society, and that cultures are shaped by language. (Relativism remains a central issue in cognitive anthropology and will be considered at length later.) From this tradition of linguistic anthropology the new field took the view that language and culture are intimately related, and that the former provides a key to understanding the latter.

Researchers in the new field resisted the more extreme versions of linguistic relativity, but they borrowed the view that the cultural orientation of society members could be reached by careful analysis of linguistic materials. For example, in an effort to discover how people in different societies conceptualize their natural environments, many studies focused on words and their relationships to cognitive categories of plants and animals. Because these studies dealt with folk botanical and zoological knowledge, the field at this earliest point in its development was dubbed *ethnoscience.* As researchers turned from studies of folk scientific knowledge to such other domains of cultural knowledge as law, medicine, and religion, the field came to be called *ethnosemantics* or *ethnographic semantics.* These labels, although not particularly elegant, aptly indicate the concern in this research with elucidating folk meaning. In addition to Goodenough, the anthropologists whose writings were most responsible for these early developments were Charles O. Frake and Harold C. Conklin. The now-classic articles of these writers (cf. Frake 1962; Conklin 1962) and several survey articles (Sturtevant 1964; Colby 1966; Kay 1970) are still the best sources of information on early cognitive anthropology. Two influential collections of early articles were published by Tyler (1969) and Spradley (1972); articles from the 1970s were reprinted in a collection edited by Casson (1981); and two collections of original articles were edited by Dougherty (1985) and Holland and Quinn (1987).

Culture and Personality is the second anthropological subfield that contributed importantly to the formation of cognitive anthropology. From its inception in the 1930s, the principal research interest of this school of psychological anthropology has been individual psychology and its relationship to culture (see Barnouw 1979; Bock 1988). Although Culture and Personality has been dominated, especially in its earlier years, by a concern with affective aspects of individual personalities, Freudian psychology being the main source of theoretical inspiration (see the chapter by Steven Piker in this volume), cognitive aspects began to receive serious attention in the 1950s and 1960s. Together with its interest in the relationship between culture and the emotional structures and processes of individual society members, Culture and Personality became concerned with the relationship between culture and the mental structures and processes of individuals. The most influential cognitive work of the period was Anthony F. C. Wallace's *Culture and Personality* (1961). This new direction of anthropological research was influenced by studies of cognition in cognitive psychology, the most important of which were *A Study of Thinking* (Bruner, Goodnow, and Austin 1956) and *Plans and the Structure of Behavior* (Miller, Galanter, and Pribram 1960).

Early cognitive anthropologists also confronted the problem of sharing and variability. This is a problem that arose in assessments of the relationship between the individual and his culture in most Culture and Personality research. A particularly incisive discussion appeared in Wallace's (1961) book, which still contains some of the best theoretical writing on the subject. The basic question stems from an apparent contradiction: culture is cognitive and therefore located in individual human minds, yet no two individuals share exactly the same system of cultural knowledge. In what sense, then, is culture a cognitive property of individuals, and in what sense is it a shared property of society members? Like relativity and universality, the sharing and variability problem remains one of the central issues in cognitive anthropology and will be considered in more detail later.

BASIC CONCEPTS

The definition of culture that guides the majority of research in cognitive anthropology, as we have seen, holds that culture is an idealized cognitive system—a system of knowledge, beliefs, and values—that exists in the minds of individual members of society (see Goodenough 1981). Culture is the mental equipment that society members use in orienting, transacting, discussing, defining, categorizing, and interpreting actual social behavior in their society. It is the means by which members of a society generate appropriate social behavior and interpret appropriately the behavior of others. Social behavior occurs in the actual physical world. It is the things people actually say and do.

Culture exists in the minds of individual human beings, but individuals do not share exactly the same cognitive model of their culture, just as they do not share exactly the same cognitive model of their language (they differ, for example, in dialect and idiolect). Because of differences in biological heritage, unique personal histories, and the different roles individuals occupy in society, individual society members have varying cognitive models of the society's culture. In the course of growing up, each individual constructs a model or theory of the society's culture. Because it is a personal model, it is only partially shared by other members of the society. The individual's model of the culture does not comprise his or her entire cognitive world. The cognitive worlds of individuals also include idiosyncratic knowledge, beliefs, and values that are the result of people's unique life experiences. As a consequence, they may regard this internal construction as having an external counterpart. So, although individuals may perceive the culture as being an autonomous system of symbols that they can use, manipulate, or change, it is ultimately a mental construct located only in individual minds (see Keesing 1974).

Cognitive models, often called *schemata*, are conceptual abstractions stored in the brain that mediate between stimuli received by the sense organs and behavioral responses (see Wallace 1961). They are abstractions that serve as a basis for all human information processing, for example, perception and comprehension, categorization and planning, recognition and recall, and problem solving and decision making. Schemata are both structures and processes. They are cognitive structures in memory that represent stereotypical concepts. Cognitive schemata represent all of our conceptual knowledge. They structure our knowledge of objects and situations, events and actions, and sequences of events and actions. General and invariant aspects of concepts are represented at higher levels in schematic structures, whereas variables (or ''slots'') that can be associated with (or ''bound by'') specific elements in the environment are represented at lower levels (see Rumelhart 1980).

The cognitive model underlying commercial events in our culture, a much-discussed schema (see Fillmore 1977; Rumelhart 1980; Casson 1983), can serve as an example. The COMMERCIAL EVENT schema has the variables BUYER, SELLER, MONEY, GOODS, and EXCHANGE (upper case here distinguishes conceptual units from words). BUYER is a person who possesses MONEY, the medium of exchange, and SELLER is a person who possesses GOODS, the merchandise for sale. EXCHANGE is an interaction in which BUYER gives MONEY and gets GOODS, and SELLER gives GOODS and gets MONEY. An event is understood as a commercial transaction when persons, objects, and subevents in the environmental situation are bound to appropriate schema variables.

Schemata are also processors that construct interpretations of behavior and experience. They are active procedures that evaluate the goodness-of-fit between schema structures and elements in the phenomenal realm (Rumelhart 1980). Expectations represented in schemata are matched with elements in the behavioral and experiential environment, and, on the basis of goodness-of-fit between expectations and elements, the instantiation process constructs accounts that make sense of occurrences in the phenomenal world.

Activity taking place in a large glass-fronted enclosure containing people and automobiles can provide an example of schema processing. A number of people are milling around, chatting, and examining the cars. The setting, people, objects, and activities suggest that the CAR DEALERSHIP cognitive model is relevant to interpreting what is going on in the enclosure. Because an expectation associated with the CAR DEALERSHIP schema is that cars will be bought and sold, one of its subschemata is the now-familiar COMMERCIAL EVENT schema. The GOODS variable may be bound by the cars, and a well-dressed man engaged in kicking tires and slamming doors is a reasonable candidate for the BUYER variable. The fact that the man is well dressed suggests financial resources, a possible binding for the MONEY variable. The presence of a broadly smiling man in a checkered sports coat who approaches the well-dressed man and engages him in hearty conversation suggests a potential binding for the SELLER variable. The binding of these variables confirms the schema expectations and eliminates from consideration alternative general cognitive models that might have been invoked at the outset of processing. One candidate would have been the AUTO SHOW schema in which the expectation is not that cars will be bought or sold, but that they will simply be exhibited.

In cognitive research, linguists often use the concept of "frames" to account for how the lexical and grammatical forms in language both structure and express underlying schematic representations (see Fillmore 1977, 1985; Chafe 1977, 1979). The basic notion in framing is that lexical items (essentially, words) and grammatical categories and rules are associated in memory with schemata and parts of schemata. Frames and schemata "activate" each other: linguistic forms bring schemata to mind, and schemata are expressed in linguistic forms. Linguistic forms label schemata and provide the means of verbalizing them. The major research strategies used in cognitive anthropology exploit this relationship between language and cognition. Linguistic expressions are the principal tools employed by virtually all researchers in discovering and studying conceptual categories and systems. As succinctly stated by D'Andrade, the program for studying cultural cognition is to "search for commonalities in knowledge systems built into language in order to find out basic characteristics of human thought" (1979:3).

A number of lexical items, for example, can activate the COMMERCIAL EVENT cultural model. *Buy, sell, pay, cost, worth, value, spend*, and *charge* are some of the words that activate this schema. Each of them selects particular aspects of the schema for highlighting or foregrounding, while leaving others in the background unexpressed (Fillmore 1977:103). *Buy* focuses on the exchange from the buyer's perspective, and *sell* from the seller's perspective. *Cost* focuses on the money part of the money-goods relationship, and *value* and *worth* focus on the goods part of the relationship. *Pay* and *spend* focus on the buyer and the money part of the money-goods relationship, and *charge* focuses on the seller and the goods part of the money-goods relationship.

Cognitive models generally include a number of subschemata as component parts, each of which interacts in its own right with elements in the phenomenal world. Schemata, in other words, are most often complex structures composed of numerous subschemata. Schemata are interrelated in complex structures in two basic ways. They are connected by hierarchical embedding, general schemata dominating specific schemata, which are bound to schema variables as subschemata, and they are connected by horizontal linkages, initial schemata preceding subsequent schemata in ordered temporal and causal sequences.

Classification systems are hierarchically ordered cognitive models in which general conceptual categories are represented at higher levels in complex schemata and specific categories are represented at lower levels. Classifications of plants, for example, are organized hierarchically: general categories, such as TREE, dominate and include more specific categories, such as OAK, ELM, and SPRUCE. Event scenarios are horizontally ordered models, in which causal conceptual scenes are sequentially linked to resultant scenes (see Minsky 1975: 234–40). Eating in a restaurant is organized horizontally: ENTERING the restaurant precedes ORDERING a meal, which occurs before EATING the meal; PAYING for the meal follows eating; and EXITING the restaurant concludes the scene sequence (see Schank and Abelson 1977:45). Hierarchical embedding and horizontal linking are not mutually exclusive in complex schemata. We will examine research on both types of cognitive structures in following sections.

Cognitive models differ in their distribution in populations: some are universal, some idiosyncratic, and some cultural (see the introduction to this volume). Universal schemata are uniform in the human species, idiosyncratic schemata are unique to particular individuals, and cultural schemata are neither unique to individuals nor shared by all humans, but rather are shared by members of particular societies (Casson 1981:20–21). Cognitive anthropologists are concerned with cultural schemata, with "the cultural part of cognition" (D'Andrade 1981). They focus on how systems of cultural knowledge are constrained and shaped by the machinery of the brain. The assumption here is that as a result of its regular transmission from generation to generation, cultural knowledge comes to be organized in such a way that it "fits" the capabilities and constraints of the human mind (D'Andrade 1981:182).

The focus of cognitive anthropologists on the interface between cultural knowledge and basic psychological factors can be illustrated by Berlin and Kay's (1969) research on color categories. Their comparative studies demonstrated that basic color categories are organized around best examples, and that these focal colors are the same across individuals and across languages. This general finding about color categorization has been shown to be the result of neurophysiological processes in human color perception that interact with cognitive mechanisms in the formation of color categories (Ratliff 1975; Kay and McDaniel 1978; Kay, Berlin, and Merrifield 1991; MacLaury 1992).

Until the advent of ethnoscience/ethnosemantics in the 1950s, anthropological research into the nature of the relationship between language and cognition was dominated by the Sapir-Whorf hypothesis. This perspective on linguistic and cultural relativism was named after Edward Sapir and Benjamin Lee Whorf,

American linguistic anthropologists of the 1920s and 1930s. The highly influential position they espoused claims that cognitive categories are not formed in response to divisions in the natural world or to universal properties of the mind, but rather in response to the organization of grammatical (including lexical) systems. Because, in their view, grammatical systems are determined by arbitrary conventions in speech communities, the cognitive systems created by grammatical systems are entirely relative to, in fact idiosyncratic to, individual communities. The complete relativist position holds that languages and cultures are, as Sapir put it, "incommensurable," that is, they have no common measure and, therefore, cannot be compared or translated.

Early work in ethnoscience/ethnosemantics was focused on perfecting new methods for the ethnographic description of cultural differences in cognitive systems. By the mid-1960s, however, a new emphasis appeared. The concern with cultural diversity continued, but an interest in comparative issues and research emerged, and the field now emphasizes uniformity as well as diversity in language and culture studies.

Cognitive anthropologists who adopt this perspective generally oppose the extreme relativist position of Sapir and Whorf. Their position, which has been termed the *limited relativist* or *universalist* position, emphasizes commonality in language and culture and the psychic unity of humankind. Diversity in language and culture is acknowledged, but the focus of research is the discovery of prime concepts—the fundamental, universal concepts underlying the variable superstructures of linguistic and cultural systems (Lounsbury 1969:10). The discovery of such concepts provides a basis for the commensurability, comparability, and translatability that is denied by proponents of the complete relativist position. The limited relativist position is thus universalist in its emphasis on primes yet relativist in its recognition of diversity in all aspects of linguistic and cultural systems above ultimate primes.

Several theoretical distinctions are basic to the study of cognitive universals. One is the distinction between formal and substantive universals (see Chomsky 1965). Formal universals are universals of form. For example, all languages have the grammatical categories noun, verb, and adjective. Substantive universals are universals of content. All languages have nouns that refer to relatives and adjectives that refer to colors. The second distinction is between absolute universals and conditional, or implicational, universals (see Greenberg 1966). The former are characteristics that occur in all languages. All languages have words for "mother" and "father," for example. The latter are characteristics that occur under certain conditions. If a language has a word for "red," for example, it always has terms for "black" and "white" as well. The presence of a term for red universally implies the presence of terms for black and white (the presence of terms for black and white, on the other hand, does not imply the presence of a term for red). Research in cognitive anthropology, as we shall see, has been more concerned with implicational universals than with absolute universals.

As stated earlier, culture exists in the minds of individuals, but the cultural models of these individuals are not identical. In much cognitive anthropological research, as in mainstream linguistic research, accounts of aspects of culture and language are idealized composite or shared models constructed from the varying cognitive models of individuals. These models attempt to capture the perfect knowledge of an ideal individual in a culturally homogeneous community.

Composite models of culture are assembled by ethnographers from numerous informants. A knowledgeable informant knows a great deal about a particular cultural domain of knowledge, but he does not know everything about it. A second informant does not know all that the first informant reported, but she knows other things that the first informant did not mention. A third informant, who does not control all the cultural knowledge provided by the first and second informants, may have specialized cultural information that neither of the others were able to contribute. An ethnographic description pieced together from these disparate contributions is a composite model of the domain. It represents the ideal knowledge of an informant in a presumably homogeneous community who knows all aspects of the cultural domain perfectly.

Shared models of culture employ a second strategy in sidestepping the problem of variability in cultural knowledge. Whereas a composite model is constructed from the varying knowledge of individual informants, a shared model is comprised only of cultural elements that are known by all informants. Of the cultural knowledge supplied by the three informants consulted in making the composite model, only information contributed by all three would be included in a shared model. A shared model specifies only the subset of cultural knowledge that is shared by members of a community.

The majority of cognitive anthropological studies of conceptual systems are composite or shared models of cultural knowledge. Both types of cognitive models omit individual variability and analyze cultural knowledge as though it were homogeneous in the community. Adopting this heuristic assumption has made significant progress possible in research and has considerably advanced our understanding of linguistic and cultural phenomena. But viewed from the perspective of individual society members, composite models overrepresent, and shared models underrepresent, the cultural knowledge that is controlled by any single member of society. No society member knows all the cultural elements represented in a composite model, but all members know more cultural elements than are represented in a shared model. This is not to say that either model is false or invalid. Both have contributed important insights into cognitive structures and processes. The data on individual variability omitted from composite and shared models are, however, crucial to an understanding both of how the diverse cognitive models of individuals are organized in societies, and of how this individual variability serves as a basis for linguistic and cultural change. (Research exploring these variability issues is described later. See also the chapter by Niko Besnier in part II.)

METHODS AND FINDINGS

The influence of linguistic anthropology and linguistics proper on the development of cognitive anthropology went beyond a basic interest in the relationship between language and culture. Ethnoscientists and ethnosemanticists also modeled the methods and techniques they used in studying conceptual systems in cultures on the procedures used by linguists in studying languages. Linguistic borrowings influenced cognitive anthropological research in the earliest stages, and they have continued to do so to the present.

The central unit in cognitive anthropology is the *conceptual category*. The structure and organization of conceptual categories in folk classification systems and the cultural meaning encoded in these systems have long been primary concerns in the field. In all societies, objects, acts, and events that are in fact different are grouped together in categories and regarded as equivalent. Every tree is in some respects unique, yet differences are ignored and trees are classed as instances of particular cultural categories, such as oak, maple, and poplar. Cultural systems contain vast numbers of conceptual categories. Some of them are specific categories that have few members, while others are general categories that have many members.

No analysis has yet been made of the full set of conceptual categories in a culture, just as no complete analysis has yet been achieved of all the conceptual units in a language. Like linguists, cognitive anthropologists have limited the scope of their investigations. Rather than attempt superficial accounts of whole cultures, they have concentrated on the study of conceptual categories called *semantic domains*. These domains are large cultural categories that include many related smaller categories. Domains that have been investigated in particular cultures include plants, animals, colors, foods, kinsmen, occupations, supernaturals, body parts, time and tide, emotions, illness and diseases, statuses and roles, activities and tasks, and situations and events.

Classification systems, as we have seen, are complex cognitive models that are structured by hierarchical embedding. Probably the most common and certainly the most studied of classification systems is the *taxonomy*. The term *taxonomy* has two meanings: in general it refers to any type of classification system, while specifically it refers to the type of classification system based on the ''kind of'' relation. The structure of a taxonomy (and all other classification systems) is determined by the semantic contrasts that distinguish its component categories. Two categories contrast when they have different memberships. They may contrast totally, in some or many respects, or in only one respect. In our culture, the categories associated with the words *hamburger* and *truck* are totally distinct. *Hamburger* and *chowder* contrast partially in that, although they both refer to food, they refer to different kinds of food. *Hamburger* and *cheeseburger* designate categories of food that differ only with respect to the presence or absence of a slice of cheese.

Taxonomic classification systems are structured on the basis of a particular type of semantic contrast, *inclusion.* Categories that contrast in one or many, but not all, respects (and are therefore semantically distinct) may stand to each other in an inclusion or "kind of" relationship: category X completely includes category Y, which is regarded as a kind of X. For example, the category labeled *tree* in English includes the *oak* category. An oak is a kind of tree. Other categories included in the *tree* category are *maple, pine, elm, spruce, poplar, walnut*, and *fir. Oak* in turn includes the subordinate categories *white oak, post oak, red oak, jack oak, scrub oak, live oak, pin oak, burr oak,* and *blue oak.* The contrastive relationships among these categories define a hierarchical taxonomic classification (cf. Berlin 1976, 1978, 1992; Berlin, Breedlove, and Raven 1973, 1974; Brown 1977, 1979, 1984, 1985, 1986; Hayes 1976, 1983; Hunn 1977, 1985).

Lexical labels are associated with conceptual categories, but semantic contrasts, as we have seen, are defined in terms of conceptual categories, not words. Categories, which are often termed *taxa* (singular *taxon*) in the study of taxonomies (in the narrow sense), are always mutually exclusive, each having a unique place in the taxonomic hierarchy. The relationships between semantic categories and their lexical representations must be determined empirically because meaning and form are not always associated in a one-to-one fashion. A single concept may be associated with more than one lexical item, and more than one concept may be associated with a single lexical item. The former relationship is known as *synonymy*, and the latter is known as *polysemy.*

Polysemy must be defined in contrast with *homonymy*, another semantic relationship. Homonymy is a relationship between two or more lexical items that have the same form but completely different meanings. *Pop* ("father") and *pop* ("sweet, carbonated beverage") and *bank* ("side of a stream") and *bank* ("repository for money") are examples. Polysemy is a relationship between the several conceptual meanings of a single lexical item. A polysemous lexical item has a single form, but multiple related meanings.

Semantic categories are not isomorphic with their lexical labels, and the structure of classification systems is defined by contrasts among categories, not lexical labels. Nonetheless, the form of lexical items is relevant to an understanding of classification systems. In their studies of classifications, cognitive anthropologists employ the concept *lexeme*, which is determined largely by semantic considerations. Whether a word or combination of words is a lexeme depends on the meaning of its component parts. It is a lexeme if it is semantically opaque or exocentric (outwardly oriented), such that its meaning is not determinable from its constituent parts. It is a nonlexemic compound or phrase if it is semantically transparent or endocentric (inwardly oriented), such that its meaning can be determined from its constituencies (cf. Conklin 1962). The following pairs of lexemic and nonlexemic forms illustrate this distinction: *blackbird* (a species of bird) versus *black bird* (a bird that is black in color), *eggplant* versus *leafy plant, red herring* versus *pickled herring, white oak* versus *ancient oak*, and *grandson* versus *oldest son.*

Several types of lexemic forms must be distinguished. Primary lexemes are either simple or complex. Simple primary lexemes consist of only a single unanalyzable constituent, for example, *bird, cat, plant, herring, oak,* and *son*. Complex primary lexemes, on the other hand, have two types of analyzable constituent structure. Unproductive complex primary lexemes have no components that refer to superordinate categories. *Red herring*, for example, does not refer to a kind of fish, and *grandson* is not a term that refers to sons who are large or grand. Productive complex primary lexemes, which do have constituent parts referring to superordinate categories, occur in contrast sets with simple and complex unproductive primary lexemes. *Eggplant*, for instance, refers to a plant category, but one that occurs in contrast with *squash, cucumber*, and *avocado*. Secondary lexemes are distinct from all types of primary lexemes. They have constituents that refer to subordinate categories, and they occur in contrast sets with other categories, each sharing the same superordinate marker. *White oak, post oak, jack oak*, and all the other members of the oak contrast set include the constituent *oak*, which is the label for the immediately dominating superordinate category *oak* (see Berlin 1976).

An important finding of cognitive anthropological research on classification systems is that categories (or taxa) in ethnobiological taxonomies are grouped into six mutually exclusive hierarchical ranks, termed "kingdom," "life-form," "generic," "specific," "varietal," and "intermediate." Taxonomic and nomenclature characteristics are the principal criteria by means of which categories are assigned to ranks, although biological and psychological considerations also play a part (see Berlin 1976, 1978; Berlin, Breedlove, and Raven 1973, 1974).

The kingdom category is the all-inclusive unique beginner, or head taxon, that delimits the entire domain. It occurs at the highest level, level 0, in taxonomic hierarchies and is often a covert category, that is, a category lacking a linguistic label. English *plant* is an overt label for our botanical domain. Life-form categories are the next most inclusive categories. They are few in number (zero to ten) and occur only at level 1 in taxonomic hierarchies. The lexemes for categories of life-form rank are always primary lexemes and nearly always simple primary lexemes. *Tree, bush, plant, grass*, and *vine* are terms for English life-form categories.

Generic rank categories comprise the core of ethnobiological taxonomies. By far the largest number of categories in taxonomic classifications are of generic rank. They are psychologically extremely salient: they are learned very early by children, and they are readily elicited from informants. The lexemes used for generic categories are generally primary lexemes, most often (but not always) simple primary lexemes, and are more frequently used than the lexemes for categories of other ranks. English examples are *oak, maple, pine, elm, spruce*, and so on. The majority of generic categories occur at level 2 and are included in life-form categories. However, a few generic categories, termed "unaffiliated generics," occur at level 1 are are directly included in the kingdom category.

Most generic categories include only one subcategory and, as such, are terminal categories. Generic categories that dominant subcategories always immediately include categories of specific rank at level 3 (or level 2 if the dominating category is an unaffiliated generic). Specific rank categories, in turn, include categories of varietal rank at level 4 (or level 3 if the dominating generic category is unaffiliated). Specific categories are few in number, and varietal categories are rare. The lexemes for both are binomial (two-name) secondary lexemes, such as *white oak, post oak, jack oak,* and *scrub oak.*

Categories of intermediate rank are categories of a special type. They are midlevel classes, occurring most commonly between level 1 life-form and level 2 generic categories, but also between categories of other adjacent ranks. Midlevel groupings of trees into ''leaf-bearing,'' ''needle-bearing,'' and ''frond-bearing'' are examples of covert intermediate categories in our ethnobotanical classification system. For many Americans, the ''needle- bearing'' intermediate category (including *pine, spruce,* and *fir*) is overtly labeled *evergreen.* Midlevel categories occur in most classification systems. They are temporary distinctions, or quasi-categories, that are especially important because they reflect the progress of ongoing change (see Dougherty 1978).

NONTAXONOMIC CATEGORIES AND SUPERCATEGORIES

In addition to taxonomies, cognitive anthropologists have studied various types of nontaxonomic classification. One of these is the constituent, or partonomic, classification system, in which higher- and lower-level categories are related not by the inclusion relation but rather by the part-whole, or ''part of,'' relation: category X is a part of category Y, and Y is the whole of which X is a part (see Frake 1964b; Casagrande and Hale 1967; Spradley 1979). The most extensively studied constituent classifications are ethnoanatomical systems, which, like taxonomies, often involve several hierarchical levels. An English example is ''*fingernail* is part of *finger, finger* and *palm* are parts of *hand, hand* and *forearm* are parts of *arm,* and *arm* is a part of *body*'' (see Andersen 1978; also Brown 1976; Burton and Kirk 1979; MacLaury 1989; Stross 1976). Other constituent classifications include membership classification systems such as *family,* which has among its members *mother, son,* and *sister,* and *baseball team,* which has the members *pitcher, shortstop,* and *manager.*

Functional classifications are constructed on the basis of the instrumental, or ''used for,'' relationship: X is the means of doing Y, and Y is what is done through the aid or application of X. One way in which shoes, for example, are classified in our culture is by function: a *jogging shoe* is a shoe used for jogging, and a *tennis shoe* is a shoe used for playing tennis. Categories in classification systems that in earlier research were treated as taxonomic categories have been shown to be functional categories (Wierzbicka 1984, 1985). For example, *vehicle* is not a taxonomic category. It is, rather, a functional concept: a *vehicle* is any kind of object that can be used as transportation. *Car, bus, moped,* and *monocycle* are all kinds of objects that function as vehicles.

Functional categories group together things of any kind that share a particular function (see Wierzbicka 1984, 1985). In addition to *vehicle*, other functional categories are *toy, weapon, tool, utensil*, and *ornament*. A *toy* is a kind of thing that children use in playing, and a *weapon* is a kind of thing that people use in fighting. Many artifacts are manufactured to be toys or weapons, but other objects can also function as toys or weapons. A rubber ball is made to be a child's *toy*, and a pistol is made to serve as a *weapon*. But children often use an old purse or tube of lipstick as a *toy*, and people occasionally employ a fireplace poker or bicycle chain as a handy *weapon* (Wierzbicka 1985:263–69).

The majority of our object categories are taxonomic concepts. Whether they are parrots, roses, horses, bottles, triangles, or cars, entities in the world are categorized as kinds of things (Wierzbicka 1984:325). In ethnobiological classifications, as we have seen, generic-level categories such as *parrot, rose*, and *horse* are subcategories of higher-level taxonomic categories, termed life-form categories, by virtue of the inclusion relation. Generic categories are the basic-level categories in ethnobiological classification systems; they are by far the most numerous and the most salient categories in these classifications. Classifications of nonbiological or "manufactured" entities have basic-level categories such as *bottle, triangle*, and *car*, but they are not generally subcategories of taxonomic superkinds, that is, life-form categories. Rather, they are most often subcategories of functional, constituent, and other types of higher-level categories. "Supercategory" is used instead of "life-form category" as the term for these higher-level categories, as "life-form" is inapplicable to nonbiological categories.

Basic categories of objects that are subcategories of functional supercategories such as *toy, weapon*, or *vehicle* are often not functional concepts. *Ball*, for instance, refers to a round or roundish thing that is used as a plaything. It is a particular kind of thing and, thus, a taxonomic concept. Some taxonomic categories are subcategories of several functional supercategories. *Knife* labels a taxonomic concept—slender, sharp-bladed object used for cutting—that is a subcategory of at least three different functional supercategories, *weapon, utensil*, and *tool.*

Knife also labels subcategories of *kitchenware* and *tableware*, which are neither taxonomic nor functional supercategories, but rather "collective supercategories" (cf. Wierzbicka 1985:269–93). There are two types of collective supercategories. "Collective-functional" supercategories group basic-level subcategories on the basis of contiguity and function. Examples of this type of collective concept are *furniture, cutlery, crockery, jewelry, kitchenware*, and *tableware*. These are all supercategories of different kinds of things that are kept or used together in a particular location for a similar purpose. *Pot, pan, bowl, knife*, and *spatula* are subcategories of *kitchenware*: they are basic-level categories of different kinds of things that are used collectively in the kitchen. *Sofa, armchair, end table*, and *lamp* are subcategories of *furniture* that include different kinds of things that are kept together to furnish a room.

"Collective-nonfunctional" supercategories group subcategories on the basis of contiguity and rationale. *Leftovers, contents, groceries, valuables, belongings, supplies, trappings, odds and ends*, and *dishes* are examples of this type. They are supercategories of different kinds of things that at some time are or were in the same location for a particular reason. *Leftovers* are different kinds of foods located in the same place because they are all left over from a meal. *Dishes*, the items that are washed in "washing the dishes," are different kinds of things (most not dishes at all) that formed a collectivity during the preparing, serving, and consuming of a meal and now need to be washed.

EVENT SCENARIOS

Event schemata, as was pointed out earlier, are complex cognitive models that are structured by horizontal linkages (see Agar 1974, 1975; Frake 1964a, 1964b, 1975, 1977; McDermott, Gospodinoff, and Aron 1978; Quinn 1985). In event schemata, scenes are horizontally linked in ordered sequences and vertically dominated by a superordinate category. Scenes in event scenarios, like object categories in taxonomic and nontaxonomic classification systems, are basic-level concepts immediately dominated by a supercategory, the scenario as a whole. Scenes are linked by way of causal, or contingency, relations. Actions and states are conditionally connected: X (a state) is usually or necessarily followed or accompanied by Y (an action), and Y (the action) is the usual or necessary consequence or concomitant of X (the state). Numerous types of causal relations have been proposed, but five are essential in event scenarios: RESULT causation (action RESULTS IN state change), ENABLE causation (state ENABLES action), DISABLE causation (state DISABLES action), INITIATION causation (state or act INITIATES mental state), and REASON causation (mental state is REASON FOR action) (Schank and Abelson 1977:24–32).

Charles O. Frake's (1975) account of "How to Enter a Yakan House" can provide an unfamiliar example of an event scenario. The Yakan are Philippine Moslems living on Basilan, an island located near Mindanao. They are agriculturalists who reside in nuclear-family dwellings dispersed in fields and groves. Yakan houses are rectangular, ridge-roofed, single-room dwellings elevated two to three meters above ground level on piles. The space within and around a Yakan house is conceptually organized into discrete settings for numerous types of social events (Frake 1975:26–28).

Social encounters between householders and outsiders are defined by the degree to which outsiders penetrate household settings. The more setting boundaries an outsider crosses, the deeper the penetration. The outsider progresses from "in the vicinity" of the house (within sight and calling distance of the house) to "at" the house (any setting closer than in the "vicinity"), from "below" the house to any setting above the porch ladder, from "outside" (on the porch) to "inside" (the main room), and from the "foot zone" (the portion of floor space adjacent to the entrance door) to the "head zone" (the portion of floor space opposite to the doorway, which is the sleeping area for household members). The head zone is the most private setting and the setting of maximal penetration (Frake 1975:29).

The progress of an outsider through these settings is guided by proper etiquette. The householder gives "invitations" to the outsider to enter the next setting and offers amenities appropriate to the social encounter in each setting—tobacco or betel quids on the porch, snacks or a meal inside. The outsider never leaves a setting before asking and receiving "permission to leave" from the householder (Frake 1975:30). At each stage (except the last) in the fixed sequence of settings, three outcomes are possible: advance, terminate, or hold. The householder can invite the outsider to advance to the next setting, but cannot request a guest to leave. The outsider can request permission to leave, but can only advance by invitation of the householder. When the householder issues an invitation and the outsider does not ask for permission to leave, their interaction moves to the next setting. When the outsider asks for permission to leave and the householder does not give an invitation, interaction is terminated. When the householder gives an invitation and the outsider asks for permission to leave (or when the householder does not invite and the outsider does not ask permission), interaction continues on hold in the same setting (Frake 1975:33).

The schema for entering a Yakan house is an event scenario. The HOUSE ENTERING event has the variables HOUSEHOLDER, OUTSIDER, SETTINGS, INVITATION, and PERMISSION TO LEAVE. HOUSEHOLDER and OUTSIDER are role variables, SETTINGS is a set of ordered location variables, and INVITATION and PERMISSION TO LEAVE are interactions between HOUSEHOLDER and OUTSIDER that guide movements through SETTINGS. As we have seen, outsider-householder interactions in Yakan house entering can result in several different outcomes.

An American scenario can provide a more familiar example. We will again take up the COMMERCIAL EVENT schema, this time to illustrate the ordering of multiple-scene RESTAURANT EVENT scenarios (Schank 1982; Schank and Abelson 1977). Whereas in the CAR DEALERSHIP event the schema variables included only BUYER and SELLER as role variables, with MONEY and GOODS as prop variables, the scenario for the RESTAURANT EVENT requires at a minimum the roles CUSTOMER, WAITER/WAITRESS, CHEF, CASHIER, and OWNER and the props MONEY, FOOD, BILL, MENU, and TABLE. The critical variable in both commercial events is EXCHANGE. In the restaurant version of the event, EXCHANGE is a transaction in which CUSTOMER gives MONEY and gets FOOD, and OWNER, CASHIER, CHEF, and WAITER/WAITRESS give FOOD and get MONEY.

To get a meal at a fancy restaurant such as Françoise's Gourmet French Restaurant or a family restaurant such as Farmer Bob's Friendly Restaurant, customers must negotiate a strict sequence of scenes. They first enter the restaurant; then they are seated, order food, eat the food, pay for the food, and finally exit the restaurant (Schank 1982:41, 133–42). The causal relations linking actions and states in this event scenario can be sketched as follows:

CUSTOMER ENTERS the restaurant (action)
  RESULTS IN
CUSTOMER being in restaurant (state change)
  ENABLES
CUSTOMER to be SEATED at a TABLE (action)
  RESULTS IN
CUSTOMER located at TABLE (state)
  ENABLES
CUSTOMER to ORDER FOOD from WAITER/WAITRESS (action)
  RESULTS IN
CUSTOMER obtaining FOOD from WAITER/WAITRESS (state change)
  ENABLES
CUSTOMER to EAT the FOOD (action)
  INITIATES
CUSTOMER owing MONEY for the FOOD (state)
  REASON FOR
CUSTOMER to PAY MONEY to CASHIER (action)
  RESULTS IN
CUSTOMER being free to EXIT restaurant (state)
  ENABLES
CUSTOMER to EXIT the restaurant (action)

This scenario is in fact more complex than shown here. For example, not all enablement conditions are specified: in the PAY scene, in addition to a debt for FOOD, the customer must have MONEY as a prerequisite to paying. Many other details are omitted, but the scenario is probably sufficiently detailed that a customer entering Farmer Bob's or Françoise's could use it to move through the sequence of scenes in the event and get a meal.

Scenes in RESTAURANT EVENT scenarios are basic-level concepts dominated by a supercategory, the RESTAURANT EVENT itself. They are general concepts that are instantiated, or colored, by "scripts." Defined as a "predetermined, stereotyped sequence of actions that defines a well-known situation" (Schank and Abelson 1977:41), scripts supply detail and specificity to scenes. The script that instantiates the ORDERING scene in fancy and family restaurants specifies that the CUSTOMER is sitting at a TABLE, a MENU is located on the TABLE (or a WAITER/WAITRESS brings a MENU to the TABLE), the CUSTOMER selects FOOD and communicates selections to the WAITER/

WAITRESS, the WAITER/WAITRESS conveys this information to the CHEF, the CHEF prepares the FOOD, and (eventually) the WAITER/WAITRESS brings the FOOD to the CUSTOMER at the TABLE. The script that instantiates the ORDERING scene in a fast-food restaurant specifies that the CUSTOMER proceeds to the COUNTER, the CUSTOMER scans the MENU BOARD located on the wall behind the COUNTER, the CUSTOMER selects FOOD and communicates selections to the COUNTER ATTENDANT, and the COUNTER ATTENDANT brings the FOOD to the COUNTER. So while the ORDERING scene is a general concept that occurs in both sit-down and fast-food restaurant scenarios, it is instantiated by scripts that provide the specific details involved in ordering in particular types of restaurants (Schank 1982:133–42).

PROTOTYPE CATEGORIES

To this point we have been concerned with the relationships among conceptual categories in classification systems and event scenarios. In turning now to prototype categories, we focus on the internal structure of conceptual categories. Prototype categories are defined in contrast to accounts of category structure that posit *digital* representations of concepts (Rosch 1978); they define conceptual meanings in terms of conjunctions of discrete properties, variously termed "distinctive features," "semantic components," and "criterial attributes" (Fillmore 1975). Elements displaying the set of distinctive features defining a concept are instances of the concept. Thus membership in categories is a "yes" or "no" matter: elements are either instances of categories or they are not, and all instances are equivalent as members.

A favorite example of categories of this type, which have been dubbed "classical categories," is *bachelor* (Fillmore 1982; Lakoff 1987). The category *bachelor* is defined by several distinctive features: MALE, ADULT, and UNMARRIED. Given cultural background information about what constitutes marriage and being married or unmarried, and about what age a male must reach to qualify as an adult eligible to marry, individuals are classed either in the category or not in the category. There is no middle ground, and all individuals classed in the category are equally members of the category.

A prototype is a stereotypic, or generic, representation of a concept that serves as a standard for evaluating typical elements that instantiate the prototype and less typical elements that bear a family resemblance to it, that is, are sufficiently similar to it (Coleman and Kay 1981; Fillmore 1977, 1982, 1985; Rosch 1973, 1977, 1978). Similarity is, of course, a matter of degree: some elements resemble prototypes more closely than others. A basic tenet of prototype theory is that the meaning of a concept "consists in a cognitive prototype to which various real and imagined events may correspond in varying degrees" (Coleman and Kay 1981:26). Prototype theories of category structure posit *analog* representations of concepts (Rosch 1978) and define conceptual meanings in terms of overall resemblance to cognitive prototypes. Elements that possess some (but not necessarily all) of the properties defining the prototype are instances of the concept. Thus membership in prototype categories is a ''more'' or ''less'' matter: elements are instances of categories to a degree, and instances differ in the degree to which they are members (Coleman and Kay 1981; Kempton 1981; Kronenfeld, Armstrong, and Wilmoth 1985; Rosch 1977, 1978).

Asymmetries among category members have been termed ''prototype effects.'' Different cognitive prototypes produce different prototype effects, but in all cases the prototype member is the ''best example,'' and other members are ranked by degree of distance from the prototype (Lakoff 1987:40–42). A robin or a sparrow is a best example of the category *bird*, an owl or an eagle is a less good example, and an emu or penguin is an even less worthy example. Prototype effects are a genuine phenomenon in conceptual categories, but they do not constitute a theory or explanation of prototype categories. Cognitive prototypes occur in many different types of prototype categories, but prototypes alone account for categories of only one type, ''graded, or scalar, categories.'' Most varieties of prototype categories are structured by the interaction of cognitive prototypes and *idealized cognitive models*, conventionally abbreviated as ICMs (Lakoff 1987:42–45).

Graded categories have degrees of membership (that is, prototype effects), and boundaries are fuzzy. Prototype effects in graded categories are produced simply by the scaling of members along a single dimension of distance from the prototype. Basic color terms are the best-studied example. Berlin and Kay's (1969) comparative research showed that the focal types, or best examples, of basic color terms are fixed and invariant, but that their boundaries are fuzzy and highly variable across societies and individuals. Focal BLUE, for example, is not only a category member, it is the central member of the blue category. Nonprototypical colors closely resembling focal BLUE are also clearly members of the category. But a color that is equally distant from focal BLUE and focal GREEN can be located in the fuzzy overlap between the blue and green categories and be a member of the blue category, the green category, or both categories to a minor degree (Kay and Kempton 1984).

The most common type of prototype category, the ''typical example'' or ''typical case'' category, has degrees of membership and strict boundaries (Lakoff 1987:86). Much of our categorization is concerned with the typicality of concrete entities. (This category type can, in fact, be regarded as the prototype of prototype categories.) Typical example categories derive from the interaction of cognitive prototypes and ICMs that impose typicality structure on category membership within discrete boundaries. Entities ranked according to typicality are prototype effects, and typical and nontypical entities are all included within category boundaries (Lakoff 1987:44, 86).

The *chair* category has been a very popular example in the cognitive literature (cf. Minsky 1975; Rumelhart 1980; Lakoff and Johnson 1980). The prototype of the *chair* category is defined in terms of distinctive features of form and function: LEGS, RUNGS, SEAT, BACK, and USED FOR SITTING. Desk chairs and kitchen chairs are best examples of the category. Nonprototypical members have some but not all of the prototypical features. Those that have most of the features rank closer to the prototype than those that have fewer of the features. Reclining chairs, swivel chairs, contour chairs, and rocking chairs are all nonprototypical but reasonably good examples of chairs, whereas beanbag chairs, hanging chairs, barber chairs, and electric chairs are weak prototypical examples. Despite their differences, however, all these objects are members of the *chair* category.

Several other types of categories structured by prototypes and ICMs deserve mention. Stereotypic prototype effects are induced when prototypes are joined with social stereotype ICMs (Lakoff 1987:85–86). The category *bachelor* can again serve as an example. *Bachelor*, as we have seen, is a bounded category with no membership grading. Everyone classed as a *bachelor* is equally a bachelor. When a stereotypic prototype imposes internal structure within the boundaries of this classical category, bachelors are ranked on the basis of how closely they match the stereotypical BACHELOR prototype. If the stereotypical bachelor is macho, promiscuous, and nondomestic, then a bachelor who is a bookworm, has a steady relationship, and enjoys housework and cooking is a nonstereotypical bachelor (Lakoff 1987:85–86). Both are members of the stereotypical *bachelor* category, but one is a prototypical example and the other is a nonprototypical example.

''Generative categories'' are structured by a special prototype called a ''generator'' and rules that account for additional nonprototypical members (Lakoff 1987:24, 88). Boundaries are neither strict nor fuzzy. They are expanded by the application of the rules. Floyd G. Lounsbury's original work initiating the study of prototype categories dealt with categories of this type. Lounsbury demonstrated that generative categories in kin classifications are organized in terms of generator prototypes (focal kintypes) and nonprototypical members (nonfocal kintypes) that are equated by means of what he called ''equivalence rules'' (Lounsbury 1964, 1965; Scheffler and Lounsbury 1971). The generator prototype of the English *aunt* category, PARENT'S SISTER, for example, is equated with nonprototypical members of the *aunt* category (e.g., PARENT'S BROTHER'S WIFE and SPOUSE'S PARENT'S SISTER) by these special equivalence rules (see Bock 1989).

''Radial categories'' include central prototypes and a number of linked noncentral concepts that can serve as subcenters for still other concepts (Lakoff 1987:74–84). Lakoff regarded radial categories as the most radical prototype phenomena (1987:153). Like generative categories, they have neither strict nor fuzzy boundaries. Unlike generative categories, they have no general rule for generating nonprototypical members, but instead form links on the basis of cultural convention and one-at-a-time learning (Lakoff 1987:91).

The English word *mother* is defined by the features FEMALE and PARENT. These features state that a mother is a child's genetrix, or female genealogical parent; that is, she is the person who gave birth to the child and contributed half of the child's genetic makeup. A range of linked noncentral mother concepts radiate around the MOTHER prototype (see Lakoff 1987:84). A stepmother is not the child's genealogical parent, but is an atypical mother by virtue of being married to the child's father. A foster mother is also not the child's genetrix, but is the child's temporary legal guardian and paid caregiver. A biological mother is the woman who gives birth to the child, but permits stepmothers and foster mothers to raise the child. An adoptive mother has no biological or genetic relationship to the child, but has become the child's legal guardian. A birth mother is the woman who gives birth to the child, but gives up the child to an adoptive mother. The birth-mother concept serves as a subcenter for at least one further radiation: a surrogate mother is a birth mother who contracts to carry a child for someone else and legally forfeits her rights to the child. These atypical mother concepts, which are conventionally linked in various ways to the MOTHER prototype and are subcenters for links to further concepts, are all members of a radial mother category (see MacLaury 1991:66).

METAPHORICAL AND METONYMIC CONCEPTS

Metaphor and metonymy are figurative processes of semantic extension that share a family resemblance but that differ in their specific processes of extension. Metaphor is based on similarity relationships, and metonymy is based on contiguity relationships (cf. Sapir 1977). Whereas metaphorical meanings derive through perceived similarities (that is, shared properties or features) between literal primary referents and figurative secondary referents, metonymic meanings are based on perceived contiguities (that is, natural or contextual associations) between literal primary referents and figurative secondary referents. English *turkey*, for example, is used to designate the unattractive and ungainly North American bird and, by metaphorical extension, a person regarded as unappealing, stupid, or inept, a misfit or loser. English *tongue*, on the other hand, is used metonymically for ''language'' or ''dialect'' by extension from the fleshy muscular organ in the mouth that is so intimately associated with the production of speech.

The metaphor ''Richard is a gorilla'' states an equivalence between a human being, Richard, and an animal, a gorilla. *Richard* is the ''tenor'' of the metaphor, the concept that is continuous with the topic of discourse, and *gorilla* is the metaphor's ''vehicle,'' its discontinuous concept (Sapir 1977:7). Placing the two concepts in juxtaposition, the metaphor forms a concept that subsumes both tenor and vehicle. In their ''wise words'' metaphor, ''Butterflies are girls,'' the Western Apache juxtapose *butterfly* (vehicle) and *girl* (tenor) to create a metaphorical concept pertaining to girls (Basso 1976:93–121). In schema theory terms, the creation of metaphors such as these depends on similarities in the values of the schemata variables underlying tenor and vehicle (Ortony 1980: 359–60). Variables that are similar are maintained in the metaphorical concept: Richard and gorillas are ANIMATE BEINGS, as are butterflies and girls.

Variables that are dissimilar are omitted from the metaphor: Richard is not FURRY, and girls are not INSECTS. Shared variables are recognized as the critical variables in the metaphorical concept: Richard and gorillas are FEROCIOUS and DANGEROUS, and butterflies and girls are BEAUTIFUL and ENTICING.

Cultural knowledge conditions the meanings of metaphorical concepts. For certain groups, such as primatologists, gorillas are not ferocious or dangerous, but gentle and passive, so for them, the metaphor characterizes Richard as an easygoing and peaceable fellow (cf. Searle 1979:102–3). Western Apache "wise words" are never complimentary, but always express mild personal criticism, so the "Butterflies are girls" metaphor does not imply that girls are beautiful and enticing, but that they are fickle and feckless, that they are flighty and flit around (Basso 1976:104–105).

The English word *lemon* literally refers to a yellowish acid citrus fruit, but additionally has two figurative senses. In the sentence, "Pat's car is a lemon," *lemon* is extended metaphorically to an object that has proven to be defective, imperfect, or in some way unsatisfactory. The metaphorical concept results from an interaction of features between the two terms based on similarity. In the sentence, "Pat's sweater is lemon," *lemon* is extended metonymically to the yellow color that is characteristic of and associated with lemons. The metonymic concept does not involve an interaction of features between the terms because the figurative sense of *lemon* is based on contiguity. The sweater is not similar to a lemon; rather, it has the color conventionally associated with a lemon. The color sense expressed in the sentence derives from a metonym that can be stated LEMON STANDS FOR LEMON'S COLOR.

This is not unique among color terms. In fact, all English secondary color terms (that is, nonbasic terms such as *russet, rose*, and *raspberry*) were innovated on the basis of a general metonymic principle, ENTITY STANDS FOR ENTITY'S COLOR. This general principle guided the unidirectional development of secondary color terms from earlier entity senses to later color senses. For English speakers, the entity senses of many secondary color terms are transparent. *Violet, olive, salmon, emerald*, and *gold* are examples. To most speakers, the entity senses of other secondary color terms are opaque, although historically these terms had metonymically related entity senses that are now obsolete. *Russet* derives from the color of cloth worn by peasants, *crimson* from a red dye obtained from the kermes insect, *buff* from the color of leather made from buffalo hides, *sepia* from the secretion of a marine mollusk used as ink, and *taupe* from the color of a mole (Casson 1994).

Another line of metaphor and metonymy research deals with complex metaphorical/metonymic systems. This pathbreaking research, initiated by Lakoff and Johnson's *Metaphors We Live By* (1980), is concerned with demonstrating that much of everyday experience is structured by metaphorical and metonymic concepts. Essentially, Lakoff and Johnson's argument is that basic abstract concepts that are not clearly delineated in experience, such as ARGUMENT, TIME,

LOVE, COLORS, and IDEAS, are metaphorically and/or metonymically structured in terms of other basic concepts that are more concrete in experience, such as WAR, MONEY, TRAVEL, ENTITIES, and FOODS. Metaphorical and metonymic structuring in this approach is not simply a matter of individual concepts, but rather of "experiential gestalts" or "multidimensional structured wholes"—that is to say, schemata—that coherently organize experience in terms of natural dimensions of experience: participants, parts, stages, causes, or purposes (Lakoff and Johnson 1980:81).

The metaphorical concept ARGUMENT IS WAR is an example. Conversation seen as an argument is understood as such on the basis of the ARGUMENT IS WAR metaphor. ARGUMENT, an abstract, not clearly delineated concept, is "partially structured, understood, performed, and talked about in terms of WAR," which is a more concrete concept that emerges naturally from the experience of physical combat (Lakoff and Johnson 1980:5). The WAR schema specifies an event in which participants are adversaries who attack and defend positions, plan strategies, maneuver, advance, retreat, counterattack, declare truces, surrender, and triumph. The ARGUMENT schema, derived systematically from the WAR schema, represents an event in which participants are adversaries embattled in a conflict of opinions (not actual combat), who struggle over positions, gain ground, win or lose, and so on. Another metaphorical example is TIME IS MONEY, and ENTITY STANDS FOR ENTITY'S COLOR is a metonymic example.

The systematicity of metaphorical and metonymic concepts such as these is reflected in the language used in talking about these concepts. As a consequence, linguistic expressions are a source of insight into and evidence for the nature of underlying conceptual systems. Everyday speech formulas, or fixed-form expressions, reflecting the ARGUMENT IS WAR metaphor are evident in the following sentences (Lakoff and Johnson 1980:4): "Your claims are *indefensible*," "He *attacked* every weak point in my argument," "His criticisms were *right on target*," "I *demolished* his argument," and "He *shot down* all my arguments."

One of the most impressive accomplishments of this line of research is the cognitive model of anger in American English formulated by Lakoff and Kovecses (1987). Too complex to be more than sketched here, the model is structured by both metaphorical and metonymic principles. A basic metonymic principle, THE PHYSIOLOGICAL EFFECTS OF AN EMOTION STAND FOR THE EMOTION, produces a system of anger metonymies (Lakoff and Kovecses 1987:196). Particular physiological effects are reflected in linguistic expressions, for example, BODY HEAT ("Don't get *hot under the collar*," "She got all *hot and bothered* and started cursing") and INTERNAL PRESSURE ("I almost *burst a blood vessel*," "Don't get a *hernia*!"). Heat and pressure cause REDNESS IN THE FACE AND NECK ("He was *flushed* with anger," "She was *scarlet* with rage"), AGITATION ("She was *shaking* with anger,'' ''He was *hopping mad*''), and INTERFERENCE WITH PERCEPTION (''She was *blind* with rage,'' ''I was so mad I *couldn't see straight*'').

Heat is the basis for the most general metaphor for anger, ANGER IS HEAT (Lakoff and Kovecses 1987:197). This metaphor combines with a general metaphor, THE BODY IS A CONTAINER FOR THE EMOTIONS (''He's *brimming* with enthusiasm,'' ''She couldn't *contain* her happiness''), to form the central anger metaphor, ANGER IS THE HEAT OF A FLUID IN A CONTAINER (''You make my *blood boil*,'' ''*Simmer* down!'' ''I had reached the *boiling point*,'' ''Let him *stew*''). Conceptual metaphors are elaborated by numerous metaphorical entailments. ''Hot fluids'' in the central metaphor have many such entailments (Lakoff and Kovecses 1987:199–200): WHEN THE INTENSITY OF ANGER INCREASES, THE FLUID RISES (''She could feel her *gorge rising*,'' ''We got a *rise* out of him''), INTENSE ANGER PRODUCES STEAM (''She got *all steamed up*,'' ''I was *fuming*'') AND PRESSURE ON THE CONTAINER (''She was *bursting* with anger,'' ''I could barely *contain* my rage''), WHEN ANGER BECOMES TOO INTENSE, THE PERSON EXPLODES (''When I told him, he just *exploded*,'' ''She *blew up* at me''), WHEN A PERSON EXPLODES, PARTS OF HIM GO UP IN THE AIR (''He *blew his top*,'' ''She *hit the ceiling*,'' ''I *went through the roof*''), and WHEN A PERSON EXPLODES, WHAT WAS INSIDE HIM COMES OUT (''His anger finally *came out*,'' ''Smoke was *pouring out of his ears*''). There is much more to this model of anger, to which we will return in the next section.

UNIVERSALS

Cognitive anthropologists not only study the details of diverse cognitive and cultural systems, they also engage in research aimed at discovering commonalities in these systems. Their methods of studying cognitive universals are empirical and comparative. Data from particular societies are viewed in cross-cultural perspective, universal structures and processes are isolated, and inferences are drawn about their historical and evolutionary development.

To illustrate this, we can elaborate an earlier example of color terminology. Comparative color-term research by Berlin and Kay (1969) has demonstrated that color categories are organized around focal colors that are the same across individuals and languages. This research has established that there are exactly eleven of these universal color categories—black, white, red, green, yellow, blue, brown, purple, orange, pink, and gray—and that although different languages have different numbers of basic color concepts, they are encoded in a strict implicational evolutionary sequence: black and white are always first; red is always third; green, yellow, and blue are then added in any order; brown, purple, orange, and pink are also added in no particular order, but only after green, yellow, and blue have all been encoded; and gray, a ''wild card,'' may appear at any point in the sequence after black, white and red (cf. Kay 1975;

Berlin and Berlin 1975; Dougherty 1977; Witkowski and Brown 1977; Kay and McDaniel 1978; MacLaury 1987, 1992; Kay, Berlin, and Merrifield 1991).

Cognitive structures are "embodied," that is, arise from and are grounded, in human bodily experience (Lakoff and Johnson 1980; Johnson 1987). Basic color categories are a prime example of physiological embodiment. Cognitive anthropologists and vision scientists agree that the universal focal color categories and the evolutionary sequence of their encoding are determined largely by neurophysiological processes in human color perception (cf. Boynton and Olson 1987, 1990; Ratliff 1975; Kay and McDaniel 1978; Kay, Berlin, and Merrifield 1991; MacLaury 1987, 1992). Kay and McDaniel (1978), for example, demonstrated that the neurobiology of color vision (as represented in the Hering theory of opponent-response cells) accounts for the primary basic color categories white, black, red, yellow, green, and blue, and they posited universal cognitive mechanisms (modeled by fuzzy set theoretical intersection and union of these primary basic categories) that account for the derived basic color categories brown, pink, purple, orange, and gray.

Emotion concepts are also physiologically embodied. Researchers have shown that various measures of heart rate and skin temperature correlate closely with six emotions: surprise, disgust, sadness, anger, fear, and happiness (Ekman, Levinson, and Friesen 1983:1208–10). As discussed earlier, Lakoff and Kovecses's cognitive model of anger rests heavily on metonymies and metaphors having to do with heat and internal pressure. The cognitive model of anger corresponds quite precisely with the physiological research. The autonomic nervous system activity that occurs with the experience of anger is increased skin temperature and increased heart rate, experienced as internal pressure (Ekman, Levinson, and Friesen 1983:1208–10; Lakoff and Kovecses 1987:219). Thus, although "getting hot under the collar" and "bursting a blood vessel" are particularly American metaphors for anger, we can expect (and Lakoff and Kovecses predicted) that when cognitive models of anger in other cultures are studied, they will universally involve heat and internal pressure.

Cognitive structures are embodied physiologically and also as a consequence of human perceptual and physical interaction with the world (Lakoff 1987:266–68). Basic-level categories are an excellent example of this type of embodiment. Generic rank categories such as *oak, maple, pine, elm,* and *spruce* are the basic-level categories in ethnobiological classifications (Berlin 1976, 1978). They are by far the most numerous category type, and they are psychologically the most salient categories: they are frequently used in everyday interaction, easily recalled by informants, and acquired early in development (see Dougherty 1978). Nontaxonomic categories such as *shoe, drum,* and *bus* are also "generic" rank categories, but they are not biological kinds and are not included in life-form, or superkind, categories. They are basic-level categories that are classed as subcategories of nontaxonomic supercategories on the basis of constituency, function, and/or contiguity. They are also the most numerous category types and most salient categories in their classification systems.

Frequency of use, ease of recall, and ontogenetic priority are what Lakoff (1987:46) called "basic-level effects." They provide overt evidence of the existence and nature of basic-level concepts, but they do not determine or account for them. Lakoff (1987:31–38) argued that basic-level concepts are determined by human capacities for gestalt perception, for rich mental imagery, and for bodily movements that interact with the physical and social world. These capacities structure our basic-level categorization of objects (oaks, horses, chairs), actions (ordering, seating, eating), and properties (tall, hot, red). Basic-level concepts are embodied: they arise from preconceptual structures and are grounded in our bodily experience of functioning in the world (Lakoff 1987: 292).

Basic-level effects are not incidental or trivial. As we have seen, lexical forms directly reflect hierarchical ranks in classification systems. Basic-level (or generic) categories are nearly always labeled by primary lexemes, whether simple or complex. Categories immediately dominating basic-level categories, that is, supercategories (or life-form categories), are always labeled by primary lexemes, and categories dominated by basic-level categories, secondary (or specific) categories, are labeled by secondary lexemes. Thus basic-level categories are located beneath categories labeled by primary lexemes and above categories labeled by secondary lexemes.

English secondary color terms illustrate embodiment in nonbasic-level concepts. The metonym ENTITY FOR ENTITY'S COLOR developed as a result of human perceptual and cognitive experience of physical entities and their associated colors. Because it is based on perceptual processes and operations that are general in human experience, the ENTITY FOR ENTITY'S COLOR metonym is the basis for the development of English secondary color terms and probably for the universal development of secondary color terms in languages and cultures (Casson 1994). This prediction awaits comparative research for verification.

Anthropologists have discovered many universals that are widely regarded as well founded, but that nonetheless excite controversy and disagreement when explanations are proposed. Kinship classification systems are probably the most studied example of this type in cognitive anthropology. There is general agreement that at the center of kinship classifications is a universal set of primitive kintypes that derive from the parent-child relationship: FATHER and MOTHER are parents, SON and DAUGHTER are children, and BROTHER and SISTER are parents' children. It is also widely agreed that relational chains of these simple kintypes structure categories in kin classification systems (Bock 1989). But controversies rage over whether these universal primitives and relational networks are genealogical constructs determined by human physiological capacities or social constructs determined by human mental and interactive abilities.

There is also controversy over explanations of another major kinship universal. Anthropologists have demonstrated that there are universally only four general types of kin classifications, Hawaiian, Eskimo, Sudanese, and Iroquois, or, alternatively, six types, if Crow and Omaha are counted as distinct classification types and not as variations of the Iroquois classification (Lounsbury 1964, 1965; Scheffler and Lounsbury 1971). It is evident that relational chains are tightly constrained in the formation of category structure in kin classifications. What is not certain is whether these universal types of kin classifications are limited by physiological requisites or experience in the world.

CONSENSUS AND CHANGE

Cognitive anthropological studies of conceptual systems, as discussed earlier, are generally composite or shared models that omit individual variability and that analyze conceptual systems as homogeneous phenomena. Although this assumption has made possible major advances in understanding of cognitive structures and processes, they do not deal with variability in the cultural knowledge of individual society members. However, individual variability in cultural knowledge is central in cognitive anthropological studies of how the diversity of individual models is organized in cultural systems, and in studies of how variability gives rise to changes in cultural systems.

Recent research has argued that the fact of individual variability does not rule out the possibility of framing coherent accounts of culture. As a supplement to composite and shared models of culture, a formal mathematical model of ''culture as consensus'' has been formulated to describe and measure individual variability in cultural knowledge within groups (Romney, Weller, and Batchelder 1986; Romney, Batchelder, and Weller 1987). This approach examines the *patterns of agreement* among group members about particular domains of cultural knowledge in order to make inferences about the organization of cognitive diversity (cf. Wallace 1970). The consensus model assumes that the degree to which any two individuals agree depends on the degree to which each individual controls culturally correct knowledge (Romney, Weller, and Batchelder 1986: 316).

Tennis players with differing degrees of knowledge about the game of tennis can illustrate this model. Interviews with experienced and novice tennis players show that experienced players agree more among themselves about answers to tennis questions than do novice players. Experienced players answer more questions correctly and therefore agree closely in their answers, whereas novice players give answers that differ from each other and from the answers of experienced players. Analysis of these patterns of agreement among players produces an estimate of the tennis knowledge of each individual player. When the degree of knowledge, or ''cultural competence,'' of each individual is calculated, the culturally correct answers are estimated by weighing individual responses (in terms of cultural competence) and aggregating them. A consensus analysis is determined by correlating each individual's responses with the culturally correct answers.

Technical details of the formal mathematical model of cultural consensus are available in several publications (Romney, Weller, and Batchelder 1986; Romney, Batchelder, and Weller 1987), and various versions of the model have been used in empirical studies (Weller 1984; Weller, Romney, and Orr 1987; Weller 1987). The model can be applied to data from cultural domains that can be explored by systematic question formats, that is, by dichotomous (e.g., true-false), multiple-choice, fill-in-the-blank, and rank-order formats, and it is currently being extended to analyze data collected by triadic comparisons. These and other data-collection formats are described in a methods monograph (Weller and Romney 1988); computer programs for these formats are available in the Anthropac 4.0 program (Borgatti 1993).

The consensus model generates both a ''correct'' version of cultural knowledge and patterns of cognitive diversity. An ethnographic study of manioc cultivation among the Aguaruna Jivaro by James Boster provides a detailed illustration. The Aguaruna, a forest tribe in northern Peru, derive the majority of their sustenance from the manioc plants they grow in their gardens. In an elaborate study of Aguaruna manioc gardens, Boster discovered that although individuals vary a great deal in their naming of manioc plants, they nonetheless maintain a consensus model of manioc classification. Analysis of patterns of agreement reveals that individuals learn a single set of manioc categories with varying degrees of success; that is, some individuals have greater cultural competence in manioc identification than others (Boster 1985:185).

Boster demonstrated that this cognitive diversity in knowledge of manioc varieties is organized by social factors. Deviations from the cultural consensus are shown to be related to the sexual division of labor, individual expertise, and membership in kin and residential groups (Boster 1985:178). The largest differences in manioc identification are between men and women: women are knowledgeable about manioc and men are not. These gross differences in agreement are attributable to the Aguaruna division of labor, in which women are cultivators of manioc gardens and men are hunters and gatherers of forest products (Boster 1985:186). As a consequence, women agree with each other more about manioc names, and men agree with each other more about bird identifications. This division of intellectual labor reflects the division of physical labor (see Berlin, Boster, and O'Neill 1981:99).

Individual expertise in manioc cultivation is a second factor that structures the pattern of cognitive diversity in knowledge of manioc identification. Boster's research shows that Aguaruna women who are expert manioc gardeners agree much more closely on an array of plant-identification tasks than other gardeners. This overall consistent agreement across tasks identifies a group of women gardeners who have more correct cultural knowledge of this domain than other Aguaruna women (Boster 1985:187–88).

The third social factor accounting for the pattern of cognitive diversity is strong agreement in manioc identification among women who are closely related by kinship bonds. Close kinswomen agree with each other on the names of manioc plants because they actively exchange manioc plants and knowledge about manioc varieties among themselves. The pattern of agreement among groups of kinswomen reflects the transmission of manioc knowledge (Boster 1985:188). The mother-daughter relationship is primary. Girls work with their mothers in the gardens from an early age, and the predominant pattern of matrilocal residence tends to keep them together after marriage. Sisters share much manioc knowledge, having grown up together working with their mother. Sisters-in-law tend to share some manioc knowledge if they are related as cross-cousins and/or they reside together because one of them moved with her husband to his native residence (Boster 1985:189).

As just shown, cultural consensus exists in patterns of individual variations in cultural knowledge, and patterns of cognitive diversity are structured by social factors. What needs to be added is that deviations from a cultural consensus are the source of change in cognitive systems. Research in sociolinguistics and linguistics proper has shown that the principal source of diachronic change in phonological and syntactic systems in synchronic variability among individuals in a speech community (cf. Labov 1972; Sankoff 1978). Paul Kay (1975) has shown that synchronic heterogeneity is the source of change in conceptual systems as well.

Kay examined data from the now-familiar domain of color categorization. Drawing a contrast between homogeneous communities in which there is little individual variability and heterogeneous communities in which there is significant individual variability, Kay made several predictions about color classifications. He predicted that individuals in homogeneous communities will share the same set of basic color terms and that the most salient secondary color terms will be the next ones in the evolutionary sequence. If, for example, community members share a two-term (black-and-white) system, the most salient secondary term will be the term for red, followed by the terms for yellow, green, and blue, in any order. He also predicted that in heterogeneous communities, individuals will not share the same set of basic color terms, but will have different sets of terms that are contiguous in the evolutionary sequence. Thus, if some community members have two-term (black- and-white) systems, others may have three-term (black, white, and red) systems or four-term (black, white, red, and yellow, green, or blue) systems, but none will have ten- or eleven-term systems. In heterogeneous communities, Kay predicted a correlation between size of color lexicon and age, the color lexicons of younger individuals being more complex than those of older individuals. Analyses of all available color-term systems confirmed Kay's predictions (1975:263–65). This strongly supports the view that synchronic variability among individuals is the source of diachronic change in cognitive systems.

Another, quite different, study sheds additional light on this issue. In his unique study of the ethnic domain in urban Ghana, Roger Sanjek (1977) examined variability and change in an extremely heterogeneous community. Sanjek collected data on "tribes" (which he termed "ethnic identities") in the

Adabraka section of Accra, a city of 650,000 people. Residents identified with twenty-three different ethnic groups, speaking fourteen different languages. Fifty-seven individuals provided highly variant tribe-classification systems: one-third of them organized the domain as widely divergent taxonomic hierarchies, and the rest used numerous other modes of organization (Sanjek 1977:604–8).

In addition to presenting shared and composite models, Sanjek considered the extreme diversity of individual models of the domain in relation to diachronic change. He argued that individual models that differ greatly from most of the other models may be regarded as "remnants of the past" or "harbingers of the future." The model of a seventy-year-old man, organized in terms of the seven traditional sections of the old town around which Accra has grown, is a "fossil" remnant of a typical classification system. The models of a few educated informants, based on ethnic categories used in the wider society (for instance, in government censuses or in the schools), will probably be common models of the ethnic domain in the future. So Sanjek's analysis of synchronic variability reveals both the course of diachronic change from the past to the present and its likely direction in the future (Sanjek 1977:616–17).

RECENT ADVANCES AND NEW DIRECTIONS

Cognitive anthropologists have achieved significant advances in their central research topics: cultural and cognitive systems, relativism and universality, sharing and variability. In the study of classification systems, linguistic concepts (e.g., the semantic relations synonymy and polysemy and a typology of primary and secondary lexemes) have been used to add precision and refinement to taxonomic analyses, particularly in the determination of category relationships and hierarchical ranks. The study of classification systems has also been advanced by the delineation of conceptual categories structured not only by inclusion relations, but additionally by constituent, functional, and contiguity relations. Equally important has been the research showing that taxonomic categories, particularly basic-level categories, are often grouped as subcategories of nontaxonomic supercategories (termed life-form categories in ethnobiological research) on the basis of constituency, function, and/or contiguity.

The recognition and exploration of nontaxonomic categories, particularly supercategories, is a development in the study of classification systems that truly qualifies as a new direction in cognitive anthropology. Whereas all classification systems were previously treated as taxonomies, cognitive anthropologists now recognize numerous types of classifications. Higher-level categories, which were thought always to be taxonomic life-form categories, or superkinds, are now most often seen to be nontaxonomic categories: constituent, functional, collective-functional, and collective-nonfunctional supercategories.

In the study of event scenarios, the positing of general scene concepts instantiated by specific scripts has also produced an important advance. The view that scripts specifying causal linkages between actions and states could account for all aspects of event schemata has been replaced by a broader theory of event schemata (Schank 1982). Scenes are now treated as general concepts that occur widely in many event scenarios. They are general, basic-level concepts that acquire specificity in two ways: they are ordered into specific sequences in particular scenarios, and they are instantiated with specific details by scripts that are now restricted to elaborating scenes. A theory of event schemata that is focused not only on the details of a particular event or type of event but is aimed as well at capturing uniformities in event schemata is a richer and more explanatory theory.

Recent cognitive research exploring prototype categorization has achieved a major leap forward in our understanding of categories and their internal structures. Prototype theory has experienced a two-step advance. The first step was the recognition that categories do not always include category members in a completely disjunctive, yes-or-no fashion. "Classical categories" of this sort exist and are important, but prototype categories that include members on a more-or-less basis are more prevalent. The second and more recent step was the wonderfully illuminating development of an array of types of prototype categories (Lakoff 1987). One type, the graded category type, structures only a simple prototype effect, that is, graded distances from the prototype of nonprototypical members. Other types, however, structure complex prototype effects by means of overlaps between prototypes and various cognitive models. There are numerous types of these complex categories, but among the most interesting are typicality, stereotypic, generative, and radial categories. An excellent review of prototype theory is available in the *Annual Review of Anthropology* (MacLaury 1991).

Two lines of metaphor and metonymy research have produced important findings that shed new light on issues in culture and cognition. The first is based on an approach derived from centuries of research in philosophy and literary studies and, more recently, from linguistics and anthropology. It is concerned with the metaphorical and metonymic meanings that arise from the interaction of the literal meanings of two terms. Recent researchers building on this tradition have focused on the cognitive processes involved in the formation of creative metaphorical and metonymic concepts and on the cultural factors that condition the meanings of these concepts. The second line of research was given its modern form by Lakoff and Johnson (1980). This line of study has focused on the complex experiential gestalts, or cognitive schemata, that guide our understanding of everyday experience. Researchers are concerned with metaphorical and metonymic concepts that structure complex cognitive systems and are reflected in everyday speech formulas and conventional expressions.

Recent research concerned with cognitive universals has achieved several important breakthroughs. A firm basis for explaining many (although certainly not all) cognitive universals has been put forward with considerable success. This is the theory of embodiment, which argues that "the body is in the mind"; that is, that cognitive structures arise from and are grounded in human bodily experience (Lakoff and Johnson 1980; Johnson 1987). Examples such as color and emotion concepts have been shown to be based in physiological embodiment, and basic-level concepts have been shown to derive from bodily experience in the physical and social world. Accounts of basic-level categories have been distinguished from basic-level effects, which provide overt evidence for underlying basic-level concepts (Lakoff 1987). Linguistic labeling is a basic-level effect that is of major importance in identifying and locating basic-level concepts and structures.

The development of the "culture as consensus" model has provided an encompassing framework that unites and organizes a large body of research in cognitive anthropology (Romney, Weller, and Batchelder 1986). The formal mathematical model establishes a solid foundation for Wallace's (1970) "organization of cognitive diversity" proposals and has been used to explore a wide range of issues and problems in the study of variability in cultural knowledge. Convincing analyses of synchronic variability among individuals show that social factors (such as gender, individual expertise, and kinship relations) account for patterns of cognitive diversity in a cultural consensus, and that deviance from a cultural consensus created by social factors (age and education) is the principal source of diachronic change in cognitive systems. The end product of diachronic changes derived from individual variability is a reformulated cultural consensus.

Few speculations about the future of cognitive anthropological research can be stated with any degree of certainty. In the area of classification systems, however, one prediction seems a good bet. As we have seen, many supercategories previously thought to be taxonomic categories are in fact nontaxonomic supercategories. The prediction here is that taxonomic supercategories will be shown to occur only in ethnobiological classification systems. Supercategories in other types of classification systems will always be nontaxonomic (Wierzbicka 1984).

In other areas of cognitive anthropology, speculations are not so much predictions as hoped-for developments. Future studies of event scenarios will hopefully be detailed ethnographic accounts employing the three-tiered event schema: overall sequencing in scenarios, general basic event concepts in scenes, and specific instantiations in scripts. Researchers will continue in the future to develop an elaborate prototype theory with a particular emphasis on expanding and refining the array of prototype category types.

The future of metaphor and metonymy research is difficult to predict. Lakoff and Johnson's theory of underlying metaphorical and metonymic schemata is still controversial, but when the dust settles, the dispute will likely have contributed significant new insights into the nature of metaphorical and metonymic concepts and their place in complex cognitive systems. Much the same can be said about the theory of embodiment and cognitive universals. The value and validity of both these enormously promising approaches will become more apparent as research proceeds.

The cultural consensus model has been highly successful in studies of individual variability in cultural knowledge. Speculating as a participant observer about the future of this area of cognitive anthropological research is indeed risky, but it seems likely that future versions of the consensus model will not only provide formal accounts of patterns of synchronic variability in cultural consensuses but will also be able to account for patterns of diachronic change that lead to a new cultural consensus.

As seen in the discussions of research, language virtually always plays an essential role in the description and analysis of cognitive structures. The basic strategy in cognitive anthropological research is to look for regularities in conceptual systems that are built into language in order to discover properties of thought. Linguistic structures are the keys to conceptual structures: metaphorical and metonymic speech formulas and conventional expressions are evidence of underlying cognitive systems, and primary and secondary lexical distinctions are guides to basic-level category structure. The advent of new linguistic approaches to thought and culture will provide a sound basis for future developments in cognitive anthropology.

REFERENCES

Agar, M. 1974. Talking about Doing: Lexicon and Event. *Language in Society* 3:83–89.

———. 1975. Cognition and Events. Pp. 41–56 in M. Sanches and B. Blount, eds., *Sociocultural Dimensions of Language Use*. New York: Academic Press.

Andersen, E. S. 1978. Lexical Universals of Body-Part Terminology. Pp. 335–68 in J. H. Greenberg, C. A. Ferguson, and E. A. Moravcsik, eds., *Universals of Human Language*, vol. 3: *Word Structure*. Stanford, CA: Stanford University Press.

Barnouw, V. 1979. *Culture and Personality*. 3rd ed. Homewood, IL: Dorsey Press.

Basso, K. H. 1976. "Wise Words" of the Western Apache: Metaphor and Semantic Theory. Pp. 93–121 in K. H. Basso and H. A. Selby, eds., *Meaning in Anthropology*. Albuquerque: University of New Mexico Press.

Berlin, B. 1976. The Concept of Rank in Ethnobiological Classification: Some Evidence from Aguaruna Folk Botany. *American Ethnologist* 3:381–99.

———. 1978. Ethnobiological Classification. Pp. 9–26 in E. Rosch and B. B. Lloyd, eds., *Cognition and Categorization*. Hillsdale, NJ: Erlbaum.

———. 1992. *Ethnobiological Classification: Principles of Categorization of Plants and Animals in Traditional Societies*. Princeton: Princeton University Press.

Berlin, B., and E. A. Berlin. 1975. Aguaruna Color Categories. *American Ethnologist* 2:61–87.

Berlin, B., J. S. Boster, and J. P. O'Neill. 1981. The Perceptual Basis of Ethnobiological Classification: Evidence from Aguaruna Jivaro Ornithology. *Journal of Ethnobiology* 1:95–108.

Berlin, B., D. E. Breedlove, and P. H. Raven. 1973. General Principles of Classification and Nomenclature in Folk Biology. *American Anthropologist* 75:214–42.

———. 1974. *Principles of Tzeltal Plant Classification: An Introduction to the Botanical Ethnography of a Mayan-Speaking People of Highland Chiapas*. New York: Academic Press.

Berlin, B., and P. Kay. 1969. *Basic Color Terms: Their Universality and Evolution*. Berkeley: University of California Press.

Bock, P. K. 1988. *Rethinking Psychological Anthropology: Continuity and Change in the Study of Human Action*. New York: W. H. Freeman.

———. 1989. "Say 'Hello' to Your (Second) Cousin Claude:" Kinship Terminology and Recursive

Rules. Pp. 447–460 in M. Key and H. Hoenigswald, eds., *General and Amerindian Ethnolinguistics: In Remembrance of Stanley Newman.* Berlin and New York: Mouton de Gruyter.

Borgatti, S. P. 1993. *Anthropac 4.0: Cultural Domain Analysis.* Columbia, SC: Analytic Technologies.

Boster, J. S. 1985. "Requiem for the Omniscient Informant": There's Life in the Old Girl Yet. Pp. 177–97 in J.W.D. Dougherty, ed., *Directions in Cognitive Anthropology.* Urbana: University of Illinois Press.

Boynton, R. M., and C. X. Olson. 1987. Locating Basic Colors in the OSA Space. *Color Research and Application* 12(2):94–105.

———. 1990. Salience of Chromatic Basic Color Terms Confirmed by Three Measures. *Vision Research* 30:1311–17.

Brown, C. H. 1976. General Principles of Human Anatomical Partonomy and Speculations on the Growth of Partonomic Nomenclature. *American Ethnologist* 3:400–424.

———. 1977. Folk Botanical Life-Forms: Their Universality and Growth. *American Anthropologist* 79:317–42.

———. 1979. Folk Zoological Life-Forms: Their Universality and Growth. *American Anthropologist* 81:791–817.

———. 1984. *Language and Living Things: Uniformities in Folk Classification and Naming.* New Brunswick, NJ: Rutgers University Press.

———. 1985. Mode of Subsistence and Folk Biological Taxonomy. *Current Anthropology* 26:43–53.

———. 1986. The Growth of Ethnobiological Nomenclature. *Current Anthropology* 27:1–19.

Bruner, J. S., J. J. Goodnow, and G. A. Austin. 1956. *A Study of Thinking.* New York: Wiley.

Burton, M. L., and L. Kirk. 1979. Ethnoclassification of Body Parts: A Three-Culture Study. *Anthropological Linguistics* 21:379–99.

Casagrande, J. B., and K. L. Hale. 1967. Semantic Relations in Papago Folk Definitions. Pp. 168–93 in D. Hymes and W. E. Bittle, eds., *Studies in Southwestern Ethnolinguistics.* The Hague: Mouton.

Casson, R. W., ed. 1981. *Language, Culture, and Cognition: Anthropological Perspectives.* New York: Macmillan.

———. 1983. Schemata in Cognitive Anthropology. *Annual Review of Anthropology* 12:429–632.

———. In press. Russett, Rose, and Raspberry: The Development of English Secondary Color Terms. *Journal of Linguistic Anthropology*: in press.

Chafe, W. L. 1977. Creativity in Verbalization and Its Implications for the Nature of Stored Knowledge. Pp. 41–55 in R. O. Freedle, ed., *Discourse Production and Comprehension.* Norwood, NJ: Ablex.

———. 1979. The Flow of Thought and the Flow of Language. Pp. 151–89 in T. Givon, ed., *Syntax and Semantics*, vol. 12: *Discourse and Syntax.* New York: Academic Press.

Chomsky, N. 1965. *Aspects of the Theory of Syntax.* Cambridge, MA: M.I.T. Press.

Colby, B. N. 1966. Ethnographic Semantics: A Preliminary Survey. *Current Anthropology* 7:3–32.

Coleman, L., and P. Kay. 1981. Prototype Semantics. *Language* 57:26–44.

Conklin, H. C. 1962. Lexicographical Treatment of Folk Taxonomies. In. F. W. Householder and S. Saporta, eds., *Problems in Lexicography.* Bloomington: Indiana University Research Center in Anthropology, Folklore, and Linguistics.

D'Andrade, R. G. 1979. Culture and Cognitive Science. Memorandum to Cognitive Science Committee, Sloan Foundation.

———. 1981. The Cultural Part of Cognition. *Cognitive Science* 5:179–95.

Dougherty, J.W.D. 1977. Color Categorization in West Futunese: Variability and Change. In B. Blount and M. Sanches, eds., *Sociocultural Dimensions of Language Change.* New York: Academic Press.

———. 1978. Salience and Relativity in Classification. *American Ethnologist* 5:66–80.

———. 1985. *Directions in Cognitive Anthropology.* Urbana: University of Illinois Press.

Ekman, P., R. W. Levinson, and W. V. Friesen. 1983. Autonomic Nervous System Activity Distinguishes between Emotions. *Science* 221:1208–10.

Fillmore, C. J. 1975. An Alternative to Checklist Theories of Meaning. *Proceedings of the Annual Meeting of the Berkeley Linguistics Society* 1:123–131.

———. 1977. Topics in Lexical Semantics. In R. W. Cole, ed., *Current Issues in Linguistic Theory.* Bloomington: Indiana University Press.

———. 1982. Frame Semantics. Pp. 111–38 in Linguistic Society, ed., *Linguistics in the Morning Calm*, Linguistic Society. Seoul: Hanshin.

———. 1985. Frames and the Semantics of Understanding. *Quaderni di Semantica* 6:222–54.

Frake, C. O. 1962. The Ethnographic Study of Cognitive Systems. In T. Gladwin and W. C. Sturtevant, eds., *Anthropology and Human Behavior.* Washington, DC: Anthropological Society of Washington.

———. 1964. How to Ask for a Drink in Subanun. *American Anthropologist* 66(6)2:127–32.

———. 1964. Notes on Queries in Ethnography. Pp. 132–45 in A. K. Romney and R. G. D'Andrade, eds., *Transcultural Studies in Cognition.* Special Publication *American Anthropologist* 66(3) pt. 2.

———. 1975. How to Enter a Yakan House. In M. Sanches and B. Blount, eds., *Sociocultural Dimensions of Language Use*. New York: Academic Press.

———. 1977. Plying Frames Can Be Dangerous: Some Reflections on Methodology in Cognitive Anthropology. *Quarterly Newsletter of the Institute for Comparative Human Development* 1(3):1–7.

Goodenough, W. H. 1957. Cultural Anthropology and Linguistics. *Georgetown University Monograph Series on Languages and Linguistics* 9:167–73. Georgetown: Georgetown University Press.

———. 1981. *Culture, Language, and Society*. 2nd ed. Menlo Park, CA: Benjamin/Cummings.

Greenberg, J. H. 1966. *Language Universals, with Special Reference to Feature Hierarchies.* The Hague: Mouton.

Hays, T. E. 1976. An Empirical Method for the Identification of Covert Categories in Ethnobiology. *American Ethnologist* 3:489–507.

———. 1983. Ndumba Folk Biology and General Principles of Ethnobotanical Classification and Nomenclature. *American Anthropologist* 85:592–611.

Holland, D., and N. Quinn, eds. 1987. *Cultural Models in Language and Thought.* Cambridge, Eng.: Cambridge University Press.

Hunn, E. S. 1977. *Tzeltal Folk Zoology: The Classification of Discontinuities in Nature.* New York: Academic Press.

———. 1985. The Utilitarian Factor in Folk Biological Classification. In J.W.D. Dougherty, ed., *Directions in Cognitive Anthropology.* Urbana: University of Illinois Press.

Johnson, M. 1987. *The Body in the Mind: The Bodily Basis of Meaning, Imagination, and Reason.* Chicago: University of Chicago Press.

Kay, P. 1970. Some Theoretical Implications of Ethnographic Semantics. In Current Directions in Anthropology. *Bulletins of the American Anthropological Association* 3(3)2:19–31.

———. 1975. Syntactic Variability and Diachronic Change in Basic Color Terms. *Language in Society* 4:257–270.

Kay, P., B. Berlin, and W. Merrifield. 1991. Biocultural Implications of Systems of Color Naming. *Journal of Linguistic Anthropology* 1:12–25.

Kay, P., and W. Kempton. 1984. What Is the Sapir-Whorf Hypothesis? *American Anthropologist* 86:65–79.

Kay, P., and C. K. McDaniel. 1978. The Linguistic Significance of the Meanings of Basic Color Terms. *Language* 54:610–46.

Keesing, R. M. 1974. Theories of Culture. *Annual Review of Anthropology* 3:73–97.

Kempton, W. 1981. *The Folk Classification of Ceramics: A Study of Cognitive Prototypes.* New York: Academic Press.

Kronenfeld, D. B., J. D. Armstrong, and S. Wilmoth. 1985. Exploring the Internal Structure of

Linguistic Categories: An Extensionist Semantic View. In J.W.D. Dougherty, ed., *Directions in Cognitive Anthropology*. Urbana: University of Illinois Press.

Labov, W. 1972. On the Mechanisms of Linguistic Change. In J. J. Gumperz and D. Hymes, eds., *Directions in Sociolinguistics*. New York: Holt, Rinehart and Winston.

Lakoff, G. 1987. *Women, Fire, and Dangerous Things*. Chicago: University of Chicago Press.

Lakoff, G., and M. Johnson. 1980. *Metaphors We Live By*. Chicago: University of Chicago Press.

Lakoff, G., and Z. Kovecses. 1987. The Cognitive Model of Anger Inherent in American English. In D. Holland and N. Quinn, eds., *Cultural Models in Language and Thought*. Cambridge, Eng.: Cambridge University Press.

Lounsbury, F. G. 1964. The Formal Analysis of Crow- and Omaha-Type Kinship Terminologies. In W. H. Goodenough, eds., *Explorations in Cultural Anthropology: Essays in Honor of George Peter Mundock*. New York: McGraw-Hill.

———. 1965. Another View of the Trobriand Kinship Categories. *American Anthropology* 67(5)2: 142–185.

———. 1969. Language and Culture. Pp. 3–29 in S. Hook, ed., *Language and Philosophy*. New York: New York University Press.

MacLaury, R. E. 1987. Color-Category Evolution and Shuswap Yellow-with-Green. *American Anthropologist* 89:107–24.

———. 1989. Zapotec Body-Part Locatives: Prototypes and Metaphoric Extensions. *International Journal of American Linguistics* 55:119–54.

———. 1991. Prototypes Revisited. *Annual Review of Anthropology* 20:55–74.

———. 1992. From Brightness to Hue: An Exploratory Model of Color-Category Evolution. *Current Anthropology* 33:137–87.

McDermott, R. P., K. Gospodinoff, and J. Aron. 1978. Criteria for an Ethnographically Adequate Description of Concerted Activities and Their Contexts. *Semiotica* 13:245–75.

Miller, G. A., E. Galanter, and K. H. Pribram. 1960. *Plans and the Structure of Behavior*. New York: Holt, Rinehart and Winston.

Minsky, M. 1975. A Framework for Representing Knowledge. Pp. 211–77 in P. H. Winston, ed., *The Psychology of Computer Vision*. New York: McGraw-Hill.

Ortony, A. 1980. Metaphor. In R. J. Spiro, B. C. Bruce, and W. F. Brewer, eds., *Theoretical Issues in Reading Comprehension*. Hillsdale, NJ: Erlbaum.

Quinn, N. 1985. "Commitment" in American Marriage: A Cultural Analysis. Pp. 291–320 in J.W.D. Dougherty, ed., *Directions in Cognitive Anthropology*. Urbana: University of Illinois Press.

Ratliff, F. 1975. On the Psychophysical Bases of Universal Color Terms. *Proceedings of the American Philosophical Society* 120:311–30.

Romney, A. K., S. C. Weller, and W. H. Batchelder. 1986. Culture as Consensus: A Theory of Culture and Informant Accuracy. *American Anthropologist* 88:313–38.

Rosch, E. 1973. On the Internal Structure of Perceptual and Semantic Categories. In T. E. Moore, ed., *Cognitive Development and the Acquisition of Language*. New York: Academic Press.

———. 1977. Human Categorization. In N. Warren, ed., *Studies in Cross-Cultural Psychology*, vol. 1. New York: Academic Press.

———. 1978. Principles of Categorization. In E. Rosch and B. B. Lloyd, eds., *Cognition and Categorization*. Hillsdale, NJ: Erlbaum.

Rumelhart, D. E. 1980. Schemata: The Building Blocks of Cognition. In R. J. Spiro, B. C. Bruce, and W. F. Brewer, eds., *Theoretical Issues in Reading Comprehension*. Hillsdale, NJ: Erlbaum.

Sanjek, R. 1977. Cognitive Maps of the Ethnic Domain in Urban Ghana: Reflections on Variability and Change. *American Ethnologist* 4:603–22.

Sankoff, D., ed. 1978. *Linguistic Variation: Models and Methods*. New York: Academic Press.

Sapir, J. D. 1977. The Anatomy of Metaphor. Pp. 3–32 in J. D. Sapir and J. C. Crocker, eds., *The Social Use of Metaphor*. Philadelphia: University of Pennsylvania Press.

Schank, R. C. 1982. *Dynamic Memory: A Theory of Reminding and Learning in Computers and People*. Cambridge, Eng.: Cambridge University Press.

Schank, R. C., and R. P. Abelson. 1977. *Scripts, Plans, Goals, and Understanding: An Inquiry into Human Knowledge Structures*. Hillsdale, NJ: Erlbaum.

Scheffler, H. W., and F. G. Lounsbury. 1971. *A Study in Structural Semantics: The Siriono Kinship System*. Englewood Cliffs, NJ: Prentice-Hall.

Searle, J. R. 1979. Metaphor. Pp. 92–123 in A. Ortony, ed., *Metaphor and Thought*. Cambridge, Eng.: Cambridge University Press.

Spradley, J. P., ed. 1972. *Culture and Cognition: Rules, Maps, and Plans*. San Francisco: Chandler.

———. 1979. *The Ethnographic Interview*. New York: Holt, Rinehart and Winston.

Stross, B. 1976. Tzeltal Anatomical Terminology: Semantic Processes. In M. McClaran, ed., *Mayan Linguistics*, vol. 1. Los Angeles: American Indian Studies Center, University of California.

Sturtevant, W. C. 1964. Studies in Ethnoscience. *American Anthropologist* 66(3)2:99–131.

Tyler, S. A., ed. 1969. *Cognitive Anthropology*. New York: Holt, Rinehart and Winston.

Wallace, A.F.C. 1960. *Culture and Personality*. New York: Random House.

———. 1970. *Culture and Personality*. 2nd ed. New York: Random House.

Weller, S. C. 1984. Consistency and Consensus among Informants: Disease Concepts in a Rural Mexican Village. *American Anthropologist* 86:966–75.

———. 1987. Shared Knowledge, Intracultural Variation, and Knowledge Aggregation. *American Behavioral Scientist* 31:178–93.

Weller, S. C., and A. K. Romney. 1988. *Systematic Data Collection*. Newbury Park, CA: Sage.

Weller, S. C., A. K. Romney, and D. P. Orr. 1987. The Myth of a Sub-Culture of Corporal Punishment. *Human Organization* 46:39–47.

Wierzbicka, A. 1984. Apples Are Not a ''Kind of Fruit'': The Semantics of Human Categorization. *American Ethnologist* 11:313–28.

———. 1985. *Lexicography and Conceptual Analysis*. Ann Arbor, MI: Karoma Publishers.

Witkowski, S., and C. H. Brown. 1977. An Explanation of Color Nomenclature Universals. *American Anthropologist* 79:50–57.

CHAPTER FIVE

THE PSYCHOCULTURAL STUDY OF EMOTION AND MENTAL DISORDER

Janis H. Jenkins

Propitious circumstances for examination of the problem of relations among culture, emotion, and psychopathology have recently coalesced in psychological anthropology. This development occurs in the wake of a proliferation of studies on emotion (Abu-Lughod 1986, 1990; Desjarlais 1992; Gaines and Farmer 1986; M. J. Good and B. Good 1988; Hollan 1988; Jenkins 1991b; Kleinman and Good 1985; Lutz 1985, 1988, 1990; Lutz and White 1986; Markus and Kitayama in press; Mathews 1992; Myers 1986; Ochs and Schieffelin 1989; Rosaldo 1980; Roseman 1991; Scheper-Hughes and Lock 1988; Schieffelin 1976; Shweder and LeVine 1984; Wellenkamp 1988; Wikan 1990) and a long-standing interest in culture and psychopathology (Bateson et al. 1956; Edgerton 1966, 1969, 1971a, 1971b; Hallowell 1938, 1955; Kennedy 1974; Sapir 1961; Scheper-Hughes 1979; Sullivan 1953; Wallace 1961). The domain of emotion has become a cultural problem in light of anthropological challenges to the assumption of a psychobiological universality of emotional life (Rosaldo 1984; Kleinman and Good 1985; Lutz 1988). Revitalization of the study of psychopathology in culturally interpreted terms has occurred in the wake of ''the new cross-cultural psychiatry'' (Kleinman 1977, 1980, 1988a) and ''meaning-centered medical anthropology'' (B. Good and M. J. Good 1982; Good 1992). This chapter explores these developments in the psychocultural study of emotion and mental disorder by drawing out conceptual issues common to each.

While implicit claims about emotion abound in classic ethnographies (Bateson 1958; Benedict 1934; Mead 1935; Hallowell 1955), explicit and sustained theorizing on emotion has emerged only in the last decade. Where studies of culture and personality once held sway, studies of culture and emotion are now numerous. Previously, suitable topics in psychological anthropology would likely include, for example, motivation, cognition, perception, dreams, and values, but not emotion (Bock 1980; Barnouw 1985; LeVine 1974; Spindler 1980).[1] Where subdisciplines of "cognitive anthropology" or "cognitive psychology" appeared, similar attention was not granted on "affective anthropology" or "affective psychology." Indeed, the sight and sound of these latter phrases may appear as preposterous as they are unfamiliar in social science.

The relative valuation of cognition at the expense of emotion is embedded in the mind-body dualisms that structure scholarly thinking on the issue. Feminist theories of emotion and social relations (Lutz 1988, 1990; Lutz and Abu-Lughod 1990; Rosaldo 1984) shed light on this dualism by revealing symbolic associations of emotion with the irrational, uncontrollable, dangerous, natural, and female (Lutz 1988).[2] Catherine Lutz's (1988) brilliant analysis of these complex cultural logics revealed contradictions among the cherished presuppositions that constitute the domain of emotion in Western scientific and popular discourse. For example, while emotional expression is generally devalued in favor of a rational, controlled demeanor, failure to demonstrate "basic" human emotions renders one "estranged" from an innate human capacity for feeling (Lutz 1986). The particular associations of emotion, the body, and women have also been examined by Emily Martin (1987).

The historic anthropological ambivalence and neglect of the cultural category of "emotion" can therefore be understood in relation to how certain scholarly topics are deemed worthy or unworthy (Ortner 1974; Lutz 1990; MacKinnon 1989). Emotion has emerged as a problem in psychological anthropology only recently because the passions have been considered secondary cultural artifacts relative to more "cognitively" conceived objects such as beliefs, propositions, and values. With feminist approaches and the expansion of the conceptual horizons of psychological anthropology, however, emotion is now regarded as properly situated within a cultural repertoire. This problem will be addressed further later in relation to the question of how the construct of culture suggests (or constrains) questions about emotion.

Current studies by psychological anthropologists cover a range of emotion topics that include child-rearing practices and the socialization of emotion (Clancy 1986; Schieffelin and Ochs 1986; Weisner 1983; LeVine 1990); the cultural constitution of the self (Csordas 1993 and his chapter in this volume; Hallowell 1955; Marsella, DeVos, and Hsu 1985; Shweder and Bourne 1984; White and Kirkpatrick 1985); cross-cultural variations in the experience and expression of emotion (Briggs 1970; Edgerton 1971a; Shweder and LeVine 1984; Levy 1973; Myers 1979; Schieffelin 1983; Wikan 1990; Roseman 1991); cognitive approaches to emotion (D'Andrade 1987; Holland 1992; Lakoff and Kovecses 1987; Lutz 1982; White 1992); linguistic studies of emotion (Beeman 1985; Schieffelin and Ochs 1986; Lutz 1988; Mathews 1992; Solomon 1984; White and Kirkpatrick 1985); and theoretical examination of Western scientific discourse on emotion (Lutz 1988; Lutz and Abu-Lughod 1990; Rosaldo 1984).

In contrast to the case of emotion, mental disorder has long been the subject of study in psychological anthropology. This long-standing interest stems in large measure from the collaboration of Edward Sapir (1961) and Harry Stack Sullivan (1962),[3] for whom the study of mental disorder was considered essential to an understanding of fundamental (and divergent) human processes. Sullivan and Sapir insisted that a person with a psychiatric disorder must be studied in interpersonal contexts, with particular attention paid to the emotional atmosphere (Jenkins 1991b). Although their collaborative program for the study of culture and mental disorder never fully reached its potential in psychological anthropology (Darnell 1990; Perry 1982; Kennedy 1974), their works still stand as an important foundation for current studies in this area. To draw a parallel between emotion and psychopathology, the early conceptualization of mental disorder as socially transacted has as its counterpart the contemporary formulation of affect as interactive construction (Lutz 1988; Jenkins 1991b).

Reconsideration of relations among culture, emotion, and psychopathology therefore requires examination of enduring and previously unexplored questions: What is particularly *cultural* about emotion and psychopathology? How are emotion and mental disorder to be conceived: as intrapsychic mental events or intersubjective social processes? As biologically natural events or sociopolitically produced reactions? Can cognitively comprised "emotion" be differentiated from bodily "feeling"? How is "illness" to be distinguished from "pathology"? In what sense might an emotion be termed "abnormal"? How are emotions to be probed in relation to "mental" disorders such as schizophrenia or depression?

CULTURAL, ETHNOPSYCHOLOGICAL, AND ETHNOBIOLOGICAL CONSIDERATIONS

Before proceeding further, it will be helpful to provide a working definition of culture as used in this chapter. This is so not merely because I wish to introduce my particular use of the term *culture* as a basis for my discussion of emotion and psychopathology, but also because the concept of culture has become so controversial of late that some may prefer to abandon it altogether. Identification of problems with the notion of culture has resulted in a significant movement to substitute the term *discourse*. Some find that the concept of culture presumes an uneasy coherence, a static and ahistorical notion that excludes agency (Abu-Lughod and Lutz 1990; White and Lutz 1992). The term *discourse*, however, has a variety of quite specific meanings in fields ranging from literary criticism to conversational analysis, and the new role for discourse sacrifices this specificity for the sake of a linguistic and textual slant on the domain subsumed under the term *culture*. It will do just as well to be clear about what counts as culture, taking advantage of the sustained revision of culture theory over the past several decades.

I take culture to be a context of more or less known symbols and meanings that persons dynamically create and re-create for themselves in the process of social interaction. Culture is thus the orientation of a people's way of feeling, thinking, and being in the world—their unself-conscious medium of experience, interpretation, and action. As a context, culture is that through which all human experience and action—including emotions—must be interpreted. This view of culture attempts to take into consideration the quality of culture as something emergent, contested, and temporal (White and Lutz 1992), thereby allowing theoretical breathing space for individual and gender variability and avoiding notions of culture as static, homogeneous, and necessarily shared or even coherent. I would argue that such a conceptualization of culture is crucial for comparative studies of psychopathology (Jenkins and Karno 1992:10). It encompasses the indeterminacy of experience and subjectivity that are submerged both by restricting the debate to discourse and by reducing it to a generalized baseline from which individuals and groups may, and often do, deviate.[4]

An essential step toward culturally informed models of emotion is the investigation of indigenous ethnopsychologies. Ethnopsychological issues include the constitution of the self; indigenous categories and vocabularies of emotion; the predominance of particular emotions within societies; the interrelation of various emotions; identification of those situations in which emotions are said to occur; and ethnophysiological accounts of bodily experience of emotions. These elements of ethnopsychology will mediate both the experience and expression of emotion, presuming the existence of an actively functioning (or dysfunctioning) psyche in transaction with the social world. Geoffrey White (1992:22) has disputed Richard Shweder's (1990) characterization of ethnopsychology as *excluding* actual psychological functioning and subjective life, suggesting that this characterization is based on a dichotomy between "abstract formal theories and ordinary understandings as used in everyday life," and that in fact (cognitively oriented) ethnopsychologists have recognized that this distinction is untenable. White seems correct that both abstract theories and everyday understandings are representational in form, but Shweder's critique must be taken seriously insofar as there are experiential realms and subjectivity beyond the strictly representational. Shweder included these as the domain of "cultural psychology" distinct from ethnopsychology.

Whether labeled as ethnopsychology or as cultural psychology, compared to psychologists' definitions of emotion within a framework of stimulus properties, physiological manifestations, and behavioral responses (Fridja 1987), anthropological frameworks appear considerably more broad-ranging. Consider Michelle Rosaldo's anthropological definition of emotion as "self-concerning, partly physical responses that are at the same time aspects of a moral or ideological attitude; emotions are both feelings and cognitive constructions, linking person, action, and sociological millieu" (see Rosaldo in Levy 1983:128). The anthropological conception of emotion as inherently and explicitly cultural (Lutz 1982, 1988; Rosaldo 1980, 1984) is designed to encompass a broader social field than psychological definitions of emotion as individual response to stimulus events. What is cultural about emotion is that emotion necessarily involves an interpretation, a judgment, or an evaluation (Solomon 1984; Rosaldo 1984). However, as Lila Abu-Lughod and Lutz (1990:26) have recently cautioned, there may be a problem with privileging cultural-cognitivist accounts of emotion "such as understanding, making sense of, judging, and interpreting, [since] these theorists may be inadvertently replicating that bias toward the mental, idealist, or cognitive that Lutz (1986) points out is such a central cultural value for us."

On the other hand, anthropologists have also disputed essentialist claims of basic, universally shared emotions based on innate, uniform processes where "brute, precultural fact" is bedrock (C. Geertz 1973).[5] The presumption of biological regularity and similarity of human emotional life has been challenged by several ethnographic accounts (Lutz 1988; Kleinman 1986; Rosaldo 1980). Plutchik (1980:78) exemplifies the natural science approach to the psychological study of emotion in his search for a set of basic emotions that are the equivalent of Mendeleyev's periodic table in chemistry or Linnaeus's system of classifications in biology. In contrast, anthropological studies are likely to highlight the cultural specificity and *situatedness* of emotion. The conceptualization of emotion as situationally constituted in social settings has been firmly established in the theoretic formulations of Lutz (1988, 1990). Her analyses of the emotional repertoire of the Ifaluk serve as a powerful retort to the notion of basic, universally recognizable emotions (see Ekman 1972). It is also within this Ifalukian ethnographic light that emotion is found not to reside within hearts or minds of individuals but instead in the mutually transacted terrain of social and political space.

Russell (1991:445) has taken issue with Lutz's assertion that Ifaluk emotion terms (*song* [or justifiable anger], for example) do not refer to a person's internal state, but rather to something external. He cited Lutz's finding that Ifaluk terms sometimes define emotions as "about our insides" and raised "the conceptual issue of how a word in any language that does not refer to an internal state could be said to be an emotion word. If *song* were a member of a class of words that, like *marriage* or *kinship*, referred to a relationship, then the reason for calling *song* an emotion word is unclear" (Russell 1991:445; italics in original). Russell interpreted the problem as a conflation of sense and reference and suggested that the proper interpretation is that *song* refers to an internal state created when certain external circumstances occur. There are two problems with this critique. First is a conceptual difficulty with the equation of marriage, kinship, and emotion in that the latter is inherently evaluative and interpretive (as formulated by Lutz), whereas the former are social categories that emotions are *about*. The assertion that emotions are located in social space (rather than individual, internal space) does not "externalize" emotion in such a way to render it conceptually similar to marriage or kinship. Second, there may be a difficulty with just what kind of self is premised here. If the self is ethnopsychologically conceived as private, bounded, and separate, the notion of "internal" states may make cultural sense. However, if the self is more social-relationally conceived, the "internal" and "external" dichotomy may prove an unsatisfactory point of comparison.

Yet Russell's concern with the theoretic representation of the ethnographic fact that Ifaluk emotion words are sometimes defined as "about our insides" may suggest a genuine dilemma, that is, the need for the representation of subjective experience in anthropological constructs for emotion. This problem is significant since emotion necessarily involves subjectivity (and intersubjectivity) in presupposing some object about which the subject is feeling (Shweder 1985; Frijda 1986). The socially constructed object might be not only a human person (or group), but also a deity, demon, animal, or landscape. The role of subjectivity for emotion cannot be confined to one ethnopsychological version of emotion, but can instead be productively employed cross-culturally in comprehensive studies of emotion. At present the problem of emotion as subjective experience is still mostly neglected by psychological anthropologists, a difficult area not much advanced beyond the pioneering work of Hallowell (1938, 1955). The difficulty, however, should not dissuade us from investigation of what must be regarded as a crucial dimension of emotion realms.

Psychological and cognitive researchers have tended to distinguish between emotion, on the one hand, and feeling, on the other (Shweder in press; Levy 1984). By *emotion*, psychologists have tended to mean cognized, behavioral response, whereas by *feeling* they have tended to mean physiologically based sensation. In contrast to the mental nature of emotion, the contemporary distinction dualistically construes feelings as physical. The consequences of this scientific dichotomy are that (1) feelings are understood as biological, while emotions are construed as cultural; and (2) feelings as biological are further construed as universal and immutable, whereas emotions alone may reasonably be thought of as cross-culturally variable. Because feelings are immutable, they are no longer problematized. However, the very notion that emotion is cultural, cognitive, and interpretive, while feeling is homogeneous, biological, and universal, is inherently problematic. An enduring contribution of William James (1884) and more recently of Michelle Rosaldo (1984) is the observation that a disembodied emotion is a nonentity. Emotion and feeling cannot be separated; emotion must involve feeling.

MEDICAL AND POLITICAL CONSIDERATIONS

In medical and psychiatric anthropology, researchers have examined cultural dimensions of dysphoria generally and affective disorders in particular. An abbreviated sampling from domains of inquiry in this area would include cultural meanings and indigenous conceptions of distress and illness (Gaines and Farmer 1986; B. Good and M. J. Good 1982; Good 1992; Jenkins 1988; Kirmayer 1984; Low 1985; Lutz 1985; Toussignant 1984); culture-bound "syndromes" (Carr and Vitaliano 1985; Simons and Hughes 1985); comparative treatments of the cultural validity of psychiatric syndromes catalogued in the American Psychiatric Association's *Diagnostic and Statistical Manual of Mental Disorders (DSM) III-R* (1987) (Good, Good, and Moradi 1985; Good 1992; Hopper 1991,

1992; Kleinman 1980, 1986, 1988a; Manson, Shore, and Bloom 1985); emotional climates and the course of mental disorder (Corin 1990; Karno et al. 1987; Jenkins 1991a; Jenkins and Karno 1992); epidemiological studies of affective and anxiety disorders (Guarnaccia, Good, and Kleinman 1990; Beiser 1985; Manson, Shore, and Bloom 1985); phenomenological accounts of embodiment and illness experience (Csordas 1990, 1993; Frank 1986; Kleinman 1988b; Ots 1990; Scarry 1985); and the medicalization of social problems and human suffering in Western scientific discourse (Fabrega 1989; Kleinman 1988a; Kleinman and Good 1985; Scheper-Hughes and Lock 1987).

Another area that has very recently emerged concerns sociopolitical analyses of emotion. Mary-Jo Good and Byron Good (1988) have introduced the idea of the "state construction of affect," that is, the production of sentiments and actions by the nation-state. They argued for the importance of the role of the state and other political, religious, and economic institutions in legitimizing, organizing, and promoting particular discourses on emotions (M. J. Good and B. Good 1988). Lutz and Abu-Lughod's (1990) analysis of the interplay of emotion talk and the politics of everyday social life is also significant here. They redirected scholarly attention away from largely privatized and culturalized representations of emotion to examination of emotion discourse in the contexts of sociability and power relations.

Kleinman's (1986) case studies from China in the period following the upheaval of the Cultural Revolution provide a convincing argument for the social and political production of affective disorders. In a case study of El Salvador, Jenkins (1991a:139) sought to extend current theorizing on emotion "by examining the nexus among the role of the state in constructing a 'political ethos,' the personal emotions of those who dwell in that ethos, and the mental health consequences for refugees." Other recent literature on the mental health sequelae of sociopolitical upheaval includes treatment of Latin America (Farias 1991; Suarez-Orozco 1989), Southeast Asia (Mollica, Wyshak, and Lavelle 1987; Westermeyer 1988), and South Africa (Swartz 1991).

Emphasis on sociopolitical aspects of affectivity expands the parameters of emotion theory beyond the biological, psychological, and cultural. Closely related to much of this current thinking is feminist theory, which has long been analytically concerned with power relations and inequities (rather than differences) in global context (Rosaldo and Lamphere 1974; Miller 1993). Feminist analyses also question the limits of cultural relativism through grounded locational perspectives on human experience and the human condition (Haraway 1991). The argument here is that the emerging agenda for studies of emotional processes and experience must take political dimensions into account in any of an array of intentional worlds, large and small.

"NORMAL" AND "PATHOLOGICAL" EMOTION: DISCONTINUOUS CATEGORIES OR POLES ON A CONTINUUM?

In what sense can we draw a distinction between "normal" and "pathological" emotion? If normal emotions are those commonly shared within cultural settings, are "abnormal" emotions those outside the range of normal human experience within a particular community? Or within the range of normal experience but inappropriate to a particular setting or event? What criteria would render an emotion or emotional state "abnormal"? Here we encounter the enduring question of whether the normal and pathological are discontinuous categories or poles of a continuum.

In the study of emotion and psychopathology, we have yet to resolve the problem of what Georges Canguilhem (1989) defined as the ontological versus positivist conceptions of disease. Is there, as the ontological view would have it, a distinct qualitative difference between depression as a normal emotion and depression as a pathological state? If so, is this based on some pathogenic alteration, or on some "inborn error" of biochemistry with a genetic origin? Or, as the positivist view would hold, is there only one depression, the intensity of which can vary quantitatively from total absence to a degree that becomes so great as to be pathological? In this view, abnormality is defined as "more" of what otherwise might be considered within the bounds of normal human experience. Canguilhem (1989:45) quoted Nietzsche as follows:

> It is the value of all morbid states that they show us under a magnifying glass certain states that are normal—but not easily visible when normal.

In a more contemporary vein, Sullivan (1962) argued that there is no definitive threshold distinguishing healthy from ill individuals. The inability to recall a name that is "right on the tip of one's tongue" is a mental disorder in the same sense as is schizophrenia, albeit much less severe. Sullivan maintained that schizophrenic illness could productively be considered as a paradigmatic case for the analysis of fundamental human processes.

Contemporary psychiatry and medicine have for some time been dominated by the quantitative perspective, with its corollary that since they are essentially the same, studies of the pathological can help us understand the normal and vice versa. However, a curious mixture of quantitative and qualitative criteria is characteristic of actual diagnostic practice in psychiatry today. The qualitative criteria revolve around the specific symptoms that comprise the symptom cluster or syndrome for a given diagnostic category. Yet the *Diagnostic and Statistical Manual or Mental Disorders (DSM III-R)* (American Psychiatric Association 1987) is unhesitatingly organized according to three kinds of quantitative criteria: (1) intensity or severity of specific experiences/symptoms (generally exceeds normal range); (2) duration of the experiences (generally longer than usual); and (3) occurrence of the symptom along with one or more other affective, cognitive, and behavioral phenomena that form a particular configuration or symptom profile. It should be obvious that the particular psychiatric symptoms selected for attention as well as the cut-off points for duration and severity of co-occurring symptoms are somewhat arbitrary. Failure to meet criteria of enough symptoms of sufficient duration is a failure to meet the parameters of particularly defined syndromes. Therefore, patients who meet some but not all of the designated classificatory category are considered "subclinical." Most persons have at least some experience of the myriad of diverse symptoms cataloged in the *DSM*. Whether this observation provokes anxiety or amusement, it is evidence of the continuous nature of such definitions of psychopathology. Much normal-range experience is cataloged in those 567 pages.

According to psychiatric diagnostic procedure, emotions are unusual or abnormal not because they are unrecognizable features of human experience. Instead, they are considered abnormal because they appear more severe and prolonged and often co-occur with an array of other behavioral or cognitive disturbances that (as a syndrome) are outside the range of culturally prescribed orientations to the world. On the other hand, when we move from diagnosis to the etiology and ontology of psychiatric disorder, the dominant (medical) paradigm argues that there is a qualitative gulf between normal and pathological. Pathology is a result of a genetically based "inborn error of metabolism," a qualitative anomaly, or even a kind of lesion.

There are other more specific ways in which the continuity or discontinuity between normal and pathological is incorporated in our thinking. Take, for example, the delusional fear that a university president wants a given male faculty member dismissed from his position. Quantitatively, such a person might find this fear becoming increasingly intense, or being just a passing notion that is extinguished when it is shrugged off as silly. On the other hand, qualitatively there would be a definite discontinuity between a mistaken idea and a fixed delusion about a university president, for given the proper evidence the former can be changed or corrected and the latter cannot. Again, although delusions can become quantitatively more or less intense and rigid, true delusions have the qualitative feature of exfoliating into a system, adding more and different and even absurd elements. The delusion that the president of the university wants one dismissed from his position can become the idea that the president, provost, dean, and the department chair are in a conspiracy, and can further come to include the fact that they especially want the faculty member's parking space taken away.

Depending on the way an emotion is formulated, it may presuppose a quantitative or qualitative notion of normal versus pathological. For example, one might conceive a qualitative continuum between happiness and sadness, with clinical mania and depression at the pathological extremes of the continuum. On the other hand, when it comes to the symptomatic "flat affect" of schizophrenia, one thinks of a quantitative continuum between flatness and expressiveness. Could one formulate a qualitative distinction between normal flat affect and pathological flat affect? The differences between quantitative and qualitative and between continuous and discontinuous easily become quite tangled. As Canguilhem observed, "The continuity between one state and another can certainly be compatible with the heterogeneity of these states. The continuity of the middle stages does not rule out the diversity of the extremes" (1989:56).

AN ORIENTATION TO EMOTION AND PSYCHOPATHOLOGY

Systematic study of emotion and psychopathology requires examination of the following questions: How are the phenomenological worlds of persons with major mental disorders culturally elaborated? What consequences ensue for cross-culturally valid diagnoses if emotions are considered as cultural objects? Are there cross-cultural variations in the emotions expressed by kin about a relative with major mental disorder? Does emotional response on the part of kin mediate the course and outcome of a psychiatric disorder? This section explores these issues in the context of the major disorders schizophrenia and depression. A cogent rationale for the productive use of specific *DSM* diagnostic categories (as opposed to generalized distress) in anthropological studies of culture and psychopathology has already been provided by Byron Good (1992). Good agreed that although they are grounded in Western cultural assumptions (Gaines 1992), the categories are systematic enough to be used as the basis for cross-cultural research and to be subject to critique as the result of that research.

With respect to the cross-cultural study of the phenomenology of psychosis, little is known about the processes whereby selves and emotional atmospheres constitute worlds of experience for persons living with schizophrenia. At issue is the fundamental question of how psychiatric illness is experienced emotionally. Is schizophrenic psychosis, for example, nearly always and everywhere devalued as a terrifying experience? While many feel that this is likely to be the case, we cannot know with certainty since the cross-cultural ethnographic and clinical record is notably thin with respect to phenomenological accounts of mental disorder (Kennedy 1974; Kleinman 1988a, 1988b). Jenkins (1991a) has summarized cross-cultural studies of "emotional atmospheres" to document not only the variation in everyday experience but also the importance of that emotional experience in mediating the course and outcome of major mental disorder.

For theoretical orientation to future phenomenological studies of psychosis, it may be useful to reconsider ideas long ago introduced by Sullivan (1953). Recall that for Sullivan, mental disorder is properly conceived not as a discrete disease entity but as an interactive process. This view has major implications if it is used as a cross-cultural starting point for investigation, since it would appear to require that mental disorder be examined within the arena of everyday social life rather than in the brain scan or clinic. For Sullivan, psychiatry "is not an impossible study of an individual suffering mental disorder; it is a study of disordered interpersonal relations nucleating more or less clearly in a particular person" (1953:258). Not sick individuals but "complex, peculiarly characterized situations" are then the target of cross-cultural research and therapy. Sullivan's theory is premised on a notion of the "self-system" as a constellation of interpersonal mechanisms in service of emotional protection against a noxious emotional milieu (Sullivan 1953). Here the self is not a discrete and fixed entity but instead a constellation of interpersonal processes developed during childhood and adolescence. This view of self as intersubjective creation leaves behind the more usual intrapsychic and individuated configuration in psychiatric science. Thus these early theoretical formulations by Sullivan provide a bridge between the subjective experience of the afflicted self and the world of everyday social interaction.

Emotion and Schizophrenic Disorders

In this section, emotion issues are examined in relation to (1) the content and form of diagnostic symptom criteria for schizophrenia and (2) illness processes relevant to the experience, the manifestation, and the course and outcome of schizophrenia. Exploration of the emotional dimensions of schizophrenia serves to underscore the point that emotion should be considered no less central to so-considered thought disorders (i.e., the schizophrenias) than to mood disorders (i.e., affective disorders).

The cross-cultural evidence appears to support the notion of important variation in both the *content* (e.g., delusions about witches rather than about popular performing artists) and *form* (e.g., visual, auditory, or tactile hallucinations) of schizophrenic symptomatology. An early report from H.B.M. Murphy et al. (1963) listed four schizophrenic symptoms as common cross-culturally: (1) social and emotional withdrawal; (2) auditory hallucinations; (3) delusions; and (4) flatness of affect. In addition, the early transcultural psychiatric reports provided documentation of significant differences in the manifestation of symptomatology. For example, "Falling toward the quiet, nonaggressive end of the continuum appear to be patients from India (Wittkower and Rin 1965), the Hutterites (Eaton and Weil 1955), and the Irish (Opler 1959). Toward the noisy, aggressive side would probably come the Africans, Americans, and Japanese (e.g., Schooler and Caudill 1964)" (Kennedy 1974:1148–49). Cross-cultural variation in the subtypes of schizophrenia—such as paranoia, hebephrenia, and catatonia—has also been widely noted (World Health Organization [WHO] 1979). The pathoplasticity of symptom formation and expression has been interpreted by Kennedy (1974:1149) as providing evidence not only of the cultural shaping of the disorder but also of the likelihood that "schizophrenia" does not denote a single disease process. It is probable that as a research and clinical construct, schizophrenia is better conceived as a plurality of disorders as opposed to a unitary diagnostic category.

Anthropological analysis of the specific symptoms from the American Psychiatric Association's (1987) *Diagnostic And Statistical Manual (DSM)* for the category of schizophrenia makes it evident that all prodromal, actively psychotic, and residual symptoms must be evaluated with reference to the patient's cultural context. Failure to do so can result in misdiagnosis. Broadly conceived, symptom criteria include the patient's sense of self, behavioral repertoire, beliefs, cognitive style, and affects. Narrowly conceived, and for the purposes of differential diagnosis, the revised *DSM-IV* (American Psychiatric Association 1994) symptom criteria are (1) delusions; (2) hallucinations; (3) disorganized speech; (4) grossly disorganized or catatonic behavior; and (5) negative symptoms (i.e., affective flattening, alogia, or avolition).[6] While delusions, hallucinations, disorganized speech, or disorganized behavior might all arguably be affective in nature (i.e., how can these have no culturally specific affective coloration?), culture in relation to the so-called negative symptoms is of particular interest to the present analysis.[7] This is particularly so in the case of ''flat'' affect, long thought to be pathognomonic for schizophrenia.

''Flat'' or ''blunted'' affect is defined as ''a disturbance of affect manifest by dullness of feeling tone'' (Freedman, Kaplan, and Sadock 1976:1280). To examine this symptom cross-culturally, I turn now to cross-cultural data on schizophrenic symptomatology as collected by the World Health Organization's (WHO) International Pilot Study of Schizophrenia (IPSS). The IPSS conducted a longitudinal study of schizophrenic symptomatology and course of illness. Psychiatric assessments were completed for 1,202 patients in nine countries (the United Kingdom, the USSR, the United States, Czechoslovakia, Denmark, China, Colombia, Nigeria, and India). Two-year follow-up data (WHO 1979) across all sites provided a striking range in the presence of flat affect: from 8 percent (Ibadan, Nigeria) to 50 percent (Moscow, Russia) of patients were so rated. A slight tendency for flat affect to be more common among patients from the more industrialized countries was noted.[8] In addition, flat affect was recorded as the second most common symptom.[9] While these longitudinal data suggest important cross-cultural differences in the presence of flat affect, methodological questions remain as to precisely how flat affect was assessed. The lack of systematic discussion by IPSS investigators on this point is troubling. The cross-cultural variation in emotional experience and expression generally and in schizophrenic symptomatology specifically renders the culturally valid assessment of flat affect a complicated undertaking.

The other two *DSM-IV* negative symptoms of schizophrenia—alogia and avolition—have been subjected to even less systematic cross-cultural examination. Alogia (speechlessness that may be resultant from psychotic confusion) is of particular cultural and sociolinguistic concern insofar as the language and ethnicity of the individual conducting the psychiatric assessment may differ from those of the patient. (Alogia may also be related to intellectual deficit.) Certainly the symptom of avolition can be expected to vary substantially in relation to culturally constituted capacities such as self, agency, motivation, and the meaning of purposeful action (Karno and Jenkins 1994).

A second area of research concerns emotion and schizophrenic illness *processes*. This processual approach to affective components of schizophrenic illness can be considered in relation to experience of emotion, on the one hand, and expression of emotion, on the other. With respect to *experience*, questions arise about everyday phenomenological constitution of affect in relation to schizophrenic illness. While a full range of affects may be experienced by the patient, fear and terror have often been a large part of schizophrenic experience (Glass 1989). The illness experience of families has been more systematically investigated in relation to emotional *expression* about the patient and his or her illness. The suggestion that kind and community emotional response to schizophrenic illness may vary cross-culturally is certainly present in early reports from transcultural psychiatry. Nancy Waxler (1974, 1977), for instance, has maintained that a greater tolerance for schizophrenic illness exists in non-Western settings. Following a systematic analysis of the WHO (1979) data on recovery from schizophrenia, Edgerton (1980) pointed out that the findings of better prognosis in non-Western settings may not reflect especially salutary conditions in those settings but instead noxious features within more industrialized nations. Alex Cohen (1992) disputed Waxler's claim and raised questions about her data on this topic. In reviews of Cohen's work, however, Hopper (1992) and Warner (1992) pointed to several limitations of Cohen's critique. Following evaluation of the overall evidence, Hopper (1992:96) called for "some careful stocktaking of the fruits of the anthropological effort in cross-cultural psychiatry," particularly in the areas of epidemiological evidence, beliefs and utilities, and the contexts of work and family. Warner (1992) also pointed to limitations of Cohen's critique and found only one example of an outcome study that failed to support the general finding (see also Warner 1985).

Three decades of research on "expressed emotion" serve as confirmation that emotional response to schizophrenic illness not only varies substantially cross-culturally but also mediates course and outcome (Brown, Birley, and Wing 1972; Vaughn and Leff 1976a; Vaughn et al. 1984; Karno et al. 1987; Jenkins and Karno 1992). In particular, the "expressed emotion" factors of criticism, hostility, and emotional overinvolvement show considerable variability (Brown, Birley, and Wing 1972; Vaughn and Leff 1976a; Karno et al. 1987; Vaughn et al. 1984).[10] Lower levels of criticism and emotional involvement have been observed among Indian, British, and Mexican-descent families than among Euro-American families (Jenkins and Karno 1992). Moreover, persons suffering from a schizophrenic illness who reside with critical, hostile, or emotionally overinvolved relatives are far more likely to suffer a relapse or exacerbation of symptoms compared to their counterparts who reside in households noteworthy by virtue of the relative absence of such factors.

To account for the link between "expressed emotion" and schizophrenic outcome, the hypothesis of a heightened vulnerability to negatively constituted family atmospheres has been put forward by Vaughn (1989). This formulation is general, however, and much remains to be examined with respect to the specific mechanisms of how such processes unfold. In addition, the specifically cultural basis of the "expressed emotion" construct has yet to be fully appreciated by psychiatric researchers (Jenkins 1991a; Jenkins and Karno 1992). Certainly the emotional response to schizophrenic illness must be understood as mediated by cultural conceptions of the nature of the problem (for example, "witchcraft," "*nervios*," "laziness," or "schizophrenia"). Such analyses draw our attention to the inherently affective nature of conceptions of mental disorder (Jenkins 1988; Fabrega 1982). To the extent that cultural conceptions of illness may partially determine which affects surround the illness and, conversely, which emotional stances may suggest the saliency of particular conceptions of the problem, we must be concerned with how such reciprocally constructed responses mediate the course of disorder.

The previously mentioned WHO's IPSS also provided evidence of a cross-culturally variable course of schizophrenia. The IPSS concluded that "on virtually all course and outcome measures, a greater proportion of schizophrenic patients in Agra [India], Cali [Colombia], and Ibadan [Nigeria] had favorable, non-disabling courses and outcomes than was the case in Aarhus, London, Moscow, Prague, and Washington" (Sartorius, Jablensky, and Shapiro 1978:106). While the IPSS investigators believed that this variation was probably accounted for by social and cultural factors, they could not submit their hypothesis to examination since sociocultural data were not systematically collected. Insights into the possible cultural sources of variation are offered in two especially careful and critical reanalyses of these data of the IPSS and "expressed emotion" data recently published by Hopper (1991, 1992). Additional evidence for the important role of the emotional environment on the course of schizophrenia comes from Ellen Corin's (1990) research in Montreal on "positive social withdrawal." Patients who regularly inhabit behavioral environments with few social demands evidence less psychotic symptomatology and a greater personal functioning than those in more demanding environments.

Emotion and Major Depressive Disorders

Viewed cross-culturally, depression is more commonly manifest in somatic than in psychological forms (Kleinman 1986, 1988a; Kleinman and Good 1985). This finding necessarily calls into question the validity of *DSM* symptoms such as "depressed mood" or "loss of pleasure" as pathognomonic symptoms of the disorder. Cultural propensities toward "psychologization" versus "somatization" are more fully reviewed elsewhere (Kirmayer 1984; Ots 1990; Kleinman 1986). Jenkins, Kleinman, and Good (1991:67) have argued that "[i]nsofar as this dichotomous approach distinguishes psyche and soma, it reproduces assumptions of Western thought and culture, [but] must from the outset be suspended in formulating a valid comparative stance.'' A key cross-cultural question is whether the clinical-research construct of ''depression'' can validly include both somatic and psychologized forms of depressive symptomatology or whether these are better considered as essentially different disorders.

Somatized versus psychologized expressions of depressive affect suggest a cultural specificity to ''sadness'' and ''suffering'' (Kleinman and Kleinman 1991). Cultural styles of dysphoria are perhaps best understood as elements of indigenous or ethnopsychological models of emotion (Lutz 1988; White and Kirkpatrick 1985), as outlined earlier. An understanding of local ethnopsychological models of depression is crucial to specification of everyday depressive affects, on the one hand, and more severely distressing depressive states, on the other.

As pointed out by Kleinman and Good (1985), there are methodological problems in differentiating depression as emotion, mood, and disorder. The parallel observation by Sullivan has already been made for normal-range behavior and that characteristic of schizophrenia. An extension of Sullivan's approach to schizophrenia as ''complex, peculiarly characterized situations'' was adopted by George Brown and Tirril Harris (1978) in their studies of depression. They found that cases of depressive illness, apparently very common among working-class women in the London area, could be predicted not by individual factors but instead by a specific set of situational factors. These factors include unemployment, dilapidated housing conditions, caring for three or more small children, the lack of a confiding relationship, and the death of the mother before age eleven. Taken together, these factors could be observed to produce depressive reactions in these English women. This careful empirical study provides powerful evidence for the conclusion that depression is more diagnostic of women's social and economic situations than women's psychobiological vulnerability.

The sociocultural feature that may be most important to cross-cultural studies of depression is gender. The relationship between depression and gender is well known: epidemiological evidence documents that women suffer disproportionately from depression relative to men (Nolan-Hoeksema 1990). This epidemiological fact with reference to North American women has been confirmed cross-culturally in virtually every case that has been investigated. Strickland (1992) has summarized these data. Jenkins, Kleinman, and Good (1991) critically reviewed the available literature on cross-cultural susceptibility to depression to conclude that the disproportionate degree of depression among women is likely to be universal. This disturbing conclusion must be accounted for in light of gender inequality conferring less power and status on women relative to men in both Western and non-Western countries (Miller 1993; Rosaldo and Lamphere 1974). Low socioeconomic status also must be examined since several studies have linked adverse life events and conditions to a vulnerability to depression, with again a disproportionate effect on poor women and children (Brown and Harris 1978). Migration (of immigrants and refugees) and social change are also implicated in the onset of a major depressive episode (Farias

1991; Jenkins 1991b; Kinzie et al. 1984; Mollica, Wyshak, and Lavelle 1987; Westermeyer 1988, 1989).

Cultural variations in socialization practices and marital discord, as well as "expressed emotion," may also contribute to differential rates of depression (Vaughn and Leff 1976a; Hooley, Orley, and Teasedale 1986). In summary, there is evidence that culture plays a strong role in the experience of depressive affects and disorder, the meaning of and social response to depression within families and communities, and the course and outcome of the disorder (Jenkins, Kleinman, and Good 1991:68).

CONCLUDING REMARKS

In this chapter, I have drawn together two critical but often separate areas within psychological anthropology, the study of the relation between culture and emotion and the study of psychopathology, in order to suggest that there is a great deal of commonality in the conceptual issues raised by each. My argument has encompassed the methodological orientations of ethnopsychology and cultural psychology, interpersonal and intrapsychic accounts of the theory of emotion, the conceptual distinction between emotion and feeling, and the problem of continuity and discontinuity between normal and pathological. I have summarized studies of dysphoric affects and emphasized the importance of experiential accounts of emotional distress and disorder in the context of power relations and considerations of the state construction of affect, formulated in intersubjective interpersonal terms and premised on a relational notion of self. Finally, I have considered cultural variability in the phenomenology, course, and outcome of the major mental disorders schizophrenia and depression and have examined contemporary psychiatric diagnostic conventions in light of anthropological theories of emotion.

Anthropological approaches to the study of emotion have come a great distance in a relatively short period of time. Nevertheless, we have yet to see the full development of what could be considered "affective anthropology" or to take seriously something that might be called "emotional anthropology." Along with Western traditional views of the superiority of mind over body, there is currently a strong bias toward cognitive science. While "cognitive anthropology" has made a powerful scientific contribution to the anthropological endeavor, relatively little anthropological attention has been directed toward the full range of emotion phenomena. As a complement to studies of emotion based on lexicon, discourse, ethnopsychological category, communication, and expression, we are in rather short supply of emotion studies based on intersubjective dimensions of culture and a theoretically elaborated concept of experience (Hallowell [1938, 1955] was a notable exception). Signs are beginning to be observable, however, that this is about to change. Kleinman and Kleinman (1991:277) offered a definition of experience as "an intersubjective medium of social transactions in local moral worlds. It is . . . the felt flow of that intersubjective medium.'' Schwartz (1992), who had previously endorsed a ''distributive'' theory of culture, called for an ''experience-processing'' model of culture. Others have begun at least to turn in a similar direction (Good 1992; White and Kirkpatrick 1985; Shweder 1990; Wikan 1990). In this movement we should expect to see a renewed interest in naturalistic observation and interpretive analyses of behavior, particularly in contexts where dynamic theoretical analyses, as introduced by Pierre Janet (1924), are brought into play. The development of such models poses a substantial challenge for the future.

NOTES

1. Much of the discourse on emotion was subsumed under the rubric of ''personality'' studies (Rosaldo 1984; White 1992). A notable exception is Hildred Geertz's excellent 1959 article ''The Vocabulary of Emotion'' published in the journal *Psychiatry*. Another important exception is Gregory Bateson's (1958:118) notion of ethos defined as ''the expression of a culturally standardized system of organization of the instincts and emotions of the individuals.'' In the revision of his text on psychological anthropology, Bock (1988) did include a new chapter on ''Self and Emotion.''

2. The counterpart of cognition (and thought) as rational, controlled, safe, cultural, and male is obvious. The scientific suitability of these adjectival descriptors has long been assumed in anthropological and psychological discourse.

3. Although the collaboration between Sullivan and Sapir is well known, it is of historic interest that Hallowell (1938) is also on record as having collaborated with Sullivan.

4. For theoretical discussion of culture, deviance (including psychopathology), and ambiguity, see Edgerton (1985). For review of a controversial thesis concerning the notion of societally widespread or institutionalized forms of deviance as constitutive of a ''sick society,'' see Edgerton (1992). For a discussion of ''explanatory models'' of discrete illness episodes as necessarily complex, dynamic, contradictory, and ambiguous, see Kleinman (1980). Both of these theorists have been preoccupied with how culture theory can account for change, heterogeneity, and disagreement in the context of individual and subgroup variability.

5. Lutz and Abu-Lughod (1990) and Kirmayer (1992) provided thoroughgoing accounts of issues surrounding essentialist presumptions in social scientific discourse.

6. The new criteria forthcoming for ''Schizophrenia and Related Psychotic Disorders'' in the *DSM-IV* are presented here as part of the author's ongoing work with the National Institute of Mental Health [NIMH] Task Force on Culture and Diagnosis.

7. So-termed negative symptoms in schizophrenia are noteworthy by virtue of their absence: for example, *lack* of appropriate affect, speech, and volition.

8. The differences between the nonindustrialized and more industrialized countries are not uniform, however: only 9 percent of London patients and 11 percent of Washington patients displayed flat affect at the time of follow-up.

9. The observation of ''lack of insight'' as the most common symptom might be indicative of a clash between professional psychiatric and popular lay formulations of the problem (e.g., as a psychiatric, nervous, mental, or personality problem). If the psychiatric interviewer had accorded a legitimacy to popular illness categories, this ''symptom'' might not have been recorded so frequently. Failure to appreciate these cross-

cultural differences in what Kleinman (1980) has termed "explanatory models" can result in an array of methodological difficulties in the assessment of symptoms.

10. Methodological definitions of these affects have been provided elsewhere (Vaughn and Leff 1976b). Briefly, criticism is any verbal statement indicating dislike, resentment, or disapproval. Emotional "overinvolvement" is indexed by a set of particular attitudes, emotions, and behaviors that are culturally determined to include overprotective or intrusive behaviors. Although affects of warmth and praise are also undoubtedly important to many qualitative dimensions of family life, these have yet to be significantly predictive of recovery from major mental disorder. The relationship between criticism, hostility, and emotional overinvolvement has also been found for depressive illness at even lower thresholds than for schizophrenia (Hooley, Orley, and Teasedale 1986; Vaughn and Leff 1976a).

REFERENCES

Abu-Lughod, L. 1986. *Veiled Sentiments: Honor and Poetry in a Bedouin Society.* Berkeley: University of California Press.

Abu-Lughod, L., and C. Lutz. 1990. Introduction: Emotion, Discourse, and the Politics of Everyday Life. In C. A. Lutz and L. Abu-Lughod, eds., *Language and the Politics of Emotion.* Cambridge, Eng.: Cambridge University Press.

American Psychiatric Association. 1987. *Diagnostic and Statistical Manual of Mental Disorders.* 3rd ed., rev. (*DSM-III-R*). Washington, DC: American Psychiatric Association.

Barnouw, V. 1985. *Culture and Personality.* 4th ed. Homewood, IL: Dorsey Press.

Bateson, G. 1958. *Naven.* Stanford, CA: Stanford University Press.

Bateson, G., D. Jackson, J. Haley, and J. Weakland. 1956. Toward a Theory of Schizophrenia. *Behavioral Science* 1:251–64.

Beeman, W. O. 1985. Dimensions of Dysphoria: The View from Linguistic Anthropology. In A. Kleinman and B. Good, eds., *Culture and Depression: Studies in the Anthropology and Cross-Cultural Psychiatry of Affect and Disorder.* Berkeley: University of California Press.

Beiser, M. 1985. A Study of Depression among Traditional Africans, Urban North Americans, and Southeast Asian Refugees. In A. Kleinman and B. Good, eds., *Culture and Depression: Studies in the Anthropology and Cross-Cultural Psychiatry of Affect and Disorder.* Berkeley: University of California Press.

Benedict, R. 1934. *Patterns of Culture.* Boston: Houghton Mifflin.

Bock, P. K. 1980. *Continuities in Psychological Anthropology: A Historical Introduction.* San Francisco: W. H. Freeman.

———. 1988. *Rethinking Psychological Anthropology: Continuity and Change in the Study of Human Action.* New York: W. H. Freeman.

Briggs, J. 1970. *Never in Anger: Portrait of an Eskimo Family.* Cambridge, MA: Harvard University Press.

Brown, G., J.L.T. Birley, and J. Wing. 1972. Influence of Family Life on the Course of Schizophrenic Disorders: A Replication. *British Journal of Psychiatry* 121:241–58.

Brown, G., and T. Harris. 1978. *Social Origins of Depression: A Study of Psychiatric Disorder in Women.* New York: Free Press.

Canguilhem, G. 1989. *The Normal and the Pathological.* New York: Zone Books.

Carr, J. E., and P. P. Vitaliano. 1985. The Theoretical Implications of Converging Research on Depression and the Culture-Bound Syndromes. Pp. 244–66 in A. Kleinman and B. Good, eds., *Culture and Depression: Studies in the Anthropology and Cross-Cultural Psychiatry of Affect and Disorder.* Berkeley: University of California Press.

Clancy, P. 1986. The Acquisition of Communicative Style in Japanese. In B. Schieffelin and E. Ochs, eds., *Language Socialization across Cultures.* Cambridge, Eng.: Cambridge University Press.

Cohen, A. 1992. Prognosis for Schizophrenia in the Third World: A Reevaluation of Cross-Cultural Research. *Culture, Medicine, and Psychiatry* 16:53–75.

Corin, E. 1990. Facts and Meaning in Psychiatry: An Anthropological Approach to the Lifeworld of Schizophrenics. *Culture, Medicine, and Psychiatry* 14:153–88.

Csordas, T. J. 1990. The 1988 Stirling Award Essay: Embodiment as a Paradigm for Anthropology. *Ethos* 18:5–47.

———. 1993. *The Sacred Self: A Cultural Phenomenology of Charismatic Healing.* Berkeley: University of California Press.

D'Andrade, R. 1987. A Folk Model of the Mind. In D. Holland and N. Quinn, eds., *Cultural Models in Language and Thought.* Cambridge, Eng.: Cambridge University Press.

Darnell, R. 1990. *Edward Sapir: Linguist, Anthropologist, Humanist.* Berkeley: University of California Press.

Desjarlais, R. 1992. *Body and Emotion: The Aesthetics of Illness and Healing in the Napal Himalayas.* Philadelphia: University of Pennsylvania Press.

Eaton, J., and R. Weil. 1955. *Culture and Mental Disorders.* Glencoe, IL: Free Press.

Edgerton, R. B. 1966. Conceptions of Psychosis in Four East African Societies. *American Anthropologist* 68:408–25.

———. 1969. On the "Recognition" of Mental Illness. In S. Plog and R. B. Edgerton, eds., *Changing Perspectives in Mental Illness.* New York: Holt, Rinehart and Winston.

———. 1971a. *The Individual in Cultural Adaptation: A Study of Four East African Peoples.* Berkeley: University of California Press.

———. 1971b. A Traditional African Psychiatrist. *Southwestern Journal of Anthropology* 27:259–78.

———. 1980. Traditional Treatment for Mental Illness. In *Africa: A Review. Culture, Medicine, and Psychiatry* 4:167–89.

———. 1985. *Rules, Exceptions, and Social Order.* Berkeley: University of California Press.

———. 1992. *Sick Societies: Challenging the Myth of Primitive Harmony.* New York: Free Press.

Ekman, P., ed., 1972. *Emotion in the Human Face.* 2nd ed. Cambridge, Eng.: Cambridge University Press.

Fabrega, H. 1982. Culture and Psychiatric Illness: Biomedical and Ethnomedical Aspects. In A. Marsella and G. White, eds., *Cultural Conceptions of Mental Health and Therapy.* Dordrecht, Holland: D. Reidel Publishing Co.

———. 1989. Cultural Relativism and Psychiatric Illness. *Journal of Nervous and Mental Disease* 177:415–30.

Farias, P. 1991. The Socio-Political Dimensions of Trauma in Salvadoran Refugees: Analysis of a Clinical Sample. *Culture, Medicine, and Psychiatry* 15:167–92.

Frank, G. 1986. On Embodiment: A Case Study of Congenital Limb Deficiency in American Culture. *Culture, Medicine, and Psychiatry* 10:189–219.

Freedman, A., H. Kaplan, and B. Sadock. 1976. *Modern Synopsis of Comprehensive Textbook of Psychiatry II.* Baltimore, MD: Williams and Wilkins Co.

Frijda, N. 1986. *The Emotions.* Cambridge, Eng.: Cambridge University Press.

Gaines, A. 1992. From DSM-I to II-R: Voices of Self, Mastery, and the Other: A Cultural Constructivist Reading of a U.S. Psychiatric Classification. *Social Science and Medicine* 35:3–24.

Gaines, A., and P. Farmer. 1986. Visible Saints: Social Cynosures and Dysphoria in the Mediterranean Tradition. *Culture, Medicine, and Psychiatry* 10:295–330.

Geertz, C. 1973. *The Interpretation of Cultures.* New York: Basic Books.

Geertz, H. 1959. The Vocabulary of Emotion: A Study of Javanese Socialization Processes. *Psychiatry* 22:225–37.

Glass, J. M. 1989. *Private Terror/Public Life.* Ithaca, NY: Cornell University Press.

Good, B. 1992. Culture and Psychopathology: Directions for Psychiatric Anthropology. Pp. 181–205 in T. Schwartz, G. White, and C. Lutz, eds., *New Directions in Psychological Anthropology.* Cambridge, Eng.: Cambridge University Press.

Good, B., and M.-J. D. Good. 1982. Toward a Meaning-Centered Analysis of Popular Illness Categories. Pp. 141–166 in M. White and G. White, eds., *Cultural Conceptions of Mental Health and Therapy*. Dordrecht, Holland: D. Reidel Publishing Co.

Good, B., M.-J. D. Good, and R. Moradi. 1985. The Interpretation of Iranian Depressive Illness and Dysphoric Affect. Pp. 369–428 in A. Kleinman and B. Good, eds., *Culture and Depression: Studies in the Anthropology and Cross-Cultural Psychiatry of Affect and Disorder*. Berkeley: University of California Press.

Good, M.-J. D., and B. Good. 1988. Ritual, the State, and the Transformation of Emotional Discourse in Iranian Society. *Culture, Medicine, and Psychiatry* 12:43–63.

Guarnaccia, P., B. Good, and A. Kleinman. 1990. A Critical Review of Epidemiological Studies of Puerto Rican Mental Health. *American Journal of Psychiatry* 147:1449–56.

Hallowell, A. I. 1938. Fear and Anxiety as Cultural and Individual Variables in a Primitive Society. *Journal of Social Psychology* 9:25–47.

———. 1955. The Self in Its Behavioral Environment. Pp. 75–111 in *Culture and Experience*. Philadelphia: University of Pennsylvania Press.

Haraway, D. 1991. *Simians, Cyborgs, and Women: The Reinvention of Nature*. New York: Routledge.

Hollan, D. 1988. Staying "Cool" in Toraja: Informal Strategies for the Management of Anger and Hostility in a Nonviolent Society. *Ethos* 16:52–72.

Holland, D. 1992. How Cultural Systems Become Desire: A Case Study of American Romance. Pp. 61–89 in R. D'Andrade and C. Strauss, eds., *Human Motives and Cultural Models*. Cambridge, Eng.: Cambridge University Press.

Hooley, J., J. Orley, and J. D. Teasedale. 1986. Levels of Expressed Emotion and Relapse in Depressed Patients. *British Journal of Psychiatry* 148:642–47.

Hopper, K. 1991. Some Old Questions for the New Cross-Cultural Psychiatry. *Medical Anthropology Quarterly* 5:299–330.

———. 1992. Cervantes' Puzzle—A Commentary on Alex Cohen's "Prognosis for Schizophrenia in the Third World: A Reevaluation of Cross-Cultural Research." *Culture, Medicine, and Psychiatry* 16:89–100.

James, W. 1884. What Is an Emotion? *Mind* 9:188–205.

Janet, P. 1924. *The Major Symptoms of Hysteria: Fifteen Lectures Given in the Medical School of Harvard University*. New York: Macmillan.

Jenkins, J. H. 1988. Ethnopsychiatric Interpretations of Schizophrenic Illness: The Problem of *nervios* within Mexican-American Families. *Culture, Medicine, and Psychiatry* 12:303–31.

———. 1991a. The State Construction of Affect: Political Ethos and Mental Health among Salvadoran Refugees. *Culture, Medicine, and Psychiatry* 15:139–65.

———. 1991b. Anthropology, Expressed Emotion, and Schizophrenia. *Ethos* 19:387–431.

Jenkins, J. H., and M. Karno. 1992. The Meaning of "Expressed Emotion": Theoretical Issues Raised by Cross-Cultural Research. *American Journal of Psychiatry* 149:9–21.

Jenkins, J. H., A. Kleinman, and B. J. Good. 1991. Cross-Cultural Aspects of Depression. In J. Becker and A. Kleinman, eds., *Psychological Aspects of Depression*. Hillsdale, NJ: Erlbaum.

Karno, M., and J. H. Jenkins. 1994. Schizophrenia and Related Disorders. In J. Mezzich et al., eds., *Cultural Proposals and Supporting Papers for DSM-IV*. NIMH-Sponsored Group on Culture and Diagnosis. Washington, DC: American Psychiatric Association.

Karno, M., J. H. Jenkins, A. de la Selva, F. Santana, C. Telles, S. Lopez, and J. Mintz. 1987. Expressed Emotion and Schizophrenic Outcome among Mexican-American Families. *Journal of Nervous and Mental Disease* 175:143–51.

Kennedy, J. G. 1974. Cultural Psychiatry. Pp. 1119–1198 in J. J. Honigmann, ed., *Handbook of Social and Cultural Anthropology*. New York: Rand McNally College Publishing Co.

Kinzie, J., D. R. Frederickson, R. Rath, J. Fleck, and W. Karls. 1984. Posttraumatic Stress Disorder among Survivors of Cambodians in Concentration Camps. *American Journal of Psychiatry* 141:645–50.

Kirmayer, L. 1984. Culture, Affect, and Somatization. Parts 1 and 2. *Transcultural Psychiatric Research Review* 21:159–88, 237–62.

Kleinman, A. 1977. Culture, Depression, and the New Cross-Cultural Psychiatry. *Social Science and Medicine* 11:3–11.

———. 1980. *Patients and Healers in the Context of Culture*. Berkeley: University of California Press.

———. 1986. *Social Origins of Distress and Disease: Depression, Neurasthenia, and Pain in Modern China*. New Haven: Yale University Press.

———. 1988a. *Rethinking Psychiatry: From Cultural Category to Personal Experience*. New York: Free Press.

———. 1988b. *The Illness Narratives: Suffering, Healing, and the Human Condition*. New York: Free Press.

Kleinman, A., and B. Good. 1985. Meanings, Relationships, Social Affects: Historical and Anthropological Perspectives on Depression: Introduction. In A. Kleinman and B. Good, eds., *Culture and Depression: Studies in the Anthropology and Cross-Cultural Psychiatry of Affect and Disorder*. Berkeley: University of California Press.

Kleinman, A., and J. Kleinman. 1991. Suffering and Its Professional Transformation: Toward an Ethnography of Interpersonal Experience. *Culture, Medicine, and Psychiatry* 15:275–301.

Lakoff, G. and Z. Kovecses. 1987. The Cognitive Model of Anger Inherent in American English. Pp. 195–211 in D. Holland and N. Quinn, eds., *Cultural Models in Language and Thought*. Cambridge, Eng.: Cambridge University Press.

LeVine, R. A. 1974. *Culture and Personality: Contemporary Readings*. Chicago: Aldine.

———. 1990. Infant Environments in Psychoanalysis: A Cross-Cultural View. In J. Stigler, R. Shweder, and G. Herdt, eds., *Cultural Psychology: Essays on Comparative Human Development*. Cambridge, Eng.: Cambridge University Press.

Levy, R. I. 1973. *Tahitians*. Chicago: University of Chicago Press.

———. 1983. Introduction. Self and Emotion. (Special Issue) *Ethos* 11:128–134.

———. 1984. Emotion, Knowing, and Culture. In R. Shweder and R. LeVine, eds., *Culture Theory: Essays on Mind, Self, and Emotion*. Cambridge, Eng.: Cambridge University Press.

Low, S. 1985. Culturally Interpreted Symptoms of Culture-Bound Syndromes: A Cross-Cultural Review of Nerves. *Social Science and Medicine* 22:187–96.

Lutz, C. 1982. The Domain of Emotion Words on Ifaluk. *American Ethnologist* 9:113–28.

———. 1985. Ethnopsychology Compared to What? Explaining Behavior and Consciousness among the Ifaluk. In G. M. White and J. Kirkpatrick, eds., *Person, Self, and Experience: Exploring Pacific Ethnopsychologies*. Berkeley: University of California Press.

———. 1986. Emotion, Thought, and Estrangement: Emotion as a Cultural Category. *Cultural Anthropology* 1:287–309.

———. 1988. *Unnatural Emotions: Everyday Sentiments on a Micronesian Atoll and Their Challenge to Western Theory*. Chicago: University of Chicago Press.

———. 1990. Engendered Emotion: Gender, Power, and the Rhetoric of Emotional Control in American Discourse. In C. A. Lutz and L. Abu-Lughod, eds., *Language and the Politics of Emotion*. Cambridge, Eng.: Cambridge University Press.

Lutz, C., and L. Abu-Lughod, eds. 1990. *Language and the Politics of Emotion*. Cambridge, Eng.: Cambridge University Press.

Lutz, C., and G. White. 1986. The Anthropology of Emotions. *Annual Review of Anthropology* 15: 405–36.

MacKinnon, C. A. 1989. *Toward a Feminist Theory of the State*. Cambridge, MA: Harvard University Press.

Manson, S., J. H. Shore, and J. D. Bloom. 1985. The Depressive Experience in American Indian Communities: A Challenge for Psychiatric Theory and Diagnosis. Pp. 331–68 in A. Kleinman and B. Good, eds., *Culture and Depression: Studies in the Anthropology and Cross-Cultural Psychiatry of Affect and Disorder*. Berkeley: University of California Press.

Markus, H., and S. Kitayama, eds. In press. *Emotion and Culture: Multidisciplinary Perspectives.* Washington, DC: American Psychological Association.

Marsella, A. J., G. DeVos, and F.L.K. Hsu, eds. 1985. *Culture and Self: Asian and Western Perspectives.* New York: Tavistock Publications.

Mathews, H. F. 1992. The Directive Force of Morality Tales in a Mexican Community. Pp. 127–62 in R. D'Andrade and C. Strauss, eds., *Human Motives and Cultural Models.* Cambridge, Eng.: Cambridge University Press.

Mead, M. 1935. *Sex and Temperament in Three Primitive Societies.* New York: William Morrow and Company.

Miller, B. D., ed. 1993. *Sex and Gender Hierarchies.* Cambridge, Eng.: Cambridge University Press.

Mollica, R., G. Wyshak, and J. Lavelle. 1987. The Psychosocial Impact of War Trauma and Torture on Southeast Asian Refugees. *American Journal of Psychiatry* 144:1567–72.

Murphy, H.B.M., E. D. Wittkower, J. Fried, and H. F. Ellenberger. 1963. A Cross-Cultural Survey of Schizophrenic Symptomatology. *International Journal of Social Psychiatry* 9:237–49.

Martin, E. 1987. *The Woman in the Body.* Baltimore: Johns Hopkins University Press.

Myers, F. 1979. Emotions and the Self: A Theory of Personhood and Political Order among Pintupi Aborigines. *Ethos* 7:343–70.

———. 1986. *Pintupi Country, Pintupi Self: Sentiment, Place, and Politics among Western Desert Aborigines.* Washington, DC: Smithsonian Institution Press.

Nolen-Hoeksema, S. 1990. *Sex Differences in Depression.* Stanford, CA: Stanford University Press.

Ochs, E., and B. Schieffelin. 1989. Language Has a Heart. *Text* 9:7–25.

Opler, M. K. 1959. Cultural Differences in Mental Disorders: An Italian and Irish Contrast in the Schizophrenias—U.S.A. Pp. 425–42 in M. K. Opler, ed., *Culture and Mental Health: Cross-Cultural Studies.* New York: Macmillan.

Ortner, S. H. 1974. Is Female to Male As Nature Is to Culture? Pp. 67–87 in M. Rosaldo and L. Lamphere, eds., *Woman, Culture, and Society.* Stanford, CA: Stanford University Press.

Ots, T. 1990. The Angry Liver, the Anxious Heart, and the Melancholy Spleen. *Culture, Medicine, and Psychiatry* 14:21–58.

Perry, H. S. 1982. *Psychiatrist of America: The Life of Harry Stack Sullivan.* Cambridge, MA: Belknap Press of Harvard University Press.

Plutchik, R. 1980. A Language for the Emotions. *Psychology Today* 13(9):68–78.

Rosaldo, M. 1980. *Knowledge and Passion: Ilongot Notions of Self and Social Life.* Cambridge, Eng.: Cambridge University Press.

———. 1984. Toward an Anthropology of Self and Feeling. Pp. 137–57 in R. A. Shweder and R. A. LeVine, eds., *Culture Theory: Essays on Mind, Self, and Emotion.* Cambridge, Eng.: Cambridge University Press.

Rosaldo, M., and L. Lamphere, eds. 1974. *Woman, Culture, and Society.* Stanford, CA: Stanford University Press.

Roseman, M. 1991. *Healing Sounds from the Malaysian Rainforest: Temiar Music and Medicine.* Berkeley: University of California Press.

Russell, J. 1991. Culture and the Categorization of Emotions. *Psychological Bulletin* 110:426–50.

Sapir, E. 1961. *Culture, Language, and Personality: Selected Essays.* Ed. D. G. Mandelbaum. Berkeley: University of California Press.

Sartorius, N., A. Jablensky, and R. Shapiro. 1978. Cross-Cultural Differences in the Short-Term Prognosis of Schizophrenic Psychosis. *Schizophrenia Bulletin* 4:102–13.

Scarry, E. 1985. *The Body in Pain: The Making and Unmaking of the World.* New York: Oxford University Press.

Scheper-Hughes, N. 1979. *Saints, Scholars, and Schizophrenics: Mental Illness in Rural Ireland.* Berkeley: University of California Press.

Scheper-Hughes, N., and M. Lock. 1987. The Mindful Body: A Prolegomenon to Future Work in Medical Anthropology. *Medical Anthropology Quarterly* 1:6–41.

Schieffelin, B., and E. Ochs, eds. 1986. *Language Socialization across Cultures*. Cambridge, Eng.: Cambridge University Press.

Schieffelin, E. 1976. *The Sorrow of the Lonely and the Burning of the Dancers*. New York: St. Martin's Press.

———. 1983. Anger and Shame in the Tropical Forest: On Affect as a Cultural System in Papua New Guinea. *Ethos* 11:181–91.

Schooler, C., and W. Caudill. 1964. Symptomatology in Japanese and American Schizophrenics. *Ethnology* 3:172–78.

Schwartz, T. 1992. Anthropology and Psychology: An Unrequited Relationship. Pp. 324–49 in T. Schwartz, G. White, and C. Lutz, eds., *New Directions in Psychological Anthropology*. Cambridge, Eng.: Cambridge University Press.

Shweder, R. A. 1985. Menstrual Pollution, Soul Loss, and the Comparative Study of Emotions. In A. Kleinman and B. Good, eds., *Culture and Depression: Studies in the Anthropology and Cross-Cultural Psychiatry of Affect and Disorder*. Berkeley: University of California Press.

———. 1990. Cultural Psychology—What Is It? Pp. 1–43 in J. Stigler, R. Shweder, and G. Herdt, eds., *Cultural Psychology: Essays on Comparative Human Development*. Cambridge, Eng.: Cambridge University Press.

———. In press. You're Not Sick, You're Just in Love. In H. Markus and S. Kitayama, eds., *Emotion and Culture: Multidisciplinary Perspectives*. American Psychological Association Press.

Shweder, R. A., and E. Bourne. 1984. Does the Concept of the Person Vary Cross-Culturally? Pp. 158–99 in R. Shweder and R. LeVine, eds., *Culture Theory: Essays on Mind, Self, and Emotion*. Cambridge, Eng.: Cambridge University Press.

Shweder, R. A., and R. A. LeVine, eds. 1984. *Culture Theory: Essays on Mind, Self, and Emotion*. Cambridge, Eng.: Cambridge University Press.

Simons, R., and C. Hughes, eds. 1985. *The Culture-Bound Syndromes: Folk Illnesses of Psychiatric and Anthropological Interest*. Boston: D. Reidel Publishing Co.

Solomon, R. C. 1984. Getting Angry: The Jamesian Theory of Emotion in Anthropology. Pp. 238–54 in R. Shweder and R. LeVine, eds., *Culture Theory: Essays on Mind, Self, and Emotion*. Cambridge, Eng.: Cambridge University Press.

Spindler, G., ed. 1980. *The Making of Psychological Anthropology*. Berkeley: University of California Press.

Strickland, B. 1992. Women and Depression. *Current Directions in Psychological Science* 1(4): 132–35.

Suarez-Orozco, M. 1989. *Central American Refugees and U.S. High Schools: A Psychosocial Study of Motivation and Achievement*. Stanford, CA: Stanford University Press.

Sullivan, H. S. 1953. *Conceptions of Modern Psychiatry*. New York: W. W. Norton.

———. 1962. *Schizophrenia as a Human Process*. New York: W. W. Norton.

Swartz, L. 1991. The Politics of Black Patients' Identity: Ward-Rounds on the "Black Side" of a South African Psychiatric Hospital. *Culture, Medicine, and Psychiatry* 217–44.

Toussignant, M. 1984. *Pena* in the Ecuadorian Sierra: A Psychoanthropological Analysis of Sadness. *Culture, Medicine, and Psychiatry* 8:381–98.

Vaughn, C. 1989. Annotation: Expressed Emotion in Family Relationships. *Journal of Child Psychology and Psychiatry* 30:13–22.

Vaughn, C., and J. Leff. 1976a. The Influence of Family and Social Factors on the Course of Psychiatric Illness. *British Journal of Psychiatry* 129:125–37.

———. 1976b. The Measurement of Expressed Emotion in the Families of Psychiatric Patients. *British Journal of Social and Clinical Psychology* 15:157–65.

Vaughn, C., K. Snyder, S. Jones, W. Freeman, and I.H.R. Falloon. 1984. Family Factors in Schizophrenic Relapse: A California Replication of the British Research on Expressed Emotion. *Archives of General Psychiatry* 41:1169–77.

Wallace, A.F.C. 1961. *Culture and Personality*. New York: Random House.

Warner, R. 1985. *Recovery from Schizophrenia: Psychiatry and Political Economy*. London: Routledge and Kegan Paul.

———. 1992. Commentary on Cohen, Prognosis for Schizophrenia in the Third World. *Culture, Medicine, and Psychiatry* 16:85–88.

Waxler, N. 1974. Culture and Mental Illness: A Social Labeling Perspective. *Journal of Nervous and Mental Disease* 159:379–95.

Weisner, T. S. 1983. Putting Family Ideals into Practice: Pronaturalism in Conventional and Nonconventional California Families. *Ethos* 11:278–304.

Wellenkamp, J. 1988. Notions of Grief and Catharsis among Toraja. *American Ethnologist* 15:486–500.

Westermeyer, J. 1988. DSM-III Psychiatric Disorders among Hmong Refugees in the United States: A Point Prevalence Study. *American Journal of Psychiatry* 145:197–202.

———. 1989. *Psychiatric Care of Migrants: A Clinical Guide*. Washington, DC: American Psychiatric Association Press.

White, G. 1992. Ethnopsychology. Pp. 21–46 in T. Schwartz, G. White, and C. Lutz, eds., *New Directions in Psychological Anthropology*. Cambridge, Eng.: Cambridge University Press.

White, G., and J. Kirkpatrick, eds. 1985. *Person, Self, and Experience: Exploring Pacific Ethnopsychologies*. Berkeley: University of California Press.

White, G., and C. Lutz. 1992. Introduction. Pp. 1–20 in T. Schwartz, G. White, and C. Lutz, eds., *New Directions in Psychological Anthropology*. Cambridge, Eng.: Cambridge University Press.

Wikan, U. 1990. *Managing Turbulent Hearts: A Balinese Formula for Living*. Chicago: University of Chicago Press.

World Health Organization. 1979. *Schizophrenia: An International Follow-Up Study*. Chichester: John Wiley and Sons.

Wittkower, E. D. and H. Rin. 1965. Recent Developments in Transcultural Psychiatry. In *Transcultural Psychiatry*, ed. A.V.S. DeReuck and R. Porter. Boston: Little, Brown & Co.

CHAPTER SIX

EVOLUTIONARY PSYCHOLOGICAL ANTHROPOLOGY

Jerome H. Barkow

No field called ''evolutionary'' or ''Darwinian'' psychological anthropology presently exists, though the call for such a field is now decades old (Barkow 1973). Its absence is remarkable. In the past, when anthropologists became aware of a powerful theory of human psychology that claimed universality, the encounter was memorable. Even today, Freudian thought is a strong influence in psychological anthropology. Evolutionary psychology is not an influence, despite the great ferment, controversy, and enthusiasm it has produced in biology and psychology, despite its rapidly multiplying successes, its claim to be transcultural, and its impressive scope. The last phrases merit emphasis: the evolutionary psychology literature includes such topics as landscape aesthetics, sibling rivalry, sex differences, ethnocentrism, Freudian defense mechanisms,[1] social stratification, gossip, and time preferences.[2] The explanation for its lack of impact on psychological anthropology no doubt has to do with the history and traditions of anthropology itself.

BRIEF HISTORY

Linking human psychological and biological evolution has never been entirely disrespectable in psychological anthropology. One thinks of A. I. Hallowell (1955, 1959, 1960, 1961, 1965; Barkow 1978) and his strong interest in the evolution of human psychology and the self, and of A.F.C. Wallace (1961, 1970) and his discussions of the interaction between biological and cultural evolution. The explicitly Darwinian work of psychoanalyst and human ethologist John Bowlby (1969) has influenced the thinking of psychological anthropologists concerned with development (particularly with attachment behavior).

Despite the examples of these and other thinkers, ''biological'' approaches to human behavior and culture have long aroused suspicion: after all, many of the crimes of the twentieth century have been and are being committed by those who justify their actions in part in terms of "evolution," "biology," "blood," and "genes." In many ways, modern sociocultural and psychological anthropology grew precisely out of the rejection of a reductionistic pseudobiology and came to flourish only by obeying the stricture that explanations in the human sciences must not rely on biological concepts.[3] Given this history, graduate students in social/cultural/psychological anthropology have seldom been expected to develop familiarity with animal ethology or evolutionary biology. Until recently, even in biological anthropology, training has been much more likely to emphasize anatomy than evolutionary biology and animal behavior.

So it was that anthropologists remained unaware of important developments in evolutionary biology taking place during the mid-1960s and early 1970s, developments associated with researchers such as Williams (1966), Maynard Smith (1964, 1971, 1976), Hamilton (1964, 1970), and Trivers (1971, 1972). The work of these and other researchers led to a dramatic change in the way in which biologists think about animal behavior. Human beings, too, are animals: absent anthropologists and other social-behavioral scientists, it was largely biologists—experts on animal and insect behavior—who first applied this new perspective to our own species, often under the rubric of "sociobiology."

Though the most widely read works by Edward O. Wilson (1975), David Barash (1982), and Richard Dawkins (1982, 1989) usually devoted relatively little attention to *Homo sapiens sapiens* (as opposed to other species), the result was furor and controversy, especially in anthropology (Barkow 1978; Segerstrale 1986, 1990). Some anthropologists rushed to fight against what they feared was a resurgence of the dark pseudoscience associated with the Nazis.[4] After all, the new theories were biological and often made use of the term "gene."

Though this controversy refuses to go away (see Lamb 1993), it is simply a distraction. There is no real connection between modern evolutionary biology and racism, sexism, conservatism, Marxism, Catholicism, or any other "ism." Of course, evolutionary biology can be and at times is distorted and abused by racists and other ideologues; but it shares this weakness with, for example, Christianity and Islam. Beginning well before the popular controversy ignited by the publication of E. O. Wilson's *Sociobiology: The New Synthesis* (1975), an increasing number of psychologists and anthropologists (but relatively few psychological anthropologists or sociologists)[5] have explored the implications for their respective disciplines of modern evolutionary biology. The resulting work challenges some fundamental assumptions of both psychology and anthropology while giving hope for an evolutionary psychological anthropology.

Anthropologists and other social and behavioral scientists influenced by this "new" evolutionary biology have given rise to at least two at times contending schools of thought. One of these is *behavioral ecology*. Human behavioral ecologists apply the same theories and models to human behavior that biologists apply to other species. They emphasize direct and indirect measures of genetic fitness, such as reproductive success or the efficiency of hunting-gathering techniques.[6] They either model behavior with the assumption that the individuals concerned are maximizing genetic fitness in a given environment, or else they take that assumption as a testable hypothesis. Behavioral ecologists have been heavily criticized by exponents of the *evolutionary psychology* approach for not paying sufficient attention to the psychological mechanisms that necessarily lie between genes (whose relative frequency is determined by the processes of biological evolution) and culturally ordered behavior (Barkow 1989b). (See also Barkow 1984; Tooby and Cosmides 1990, 1992; Symons 1989, 1992.) Thus, while behavioral ecology is of keen interest to those concerned with culture and ecology, evolutionary psychology is more likely to be of interest to the psychological anthropologist.

More will be said about evolutionary psychology in a moment. First, a caveat: this chapter attempts to place the study of *Homo sapiens sapiens* within the broad framework of animal behavior and evolution. How does one describe the early stages of such a movement? The answer is, tentatively and per force, personally. The views expressed here are my own and are not necessarily characteristic of any particular university, network of researchers, past or present collaborators, or school of thought.

BASIC CONCEPTS OF EVOLUTIONARY PSYCHOLOGY

Learning to think from an evolutionary perspective is largely a matter of practice. Ideally, one would first study a textbook (such as Trivers 1985) and then read widely in the animal behavior literature; or at least read the excellent account written for the layperson by Helena Cronin (1991). Alternatively, one might read my own effort to introduce anthropologists to recent developments (Barkow 1989a). What follows can only be a bare-bones account that biologists will definitely find oversimplified, but it should suffice for present purposes.

Evolutionary Psychology and Psychological Complexity

Psychology that is explicitly compatible with and informed by what we know of human evolution is sometimes called *evolutionary psychology*. It has been argued (e.g., by Cosmides, Tooby, and Barkow 1992) that an evolutionary psychology is necessarily a complex psychology. Rather than resting on "general laws" of psychology that assume that learning is a simple process that is fundamentally the same across species—an evolutionary improbability—it begins with the assumption that natural selection favors specific information-processing mechanisms with specific decision rules (some would say "algorithms") that evolve in response to specific adaptive problems. The result is a complex psychology that contrasts sharply with the simple psychology of many learning theorists (e.g., B. F. Skinner). Evolutionary psychologists generally take the stance that assuming that a human psychological ability or attribute is due to some kind of general ability (such as a vague notion of "learning") is a last resort. Selection, they argue, is more likely to result in specialized "mental organs" that serve specific adaptive purposes than it is to produce generalized abilities that cut across information domains and rely on extremely broad decision rules.[7]

Behavior Genetics

Evolutionary psychology is not to be confused with behavior genetics. The latter field seeks to understand differences and similarities in behavior between individuals (and, for some researchers, between groups) on the basis of genetic differences. Evolutionary psychology focuses on what are presumed to be specieswide "mental organs" or psychological processes (Cosmides and Tooby 1987; Tooby and Cosmides 1992) that are thought to have evolved as adaptations to previous environments. To use the eye as an analogy, the primary analysis of this obviously adaptive organ of distal perception would involve not possible gene-based differences across individuals and populations but, rather, what the eyes of most members of our species have in common. So it is, evolutionary psychologists assume, with the "mental organs" underlying social exchange, or landscape preference, or sexual attraction, or gossip. The point is not to denigrate the field of behavior genetics but simply to distinguish between it and evolutionary psychology. (Of course, it is possible to be interested in both behavior genetics and evolutionary psychology.)

Inclusive Fitness

One way to think about natural selection is that it favors an organism's acting so as to increase its genetic representation in future generations.[8] All things being equal,[9] organisms share genes with one another, and the closer the degree of consanguinity, the greater the proportion of shared genes. For example, each offspring represents one-half of an individual's genes, as does each sibling, while half-siblings, nieces/nephews, and grandchildren represent one-quarter of the individual's genes, and first cousins one-eighth. An organism may be thought of as "acting so as to increase its genetic representation in future generations" by acting to increase the number of its relatives, with emphasis on closer rather than more distant kin. This idea of "inclusive fitness" contrasts with old notions of selection favoring "the good of the species" or "good of the group." Thus biologists now understand that an animal gives an alarm call not for the "benefit of the group" but for the benefit of its own relatives, including, for example, its own offspring. Because the offspring share its genes, by aiding them an animal is likely to be enhancing its own inclusive fitness. What is involved is not "altruism" in its ordinary sense but a sort of "genetic selfishness."

A corollary of the idea of inclusive fitness is that aside from identical twins and clones, different individuals have different fitness interests. This is true in mating pairs and even in the case of the closest of relatives. Thus evolutionary biologists account for parent-offspring conflict on the basis of selection favoring the parent seeking to transfer investment to additional offspring (actual or potential) well before the existing progeny are ready to give it up. After all, an infant at the breast is risking 100 percent of its genes when it is being weaned, with the benefit being a potential additional 25 percent or 50 percent of its genes in the gene pool (depending on whether the new sibling will be a full sibling, sharing 50 percent of its genes, or a half-sibling, sharing 25 percent of its genes). For the mother, the equation is the value of the milk to the 50 percent of her genes represented by the infant at the breast versus the value of transferring that investment to a new 50 percent of her genes represented by a potential new child. In terms of inclusive fitness, the infant at the breast has more to lose than does the mother. Though these words embarrassingly oversimplify an equation better expressed mathematically in terms of the relative probabilities of a gene's replicating itself in the gene pool, the solution in either case yields selection favoring the mother forcing weaning before the older infant is ready to self-wean. (The infant will self-wean because eventually the additional value of the milk to the nursing infant is so low relative to its overall needs that it is in its fitness interests, too, for the mother to transfer the investment involved in producing milk to the production of a new infant.) Similar mathematics account for sibling rivalry (Trivers 1972).

Past, Not Present, Adaptiveness

Evolutionary psychology generally assumes past adaptiveness of a particular "organ" or ability. The emphasis is on the past, so that, unlike the behavioral ecologist, the evolutionary psychologist places small stress on current adaptiveness (as was mentioned earlier). After all, a trait may be adaptive today (result in large families, say) without being an adaptation (that is, without having been specifically selected for in the past). Similarly, it is entirely possible that traits that may have been highly adaptive in the past are in today's world maladaptive (e.g., freezing in fright in the face of a predator, possibly adaptive when an ancestor was confronted with a smilodon but distinctly maladaptive in the face of a tractor trailer).

The Chief Weakness of Evolutionary Psychology

Evolutionary psychology produces hypotheses based on suppositions about the adaptive problems our distant ancestors are likely to have faced. This emphasis on presumed past adaptiveness entails an inescapable methodological weakness: without a time machine, how can we verify the past adaptiveness of any trait? Even worse, while evolutionary psychologists generally speak of adaptation to "a Pleistocene environment," the fact is that there is much controversy concerning the details of that environment, which, moreover, would have varied both over time and over geography. Looking at contemporary models is of limited utility: no extant human or nonhuman primate society has any claim to be a survival of our Pleistocene past. Yes, our ancestors no doubt hunted and gathered, but contemporary hunting-gathering peoples are just that, contemporaries and not ancestors.

Evolutionary psychologists use their assumptions about Pleistocene conditions and the adaptive problems faced by our ancestors to generate hypotheses. Like any other hypotheses, these require empirical verification. If assumptions about Pleistocene conditions are wrong, then the hypotheses presumably will fail. Fortunately, even very conservative judgments about the Pleistocene period yield an abundance of related hypotheses. For example, simply taking account of the fact that human females necessarily provide more parental investment than do males, and assuming that males and females competed for mates in the past much as they do now, has permitted evolutionary psychologists to develop a series of specific hypotheses about human male-female differences in sexuality, conceptions of attractiveness, and even derogation of rivals. A growing body of evidence supports these predictions (Buss 1992; Ellis 1992).

Some would argue that an additional weakness of evolutionary psychology is its usual (and often implicit) assumption that evolution since the end of the Pleistocene can safely be ignored. While there is no reason to believe that natural selection suddenly ceases the day our ancestors became sedentary cultivators, the evolutionary psychologist's response to this criticism is that there is no reason to believe that we have developed new "mental organs" or cognitive abilities since the end of the Pleistocene. Perhaps some genetic differences in the bases of behavior have developed in response to natural selection or simply to statistical processes involving small founder populations, but such differences would not be fundamental. While local populations might come to differ slightly in visual, auditory, and olfactory abilities, they are unlikely to have developed novel senses distinct from those of other populations. Similarly, even if genetic variation that affects our psychology does exist across human populations (a controversial conjecture in any event), it is very unlikely that such differences would involve new "mental organs" or specialized psychological abilities (Cosmides and Tooby 1989; Tooby and Cosmides 1990). There is certainly no evidence of novel psychological traits or abilities in any human population, even though various groups left Pleistocene living conditions behind at different times.

Adaptive Problems and Evolved Mechanisms

It is useful to think of evolution as in effect working to solve particular adaptive problems. The adaptive problems that would have faced our Pleistocene ancestors seem endless, in part because many are shared by other species, in part because many are not. Here is a random selection of adaptive problems whose evolved solutions are likely to have shaped our psychology.

An organism will enhance its inclusive fitness if it preferentially aids kin rather than nonkin, and close kin rather than distant. But how is it to distinguish among them, and between kin and nonkin in general? This question, when asked about our own species, has led to hypotheses and research on the ethnocentrism phenomenon and our ability to identify with a group.[10]

Another adaptive problem is that an individual who provides aid primarily to individuals with a high probability of reciprocating it will have a higher genetic fitness than one who aids indiscriminately: for any given species exhibiting this "reciprocal altruism," how is the organism to differentiate between reciprocators and "cheaters"? The evolved mechanisms helping to solve this problem are crucial to any discussion of social exchange in human beings (Cosmides and Tooby 1992).

Furthermore, in many species, a female will enhance her genetic fitness if she mates preferentially with a male who will provide some "parental investment" by staying to provide food and protection for her and her offspring rather than leaving immediately after fertilization; but how can she distinguish between one likely to stay and one likely to depart early? This evolutionary analysis, when applied to our own species, has led to various hypotheses concerning the mechanisms underlying courtship and sexual attractiveness.[11] To rephrase more vividly, an evolutionary perspective readily explains the so-called battle of the sexes, shedding light on phenomena such as rape and the pain of rape (Ellis 1989; Thornhill and Thornhill 1989).

A similar adaptive problem for males of many species is that providing parental investment for a female's offspring will enhance the male's fitness only if he can prevent her from copulating with others. How can he do so? For our own species, the evolutionary solution to this problem may involve male sexual jealousy (Daly, Wilson, and Weghorst 1982).

In many species, aid to relatively young kin will result in greater inclusive fitness than aid to those who may no longer be capable of successfully rearing offspring to independence (or even of reproducing at all). How is the organism to assess the "reproductive potential" of both kin and nonkin in order to apportion its aid accordingly? This evolutionary question leads to hypotheses about the nature of altruism (Trivers 1971; Barkow 1989c).

Finally, there is the adaptive problem of habitat selection: members of any given species will have higher inclusive fitness in some habitats than in others. How is the individual to select the optimum habitat? Research stemming from this question is leading to a transcultural theory of landscape aesthetics (Orians and Heerwagen 1992; Kaplan 1992).

Evolutionary Psychology Can Be Boring

The psychologist's counterpart to the anthropologist's search for the exotic has been the pursuit of the counterintuitive—the omnipresent sexuality of the Freudians, the grand reductionism of the learning theorists, and so forth. An evolutionary psychology, in contrast, presents a view of human nature that is not too far from the shared folk psychology of many cultures. Human beings are portrayed as more self-interested than altruistic, as obsessed with relative standing and with managing the impressions others have of them, as deeply concerned with sexuality and with family, endlessly capable of self-deception and frequently suspicious of being cheated. Males are generally presented as following several reproductive strategies but with opportunistic copulation always an option, whereas females have been selected to be more discriminating among potential mates than are males and to seek parental investment from their mates. Many a mother counseling her daughters would have little difficulty in agreeing with the conclusions of evolutionary psychology. This is not a criticism: the strength of evolutionary psychology is that it does portray human nature in a way made familiar to us by our lived experience and by our reading of great literature.

Vertical (Conceptual) Integration

An evolutionary psychological anthropology is necessarily part of a vertically integrated knowledge structure. Compare the natural and the human sciences: the natural sciences are "vertically integrated" in that theories and laws from one discipline and/or level of organization are necessarily compatible with theories and laws from other disciplines and levels (Barkow 1980, 1983, Cosmides, Tooby, and Barkow 1992). For example, the laws of physics apply equally to chemistry, biology, astronomy, geology, and so forth. Reductionism is not involved here: physicists are not accused of trying to do away with chemistry or of reducing all chemistry to physics when they assert that the principle of conservation of matter and energy applies to chemical as well as to subatomic processes. In similar fashion, the notion of a biologist unfamiliar with basic chemistry would be bizarre.

Lack of vertical integration is, however, typical of the human sciences. Psychologists do not ask themselves if their theories are compatible with evolutionary biology and the fossil record of human evolution, or if they are positing phenomena that, from the perspectives of these related disciplines, are unlikely or impossible. Indeed, graduate students in psychology for the most part are not expected even to be familiar with these fields. Social scientists often do not even bother to make their psychological assumptions explicit, let alone ask if they are compatible with the conclusions of psychologists (Bock 1988:2).

If a theory in biology violates a law of chemistry or physics, either that theory is in error or else the "law" is false, and the theorist at least knows that further research will be needed to determine where the problem lies. Of course, most of the time the biologist simply does not waste time pursuing theories that involve contradictions of widely accepted principles. In the human sciences, unfortunately, psychologists regularly discuss human beings who could never have evolved, while social scientists build societies on impossible psychologies.[12] Many human scientists seek to emulate the natural sciences by emphasizing quantification and the search for general laws or principles, but it is very unusual for social or behavioral scientists to emulate the vertical conceptual integration of the "hard" sciences.

An evolutionary psychological anthropology analyzes culturally ordered behavior in a manner compatible with evolutionary psychology, which itself is compatible with evolutionary biology and with our understanding of human evolution in particular. It thus forms part of a vertically integrated knowledge structure. What, however, is distinctive about the way in which it treats culture?

EVOLUTIONARY PSYCHOLOGY AND CULTURE

Culture is an information pool and the individual an active swimmer. From the viewpoint of evolutionary psychology, culture is a pool of different categories of information likely to be processed by the brain in different ways (Barkow 1989b). The individual selects information items, edits them, revises them, and, above all, uses them. How does the individual use cultural information?

We use culture in a self-interested manner. From an evolutionary perspective, humans must be genetically selfish. To be somewhat tautological, our ancestors were selected to act in a manner that increased the relative frequency of the genes they themselves carried in later generations. To act in such a way is to be genetically selfish. Individuals who aided others who were neither gene-sharers nor likely to return that aid left fewer of their genes in our gene pool than did individuals who were genetically selfish (e.g., aiding relatives or those who were likely to return that aid to themselves or their close relatives). It therefore follows that we have been selected to use culture in a genetically selfish way, that is, in a manner that, at least in earlier environments, would have been likely to increase our own inclusive fitness.

It follows further that selection has favored our inventing, accepting, and promulgating arguments and ideologies (including the ideological components of religions and philosophies) that would have been likely to enhance our fitness at least since the Pleistocene. It also follows that culture is an arena for conflict because individuals and factions have been selected to attempt to "input" ideological information conducive to their interests while trying to convince others that these ideologies serve them. The implication here is not that human beings are conscious hypocrites; rather, we have been selected to be unself-conscious self-deceivers (self-deception being highly adaptive in attempts to influence the behavior of others).

Information in a cultural pool may be maladaptive (Barkow 1989b; Edgerton 1992). This also follows from the reasoning in the preceding two paragraphs. For any given individual, some of the socially transmitted information of which a culture consists may be in the fitness interests of others rather than of self (e.g., "The power of the aristocrats represents the will of the gods" or "Trickle-down economics will help the poor"). Other processes may also result in maladaptive cultural information, as when ecologies alter or when apparently adaptive strategies have negative long-term consequences (e.g., net fishing may work well for a time but eventually lead to depletion of the fishery). That some cultural information is likely to be maladaptive for some or all individuals implies selection in favor of correcting such information.

Enculturation is not a passive process. If some cultural information is likely to be maladaptive, then the passive and automatic absorption of culture must have been selected against. The solution to the adaptive problem of keeping cultural information adaptive appears to be a testing/editing mechanism. The "rebelliousness" of the child and adolescent may in part represent the operation of such a mechanism. The "status consciousness" of the adolescent (Weisfeld and Billings 1988; Weisfeld 1991) and his or her tendency to learn preferentially from the prestigious and from "popular" peers may also represent cultural editing in which behavioral strategies resulting in power and control of resources are more likely to be imitated than are others. However, different categories of cultural information have different fitness consequences for the individual and are therefore likely to involve different evolved mechanisms; some kinds of cultural information are apparently more subject to editing, revision, and even rejection than are others (Barkow 1989a). For example, prestige strategies receive more editing than does the grammatical structure of one's native language.

An important implication of this stance is that the "transmission" of cultural information is always problematic. Where cultures seem relatively unchanging from generation to generation, it would appear that our evolved editing mechanisms are operating in such a way as to "re-create" much information with each generation. For example, if the "imitate-the-high-in-status" mechanism previously suggested is valid, then in "stable" cultures, adolescents must be perceiving the holders of traditional statuses as high in prestige. In any event, any theory of "culture change" that is not simultaneously a theory of "culture stability" is at best incomplete. A single theory must account for both stability and change, given that the underlying evolved mechanisms mediating information extraction from and addition to the cultural information pool must always be the same.

Old psychology lies beneath new culture (Barkow 1992). We are not in the Pleistocene. Mechanisms evolved to cope with Pleistocene problems can underlie entirely new sociocultural phenomena. Listening to gossip would have been part of the solution to several adaptive problems: how to know if someone is trustworthy as a partner in social exchange, or would make a reliable mate for self or close kin, or is likely to make either a useful ally or dangerous rival. We appear to listen preferentially to information about members of our community that is relevant to these problems, information about sexual activities and availability, changes in health status, changes in relative power and influence, or signs of lack of trustworthiness in social exchange ("cheating"). We also use gossip as part of the solution of the adaptive problem of how to handicap rivals (our own and those of our close kin) for mates and for other resources needed to enhance our genetic fitness. Thus we readily pass on and elaborate information as to the lack of trustworthiness in social exchange of our rivals: if we are males, we denigrate the relative standing of other males; if we are females, we exaggerate the number of sexual partners of rivals (thereby in effect warning males for whom we are competing that these females would be likely to present them with someone else's offspring); and we counter "libels" against allies and close relatives.

Today's gossip is often much less likely to influence our genetic fitness than it probably once was. Today, we often take media figures, many of whom are in whole or part fictitious (e.g., characters in television soap operas) for important members of our community. We purchase tabloids with often entirely fictitious "gossip" about their activities. We avidly seek and discuss with friends information about their trustworthiness, health, and sexual activities. Old gossip mechanisms fuel an entirely new and modern phenomenon, the tabloid press and its paparazzi. More than that, these old mechanisms underpin much of the modern phenomenon of celebrity, of "star" and "fan." Thus an analysis of a Pleistocene information problem ultimately helps explain historically recent social phenomena.

If this perspective is to be applied across the board, then we should expect that a routine task for future ethnography informed by evolutionary psychology will be the analysis of the particular psychological mechanisms underpinning a society's particular social institutions and the roles and statuses of which they are composed. One might even anticipate an ethnology focused on how diverse social institutions across many societies are underpinned by the same (evolved) psychology (see the chapter by Philip Bock, "Social Structure and Personality," in this volume).

The emphasis is more on universality than on exoticism. Anthropology has often been accused of emphasizing the exotic, of denying our common humanity in constant creation of the other, of ignoring the fact that across all cultures, our similarities are so vast that they permit us to practice a methodology entirely dependent upon shared humanness, that of participant observation (cf. Brown 1991). An evolutionary psychological anthropology will no doubt be a rather mundane field with little of the exotic and of the counterintuitive because, as was just suggested, it will find that underlying the apparently exotic and even the unique is simply our familiar, evolved psychology. For example, the idioms of gossip differ, but the essential concerns will always be the same. The nature of ethnocentric groupings differ immensely, sometimes along racial lines, sometimes occupational, sometimes linguistic, but always and in every society, people will form into ethnocentric groups that develop ideologies justifying their claim to superiority over other groups. Similarly, while the details of social stratification and the structuring of prestige differ across human societies, as does the symbolic communication of relative status, every analysis must begin with the evolutionary psychology fact that human beings strive for higher relative standing for themselves and their children, that status plays a key role in mate choice and in the amount of parental investment that can be provided for offspring, and that facility in social exchange is one of the key skills involved in acquiring and maintaining standing (Barkow 1992).

What would a political anthropology informed by evolutionary psychology look like? It would assume that we will find politics to be ubiquitous, with individuals and coalitions vying for relative standing at the local level, and at the higher levels leaders attempting to promulgate ideologies that redefine the solidary group and its problems in such a way as to convince others to follow them. We would also expect frequent and self-serving efforts to trigger the ethnocentrism mechanism so that potential followers are motivated to set aside internal disputes and transfer loyalty to the solidary group headed by the would-be leader. Everywhere, we seem to find the same politician's speech: "We are a great and noble and naturally superior group, but lately we have been letting things slide. We face an external enemy/threat that challenges our natural position of superiority. If you eschew other group solidarities and bond closely with one another, accepting me as leader and doing what I say, we will win out against the threat and resume our natural position of dominance/superiority." From Moses to ministers of the environment, one hears this same message.

CONCLUSION

It would be very premature to use the headings "characteristic methods" or even "major findings" or "critique and lasting contributions," used or implied by other contributors to this volume. There is as yet no "evolutionary psychological anthropology," though there soon will be. However scant the attention psychological anthropologists pay to evolutionary biology, they do attend to the discipline of psychology. Within that discipline, the evolutionary psychology approach is still young and highly controversial, but its use is burgeoning (particularly in cognitive and developmental psychology). Psychological anthropologists cannot help but be influenced.

Ultimately, what evolutionary psychology has to offer to psychological anthropology is what psychoanalysis once seemed to make available: a respected if controversial scientific theory, generating much excitement in a host of intellectual domains, claiming applicability to all human societies and perhaps to all of human behavior, at a point in history when competing paradigms are, in the opinion of many, moribund. The next decade or two will be interesting ones for psychological anthropology.

NOTES

1. There are those who argue that an evolutionary perspective and psychoanalytic thought are complementary or even form a unitary body of thought. Though I am myself unpersuaded, the interested reader may wish to see some of the following: Badcock

(1989); Glantz and Pearce (1989); MacDonald (1986); Nesse (1987, 1989, 1990); Nesse and Lloyd (1992); Slavin (1987, 1988); and Slavin and Kriegman (1992).

2. Citations to these topics will be supplied elsewhere in this chapter, with the exception of the subject of time preferences (Rogers, in press).

3. Of course, many sociocultural anthropologists were and remain Durkheimians and for that reason react negatively to any suggestion that either biology or psychology are essential parts, or even nonessential parts, of social theories. I have discussed the negative effects of Durkheimian influence elsewhere (1989a), but the present focus is largely on psychological anthropology, and so here I omit Durkheim.

4. Certain biologists were also very active in criticizing early applications of evolutionary biology to the human species. See Segerstrale (1986) for an insightful sociological analysis of their opposition, particularly with respect to Stephen Jay Gould and Richard Lewontin.

5. For important exceptions to this generalization about sociologists, see the evolutionarily informed work of Lee Ellis (1989, 1991, 1993) and of Pierre van den Berghe (1990).

6. For recent work in behavioral ecology, see Standen and Foley (1989); Cronk (1991); and Smith and Winterhalder (1992). For a well-respected reader in the behavioral ecology of nonhuman species, see Krebs and Davies (1991).

7. This approach reflects modern cognitive science and the experience of the field of artificial intelligence. Artificial intelligence can handle domain-specific problems with relative ease, but extremely broad problem-solving capabilities that cut across many domains are much more difficult.

8. There are other ways in which to think about natural selection. The topic of the "unit of selection" is a controversial one in evolutionary biology, and evolution actually takes place at multiple levels (e.g., gene, individual organism, deme, species, ecology). For the reader with an interest in this debate, varying views are available (Dawkins 1982; Shanahan 1990). I have deliberately ignored the complexities of the topic and emphasized the individual (rather than the gene) because it appears to be the level most quickly grasped by those previously unfamiliar with evolutionary biology and population genetics and because it is the individual that is most relevant for the field of psychological anthropology. I believe that any distortions caused by this emphasis are minimal.

9. I am deliberately neglecting the very large proportion of genes any two individuals are likely to share by virtue of being members of the same species. See Barkow (1989a) for discussion.

10. For discussion of identity and of ethnocentrism in an evolutionary context, see, for example, Barkow (1989c); Shaw and Wong (1988); Vine (1987); and Warnecke, Masters, and Kempter (1992).

11. See the reference cited in note 10.

12. As was mentioned earlier, evolutionary psychologists generally consider the kind of domain-general learning mechanism posited by, for example, Skinner as being incompatible with current understanding of evolutionary biology. Social scientists very frequently (if tacitly) accept this simplistic psychology, leading to the erroneous assumption that enculturation is a passive process and that only culture change rather than both stability and change is in need of explanation. In similar fashion, I have argued elsewhere (1992) that the Marxist notion of a classless society is incompatible with the evolved human psychological traits of nepotism and of social exchange.

REFERENCES

Badcock, C. R. 1989. *Oedipus in Evolution: A New Theory of Sex*. Oxford: Basil Blackwell.

Barash, D. P. 1982. *Sociobiology and Behavior*. 2nd ed. New York: Elsevier.

Barkow, J. H. 1973. Darwinian Psychological Anthropology: A Biosocial Approach. *Current Anthropology* 14:373–88.

———. 1978. Culture and Sociobiology. *American Anthropologist* 80:5–20.

———. 1980. Sociobiology: Is This the New Theory of Human Nature? Pp. 171–92 in A. Montagu, ed., *Sociobiology Examined*. New York and London: Oxford University Press.

———. 1983. Begged Questions in Behavior and Evolution. Pp. 205–22 in G. Davey, ed., *Animal Models of Human Behavior*. Chichester and New York: John Wiley.

———. 1984. The Distance between Genes and Culture. *Journal of Anthropological Research* 40: 367–79.

———. 1989a. *Darwin, Sex, and Status: Biological Approaches to Mind and Culture*. Toronto: University of Toronto Press.

———. 1989b. The Elastic between Genes and Culture. *Ethology and Sociobiology* 10:111–29.

———. 1989c. Overview. *Ethology and Sociobiology* 10:1–10.

———. 1992. Beneath New Culture Is Old Psychology. Pp. 626–37 in J. H. Barkow, L. Cosmides, and J. Tooby, eds., *The Adapted Mind: Evolutionary Psychology and the Generation of Culture*. New York: Oxford University Press.

Bock, P. K. 1988. *Rethinking Psychological Anthropology. Continuity and Change in the Study of Human Action*. New York: Freeman.

Bowlby, J. A. 1969. *Attachment and Loss*, vol. 1: *Attachment*. New York: Basic Books.

Brown, D. E. 1991. *Human Universals*. New York: McGraw-Hill.

Buss, D. M. 1992. Mate Preference Mechanisms: Consequences for Partner Choice and Intrasexual Competition. Pp. 249–66 in J. H. Barkow, L. Cosmides, and J. Tooby, eds., *The Adapted Mind: Evolutionary Psychology and the Generation of Culture*. New York: Oxford University Press.

Cosmides, L., and J. Tooby. 1987. From Evolution to Behavior: Evolutionary Psychology as the Missing Link. Pp. 277–306 in J. Dupré, ed., *The Latest on the Best: Essays on Evolution and Optimality*. Cambridge, MA: MIT Press.

———. 1989. Evolutionary Psychology and the Generation of Culture, II. Case Study: A Computational Theory of Social Exchange. *Ethology and Sociobiology* 10:51–97.

———. 1992. Cognitive Adaptations for Social Exchange. Pp. 163–228 in J. H. Barkow, L. Cosmides, and J. Tooby, eds., *The Adapted Mind: Evolutionary Psychology and the Generation of Culture*. New York: Oxford University Press.

Cosmides, L., J. Tooby, and J. H. Barkow. 1992. Introduction. Pp. 3–15 in J. H. Barkow, L. Cosmides, and J. Tooby, eds., *The Adapted Mind: Evolutionary Psychology and the Generation of Culture*. New York: Oxford University Press.

Cronin, H. 1991. *The Ant and the Peacock: Altruism and Sexual Selection from Darwin to Today*. Cambridge, Eng., and New York: Press Syndicate of the University of Cambridge.

Cronk, L. 1991. Human Behavioral Ecology. *Annual Review of Anthropology* 20:25–54.

Daly, M., M. I. Wilson, and S. J. Weghorst. 1982. Male Sexual Jealousy. *Ethology and Sociobiology* 3:11–27.

Dawkins, R. 1989. *The Selfish Gene*. 2nd ed. Oxford: Oxford University Press.

———. 1982. *The Extended Phenotype: The Gene as the Unit of Selection*. Oxford and San Francisco: W. H. Freeman.

———. 1989. *The Selfish Gene*. 2nd ed. New York: Oxford University Press.

Edgerton, R. B. 1992. *Sick Societies: Challenging the Myth of Primitive Harmony*. New York: Free Press.

Ellis, B. J. 1992. The Evolution of Sexual Attraction: Evaluative Mechanisms in Women. Pp. 267–88 in J. H. Barkow, L. Cosmides, and J. Tooby, eds., *The Adapted Mind: Evolutionary Psychology and the Generation of Culture*. New York: Oxford University Press.

Ellis, L. 1989. *Theories of Rape: Inquiries into the Causes of Sexual Aggression*. New York: Hemisphere Publishing Corporation.

———. 1991. A Biosocial Theory of Social Stratification Derived from the Concepts of Pro/Antisociality and r/K Selection. *Politics and the Life Sciences* 10:5–23.

———. 1993. *Social Stratification and Socioeconomic Inequality*, vol. 1: *A Comparative Biosocial Analysis*. Westport, CT: Praeger.

Glantz, K., and J. K. Pearce. 1989. *Exiles from Eden: Psychotherapy from an Evolutionary Perspective*. Scranton, PA: W. W. Norton.

Hallowell, A. I. 1955. *Culture and Experience*. Philadelphia: University of Pennsylvania Press.

———. 1959. Behavioral Evolution and the Emergence of the Self. Pp. 36–60 in B. J. Meggers, ed., *Evolution and Anthropology: A Centennial Appraisal*. Washington, DC: Anthropological Society of Washington.

———. 1960. Self, Society, and Culture in Phylogenetic Perspective. Pp. 309–71 in S. Tax, ed., *Evolution after Darwin*, vol. 2: *The Evolution of Man*, Chicago: University of Chicago Press.

———. 1961. The Protocultural Foundations of Human Adaptation. Pp. 429–509 in S. L. Washburn, ed., *Social Life of Early Man*. New York: Viking Fund Publications in Anthropology.

———. 1965. Hominid Evolution, Cultural Adaptation, and Mental Dysfunctioning. Pp. 26–54 in A.V.S. de Reuck and R. Porter, eds., *CIBA Foundation Symposium on Transcultural Psychiatry*. London: J. and A. Churchill.

Hamilton, W. D. 1964. The Evolution of Social Behavior. *Journal of Theoretical Biology* 7:1–52.

———. 1970. Selfish and Spiteful Behavior in an Evolutionary Model. *Nature* 228:1218–20.

Kaplan, S. 1992. Environmental Preference in a Knowledge-Seeking, Knowledge-Using Organism. Pp. 581–98 in J. H. Barkow, L. Cosmides, and J. Tooby, eds., *The Adapted Mind: Evolutionary Psychology and the Generation of Culture*. New York: Oxford University Press.

Krebs, J. R., and N. B. Davies. 1991. *Behavioural Ecology*. 3rd ed. Oxford: Blackwell Scientific Publications.

Lamb, M. E. 1993. Nazism, Biological Determinism, Sociobiology, and Evolutionary Theory: Are They Necessarily Synonymous? *International Journal of Comparative Psychology* 6(3):149–57.

MacDonald, K. 1986. Civilization and Its Discontents Revisited: Freud as an Evolutionary Biologist. *Journal of Social and Biological Structures* 9:307–18.

Maynard Smith, J. 1964. Group Selection and Kin Selection. *Nature* 201:1145–47.

———. 1971. The Origin and Maintenance of Sex. Pp. 163–75 in G. C. Williams, ed., *Group Selection*. Chicago: Aldine-Atherton.

———. 1976. Evolution and the Theory of Games. *American Scientist* 64:41–45.

Nesse, R. M. 1987. An Evolutionary Perspective on Panic Disorder and Agoraphobia. *Ethology and Sociobiology* 8:73s–85s.

———. 1989. Evolutionary Explanations of Emotions. *Human Nature* 1:261–89.

———. 1990. The Evolution of Repression and the Ego Defenses. *Journal of the American Academy of Psychoanalysis* 18:260–86.

Nesse, R. M., and A. T. Lloyd. 1992. The Evolution of Psychodynamic Mechanisms. Pp. 601–25 in J. H. Barkow, L. Cosmides, and J. Tooby, eds., *The Adapted Mind: Evolutionary Psychology and the Generation of Culture*. New York: Oxford University Press.

Orians, G. H., and J. H. Heerwagen. 1992. Evolved Responses to Landscapes. Pp. 555–79 in J. H. Barkow, L. Cosmides, and J. Tooby, eds., *The Adapted Mind: Evolutionary Psychology and the Generation of Culture*. New York: Oxford University Press.

Rogers, A. R. In press. Evolution of Time Preference by Natural Selection. *American Economic Review.*

Segerstrale, U. 1986. Colleagues in Conflict: An "In Vivo" Analysis of the Sociobiology Controversy. *Biology and Philosophy* 1:53–87.

———. 1990. The Sociobiology of Conflict and the Conflict about Sociobiology. Pp. 273–85 in J. vander Dennen and V.S.E. Falger, eds., *Sociobiology and Conflict.* New York: Chapman and Hall.

Shanahan, T. 1990. Evolution, Phenotypic Selection, and the Units of Selection. *Philosophy of Science* 57:210–26.

Shaw, R. P., and Y. Wong. 1988. *Genetic Seeds of Warfare: Evolution, Nationalism, and Patriotism.* Winchester, MA: Unwin Hyman.

Slavin, M. O. 1988. The Origins of Psychic Conflict and the Adaptive Functions of Repression: An Evolutionary Biological View. *Psychoanalysis and Contemporary Thought* 8:407–40.

———. 1988. Self Psychology from the Perspective of Evolutionary Biology: Toward a Biological Foundation for Self Psychology. *Progress in Self Psychology* 3:253–74.

Slavin, M. O., and D. Kriegman. 1992. *The Adaptive Design of the Human Psyche.* New York and London: Guilford Press.

Smith, E. A., and B. Winterhalder, eds., 1992. *Evolutionary Ecology and Human Behavior.* Hawthorne, NY: Aldine de Gruyter.

Standen, V., and R. A. Foley. 1989. *Comparative Socioecology: The Behavioural Ecology of Humans and Other Mammals.* Special Publication no. 8 of the British Ecological Society. Oxford: Blackwell Scientific Publications.

Symons, D. 1989. A Critique of Darwinian Anthropology. *Ethology and Sociobiology* 10:131–44.

———. 1992. On the Use and Misuse of Darwinism in the Study of Human Behavior. Pp. 137–62 in J. H. Barkow, L. Cosmides, and J. Tooby, eds., *The Adapted Mind: Evolutionary Psychology and the Generation of Culture.* New York: Oxford University Press.

Thornhill, R., and N. W. Thornhill. 1989. The Evolution of Psychological Pain. In R. W. Bell, and N. J. Bell, eds., *Sociobiology and the Social Sciences.* Lubbock: Texas Tech University Press.

Tooby, J., and L. Cosmides. 1990. On the Universality of Human Nature and the Uniqueness of the Individual: The Role of Genetics and Adaptation. *Journal of Personality* 58:17–68.

———. 1992. The Psychological Foundations of Culture. Pp. 19–136 in J. H. Barkow, L. Cosmides, and J. Tooby, eds., *The Adapted Mind: Evolutionary Psychology and the Generation of Culture.* New York: Oxford University Press.

Trivers, R. L. 1971. The Evolution of Reciprocal Altruism. *Quarterly Review of Biology* 46:35–37.

———. 1972. Parental Investment and Sexual Selection. Pp. 136–39 in B. Campbell, eds., *Sexual Selection and the Descent of Man, 1871–1971.* Chicago: Aldine.

———. 1985. *Social Evolution.* Menlo Park, CA: Benjamin/Cummings.

Van den Berghe, P. 1990. Why Most Sociologists Don't (and Won't) Think Evolutionarily. *Sociological Forum* 5:173–86.

Vine, I. 1987. Inclusive Fitness and the Self-System: The Roles of Human Nature and Sociocultural Processes in Intergroup Discrimination. Pp. 60–80 in V. Reynolds, V. Falger, and I. Vine, eds., *The Sociobiology of Ethnocentrism: Evolutionary Dimensions of Xenophobia, Discrimination, Racism, and Nationalism.* Beckenham, Kent: Croom Helm.

Wallace, A.F.C. 1961. The Psychic Unity of Human Groups. Pp. 129–63 in B. Kaplan, ed., *Studying Personality Cross-Culturally.* New York: Harper and Row.

———. 1970. *Culture and Personality.* 2nd ed. New York: Random House.

Warnecke, A. M., R. D. Masters, and G. Kempter. 1992. The Roots of Nationalism: Nonverbal Behavior and Xenophobia. *Ethology and Sociobiology* 13:267–82.

Weisfeld, G. E. 1991. Biosocial Models of Human Social Stratification. *Politics and the Life Sciences* 10:24–28.

Weisfeld, G. E., and R. L. Billings. 1988. Observations on Adolescence. Pp. 207–33 in K. B. MacDonald, ed., *Sociobiological Perspectives on Human Development.* New York: Springer-Verlag.

Williams, G. C. 1966. *Adaptation and Natural Selection: A Critique of Some Current Evolutionary Thought.* Princeton: Princeton University Press.

Wilson, E. O. 1975. *Sociobiology: The New Synthesis.* Cambridge, MA: Belknap Press of Harvard University Press.

CHAPTER SEVEN

CULTURAL PSYCHOLOGY: BRIDGING DISCIPLINARY BOUNDARIES IN UNDERSTANDING THE CULTURAL GROUNDING OF SELF

Joan G. Miller

Cultural psychology may be defined from multiple perspectives, and any one gloss is invariably incomplete.[1] From a categorical perspective, cultural psychology may be understood as an interdisciplinary field that has historical roots in anthropology, psychology, and linguistics, with these roots presently undergoing both rediscovery and transformation. From a teleological perspective, cultural psychology may be understood as a direction for future theory and research, with present work from a cultural psychology perspective failing fully to realize the goals of the field. From a polythetic perspective, cultural psychology may be understood as a set of approaches that share many but not all of their core conceptual presuppositions and that, in many cases, maintain presuppositions that are mutually incompatible.

THE EMERGENCE OF CULTURAL PSYCHOLOGY

The term *cultural psychology* has been employed in several different contexts (e.g., Boesch 1991; Howard 1985; Kantor 1982; Price- Williams 1980).[2] Many of the core ideas now associated with the approach are discussed in expositions that have not employed the term (e.g., Bronfenbrenner, et al. 1986; Geertz 1973; Kessen 1990; Lutz and White 1986; Misra and Gergen 1993; Pepitone 1976; Pepitone and Triandis 1987; Price-Williams 1980; Schwartz 1981). Certain recent theoretical writings may be noted in particular as marking the emergence of cultural psychology as a distinct viewpoint.

In a seminal chapter, Shweder (1990) noted that cultural psychology represents an interdisciplinary approach whose assumptions and agenda depart from those in closely related fields, such as general psychology, cross-cultural psychology, ethnopsychology, and traditional psychological anthropology (see also Shweder and Sullivan 1990, 1993). The perspective is portrayed as one whose focus includes individual psychology, but which treats this psychology as, in part, culturally constituted and as at least potentially culturally variable. In another important theoretical exposition, Cole (1990) emphasized the roots of cultural psychology in the sociohistorical approach associated with such figures as Vygotsky, Luria, and Leontiev (see also Cole 1988; Laboratory of Comparative Human Cognition 1983). Central to this approach is a view that psychological processes are culturally mediated, historically developing, contextually specific, and both embedded in and arising from practical activity. In still another major formulation of the agenda of the field, Bruner (1990) argued for a psychology that treats individuals as participants in culturally constituted worlds that are fundamental to the development of their capacities (see also Bruner 1986). From this perspective, cultural meanings are seen as negotiated in interaction and as necessarily integral to any psychological theory formulated to account for human behavior.

Many different accounts might be written of the origins of cultural psychology (for a historical overview, see, e.g., Jahoda 1990, 1992). It may be seen to have emerged from theoretical and methodological shifts within anthropological, psychological, and language socialization approaches.[3]

Anthropological Approaches

Early work in cognitive anthropology both assumed and verified a view of cultural knowledge as paradigmatically and taxonomically organized (e.g., Berlin, Breedlove, and Raven 1973; Tyler 1969). Advances in the field occurred at least partially in response to new theories regarding the organization and content of culture. In parallel with the changing views of categorization in cognitive psychology (e.g., Rosch 1975; Schank and Abelson 1977; Vygotsky 1962), cultural knowledge came to be understood as structured, in part, in terms of schematic and prototypical modes of organization (Berlin and Kay 1969; Needham 1975). Cultural information was also appreciated as presupposing particular models or theories of the world and as embodying affective and social meanings, rather than as including only referential content (Besnier 1990; D'Andrade 1984; Geertz 1973, 1984; Lave, Stepick, and Sailer 1977; Shweder 1984a; Sperber 1975). Reflecting these shifts, greater research attention came to be directed to meaning-based aspects of culture and to psychological states as culturally defined elements in social life (e.g., Carrithers, Collins, and Lukes 1985; Holland and Quinn 1987; Marsella and White 1982; White and Kirkpatrick 1985).

Insufficient attention had been directed to the cognitive processing entailed in cultural learning, the distribution of cultural understandings, the relationship of cultural meanings to the political order, and the conflicting nature of cultural messages, as well as to the process through which cultural meanings obtain motivational force (D'Andrade 1984; LeVine 1984; Schwartz 1981). These topics are presently being addressed in research that examines the impact of culture on individual subjectivity and behavior (e.g., D'Andrade and Strauss 1992; Lutz and Abu-Lughod 1990). Studies in this tradition are not only challenging the universality of Western models of psychological processes but are showing culture to be constitutive of the patterning of individual psychology (Lutz and White 1986; Lutz 1988; M. F. Rosaldo 1984).

Psychological Approaches

Investigators in cross-cultural psychology have typically focused either on verifying the hypothesis that psychological structures and process are universal or on testing the causal relationships that are presumed to exist between the ecological setting, individual psychological processes, and expressive culture (e.g., Dasen 1977; Ekman 1972; Ford 1967; LeVine 1973; Whiting and Child 1953; Whiting and Whiting 1975). In general, investigators have interpreted their results as indicating that psychological processes are invariant, with culture influencing the rate of psychological development or the highest developmental level attained, but not its course.

In contrast to cross-cultural psychology, the sociohistorical school of Soviet psychology rejects the postulate of psychic unity (Leontiev 1964; Vygotsky 1929, 1962, 1978), assuming rather that the development of higher-order psychological processes depends on historically variable and culturally mediated practical activity. Although this approach makes no claim either that ontogenetic development recapitulates societal development or that psychological processes are global in nature (see Cole 1988), these assumptions guided the first empirical studies based on this viewpoint—studies that showed that higher levels of cognitive development are attained only in more technologically advanced societies (e.g., Bruner, Olver, and Greenfield 1966; Luria 1976).

Shifts in culturally oriented psychological research have taken place in response to perceived methodological limitations in past studies as well as to certain empirical findings. It has been shown, for example, that when culturally sensitive procedures are employed, basic cognitive competencies can be demonstrated to exist among adults who do not evidence such abilities in response to more conventional experimental methods (Cole and Scribner 1974). Research has also revealed that cognitive and personality processes are highly dependent on context (Donaldson 1978; Gelman 1978; Mischel 1968; Scribner and Cole 1981; Shweder 1979a; Wason and Johnson-Laird 1972). Recent studies in this tradition approach cognition in terms of local culturally constituted functional systems (e.g., Rogoff 1990; Lave 1990; Lave and Wenger 1991).

Shifts in psychologically oriented cultural research have also occurred with the recognition that psychological theories have been informed by Western cultural conceptions and thus may not be applicable to other populations. Work motivated by this insight may be seen in the development of indigenous psychologies as well as in efforts by Western psychologists to formulate psychological theories based on views of the self emphasized in various non-Western cultures (Enriquez 1990; Markus and Kitayama 1991; Moghaddam 1987; Paranjpe, Ho, and Rieber 1988; Roland 1988; Serpell 1984).

Language Socialization Approaches

Early work on language socialization focused on the role of environmental input in language learning (e.g., Bates and Benigni 1979; Snow and Ferguson 1977). Evidence that language socialization processes are highly variable in different cultural traditions was of interest primarily for supporting innatist theories of language acquisition (Chomsky 1975; Fodor 1979) and for documenting the robustness of the language-learning process.

Recently, it has been recognized that socialization is occurring not only to use language but also through language, with cultural meanings simultaneously created, negotiated, and communicated in everyday discourse (P. Miller et al. 1990; Schieffelin and Ochs 1986a, 1986b). Focusing on both formal and pragmatic features of discourse, recent research in this tradition has exploited the development of alternative culturally grounded conceptions of self through language practices (e.g., P. J. Miller 1982; Heath 1983; Kulick 1992; Ochs 1988; Ochs and Schieffelin 1984; Schieffelin 1990).

BASIC CONCEPTS

Despite the divergent foci of concern associated with the approaches discussed, marked consensus exists concerning some of the core concepts of what is coming to constitute cultural psychology. The discussion here will attempt to highlight this consensus by identifying some widely shared assumptions in this emerging tradition, and to underscore the fluid nature of the tradition by noting points of controversy. The assumptions considered here as central to cultural psychology include (1) a focus on individual subjectivity; (2) a nonreductionist view of the relationship between culture, psychology, and experience; (3) a monistic perspective on culture and psychology; (4) a recognition of the need for culturally diverse psychologies; and (5) an emphasis on language and interaction.

A Focus on Individual Subjectivity and Behavior

Whereas the term *cultural psychology* is misleading when it is interpreted to imply that the field is located exclusively within the discipline of psychology (Shweder and Sullivan 1990), it conveys the focus of the approach on explaining behavior at the individual level. The subject matter of cultural psychology then overlaps with that of general psychology. Despite their widely divergent theoretical presuppositions and methodological commitments, both cultural psychology and general psychology share an interest in explaining individual subjectivity and individual behavior (e.g., D'Andrade 1981; Schwartz 1981, 1992). One important implication of acknowledging this point of commonality, as will be argued later, is to highlight the value of increased collaboration between investigators in each discipline.

Antireductionism

Within cultural psychology, it is assumed that the objective world, individual subjectivity, and cultural meanings cannot be reduced to each other. In particular, the approach rejects the reductionism associated with realism or with either cultural or psychological determinism (Shweder 1979b).

In general psychology, there has been a tendency to treat the categories employed in interpreting experience as self-evident. It is maintained that to explain social inference requires taking into account merely the objective patterns of covariation to which the individual has been exposed as well as the individual's abilities to process this information inductively or deductively (e.g., Kelley 1973). The present stance, in contrast, assumes that experience is indeterminate as to how it is conceptualized. Rejecting both the essentialist presupposition that there is only one true representation of a given pattern of events as well as the encyclopedic presupposition that there is one most complete representation of a given pattern (Mandelbaum 1977; Gardiner 1974), the present perspective assumes that interpretation of experience always involves arbitrary weighing of information. It is maintained that although there may be a universal human tendency to imbue the world with an objective status (Feldman 1987), reality itself can never be known from an observer-independent perspective (Goodman 1968, 1972, 1978; Nagel 1986).

Cultural psychology also involves a rejection of the cultural determinism found not only in the Durkheimian structuralist tradition and in early sociological models but also in work in anthropology that has adopted a ''transmission'' or ''fax'' model of cultural learning (e.g., Bendix 1952; Durkheim 1961; Parsons 1968). In these latter approaches, individual subjectivity and behavior are seen as fully determined by cultural beliefs and expectations, and the processes of cultural communication and of cultural conformity are treated as total and nonproblematic (see the discussions in D'Andrade 1984; Strauss 1990, 1992). Such determinism is rejected for its passive view of the agent—a view that, as some general psychological critics have charged, resembles that portrayed in behaviorist or social learning theories (Turiel 1983). It is argued alternatively that although individual subjectivity is never formed outside of or independently of culture, it does not stand in a one-to-one relationship with culture. Individuals are seen as not only actively involved in interpreting the meaning of experiences but as collectively creating intentional worlds. In recognizing that individuals come to construct multiple sociohistorically grounded realities rather than one observer-independent reality, cultural psychology gives greater weight to human agency than do traditional cognitive developmental approaches (J. G. Miller in press a).

Finally, cultural psychology rejects psychological determinism as reflected in attempts to explain the nature of cultural forms by reference to psychological dispositions. Psychological determinism may be seen, for example, in early research on culture and personality, as well as in various structuralist anthropological approaches (Lévi–Strauss 1966; Fiske, 1991). Forwarding a psychological interpretation of culture, Spiro (1965), for instance, maintained that cultural forms evolved to serve as culturally constituted defense mechanisms. In another example, Fiske (1991) suggested that social practices conform to four general types that are structured by universal properties of the human psyche. Although illuminating in many ways, psychological explanations of culture are considered somewhat limited from a cultural psychology perspective in that they are frequently based on circular functionalist arguments and/or gloss over important differences in indigenous meanings and practices in their efforts to identify deep structural equivalences.

A Monistic Perspective on Culture and Psychology

Whereas from a cultural psychology perspective culture and psychology are conceptualized as distinct phenomena, they are not treated as independent of each other. Rather, culture and psychology are assumed to be mutually constitutive.

The view that psychology is, at least in part, culturally constituted follows from the recognition, with the cognitivist revolution in psychology, that agents play an active role in constructing the meaning of experience, and the recognition, with developments in culture theory, that such construction proceeds in terms of culturally constituted presuppositions (Bruner 1990; Shweder and LeVine 1984). Thus, for example, to the extent that emotion is understood on cognitive appraisals of experience, it also is seen as necessarily a culturally grounded process (Lutz and White 1986). Similarly, to the extent that behavior is assumed to reflect the agent's goals, it also is viewed as necessarily culturally based (D'Andrade and Strauss 1992; Markus and Kitayama 1991). As noted earlier, the present stance does not imply that individual subjectivity matches cultural schemata and does not deny the possibility of individual differences in behavior. Rather, as in the case of the prototypical contrast of nature and nurture, it is assumed that the individual is always a participant in a culture, with his/her subjectivity informed by cultural meanings and practices, and thus that no sharp dichotomy can be drawn between what is psychology and what is culture (Paul 1990; Shweder 1990; Shweder and Sullivan 1990). It is also widely argued that individual subjectivity must be taken into account in understanding cultural meanings. Cultural symbols and practices, it is maintained, can only be understood in terms of the individuals for whom the meanings exist and for whom they have motivational force.

Need for Multiple Culturally Diverse Explanatory Theories

Rejecting the postulate of psychic unity, cultural psychology perspective argues that multiple culturally diverse explanatory theories are needed to account for individual psychological development. This position follows from the recognition that psychological processes are culturally constituted and thus may be expected to vary with differences in cultural meanings and practices.

The present perspective does not deny the possibility of universal psychological processes or assume that psychological universals necessarily result from noncultural effects. Rather, it is maintained that universals may occur because of similar cultural meanings and practices that support them. Equally, this position does not assume that a biological propensity to engage in a particular behavior or to perceive experience in a particular way implies that the behavior or perception is unaffected by culture. Rather, biological processes are regarded as constraints whose meaning and significance are culturally dependent (Rozin 1982; Sahlins 1976a, 1976b). In a well-known example from Whorf (1956), although there appears to exist a universal tendency for the acoustic patterns of "peep," "veep," "treep," and "queep" to have the connotations of bright, sharp, and quick, the English word "deep," with its associations of dark, warm, heavy, and so on, is able to override this biologically based connotation. In another example, even if temperamental dispositions such as introversion/extraversion are, in part, genetically based (e.g., Kagan and Snidman 1991), these dispositions are likely to be accorded varied meanings and importance in different cultural contexts and to be associated with contrasting developmental outcomes (Markus and Kitayama 1991; Misra and Gergen 1993).

The possibility of multiple culturally diverse explanatory theories raises the issue of how many theories are necessary. Pushed to an extreme, it could be argued that there needs to be a unique psychology for each cultural group or—pushed to an even greater extreme—for each individual. To date, the answer to this question has tended to vary along disciplinary lines, with anthropologists prone to limit their accounts of psychological processes to a specific subgroup or even to an individual under study (e.g., Holland, 1992; Lutz 1988; Quinn 1992; Rosaldo 1984; Strauss 1992), and psychologists more prone to formulate accounts at a level of generality that applies to a whole cultural tradition such as Hindu India or Japan (e.g., Roland 1988; Kakar 1978; J. G. Miller and Bersoff 1992) or to a series of types of cultures such as individualistic versus collectivist (Markus and Kitayama 1991; Triandis 1989; Triandis et al. 1988). While there need be no one answer to this question, it raises the issue of whether a cultural psychology can retain nomothetic goals or whether it is necessarily idiographic.

An Emphasis on Language and Interaction

Cultural psychology theorists agree on the importance of language and interaction as vehicles through which cultural meanings are created, communicated, sustained, and transformed. The code of language (e.g., whether it marks rank) and the pragmatics of language use (e.g., who is treated as a communicative partner) are regarded as fundamental in creating and sustaining social realities (the chapter by Niko Besnier in part II of this handbook; Ochs and Schieffelin 1984; Schieffelin and Ochs 1986a, 1986b). Experience with cultural artifacts and participation in institutionalized cultural practices are also seen as leading to powerful regularities in thought and behavior (Bourdieu 1977, 1990; Gergen 1989). For example, what may be even more important for development than a caregiver's deliberate enculturation efforts (e.g., a mother's admonishing a child who appears to lack sufficient independence) are the myriad cultural practices that communicate that individual autonomy and independence are valued (e.g., expecting babies to sleep alone in their own beds from birth; see Gorer 1964; Harkness 1992; Harkness and Super 1992; Mead 1949, 1953; Nuckolls 1993).

Some Points of Controversy

An important area of theoretical disagreement in work in this tradition concerns the role of individual subjectivity in explaining both culture and psychology. Within the tradition of cognitive anthropology, as well as within most psychological and language socialization perspectives, it is maintained that individual subjectivity must be taken into account to understand the nature of cultural meanings as well as to explain individual conformity with cultural practices. It is also assumed that whereas both culture and psychology are mutually constitutive, they are analytically distinct and cannot be reduced to each other (e.g., D'Andrade and Strauss 1992; Quinn and Strauss 1993; Schwartz, White, and Lutz 1992). Perspectives adopting these assumptions are concerned with individual meanings and their relationship to general cultural schemata.

Although they share many of the goals and assumptions described here as part of cultural psychology, perspectives such as symbolic action theory, social constructionism, and situated cognition do not treat individual subjectivity as important in explaining either culture or individual behavior (e.g., Boesch 1991; Gergen 1989; Harré 1986; R. Rosaldo 1989; Clifford 1988; Lave 1988; Lave and Wenger 1991). Rather, regularities in behavior are seen as explicable by reference to normative expectations and constraints in the sociocultural environment without reference to processes occurring within persons or to agents' conscious reflections. Such perspectives then reject, as misleading, constructs such as internalization or enculturation, if not the notion of individual psychology itself.

Although marked differences exist in the viewpoints contrasted here, it is important not to overstate the significance of the present points of controversy. As various investigators have suggested, it may not be crucial to resolve issues concerning the locus of culture or even to speak of culture as having a locus to conduct worthwhile research on topics in cultural psychology (Shweder 1984b; G. White 1992). Similarly, whether or not a focus on routine practices is sufficient to explain individual behavior, attention to such practices and to the tacit or uncommented-upon cultural messages embedded in everyday social activities must be considered critical in any cultural psychology (D'Andrade 1992a).

CHARACTERISTIC METHODS

Ethnographic techniques are prototypical of approaches assuming a cultural psychology perspective, but a wide range of methodological strategies are utilized. This eclecticism reflects the interdisciplinary nature of the field. Particularly in the tradition of cognitive anthropology, the typical methodologies employed tend to include a combination of ethnography, discourse analysis, and person-centered unstructured interviews (e.g., D'Andrade and Strauss 1992; Holland and Quinn 1987; Lutz and Abu-Lughod 1990; Rosenberger 1992; Schwartz, White, and Lutz 1992; Watson-Gegeo and White 1990; White and Kirkpatrick 1985).

Quinn's analysis of Americans' understanding of marriage may be considered a sophisticated example of this type of methodological approach (Quinn 1981, 1987, 1992). In her research, husbands and wives in eleven marriages were interviewed separately for extended periods (fifteen or sixteen hours each) on the general topic of their marriage, with the interviewer asking questions to follow up on the concerns raised. Analyses of the syntax, metaphorical usages, formulaic language, and sense of utterances were undertaken to identify a cultural model of marriage assumed to underlie the discourse and make it intelligible. Among its findings, this work revealed the existence of a general cultural scheme for marriage that centered on the concept of "commitment," with its three subordinate polysemous senses of "promise," "dedication," and "attachment." Case analyses also clarified some of the processes through which this and other cultural schemata obtain motivational force for individuals. For example, it was demonstrated that the general American cultural goal of equal rights is differentially linked to more specific individual goals; for example, the goal of equal rights was linked by one female informant to her desire for equal division of housework and by another female informant to her desire for reciprocal emotional support from her husband.

In other cases, ethnographic techniques have been used in conjunction with traditional experimental methodologies to examine the impact of cultural practices on psychological processes (Scribner 1984; Stigler 1984). In their study testing the "great divide" theory of literacy (Goody 1968; Luria 1976), for example, Scribner and Cole (1981) employed ethnographic techniques to identify the literary practices of the Vai community. On the basis of the information obtained, experimental tasks were designed to tap the cognitive capacities associated with this practical activity. Thus, for example, it was shown that Vai literates' experience in writing and receiving letters was associated with their being more skilled than Vai nonliterates in giving clear instructions on a referential communication task and in analyzing oral speech.

Work from a cultural psychology perspective has also made productive use of cross-cultural comparative methodologies (Markus and Kitayama 1991). For example, in a highly influential study, Shweder and Bourne (1984) utilized content analysis to compare the person attributions made by samples of American and Oriyan adults. Employing a common set of content categories, they analyzed informants' responses according to the relative emphasis placed on traits (e.g., "she is friendly") versus actions (e.g., "she brings cakes to my family on festival days") as well as according to the usage of qualified versus unqualified references (e.g., "he gets angry [with his father]"). Statistical analysis revealed that as compared with Americans, Oriyans made greater reference to actions and less reference to contexts and that they qualified their attributions more frequently. Such results were interpreted as demonstrating that person attribution cannot be explained merely in cognitive or experiental terms, as previously assumed, but rather reflects the conceptions of the person emphasized in particular cultural traditions.

In sum, there is no bounded set of methodologies associated with cultural psychology or one type of strategy (e.g., interpretive versus quantitative; comparative versus noncomparative; naturalistic versus experimental) crucial to progress in the field. Most critical in identifying an approach as a part of the present tradition are its theoretical goals and conceptual presuppositions, not a particular methodology.

SOME MAJOR FINDINGS

This section will provide a selective review of some of the major findings that are emerging in cultural psychology. An effort will be made to focus on a few representative results in each area under consideration rather than to survey the available literature. As will be argued, work from a cultural psychology perspective is contributing to the deparochialization of psychological theory, is enhancing current understanding of the cultural grounding of psychological processes, and is providing new frameworks in which to understand the processes of development and of culture learning. The discussion in this section is organized in terms of the topical areas addressed, with issues of development considered in all of the sections.

Self

Highly influential throughout the social sciences, psychoanalytical theory represents a maturationally based model of human development (e.g., Hartmann 1958; Kohut 1971). Focusing on discourse, interaction, and practice, recent work in cultural psychology has been devoted to reformulating psychoanalytic theory in culturally sensitive ways as well as to applying the theory to understand psychological dimensions of cultural beliefs and practices (Doi 1973, 1986; Ewing 1990; Herdt 1981; Kakar 1978; Kracke and Herdt 1987; Obeyesekere 1981; Roland 1988; Rosenberger 1992; Spiro 1981, 1987).[4]

Based on comparative psychoanalytic research undertaken in the United

States, India, and Japan, Roland (1988) provided evidence to suggest that whereas universally individuals come to develop an "individualized self," a "familial self," and a "spiritual self," as well as an "expanding self," the qualitative nature of these selves and their importance is culturally variable. Thus the individualized self, with its associated emotional strengths and limitations, comes to predominate for Americans, whereas the familial and spiritual selves, with their alternative strengths and limitations, are more central among Indians and Japanese.

LeVine (1990), in turn, argued that the psychoanalytical concept of "average expectable environment" is culturally biased. From a psychoanalytical perspective, acceptable caregiving is seen as encompassing such practices as conversing with infants and giving infants considerable praise and attention—behaviors that are modal for Western middle-class populations. In contrast, reflecting their contrasting cultural conceptions of the child, the Gusii do not treat infants as conversational partners or single infants out for praise or attention. From the perspective of psychoanalytic theory, Gusii practices fall outside the normal range and would be expected to lead to pathological outcomes. However, such a conclusion arises from a failure to appreciate the normative grounding of Gusii caregiving routines and their association with successful adaptive outcomes. LeVine proposed alternatively that the psychoanalytic concept of "normal expectable environment" must be broadened to include the range of behaviors considered appropriate in different cultural contexts.

Recent psychoanalytically grounded ethnographic research (e.g., Rosenberger 1992) has also challenged various dichotomies drawn between what have been portrayed as Western individualistic as contrasted with non-Western collectivist experiences of self. Extending seminal work by Doi on the Japanese conception of dependent love or *amae* (Doi 1973), Kumagai and Kumagai (1986), for example, highlighted the active elements in *amae*, with an affirming self seen as expressed in entering into formalized interactions. Contrary to certain previous claims, it was shown that the Japanese neither lack a sense of self nor maintain a totally passive self. In another example, Ewing (1990) argued that cultures cannot be distinguished on the basis of whether the self is experienced as bounded as contrasted with being open to the surround. Rather, her evidence suggested that although traditional psychoanalytical accounts are biased in their reification of certain Western cultural representations of self, the cohesive sense of self described in such accounts appears to be universal. (See D. W. Murray 1993 and Spiro 1993 for discussion of the heterogeneity of Western cultural conceptions of self.)

Emotions

In general psychology, emotions are commonly defined as including such aspects as (1) eliciting stimulus events; (2) biologically based emotional receptors and emotional states; (3) modes of overt emotional expression; and (4) emotional experiences or evaluations (e.g., Lewis and Saarni 1985). Although it is acknowledged that certain aspects of emotion are culturally variable—such as the kinds of eliciting situations or modes of emotional expression and evaluation—the types of emotions available and their component processes are generally assumed to be universal (e.g., Buck 1988; Izard 1971). These assumptions of universality are challenged by recent research from a cultural psychology perspective.

Studies that have provided evidence for universal emotion categories are limited due to their reliance on English-language labels and their neglect of the varied connotations of emotion terms (Solomon 1984; Wierzbica 1986, 1992). Recent ethnographic reports suggest, in contrast, that certain languages do not clearly distinguish the emotion categories identified in English or may have emotion categories that are not present in English (Gerber 1985; Russell 1991). For example, the Utku have no general term for *fear*, but rather a fear of physical injury, *ighi*, which is distinguished from a fear of social injury, *ilira* (Briggs 1970), whereas the Japanese identify an emotion associated with respect, *sungkan*, that does not exist in English (Geertz 1959). In addition, anthropological evidence indicates that many cultures do not share the concept of emotion assumed in psychological theory, and that various cultures link what might be considered to constitute emotional elicitors only to physical illness, making no distinction between thoughts and feelings or objectifying emotions (Gerber 1985; Levy 1973; Lutz 1988; Lutz and Abu-Lughod 1990; Lynch 1990; Potter 1988; Shweder in press).

Taking into account this cultural variety, some theorists have argued that cultures differ in the degree to which they elaborate particular emotions. Levy, for example, maintained that in all cultures, certain emotions are "hypercognized" as reflected in there being many lexical labels for the emotion and marked cultural elaboration of the emotion, whereas other emotions are "hypocognized" as reflected in there being relatively few lexical labels for the emotion and little cultural elaboration of it (Levy 1973, 1983). He illustrated that among the Tahitians, anger is a hypercognized emotion, with forty-six separate lexical items referencing it, whereas sadness is a hypocognized emotion, with no lexical item referring to sadness but only a more generic label that references feeling ill, troubled, or fatigued.

Other research radically challenges the existence of universal emotions and suggests that the nature of emotion differs qualitatively in different cultural contexts (Harré 1986; Kitayama and Markus in press; Lutz 1988; Solomon 1976, 1984). M. Z. Rosaldo (1980, 1983, 1984), for example, presented evidence to suggest that the hydraulic view of emotion assumed in many traditional accounts may be reflective of dualisms characterizing Western cultural views of the self and may not characterize emotions in other cultures. She showed that anger is both spoken about and experienced among the head-hunting tribe of the llongots as something that occurs and is negotiated between persons. Thus, rather than experiencing the "anger" associated with an affront as an internal press that must be given expression, anger is treated as a process that may be negotiated and "paid back" between persons. Equally, she reported that the Ilongots do not experience emotions such as guilt or shame when they engage in head-hunting—emotions assumed in most psychological accounts to be universally associated with acts of this type.

Ethnographic research has also explored the ways in which children are provided with experiences that lead to the development of distinct affective repertoires (e.g., Harkness and Super 1985; Kilbride and Kilbride 1983; P. J. Miller 1982; P. J. Miller and Sperry 1987). Focusing on the universal affective display of crying, Harkness and Super (1985) illustrated how, at different points in development, responses to crying both reflect and create contrasting cultural conceptions of the self. Thus, among the Kipsigis, caregiver responses to crying involve a goal of redirecting the young child's attention to an external focus, whereas among Americans, responses to this behavior involve reorienting the child's attention to his or her inner experiences.

Social Inference

Psychological research on social inference has typically assumed that attributional effects assume a universal form and can be explained exclusively in information-processing terms (e.g., Harvey, Ickes, and Kidd 1976; Jones et al. 1972; Kelley 1973). In contrast, recent research from a cultural psychology perspective documents that many attributional effects do not occur in non-Western cultural groups and highlights their implicit cultural grounding (Markus and Kitayama 1991; Pepitone and Triandis 1987).

Comparative research (Markus and Kitayama 1991) showed, for example, that Indian adults do not display what had been assumed to be a universal tendency for the self to be judged as more dissimilar to others than others are to the self, but rather tend to display the reverse asymmetry. Challenging the previous assumption that the relative salience of self-other representations is universal, these results suggest that the independent cultural view of self emphasized among Americans leads to a high degree of self-attention and elaboration of self-schemata, whereas the more interdependent cultural view of self emphasized among Indians leads to a greater concern with the self in relation to others and a greater elaboration of information about others.

Comparative research has demonstrated that adults from India, Hong Kong, and Japan tend to place less emphasis on individual psychological traits and more emphasis on aspects of the social context when describing self and others than do Americans (Bond and Cheung 1983; Cousins 1989; J. G. Miller 1984; Shweder and Bourne 1984). Reflecting culturally grounded views of the self rather than merely cognitive or informational effects, these cross-cultural attributional differences have been shown to vary with context. In assuming that autonomy from the context is natural, Americans tend to utilize more abstract modes of attribution on a decontextualized person-description task, in which the situation-free nature of behavior is assumed, than on a contextualized person-description task, in which they feel compelled to make it clear that their behavior is not situationally bound (Cousins 1989). In contrast, Japanese respondents tend to be more abstract on a contextualized task in which the situational dependency of behavior is presupposed and need not be mentioned.

Research exploring the cultural grounding of social cognitive development demonstrates that whereas a significant increase with increasing age occurs among Americans in reference to abstract traits but not in reference to contextual factors, among Indians there is a significant increase with increasing age in reference to contextual factors but not in reference to abstract traits (J. G. Miller 1984, 1986). Also, whereas Americans' attributions tend to become less self-involved with increasing age, Indians' attributions tend to become more self-involved (J. G. Miller 1987). It is concluded that developmental change needs to be understood not merely as a matter of the child developing cognitively or gaining increased experience but as patterned by the dominant cultural views of the self. This work also implies that there are cross-cultural commonalities in the processes entailed in cultural learning, with American and Hindu Indian children showing extensive similarities in their attributions, despite the markedly different cultural conceptions of the child and normative expectations of children maintained in each culture (see also Shweder and LeVine 1975).

Motivation

Cultural beliefs and values are traditionally seen in psychology as influencing specific goals of socialization but not as necessary to explain an assumed set of basic human motives (Dienstbier 1991; Mook 1986; H. A. Murray 1938; Reykowski 1982). These basic motives tend to be formulated in individualistic terms, with an emphasis on the agent's desires to master the environment, control his/her own actions, seek self-actualization, and so on (Deci and Ryan 1985; Rodin 1990; Ryan and Connell 1989; R. W. White 1959). Demonstrating that many of the present motivational constructs in psychology may not be adequate to understand modes of motivation in various non-Western cultures, work from a cultural psychology perspective is contributing to an understanding of the processes through which cultural meanings motivate behavior.

It has been shown, for example, that in cultures emphasizing interdependent cultural views of the self, achievement is predominantly other oriented (Bond 1986; Maehr and Nicholls 1980) rather than predominantly ego oriented (Atkinson 1964; McClelland 1953; H. A. Murray 1938). Among Indian adults, such social concerns as the well-being of others and fulfilling one's duty constitute the predominant part of achievement goals, and social skills such as respecting elders or helping others constitute the predominant means of achieving these goals (Dalal, Singh, and Misra 1988). Similarly, the psychological construct of internal locus of control, with its individualistic emphasis, does not account for the modes of self-control emphasized in various Eastern cultures that focus on control over internal states that may interfere with harmonious interpersonal transactions and exchange (Markus and Kitayama 1991; Marriott 1976; Misra and Gergen 1993; Ramanujan 1990). Traditional psychological research has overlooked the concept of shared locus of control—a concept that is more salient and accorded more value in non-Western cultural groups (Weisz, Rothman, and Blackburn 1984).

Work in this area also calls into question the presumed universal tendency for endogenous motivation to be experienced as opposed to exogenous motivation, that is, for agents to perceive themselves and others as less spontaneously motivated to undertake a behavior when this behavior is compelled by normative expectations as contrasted with when it is not (e.g., Clark and Mills 1979; Deci and Ryan, 1985; Schoenrade et al. 1986). Given their monistic cultural views of the self, Hindu Indians treat individual inclination as consonant with social duty or *dharma* (J. G. Miller and Bersoff in press). In another illustration, the self-serving biases documented repeatedly among Americans (e.g., Greenwald 1980; Steele 1988; Tesser 1986) are shown not to occur in cultural groups emphasizing more interdependent cultural views of the self (Markus and Kitayama 1991). In contrast to Americans, for example, Japanese do not show the false-uniqueness bias (in which the self is rated on average as better than others) and tend to show self-effacing rather than self-enhancing response biases (Markus and Kitayama in press; Takata 1987).

Research on the cultural grounding of individual motivation demonstrates that cultural schemata for such general concepts as "love," "work," or "marriage" function as high-level goals in individual goal hierarchies, with individuals drawing selectively from the cultural repertoire of schemata available to them in formulating their images of self (Quinn 1992; Strauss 1990, 1992). Cultural schemata are conveyed through a wide range of cultural artifacts, such as morality tales and proverbs (Mathews 1992; G. White 1987), as well as through informal and expert sources of knowledge (Harkness, Super, and Keefer 1992). Work in this area is also building on neo-Vygotskyan theory to examine the processes through which individuals learn particular cultural schemata (D'Andrade and Strauss 1992). Treating romantic relationships as an area of cultural expertise, Holland (1992) explored the ways in which this cultural practice becomes salient for individuals. In her account, social action and experience in applying a cultural schema are seen as developing first, with explicit or abstract knowledge of the schema coming later, if at all. In its emphasis on the grounding of cultural learning in social activity, this type of perspective then extends approaches to cultural learning focused exclusively on changes in cognitive representations. In highlighting the existence of marked differences within populations in the degree to which particular cultural schemata are understood and have emotional salience, this type of approach calls into question past monolithic views of culture learning.

Morality

The Kohlbergian approach to morality maintains that moral codes center exclusively on issues of individual rights and justice (Kohlberg 1971, 1981; see also Turiel 1983). More recently, in the approach of Gilligan, morality has been viewed as also encompassing issues of caring—a moral perspective assumed to be emphasized more by females than by males (Gilligan 1982). The morality of caring is assumed to be linked to gender-related developmental tasks as well as gender-related socialization experiences.

Recent research has highlighted the cultural grounding of moral systems (see also Huebner and Garrod 1991; Ma 1992; Snarey 1985). An investigation by Shweder, Mahapatra, and Miller (1987), for example, demonstrated that traditional Brahmins from Bhubaneswar accord full moral status to various practices that Americans treat as matters of social convention or of personal choice. These include such behaviors as a widow eating fish, a wife eating with her husband's elder brother, or a son cutting his hair and eating chicken after his father's death. This research and related studies (Shweder and Much 1987) not only uncovered cross-cultural variability in the degree to which everyday practices are viewed in conventional terms, but identified spiritual concerns as a content domain that is invested with full moral force.

Recent cross-cultural research also has shown that understanding a morality of caring requires attention to cultural beliefs and values and cannot be explained merely in terms of gender-related experiences (J. G. Miller in press b). Qualitatively distinct views of interpersonal responsibilities develop in American as contrasted with Hindu Indian populations, and these differences reflect the contrasting views of the self emphasized in each culture. Reflecting the individualism of American culture, Americans tend to develop a morality of caring that emphasizes personal freedom of choice, a contractual view of social relationships, and individual responsibility for action (Bersoff and Miller 1993; J. G. Miller and Luthar 1989; J. G. Miller, Bersoff, and Harwood 1990; J. G. Miller and Bersoff 1992). In contrast, reflecting the more monistic and relationally oriented cultural views emphasized in Hindu Indian culture, Indians tend to develop a morality of caring that emphasizes broad and relatively noncontingent interpersonal obligations, a familial view of interpersonal relationships, and contextual sensitivity.

Language Socialization

Theorists concerned with language socialization have assumed that caregivers universally modify their speech to children in ways that facilitate language learning. Thus, for example, it has been shown in American populations that mothers use higher intonation, less complex syntax, expansion of speech, and other simplifying techniques when they address infants as compared with adults. This type of speech has been referred to by researchers as "motherese" (Newport

1976; Snow and Ferguson 1977). In this view, it is assumed that the mother is responding to the child merely as a partner who lacks full conversational competence, with motherese serving the functional purposes both of communication and of promoting language acquisition. Highlighting the importance of language practices in cultural communication, recent work in this area has challenged both the presumed universality of motherese and the limitations of a purely functional language-learning framework (see the chapter by Niko Besnier in part II).

Ochs and Schieffelin (1984), for example, revealed the existence of three discrete styles of speech to infants. "Motherese" was found only in American samples and not in samples either from the Kaluli of Papua New Guinea or from Samoa. The authors documented that the patterns of infant-caregiver speech observed in these three contexts can be understood by reference to the cultural meaning systems and practices emphasized in each setting. Thus the use of motherese is seen as expressing Western cultural views of the person that centralize a conception of children as equal in status to adults, at least on an ideological level. The tendency of Samoans not to speak directly to infants but to do so through sibling caregivers is seen as communicating the Samoan emphasis on hierarchically ordered relations. In a similar vein, the Kaluli practice of using no baby-talk lexicon and their avoidance of saying what the child may be thinking or feeling are viewed as expressive of the adult cultural conventions that stipulate the avoidance of gossip and emphasize face-to-face egalitarian interactions.

Cognitive Development

Past cross-cultural research on cognitive development has revealed that whereas individuals frequently appear incapable of abstract modes of cognition when confronted with unfamiliar materials or procedures with low practical utility, they display such capacities in experimental settings that are more meaningful as well as in certain naturalistic situations (Cole and Scribner 1974; Hutchins 1980; Laboratory of Comparative Human Cognition 1983). Findings of this type have led to the important, but also somewhat unsatisfying conclusion (Schwartz 1981) that cognitive capacities are universal, and that variability in their display depends on the task content. Research in this area is moving to a more localized view of cognition and to a view that treats the products and processes of thought as mutually constitutive. Also, learning is being treated as a culturally supported process occurring in interaction rather than as an individual achievement.

Considerable research attention in this area is focusing on *domain-specific cultural expertise* (e.g., Stigler 1984). For example, in a study of the cognitive consequences of working in a milk factory, Scribner (1984) demonstrated that individuals who carry out different jobs in this factory develop particular heuristic strategies to enhance their efficiency. Individuals who work as milk preloaders but have less formal education than white-collar workers not only solve a simulated loading task more rapidly than do white-collar workers but solve it in a different way, that is, by using a more effective perceptual solution strategy as contrasted with a slower enumerative technique. In another examination of expertise, Chi revealed that child chess experts are more proficient than adult novices in their memory for chess positions and use more complex clustering strategies in organization and retrieval of chess information (Chi 1978; see also Chi and Koeske 1983). This research implies that expertise represents an important source of adult differences in cognitive performance and can reverse the common developmental tendency for adults to be more competent than children. Work in this tradition also highlights the ideological and political nature of orthodox measures of cognitive abilities.

A second important thrust of cognitively oriented research from a cultural psychology perspective has been to understand the processes through which development occurs as forms of apprenticeship or of guided participation (Holland and Valsiner 1988; Rogoff 1990; Rogoff and Lave 1984; Rogoff and Wertsch 1984; Valsiner 1988). Drawing on the Vygotskyan concept of the "zone of proximal development" as the difference between what a learner can achieve on his/her own as contrasted with what he or she can achieve with cultural support, researchers have studied how everyday interactions are structured to sustain cultural learning (Wertsch 1985b, 1991). Learning may be supported through processes such as determining the activities and roles available to children and caregivers, adjusting tasks and materials to children's interests and skills, joint problem solving, and transfer of responsibility for managing activities (Rogoff 1990).

Recent work on situated cognition has challenged the view of learning as a distinct activity or end in itself set off from daily life and has emphasized its embeddedness in everyday activities, purposes, and contexts (Goodnow 1990; Lave 1988, 1990). Maintaining that individual internalization may not be the major vehicle for transmission of cultural messages, this viewpoint underscores the importance of cultural practices in sustaining cultural learning (Bourdieu 1977, 1990). For example, Lave showed that individuals involved in the Weight Watchers Program generate solutions to math problems as a function of the practical problems that they encounter in their everyday experiences, for example, solving the conflict between gaining control of food portions versus getting food efficiently on the table by using everyday serving utensils as measuring devices. It is argued that legitimate peripheral participation in social practices is primary, and that learning is part of this practice (Lave and Wenger 1991).

A CRITIQUE OF CULTURAL PSYCHOLOGY

A significant limitation in work undertaken to date from a cultural psychology perspective has been the disciplinary insularity between investigators associated with the more positivist empirical traditions of psychology as contrasted with investigators associated with the more interpretive ethnographic traditions of sociocultural and linguistic anthropology. This has resulted in one set of researchers ignoring conceptual and methodological insights of the other tradition and producing findings considered of relatively little importance from the perspective of the other tradition. However, given the overlap in concerns across these traditions and given their contrasting strengths, greater interdisciplinary exchange can only serve to enhance progress in the field.

Psychological theories are at times incorporated into anthropological accounts without recognition of their limitations. As one example, in an award-winning paper that offered a highly insightful ethnographic account of the sense of self among Brahmin men, Derne (1992) gave a psychological grounding to his claims by drawing on both cognitive dissonance theory (Festinger 1957) and on Gilligan's (1982) theory of a distinctive view of self and morality among American women. From the perspective of current research in psychology, however, this grounding appears weak. After a period of intense initial interest in cognitive dissonance, enthusiasm for the theory has waned since the 1970s as numerous alternative and in many cases competing motivational effects have been identified (Kunda 1992; Lord 1992; Schlenker 1992). Similarly, recent research has shown extremely weak empirical support for Gilligan's claims of gender differences (Brabeck 1983; Thomas 1986; Walker 1984) and has suggested that the model itself may be culturally biased (J. G. Miller and Bersoff 1992; J. G. Miller in press b).

In other cases, select psychological theories are embraced in an uncritical way, with inadequate recognition of their weaknesses. For example, psychoanalytic theory is treated in many recent anthropological studies as a successful explanatory theory, notwithstanding its vulnerability to the same empirical failings that seriously undermined past research in culture and personality (Shweder 1979a). Equally, although the current embrace of connectionism in cognitive anthropology appears thoughtful (e.g., D'Andrade 1992b; Quinn and Strauss 1993), it may be argued that there has been insufficient consideration of the implications of the associationist roots of connectionism and its possible antithesis to a concern with cultural meaning (Bruner 1990).

Finally, as anthropological work begins to address questions that are psychological in nature and to employ procedures that closely resemble those utilized in psychology, some of the same methodological concerns that are relevant to psychological inquiry need to be given greater attention. For example, the talking-diary or life-history procedures that have been adopted in recent anthropological investigations resemble the unstructured interviews commonly employed in general psychology. In employing such procedures, it is important, then, to be sensitive to the methodological issues of concern in general psychological research. These include the need to reduce social desirability effects and other potential response biases and to pay greater attention to the limitations of self-report data, for example, the limited access that individuals have to their own motives (Nisbett and Wilson 1977). Given the documented capacity of observers to make sense of virtually any pattern of events (Garfinkel 1967; Ross et al. 1977), attention must also be given to the ways in which clinical assessment procedures may be falsified or to establishing criteria whereby one autobiographical interpretation of experience may be judged to be more adequate, if not more accurate, than another (see the discussion in D'Andrade 1991). These issues, it may be noted, are particularly important because the goal of the inquiries is not merely to describe the meanings held by particular cultural groups but to understand individual motivation and behavior.

A limitation of at least some cross-cultural research in the cultural psychology tradition has been its focus on describing cultural meanings at highly global levels and its attention primarily to formal sources of cultural knowledge. Cultural meanings are often portrayed as characteristic of entire populations (e.g., the Indians or the Japanese), with cultural knowledge treated as consistent and widely shared. Descriptions at this level may serve the purpose of enabling the successful prediction of contrasting patterns of cognition and behavior among individuals from markedly different groups (e.g., in discriminating the moral judgments of Americans from those of Indians). However, they are deficient in their failure to take into account within-culture diversity in cultural meanings as well as the varied sources of cultural messages—issues given considerable attention in recent anthropological writings.

Another weakness in at least some psychologically oriented research from a cultural psychology perspective has been the tendency to focus on cultural meanings independent of cultural practices. In this work, culture is treated primarily as an ideational system, and relatively little attention is given to the everyday routines and modes of interaction through which culture acquires motivational force and impacts on behavior, if not on individual subjectivity. This neglect of cultural practices may result from the reluctance of some researchers in this tradition to consider processes that cannot be measured through traditional empirical methods of inquiry. However, it may be argued that it is only through attention to everyday practices that it will be possible to understand the cultural grounding of action (Misra and Gergen 1993).

In sum, whereas cultural psychology is presently an interdisciplinary enterprise, a valuable direction for future work in this area is to become even more interdisciplinary (Harris 1991; J. G. Miller 1988, in press a; Schwartz 1981, 1992). This means that greater effort should be made to integrate conceptual and methodological perspectives associated with one disciplinary tradition into work that has its roots in another tradition. It is important, however, to note that such interchange does not imply a homogenization in goals, methods, or concepts. It becomes important to appreciate that multiple questions need to be addressed with multiple methodologies and approaches, each of which has its own strengths and limitations.

The empirical focus of psychological research can prove useful in testing claims that may pertain to the generality of an effect across contexts and/or across persons within a population—claims that individual case analyses or ethnographies may not be well suited to answer. Conversely, ethnographic analyses can serve as a source of rich insights and hypotheses about the nature of cognition, emotion, and motivation in different cultural contexts, revealing phenomena that are frequently not apparent from traditional psychological modes of inquiry alone. As greater recognition is accorded to the cultural and contextual grounding of behavior, ethnographic modes of inquiry may be necessary to gain insight into the processes of everyday interaction through which culture forms individual psychology.

CONCLUSION

As many theorists have long recognized (e.g., Bock 1980, 1988; Bruner 1990; Cole 1990; Jahoda 1992; Shweder 1991), psychology has always been cultural psychology and always will be cultural psychology. To paraphrase Geertz (1973), there is no such thing as a human nature independent of culture. Individuals always operate within socially constituted worlds that are essential to and constitutive of their being. The field of cultural psychology represents an attempt to explore the implications of this proposition and to make an awareness of the cultural grounding of psychological processes overt rather than covert, as it has been in the past and remains in much work conducted in the disciplines of anthropology, psychology, and linguistics today.

What cultural psychology aims to achieve, and what it has already accomplished in many respects, is more than to lead investigators to treat psychological findings and processes as limited in generality. Its major contributions and promises are conceptual, leading to new understandings of development, a rethinking of the concept of culture, and the formulation of new topics for theory and research.

In a challenge to the notion of progress that has dominated developmental psychology, age changes are now being treated as oriented toward local rather than universal goals. At all points in the life course, not merely in childhood, development is being viewed as involving the acquisition of expertise in particular socially constructed domains. Whereas there is much to be done to go beyond the fax model of cultural transmission and to understand culture learning as a process patterned both by an active agent and an active culture (e.g., Harris 1991; J. G. Miller 1986; Sperber 1985), the field is succeeding in expanding current conceptions of the possibilities of development.

Thoughtful debates are also being stimulated on key conceptual issues, such as whether individual subjectivity needs to be taken into account in understanding the impact of cultural practices on behavior, how important explicit processes of cultural transmission are as contrasted with implicit cultural practices, and whether it is necessary (or even possible) to distinguish analytically between culture and psychology. The specific outcomes of these debates may be less crucial than their effect in broadening present visions of culture and in challenging the adequacy or completeness of visions that have dominated theory and research in the past.

Finally, cultural psychology is proving a rich source of conceptual questions. New models are being explored to account for the nature of emotions, cognition, and motivation, and the field is generating rich hypotheses for investigation by varied methodological means. Psychological phenomena that did not appear explicable when the exclusive focus was individual subjectivity or individual behavior alone—such as successful adaptation in the face of individual cognitive shortcomings—are becoming explicable when the unit of analysis is treated as the dyad or larger social unit (D'Andrade 1981).

Although cultural psychology is in a marginal position within the disciplines of anthropology, psychology, and linguistics, it is coming to have an importance in all three fields due to the freshness of its ideas and its relevance to multiculturalism as well as its promise of taking into account indigenous psychologies developed by non-Western social scientists. Not as a new orthodoxy but as a field that is suggesting new ways to think about culture and psychology, cultural psychology is emerging as an approach of importance throughout the social sciences.

NOTES

Thanks are expressed to Niko Besnier, Sara Harkness, William Kessen, Fathali Moghaddam, Paul Rozin, and Geoffrey White for their comments on an earlier version of this chapter. Preparation of the manuscript was supported by grants to the author from the National Science Foundation (DBS-9108924) and the National Institute of Mental Health (MH42940).

1. It should be emphasized that there are presently no widely agreed-on definitions of cultural psychology and that the construction offered in this chapter represents only one of many possible interpretations of the field.

2. The term *cultural psychology* has at times been utilized in different senses than that under consideration here (e.g., Berry 1985).

3. It is recognized that this division is arbitrary and fails to take into account the considerable overlap in the various perspectives.

4. It is likely that the appeal of psychoanalytic theory in cultural psychology relates not merely to the richness of its theoretical insights but to the compatibility of its emphasis on interpretive methodological techniques with traditional ethnographic modes of inquiry.

REFERENCES

Atkinson, J. W. 1964. *An Introduction to Motivation*. Princeton: D. Van Nostrand.

Bates, E. L., with the collaboration of L. Benigni. 1979. *The Emergence of Symbols*. New York: Academic Press.

Bendix, R. 1952. Compliant Behavior and Individual Personality. *American Journal of Sociology* 58:292–302.

Berlin, B., D. E. Breedlove, and P. H. Raven. 1973. General Principles of Classification and Nomenclature in Folk Biology. *American Anthropologist* 75:214–42.

Berlin, B., and P. Kay. 1969. *Basic Color Terms: Their Universality and Evolution.* Berkeley: University of California Press.

Berry, J. W. 1985. Cultural Psychology and Ethnic Psychology: A Comparative Analysis. Pp. 3–15 in I. R. Lagunes and Y. H. Poortinga, eds., *From a Different Perspective: Studies of Behavior across Cultures.* Lisse, Netherlands: Swets and Zeitlainger.

Bersoff, D. M., and J. G. Miller. 1993. Culture, Context, and the Development of Moral Accountability Judgments. *Developmental Psychology* 29:664–76.

Besnier, N. 1990. Language and Affect. *Annual Review of Anthropology* 19:419–51.

Bock, P. K. 1980. *Continuities in Psychological Anthropology: A Historical Introduction.* San Francisco: W. H. Freeman.

———. 1988. *Rethinking Psychological Anthropology: Continuity and Change in the Study of Human Action.* New York: W. H. Freeman.

Boesch, E. E. 1991. *Symbolic Action Theory and Cultural Psychology.* Berlin: Springer-Verlag.

Bond, M. H., ed. 1986. *The Psychology of the Chinese People.* New York: Oxford University Press.

Bond, M. H., and T. Cheung. 1983. College Students' Spontaneous Self-Concept: The Effect of Culture among Students in Hong Kong, Japan, and the United States. *Journal of Cross-Cultural Psychology* 14:153–71.

Bourdieu, P. 1977. *Outline of a Theory of Practice.* Trans. R. Nice. Cambridge, Eng.: Cambridge University Press.

———. 1990. *The Logic of Practice.* Trans. R. Nice. Stanford, CA: Stanford University Press.

Brabeck, M. 1983. Moral Judgment: Theory and Research on Differences between Males and Females. *Developmental Review* 3:274–91.

Briggs, J. L. 1970. *Never in Anger: Portrait of an Eskimo Family.* Cambridge, MA: Harvard University Press.

Bronfenbrenner, U., F. Kessel, W. Kessen, and S. White. 1986. Toward a Critical History of Developmental Psychology: A Propaedeutic Discussion. *American Psychologist* 4:1218–30.

Bruner, J. S. 1986. *Actual Minds, Possible Worlds.* Cambridge, MA: Harvard University Press.

———. 1990. *Acts of Meaning.* Cambridge, MA: Harvard University Press.

Bruner, J. S., R. R. Olver, and P. M. Greenfield. 1966. *Studies in Cognitive Growth.* New York: Wiley.

Buck, R. 1988. *Human Motivation and Emotion* 2nd ed. New York: Wiley.

Carrithers, M., S. Collins, and L. Lukes, eds. 1985. *The Category of the Person: Anthropology, Philosophy, History.* Cambridge, Eng.: Cambridge University Press.

Chi, M. 1978. Knowledge Structures and Memory Development. Pp. 73–96 in R. Siegler, ed., *Children's Thinking: What Develops?* Hillsdale, NJ: Erlbaum.

Chi, M., and R. Koeske. 1983. Network Representation of a Child's Knowledge. *Developmental Psychology* 19:29–39.

Chomsky, N. 1975. *Reflections on Language.* New York: Pantheon.

Clark, M. S., and J. Mills. 1979. Interpersonal Attraction in Exchange and Communal Relationships. *Journal of Personality and Social Psychology* 37:12–24.

Clifford, J. 1988. *The Predicament of Culture: Twentieth-Century Ethnography, Literature, and Art.* Cambridge, MA: Harvard University Press.

Cole, M. 1988. Cross-Cultural Research in the Sociohistorical Tradition. *Human Development* 31: 137–57.

———. 1990. Cultural Psychology: A Once and Future Discipline? Pp. 279–335 in R. A. Dienstbier and J. Berman, eds., *Nebraska Symposium on Motivation.* Lincoln: University of Nebraska Press.

Cole, M., and S. Scribner. 1974. *Culture and Thought.* New York: Wiley.

Cousins, S. 1989. Culture and Self-Perception in Japan and the United States. *Journal of Personality and Social Psychology* 56:124–31.

Dalal, A. K., A. K. Singh, and G. Misra. 1988. Reconceptualization of Achievement Behavior: A Cognitive Approach. Pp. 82–97 in A. K. Dalal, ed., *Attribution Theory and Research*. New Delhi: Wiley Eastern.

D'Andrade, R. G. 1981. The Cultural Part of Cognition. *Cognitive Science* 5:179–95.

———. 1984. Cultural Meaning Systems. Pp. 88–119 in R. A. Shweder and R. A. LeVine, eds., *Culture Theory: Essays on Mind, Self, and Emotion*. Cambridge, Eng.: Cambridge University Press.

———. 1991. The Identification of Schemas in Naturalistic Data. Pp. 279–301 in M. J. Horowitz, ed., *Person Schemas and Maladaptive Interpersonal Patterns*. Chicago: University of Chicago Press.

———. 1992a. Afterword. Pp. 225–32 in R. G. D'Andrade and C. Strauss, eds., *Human Motives and Cultural Models*. Cambridge, Eng.: Cambridge University Press.

———. 1992b. Cognitive Anthropology, Pp. 47–58 in T. Schwartz, G. M. White, and C. A. Lutz, eds., *New Directions in Psychological Anthropology*. Cambridge, Eng.: Cambridge University Press.

D'Andrade, R. G., and C. Strauss, eds. 1992. *Human Motives and Cultural Models*. Cambridge, Eng.: Cambridge University Press.

Dasen, P. R., ed. 1977. *Piagetian Psychology: Cross-Cultural Contributions*. New York: Gardner Press.

Deci, E. L., and R. M. Ryan. 1985. *Intrinsic Motivation and Self-Determination in Human Behavior*. New York: Plenum Press.

Derne, S. 1992. Beyond Institutional and Impulsive Conceptions of Self: Family Structure and the Socially Anchored Real Self. *Ethos* 20:259–88.

Dienstbier, R., ed. 1991. *The Nebraska Symposium on Motivation 1990: Perspectives on Motivation*. Lincoln: University of Nebraska Press.

Doi, T. 1973. *The Anatomy of Dependence*. Tokyo: Kodansha.

———. 1986. *The Anatomy of Self: The Individual versus Society*. Tokyo: Kodansha.

Donaldson, M. 1978. *Children's Minds*. New York: W. W. Norton.

Durkheim, E. 1961. *Moral Education*. Glencoe, IL: Free Press.

Ekman, P. 1972. Universals and Cultural Differences in Facial Expressions of Emotion. Pp. 207–83 in J. K. Cole, ed., *Nebraska Symposium on Motivation*. Lincoln: University of Nebraska Press.

Enriquez, V. 1990. Indigenous Psychology: A Book of Readings. Quezon City, Philippines: New Horizons Press.

Ewing, K. 1990. The Illusion of Wholeness: Culture, Self, and the Experience of Inconsistency. *Ethos* 18:251–78.

Feldman, C. F. 1987. Thought from Language: The Linguistic Construction of Cognitive Representation. Pp. 131–46 in J. Bruner and H. Haste, eds., *Making Sense: The Child's Construction of the World*. London: Methuen.

Festinger, L. 1957. *A Theory of Cognitive Dissonance*. Stanford, CA: Stanford University Press.

Fiske, A. P. 1991. *Structure of Social Life: The Four Elementary Forms of Human Relations*. New York: Free Press.

Flavell, J. H. 1963. *The Developmental Psychology of Jean Piaget*. Princeton: Van Nostrand.

Fodor, J. 1979. *The Language of Thought*. Cambridge, MA: Harvard University Press.

Ford, C. S., ed. 1967. *Cross-Cultural Approaches: Readings in Comparative Research*. New Haven: HRAF Press.

Gardiner, P., ed. 1974. *The Philosophy of History*. Oxford: Oxford University Press.

Garfinkel, H. 1967. *Studies in Ethnomethodology*. Englewood Cliffs, NJ: Prentice-Hall.

Geertz, C. 1973. *The Interpretation of Cultures*. New York: Basic Books.

———. 1984. From the Native's Point of View: On the Nature of Anthropological Understanding. Pp. 123–36 in R. A. Shweder and R. A. LeVine, eds., *Culture Theory: Essays on Mind, Self, and Emotion*. Cambridge, Eng.: Cambridge University Press.

Geertz, H. 1959. The Vocabulary of Emotion: A Study of Javanese Socialization Processes. *Psychiatry* 22:225–37.

Gelman, R. 1978. Cognitive Development. *Annual Review of Psychology* 29:297–332.

Gerber, E. 1985. Rage and Obligation: Samoan Emotions in Conflict. Pp. 121–67 in G. M. White and J. Kirkpatrick, eds., *Person, Self, and Experience: Exploring Pacific Ethnopsychologies.* Berkeley: University of California Press.

Gergen, K. J. 1989. Realities and Their Relationships. Pp. 51–62 in W. J. Baker, M. E. Hyland, R. van Hezewizk, and S. Terwee, eds., *Recent Trends in Theoretical Psychology.* New York: Springer-Verlag.

Gilligan, C. 1982. *In a Different Voice: Psychological Theory and Women's Development.* Cambridge, MA: Harvard University Press.

Goodman, N. 1968. *Languages of Art.* Indianapolis: Bobbs-Merrill.

———. 1972. Seven Structures on Similarity. Pp. 437–47 in N. Goodman, ed., *Problems and Projects.* Indianapolis: Bobbs-Merrill.

———. 1978. *Ways of Worldmaking.* New York: Hackett.

Goodnow, J. J. 1990. The Socialization of Cognition: What's Involved? Pp. 259–86 in J. W. Stigler, R. A. Shweder, and G. Herdt, eds., *Cultural Psychology: Essays on Comparative Human Development.* Cambridge, Eng.: Cambridge University Press.

Goody, J. ed. 1968. *Literacy in Traditional Societies.* New York: Cambridge University Press.

Gorer, G. 1964. *The American People.* New York: Norton.

Greenwald, A. G. 1980. The Totalitarian Ego: Fabrication and Revision of Personal History. *American Psychologist* 35:603–18.

Harkness, S. 1992. Human Development in Psychological Anthropology. Pp. 102–22 in T. Schwartz, G. M. White, and C. A. Lutz, eds., *New Directions in Psychological Anthropology.* Cambridge, Eng.: Cambridge University Press.

Harkness, S., and C. M. Super. 1985. Child-Environment Interactions in the Socialization of Affect. Pp. 21–36 in M. Lewis and C. Saarni, eds., *The Socialization of Emotions.* New York and London: Plenum Press.

———. 1992. The Cultural Foundations of Fathers' Roles: Evidence from Kenya and the United States. Pp. 191–211 in B. S. Hewlett, ed., *Father-Child Relations: Cultural and Biosocial Contexts.* New York: Aldine de Gruyter.

Harkness, S., C. M. Super, and C. H. Keefer. 1992. Learning to Be an American Parent: How Cultural Models Gain Directive Force. Pp. 163–78 in R. D'Andrade and S. Strauss, eds., *Human Motives and Cultural Models.* Cambridge, Eng.: Cambridge University Press.

Harré, R. 1986. An Outline of the Social Constructionist Viewpoint. Pp. 220–33 in R. Harré, ed., *The Social Construction of Emotions.* Oxford: Basil Blackwell.

Harris, P. L. 1991. Uneasy Union and Neglected Children: Cultural Psychology and Its Prospects. *Current Anthropology* 32:82–89.

Hartmann, H. 1958. *Ego Psychology and the Problem of Adaptation.* New York: International Universities Press.

Harvey, J. H., W. J. Ickes, and R. F. Kidd, eds. 1976. *New Direction in Attribution Research.* Vol. 1. Hillsdale, NJ: Erlbaum.

Heath, S. B. 1983. *Ways with Words: Language, Life, and Work in Communities and Classrooms.* Cambridge, Eng.: Cambridge University Press.

Herdt, G. 1981. *Guardians of the Flutes: Idioms of Masculinity.* New York: McGraw-Hill.

Holland, H. C. 1992. How Cultural Systems Become Desire: A Case Study of American Romance. Pp. 61–89 in R. D'Andrade and C. Strauss, eds., *Human Motives and Cultural Models.* Cambridge, Eng.: Cambridge University Press.

Holland, D. C., and N. Quinn. 1987. *Cultural Models in Language and Thought.* Cambridge, Eng.: Cambridge University Press.

Holland, D.C., and J. Valsiner. 1988. Cognition, Symbols, and Vygotsky's Developmental Psychology, *Ethos* 16:247–72.

Howard, A. 1985. Ethnopsychology and the Prospects for a Cultural Psychology. Pp. 401–20 in G. M. White and J. Kirkpatrick, eds., *Person, Self, and Experience: Exploring Pacific Ethnopsychologies*. Berkeley: University of California Press.

Huebner, A., and A. Garrod. 1991. Moral Reasoning and a Karmic World. *Human Development* 34:341–52.

Hutchins, E. 1980. *Culture and Inference*. Cambridge, MA: Harvard University Press.

Izard, C. E. 1971. *The Face of Emotion*. New York: Appleton-Century-Crofts.

Jahoda, G. 1990. Our Forgotten Ancestors. Pp. 1–40 in R. A. Dienstbier and J. Berman, eds., *Nebraska Symposium on Motivation*. Lincoln: University of Nebraska Press.

———. 1992. *Crossroads between Culture and Mind: Continuities and Change in Theories of Human Nature*. London: Harvester Wheatsheaf.

Jones, E. E., et al., eds. 1972. *Attribution: Perceiving the Causes of Behavior*. Morristown, N.J.: General Learning Press.

Kagan, J., and N. Snidman. 1991. Temperamental Factors in Human Development. *American Psychologist* 46:856–62.

Kakar, S. 1978. *The Inner World: A Psycho-Analytic Study of Childhood and Society in India*. Delhi: Oxford University Press.

Kantor, J. R. 1982. *Cultural Psychology*. Chicago: Princicpia Press.

Kelley, H. H. 1973. The Process of Causal Attribution. *American Psychologist* 289:107–28.

Kessen, W. 1990. *The Rise and Fall of Development*. Worcester, MA: Clark University Press.

Kilbride, P. L., and J. E. Kilbride. 1983. Socialization for High Positive Affect between Mother and Infant among the Baganda of Uganda. *Ethos* 11:323–45.

Kitayama, S., and H. Markus, eds. In press. *Emotion and Culture*. Washington, DC: American Psychological Association.

Kohlberg, L. 1971. From Is to Ought: How to Commit the Naturalistic Fallacy and Get Away with It in the Study of Moral Development. Pp. 151–232 in T. Mischel, ed., *Cognitive Development and Epistemology*. New York: Academic Press.

———. 1981. *Essays on Moral Development*, Vol. 1: *The Philosophy of Moral Development: Moral Stages and the Idea of Justice*. New York: Harper and Row.

Kohut, H. 1977. *The Restoration of the Self*. New York: International Universities Press.

Kracke, W., and G. Herdt, eds. 1987. Interpretation in Psychoanalytic Anthropology [Special Issue] *Ethos* 15:3–143.

Kulick, D. 1992. *Language Shift and Cultural Reproduction: Socialization, Self, and Syncretism in a Papua New Guinea Village*. Studies in the Social and Cultural Foundations of Language, 14. Cambridge, Eng.: Cambridge University Press.

Kumagai, H. A., and A. K. Kumagai. 1986. The Hidden "I" in Amae: "Passive Love" and Japanese Social Perception. *Ethos* 14:305–20.

Kunda, Z. 1992. Can Dissonance Theory Do It All? *Psychological Inquiry* 3:337–39.

Laboratory of Comparative Human Cognition. 1983. Culture and Cognitive Development. Pp. 295–356 in W. Kessen, ed., *Mussen's Handbook of Child Psychology: History, Theory, and Method*. 4th ed. New York: Wiley.

Lave, J. 1988. *Cognition in Practice: Mind, Mathematics, and Culture in Everyday Life*. Cambridge, Eng.: Cambridge University Press.

———. 1990. The Culture of Acquisition and the Practice of Understanding. Pp. 309–27 in J. W. Stigler, R. A. Shweder, and G. Herdt, eds., *Cultural Psychology: Essays on Comparative Human Development*. Cambridge, Eng.: Cambridge University Press.

Lave, J. A., Stepick, and L. Sailer. 1977. Extending the Scope of Formal Analysis. *American Ethnologist* 4:321–39.

Lave, J., and E. Wenger. 1991. *Situated Learning: Legitimate Peripheral Participation*. Cambridge, Eng.: Cambridge University Press.

Leontiev, A. N. 1964. *Problems of the Development of Mind*. Moscow: Progress.

LeVine, R. A. 1973. *Culture, Behavior, and Personality*. Chicago: Aldine.

———. 1984. Properties of Culture: An Ethnographic View. Pp. 67–87 in R. A. Shweder and R. A. LeVine, eds., *Culture Theory: Essays on Mind, Self, and Emotion*. Cambridge, Eng.: Cambridge University Press.

———. 1990. Infant Environments in Psychoanalysis: A Cross-Cultural View. Pp. 454–74 in J. W. Stigler, R. A. Shweder, and G. Herdt, eds., *Cultural Psychology: Essays on Comparative Human Development*. Cambridge, Eng.: Cambridge University Press.

Lévi-Strauss, C. 1966. *The Savage Mind*. Chicago: University of Chicago Press.

Levy, R. I. 1973. *Tahitians*. Chicago: University of Chicago Press.

———. 1983. Introduction: Self and Emotion. *Ethos* 11:128–34.

Lewis, M., and C. Saarni. 1985. Culture and Emotions. Pp. 1–17 in M. Lewis and C. Saarni, eds., *The Socialization of Emotions*. New York and London: Plenum Press.

Lord, C. G. 1992. Was Cognitive Dissonance Theory a Mistake? *Psychological Inquiry* 3:339–42.

Luria, A. R. 1976. *Cognitive Development*. Cambridge, MA: Harvard University Press.

Lutz, C. 1988. *Unnatural Emotions: Everyday Sentiments on a Micronesian Atoll and Their Challenge to Western Theory*. Chicago: University of Chicago Press.

Lutz, C., and L. Abu-Lughod, eds. 1990. *Language and the Politics of Emotion*. New York: Cambridge University Press.

Lutz, C., and G. M. White. 1986. The Anthropology of Emotions. *Annual Review of Anthropology* 15:405–36.

Lynch, O. M. 1990. *Divine Passions: The Social Construction of Emotion in India*. Berkeley: University of California Press.

Ma, H. K. 1992. The Moral Judgment Development of the Chinese People: A Theoretical Model. *Philosophica* 49(1):55–82.

Maehr, M., and J. Nicholls. 1980. Culture and Achievement Motivation: A Second Look. Pp. 221–67 in Warren, ed., *Studies in Cross-Cultural Psychology*, vol. 2. New York: Academic Press.

Mandelbaum, M. 1977. *The Anatomy of Historical Knowledge*. Baltimore: Johns Hopkins University Press.

Markus, H., and S. Kitayama. 1991. Culture and the Self: Implications for Cognition, Emotion, and Motivation. *Psychological Review* 98:224–53.

———. In press. Cultural Variation in the Self-Concept. Pp. 100–27 in M. Crawford and M. Hamilton, eds., *Multidisciplinary Perspectives on the Self*. New York: Springer-Verlag.

Marriott, M. 1976. Hindu Transactions: Diversity without Dualism. Pp. 109–42 in B. Kapferer, ed., *Transaction and Meaning: Directions in the Anthropology of Education and Symbolic Behavior*. Philadelphia: Institute for the Study of Human Issues.

Marsella, A., and G. White. 1982. *Cultural Conceptions of Mental Health and Therapy*. Dordrecht, Holland: D. Reidel Publishing Company.

Mathews, H. F. 1992. The Directive Force of Mortality Tales in a Mexican Community. Pp. 127–62 in R. D'Andrade and C. Strauss, eds., *Human Motives and Cultural Models*. Cambridge, Eng.: Cambridge University Press.

McClelland, D. C. 1953. *The Achievement Motive*. New York: Appleton-Century Crofts.

Mead, M. 1949. *Coming of Age in Samoa*. New York: Mentor.

———. 1953. *Growing Up in New Guinea*. New York: Mentor.

Miller, J. G. 1984. Culture and the Development of Everyday Social Explanation. *Journal of Personality and Social Psychology* 46:961–78.

———. 1986. Early Cross-Cultural Commonalities in Social Explanation. *Developmental Psychology* 22:514–20.

———. 1987. Cultural Influences on the Development of Conceptual Differentiation in Person Description. *British Journal of Developmental Psychology* 5:309–19.

———. 1988. Bridging the Content-Structure Dichotomy: Culture and the Self. Pp. 266–81 in M. Bond, ed., *The Cross-Cultural Challenge to Social Psychology*. Newbury Park, CA: Sage.

———. In press. Taking Culture into Account in Social Cognitive Development. In G. Misra, ed., *Socialization and Social Development in India*. Delhi: Sage Publications.

———. 1994. Cultural Diversity in the Morality of Caring: "Individually-Oriented Versus Duty-Based" Interpersonal Moral Codes. *Cross-Cultural Research* 28:3–39.

Miller, J. G., and D. M. Bersoff. 1992. Culture and Moral Judgment: How Are Conflicts between Justice and Interpersonal Responsibilities Resolved? *Journal of Personality and Social Psychology* 62:541–54.

———. In press. Cultural Influences on the Moral Status of Reciprocity and the Discounting of Endogenous Motivation. *Personality and Social Psychology Bulletin.* Special Issue on The Self and the Collective: Groups Within Individuals.

Miller, J. G., D. M. Bersoff, and R. Harwood. 1990. Perceptions of Social Responsibilities in India and the United States: Moral Imperatives or Personal Decisions? *Journal of Personality and Social Psychology* 58:33–47.

Miller, J. G., and S. Luthar. 1989. Issues of Interpersonal Responsibility and Accountability: A Comparison of Indians' and Americans' Moral Judgments. *Social Cognition* 7:237–61.

Miller, P. J. 1982. *Amy, Wendy, and Beth: Learning Language in South Baltimore.* Austin: University of Texas Press.

Miller, P. J., Potts, H., H. Fung, L. Hoogstra, and J. Mintz. 1990. Narrative Practices and the Social Construction of Self in Childhood. *American Ethnologist* 17:292–311.

Miller, P. J., and L. L. Sperry. 1987. The Socialization of Anger and Aggression. *Merrill-Palmer Quarterly* 33(1):1–31.

Mischel, W. 1968. *Personality and Assessment.* New York: Wiley.

Misra, G., and K. J. Gergen. 1993. On the Place of Culture in Psychological Science. *International Journal of Psychology* 28:225–43.

Moghaddam, F. 1987. Psychology in the Three Worlds: As Reflected by the Crisis in Social Psychology and the Move toward Indigenous Third-World Psychology. *American Psychologist* 42:912–20.

Mook, D. G. 1986. *Motivation: The Organization of Action.* New York: Norton.

Murray, D. W. 1993. What Is the Western Concept of the Self? On Forgetting David Hume. *Ethos* 21:3–23.

Murray, H. A. 1938. *Explorations in Personality.* New York: Oxford University Press.

Nagel, T. 1986. *The View from Nowhere.* New York: Oxford University Press.

Needham, R. 1975. Polythetic Classification: Convergence and Consequences. *Man* 10:349–69.

Newport, E. L. 1976. Motherese: The Speech of Mothers to Young Children. Pp. 177–217 in N. J. Castellan, D. B. Pisoni, and G. R. Potts, eds., *Cognitive Theory,* vol. 2. Hillsdale, NJ: Erlbaum.

Nisbett, R., and T. D. Wilson. 1977. Telling More Than We Can Know: Verbal Reports on Mental Processes. *Psychological Review* 84:231–59.

Nuckolls, C., ed. 1993. *Siblings in South Asia.* New York: Guilford Press.

Obeyesekere, G. 1981. *Medusa's Hair: An Essay on Personal Symbols and Religious Experience.* Chicago: University of Chicago Press.

Ochs, E. 1988. *Culture and Language Development: Language Acquisition and Language Socialization in a Samoan Village.* Cambridge, Eng.: Cambridge University Press.

Ochs, E., and B. B. Schieffelin. 1984. Language Acquisition and Socialization: Three Developmental Stories and Their Implications. Pp. 276–320 in R. A. Shweder and R. A. LeVine, eds., *Culture Theory: Essays on Mind, Self, and Emotion.* Cambridge, Eng.: Cambridge University Press.

Paranjpe, A. C., D.Y.F. Ho, and R. W. Rieber, eds. 1988. *Asian Contributions to Psychology.* New York: Praeger.

Parsons, T. 1968. *The Structure of Social Action,* vol. 1. New York: Free Press.

Paul, R. A. 1990. What Does Anybody Want? Desire, Purpose, and the Acting Subject in the Study of Culture. *Cultural Anthropology* 5:431–51.

Pepitone, A. 1976. Toward a Normative and Comparative Biocultural Social Psychology. *Journal of Personality and Social Psychology* 34:641–53.

Pepitone, A., and H. Triandis. 1987. On the University of Social Psychological Theories. *Journal of Cross-Cultural Psychology* 18:471–98.

Potter, S. H. 1988. The Cultural Construction of Emotion in Rural Chinese Social Life. *Ethos.* 16: 181–208.

Price-Williams, D. 1980. Toward the Idea of a Cultural Psychology: A Superordinate Theme for Study. *Journal of Cross-Cultural Psychology* 11:75–88.

Quinn, N. 1981. "Commitment" in American Marriage: A Cultural Analysis. *American Ethnologist* 9:775–98.

———. 1987. Convergent Evidence for a Culture Model of American Marriage. Pp. 173–92 in D. Holland and N. Quinn, eds., *Cultural Models in Language and Thought.* Cambridge, Eng.: Cambridge University Press.

———. 1992. The Motivational Force of Self-Understanding: Evidence from Wives' Inner Conflicts. Pp. 90–126 in R. D'Andrade and C. Strauss, eds., *Human Motives and Cultural Models.* Cambridge, Eng.: Cambridge University Press.

Quinn, N., and C. Strauss. 1993. A Cognitive Framework for a Unified Theory of Culture. Unpublished manuscript.

Ramanujan, A. K. 1990. Is There an Indian Way of Thinking? An Informal Essay. Pp. 41–58 in M. Marriott, ed., *India through Hindu Categories.* New Delhi: Sage Publications.

Reykowski, J. 1982. Social Motivation. *Annual Review of Psychology* 33:123–54.

Rodin, J. 1990. Control by Any Other Name: Definitions, Concepts, and Processes. Pp. 1–17 in J. Rodin, C. Schooler, and K. W. Schaie, eds., *Self-Directedness: Causes and Effects throughout the Life Course.* Hillsdale, NJ: Erlbaum.

Rogoff, B. 1990. *Apprenticeship in Thinking: Cognitive Development in Social Context.* New York: Oxford University Press.

Rogoff, B., and J. Lave, eds. 1984. *Everyday Cognition: Its Development in Social Context.* Cambridge, MA: Harvard University Press.

Rogoff, B., and J. V. Wertsch, eds. 1984. Children's Learning in the "Zone of Proximal Development." In *New Directions for Child Development,* no. 23. San Francisco: Jossey-Bass.

Roland, A. 1988. *In Search of Self in India and Japan: Toward a Cross-Cultural Psychology.* Princeton: Princeton University Press.

Rosaldo, M. Z. 1980. *Knowledge and Passion: Ilongot Notions of Self and Social Life.* Cambridge, Eng.: Cambridge University Press.

———. 1983. The Shame of Headhunters and the Autonomy of Self. *Ethos* 11:135–51.

———. 1984. Toward an Anthropology of Self and Feeling. Pp. 137–57 in R. A. Shweder and R. A. LeVine, eds., *Culture Theory: Essays on Mind, Self, and Emotion.* Cambridge, Eng.: Cambridge University Press.

Rosaldo, R. 1989. *Culture and Truth: The Remaking of Social Analysis.* Boston: Beacon Press.

Rosch, E. 1975. Universals and Cultural Specifics in Human Categorization. Pp. 177–206 in R. W. Brislin, S. Bochner, and W. J. Lonner, eds., *Cross-Cultural Perspectives on Learning.* Beverly Hills, CA: Sage.

Rosenberger, N. R. 1992. *Japanese Sense of Self.* New York: Cambridge University Press.

Ross, L., M. R. Lepper, F. Strack, and J. Steinmetz. 1977. Social Explanation and Social Expectation: Effects of Real and Hypothetical Explanations on Subjective Likelihood. *Journal of Personality and Social Psychology* 35:817–29.

Rozin, P. 1982. Human Food Selection: The Interaction of Biology, Culture, and Individual Experience. Pp. 225–54 in L. M. Barker, ed., *The Psychobiology of Human Food Selection.* Westport, Conn.: Avi Publishing.

Russell, J. A. 1991. Culture and the Categorization of Emotions. *Psychological Bulletin* 110:426–50.

Ryan, R. M., and J. P. Connell. 1989. Perceived Locus of Causality and Internalization: Examining Reasons for Acting in Two Domains. *Journal of Personality and Social Psychology* 57:749–61.

Sahlins, M. 1976a. *Culture and Practical Reason.* Chicago: University of Chicago Press.

———. 1976b. *The Use and Abuse of Biology.* Ann Arbor: University of Michigan Press.

Schank, R. C., and R. P. Abelson. 1977. *Scripts, Plans, Goals, and Understanding: An Inquiry into Human Knowledge Structures.* Hillsdale, NJ: Erlbaum.

Schieffelin, B. 1990. *The Give and Take of Everyday Life: Language Socialization of Kaluli Children.* Studies in the Social and Cultural Foundations of Language, 9. Cambridge, Eng.: Cambridge University Press.

Schieffelin, B. B., and E. Ochs. 1986a. Language Socialization. *Annual Review of Anthropology* 15: 163–91.

———, eds. 1986b. *Language Socialization across Culture.* Cambridge, Eng.: Cambridge University Press.

Schlenker, B. R. 1992. Of Shape Shifters and Theories. *Psychological Inquiry* 3:342–44.

Schoenrade, P. A., C. D. Batson, J. R. Brandt, and R. E. Loud, Jr. 1986. Attachment, Accountability, and Motivation to Benefit Another Not in Distress. *Journal of Personality and Social Psychology* 51:557–63.

Schwartz, T. 1981. The Acquisition of Culture. *Ethos* 9:4–17.

———. 1992. Anthropology and Psychology: An Unrequited Relationship. Pp. 324–49 in T. Schwartz, G. White, and C. Lutz, eds., *New Directions in Psychological Anthropology.* Cambridge, Eng.: Cambridge University Press.

Schwartz, T., G. M. White, and C. A. Lutz, eds. 1992. *New Directions in Psychological Anthropology.* Cambridge, Eng.: Cambridge University Press.

Scribner, S. 1984. Studying Working Intelligence. Pp. 9–40 in B. Rogoff and J. Lave, eds., *Everyday Cognition: Its Development in Social Context.* Cambridge, MA: Harvard University Press.

Scribner, S., and M. Cole. 1981. *The Psychology of Literacy.* Cambridge, MA: Harvard University Press.

Serpell, R. 1984. Commentary: The Impact of Psychology on Third World Development. *International Journal of Psychology* 19:179–92.

Shweder, R. A. 1979a. Rethinking Culture and Personality Theory, Part I: A Critical Examination of Two Classical Postulates. *Ethos* 7:255–78.

———. 1979b. Rethinking Culture and Personality Theory, Part I: A Critical Examination of Two More Classical Postulates. *Ethos* 7:279–311.

———. 1984a. Anthropology's Romantic Rebellion against the Enlightenment; or, There's More to Thinking Than Reason and Evidence. Pp. 27–66 in R. A. Shweder and R. A. LeVine, eds., *Culture Theory: Essays on Mind, Self, and Emotion.* Cambridge, Eng.: Cambridge University Press.

———. 1984b. Preview: A Colloquy of Culture Theorists. Pp. 1–24 in R. A. Shweder and R. A. LeVine, eds., *Culture Theory: Essays on Mind, Self, and Emotion.* Cambridge, Eng.: Cambridge University Press.

———. 1990. Cultural Psychology—What Is It? Pp. 1–43 in J. W. Stigler, R. A. Shweder, and G. Herdt, eds., *Cultural Psychology: Essays on Comparative Human Development.* Cambridge, Eng.: Cambridge University Press.

———. 1991. *Thinking through Cultures: Expeditions in Cultural Psychology.* Cambridge, MA: Harvard University Press.

———. In press. Fundamental Issues and Questions about Emotion. in P. Ekman and R. Davidson, eds., *Questions about Emotion.* New York: Oxford University Press.

Shweder, R. A., and E. J. Bourne. 1984. Does the Concept of the Person Vary Cross-Culturally? Pp. 158–99 in R. A. Shweder and R. A. LeVine, eds., *Culture Theory: Essays on Mind, Self, and Emotion.* Cambridge, Eng.: Cambridge University Press.

Shweder, R. A., and R. A. LeVine. 1975. Dream Concepts of Hausa Children: A Critique of the "Doctrine of Invariant Sequence" in Cognitive Development. *Ethos* 3:209–30.

———, eds. 1984. *Culture Theory: Essays on Mind, Self, and Emotion.* Cambridge, Eng.: Cambridge University Press.

Shweder, R. A., M. Mahapatra, and J. G. Miller. 1987. Culture and Moral Development. Pp. 1–89 in J. Kagan and S. Lamb, eds., *The Emergence of Morality in Young Children.* Chicago: University of Chicago Press.

Shweder, R. A.,, and N. C. Much. 1987. Determinations of Meaning: Discourse and Moral Socialization. Pp. 197–244 in W. M. Kurtines and J. L. Gewirtz, eds., *Moral Development through Social Interaction.* New York: Wiley.

Shweder, R. A., and M. A. Sullivan. 1990. The Semiotic Subject of Cultural Psychology. Pp. 399–416 in L. A. Pervin, ed., *Handbook of Personality Theory and Research.* New York: Guilford Press.

———. 1993. Cultural Psychology: Who Needs It? *Annual Review of Psychology* 44:497–527.

Snarey, J. R. 1985. Cross-Cultural Universality of Social-Moral Development: A Critical Review of Kohlbergian Research. *Psychological Bulletin* 97:202–32.

Snow, C., and C. Ferguson, eds. 1977. *Talking to Children: Language Input and Acquisition.* Cambridge, Eng.: Cambridge University Press.

Solomon, R. C. 1976. *The Passions.* Garden City, NJ: Anchor Press.

———. 1984. Getting Angry: The Jamesian Theory of Emotion in Anthropology. Pp. 238–54 in R. A. Shweder and R. A. LeVine, eds., *Culture Theory: Essays on Mind, Self, and Emotion.* Cambridge, Eng.: Cambridge University Press.

Sperber, D. 1975. *Rethinking Symbolism.* Cambridge, Eng.: Cambridge University Press.

———. 1985. Anthropology and Psychology: Towards an Epidemiology of Representations. *Man* 20:73–87.

Spiro, M. E. 1965. Religious Systems as Culturally Constructed Defense Mechanisms. Pp. 100–13 in M. E. Spiro, ed., *Context and Meaning in Cultural Anthropology.* New York: Free Press.

———. 1982. *Oedipus in the Trobriands.* Chicago: University of Chicago Press.

———. 1987. *Culture and Human Nature: Theoretical Papers of Melford E. Spiro.* Ed. B. Kilbourne and L. L. Langness. Chicago: University of Chicago Press.

———. 1993. Is the Western Conception of the Self "Peculiar" within the Context of the World Cultures? *Ethos* 21:107–53.

Steele, C. 1988. The Psychology of Self-Affirmation: Sustaining the Integrity of the Self. Pp. 181–227 in L. Berkowitz, ed., *Advances in Experimental Social Psychology.* San Diego, CA: Academic Press.

Stigler, J. W. 1984. "Mental Abacus": The Effect of Abacus Training on Chinese Children's Mental Calculation. *Cognitive Psychology* 16:145–76.

Strauss, C. 1990. Who Gets Ahead? Cognitive Responses to Heteroglossia in American Political Culture. *American Ethnologist* 17:312–28.

———. 1992. Models and Motives. Pp. 1–20 in R. G. D'Andrade and C. Strauss, eds., *Human Motives and Cultural Models.* Cambridge, Eng.: Cambridge University Press.

Takata, T. 1987. Self-Deprecative Tendencies in Self-Evaluation through Social Comparison. *Japanese Journal of Experimental Social Psychology* 27:27–36.

Tesser, A. 1986. Some Effects of Self-Evaluation Maintenance on Cognition and Action. Pp. 435–64 in R. M. Sorrentino and E. T. Higgins, eds., *Handbook of Motivation and Cognition: Foundations of Social Behavior.* New York: Guilford Press.

Thomas, S. J. 1986. Estimating Gender Differences in the Comprehension and Preference of Moral Issues. *Developmental Review* 6:165–80.

Triandis, H. C. 1989. The Self and Social Behavior in Differing Cultural Contexts. *Psychological Review* 96:506–20.

Triandis, H. C., R. Bontempo, M. Villareal, M. J. Asai, and N. Lucca. 1988. Individualism and Collectivism: Cross-Cultural Perspectives on Self-Ingroup Relationships. *Journal of Personality and Social Psychology* 54:323–38.

Turiel, E. 1983. *The Development of Social Knowledge: Morality and Convention.* Cambridge, Eng.: Cambridge University Press.

Tyler, S. A., ed. 1969. *Cognitive Anthropology.* New York: Holt, Rinehart and Winston.

Valsiner, J., ed. 1988. *Child Development within Culturally Structured Environments*, Vol. 2: *Social Co-Construction and Environmental Guidance in Development*. Norwood, NJ: Ablex.

Vygotsky, L. S. 1929. The Problem of the Cultural Development of the Child, II. *Journal of Genetic Psychology* 36:414–34.

———. 1962. *Thought and Language*. Cambridge, MA: M.I.T. Press.

———. 1978. *Mind in Society: The Development of Higher Psychological Processes*. Cambridge, MA: Harvard University Press.

Walker, L. J. 1984. Sex Differences in the Development of Moral Reasoning: A Critical Review. *Child Development* 55:677–91.

Wallace, A.F.C. 1961. *Culture and Personality*. New York: Random House.

Wason, P. C., and P. N. Johnson-Laird. 1972. *The Psychology of Reasoning*. London: Batsford.

Watson-Gegeo, K. A., and G. M. White, eds. 1990. *Disentangling: Conflict Discourse in Pacific Societies*. Stanford, CA: Stanford University Press.

Weisz, J., F. M. Rothbaum, and T. C. Blackburn. 1984. Standing Out and Standing In: The Psychology of Control in America and Japan. *American Psychologist* 39:955–69.

Wertsch, J. V., ed. 1985b. *Culture, Communication, and Cognition: Vygotskian Perspectives*. Cambridge, Eng.: Cambridge University Press.

———. 1991. *Voices of the Mind: A Sociocultural Approach to Mediated Action*. Cambridge, Eng.: Cambridge University Press.

White, G. 1987. Proverbs and Cultural Models: An American Psychology of Problem Solving. Pp. 151–72 in D. Holland and N. Quinn, eds., *Cultural Models in Language and Thought*. Cambridge, Eng.: Cambridge University Press.

———. 1992. Ethnopsychology. Pp. 21–46 in T. Schwartz, G. M. White, and C. A. Lutz, eds., *New Directions in Psychological Anthropology*. Cambridge, Eng.: Cambridge University Press.

White, G., and J. Kirkpatrick, eds. 1985. *Person, Self, and Experience: Exploring Pacific Ethnopsychologies*. Berkeley: University of California Press.

White, R. W. 1959. Motivation Reconsidered: The Concept of Competence. *Psychological Review* 66:297–333.

Whiting, B. B., and J.W.M. Whiting. 1975. *Children of Six Cultures: A Psycho-Cultural Analysis*. Cambridge, MA: Harvard University Press.

Whiting, J.W.M., and I. L. Child. 1953. *Child Training and Personality: A Cross-Cultural Study*. New Haven: Yale University Press.

Whorf, B. L. 1956. *Language, Thought, and Reality*. Cambridge, Mass.: M.I.T. Press.

Wierzbicka, A. 1986. Human Emotions: Universal or Cultural-Specific? *American Anthropologist* 88:584–94.

———. 1992. *Semantics, Culture, and Cognition*. New York: Oxford University Press.

PART 2
THE EVIDENCE

CHAPTER EIGHT

PRIMATE ETHOLOGY: A PERSPECTIVE ON HUMAN AND NONHUMAN HANDEDNESS

William C. McGrew and Linda F. Marchant

The ethological approach to understanding behavior is usually associated with biology rather than anthropology. The three Nobel-winning founders of the field (Karl von Frisch, Konrad Lorenz, and Niko Tinbergen) were all zoologists who concentrated on insects, fishes, and birds. Yet for one order of mammals, the Primates, ethological methods have proven to be central to a multidisciplinary synthesis that is unique among nonhuman animals and that integrates human animals too.

Behavioral primatology has been cross-fertilized from three main directions: Anthropology has contributed a comparative focus on apes and monkeys as sources for modeling human origins, both by homology and by analogy. Psychology has fostered experimental rigor and statistical sophistication, emphasis on individual differences, and means for inferring the cognitive processes underlying behavior. Zoology has embedded primatology in nature through detailed socioecology and, most important, has supplied the unifying theory in the form of Darwinian evolution.

The result is a potent intellectual blend that has burgeoned in the last thirty years in Europe, Japan, and North America. (Interestingly, emphases differ geographically: Field primatology based in America comes mostly from biological anthropology, under the pioneering influence of Sherwood Washburn. In Europe, zoologists and psychologists predominate, prompted by figures like Hans Kummer and Robert Hinde. In Japan, the ecologist Kenji Imanishi preceded all others elsewhere in laying the discipline's foundations in the 1950s.) Moreover, behavioral primatology is increasingly interdisciplinary as anthropologists extend research into captive colonies of primates and psychologists take to the field to test the validity of hypotheses posed from the laboratory.

Contemporary behavioral primatology is mostly *observational* of spontaneous activities (as opposed to induced, artificial responses), takes place in *naturalistic* settings (if not in the wild, at least in captive environments that seek to stimulate key features of nature), is both richly descriptive and carefully *quantitative* (having gone beyond natural history), and is *theory-driven*, based on the assumption that organisms maximize their genetic fitness by optimal decision making. Thus proximate factors of immediate causation grade unto ultimate factors of selection and so obviate the sterile but persistent dichotomy of nature versus nurture. Finally, behavioral primatology is *comparative*, contrasting individuals, groups, populations, and species. The extent to which this approach applies usefully to the behavior of human primates remains to be seen. It will likely prove to be a utilitarian matter: If human ethology "works," it will take its place alongside the more traditional methods and approaches of the other human sciences (Eibl-Eibesfeldt 1989).

Behavioral primatology has always been at the interface of the natural and social sciences: Japanese macaques inventing and disseminating techniques of processing food, such as sweet-potato-washing (Itani 1958), are in every introductory textbook. Harlow's (1971) devastating experiments on the long-lasting effects of social deprivation on monkeys emphasized the fragility of basic processes underpinning reproductive success. Marmosets and tamarins in South American forests practice familial division of labor that is both flexible (monogamy or polygamy) and complex (communal child rearing) (Goldizen 1989). Finally, field studies of African apes, most notably Jane Goodall's (1986) research on wild chimpanzees in the Gombe National Park, Tanzania, have changed our conception of ourselves as a species.

The latter point is sufficiently grandiose and provocative to require elaboration. Before Goodall's work began in 1960, human nature was clearly enough demarcated that people were able to say that of all the living species, only human beings thought rationally, made tools, uttered words, murdered enemies, recognized kin, practiced medicine, attributed intentions, and conceived of themselves. All of these defining traits of humanity are now known or strongly suggested in at least our sibling species, the African great apes, if not in our most distant cousins, the monkeys. Unlike the anecdotal speculations of past anthropomorphism, there is empirical evidence for each of these traits, often gathered with technological aids such as controlled playback of high-quality recordings to test the meaning of vocalizations (Cheney and Seyfarth 1990).

Each finding that narrows the phylogenetic gap between human and nonhuman primates adds flesh to the bones of reconstructuring hominid evolution (McGrew 1992). Scenarios of hominization can now be more firmly anchored: meat-eating chimpanzees are both predators and scavengers, but without flaked stone tools. They show sex differences in diet that presage female gathering and male hunting, but lack the reciprocal exchange of the products of these labors, which may depend on gender differentiation. Wild chimpanzees ingest medicinal plants, but do not administer them to others (Wrangham and Nishida 1983). Cooperating males may cold-bloodedly kill counterparts from a neighboring

Table 8.1
Laterality of Hand Function in Terms of Tasks and Subjects

		SUBJECT(S)	
		WITHIN	ACROSS
TASK(S)	WITHIN	Hand preference	Task Specialization?
	ACROSS	Manual Specialization?	Handedness

community, but rarely kill members of their own community, unless cuckoldry is suspected.

Referential modeling that bases extinct hominids on living hominoids has its pitfalls (as, after all, chimpanzees are not humans and never have been), but our present-day reconstructions of the extinct lives of our ancestors are far less fanciful and far more constrained than before, thanks to recent advances in behavioral primatology. To exemplify the usefulness as well as the shortcomings of the ethological approach to the behavior of human and nonhuman primates, we turn to a cast study.

LATERALITY

Laterality of function is a basic feature of all bilaterally symmetrical organisms, including *Homo sapiens* (Ciba Foundation 1991). Its most obvious manifestation is in the differential use of the forelimbs, and this has long been linked with asymmetry of cerebral structure (Springer and Deutsch 1989). This congruence of structure and function is often linked to the evolution of humankind's most distinctive and also lateralized trait, language (Corballis 1991). At the same time, the symbolic significance of left versus right in human culture is manifest, for example, when Westerners clasp and shake their right hands in greeting (Needham 1973). Thus handedness is an appropriate focus for ethological analysis, and this generates two general topics: *species-specificity* or uniqueness, and *species-typicality* or universality. We will target each of these in turn, emphasizing methodological strengths and weaknesses and proposing new knowledge needed to fill existing gaps.

A useful way to visualize the logical possibilities for species is to generate a 2 x 2 matrix, using the extent to which hand use varies within and across task(s) and within and across subject(s) (see table 8.1). The two extreme, or homogenous, conditions are straightforward. If the same hand predominates over most subjects in a population or culture or species and over most tasks performed, then *handedness* is proven. If hand predominance is shown only for individual subjects on one task, then it is *hand preference.* The two heterogenous conditions are more problematical. Consistency across subjects but within one task usually is also called handedness, but might be better termed *task specialization.* Finally, consistency across tasks within a subject is stronger than hand preference and so amounts to *manual specialization.* (Unfortunately, most of these terms have varying and sometimes contradictory meanings in the literature, cf. Fagot and Vauclair 1991, and usually only the first two are commonly used.)

Species Specificity

The received wisdom in textbooks is that handedness is unique to the human species, in contrast to all others (e.g., Springer and Deutsch 1989:251). Mice, cats, monkeys, apes, and other creatures may or may not show individual hand preferences or (more rarely) manual specialization, but taken as a population or species they are thought to be evenly distributed between left- and right-preferent. Or, in any given study, any or all subjects may be ambipreferent. This random or 50/50 model for nonhumans at the population or species level is most forcefully associated, empirically and theoretically, with the late J. M. Warren (1980), who focused on other primates, especially rhesus monkeys.

This view was challenged in a provocative reevaluation of existing data by MacNeilage, Studdert-Kennedy, and Lindblom (1987), who revived interest in the issue of species-specificity. They claimed that handedness is widespread in primates, especially prosimians, and provided a ''postural origins theory'' to account for it (MacNeilage, Studdert-Kennedy, and Lindblom 1991). According to this rationale, primitive arboreal primates needed their right hands for postural support, and so their left hands became specialized for simple, visually guided reaching (see photograph 8.1). Their more terrestrial successors used their freed right hands for more complex object manipulation, and so right-handedness became habitual, especially for skilled tasks. Such assertions spurred further empirical investigation that strengthened the claim (MacNeilage, Studdert-Kennedy, and Lindblom 1988), so that recently it could be said that gorillas showed ''for the first time in primates, a significant human-like pattern consisting of a greater number of animals which preferred the right hand for *all acts*'' (MacNeilage, Studdert-Kennedy, and Lindblom 1991:344).

Who is right, Warren or MacNeilage? The most likely candidates for human-like handedness would seem to be our nearest living relations, the apes. We shared a common ancestor with the African great apes perhaps as recently as five million years ago, according to molecular anthropological evidence. The likelihood of laterality of hand function is enhanced by findings of the last twenty years that show asymmetry of brain structure (Falk 1987). In some cases, apparent handedness (in chest beating) and asymmetry (in cranial dimensions) have been shown in the same population, for example, the mountain gorillas of the Virunga Volcanoes of Rwanda (Schaller 1963; Groves and Humphrey 1973).

Marchant and McGrew (1991) carried out an exhaustive meta-analysis of

Photograph 8.1

A male chimpanzee holds on with three limbs while reaching for a fig with his left hand.
(*Photograph by W. C. McGrew*)

Table 8.2
Variables for Analysis of Laterality of Function

Variable	Definition
Function	Bilaterally symmetrical organs noted, e.g. hands
Context	Captivity or wild
Sample	Number of subjects in study
Age	Age of subjects
Task	Induced or spontaneous
Number	Number of tasks in study
Trials	Number of trials per subject per task
Complexity	Degree of difficulty or intellectual demand

Source: From Marchant and McGrew 1991.

laterality of function in apes, focusing on methods used. We coded fifty-eight published sources on eight variables: function, context, sample, age, task, number, trials, and complexity (see table 8.2). We found that most studies focused on hands rather than other organs, captive rather than wild subjects, small rather than large samples of subjects, youngsters rather than adults, spontaneous rather than induced measures, few rather than many tasks and trials, and simple rather than complex tasks. Such are the gaps in the literature published to date that in only a few studies have hand preference and task specialization been tested, and in no studies have handedness and manual socialization been adequately addressed (see photographs 8.2 and 8.3). Thus the typical study for assessing laterality was done in captivity with a small number of young chimpanzees, and the usual task was one-handed, nonsequential, and gross in movement.

For MacNeilage, Studdert-Kennedy, and Lindblom's (1991) best candidate, *Gorilla gorilla*, the picture is equally unclear from twenty-two studies of a total of 227 subjects (McGrew and Marchant 1992). If one chooses to focus on the most right-sided (''best right'') results from the array of measures, then gorillas look to be right-handed, but focus on the ''best left'' results make them out to be left-handed. Inclusion of all measures from all studies show gorillas to be unlateralized for hand use.

In summary, nothing can yet be said confidently about the species-specificity of human handedness. Tentative conclusions suggest strong hand preferences and weak task specialization in other primates, at least for tool-use tasks in chimpanzees, but no compelling signs of manual specialization or handedness.

Photograph 8.2

Two chimpanzees engage in a grooming handclasp with right hands while grooming each other's underarms with left hands. (*Photograph by C. Tutin*)

Photograph 8.3

Four chimpanzees fish for driver ants; each inserts a fishing wand into the ants' nest, using one hand. (*Photo by D. Bygott*)

Table 8.3
Primary Ethnography on Proportion of Left- and Right-Handers across Cultures

Culture	N	% Left	% Right	Reference
Katanga, Zaire	1047	0.5	99.5	Verhaegen and Ntumba 1964
Solomon Islands	1352	2.8	97.2	Rhoads and Damon 1973
Temne, Sierra Leone	204	3.4	96.6	Dawson 1972
Sweden	981	5.4	94.6	Beckman and Elston 1962
Jimi, Western Highlands Papua New Guinea	180	8.8	91.1	Connolly and Bishop 1992
Berkeley, California, USA	7688	9.6	90.4	Hardyck et al. 1975
Kyoto, Japan	16,947	11.5	88.5	Komai and Fukuoka 1934
Kwakiutl, British Columbia, Canada	180	22.8	77.2	Marrion 1986

Species-Typicality

Laterality of hand function would be species-typical if we found universal patterns across all or most human populations or cultures. (These need not be the same, insofar as biological anthropologists tend to think of the species divided into populations, while sociocultural anthropologists divide it into cultures.) Thus we might ask if the Yanomami are as predominantly right-handed as the Hadza, or if New Yorkers are as right-handed as Djakartans. In wider comparative exercises, two or more species may be contrasted: are gorillas more right-handed than chimpanzees?

Textbooks make clear the answer: human beings are right-handed. Buchanan (1862) felt able to state qualitatively that all nations, races, and tribes prefer to use the right hand rather than the left. However, quantitative generalizations of extent vary considerably: McManus (1991:251) put the proportion of left-handers at 8 percent, Springer and Deutsch (1989:151) estimated it at 10 percent, and Corballis (1991:90) had it topping out at 12 to 13 percent. All of these pronouncements turn out to be wrong when reference is made to the primary ethnography from whence the original data came.

Table 8.3 lists a selected sample of human populations or cultures for which primary data are published. The actual extent of left-hand use varies from almost nil (5 of 1,047 subjects in Katanga) to up to 22 percent for the Kwakiutl. (Figures of up to 30 percent left-handedness are reported in secondary sources, e.g., Wile 1934). The number of subjects tested varies almost a hundredfold, from 180 New Guinean highlanders to almost 17,000 Japanese schoolchildren, and the studies span almost sixty years. Even this limited sample suggests that the variation cannot be explained simply as a function of geography, as the Amer-

Table 8.4
Methods and Subjects of Studies of Handedness across Cultures

Culture	No. of Measures	Age of Subjects	Type of Measure[a]	Measure(s) Used
Katanga	3	children	IT	Erase, scissors, unscrew
Solomon	1	all ages	IT	Trace with brush
Temne	3	adults	IT	Write, scissors, receive object
Sweden	?	?	?	?
New Guinea	9	children adults	IT	Pencil, scissors, hammer, blocks, thread, throw, spoon, match, deal
Berkeley	3	children	IT	Write, scissors, held
Japan	6	children	SR	Write, scissors, pen knife, throw, chop-sticks, match
Kwakiutl	2	all ages	SR,IT	Write

[a]IT = induced task, SR = self report

ican figure is closer to the New Guinean one than to the Canadian one. Nor are the differences likely to be a reflection of schooling, as the First World Swedish figure is more like the Third World Sierra Leonean one than the First World Japanese one. Degree of left-handedness is not correlated with the size of the sample or with the recency of the research. These may be genuine cross-cultural or populational differences that disprove the hypothesized claims of species-typicality, or it may be that confounding factors will otherwise explain the diversity. Methodology is a prime suspect for the latter.

Table 8.4 presents data on selected aspects of methodology in research on human handedness from the same studies listed in table 8.3. First, few measures or tasks were used to assess hand use. The greatest number, nine, came from the most recent data, from New Guinea (and from the only study done by an ethologist, Kevin Connolly).

Second, most subjects were children tested at school. Laterality in the motor skills of immature subjects may not adequately represent the performance of all age grades in a population, especially adults. (However, there is no apparent correlation here between the age composition of subjects and the extent of left-handedness reported.) Furthermore, "forced" laterality, such as training children to write with their right hands, may bias their hand use, although this appears not to generalize to other activities. Teng et al. (1976) found that although children were drilled to write and to eat with their right hands, this did not transfer to other patterns, such as brushing their teeth.

Third, all but two of the studies relied upon induced demonstration of requested tasks, usually as part of a standardized protocol. Typically the tester would take each subject through a series of tasks, giving verbal instructions, and then score responses. (No studies reported the hand preference of the testers, but two controlled for the tester's hand use in administration [Connolly and Bishop 1992; Rhoads and Damon 1973].) Komai and Fukuoka (1934) used self-report in response to a questionnaire, but no study collected observational data on spontaneous hand use in everyday activities.

Fourth, the measures or tasks chosen were not a random sample of manual activity. All included use of a pencil or brush, usually in writing. Revealingly, in the Katangan study, after all of the children wrote their names with their right hands, some then erased them with their left. Unexpectedly, the second most frequent task was the use of scissors, a Western cutting tool of specialized function. (No study reported if the scissors used were biased or neutral in design with regard to handedness.) All studies in this limited sample used measures only of object manipulation, and other hand usage such as gesture or mannerism was ignored.

Any or all of these four factors present potential problems of validity of measures. All but one study, Connolly and Bishop 1992, also present problems of reliability, as they tested each subject only once.

In summary, the only safe generalization about species-typicality that can be made echoes the one put forward by Buchanan (1862), that all known human societies show right-hand predominance for task specialization. Handedness seems likely, but hand preference and manual specialization are largely unexplored. Recall that hand preference and manual specialization are within subjects and either within or across tasks. The published literature rarely provides any information about individuals' preferences. Thus, in contrast to what textbooks and other secondary sources assert, neither the uniqueness nor the universality of human handedness is yet proven.

Of primary importance is ethological study of human manual behavior in everyday life. Standard human ethological techniques (Eibl-Eibesfeldt 1989) should be brought to bear on the widest repertoire of such motor patterns, going beyond object manipulation to include both idiosyncratic and conventional communicatory gestures, mannerisms, habitual self-directed acts, and so on. Observations should take place in the full range of settings, from playground to workplace and in solitude or while socializing. Such research should encompass a wide array of cultures, focusing especially on traditional societies, particularly those in which Western educational practices have not yet been introduced. If a society is no longer available for direct observation, then cinematic archives should be explored. The implicit hierarchy of validity is that spontaneous acts are more useful than induced ones, and that induced ones are more useful than verbal self-report of acts.

Comparable research is needed on nonhuman species, especially apes. More field studies are wanted that cover the full array of manual behavior patterns. (Surprisingly, this has not yet been done for any species of primate.) However, studies of induced laterality of function in other species also need tighter experimental designs to clarify some of the apparent cross-species contrasts in performance. No study of nonhuman primates matches the methodological rigor of some of the human experimental psychological ones (Connolly and Bishop 1992; Seltzer, Forsythe, and Ward 1990). For example, many apes tested in captivity were human reared, and given the imitational capacities of our nearest relations, their lateralized performances might mimic their human models.

Finally, standardized methods of recording both induced and spontaneous hand use should be devised and implemented systematically for apes and humans. Not just differential preference of hands needs recording, but also variation in grips employed in skillfulness of techniques (Annett 1985). Solar battery rechargers, minicam video recorders, and hand-held computers make feasible even the most sophisticated technology of data recording under field conditions.

CONCLUSIONS

Ethological studies of primates in general, and of laterality of function in particular, exemplify a fruitful meeting point of anthropology and psychology. Neuropsychologists need the diversity of the ethnographic record just as much as sociocultural anthropologists need to know about the hardware of the brain. Whether the origins of laterality of function lie in the spatial skills of navigation, the motor skills of gestural (sign) language, or the cognitive division of labor of hemispheric asymmetry, all of these capacities are expressed as behavior and so are the province of ethology. Even the most ticklish problems of linguistic meaning in laterality, of the symbolic connotations of the sinister left versus the adroit right, are addressable in principle in nonhuman primates. Finally, the most challenging arena is that of palaeoethology, of reconstructing behavior from its products, as in archaeology, and mental process from its imprints, as in palaeontology. Both artifacts and endocasts are mute, but their laterality of form may speak to us from both sides.

NOTE

We thank Phillip Bock, Kevin Connolly, and Jeanette Ward for critical comments on the manuscript, although of course all responsibility for any errors remains with us; Cathie Francis and Fay Somerville for manuscript preparation; and David Bygott and Caroline Tutin for photographs.

REFERENCES

Annett, M. 1985. *Left, Right, Hand, and Brain: The Right Shift Theory*. London: Lawrence Erlbaum Associates.

Beckman, L., and R. Elston. 1962. Data on Bilateral Variation in Man: Handedness, Hand Clasping, and Arm Folding in Swedes. *Human Biology* 34:99–103.

Buchanan, A. 1862. Mechanical Theory of the Preponderance of the Right Hand over the Left; or, More Generally, of the Limbs of the Right Side over the Left Side of the Body. *Proceedings of the Philosophical Society of Glasgow* 5:142–67.

Cheney, D. L., and R. M. Seyfarth. 1990. *How Monkeys See the World*. University of Chicago Press.

Ciba Foundation. 1991. *Biological Asymmetry and Handedness*. Chichester: John Wiley and Sons.

Connolly, K. J., and D.V.M. Bishop. 1992. The Measurement of Handedness: A Cross-Cultural Comparison of Samples from England and Papua New Guinea. *Neuropsychologia* 30:13–26.

Corballis, M. C. 1991. *The Lopsided Ape*. New York: Oxford University Press.

Dawson, J.L.M. 1972. Temne-Arunta Hand-Eye Dominance and Cognitive Style. *International Journal of Psychology* 7:219–33.

Eibl-Eibesfeldt, I. 1989. *Human Ethology*. New York: Aldine de Gruyter.

Fagot, J., and J. Vauclair. 1991. Manual Laterality in Nonhuman Primates: A Distinction between Handedness and Manual Specialization. *Psychological Bulletin* 109:76–89.

Falk, D. 1987. Brain Lateralization in Primates and Its Evolution in Hominids. *Yearbook of Physical Anthropology* 30:107–25.

Goldizen, A. W. 1989. Social Relations in a Cooperatively Polyandrous Group of Tamarins (*Saguinus fuscicollis*). *Behavioral Ecology and Sociobiology* 24:79–80.

Goodall, J. 1986. *The Chimpanzees of Gombe*. Cambridge, MA: Belknap Press of Harvard University Press.

Groves, C. P., and N. K. Humphrey. 1973. Asymmetry in Gorilla Skulls: Evidence of Lateralised Brain Function? *Nature* 244:53–54.

Hardyck, C., R. Goldman, and L. Petrinovich. 1975. Handedness and Sex, Race, and Age. *Human Biology* 47:369–75.

Harlow, H. F. 1971. *Learning to Love*. New York: Ballantine Books.

Itani, J. 1958. On the Acquisition and Propagation of a New Food Habit in the Natural Group of the Japanese Monkey at Takasaki Yama. *Primates* 1:84–98.

Komai, T., and G. Fukuoka. 1934. A Study on the Frequency of Left-Handedness and Left-Footedness among Japanese School Children. *Human Biology* 6:33–42.

MacNielage, P. F., M. G. Studdert-Kennedy, and B. Lindblom. 1987. Primate Handedness Reconsidered. *Behavioral and Brain Sciences* 10:247–303.

———. 1988. Primate Handedness: A Foot in the Door. *Behavioral and Brain Sciences* 11:720–46.

———. 1991. Primate Handedness: The Other Theory, the Other Hand, and the Other Attitude. *Behavioral and Brain Sciences* 14:338–49.

Marchant, L. F., and W. C. McGrew. 1991. Laterality of Function in Apes: A Meta-Analysis of Methods. *Journal of Human Evolution* 21:425–38.

Marrion, L. V. 1986. Writing-Hand Differences in Kwakiutls and Caucasians. *Perceptual and Motor Skills* 62:760–62.

McGrew, W. C. 1992. *Chimpanzee Material Culture: Implications for Human Evolution*. Cambridge, Eng.: Cambridge University Press.

McGrew, W. C., and L. F. Marchant. 1993. Are Gorillas Right-Handed or Not? *Human Evolution* 8:17–23.

McManus, J. C. 1991. The Inheritance of Left-Handedness. *Ciba Foundation Symposium* 162:251–67.

Needham, R., ed. 1973. *Right and Left: Essays on Dual Symbolic Classification*. Chicago: University of Chicago Press.

Rhoads, J. G., and A. Damon. 1973. Some Genetic Traits in Soloman Island Populations. II. Hand Clasping, Arm Folding, and Handedness. *American Journal of Physical Anthropology* 39:179–83.

Schaller, G. B. 1963. *The Mountain Gorilla*. Chicago: University of Chicago Press.

Seltzer, C., C. Forsythe, and J. P. Ward. 1990. Multiple Measures of Motor Lateralization in Human Primates (*Homo sapiens*). *Journal of Comparative Psychology* 104:159–66.

Springer, S. P., and G. Deutsch. 1989. *Left Brain, Right Brain*. 3rd ed. New York: W. H. Freeman.

Teng, E. L., P.-H. Lee, K. Yang, and P. C. Chang. 1976. Handedness in a Chinese Population: Biological, Social, and Pathological Factors. *Science* 192:1148–50.

Verhaegen, P., and A. Ntumba. 1964. Note on the Frequency of Left-Handedness in African Children. *Journal of Educational Psychology* 55:89–90.

Warren, J. M. 1980. Handedness and Laterality in Human and Other Animals. *Physiological Psychology* 8:351–59.

Wile, I. S. 1934. *Handedness: Right and Left.* Boston: Lothrop, Lee and Shepard.

Wrangham, R. W., and T. Nishida. 1983. *Aspilla* spp. Leaves: A Puzzle in the Feeding Behavior of Wild Chimpanzees. *Primates* 24:276–82.

CHAPTER NINE

RETHINKING DEVELOPMENT

Susan Oyama

Certain features of human populations appear reliably in successive generations. It is customary to attribute this to two kinds of "transmission": bodies and "biologically based" aspects of the mind are transmitted in the genes, while culture is perpetuated by learning, typically by language and imitation (see Barnouw 1985:5, for instance). In this framework of dual transmission (one channel for nature and another for nurture), psychology holds an ambiguous position. To biologists, "psychology" usually signals the impact of experience and so is associated with the variable, contingent outer world. For the social sciences and humanities, however, the psychological is often identified with universal, internal mechanisms. To some extent this is also true of the concept of development itself. Schneiderman (1979:215), for instance, said that a "nativist" approach to morality would emphasize ontogenetic sequences, unlike an approach that considers "internalized, culturally-patterned" ways of responding. Ontogeny is thus associated with the universal rather than the variable.

These are gross generalizations, of course, for at each level there are finer-grained distinctions between internal and external formation, so that aspects of the body are "acquired" (suntans, muscles built up by exercise), whereas aspects of culture may be innate or "phylogenetically derived" (the universal grammar of formal linguistics or the biologically natural political systems of sociobiology, as in Masters 1986; Peterson and Somit 1978; Wilson 1978:190; see also Tiger and Fox 1971 on war, hierarchy, and male dominance, and my critique, Oyama 1991b). In recent years, dichotomies have become almost universally condemned, having been replaced by compromise formulations in which nature and nurture "combine" or "interact" (behavior is partly biological and partly cultural, or biology defines potential while the environment acts within these constraints). If, however, there are problems with the very concepts of nature and nurture (and thus a need for new formulations), little is gained by declaring that both are important. Such compromises retain the belief that some things develop (largely) under genetic control and others are formed (largely) from without (Oyama 1985, 1989).

Nature-nurture distinctions seem to require an integrating discipline to bring biology and culture together. Yet the same distinctions prevent psychology, the obvious candidate, from fulfilling this role. I suggest that integration is possible only if the notions of biological and cultural transmission, which present similar problems for a satisfactory account of human life, are replaced by what I call a developmental systems perspective. Emphases on systemic relationships, mutual constraint and influence, and interactive construction offer the means to rethink development as well as other relationships between persons and their environments. Such an alternative approach would enable anthropologists to overcome the biology-culture divide, rather than being constrained by history, conceptual inertia, and disciplinary politics to maintain it.

CAUSES AND AGENTS

An important aspect of traditional conceptions of development is that they tend to erode our notions of human intentionality and agency. Genetic and cultural transmission are thought to shape, explain, or determine behavior. But if people are programmed by their genes and their societies, how do they ever act as persons?

It is difficult to integrate science's language of causes with the humanities' language of intentions and accountability (Oyama 1991a, in press). Even though they allow compromises of the sort mentioned earlier, nature-nurture distinctions are antithetical to productive thinking about action. Competing determinisms and imperialistic moves prompt one to ask which kind of cause is more important in producing an outcome. One need only think of early cultural anthropologists' challenges to eugenicists' and racists' appeals to biology in order to see how tempting it is to counter one prime factor with another. Agency fades into the background in such stories of contending determinants, because the language of transmission neglects the active role of the person. Spiro (1984:323) distinguished between the individual construction of private experience and the social transmission of culture, but even imitation is an active process to which the actor's beliefs and feelings about model and setting are relevant; and students of language acquisition have long pointed out that we need considerable mastery of a tongue in order to imitate an utterance in it. Beliefs and values that are common to a culture must still be developmentally constructed in each lifetime, and they both change with time.

HOMUNCULOID GENES

In the usual accounts of development, genes are treated as autonomous sources of organizing power, repositories of an evolutionary legacy of information, or programs that are supposed to control the unfolding of the "biological bases" on which culture is superimposed. What goes largely unnoticed is that this conception is covertly intentional, though computer metaphors encourage the feeling that one is being properly hardheaded. The genes are thought to plan and execute astounding feats of biological engineering, manipulating raw materials and making organisms out of them, even guiding those organisms' behavior. An ironic consequence of this is that as the homunculoid gene increases in intelligence and power, the organism becomes inert—made, pushed, and pulled by its genes.

Theorists from both the biological and cultural camps, of course, tend to eskew naked determinism, acknowledging all manner of "other factors." I would argue, though, that including more factors in an unsatisfactory framework hardly corrects the framework itself. An example is Scarr and McCartney's behavior-genetic view of development. These authors acknowledged that environmental factors are necessary, but reserved primary power for the genes, claiming that "genotypes are the driving force behind development," determining which environments an individual experiences or chooses (1983:424, 428). Part of their point seems to be that people have varying preferences and ways of responding. This is certainly true, though nothing is explained by replacing people by their DNA. An experience, they continued, cannot itself give rise to a new adaptation (p. 425). True again. What they missed is the necessary counterpart to this claim and the implications that follow: that the genes alone cannot give rise to anything, either; that development requires that genes be embedded in a living organism, itself moving through a set of changing environments; and that no element alone can be considered determining (or, as they said of the genotype, "*conceptually prior* to both phenotype and the rearing environment," p. 425). The need to include nongenetic factors in their account led them to use an interactionist vocabulary of sorts, but their commitment to the gene as prime mover required them to subvert that vocabulary with stories of insides dominating outsides.

Giving genes priority over phenotypes and environments is a bit like saying that persons are conceptually prior to cultures. It is therefore ironic that Shweder (1990), who spoke of the interdependence and reciprocal constitution of persons and their worlds, used Scarr and McCartney's scheme of gene-environment relations in discussing interactions between individuals and their environments. To be sure, he said that the scheme can be dissociated from behavior genetics by referring to persons instead of genotypes, but I believe that there are better ways of making good on his vision of interdefining persons and worlds. One problem is that Scarr and McCartney have already accomplished a kind of dissociation by confusing the genotype with the phenotype. It is this confusion that allowed them to give the genotype the power to select experiences, when it is obviously people who experience, choose, and act.

Genes interact selectively with the chemical environments that regulate their functioning. Here, as at higher levels, selection is reciprocal, and outcomes cannot be attributed more to one interactant than another. A bit of DNA does not interact equally with all surrounding molecules or under all conditions, and the same may be said of other participants in a biochemical interaction—an enzyme, for example, does not facilitate all reactions. If one insists on giving selective power to only some interactants, or on allocating causal responsibility for outcomes, one cannot give more than lip service to interactionism; it is common to criticize dichotomous thinking without being willing fully to give it up (Johnston 1987; Lehrman 1970).

By insisting that genes have the ultimate determining power in development, Scarr and McCartney used an "imperial premise" similar to the one Shweder (1990:15) found in some psychological anthropology, that the sociocultural world is shaped by the abstract "central processing mechanism" of human cognition. In this case, it is genetic, not psychological, imperialism (Oyama 1989, 1992a).

CONSTRUCTING MEANING

The preoccupation with insides organizing outsides is not best combatted with outside-in stories, which is the cultural or social determinist move, in which collectivities are given a quasi-intentional ability to mold and control their members. As pointed out earlier, these competing determinisms threaten to render the person passive. Because the genes are associated with fixity and inevitability, whereas environmental influences connote malleability, it may be easier to see how biological arguments usurp human agency than to see how psychological or social science accounts can do so. However, many attempts have been made in anthropology, sociology, and social psychology to show how individual behavior is controlled by reified social forces, collective representations, and the like, acting on persons from the outside or being "internalized" (Giddens 1987; Jahoda 1982). Sampson (1991:29–30, 48), for instance, spoke of the "social world that creates the various programs that people learn" and said that cognitive processes are organized by the social environment, not by individual minds. Minds exist only in and through social worlds; however, the converse is also true, and cognitive processes must be organized in the organism-environment and intraorganismic exchanges of development. In these exchanges, organization is not imposed by one element on another, but rather arises in interactive processes.

As noted earlier, theories emphasizing social determinants have often arisen in opposition to biological or psychological determinism. The developmental systems approach is perhaps better known for its critique of biological determinism than of environmentalism, but it rejects both and for the same reasons. Shweder (1990:21) claimed that as anthropologists sought to show the primacy of the sociocultural environment over individual psychology, persons disappeared from ethnography. The difficulty is not just that both determinisms focus primarily on one set of factors, neglecting others. If it were this simple, the "both are important" style of ecumenism would be an adequate corrective. Rather, the causal privileging of one set of factors ensures that others become secondary—supportive but not formative, or accounting only for minor variation. This in turn depends on seldom-articulated assumptions about "information": that it has independent existence in particular loci or causal entities, such as genes and environments, and that it can be "transmitted" to developing organisms. Hence the persistence of dual-channel notions of ontogeny, despite many declarations that the nature-nurture dichotomy is dead. The organism becomes little more than a conduit for "information" (Oyama 1989).

A different approach is seen in a relatively recent discourse analysis of moral reasoning (Shweder and Much 1991). The controversy over cognitive versus emotive views of morality mentioned by these authors is a version of the objective-subjective, outside-inside dichotomies that appear repeatedly in the present discussion, and it is related to the mind-body dualism implicated in most nature-nurture oppositions (Oyama 1991a, in press). According to Stein (1979), the opposition between emotion and intellect comes from the "anthropological and psychological distinction between nature and culture." Bock (1988:195) called for the synthesis of cognition and emotion in psychological anthropology; such a synthesis follows quite readily from the reciprocal relationship between organism and stimulus in developmental systems.

Shweder and Much found a systems approach useful in overcoming these dualities. In what follows, I use certain aspects of their analysis to demonstrate what seems to me a striking kinship with the developmental systems perspective. The problems with dichotomous or reductive explanation are general ones, and similar responses, it appears, are being articulated by workers from quite different backgrounds. When Shweder and Much said, for instance, that "ordinary talk means far more than it says" (1991:196), they were emphasizing the importance of context, of shared assumptions, of implication: in short, all the things that are needed to make sense of an utterance. (For a thoughtful exploration of talk in ethnographic interviews, see Briggs 1986:12, who described contexts as interactively constructed. In this way and in others, his treatment is very congenial to the one sketched here.) Though propositions are credited with transmitting cultural meaning (Spiro 1984:323), just as genes are credited with carrying developmental meaning, nothing can be "transmitted" at all without a richly elaborated structure.

Within such a structure, a message can take on meaning, semantic or developmental. If the rest of a system is stable, a gene may be "for" a given trait, that is, predictably associated with it under defined circumstances. If the complex of interacting influences is different, however, the gene may be "for" something else or may have no reliable correlate at all. In no case is the result preformed or prefigured in the DNA. The effect of any internal or external influence depends on the larger system, and the system's next state depends on those influences.

Shweder and Much expanded the text of an ethnographic interview beyond the customary transcript to show what, besides the utterance itself, must be taken into account if one is to understand what is said. Similarly, a developmental systems theorist expands a developmental story to include all the nested contexts within which a snippet of DNA or an environmental event may have an ontogenetic impact. Meanings, like other developmental outcomes, are context-sensitive and constructed in interaction, and contexts are constitutive, not just supportive (Oyama 1992b). If a meaning appears to be "transmitted," it is because the requisite processes are reliably associated, so that similar outcomes are constructed again and again: I say "psychological anthropology" and you understand what I intend (or, as is more likely, your history will be different from mine in ways that will make it hard for you to "receive" what I "transmit"). The information-theoretic language assumes reliable processes; it does not explain them (Oyama 1992a).

A second point made in Shweder and Much's analysis of moral talk is that the person receiving a message must already know a great deal in order to make adequate inferences (1991:197). Similarly, an organism must have had a certain kind of developmental history for any event, internal or external, to have a particular effect. (Exceptions are things like being run over by a truck, though one can readily think of exceptions to this exception; it takes more to disable or kill some individuals than others.) It is easy to ignore such histories if they are extremely common, but they are indispensable nevertheless. A person's present state, including emotional state, is the embodiment of past experiences as well as concurrent ones, and this state enters importantly into present encounters with the world.

The third main lesson follows from the first two: "the relevant unit of analysis is the entire communicative array," including the utterance, the context, and the prior knowledge of the participants in "a mutually constraining relationship" (Shweder and Much 1991:198). This is in accord with the developmental systems claim that one must investigate organism-environment complexes to understand development and behavior. Neither "inside" nor "outside" is specifiable independently of the other.

THE DEVELOPMENTAL SYSTEMS PERSPECTIVE

These communicative systems are not just like developmental systems, they are a type of developmental system. That is, the construction of moral and other meanings is an important aspect of human development. Though the language of transmission makes the process seem simple, linear, and automatic, the simplicity is illusory. The developmental systems perspective offers an alternative to oppositions like biology and culture, genes and environment, or physical and mental. Dual-transmission metaphors and their associated developmental dualism (maturation driven from the inside and experience shaped from the outside) can be replaced by progressive construction in systems of interdependent influences. Developmental "information" is not supplied either by genes or environment, but is generated in interaction. If information is a difference that makes a difference (Bateson 1972:315; Oyama 1985:3, 43–44), then it does not reside in particular locations, but is our way of marking a result: an interaction has made a difference for an entity or process (by influencing or informing it). Information always implies a point of view, because it is only in a particular frame of reference that such a difference may be marked.

What kind of difference is made depends on the interactants and their relations, that is, on the configuration of the system as a whole. A gene has one effect in one cell, another in a second, and no effect in a third. The characteristics of the cell, in turn, can depend on its location in the organism and on the organism's developmental and motivational state, which reflects that organism's history and immediate surroundings. The nested developmental systems that give rise to an organism include the cell and its constituents, including the DNA. They also include the environment of that cell, larger-scale physiological interactions, and relations between the organism and its animate and inanimate surround. Phenomena at one scale can influence phenomena at other scales; social interactions may alter hormonal and neurotransmitter levels, for instance. These systems include all the myriad factors that can influence development, and they may be studied at a variety of scales.

Similarly, a spoken command or question may have a specific meaning to one person and a different one to another, or to the same person in a different situation. In each case, the listener and the speaker, engaged in a particular relationship under particular circumstances, determine what, if anything, the command means (and they need not agree). Meaning, then, does not exist in the words or in the listener's head. Nor does it live in the situation, independently of the people in it. It is interactively constructed, and the context is as much a part of this process as the people are. Agency is part of this picture, though it is an agency of causally embedded creatures, not of beings that somehow act from outside the causal stream, as some ideas of free will require (Oyama in press). Persons reciprocally constitute and are constituted by their worlds, and it is persons, with their unique histories, who select, construe, and act in these worlds, rather than their genes, their personality traits, or their internalized cultures.

One can provisionally draw a boundary in any of these systems, creating an inside and outside for the sake of an analysis, even though there are always other ways to draw the line and the territories on either side are interdefined. In like manner, the analyst can treat one factor as a cause and another as an effect, even though the causal story can be told in a variety of ways and even though causes are themselves subject to other influences. When one views the system as a whole, one does not find discrete causes and effects but ongoing dynamic processes. Nature and nurture, in fact, can be reformulated to eliminate the causal opposition: natures result from the developmental construction we call nurture—they are concretely phenotypic, rather than being occult and abstract, somehow encoded in the DNA. Natures are thus multiple (even organisms with the same genotype are phenotypically different and so have different ''natures'') and mutable (''natures'' change with time). This unifying perspective could aid in rethinking some of the problematic assumptions that have been so influential in psychological anthropology.

TWO CRITIQUES: RETHINKING ASSUMPTIONS

That there are concerns about these matters in anthropology is evidenced by two overlapping critiques, one of psychological anthropology as a whole and the other of the Culture and Personality tradition. In them, Philip Bock and Richard Shweder raised a variety of questions about the reigning assumptions in these fields, which themselves overlap. Insofar as they have identified issues of general concern, they confirm my sense that the problems I have detailed in biology and psychology are also prevalent in anthropology. Bock's (1988) discussion centered on (1) developmental continuity, (2) uniformity of personality within cultures, (3) personality as a cause of institutions, (4) the validity of projective tests, and (5) the possibility of studying other cultures objectively. Shweder's (1979) list included (1) childhood origins of the adult psyche, (2) global personality and cultural traits, (3) individual-difference models of cultural differences, and (4) explanation of learning and evolution by consequences.

I cannot, obviously, treat these critiques exhaustively, but it seems fair to say that all the points turn on aspects of the problems I have been discussing in development, adaptation, and cognition: the relationship between insides and outsides in complex processes (Oyama 1992b). The first three points in each list (I have rearranged items to facilitate comparison) concern personality. They refer to the difficulty of conceptualizing the relationship between the behavioral differences that we tend to attribute to persons and the cross-cultural ones we attribute to cultures themselves. (A calm Japanese and a volatile one are said to have different personalities, but a calm Japanese and a volatile Italian may instead be said to differ because they come from different cultures.)

Is the ''external'' world of culture generated by the ''internal'' reality of personality? Is it the other way around? Shweder's questions about shaping by consequences are also about organism-environment relationships. Do environments have characteristics and requirements that can be specified independently of the organisms that are reinforced (in learning) or selected (in evolution) by them? Bock's doubts about projective tests and anthropological objectivity, finally, focused on inside-outside boundaries in the cognitive processes of the informant and the anthropologist. Are people's psyches projected into the world in such a way that their reports of their perceptions can be treated as revelations of their inner lives? While many scientists assume that perception and knowledge are ''subjective'' in this sense, they tend to exempt themselves, believing that they can obtain knowledge that is uncontaminated by such subjectivity.

Only if this is true can anthropologists describe other cultures from a neutral, objective standpoint.

Personalities and Cultures

These questions about development, adaptation, and cognition reflect some rather broad changes in a variety of fields. The reconceptualizations I have advocated, in fact, are at least partially implied in the two critiques cited earlier, even though my work has grown more out of biology and psychology than anthropology. It is possible to take a more dynamic, systemic view of persons and their cultures (Valsiner in press). First, the assumptions that personality is formed early and remains stable throughout life can be questioned. If development is a continuous process, and phenotypic stability depends to some degree on environmental stability, the patterns of thought, feeling, and behavior we call personality may change over time.

Personality here is construed not as internal forces (as in Barnouw 1985:8) but as a pattern of relations with one's surroundings, especially relations with other people, but with other organisms and objects as well. As such, it would be interpreted from the developmental systems point of view as a joint product of the person and the immediate situation. These are not definable independently, however, since the "situation" responded to is the one the person experiences and interprets and is thus a partial function of that person's state and history, and the response is a partial function of the situation.

Commenting on his own critique over a decade later, in fact, Shweder (1991: 364 n.1) remarked that it does not now seem useful to think in terms of autonomous internal dispositions. Rather than attributing regularities to either personality or culture, we can follow Bock (1988:43) in explicitly acknowledging the relativity of our conclusions to the questions being asked and to the explanatory framework chosen. In explaining behavior by looking at some event peculiar to an individual life, we are likely to speak of personality, because personalities imply individual variation, whereas cultural explanation often emphasizes factors common to a group. In taking one or the other point of view, however, we are not discovering phenomena that exist either inside or outside of persons (recall the earlier discussion of research on developmental systems). What changes is the question asked and the background against which the comparison is made. When we wonder, then, whether Jean is more fearful than her friend Joan because Jean grew up in a violent household, we try to imagine Jean with a different family, but within the same broader cultural and historical context. In comparing cultures, however, differences within each one are less salient, because within-culture similarities are more useful in highlighting the differences between the larger aggregates. This is very similar to the investigatory world of the experimentalist, where what is treated as an independent variable in one study may be controlled or treated as error in another.

Shaping by Consequences

In questioning scientists' habit of invoking the shaping power of consequences to explain behavioral or evolutionary changes (operant reinforcement, natural selection), Shweder (1979) raised doubts about the wisdom of considering environments independently of organisms. If organisms and their environments select, shape, and define each other over both ontogenetic and evolutionary time, then adaptational requirements must be assessed in relation to the adapting entities (Lewontin 1982; Midgley and Morris 1988). This is presumably one of the points Scarr and McCartney (1983) were trying to make, that situations are not simply imposed on organisms, ready-made. Instead, organisms are selective in their interactions, and two people in the same room may only apparently be in the same situation. (By extension, different cultures may exist in truly different worlds.) As we saw, however, these psychologists' ability to make their point was compromised by their allegiance to an explanatory system in which some causes must dominate others, and in which the selectivity that really counts is reserved for internal causes.

It is hardly accidental that behavior geneticists have long privileged insides to counter the environmentalist privileging of outsides (the shaping by consequences that Shweder objected to). To go further back in time, behaviorism and cultural anthropology were allies in the battle against various biological claims. Perhaps it is time to stop the pendulum.

Objectivity and Subjectivity

We may finally doubt the assumptions supporting anthropologists' use of projective tests. Such tests are thought to have cross-cultural validity if subjects reliably project their ''internal'' preoccupations on ''external'' stimuli and if these can be objectively interpreted (that is, without projections from the interpreter). But if cognition, like the other organism-environment relationships we have discussed, is jointly determined, perhaps these are not safe assumptions. (See Longino 1990 for a concept of objectivity that includes the observer's perspective.) Though individually variable characteristics may well be discernible in a person's responses to a projective test, there may not be a single decoding system that will allow us to decipher their meaning. Moreover, if we can reliably expect others' subjectivities to be present in their interpretations of stimuli, why should our own responses be different?

CONCLUSION: GENES, CULTURES, PERSONS

The person is an active participant in his or her own developmental construction and in the construction of meaning. The psychological anthropologist wishing to do justice to the complexity of cultural persons and their cultural worlds would do well to resist the forced choices that have long been required of students of behavior: emotion or reason, body or mind, personality or society, biology or culture, subjectivity or objectivity. These have informed anthropologists' constructions of similarity and difference in human life and are themselves badly in need of reconstruction.

One benefit of the developmental systems perspective is that it gives psychological anthropologists a way of acknowledging people's impact on their own development, including their acculturation, without falling into reductive arguments or the voluntarism of causally autonomous agents. Those who are dismayed by the disappearance of full persons from their theoretical schemes, who believe that it is people who act intentionally, not genes or cultures, but that such action is always embedded and constrained, and that possibilities and constraints change with the continuous interactions that constitute human life, may find in this perspective a way of integrating biology and culture. This requires, of course, a reconceptualization of both so that they are no longer attached to a framework that opposes them as the necessary to the contingent, the timeless to the historical, the deep to the superficial. But it seems to me that such rethinkings have been going on in anthropology for some time.

REFERENCES

Barnouw, V. 1985. *Culture and Personality*. 4th ed. Homewood, IL: Dorsey Press.

Bateson, G. 1972. *Steps to an Ecology of Mind*. New York: Ballantine Books.

Bock, P. K. 1988. *Rethinking Psychological Anthropology: Continuity and Change in the Study of Human Action*. New York: W. H. Freeman.

Briggs, C. L. 1986. *Learning How to Ask: A Sociolinguistic Appraisal of the Role of the Interview in Social Science Research*. Cambridge, Eng.: Cambridge University Press.

Giddens, A. 1987. *Social Theory and Modern Sociology*. Stanford, CA: Stanford University Press.

Jahoda, G. 1982. *Psychology and Anthropology: A Psychological Perspective*. London and New York: Academic Press.

Johnston, T. D. 1987. The Persistence of Dichotomies in the Study of Behavioral Development. *Developmental Review* 7:249–82.

Lehrman, D. S. 1970. Semantic and Conceptual Issues in the Nature-Nurture Problem. Pp. 17–52 in L. R. Aronson, E. Tobach, D. S. Lehrman, and J. S. Rosenblatt, eds., *Development and Evolution of Behavior*. San Francisco: W. H. Freeman.

Lewontin, R. C. 1982. Organism and Environment. Pp. 151–70 in H. C. Plotkin, ed., *Learning, Development, and Culture*. New York and London: Wiley.

Longino, H. 1990. *Science as Social Knowledge: Values and Objectivity in Scientific Inquiry*. Princeton: Princeton University Press.

Masters, R. D. 1986. Ostracism, Voice, and Exit: The Biology of Social Participation. *Ethology and Sociobiology* 7:379–95.

Midgley, B. D., and E. K. Morris. 1988. The Integrated Field: An Alternative to the Behavior-Analytic Conceptualization of Behavioral Units. *Psychological Record* 38:483–500.

Oyama, S. 1985. *The Ontogeny of Information: Developmental Systems and Evolution*. Cambridge, Eng.: Cambridge University Press.

———. 1989. Ontogeny and the Central Dogma: Do We Need the Concept of Genetic Programming in Order to Have an Evolutionary Perspective? Pp. 1–34 in M. R. Gunnar and E. Thelen, eds., *Systems and Development*. Minnesota Symposia on Child Psychology, vol. 22. Hillsdale, NJ: Erlbaum.

———. 1991a. Bodies and Minds: Dualism in Evolutionary Theory. *Journal of Social Issues* 47(3): 27–42.

———. 1991b. Essentialism, Women, and War: Protesting Too Much, Protesting Too Little. Pp. 64–76 in A. E. Hunter, ed., *Genes and Gender VI. On Peace, War, and Gender: A Challenge to Genetic Explanations*. New York: Feminist Press.

———. 1992a. Ontogeny and Phylogeny: A Case of Metarecapitulation? Pp. 211–39 in P. Griffiths, ed., *Trees of Life*. Dordrecht: Kluwer Academic Publishers.

———. 1992b. Pensare d'evoluzione: L'integrazione del contesto nell'ontogenesi, nella filogenesi, nella cognizione (Thinking about evolution: Integrating the context in ontogeny, phylogeny, and cognition). Pp. 47–60 in M. Ceruti, ed., *Evoluzione e cognizione: L'epistemologia genetica di Jean Piaget e le prospettive del construttivismo*. Bergamo: Lubrina Editore.

———. 1993. How Shall I Name Thee? The Construction of Natural Selves. *Theory and Psychology* 34.

Peterson, S. A., and A. Somit. 1978. Sociobiology and Politics. Pp. 449–61 in A. L. Caplan, ed., *The Sociobiology Debate*. New York: Harper and Row.

Sampson, E. E. 1991. *Social Worlds, Personal Lives*. San Diego: Harcourt Brace Jovanovich.

Scarr, S., and K. McCartney. 1983. How People Make Their Own Environments: A Theory of Genotype → Environment Effects. *Child Development* 54:424–35.

Schneiderman, L. 1979. Moral Judgment and Social Structure. *Journal of Psychological Anthropology* 2(2):213–33.

Shweder, R. A. 1979. Rethinking Culture and Personality Theory. Parts 1 and 2. *Ethos* 7:255–311.

———. 1990. Cultural Psychology—What Is It? Pp. 1–43 in J. W. Stigler, R. A. Shweder, and G. Herdt, eds., *Cultural Psychology: Essays on Comparative Human Development*. Cambridge, Eng.: Cambridge University Press.

Shweder, R. A., and N. Much. 1991. Determinations of Meaning: Discourse and Moral Socialization. Pp. 186–240 in *Thinking through Cultures: Expeditions in Cultural Psychology*. Cambridge, MA: Harvard University Press.

Spiro, M. E. 1984. Some Reflections on Cultural Determinism and Relativism with Special Reference to Emotion and Reason. Pp. 323–46 in R. A. Shweder and R. A. LeVine, eds., *Culture Theory: Essays on Mind, Self, and Emotion*. Cambridge, Eng.: Cambridge University Press.

Stein, H. F. 1979. Review of Family Therapy in Clinical Practice, by M. Bowen. *Journal of Psychological Anthropology* 2(2):235–43.

Tiger, L., and R. Fox. 1971. *The Imperial Animal*. New York: Holt, Rinehart and Winston.

Valsiner, J. In press. Culture and Human Development: A Co-Constructivist Perspective. In P. van Geert and L. Mos, eds., *Annals of Theoretical Psychology*, vol. 10. New York: Plenum Press.

Wilson, E. O. 1978. *On Human Nature*. Cambridge, MA: Harvard University Press.

CHAPTER TEN

THE EVIDENCE FROM DISCOURSE

Niko Besnier

In recent decades, scholars working in a variety of traditions of inquiry have made the relationship between discourse and its ethnographic context the object of their scrutiny. They argue that the complexity of this relationship and the problems associated with it must become an integral part of the focus of anthropology. These scholars show that meaning cannot be solely and unproblematically found in the content of talk; rather, meaning resides equally, if not more importantly, in the medium through which verbal communication takes place (e.g., discourse form, participant structure in interaction, linguistic ideology). This chapter is an overview of how "discourse-centered approaches" (Sherzer 1987) integrate a focus on cultural dynamics and categories of concern to psychological anthropology, on the one hand, and analytic attention to linguistic practices and their sociocultural context, on the other hand.

This survey is highly selective, being based on the premise that details on a handful of studies provide greater insight into approaches and methodologies than brief mentions of a large number of works. However, when relevant, I will provide references to survey articles with broader scope than this chapter. Furthermore, this chapter focuses principally on two areas of inquiry commonly identified as central topics for research in contemporary psychological anthropology, namely, emotion and personhood (cf. White 1992, 1993). The particular success that discourse-centered approaches have had in furthering our understanding of these two notions also motivates this choice of focus.

Traditionally, psychological anthropologists have relied heavily on language as an ethnographic tool and heuristic device. Responses to interview questions, talk produced in therapy and comparable contexts, and the structure of the lexicon and metaphors are examples of the type of data scholars concerned with psychological anthropological issues seek during field research. These data enable anthropologists to draw analytic inferences about the psychological world of their informants. For example, a central concern of Rosaldo's (1980) masterful ethnography of the Ilongot was to unravel the cultural significance of key emotion concepts in the lives of this Philippine people, such as *liget*, commonly glossed as "anger." In this task, Rosaldo emphasized the importance of context in understanding words and the concepts that they denote. She thus based her analysis on interpretations of a rich array of linguistic data (provided mostly in English translation), including Ilongot sayings, songs, metaphors, explanations of particular events, theoretical statements about emotion categories, and scripts for social actions that she elicited from her informants.

In a trenchant exegesis of Rosaldo's and other works in psychological anthropology and cultural psychology, Rosenberg (1990) demonstrated that the insistence that language be studied in context proclaimed in works such as Rosaldo's falls short of its goal. While emphasizing the cultural specificity of notions like personhood and emotionality, psychological anthropologists assume, paradoxically, that the meaning of discourse can be read off, translated, and paraphrased unproblematically across languages and speech communities. For example, when field researchers elicit from their informants responses to definitional questions (e.g., "What is *liget*?"), they only subject to analysis the glossing of terms. Left untouched are such questions as respondents' understanding of what a definition is, the nature of the discourse that provides an environment for the definition, and local conceptualization of the relationship between form and meaning. Yet the mapping of meaning onto form, to focus on only one problem, is conceptualized diversely in different cultures, being dependent on such culture-specific notions as the nature of intentionality and the role of language in social life (cf. Duranti 1988; Friedrich 1990; Rumsey 1990; Silverstein 1979; Stroud 1992). In practice, then, even language-oriented works in orthodox psychological anthropology narrowly focus on decontextualized language (e.g., the "meaning" of words) rather than contextualized language use.

At the other extreme, sociolinguistic approaches to language commonly fail to address issues of concern to psychological anthropologists by ignoring or even denying the possibility of discourse being related to culture. Research stemming from linguistic approaches to interaction typically seeks explanatory links between structural characteristics and such psychological processes as constraints on memory, the nature of processing mechanisms, and ease of acquisition (see Coulthard 1977; Stubbs 1983; and Van Dijk 1985 for overviews). Even works that focus on social aspects of interaction appeal uncritically to allegedly universal sociocognitive notions like "interpersonal involvement," which are taken to transcend situational, social, and cultural boundaries (cf. Besnier 1994 for a discussion of problems with such analytic categories). While the possibility that culture can "influence" the structure of discourse is sometimes recognized, it is commonly shown to affect only "superficial" and least significant features of discourse and is rarely seen as playing a mediating role in the construction of meaning. In short, the insignificant role accorded to culture in the structuring of discourse in these frameworks is symptomatic of the "cognitive bias" extant in general linguistics (Ochs 1979).

THE MEANING OF DISCOURSE FOR PSYCHOLOGICAL ANTHROPOLOGY

Discourse is one of the most commonly invoked and least frequently defined terms in contemporary scholarship (as discussed in Macdonnell 1986). The multiplicity of meanings variously attached to the term is partly the consequence of the large number of disciplines in the human sciences, social sciences, and humanities claiming the study of communication in its various guises as their area of expertise. While all definitions seem to agree that talk and writing reside at the center of discourse, they diverge dramatically over which aspects of talk and writing should constitute an object of study: at one extreme, "postmodern" theory, inspired principally by Foucault (1981), views discourse as the historically situated symbolic order that frames and sanctions certain types of social action and statements (Frank 1992); at the other extreme, sociolinguists understand "discourse analysis" as the microscopic investigation of the linguistic form of talk and writing beyond sentence level. However, that the various entities of concern to different disciplines are called by the same term is not a happenstance. Indeed, there is a compelling, if complex, connection between discourse as symbolic order and discourse as linguistic form, in that the two constantly inform one another and depend on one another's existence. In other words, linguistic practice, even in the most mundane of contexts, is always grounded in symbolic matrices for social action and cultural understanding; in return, these matrices are constantly informed by social practice (Bourdieu 1977b), linguistic practice in particular.

Neither orthodox Foucaultian nor narrowly sociolinguistic agendas are of compelling relevance to the concerns of psychological anthropologists. Of greater analytic value are approaches based on a hybrid (and somewhat vague) definition of discourse that consider as their object of inquiry the relationship between linguistic practices and the social and cultural world in which these practices emerge. While they do not constitute an integrated theory with a distinctive methodology (hence my use of the plural form "approaches"), works in this vein share a number of characteristics. First, from a methodological standpoint, they are based on painstakingly transcribed recordings of (often naturalistic) language in use, rather than translations or impressionistic paraphrases, but remain keenly aware of the interpretive nature of recording and transcribing (cf. Tedlock 1983). Second, they view meaning as created through the interaction of microscopic features of linguistic form, semantic content, and sociocultural context, rather than just form, as in the work of sociolinguists, or just content and context, as advocated by Grillo (1989:19), among others. Third, they view the interaction between discourse and context as dynamic, dialogic, and potentially problematic (Goodwin and Duranti 1992). Finally, they analyze linguistic action as one instance of social action and recognize that linguistic action shares numerous characteristics with other instances of social action (e.g., it can function as an instrument of power). What follows develops and illustrates these premises.

DISCOURSE IN SEMIOTIC PERSPECTIVE

Most of our understanding of the relationship between discourse and the psychological world derives from research that adopts, either overtly or tacitly, a semiotic perspective. The semiotic model developed by C. S. Pierce, which has proved most useful in the anthropological analysis of discourse, is based on a three-way classification of signs: symbols, arbitrarily and conventionally related to their referent; icons, which refer by physical resemblance; and indexes, whose relationship to that for which they stand is established by pointing, either physically or metaphorically. Of these three types, indexes are the most "slippery": not only does an index lack a specific meaning outside of a context, but, when embedded in a particular context, it commonly has many potential meanings. Furthermore, indexes usually work in conjunction with one another, so that their meaning is derived from the intersection of the possible meanings of each individual index.

The relationship between discourse and its sociocultural context is primarily indexical (Silverstein 1992), although it can also have iconic characteristics (Caton 1986; Irvine 1989; Urban 1988). For example, interactors rarely communicate emotional experience simply by naming emotion categories, an action that itself would have indexical characteristics and is thus more complex than usually assumed (as Crapanzano 1989 suggested); rather, they do so more opaquely, through such linguistic devices as word choice, syntactic structure, hesitations, tempo, and pitch, and through such interactive strategies as gestures and their alignment with talk (Goodwin 1981). Similarly, writing offers many comparable indexical tools, such as punctuation and writing material: the "same" message has widely divergent emotional qualities when it is printed on the page of a book published by a prestigious academic press and when it is spray-painted on a concrete wall (Street and Besnier 1994). The result is that any aspect of the structure of language and interaction can index emotion. Furthermore, a linguistic or interactional feature, such as particular intonational contours, the use of reported speech, or the strategic exploitation of vagueness and ambiguity, can index different emotions across different contexts, and, within the confines of a specific context, indexical relations are frequently ambiguous and open to negotiation and conflict (Besnier 1990).

In the light of such indeterminacy, what can a semiotic approach achieve? An illustration of the type of argument that such an approach can aim for is provided by Stroud's (1992) analysis of code switching in Gapun, Papua New Guinea. In multilingual communities, code switching obtains when speakers change languages in midtalk. There is a long tradition of inquiry into the meaning of code switching in sociolinguistics, which has sought to provide a symbolic and hence essentially nonequivocal meaning to every instance of code switching. This literature has attempted to establish that code switches can variously express solidarity, informality, or emotional involvement, among many other things. In this body of work, interdeterminacy of meaning is presented as a problem, which both analysts and interactors must strive to resolve. Through a microscopic analysis of code switching between Tok Pisin (Neo-Melanesian) and Taiap, the language of Gapun, in an oratorical performance, Stroud showed that each code switch can have a broad variety of meanings, and that the resulting ambiguity *is* the meaning of code switching in Gapun. It is thus necessary to speak of the "cultural" meaning of code switching, that is, meaning that is irreducible to a one-to-one relation, but instead consists of an indexical relationship between the form of interaction and a broader cultural context. Gapun villagers view the meaning of talk as polysemic and interactionally constructed: multiple layers of meaning and intentionality can "hide" under the surface of discourse, and their "retrieval" (often characterized by a great deal of uncertainty) can only take place through the collaboration of all participants. This linguistic ideology is in turn embedded in a cultural definition of the person as a complex composite of various facets, some of which are displayed in particular contexts while others remain hidden from the scrutiny of others. Code switching, which is very frequent in Gapun, is one of the many ways in which the cultural definition of personhood and concomitant categories (e.g., an egalitarian ideology, the nature of intentionality, and so on) are displayed, enacted, and reproduced in discourse.

THE CONSTITUTIVE RELATIONSHIP OF DISCOURSE AND ETHNOPSYCHOLOGY

Stroud's analysis illustrates several points. First, discourse and culture are constitutively related. This point may be paraphrased as follows: linguistic practices provide a locus in which culture is created, confirmed, and perhaps debated at the same time that they result from cultural order. Thus the relationship between discourse and context is best understood as an ongoing process of dialogic negotiation, one that Bauman and Briggs (1990) called "contextualization." Second, the way in which Gapun villagers map code switching and meaning highlights the indexical nature of the relationship between discourse and context: Gapun villagers themselves view meaning as indexically derived, and their linguistic ideology is indexically related to the way in which personhood is constructed in their culture. Last, the Gapun notion of personhood affects not simply the referential aspects of discourse (i.e., the "content" of what is said), but, more crucially, the form of discourse and its relationship to linguistic ideology.

The constitutive relationship between language use and personhood is most evident in social contexts in which personhood and identity play a particularly salient role. Examples of such contexts are greetings and other interaction-initiating moves (as well as farewells and closings, although these have not been subjected to the same detailed scrutiny). Generally speaking, at the beginning of an interaction, interlocutors need to align themselves metaphorically, or, to use Goffman's (1979) apt term, to establish the footing of the interaction. Footing is constituted by the way in which those facets of identity that interlocutors foreground fall into place. Thus greetings can be thought of as contexts in which interactors establish and negotiate their social identities. Caton's (1986) study of greetings in Highland Yemen provides a striking instantiation of this analysis. Caton compared the structure of greeting formulae across two Yemeni ethnic groups, the *sayyid*, reputed descendants of the Prophet, and the *gabīlī*, a "tribal" group. For both groups, piety and *ṣāraf*, usually translated as "honor," are important aspects of personhood; however, the *sayyid* value piety over *ṣāraf*, while for the tribesmen the latter encompasses the former. Caton found that these differing emphases are reflected in the structure of formulaic greeting exchanges. The *sayyid* greet one another in a soft voice, invoking God's name and echoing the greeting formulae uttered by their interlocutors with greater intensity; these features foreground humility and godliness, both manifestations of piety. In contrast, tribesmen exchange structurally symmetrical formulae in a forceful voice; the form of their greetings thus stresses interpersonal equality and assertiveness, qualities associated with *ṣāraf*. The discourse structure of greetings is determined by ideals of personhood among these two groups, but also reinforces these idealizations. The importance of the greeting as a locus for the definition and negotiation of personhood has been stressed in many other studies, such as Irvine's (1974) analysis of status negotiation in the Wolof greetings. In all of these works, the relationship between the social uses of language in everyday contexts and the cultural construction of personhood emerges as a fundamentally dialogic process.

This dialogic relationship is presumably learned early in infancy as part of the cultural equipment that children acquire through language socialization. But there are many contexts in the course of an individual's life that call for a transformation of some aspects of personhood, even in cultures that place a great deal of ideological emphasis on psychological continuity and constancy. For example, in middle-class American society, acknowledging that one has a drinking problem in the context of Alcoholics Anonymous (AA) meetings involves learning how to construct oneself as a new person, one who is overpowered by addiction (Erchak 1992:154–59). Again, the greeting is an important index of this new identity. At AA meetings, where members affirm the efficacy of the group's ideology by narrating their biographies, a peculiar routine precedes each testimony: the speaker gets up, declares being an alcoholic, and introduces himself or herself by first name, to which the audience responds with a loud and cheerful "Hi, X!" This seemingly simple formulaic routine in fact has complex meanings: at the very least, it establishes membership in the group (and thus has a shibboleth-like quality); the exclusive use of first names also indexes the emphasis that the group places on anonymity; and, perhaps most important, it foregrounds alcoholism as the central feature of the speaker's identity, in accordance with a major ideological tenet of AA. In other words, the structure of the routine enacts a very specific ideological agenda and constructs the person according to this agenda.

The pièce de résistance of AA meetings is the autobiographical narrative. Cain (1991) masterfully showed that a narrow range of topics and interpretations is allowed in these narratives; for example, when a novice speaker gives a "wrong" interpretation of a past event in his or her life, more experienced members subtly "correct" the "mistake" in a narrative of their own life story. In other words, becoming a member of AA means learning a particular way of structuring one's autobiography according to specific ideological principles. A fine-grained analysis of this process can shed light on the nature of these principles, on their grounding in the broader cultural context, and on how AA members (and Americans in general) understand personhood.

Stromberg's (1990, 1993) analysis of conversational narratives of religious conversions among American Evangelical Christians is another illustration of how discourse-centered psychological anthropology can unravel the complexities of the linkage between linguistic and psychological behavior. Focusing on autobiographical narratives of conversion experiences, Stromberg identified a number of recurrent themes, including the contextualization of conversion in times of moral and emotional ambivalence (e.g., conflicts between desire and duty, or body and soul). This ambivalence is not solved by conversion, but rather remains with the experiencer, who needs to resolve it repeatedly, and who uses the conversion narrative as an avenue for this resolution. Stromberg demonstrated how moral and emotional ambivalence is subtly indexed in narrative structure. For example, structural features of spoken discourse such as changes in voice quality occur at strategic points in the deployment of the narrative and index the speaker's stance vis-à-vis the narrated events.

Similar findings were reported in Hill (1989), a fine-grained analysis of weeping in a Mexicano (Nahuatl) woman's narrative of the injustices to which she had been subjected in the course of her life. In general, narratives constantly foreground and background different aspects of individuals' identities as they move across time, space, and social contexts, and narrators must negotiate between these various aspects. At the same time, narrators need to provide a connection between the various manifestations of their identities, particularly when they are the protagonist of their story, and they do so by distancing themselves from certain past identities, or by binding together different manifestations of their person. These negotiations take place at levels of meaning other than the referential or literal level. In the case that Hill analyzed, the speaker connected her various identities by skillfully coordinating weeping and narration; for example, she overlay changes in temporal frame (e.g., between past events and the context of narration, between various reported turns at speaking) with weeping, thus securing a sense of continuity across contexts and quoted speakers. In short, members of all societies and cultures are constantly involved in creating reality, particularly psychological aspects of reality, and discourse is centrally involved in this process. As a genre that decontextualizes the reality of one context and recontextualizes it in another, the narrative is singularly well suited for the discursive construction of reality (Bauman and Briggs 1990).

THE PARTICULARISM OF DISCOURSE-CENTERED APPROACHES

Discourse-centered research on psychological anthropological issues is most successful when it focuses on particular strips of social life, rather than on the social life of a group in general. Even in very small-scale societies, individuals are complex entities, whose makeups, behaviors, and experiences vary from one social sphere or activity to the next (Poole 1991). Thus, rather than seeking broad generalizations about personhood and emotions that are allegedly consistent across all social situations (an enterprise that tacitly presumes that the "other" leads a homogeneous, variation-free life), discourse-centered approaches focus on specific social events, particular practices, and other types of social arrangements and seek to understand how discourse is constitutive of participants' actions and experiences in these particular settings. (See the chapter by Janis Jenkins in part I.)

Areas of social life that have yielded particularly rich material are what can be loosely termed "transformations," that is, settings in which aspects of ethnopsychological processes and categories are foregrounded, defined, modified, or reproduced. The prototypical example of a transformative context is the Western-style therapeutic encounter (Labov and Fanshel 1977; Wodak 1986). In non-Western cultures, many situations are bracketed for similar purposes: analyses of the discourse of conflict resolution and mediation, for example, can provide the analyst rich insights into ethnotheories of person and emotion, and the articulation of these theories with social practice (Brenneis 1988; Briggs 1988; Grimshaw 1990; Watson-Gegeo and White 1990). Spirit possession and mediumship (cf. the chapter by Erika Bourguignon in this volume) are other examples of transformative contexts in which local notions of personhood are foregrounded in a particularly dramatic way; unfortunately, possession and mediumship have been subjected to very little discourse-centered research. Also of interest to discourse-centered psychological anthropology are social situations in which psychological categories and processes are foregrounded in more subtle ways. For example, an examination of the oratorical, argumentative, and persuasive discourse that takes place in political or legal contexts can illuminate local theories of intentionality and agency (e.g., Duranti 1990), among other things. Situations of interest to discourse-centered approaches also include the mundane happenings of everyday life in which ritualization is less obvious (although it is never absent, as Goffman demonstrated); these include contexts in which biographical narratives play an important role, such as gossip.

One aspect of social life that has lent itself to particularly successful discourse-centered analysis is socialization. Research in the emergent "language socialization" framework (e.g., Kulick 1992; Ochs 1988; Schieffelin 1990) has shown that the linguistic practices that children are exposed to and immersed in from early childhood play a pivotal role in their social development. For example, it is through the structure, content, and context of the utterances that caregivers address to them that children learn to think and feel in socially sanctioned ways and derive a sense of what society expects of them and of what they can expect in return. The relationship between language use and the "messages" that adults and children exchange about the role of the person in the sociocultural context is complex and easy to dismiss, as Bloch (1991) did, without a proper understanding of the nature of linguistic practice and its articulation with social action and culture. By focusing on the ontogeny of the categories that concern psychological anthropologists, language socialization research provides a better understanding of how emotionality and personhood are constituted through everyday discursive practices (cf. the chapter by Joan Miller in this volume).

In making sense of transformative contexts, discourse can be centralized in various ways. First, the ethnographer can arrive at a fine-grained analysis of the linguistic behavior that takes place during transformation and tease out an understanding of how this behavior reflects and constructs psychological processes. For example, the content and form of a spirit medium's utterances can provide important insights into the dynamics at play between the various voices copresent in the mediumship session. A second approach consists in examining verbal accounts of transformational situations, for example, in narratives or explanations that members of social groups generate either spontaneously or in interview situations. Discourse-centered approaches to these materials foreground the semiotic complexity of the relationship between verbal accounts, the events that these accounts purportedly represent, and the context in which accounts are produced, rather than simply viewing the account as the straightforward representation of a discourse-independent reality.

DISCOURSE, PSYCHOLOGICAL PROCESSES, AND SOCIAL FORMATIONS

Some of the more promising discourse-centered work in contemporary psychological anthropology has addressed the relationship between discursive, psychological, and social processes. This body of research recognizes that personhood, emotions, and related categories are embedded in social structures and political contexts from which they cannot be divorced. Hence the attributions of certain psychological characteristics to particular groups or individuals can place these groups and individuals on the social map and provide a justification for resulting patterns of social inequality. Certain emotions and general "demeanors" (in Goffman's terminology, presentations of self) can be given prestige, while others can be devalued; these evaluations can in turn give greater prestige to groups and individuals associated with valued emotions and demeanors at the expense of other groups (e.g., Hochschild 1983; Sennett and Cobb 1972). It is frequently through linguistic practice, the common locus of social legitimization and devaluation (cf. Bourdieu 1977a; Gal 1989), that psychological processes interact with social and political practice. For instance, among the Wolof of Senegal, members of the noble caste commonly display, particularly in social situations where rank is foregrounded, an emotional composure that contrasts sharply with the highly emotional communicative style of the low-ranking griots (Irvine 1990). In Wolof ideology, particularly as articulated by high-ranking individuals, these differences in presentation of self explain why the society is hierarchically structured. Even though rank manifests itself in many other ways, the Wolof view other manifestations as secondary and isolate emotionality and personhood as the primordial motivations for rank.

Ethnographic research on discourse and the politics of gender and emotion (reviewed in Gal 1991) illustrates how discourse-centered approaches can shed light on the interface of psychological and sociopolitical processes. For example, Briggs's (1992) analysis of Warao women's emotionally charged ritual wailing demonstrated how this genre affords women in this South American society a rare chance to present their perspective on the events that lead to the death of a mourned relative. The overtly stated purpose of wailing is to enable the wailer to express the sorrow and rage that the death occasioned. But wailing is unusual in being the only context in which women can claim a public voice in Warao society. In their wailed narratives, through strategic choices of kin terms and reported-speech constructions, for example, women often represent social relations and past events differently from the way men do in other contexts. These wailed accounts thus challenge received accounts and, at the same time, the legitimacy of men's versions of reality. Their effects can be far-reaching. Crucially, women employ a genre in which emotions play a central role to protest against and resist men's dominance. The emotions articulated in a particular performative genre, and the manner in which they are articulated, become intimately associated with counterhegemonic action in Warao culture, as well as in other cultures (e.g., Abu-Lughod 1986). In sum, by paying equal attention to microscopic aspects of social practice and to macroscopic processes at play in society and culture, discourse-centered approaches address the relationship between the various meanings of the term *discourse*.

Are the approaches I have described in this chapter appropriate to all cultural contexts? It is commonly recognized in anthropology (and, increasingly, in some subfields of psychology) that Western societies conceptualize person and emotions as bounded, cross-contextually consistent, and situated in the individual. This view is often contrasted with understandings attributed to most other cultures, in which these categories are context-bound and constructed in interaction (e.g., Geertz 1984; Heelas 1986; Markus and Kitayama 1991; Shweder and Bourne 1984). At first glance, discourse-centered approaches seem best suited to the study of cultures where the "psychological" is viewed in transactional terms if one holds the view that ethnographic analysis is most successful when it closely resembles local assumptions about the construction of the world (a stance that itself is open to debate). Indeed, if personhood and emotions are located (or at least constructed) in interaction, then it is to interaction and discourse that the investigator must look for an understanding of their nature and ontogeny. Presumably, in cultures where psychological categories are located within the individual, interaction and discourse can only be taken as "symptoms" or "manifestations" of that which is hidden inside the person.

However, methodologies that pay particular attention to discourse have proved equally useful in studying communities that maintain classically individualistic conceptions of the person and emotions. In particular, discourse-centered approaches can demonstrate that social practice in the West betrays a considerably more diverse picture than the traditional individualistic model depicts. As argued by scholars of different persuasions (feminism, critical theory, social constructionism), individualism does play a pivotal role in Western (particularly North American) ethnopsychological models; but it does so in the context of a specific ideology that is related in a complex manner to social practice and to other ideologies with which it competes. An individualistic ideology reflects and enables the middle-class idealization of self-reliant upward mobility; however, these values are not necessarily shared by members of other social classes (cf. Bellah et al. 1985; Ehrenreich 1989; Ortner 1991; Sennett and Cobb 1972; and many others). In other words, the individualism of Western personhood and emotionality is of an ideological nature, and its promotion to the status of key symbol of the West in anthropological thinking instantiates the tendency to reify Western culture that Carrier (1992) aptly termed "occidentalism." Furthermore, the West does not have a monopoly on individualistic theories of psychological processes, as shown by Poole (1991) and Hollan (1992). Discourse-centered approaches are particularly well equipped to deconstruct current anthropological models of Western ethnopsychology (cf. Carbaugh 1989; Lutz 1990; Miller et al. 1990; Ochs, Smith, and Taylor 1989, among others), and to unravel the conflicts, ambiguities, and contradictions that arise across competing ideologies, between ideology and practice, and between discourse and social action in Western settings.

NOTE

This chapter benefitted greatly from comments provided by Philip Bock, Susan Brownell, Ian Condry, Joan Miller, and Peter Stromberg.

REFERENCES

Abu-Lughod, L. 1986. *Veiled Sentiments: Honor and Poetry in a Bedouin Society*. Berkeley: University of California Press.

Bauman, R., and C. L. Briggs. 1990. Poetics and Performance as Critical Perspectives on Language and Social Life. *Annual Review of Anthropology* 19:59–88.

Bellah, R., R. Madsen, W. M. Sullivan, A. Swindler, and S. M. Tipton. 1985. *Habits of the Heart: Individualism and Commitment in American Life*. Berkeley: University of California Press.

Besnier, N. 1990. Language and Affect. *Annual Review of Anthropology* 19:419–51.

——— 1994. Involvement in Linguistic Practice: An Ethnographic Appraisal. *Journal of Pragmatics*.

Bloch, M. 1991. Language, Anthropology, and Cognitive Science. *Man* 26:183–98.

Bourdieu, P. 1977a. The Economics of Linguistic Exchanges. *Social Science Information* 16:645–68.

———. 1977b. *Outline of a Theory of Practice*. Trans. R. Nice. Cambridge, Eng.: Cambridge University Press.

Brenneis, D. 1988. Language and Disputing. *Annual Review of Anthropology* 17:221–37.

Briggs, C. L. 1992. "Since I Am a Woman, I Will Chastise My Relatives": Gender, Reported Speech, and the (Re)production of Social Relations in Warao Ritual Wailing. *American Ethnologist* 19:337–61.

———. ed. 1988. Narrative Resources for the Creation and Mediation of Conflict [Special Issue]. *Anthropological Linguistics* 30(3/4).

Cain, C. 1991. Personal Stories: Identity Acquisition and Self-Understanding in Alcoholics Anonymous. *Ethos* 19:210–53.

Carbaugh, D. 1988. *Talking American: Cultural Discourses on Donahue*. Norwood, NJ: Ablex.

Carrier, J. 1992. Occidentalism: The World Turned Upside-Down. *American Ethnologist* 19:195–212.

Caton, S. C. 1986. *Salam Tahiiyah*: Greetings from the Highlands of Yemen. *American Ethnologist* 13:290–308.

Coulthard, M. 1977. *An Introduction to Discourse Analysis*. London: Longman.

Crapanzano, V. 1989. Preliminary Notes on the Glossing of Emotions. *Kroeber Anthropological Society Papers* 69–70:78–85.

Duranti, A. 1988. Intentions, Language, and Social Action in a Samoan Context. *Journal of Pragmatics* 12:13–33.

———. 1990. Politics and Grammar: Agency in Samoan Political Discourse. *American Ethnologist* 17:646–66.

Ehrenreich, B. 1989. *Fear of Falling: The Inner Life of the Middle Class*. New York: Pantheon.

Erchak, G. M. 1992. *The Anthropology of Self and Behavior*. New Brunswick, NJ: Rutgers University Press.

Foucault, M. 1981. The Order of Discourse. Pp. 48–78 in R. Young, ed., *Untying the Text: A Post-Structuralist Reader*. Boston: Routledge and Kegan Paul.

Frank, M. 1992. On Foucault's Concept of Discourse. Pp. 99–116 in T. J. Armstrong, ed., *Michel Foucault, Philosopher*. New York: Routledge.

Friedrich, P. 1990. Language, Ideology, and Political Economy. *American Anthropologist* 92:295–312.

Gal, S. 1989. Language and Political Economy. *Annual Review of Anthropology* 18:345–67.

———. 1991. Between Speech and Silence: The Problematics of Research on Language and Gender. Pp. 175–203 in M. di Leonardo, ed., *Gender at the Crossroads of Knowledge: Feminist Anthropology in the Postmodern Era*. Berkeley: University of California Press.

Geertz, C. 1984. From the Native's Point of View: On the Nature of Anthropological Understanding. Pp. 123–36 in R. A. Shweder and R. A. LeVine, eds., *Culture Theory: Essays on Mind, Self, and Emotion*. Cambridge, Eng.: Cambridge University Press.

Goffman, E. 1979. Footing. *Semiotica* 25:1–29.

Goodwin, C. 1981. *Conversational Organization: Interaction between Speakers and Hearers*. New York: Academic Press.

Goodwin, C., and A. Duranti. 1992. Rethinking Context: An Introduction. Pp. 1–42 in A. Duranti and C. Goodwin, eds., *Rethinking Context: Language as an Interactive Phenomenon.* Studies in the Social and Cultural Foundations of Language, 11. Cambridge, Eng.: Cambridge University Press.

Grillo, R. 1989. Anthropology, Language, Politics. Pp. 1–24 in R. Grillo, ed., *Social Anthropology and the Politics of Language.* Sociological Review Monographs, 36. London: Routledge.

Grimshaw, A. D., ed. 1990. *Conflict Talk: Sociolinguistic Investigations of Arguments in Conversations.* Cambridge, Eng.: Cambridge University Press.

Heelas, P. 1986. Emotion Talk across Cultures. Pp. 234–66 in R. Harré, ed., *The Social Construction of Emotions.* Oxford: Basil Blackwell.

Hill, J. H. 1989. Weeping as a Meta-Signal in a Mexicano Woman's Narrative. *Journal of Folklore Research* 27:29–47.

Hochschild, A. R. 1983. *The Managed Heart: Commercialization of Human Feeling.* Berkeley: University of California Press.

Hollan, D. 1992. Cross-Cultural Differences in the Self. *Journal of Anthropological Research* 48: 283–300.

Irvine, J. T. 1974. Strategies of Status Manipulation in the Wolof Greeting. Pp. 167–91 in R. Bauman and J. Sherzer, eds., *Explorations in the Ethnography of Speaking.* Cambridge, Eng.: Cambridge University Press.

———. 1989. When Talk Isn't Cheap: Language and Political Economy. *American Ethnologist* 16: 248–67.

———. 1990. Registering Affect: Heteroglossia in the Linguistic Expression of Emotion. Pp. 126–61 in C. A. Lutz and L. Abu-Lughod, eds., *Language and the Politics of Emotion.* Studies in Emotion and Social Interaction. Cambridge, Eng.: Cambridge University Press; Paris: Editions de la Maison des Sciences de l'Homme.

Kulick, D. 1992. *Language Shift and Cultural Reproduction: Socialization, Self, and Syncretism in a Papua New Guinea Village.* Studies in the Social and Cultural Foundations of Language, 14. Cambridge, Eng.: Cambridge University Press.

Labov, W., and D. Fanshel. 1977. *Therapeutic Discourse: Psychotherapy as Conversation.* New York: Academic Press.

Lutz, C. A. 1990. Engendered Emotion: Gender, Power, and the Rhetoric of Emotional Control in American Discourse. Pp. 69–91 in C. A. Lutz and L. Abu-Lughod, eds., *Language and the Politics of Emotion.* Studies in Emotion and Social Interaction. Cambridge, Eng.: Cambridge University Press; Paris: Editions de la Maison des Sciences de l'Homme.

Macdonnell, P. 1986. *Theories of Discourse: An Introduction.* Oxford: Basil Blackwell.

Markus, H. R., and S. Kitayama. 1991. Culture and the Self: Implications for Cognition, Emotion, and Motivation. *Psychological Review* 98:224–53.

Miller, P. J., R. Potts, H. Fung, L. Hoogstra, and J. Mintz. 1990. Narrative Practices and the Social Construction of Self in Childhood. *American Ethnologist* 17:292–311.

Ochs, E. 1979. Social Foundations of Language. Pp. 207–21 in R. O. Freedle, ed., *New Directions in Discourse Processing.* Advances in Discourse Processes, 2. Norwood, NJ: Ablex.

———. 1988. *Culture and Language Development: Language Acquisition and Language Socialization in a Samoan Village.* Studies in the Social and Cultural Foundations of Language, 6. Cambridge, Eng.: Cambridge University Press.

Ochs, E., R. Smith, and C. Taylor. 1989. Detective stories at Dinnertime: Problem-Solving through Co-Narration. *Cultural Dynamics* 2: 238–57.

Ortner, S. 1991. Reading America: Preliminary Notes on Class and Culture. Pp. 163–89 in R. G. Fox, ed., *Recapturing Anthropology: Writing in the Present.* Santa Fe, NM: School of American Research Press.

Poole, F. J. P. 1991. Cultural Schemas and Experiences of the Self among the Bimin-Kuskusmin of Papua New Guinea. *Psychoanalytic Study of Society* 16:55–85.

Rosaldo, M. Z. 1980. *Knowledge and Passion: Ilongot Notions of Self and Social Life.* Cambridge, Eng.: Cambridge University Press.

Rosenberg, D. V. 1990. Language in the Discourse of the Emotions. Pp. 162–85 in C. A. Lutz and L. Abu-Lughod, eds., *Language and the Politics of Emotion*. Studies in Emotion and Social Interaction. Cambridge, Eng.: Cambridge University Press; Paris: Editions de la Maison des Sciences de l'Homme.

Rumsey, A. 1990. Wording, Meaning, and Linguistic Ideology. *American Anthropologist* 92:346–79.

Schieffelin, B. 1990. *The Give and Take of Everyday Life: Language Socialization of Kaluli Children*. Studies in the Social and Cultural Foundations of Language, 9. Cambridge, Eng.: Cambridge University Press.

Sennett, R., and J. Cobb. 1972. *The Hidden Injuries of Class*. New York: Alfred A. Knopf.

Sherzer, J. 1987. A Discourse-centered Approach to Language and Culture. *American Anthropologist* 89:295–309.

Shweder, R. A., and E. J. Bourne. 1984. Does the Concept of the Person Vary Cross-Culturally? Pp. 158–99 in R. A. Shweder and R. A. LeVine, eds., *Culture Theory: Essays on Mind, Self, and Emotion*. Cambridge, Eng.: Cambridge University Press.

Silverstein, M. 1979. Language Structure and Linguistic Ideology. Pp. 193–247 in P. R. Clyne, W. Hanks, and C. L. Hofbauer, eds., *The Elements: A Parasession on Linguistic Units and Levels*. Chicago: Chicago Linguistic Society.

———. 1992. The Indeterminacy of Contextualization: When Is Enough Enough? Pp. 55–76 in P. Auer and A. di Luzio, eds., *The Contextualization of Language*. Pragmatics and Beyond, New Series, 22. Amsterdam: John Benjamins.

Street, B. V., and N. Besnier. 1994. Aspects of Literacy. Pp. 527–62 in T. Ingold, ed. *Companion Encyclopedia of Anthropology, Humanity, Culture, and Social Life*. London: Routledge.

Stromberg, P. G. 1990. Ideological Language in the Transformation of Identity. *American Anthropologist* 92:42–56.

———. 1993. *Language and Self-Transformation: A Study of the Christian Conversion Narrative*. Cambridge, Eng.: Cambridge University Press.

Stroud, C. 1992. The Problem of Intention and Meaning in Code-Switching. *Text* 12:127–55.

Stubbs, M. 1983. *Discourse Analysis: The Sociolinguistic Analysis of Natural Language*. Language in Society, 4. Oxford: Basil Blackwell.

Tedlock, D. 1983. *The Spoken Word and the Work of Interpretation*. Philadelphia: University of Pennsylvania Press.

Urban, G. 1988. Ritual Wailing in Amerindian Brazil. *American Anthropologist* 90:385–400.

van Dijk, T. A., ed. 1985. *Handbook of Discourse Analysis*. 4 vols. Orlando, FL: Academic Press.

Watson-Gegeo, K. A., and G. M. White, eds. 1990. *Disentangling: Conflict Discourse in Pacific Societies*. Stanford, CA: Stanford University Press.

White, G. M. 1992. Ethnopsychology. Pp. 21–46 in T. Schwartz, G. M. White, and C. A. Lutz, eds., *New Directions in Psychological Anthropology*. Cambridge, Eng.: Cambridge University Press.

———. 1993. Emotions Inside Out: The Anthropology of Affect. Pp. 29–39 in M. Lewis and J. Haviland, eds., *Handbook of Emotions*. New York: Guilford Press.

Wodak, R. 1986. *Language Behavior in Therapy Groups*. Berkeley: University of California Press.

CHAPTER ELEVEN

MYTH AS EVIDENCE OF PSYCHOSOCIAL PROCESSES

Robin Fox

Wherever and whenever myth is gathered in space and time, it can be treated as "contemporary" and used as evidence of universal psychological processes. Alternatively, a historical or evolutionary view can be taken in which myth shows definite changes over time reflecting different stages in the development of consciousness, or at least reflecting a different psychic reality at different times, a reality corresponding to different sociocultural situations. A good example of the latter approach is Joseph Campbell's *Transformations of Myth through Time* (1990), which starts with selected myths of hunter-gatherers and moves through the Neolithic agricultural myths to the myths of the great civilizations and then to the period of "creative mythology"—the Middle Ages. In this chapter, we shall examine myth as evidence of universal processes, with a few side glances at the developmental approach. For convenience we shall list these processes under nine headings, while understanding that the categories overlap and are heuristic rather than objective. One may either view these headings as psychological processes or as social and psychological functions. It is simply a matter of emphasis. Each of the processes mentioned serves some social or psychological function, or both.

The material for the study of myth comes from three basic sources: the collections of mythical tales by folklorists, anthropologists, and philologists, spurred in many cases, such as the brothers Grimm in Germany and Lonnrot in Finland, by nineteenth-century nationalism; the classical texts of literate societies that give us the myths of Rome, Greece, Egypt, Persia, India, and China, for example; the medieval and later transcriptions of oral traditions that give us the myths of Scandinavia, Iceland, Finland, Ireland, and Central America; and finally, archaeological evidence that these societies leave behind, such as monuments and inscriptions. The material is vastly uneven, of course, but even more impressive is the evidence of the universality of themes. The greatest attempt to find order in these myths is in the work of Aarne and Thompson (1961). The greatest previous attempt at synthesis was that of Frazer (1891), but this represented a particular theory now much disputed, and the same can be said of the massive synthesis by Lévi-Strauss in his four volumes (1964–71) of *Mythologiques*.

MYTH AS EXPLANATION

This is perhaps the commonest suggested sociopsychological function of myth and the one most readily invoked by common sense. Myths are seen as stories that explain natural phenomena, social institutions, or psychological dispositions. A typical example of such theories is the rationalistic evolutionary theory of Sir James Frazer in *The Golden Bough* (first published in 1891). For Frazer, myths represented primitive man's attempt to explain the universe and its origins and nature. He gathered myths from primitive and peasant people the world over and used them to illustrate the passage in mentality from magic through religion to science. The magical element in myths involved a primitive theory of causation in which either like produced like or in which separated parts of a thing were supposed still to be connected to it. Frazer used myths connected with vegetation ceremonies to show that these two basic ways of thinking lay behind most magical and ritual practices. Most famous among these were the various myths of dying and rejuvenating gods and their mother-lover consorts: Venus (Aphrodite) and Adonis; Attis and Tammuz; Isis and Osiris; and others. The "high" versions of these myths were concentrated in the areas of original cultivation: the Fertile Crescent, the Near East and Egypt; but similar stories are found, connected with the idea of the death and rebirth of nature, in all agricultural societies. Thus the annual cycle of nature is, in this view, explained as the cosmic working out of the death and rebirth of the gods, as with Persephone's six months in Hades and six months with her mother Ceres (the corn goddess) on earth. Frazer also pointed to the profound identification of the ruler (who developed from a rain magician) with the health of his people and particularly their land. This magical connection between the king and the land was a basic theme among agriculturalists to the extent that if a king's health were to fail or if he showed weakness or impotence, he would often be put to death. The theme of the waste land, devastated by the king's illness or insufficiency, was the basic inspiration for the great poem of that name by T. S. Eliot—a poem redolent with mythological themes that in turn became a kind of defining myth of modernism.

Another theory that gained wide currency was that of Evans-Pritchard (1937), who studied magical explanations among the Azande of the southern Sudan. The Azande understood that bad luck could happen but needed an explanation of why it happened to some people at certain times. The answer to this they found in the practice of sorcery. Termites may have eaten through the supports of a granary, but why did it fall on this particular man at this time? The answer was sorcery practiced by an enemy. Evans-Pritchard pointed out that the system, like any conspiracy theory, was self-reinforcing. If one could not find the sorcerer, for example, this only served to show how cunning he was and hence how dangerous. Myths explained the origin and nature of the powers of sorcery. Again, the stress here is on the explanatory function.

Myths have been seen as having a whole range of functions in explaining the origins of things. Myths of the origin of the world itself and of mankind, whether from the actions of an "earth diver," the fiat of a high god, or the union of a sky father with an earth mother, have been taken as essentially explanatory.

The problem with attributing a primarily explanatory function to myths lies in their failure to disappear when more rational and scientific explanations are available. These should, in theory, as Frazer expected, supplant the inadequate "explanations" provided by myths. But myths continue to flourish, and new ones are constantly invented. This suggests that something other than simple explanation lies behind the persistence of mythology.

MYTH AS CHARTER

The view of myth as a social or cultural charter was popularized by Malinowski (1926, 1948), who was impressed by the Trobriand myths of clan origins. In each case, the totemic ancestors of the clans were seen to have originated in certain specific places, and their origin there validated the clan's claim to the territory. This was the "mythological charter" of the clan. Many myths provided this kind of validation. Thus among the Hopi (Waters 1963) there is a ritual hierarchy of clans, and this hierarchy is validated with reference to the original wanderings of the clans after they left the original underworld and came up into this one, and to the order of their eventual arrival on the Hopi mesas. These of course are the "origin myths" that we have seen under the heading of "explanation," but here they are seen as fulfilling the function not so much of explanation as of validation, of staking a legitimate claim to territory in particular. Thus the Jewish claim to Israel (Palestine) is based on a validating myth in which the land was given to them in perpetuity by Yahweh as part of their covenant with him. This does not so much explain why the Jews are there as validate their claim to be there legitimately. The "charter" validates not only territorial claims but also succession in royal houses and the proper performance and power of ritual. Every Navaho ritual, embodied in a sand painting, has its validating myth, which the sand painting symbolically represents.

MYTH AS RATIONALIZATION

Proponents of this approach do not stress so much the validating function of myth as its attempt to make sense of the phenomena created by ritual and religion itself. The famous "myth versus ritual" quarrel occupied a great deal of effort from anthropologists and classicists (see Versnel 1990). One side saw myth as primary and ritual simply as the playing out of mythical themes in dramatic fashion. The other saw ritual as growing up out of magical practices in an ad hoc fashion and myth coming along later to rationalize the practices. Since the origins of both the myths and the rituals are unknown, it is often impossible to prove one or the other; indeed, there must be constant feedback.

But some investigators have taken a particularly firm stand in favor of myth as rationalization of ritual. One of the most extreme of these was Lord Raglan (1936), for whom all myth was a rationalization of ritual drama. The ritual drama itself did not have a "story" but was simply a set of magical formulae: for example, the installation ceremonies of a god-king or the ritual sacrifice of a victim at the spring equinox. What later "tradition" did was to render these formulae more meaningful as tales of actual adventures of hero figures. Thus, according to Raglan, arose most of the famous "hero" myths: Robin Hood, King Arthur, Cuchulainn, Oedipus, Theseus, Perseus, and Jason; in the Bible, Joseph, Moses, and Elijah; and among primitive tribes, Watu Gunung (Java) and Nyikang (Shilluk). He showed that a fairly tight pattern of events characterizes the lives of all the heroes and scored them on a twenty-two-point scale from birth from a royal virgin, through victory over giant, dragon, or wild beast, to eventual mysterious death or assumption to heaven. All these correspond, he claimed, to stages in ritual drama. He was mostly concerned with proving that such heroes are completely unhistorical and thus refuting the "myth as distorted history" school. His method (first promulgated in 1936) interestingly anticipated the "structural" approach that we shall examine later and is suggestive of a psychological need to render ritual into narrative.

An even more unusual version of the rationalization theme is Robert Graves's (1946) theory of "iconotropy," in which many myths are the attempts by a conquering people to rationalize the icons of the conquered and bring them into line with their own beliefs. Many biblical myths are Hebrew attempts thus to rationalize icons of the earlier Canaanites. Similarly, many classical Greek myths confirmed Olympian myths at the expense of displaced Minoan ones. "For example, the story of the unnatural union of Pasiphae ('She who shines for all') and the bull, the issue of which was the monstrous Minotaur, seems to be based on an icon of the sacred marriage between Minos, the king of Cnossos (pictured with a bull's head), and the representative of the Moon-goddess, in the course of which a live bull was sacrificed." Similarly, Europa, Oedipus, and Lot's intercourse with his own daughters were all rationalizations of indigenous icons. The psychological process involved seems to be the need to rationalize alien symbolic expressions that one wishes to assimilate. The alien cannot simply be left alien; it has to be reinterpreted and then integrated into one's own idiom.

MYTH AS CODE

Known as the "structuralist" approach to myth and associated primarily with Claude Lévi-Strauss (1958), the approach of myth as code has as its main feature the abandonment of the idea of narrative as essential to myth. A myth, in this view, is a "story," but its meaning lies not in the plot but in the underlying relationships of the basic elements of the plot, or "mythemes," relationships that are revealed by looking for "structural contrasts" between the elements. Thus in the story of Oedipus, several "mythemes" are in play throughout the plot. Lévi-Strauss saw them as pairs of opposites, for example:

Overvaluation of kinship versus undervaluation of kinship

Bisexual origins of man versus autochthonous origins of man

Thus in the Oedipus legend, when Cadmus refuses to search further for his sister Europa (who has been raped by Zeus), he undervalues kinship, while when Oedipus marries his mother Jocasta, he overvalues kinship, but in each case the result is bisexual human reproduction. When Cadmus kills the Dragon or when Oedipus kills the Sphinx, they are "denying the autochthonous origins of man." This is further reflected in the fact that all the male members of Oedipus's lineage have names referring to difficulty in walking, a feature of autochthonous origins in most myth, and that male relatives kill each other throughout the cycle.

The "meaning" of the myth then lies not in some moral tale about patricide and incest, but in a "resolution" of the contradictions between the theories of autochthonous human origins (held by most agricultural peoples on the model of plant emergence) and the knowledge that they are in fact the product of bisexual union between humans themselves. Myths also show that humans must value kinship but not to the extent of investing genes in kin who are too close (this is my formulation, not his). Ultimately, all myth is reducible to the resolution of the contradiction between nature and culture—the constant in the web of human puzzlement. We are part of nature and yet defiantly different from nature. Lévi-Strauss often used the following formula to illustrate this:

Nature : Culture :: Raw : Cooked,

that is, Nature is to Culture as Raw is to Cooked. This formula lies behind many South American myths of the origins of humanity characterized by the cooking of food (and hence the invention of fire) as opposed to the eating of it raw. Myths of the origin of fire characterize all cultures, and, in the structuralist version, have to do with the resolution of this basic contradiction (Lévi-Strauss 1964).

The essence of this theory is that no meaning resides in the items and symbols and plots of myth in and of themselves. Myths are a code, and the various elements can be arranged and rearranged in different ways to produce "messages" about basic human dilemmas and their resolution. The mind is compared to a "bricoleur" who cobbles together useful objects out of whatever material is at hand. The psychological process here is essentially "intellectualistic" rather than emotional. It is as though these problems produce a strain for resolution, and the myth provides the resolution, although with a covert rather than an overt answer. The resolution is "understood" by the audience not at the overt level of plot and story, but at the subconscious level of the resolution of contradictions. Also important is the issue of "transformations" of myths. Thus neighboring peoples often take the theme of a myth and transform it into its opposite, as with the myth of the star-husband in North America and the myth of the bird fallen from its nest in South America. The essential similarity between two myth "series" may lie in their opposite statements of the same theme.

Perhaps the clearest example of the structural approach lies in Lévi-Strauss's (1962) treatment of totemic myths. The gods of ancient Egypt are almost always presented as having animal or bird heads, and this probably derives from their origins as clan totems in the previous tribal stage of Egyptian existence. The gods of the ancient Semitic tribes before the advent of the monotheistic Yahweh (Jehovah) cult were similarly "totemistic" according to Robertson Smith (1957 [1889]). The totem represented the original animal ancestor of the tribe or clan—the bridge between nature and culture—and so could be seen as an explanatory myth or an origin or charter myth.

Such totemic myths are extremely widespread, cropping up on most continents, often accompanied by rituals involving the reenactment of the myths and by food taboos that prevent the "descendants" of the totem creature from eating the animal (or plant or whatever) in question. Freud traced this back to the "primal crime" of killing the horde father, who is now represented by the totem. Several other commentators (including Radcliffe-Brown), however, had seen the interest in the natural world shown in totemic myths as essentially utilitarian, especially as members of the totem clans, among the Australian aboriginals, for example, held regular "increase ceremonies" to promote the fertility of the totem.

Lévi-Strauss saw it differently. From his intellectualist point of view, such explanations do not take into account the universal features of totemism, which, he said, boil down to the *classificatory* functions of the totems. Often, totems are inedible things, or supernatural things, or objects of no utilitarian concern. But by using opposed species (e.g., raven versus wolf, eaglehawk versus crow, emu versus crocodile, and so on) to classify moieties, for example, people are setting up metonymical systems of classification of their social worlds. This leads to his famous formula that totems are not so much "good to eat" as "good to think." Totemic myths serve to emphasize the separate but totally interdependent nature of the social units involved.

MYTH AS PROJECTION

Psychoanalytic theories differ from the structuralist approach in that they are primarily concerned with emotions rather than the intellectual solution of contradictions. Thus Freud (1938, 1957 [1943]) saw in the Oedipus myth not some code about human cognitive dilemmas, but a ''projection'' onto the mythical figures (Oedipus, Laius, Jocasta, and others) of real human anxieties. These anxieties, stemming from our own ''unresolved Oedipal conflicts'' in the sexual dilemmas of the human family, could not be dealt with directly, but could be displaced into the figures of myth, where their consequences could be played out. Thus the ubiquity of incest myths, and particularly of the awful consequences of incest, illustrates the constant human state of anxiety over incest temptations projected onto mythical personages. (Still one of the best summaries of the psychoanalytical approach to the Oedipus myth is Mullahy 1952.)

In a bold but much-misunderstood work (1952 [1913]), Freud attempted to show how this anxiety might stem from deep-rooted biological memories of events in human evolution—the primal horde and primal crime that we have already mentioned. His followers have been happier with the idea that there is a recurrent human family drama in each generation, with the unresolved conflicts handled by myth and religion. Thus children have their first libidinous attachments to their parents, and this causes intense same-sex rivalry, especially between fathers and sons. This rivalry has to be suppressed by the sons, who must both strive to identify with their fathers and at the same time try to achieve sexual and social independence. The ''hero cycle'' for the Freudians is a retelling, with larger-than-life mythical figures, of the family drama wherein the boy struggles to reach maturity. The Oedipal version, for example, shows the consequences of not suppressing the urge to murder the father and the libidinous urge toward the mother. At the same time, it shows how Oedipus, in finally recognizing and atoning for his crimes, reaches maturity and heroic stature. It is fair to say that no culture so far studied has not produced a myth, or series of related myths, of this kind, and this the psychoanalysts would take as evidence of the projective realization of a universal human anxiety.

The Culture and Personality school of anthropology attempted to blend the hypotheses of psychoanalysis with the rigors of experimental behaviorism. The basic theory can be found in Whiting and Child (1953). Using the method of cross-cultural statistical comparison, they tested a series of hypotheses derived from psychoanalytic theory and showed how these are reflected in belief systems about illness. Thus they claim that certain child-rearing practices lead to the intensification of various anxieties, which are then projected onto mythical figures. Early indulgence by the mother followed by later rejection will result in paranoid personalities who will project their paranoia into myths of aggressive witches. Others of this school have posited that severe fathering will lead to strong castration anxiety in men, producing myths that are either quite literal—like that of Cronos castrating Uranos (and giving birth—obliquely—to Aphrodite, or more disguised, like the common myth of the vagina dentata with its castrating potential. Severe toilet training will produce myths concerned with anal functions either directly or in disguised forms such as myths of miserliness—Midas, Scrooge, and others. In the projective scheme of things, as with structuralism, the processes are subconscious and disguised. The Freudians do not see the symbols and persons of myth as arbitrary elements in codes, but take them to have substantive meaning. Incest is incest, not one sign in a code to be read as "overvaluation of blood relationships."

We cannot leave the Freudian scheme without mentioning the importance of dreams. Anthropologists had always recognized the importance of dreams as sources of myth material, and "primitive" people had always recognized the connection. But Freud made them absolutely central: they were the "royal road to the unconscious." Dream symbolism was the source of myth symbolism. Part of the "dream work" was to translate primary material into symbols so that repressed material could be experienced in a disguised form in the dream. Thus a problem with one's parents that could not be faced in consciousness could be realized in a dream of giants and monsters or kings and queens, sexual problems could be translated into dreams of flying or of phallic snakes, and the like. Now that we understand the crucial importance of dreaming for long-term memory storage (see Winson 1985) and the direct involvement of the emotional centers of the brain in the dream (REM sleep) process, Freud's observations take on new strength. Myths become a kind of prepackaged dream work, readied for long-term memorization. This is extremely important when myths are used as methods of education in adolescents, as we shall see (Fox 1980: chap. 7; 1989: chap. 8; see also the chapter by Barbara Tedlock in this volume).

MYTH AS ARCHETYPE

Closely related to the Freudian school is that deriving from Jung (1971) and his followers. It starts from much the same premises but differs sharply on the meaning of the symbolic content of myths. For the projectionists, meaning is in a sense created in each generation when the basic personality patterns are set down in child training. The universal patterns observed are the result of universal human features, but their translation into myth has to be achieved anew in each generation, and meaning can change as child-training practices change. The relative conservatism of such practices usually means that there is a constancy in projective myths over time. The Jungian approach disputes this.

For Jungians, myths are not primarily reflections of childhood experiences but constants stemming from the inherited experiences of the human species itself. Calling this the "collective unconscious" has somewhat confused the idea, but Jung was simply stressing that the archetypes were the common property of the species occurring in all individuals. In an example we used earlier, the "hero" theme is indeed universal and does have to do with the boy's saga of maturation into manhood, but it is not created anew in each generation: its basic symbols and symbolic themes are part of the genetic heritage of the species. Thus we do not "project" our anxieties in the creation of heroes and villains, tricksters and witches, demigods and fatal enchantresses, and the like.

They are there, in dream material, waiting to be realized in story. We may project onto them, but we do not bring them into being.

A Jungian would ask, with some reason, how it is that despite the huge variation in human cultures, certain quite definite and recognizable characters and situations crop up universally if these are supposed to be constant "re-creations" in the form of projections of childhood anxieties. The fixed characters and situations and their accompanying symbols Jung called "archetypes," and he saw them as having explicit meanings that could be recognized quite easily. The witch or wicked stepmother was a "split" of the mother—her evil side feared by the child—while the good queen or fairy godmother was the mirror opposite, the good qualities of the mother. There is a "code" here, but its message is not to be deduced from intellectual combinatorial properties; rather, it is to be directly read off from the actual content of the myth: wicked uncle = feared aspects of father. In the Hamlet myth—which long antedates Shakespeare's version of it—the wicked uncle becomes the (step)father. These meanings do not change. The archetype is eternal.

Archetypes should not be confused with "innate ideas." They are more like the "innate releasing mechanisms" of the ethologists: instinctive responses that arise in response to certain environmental stimuli. (For an excellent discussion of the relation of archetypes to biopsychological processes, see Stevens 1982.) The major ones have to do with the same aspects of the family drama as in the Freudian version; but for Jung, the "mother archetype" existed in the human psyche *ab origine*. Individual or group experience achieved a particular realization of the archetype, with emphasis on the good or punitive sides of the mother, for example. In myth, the mother could be symbolized as Mother Earth in her various manifestations (the corn goddess, the fertility goddess, the divine queen, the mistress of the animals, Spider Woman, and so on); or as the feared version in the death goddess (Kali), the evil enchantress, the Gorgon, the dragon or sea monster, and so on. The creative Greeks split the mother-female archetype many ways, from the sexual Aphrodite through the virgin Artemis to the motherly Demeter and the dominating Hera (see Friedrich 1978, who viewed this as a way of dealing with a "repressed mother-lover archetype"). Robert Graves (1948) put forth the idea of the "triple goddess" who, while the same person, appears as the young girl, the mature woman, and the old crone in different manifestations of the stages of womanhood. The father, in turn, appears as the sun god (Aztecs), the sky god (Yahweh, Zeus), or the divine king (Caesar) and in his bad forms as the vengeful deity or god of wrath or evil magician (sorcerer). The split between bad and good fathers is at the base of many successful modern myths, such as that expressed in the conflict between Bram Stoker's Count Dracula and his nemesis, Dr. Van Helsing. (For other good examples of this "splitting" in English literature, see Brewer 1988.) One might even see the rise of the idea of Satan in Judeo-Christian mythology as an attempt to overcome the impossibility of trying to contain both the good and evil father archetypes in one father god, as demanded by strict theology. The rise of Marianism equally represents, in this view, an insistence on reinstating the mother (and especially the mater dolorosa—the sorrowing mother-goddess with her dead-but-to-be resurrected son) archetype in a religion in which she had been seriously demoted by celibate misogynist male priests (Carroll 1986).

Jung also postulated various other aspects of the archetypal psyche, all of which emerge in myth (as they do in religion and politics, music, and popular culture). Thus the psyche is always split into the *animus* and the *anima*: the masculine and feminine aspects. In Greek myth, Athena springs full-born from the head of Zeus, representing his feminine aspect; and many gods and goddesses have a decidedly androgynous aspect. Especially compelling is the archetype of the *shadow*: the evil side of the self that is rejected and feared. The fascination in legend with twins (and the real fear of twins in many societies) reflects this notion of two sides of the self that are at once identical and antithetical to each other. The fascination moves from the hero twins of primitive myth through Cain and Abel and Castor and Pollux to the constant use of the "good and evil twin" theme in modern soap operas and miniseries and was evident in much folklore as the *Doppelgänger* or exact-double theme. Its most graphic modern mythological expression is in the tale of Dr. Frankenstein and his "monster," whom he must destroy and by whom he must be destroyed. (See Twitchell 1985 for an extended discussion of such themes in modern "horror" literature and films.)

It would be wrong to think of archetypes as solely concerned with personages; they can equally be places (magical islands like the Hesperides or Atlantis, gardens like Eden, and forests and underworlds) or events and processes like the quest or the monster struggle. The major processes represented are of course individual maturation and the life-death barrier. The "death and resurrection" theme that Frazerians would see as a magical-explanatory fertility myth, or the structuralists as overcoming an intellectual contradiction, would be seen by the Jungians as a major archetype dealing with any life transition involving the death of one self and the re-creation of another. A beautiful modern mythical expression of this is the final act of Mozart's *Magic Flute*, where the young hero and heroine survive trial by fire and water to be reborn into a new life. This sequence is based on Masonic mythology, itself derived from the great mystery religions in which Christianity also has roots. The hero or heroine's triumph over death, and the promise of eternal life to believers who follow the same "path," is a powerful archetypal theme.

The Jungian tradition has been carried on by mythographers like Joseph Campbell (1949, 1959), especially on the hero theme. His essentially Jungian analysis of the hero archetype (as we have seen, the basic story of male maturation) was the source for Stephen Spielberg's highly successful movie trilogy of *Star Wars*, a spectacular cinematographic tribute to archetypal theory, which followed to the letter the "good father/bad father" and "older brother/younger brother" (hero-twin) themes, and even included the princess-*anima* and the "animal helper" themes.

It is probably useful to include under this general heading the influential work of Eliade (1965) rather than give it a separate section, such as "Myth as Education." What Campbell did for the hero, Eliade did for the process of initiation, which he linked closely to the death and rebirth theme. It is during this process that young boys particularly are introduced to the basic wisdom of the tribe, and this information is conveyed largely by myth. This is true in primitive tribes and modern societies; the latter have a tendency to convey important messages about behavior and conduct through myths (for example, of sports heroes or rock stars) as well as through direct instruction.

Myth exerts a peculiar kind of power over the developing psyche that makes it a suitable vehicle for impressing eternal (or parochial) verities on impressionable minds. This is particularly true when it is conveyed through music and drama, and for this reason Plato wanted both banned from his ideal, rational republic. He would thoroughly have understood and deplored the powerful appeal of MTV. The role of graphic imagery in producing dreams and of dreams as producing long-term selective memory, which we have previously discussed, is clearly important here. Graphic, even terrifying, myths and rituals for adolescents will have the actual physical effect of "stamping in" the messages conveyed by the myths. (See the chapter by Simon Ottenberg in this volume.)

We might briefly look at one of the most powerful archetypes that fascinated Jung, namely, the enigmatic figure of Trickster. Trickster was viewed by Campbell as one of the "primordial" myths, dating from the depths of the Paleolithic. Trickster can come in many forms in these ancient versions. He is sometimes an old man or old chief, as among the Winnebago, whose version, recorded by Radin (1956), was the source of Jung's fascination, or among the Hopi a coyote (Malotki 1985), or sometimes a hare or a raven among other North American Indians. One of his characteristics is that he is a shape-changer and sex-changer. He appears as the spider Anansi in West Africa (and in Caribbean derivations) and in Europe as Reynard the Fox. In Polynesia he is Maui, at once Trickster and Creator, who has an island in the Hawaiian chain named after him.

In the primordial version, Trickster is at once stupid and gullible, cunning and devious. He is the embodiment of chaos and yet can be an important deity of creation; he is totally amoral and yet often the founder of society and moral order; he is relentlessly libidinous and yet cannot control his own penis, which wanders off and has its own adventures. He is scatological in the extreme, and his anus, like his penis, seems to have a life of its own; he is basically male but can change sex and live as a female. He is asocial, and yet he steals fire from the gods for man. Above all, he is funny. Trickster stories are always told for amusement, and many "dirty jokes" have their origins in his adventures.

This primordial figure, who seems to us to have such a rash of contradictions built in, springs from homogeneous hunting groups, themselves equally undifferentiated and "compact." One could see him as a symbolic representative of the basic psychological process of "cheating" so important in the process of evolution itself (Trivers 1985). As society grew in complexity, so the bundle of archetypal material that was Trickster began to unravel and separate out into distinct characters. We can only sketch an outline here.

In the great Iron and Bronze Age myths, Trickster keeps some of his identity, but already is beginning to appear as more than one god or hero with different characteristics. The Greeks, for example, have their "official" trickster in Hermes (Brown 1969), who was indeed the god of trickery, and whose name derives from the herms or phallic statues used as boundary markers. He was thus the god of boundaries, but also the god of thieves and, interestingly, of merchants and craftsmen. He was the messenger of the gods and brought luck to men. Despite his phallic representations, he was not a particularly libidinous god; this aspect of him was taken over by his son Pan—half animal, half human—and by Dionysus, god of wine but basically an ancient fertility deity who was lord of orgiastic ecstasy and the period of "misrule." The human-heroic aspects of Trickster are summed up best in the person of Odysseus, with his exploits of trickery, deceit, and triumph. The Norse myths kept Trickster more intact in the person of Loki, but he is here transformed into a devil-like figure of ambiguous sexuality who is ultimately responsible for the death of Balder and the doom of the gods.

The violence and deceit of Trickster were never lost on the "folk" audience. They show up in the figure of the Devil in medieval mystery plays and in successor figures like Til Eulenspiegel, Punch, and Pierrot. We have perhaps forgotten the enormous popular appeal of these characters. Punch is highly stereotyped but clearly Trickster, while Pierrot developed an interesting complexity as the "gullible fool" or "foolish innocent" side of the Trickster equation, sometimes with sinister undertones—*Pierrot assassin de sa femme*. (On Punch see Twitchell 1985; on Pierrot see Storey 1978.)

The scatological side of Trickster, along with his gluttony and lust, was kept alive by Rabelais in *Gargantua and Pantagruel*, as was his "outlaw" status with Robin Hood and his gluttonous cowardice by Falstaff, for example. The libidinous aspects of Trickster became woven into the legends or semilegends of Don Juan, Casanova, and Cellini, for example (with perhaps Carmen as the female counterpart), with the sexual violence taken up by de Sade. The amoral "con man" aspects were taken up by such figures as Tom Jones or Barry Lyndon (who had their libidinous and gluttonous sides as well, of course).

Rapid social changes after the mid-nineteenth century in both Europe and America saw further fragmentation as more varied social types became available to take up the different aspects of Trickster's multifaceted character. Thus the "con man" theme was elaborated in various directions, including the gentleman thief, the gallant highwayman, and the unscrupulous social climber. The enormous popularity of such movies as *The Hustler* and *The Sting* shows that this part of Trickster's character continues to fascinate—as do the portrayals of all such "outlaws" as long as they amuse and the people they "take" are deserving dupes.

Just being funny does not qualify one for Trickster status. Circus clowns, for example, have a different lineage, equally steeped in mythology, while stand-up comics and funny characters need have no Trickster characteristics at all. Some cartoon characters, however, seem to be exactly in the Trickster tradition, led, appropriately, by Wile E. Coyote in his hopeless pursuit of Roadrunner. A true Trickster for grown-ups has emerged in the work of English Poet Laureate Ted Hughes. His *Crow* (1972) is all Trickster, and quite consciously so—and alternately hilarious and terrifying, as Trickster should be. One could go on almost endlessly, but the point is simple. Our archetypal mentalities retain the need for the Trickster "stuff," but we are no longer able to think of him as a single character, as our Paleolithic ancestors did, or even as three or four characters, as our Iron Age forebears could. We have fragmented him into dozens of specialized roles to match our own sociopsychological reality. Our modern modes of thinking and feeling require Trickster to be revealed to us through a kaleidoscope of roles and fragments that we must somehow imaginatively reassemble to reach the figure of Old Man Coyote, lurking somewhere in our still-Paleolithic brain.

MYTH AS INTEGRATION

A powerful school of sociological thought has stressed the sociopsychological integrative functions of myth for the society as a whole. This school, founded by Emile Durkheim (1915) and carried on by Radcliffe-Brown (1952), sees myth and ritual as inextricably mixed and indeed regards the ritual performance of the myth as far more important than the actual content. The sociological school is concerned with the local expressions of mythical ideas in ritual. If there are any general psychological functions for the Durkheimians, they lie in the functions, not the content, of myth.

Myth and ritual together serve to promote the integration of the individual into his or her society. The individual is in a sense always "alone" in his or her own perceptions, but he or she has to be in some sense in concert psychologically and socially with his or her fellows in order for society to function. This is not achieved simply by coercion or contract, but by the sharing of myths in ritual experience. Myths contain the collective wisdom of the tribe or society. In coming together in ritual to enact the myths, the members share not only information but a common psychological experience of being together under the almost objective or external authority of the society itself. This is the source, Durkheim claimed, of the power of the moral imperative that had eluded Kant. It comes from society itself. The ritual, as Radcliffe-Brown phrased it, sustains certain common sentiments in the believers, and so powerful is their experience that they attribute it to an external source or sources: a god or gods in some form or another. But these are nothing more than society itself acting through its rituals on the individual.

Durkheim turned for his major demonstration to the myths and rituals of the Australian aborigines. These have largely to do with many of the things we have been discussing: initiation of youths, for example, and increase and fertility of the animals of the hunt. The myths derive from the "dream time"—the ultimate beginnings of aboriginal society when the totemic ancestors laid down the territories, rules of marriage and initiation, rites of passage and hunting rituals, and other societal regulations. Whatever the psychologists might think of these myths, the sociological view of them sees them as functioning to integrate the individual aborigine into his or her larger society and to keep that society integrated by its common commitment to these ancestral myths. This was especially clear with the aborigines who lived for most of the year in small wandering families or bands and came together periodically for their great "collective" ceremonies like the Intichiuma of the Aranda. Radcliffe-Brown was fond of quoting Confucius on ceremonies, to the effect that it didn't matter much what the ceremonies were about, and certainly not whether the myths on which they were based were "true"; what mattered was that they were performed. Their function was to bring people together with reverence for a body of beliefs and thus reinforce their "common sentiments."

One of the more popular and easily most expressive of such forms of integrative mythology/ritual is ancestor worship. Societies that stress the worship of ancestors either stress the belief in a general body of ancestors, as do the Kachinas among the Pueblo Indians, or actually worship specific ancestors, as do the Chinese, whose ancestors are recorded in temples on ancestral tablets for as many as twenty or more generations. Reverence toward the ancestors and beliefs and rituals concerned with placating them and ensuring their continued benevolence are powerful supports for the family hierarchy and system of values it embodies. For Durkheimians, the holding of common beliefs and practice of common rituals ensure the social solidarity of the clan itself.

MYTH AS EXPRESSION

All the theories previously discussed have in common that they see myth as having some instrumental or functional purpose for the believers. But there is another aspect to myth that might be called the expressive, which sees myth as more akin to poetry or drama or opera or even science fiction and downplays the utilitarian explanations (Turner 1969). Tedlock (1972) saw Zuni myths not as explanations or projections (although they may be both these things), but as poetic expressions of Zuni concerns. Written out in a raw prose form, many myths make little sense, a fact that led early mythographers to dismiss them as examples of "pre-logical mentality" or later structuralists to seek the hidden messages behind the rambling narrative. But, said Tedlock, a good deal of expressionist poetry would make equally little sense if it were treated as a version of rational narrative. We do not treat it as such, but realize that it aims only to express a particular emotion or sentiment or feeling: to say something poetic about the world. That such an expression has "power" is a common belief, of course—the bard's poetic curse was feared even by the high kings of Ireland—

but the aim is essentially expressive. One of the most quoted Navaho ritual "chants" is certainly used in conjunction with a curing ritual, itself the reenactment of a myth, but it is also a powerful piece of expressive poetry:

> House made of the dawn
> House made of evening light
> House made of the dark cloud
> House made of male rain
> House made of dark mist
> House made of female rain
> House made of pollen
> House made of grasshoppers
> Dark cloud is at the door
> The outward trail is dark cloud
> The zigzag lightning stands high upon it
> . . .
> May it be beautiful before me
> May it be beautiful behind me
> May it be beautiful below me
> May it be beautiful above me
> May it be beautiful around me
> In beauty it is finished
> In beauty it is finished (Matthews 1907)

It would make no sense, for example, to try to interpret this chant as explanatory or projective. Rather, it expresses something to do with a central emotion of the culture in which it occurs, and it may have no function beyond that expression. (For a vivacious but insightful view of opera as a kind of "alternative mythology" to Western Christian orthodoxy, see Conrad 1987.)

MYTH AS ASTRONOMY

We have suggested both that myth has strong mnemonic properties and that it may contain a hidden "code." These two properties combine in the view that myth is in fact a form of knowledge passed on in code, but that the knowledge is not archetypal or structural but astronomical. It is, as we like to say, "star lore." We rather take for granted that all the visible planets and constellations are named for various Graeco-Roman gods, goddesses, nymphs, and heroes, but we have lost touch with the idea that this is their essential meaning. That is, they *are* the constellations and the stars and planets. Their various wanderings, risings and falls, and triumphs and deaths and resurrections are in fact encoded versions of their passage through the heavens. Yet this was indeed the common view of the literate minorities of the great civilizations throughout the world; and there is plenty of evidence that the roots of such astronomical knowledge went deeper into the Paleolithic world of the hunters. Marshack (1972) made a good case for Paleolithic recording of phases of the moon, for example. The astronomical functions of the great megalithic monuments have been postulated, and from Yucatan to China and from Polynesia to Persia, a vast system of astronomical information and its accompanying astrological lore was universally known and codified in mythic symbols (Santillana and von Dechend 1977). A great deal of this lore concerns the world axis or world tree or world mountain, sometimes pictured as a mill or quern or churn on which the whole of creation turns (or is turned by various heroes like Horus and Seth in Egypt or Vishnu in India, or even Hamlet in his pre-Shakespearean incarnations as Amlodhi in Icelandic myth) and that eventually falls into disuse or becomes a whirlpool or maelstrom. This is seen, with accompanying stories of gods dominant, gods twilit, and gods destroyed, as a coded message about the "precession of the equinoxes" (based on the tilt of the earth and the discrepancy between the global and solar equators of 23.5 degrees), subsequent "world ages" defined according to the zodiac and taking some 2,400 years to "revolve," and a "great year" of approximately 26,000 years. Thus the sun "progresses" through the zodiac from Gemini in, say, 5000 B.C. through Taurus into Aries into Pisces, where it stands now (Christ the Fish inaugurated the present age) before moving into the "Age of Aquarius" in about 200 years time.

Let us take one example from one of the most famous icons of Near Eastern religion: Mithras slaying the bull. The bullfight survives as a popular ritual, but Mithraism was one of the great mystery cults that challenged Christianity for dominance of the Roman world, and probably only the intervention of the emperor Constantine prevented it from triumphing. The astrological belief that lay at the foundation of Mithraism (revealed only to the highest order of initiates) was precisely the precession of the equinoxes rediscovered by Hipparchus about 128 B.C. (Ulansey 1989). Its great central icon shows Mithras kneeling on the back of a bull, looking away and stabbing the bull in the shoulder. Wheat ears sprout from the wound (or the tail), and various animals are in attendance—a dog, a snake, a raven, and a scorpion, and sometimes a cup and a lion.

For a Jungian "decipherment" one may look to Campbell (1964: vol. 3, p. 257); but the astrological interpretation suggests that this represents the passage of the sun from Taurus (the bull) when the constellation Perseus was directly over it. This ended the "Age of Taurus" (killed the bull) and ushered in a new astrological age. Only a very powerful "god" could have ordained this change; he was personified as Perseus/Mithras. The attendant "animals" are all constellations that were under the celestial equator and thus "under" Perseus/Mithras when the change occurred; and the cup is Aquarius, the water bearer, while the lion (Leo) represents the summer solstice, and the wheat ears are the spring equinox.

The curious reader must look at the sources and follow out the details, which, while strange on first reading, become convincing in accumulation of detail. I have dwelt on this aspect of myth at some length because it has been the most neglected by anthropologists, if it has been paid any heed at all. It is in no way incompatible with other interpretations, since the astronomical, significance of the myths was probably never widespread knowledge, and the icons and star lore rapidly degenerated into "myths, legends, and folktales." But if, for example, we see the Greeks as the crossroads between the ancient mythical world and the modern scientific one, and the Stoics and Pythagoreans as the first "scientists," then we should remember that both were steeped in the ancient "star lore" that was the basis of their science and the origin of mathematics, astronomy, navigation, and geography, and as late as Kepler and Newton, "scientists" were still steeped in this lore, kept alive by the alchemists in the Middle Ages.

CONCLUSION

It has been stressed throughout that there is no necessary conflict between these various theories of the psychological origins and functions of myth. They are different "readings" of the same material, and each has its own validity within its own assumptions and for its own purposes. But the very persistence of the mythological mode of thinking and its resistance to rationalist onslaughts and refusal to go down in the face of "scientific" alternatives suggest that we must ask the more ultimate question of its possible adaptive functions in a Darwinian sense. Born of self-consciousness and language, themselves the products of the rapid expansion of the human neocortex over the last two million years, yet drawing on phyletically old material in the limbic system—dreams, memory, and emotion—myths are clearly in some way "necessary" to the adaptation and survival of creatures who deal with the world as their language-consciousness redefines it. We live, in a sense, inside our own heads, and living there with us is the myth material that makes it possible for us to survive and interpret the strange world-as-we-see-it that is peculiar to our species. Myths are, after all, fantasy, and nature knows no fantasy, with the startling exception of one genus, *Homo*. Myths are coterminous with language and consciousness in a way that, for example, logic (a late developer) is not. Myths are a more powerful and satisfying way of apprehending the world than logic and, for most people, science. This can be either dangerous or benign, but the truth of it should be the focus of any integrated theory of myth and psychology.

REFERENCES

Aarne, A., and S. Thompson. 1961. *The Types of the Folktale*. Helsinki: Suomalainen Tiedeakatemia, Academia Scientarum Fennica.

Brewer, D. 1988. *Symbolic Stories*. London: Longman.

Brown, N. 1969. *Hermes the Thief*. New York: Vintage.

Campbell, J. 1949. *The Hero with a Thousand Faces*. Bollingen Series 17. Princeton: Princeton University Press.

———. 1959–68. *The Masks of God*. 4 vols. New York: Viking.

———. 1990. *Transformations of Myth through Time*. New York: Harper and Row.

Carroll, M. 1986. *The Cult of the Virgin Mary.* Princeton: Princeton University Press.

Conrad, P. 1987. *A Song of Love and Death: The Meaning of Opera.* New York: Poseidon.

Durkheim, E. 1915. *The Elementary Forms of the Religious Life.* Trans. J. W. Swain. London: Allen and Unwin.

Eliade, M. 1965. *Rites and Symbols of Initiation.* New York: Harper and Row.

Evans-Pritchard, E. E. 1937. *Witchcraft, Oracles, and Magic among the Azande.* Oxford: Clarendon Press.

Fox, R. 1980. *The Red Lamp of Incest.* New York: Dutton. 2nd ed.: Notre Dame, IN: University of Notre Dame Press, 1983.

———. 1989. *The Search for Society.* New Brunswick, NJ: Rutgers University Press.

Frazer, J. 1890. *The Golden Bough.* London: Macmillan.

Freud, S. 1938. *The Basic Writings of Sigmund Freud.* Ed. A. A. Brill. New York: Random House.

———. 1952. *Totem and Taboo.* Trans. J. Strachey. New York: W. W. Norton. (First published 1913, Vienna.)

Freud, S. 1957. *The Future of an Illusion.* Trans. W. D. Robson- Scott. Garden City, NY: Doubleday. (First published 1943.)

Friedrich. P. 1978. *The Meaning of Aphrodite.* Chicago: Chicago University Press.

Graves, R. 1946. *King Jesus.* New York: Farrar Straus.

———. 1948. *The White Goddess: A Historical Grammar of Poetic Myth.* New York: Farrar Straus.

Hughes, T. 1972. *Crow: From the Life and Songs of the Crow.* London: Faber.

Jung, C. G. 1971. *The Portable Jung.* Ed. Joseph Campbell. New York: Viking.

Lévi-Strauss, C. 1958. *Anthropologie structurale.* Paris: Plon.

———. 1962. *Le totemisme aujourd'hui.* Paris: Presses Universitaires de France.

———. 1964. *Le cru et le cuit.* Paris: Plon.

———. 1964–71. *Mythologiques.* 4 vols. Paris: Plon.

Malinowski, B. 1926. *Myth in Primitive Psychology.* London: Kegan Paul.

———. 1948. *Magic, Science, and Religion, and Other Essays.* Glencoe, IL: Free Press.

Malotki, E. 1985. *Gullible Coyote/Una'ihu: A Bilingual Collection of Hopi Coyote Stories.* Tucson: University of Arizona Press.

Marshack, A. 1972. *The Roots of Civilization: The Cognitive Beginnings of Man's First Art, Symbol, and Notation.* New York: McGraw-Hill.

Matthews, W. 1907. *Navaho Myths, Prayers and Songs with Texts and Translations.* Berkeley, CA: University of California Publications in American Archaeology and Ethnology. Vol. 5, no. 2.

Mullahy, P. 1952. *Oedipus: Myth and Complex.* New York: Hermitage Press.

Radcliffe-Brown, A. R. 1952. *Structure and Function in Primitive Society.* London: Cohen and West.

Radin, P., with commentaries by K. Karenyi and C. G. Jung. 1956. *The Trickster: A Study in American Indian Mythology.* London: Routledge.

Raglan, Lord. 1936. *The Hero.* London: Methuen.

Santillana, G. de, and H. von Dechend. 1977. *Hamlet's Mill: An Essay on Myth and the Frame of Time.* Boston: Godine.

Smith, W. R. 1957. *The Religion of the Semites.* New York: Meridian Books. (First published 1889.)

Stevens, A. 1982. *Archetype.* London: Routledge.

Storey, R. 1978. *Pierrot: A Critical History of a Mask.* Princeton: Princeton University Press.

Tedlock, D. 1972. *Finding the Center: Narrative Poetry of the Zuni Indians.* New York: Dial.

Trivers, R. 1985. *Social Evolution.* Menlo Park, CA: Benjamin/Cummings.

Turner, V. 1969. The Ritual Process: Structure and Anti-Structure. Chicago: Aldine.

Twitchell, J. 1985. *Dreadful Pleasures: An Anatomy of Modern Horror.* New York: Oxford University Press.

Ulansey, D. 1989. *The Origins of the Mithraic Mysteries: Cosmology and Salvation in the Ancient World.* New York: Oxford University Press.

Versnel, H. S. 1990. What's Sauce for the Goose Is Sauce for the Gander: Myth and Ritual Old and New. In L. Edmunds, ed., *Approaches to Greek Myth*. Baltimore: Johns Hopkins University Press.

Waters, F. 1963. *The Book of the Hopi*. New York: Viking Press.

Whiting, J.W.M. and I. L. Child. 1953. *Child Training and Personality: A Cross-Cultural Study*. New Haven: Yale University Press.

Winson, J. 1985. *Brain and Psyche: The Biology of the Unconscious*. Garden City, NY: Doubleday.

CHAPTER TWELVE

CROSS-CULTURAL PERSPECTIVES ON CHILDREN'S DEVELOPMENT

Barbara Rogoff and Gilda A. Morelli

Research with children of different cultures provides a broader perspective on human development than is available if one considers human behavior in a single cultural group. In this chapter, we discuss the role of specific cultural practices in organizing all human endeavors. This perspective has influenced the direction of mainstream research, encouraging the advancement of our ideas of the domain-specific nature of psychological processes and their relation to sociocultural practices. We provide a brief description of Vygotsky's theoretical approach, a perspective comfortable for many working within this tradition. Finally, we suggest that the cultural perspective can be useful in advancing research on issues involving American children varying in cultural background.[1]

LESSONS LEARNED FROM CROSS-CULTURAL STUDIES OF DEVELOPMENT

Investigations of the role of culture in development have taken advantage of the impressive variations in the human condition, which occur around the world, to advance understanding of human adaptation. Reviews and discussion of cross-cultural developmental research appear in Bornstein (1980); Dasen (1977); Field et al. (1981); Harkness (1992); Laboratory of Comparative Human Cognition (1979, 1983); Leiderman, Tulkin, and Rosenfeld (1977); LeVine (1989); Munroe and Munroe (1975); Munroe, Munroe, and Whiting (1981); Rogoff, Gauvain, and Ellis (1984); Rogoff and Mistry (1985); Schieffelin and Ochs (1986); Serpell (1976); Super and Harkness (1980); Triandis and Heron (1981); Wagner and Stevenson (1982); Werner (1979); and Whiting and Edwards (1988).

[1]Adapted with permission from *American Psychologist* 44(2):343–48, February 1989.

Cross-cultural studies have focused especially on children in nontechnological (non-Western) societies because these children contrast in important ways with children from the United States and other Western nations. This first section thus describes lessons learned from cross-cultural studies involving children around the world; psychological research on minorities in the United States has followed a somewhat different course, described later.

Perspectives Offered by Cross-Cultural Research

An important function of cross-cultural research has been to allow investigators to look closely at the impact of their own belief systems (folk psychology) on scientific theories and research paradigms. When subjects and researchers are from the same population, interpretations of development may be constrained by implicit cultural assumptions. With subjects who share researchers' belief systems, researchers are less aware of their own assumptions regarding the world of childhood, the involvement of others in child development, and the physical and institutional circumstances in which development is embedded. Working with people from a quite different background can make one aware of aspects of human activity that are not noticeable until they are missing or differently arranged, as with the fish who reputedly is unaware of water until it is removed from it. Viewing the contrasts in life's arrangements in different cultures has enabled scholars to examine very basic assumptions regarding developmental goals, the skills that are learned, and the contexts of development.

Cross-cultural research also allows scholars to use cultural variation as a natural laboratory to attempt to disentangle variables that are difficult to tease apart in the United States and to study conditions that are rare in the United States. For example, one can examine how gender differences manifest themselves in differing cultural circumstances (Whiting and Edwards 1988). Cross-cultural studies have examined the extent to which advances in intellectual skills are related to schooling versus children's age, a comparison that cannot be made in a country with compulsory schooling (Laboratory of Comparative Human Cognition 1979; Rogoff 1981). Other research examines conditions that are seen as normal in other cultures but carry connotations of being problematic in the United States. For example, studies have been made of gender roles in polygynous societies in which fathers are absent from the household because they have several wives (Munroe and Munroe 1975), and of child care and infant psychological development in societies in which nonmaternal care (care by other adults or by child nurses) is valued and expected (Fox 1977; Tronick, Morelli, and Winn 1987; Zaslow 1980).

Another function of cross-cultural studies is to examine the generality of theories of development that have been based on Western children. Examples include investigations of the universality of the stages of development proposed by Piaget, the family role relations emphasized by Freud, and patterns of mother-infant interaction taken to index security of attachment (Bretherton and Waters

1985; Dasen 1977; Dasen and Heron 1981; Greenfield 1976; Malinowski 1927; Price-Williams 1980). In such research, modifications to the assumptions of generality have often been suggested by cross-cultural findings. For example, findings that the highest stage of Piaget's theory, formal operations, seldom can be seen in non-Western cultures prompted Piaget to modify his theory in 1972 to suggest that the formal operational stage may not be universal but rather a product of an individual's expertise in a specific domain.

Research in a variety of cultures has also provided evidence of impressive regularities across cultures in developmental phenomena. For instance, there is marked similarity across cultures in the sequence and timing of sensorimotor milestones in infant development, smiling, and separation distress (Gewirtz 1965; Goldberg 1972; Konner 1972; Super 1981; Werner 1988) and in the order of stages in language development (Bowerman 1981; Slobin 1973).

An Emphasis on Understanding the Context of Development

An important contribution resulting from cultural challenges to researchers' assumptions is the conceptual restructuring emphasizing that human functioning cannot be separated from the contexts of their activities. Although there are other sources of contextual theorizing in the field of psychology, an important impetus has been the consistent findings that behavior and development vary according to cultural context.

Developmental researchers who have worked in other cultures have become convinced that human functioning cannot be separated from the cultural and more immediate context in which children develop. They observed that skills and behavior that did not appear in laboratory situations appeared in the same individuals in everyday situations. A subject whose logical reasoning or memory in a laboratory task seemed rudimentary could skillfully persuade the researcher or remind the researcher of promises outside the laboratory, or might be very skilled in a complex everyday task such as navigation or weaving (Cole 1975; Cole, Hood, and McDermott 1978; Gladwin 1970; Laboratory of Comparative Human Cognition 1979; Rogoff 1981; Scribner 1976). Such informal observations called into question the widespread assumption that individuals' skills and behaviors have a generality extending across contexts.

Systematic studies noted the close relation between the skills or behavior exhibited by an individual and the contexts of elicitation and practice (Lave 1977; Saxe 1988). Children's nurturance and aggression varied as a function of the age and gender of the people with whom they interacted (Wenger 1983; Whiting and Whiting 1975). Perceptual modeling skills of Zambian and English children varied as a function of the cultural familiarity of the specific modeling activity (Serpell 1979). Literacy provided practice with specific cognitive activities, leading to advances in particular skills rather than conferring general cognitive ability (Scribner and Cole 1981). Such results point to the importance of considering the contexts in which people practice skills and behaviors, as well as those in which we as researchers observe them.

Many of the cognitive activities examined in developmental research, such as memory, perception, logical reasoning, and classification, have been found in cross-cultural studies to relate to children's experience of schooling (Lave 1977; Rogoff 1981; Sharp, Cole, and Lave 1979). The extensive studies of the relation between school and cognitive skills call attention to a context of learning that is easily overlooked as an influence on cognitive development in the United States, where school is ubiquitous in the lives of children.

Remembering or classifying lists of unrelated objects may be unusual activities outside of literate or school-related activities (Goody 1977; Rogoff and Waddell 1982). The taxonomic categories seen as most appropriate in literate situations may not be valued in other circumstances, as is illustrated by Glick's (1975) report of Kpelle subjects' treatment of a classification problem. They sorted the twenty objects into functional groups (e.g., knife with orange, potato with hoe) rather than into categorical groups that the researcher considered more appropriate. When questioned, they often volunteered that that was the way a wise man would do things. "When an exasperated experimenter asked finally, 'How would a fool do it,' he was given back sorts of the type that were initially expected—four neat piles with food in one, tools in another, and so on" (p. 636).

People who have more schooling, such as older children and Western peoples, may excel on many kinds of cognitive tests because not only the skills but also the social situations of testing resemble the activities specifically practiced in school. In contrast with everyday life, where people classify and remember things in order to accomplish a functional goal, in schools and tests they perform in order to satisfy an adult's request to do so (Skeen, Rogoff, and Ellis 1983; Super, Harkness, and Baldwin 1977). Individuals with experience in school are likely to have more experience carrying out cognitive processes at the request of an adult without having a clear practical goal (Cazden and John 1971; Rogoff and Mistry in press).

Similar emphasis on contexts of development has come from other domains of cross-cultural research. In the area of infant sensorimotor development, Super (1981) and Kilbride (1980) have argued that the controversy over precocious development in African infants is best resolved by considering the practices of the cultural system in which the babies develop. African infants routinely surpass American infants in their rate of learning to sit and to walk, but not in learning to crawl or to climb stairs. African parents provide experiences for their babies that are apparently intended to teach sitting and walking—propping young infants in a sitting position supported by rolled blankets in a hole in the ground, exercising the newborn's walking reflex, and bouncing babies on their feet. But crawling is discouraged, and stair-climbing skills may be limited by the absence of access to stairs. Infant sensorimotor tests assess an aggregate of skills varying in rate of development according to the opportunity or encouragement to practice them.

Even infant sleep patterns vary as a function of culturally determined sleeping arrangements (Super 1981). In the United States, the common developmental milestone of sleeping for eight uninterrupted hours by age four to five months is regarded as a sign of neurological maturity. In many other cultures, however, the infant sleeps with the mother and is allowed to nurse on demand with minimal disturbance of adult sleep. In such an arrangement, there is less parental motivation to enforce "sleeping through the night," and Super reported that babies continue to wake about every four hours during the night to feed, which is about the frequency of feeding during the day. Thus it appears that this developmental milestone, in addition to its biological basis, is a function of the context in which it develops.

Cross-cultural studies demonstrating that individuals' behavior and skills are closely tied to specific activities have contributed to examination of important questions regarding the generality of the development of skills and behavior, the structure of the ecology of development, and how to conceptualize the sociocultural context of practice of skills and behavior. These issues have recently pervaded the study of developmental psychology, with some large measure of influence from research on culture.

Conceptualizing the Sociocultural Context

Many researchers in the field of culture and development have found themselves comfortable with Vygotsky's theory, which focuses on the sociocultural context of development. Vygotsky's theory, developed in the 1930s in the Soviet Union, has gradually become more accessible to English-speaking researchers, with a rapid upsurge of interest following the publication of *Mind in Society* in 1978 (see also Laboratory of Comparative Human Cognition 1983; Rogoff 1982; Scribner and Cole 1981; Wertsch 1985a, 1985b). Although Vygotsky's theory focuses on cognitive development, it is gaining interest among researchers in emotional and social development as well, perhaps due to its integration of cognitive and social processes, as well as its emphasis on socialization (see, for example, Newson and Newson 1975).

Vygotsky's theory offers a picture of human development that stresses how development is inseparable from human social and cultural activities. This contrasts with the image of the solitary little scientist provided by Piaget's theory. Vygotsky focused on how the development of higher mental processes such as voluntary memory and attention, classification, and reasoning involve learning to use inventions of society (such as language, mathematical systems, and memory devices) and how children are aided in development by guidance provided by people who are already skilled in these tools. Central to Vygotsky's theory is a stress on both the institutional and the interpersonal levels of social context.

The institutional level. Cultural history provides organizations and tools useful to cognitive activity (through institutions such as schools and inventions such as the calculator or literacy) along with practices that facilitate socially appropriate solutions to problems (e.g., norms for the arrangement of grocery shelves to aid shoppers in locating or remembering what they need; common mnemonic devices). Particular forms of activity are practiced in societal institutions such as schools and political systems.

For example, Kohlberg's hierarchy of moral development can be tied to the political system of a society, with the bureaucratic systems' perspective (stage four) appropriate for people whose political frame of reference is a large industrialized society, but inappropriate for people in small traditional tribal societies: "The two types of social systems are very different (though of course both are valid working types of systems), and thus everyday social life in them calls forth different modes of moral problem solving whose adequacy must be judged relative to their particular contexts" (Edwards 1981:524). The political institutions of a society may channel individual moral reasoning by providing standards for the resolution of moral problems.

The cultural institution of Western schooling provides norms and strategies for performance that are considered advanced in cognitive tests. Goodnow (1976) has suggested that differences between cultural groups may be ascribed largely to the interpretation of what problem is being solved in the task and to different values regarding "proper" methods of solution (e.g., speed, reaching a solution with a minimum of moves or redundancy, physically handling materials versus mental shuffling). The cultural tools and techniques used in school involve specific conventions and genres, such as conventions for representing depth in two-dimensional pictures and story-problem genres (similar to logical syllogisms) in which one must rely only on information given in the problem to reach the answer. Cross-cultural studies indicate that nonschooled subjects are unfamiliar with such conventions and genres. For example, they are uncomfortable having to answer questions for which they cannot verify the premises (Cole et al. 1971; Scribner 1977).

The interpersonal level. In Vygotsky's theory (1978), children develop skills in higher mental processes through the immediate social interactional context of activity, as social interaction helps structure individual activity. Information regarding tools and practices is transmitted through children's interaction with more experienced members of society during development, and patterns of interpersonal relations are organized by institutional conventions and the availability of cultural tools. For example, social aspects of experimental and observational situations relate to cultural practices. The relation between experimenter and subject may be rapidly grasped by Western children familiar with testing in school, but it may be highly discrepant from familiar adult-child interactions for non-Western children and young Western children. In some cultural settings, it is unusual for an adult who already knows an answer to request information from a child who may only partially know the subject matter, and it may be inappropriate for children to show off knowledge (Cazden and John 1971; Irvine 1978; Rogoff, Gauvain, and Ellis 1984).

Similarly, in observational situations such as mother-child interaction, culturally varying agendas for public behavior may influence what people do in the presence of an observer (Zaslow and Rogoff 1981). "It seems likely that one influence of the observer on parents is to produce a heightened frequency of behavior that the participants judge to be more socially desirable and inhibit behavior considered socially undesirable" (Pedersen 1981:181). Graves and Glick (1978) found that exchanges between middle-class mothers and their toddlers varied as a function of whether mothers thought that they were being videotaped. Mothers spoke more, used indirect directives more often, and spent more time in joint interactive focus with their children when they thought that they were being observed. Clearly, people's interpretation of the goals of a task and cultural rules guiding social behavior influence the display of public behavior. Values regarding interpersonal relations may be inseparable from the activities observed for research purposes.

In addition to the cultural structuring of social interaction that has importance for research into human development, social interaction provides an essential context for development itself. Vygotsky stressed that interpersonal situations are important for guiding children in their development of the skills and behaviors considered important in their culture. Working within the "zone of proximal development," adults guide children in carrying out activities that are beyond the children's individual skills, and this joint problem solving provides children with information appropriate to stretch their individual skills. Cole (1981) argued that the zone of proximal development is "where culture and cognition create each other." Thus Vygotsy's conceptualization of how individual efforts are embedded in the interpersonal and institutional contexts of culture is proving useful for understanding the relation between culture and the individual.

RESEARCH ON CULTURE INVOLVING MINORITIES IN THE UNITED STATES

Historically, research on minorities in the United States has followed a different course than the cross-cultural investigations discussed earlier. For many years, researchers were intent on comparing the behavior and skills of minority children with those of mainstream children without taking into consideration the cultural contexts in which minority and mainstream children develop. This approach involved "deficit-model" assumptions that mainstream skills and upbringing are normal and that variations observed with minorities are aberrations that produce deficits; intervention programs were designed to provide minority children with experiences to make up for their assumed deficits (Cole and Bruner 1971; Hilliard and Vaughn-Scott 1982; Howard and Scott 1981; Ogbu 1982).

The deficit model previously used in research on minority children contrasts sharply with the assumptions of the cross-cultural approach, which attempts to avoid ethnocentric evaluation of one group's practices and beliefs as being superior without considering their origins and functions from the perspective of the reality of that cultural group. With research in their own country, however, researchers have had more difficulty avoiding the assumption that the majority practices are proper (Obbu 1982). Variations have been assumed to account for the generally lower social status of the minority-group members. It is only recently, and largely through the efforts of researchers with minority backgrounds, that deficit assumptions have been questioned in research on minority children.

The working model that appears to predominate in current minority research is one in which the positive features of cultural variation are emphasized. Although this is a valuable shift, we feel that research on minorities must move beyond reiterating the value of cultural diversity and begin more seriously to examine the source and functioning of the diversity represented in the United States to increase our understanding of the processes underlying development in cultural context.

Not only is the diversity of cultural backgrounds in our nation a resource for the creativity and future of the nation, it is also a resource for scholars studying how children develop. To make good use of this information, cultural research with minorities needs to focus on examining the processes and functioning of the cultural context of development. This focus requires "unpackaging" culture or minority status (Whiting 1976) so as to disentangle the workings of the social context of development. This has become a central effort of cross-cultural research on non-Western populations.

Pioneering researchers of minorities also look at the contexts in which children from different cultures develop, and these efforts provide a basis for a greater understanding of how culture channels development. (Examples include Brown and Reeve 1985; Cazden, John, and Hymes 1975; Chisholm 1983; Erickson and Mohatt 1982; Laboratory of Comparative Human Cognition 1986; Ogbu 1982.) It is notable that some of the most interesting efforts involve combining approaches from anthropology and education with those of psychology (see also recent issues of *Anthropology and Education Quarterly*).

The potential from research on cultural groups around the world as well as down the street lies in its challenge to our systems of assumptions and in the creative efforts of scholars to synthesize knowledge from observations of differing contexts of human development. Such challenge and synthesis are fruitful in the efforts to achieve a deeper and broader understanding of human nature and nurture.

NOTE

The authors express their thanks to Ana Estrada for her comments on this chapter.

REFERENCES

Bornstein, M. H. 1980. Cross-Cultural Developmental Psychology, Pp. 231–81 in M. H. Bornstein, ed., *Comparative Methods in Psychology*. Hillsdale, NJ: Erlbaum.

Bowerman, M. 1981. Language Development. Pp. 93–185 in H. C. Triandis and A. Heron, eds. *Handbook of Cross-Cultural Psychology*, vol. 4. Boston: Allyn and Bacon.

Bretherton, I., and E. Waters, eds. 1985. Growing Points of Attachment Theory and Research. *Monographs of the Society for Research in Child Development* 50.

Brown, A. L., and R. A. Reeve. 1985. Bandwidths of Competence: The Role of Supportive Contexts in Learning and Development. Technical Report no. 336. Champaign: University of Illinois at Urbana-Champaign, Center for the Study of Reading.

Cazden, C. B., and V. P. John. 1971. Learning in American Indian Children. Pp. 252–72 in M. L. Wax, S. Diamond, and F. O. Gearing, eds., *Anthropological Perspectives on Education*. New York: Basic Books.

Cazden, C. B., V. P. John, and D.Hymes, eds. 1975. *Functions of Language in the Classroom*. New York: Teachers College Press.

Chisholm, J. D. 1983. *Navajo Infancy: An Ethological Study of Child Development*. Hawthorne, NY: Aldine.

Cole, M. 1975. An Ethnographic Psychology of Cognition. Pp. 157–75 in R. W. Brislin, S. Bochner, and W. J. Lonner, eds., *Cross-Cultural Perspectives on Learning*. Beverly Hills, CA: Sage.

———. 1981. The Zone of Proximal Development: Where Culture and Cognition Create Each Other. Report no. 106. San Diego: University of California, Center for Human Information Processing.

Cole, M. J. Gay, J. A. Glick, and D. W. Sharp. 1971. *The Cultural Context of Learning and Thinking*. New York: Basic Books.

Cole, M., and J. S. Bruner. 1971. Cultural Differences and Inferences about Psychological Processes. *American Psychologist* 26:867–76.

Cole, M., L. Hood, ant R. P. McDermott. 1978. Concepts of Ecological Validity: Their Differing Implications for Comparative Cognitive Research. *Quarterly Newsletter of the Institute for Comparative Human Development* 2:34–37.

Dasen, P. R., ed. 1977. *Piagetian Psychology: Cross-Cultural Contributions*. New York: Gardner Press.

Dasen, P. R., and A. Heron. 1981. Cross-Cultural Tests of Piaget's Theory. Pp. 295–341 in H. C. Triandis and A. Heron, eds., *Handbook of Cross-Cultural Psychology*, vol. 4. Boston: Allyn and Bacon.

Edwards, C. P. 1981. The Comparative Study of the Development of Moral Judgment and Reasoning. Pp. 501–28 in R. H. Munroe, R. L. Munroe, and B. B. Whiting, eds., *Handbook of Cross-Cultural Human Development*. New York: Garland.

Erickson, F., and G. Mohatt. 1982. Cultural Organization of Participation Structures in Two Classrooms of Indian Students. Pp. 132–74 in G. Spindler, ed., *Doing the Ethnography of Schooling*. New York: Holt, Rinehart and Winston.

Field, T. M., A. M. Sostek, P. Vietze, and P. H. Leiderman, eds. 1981. *Culture and Early Interactions*. Hillsdale, NJ: Erlbaum.

Fox, N. A. 1977. Attachment of Kibbutz Infants to Mother and Metapelet. *Child Development* 48: 1228–39.

Gewirtz, J. L. 1965. The Course of Infant Smiling in Four Child-Rearing Environments in Israel. Pp. 205–48 in B. M. Foss, ed., *Determinants of Infant Behavior*, vol. 3. London: Methuen.

Gladwin, T. 1970. *East Is a Big Bird*. Cambridge, MA: Harvard University Press.

Glick, J. 1975. Cognitive Development in Cross-Cultural Perspectives. Pp. 595–654 in F. Horowitz, ed., *Review of Child Development Research*, vol. 4. Chicago: University of Chicago Press.

Goldberg, S. 1972. Infant Care and Growth in Urban Zambia. *Human Development* 15:77–89.

Goodnow, J. J. 1976. The Nature of Intelligent Behavior: Questions Raised by Cross-Cultural Studies. Pp. 169–88 in L. B. Resnick, ed., *The Nature of Intelligence*. Hillsdale, NJ: Erlbaum.

Goody, J. 1977. *The Domestication of the Savage Mind*. Cambridge, Eng.: Cambridge University Press.

Graves, Z. R., and J. Glick. 1978. The Effect of Context on Mother-Child Interaction. *Quarterly Newsletter of the Institute for Comparative Human Development* 2:41–46.

Greenfield, P. M. 1976. Cross-Cultural Research and Piagetian Theory: Paradox and Progress.

Pp. 322–45 in K. F. Riegel and J. A. Meacham, eds., *The Developing Individual in a Changing World*, vol. 1. Chicago: Aldine.

Harkness, S. 1992. Human Development in Psychological Anthropology. Pp. 102–22 in T. Schwartz, G. White, and C. Lutz, eds., *New Directions in Psychological Anthropology*. Cambridge, Eng.: Cambridge University Press.

Hilliard, A. G., III, and M. Vaughn-Scott. 1982. The Quest for the "Minority" Child. Pp. 175–89 in S. G. Moore and C. R. Cooper, eds., *The Young Child: Reviews of Research*, vol. 3 Washington, DC: National Association for the Education of Young Children.

Howard, A., and R. A. Scott. 1981. The Study of Minority Groups in Complex Societies. Pp. 113–52 in R. H. Munroe, R. L. Munroe, and B. B. Whiting, eds., *Handbook of Cross-Cultural Human Development*. New York: Garland.

Irvine, J. T. 1978. Wolof "Magical Thinking": Culture and Conservation Revisited. *Journal of Cross-Cultural Psychology* 9:300–10.

Kilbride, P. L. 1980. Sensorimotor Behavior of Baganda and Samoa Infants. *Journal of Cross-Cultural Psychology* 11:131–52.

Konner, M. 1972. Aspects of Developmental Ethology of a Foraging People. Pp. 285–304 in N. Blurton Jones, ed., *Ethological Studies of Child Behavior*. Cambridge, Eng.: Cambridge University Press.

Laboratory of Comparative Human Cognition. 1979. Cross-Cultural Psychology's Challenges to Our Ideas of Children and Development. *American Psychologist* 34:827–33.

———. 1983. Culture and Cognitive Development. Pp. 294–356 in W. Kessen, ed., *Handbook of Child Psychology: Vol. I. History, Theory and Methods*. New York: Wiley.

———. 1986. Contributions of Cross-Cultural Research to Educational Practice. *American Psychologist* 41:1049–58.

Lave, J. 1977. Tailor-Made Experiments and Evaluating the Intellectual Consequences of Apprenticeship Training. *Quarterly Newsletter of the Institute for Comparative Human Development* 1:1–3.

Leiderman, P. H., S. R. Tulkin, and A. Rosenfeld, eds., 1977. *Culture and Infancy: Variations in Human Experience*. New York: Academic Press.

LeVine, R. A. 1989. Environments in Child Development: An Anthropological Perspective. In W. Damon, ed., *Child Development Today and Tomorrow*. San Francisco: Jossey-Bass.

Malinowski, B. 1927. *The Father in Primitive Psychology*. New York: Norton.

Munroe, R. L., and R. H. Munroe. 1975. *Cross-Cultural Human Development*. Monterey, CA: Brooks/Cole.

Munroe, R. H., R. L. Munroe, and B. B. Whiting, eds. 1981. *Handbook of Cross-Cultural Human Development*. New York: Garland.

Newson, J., and E. Newson. 1975. Intersubjectivity and the Transmission of Culture: On the Social Origins of Symbolic Functioning. *Bulletin of the British Psychological Society* 28:437–46.

Ogbu, J. U. 1982. Socialization: A Cultural Ecological Approach. Pp. 253–67 in K. M. Borman, ed., *The Social Life of Children in a Changing Society*. Hillsdale, NJ: Erlbaum.

Pedersen, F. A., ed., 1980. *The Father-Infant Relationship: Observational Studies in the Family Setting*. New York: Praeger.

Piaget, J. 1972. Intellectual Evolution from Adolescence to Adulthood. *Human Development* 15:1–12.

Price-Williams, D. R. 1980. Anthropological Approaches to Cognition and Their Relevance to Psychology. Pp. 155–84 in H. C. Triandis and W. Lonner, eds., *Handbook of Cross-Cultural Psychology*, vol. 3. Boston: Allyn and Bacon.

Rogoff, B. 1981. Schooling and the Development of Cognitive Skills. Pp. 233–94 in H. C. Triandis and A. Heron, eds., *Handbook of Cross-Cultural Psychology*, vol. 4. Boston: Allyn and Bacon.

———. 1982. Integrating Context and Cognitive Development. Pp. 125–70 in M. E. Lamb and A. L. Brown, eds., *Advances in Developmental Psychology*, vol. 2. Hillsdale, NJ: Erlbaum.

Rogoff, B., M. Gauvain, and S. Ellis. 1984. Development Viewed in its Cultural Context. Pp. 533–71 in M. H. Bornstein and M. E. Lamb, eds., *Developmental Psychology*. Hillsdale, NJ: Erlbaum.

Rogoff, B., and J. J. Mistry. 1985. Memory Development in Cultural Context. Pp. 117–42 in M. Pressley and C. Brainerd, eds., *Cognitive Learning and Memory in Children: Progress in Cognitive Development Research*. New York: Springer-Verlag.

———. In press. The Social and Motivational Context of Children's Memory Skills. In R. Fivish and J. Hudson, eds., *What Young Children Remember and Why*. Cambridge, Eng.: Cambridge University Press.

Rogoff, B., and K. J. Waddell. 1982. Memory for Information Organized in a Scene by Children from Two Cultures. *Child Development* 53:1224–28.

Saxe, G. B. 1988. Mathematics in and out of School. Unpublished manuscript, University of California at Los Angeles.

Schieffelin, B. B., and E. Ochs, eds. 1986. *Language Socialization across Cultures*. Cambridge, Eng.: Cambridge University Press.

Scribner, S. 1976. Situating the Experiment in Cross-Cultural Research. Pp. 310–21 in K. F. Riegel and J. A. Meacham, eds., *The Developing Individual in a Changing World*, vol. 1. Chicago: Aldine.

———. 1977. Modes of Thinking and Ways of Speaking: Culture and Logic Reconsidered. Pp. 483–500 in P. N. Johnson-Laird and P. C. Wason, eds., *Thinking*. Cambridge, Eng.: Cambridge University Press.

Scribner, S., and M. Cole. 1981. *The Psychology of Literacy*. Cambridge, MA: Harvard University Press.

Serpell, R. 1976. *Culture's Influence on Behaviour*. London: Methuen.

———. 1979. How Specific Are Perceptual Skills? A Cross-Cultural Study of Pattern Reproduction. *British Journal of Psychology* 70:365–80.

Sharp, D., M. Cole, and C. Lave. 1979. Education and Cognitive Development: The Evidence from Experimental Research. *Monographs of the Society for Research in Child Development* 44.

Skeen, J., B. Rogoff, and S. Ellis. 1983. Categorization by Children and Adults in Communication Contexts. *International Journal of Behavioral Development* 5:213–20.

Slobin, D. I. 1973. Cognitive Prerequisites for the Development of Grammar. Pp. 175–200 in C. A. Ferguson and D. I. Slobin, eds., *Studies of Child Language Development*. New York: Holt, Rinehart and Winston.

Super, C. M. 1981. Behavioral Development in Infancy. Pp. 181–270 in R. H. Munroe, R. L. Munroe, and B. B. Whiting, eds., *Handbook of Cross-Cultural Human Development*. New York: Garland.

Super, C. M., and S. Harkness, eds., 1980. *Anthropological Perspectives on Child Development*. San Francisco: Jossey-Bass.

Super, C. M., S. Harkness, and L. M. Baldwin. 1977. Category Behavior in Natural Ecologies and in Cognitive Tests. *Quarterly Newsletter of the Institute for Comparative Human Development* 1:4–7.

Triandis, H. C., and A. Hero, eds. 1981. *Handbook of Cross-Cultural Psychology*, vol. 4. Boston: Allyn and Bacon.

Tronick, E. Z., G. A. Morelli, and S. Winn. 1987. Multiple Caretaking of Efe (Pygmy) Infants. *American Anthropologist* 89:96–106.

Vygotsky, L. S. 1978. *Mind in Society: The Development of Higher Psychological Processes*. Cambridge, MA: Harvard University Press.

Wagner, D. A., and H. W. Stevenson, eds. 1982. *Cultural Perspectives on Child Development*. San Francisco: W. H. Freeman.

Wenger, M. 1983. Gender Role Socialization in East Africa: Social Interactions between 2-to-3-Year Olds and Older Children, A Social Ecological Perspective. Ph.D. diss., Harvard University.

Werner, E. E. 1979. *Cross-Cultural Child Development.* Monterey, CA: Brooks/Cole.

———. 1988. A Cross-Cultural Perspective on Infancy. *Journal of Cross-Cultural Psychology* 19: 96–113.

Wertsch, J. V., ed. 1985a. *Culture, Communication, and Cognition: Vygotskian Perspectives.* Cambridge, Eng.: Cambridge University Press.

———. 1985b. *Vygotsky and the Social Formation of Mind.* Cambridge, Ma: Harvard University Press.

Whiting, B. B. 1976. The Problem of the Packaged Variable. In K. F. Riegel and J. A. Meacham, eds., *The Developing Individual in a Changing World.* Chicago: Aldine.

Whiting, B. B., and C. P. Edwards. 1988. *Children of Different Worlds.* Cambridge, Ma: Harvard University Press.

Whiting, B. B., and J.W.M. Whiting. 1975. *Children of Six Cultures: A Psycho-Cultural Analysis.* Cambridge, MA: Harvard University Press.

Zaslow, M. 1980. Relationships among Peders in Kibbutz Toddler Groups. *Child Psychiatry and Human Development* 10:178–89.

Zaslow, M., and B. Rogoff. 1981. The Cross-Cultural Study of Early Interaction: Implications from Research in Culture and Cognition. Pp. 237–56 in T. M. Field, A. M. Sostek, P. Vietze, and P. H. Leiderman, eds., *Culture and Early Interactions.* Hillsdale, NJ: Erlbaum.

CHAPTER THIRTEEN

THE EVIDENCE FROM THE ARTS

Philip K. Bock

A central topic of all the humanities is the relationship between the arts (including verbal and written forms) and human psychology. Alex Alland (1983) has suggested that "playing with form" is a critical attribute of being human, and all societies seem to possess some types of aesthetic expression. Only the tragically deprived "Ik" were claimed by Turnbull (1972) to "have no music"; if true, this could be understood as a pathological exception. The universality of at least graphic, musical, and verbal arts seems to be well established (Brown 1991:140), and attempts have been made to discover the biological basis of this panhuman activity (Dissanayake 1988).

Our concern in this chapter is less with the universals of artistic expression than with the evidence such works provide of group and individual differences in perception, motivation, and cognition. This is an extremely difficult topic, and a naive approach that tries to move from a work of art to the psychology (or pathology) of its maker will not do. Culture is always present, selecting topics and media, teaching techniques and standards, and providing models for the artist to use or to rebel against. It would be well to make explicit the assumption that art always performs both social and personal functions, but that these can be inferred from art products only with the greatest of care.

For example, Nancy Munn's remarkable study, *Walbiri Iconography* (1986), examined graphic signs employed in this central Australian society to represent social groups, animal species, geographic locations, and many other things. She discussed differences in the signs and media employed by men and women, pointing out that apparently simple geometric forms are interpreted by Walbiri according to context to yield quite different meanings. Thus an arch and a circle drawn in the sand may represent a person sitting at a water hole or a woman sitting digging for yams, while an oval with a line along its axis represents a sleeper in a "bed" (traditionally, an oval depression in the earth). These figures are drawn by women as they tell stories. Women also use charcoal, red ochre, and white pigment to paint their bodies on ceremonial occasions, and these designs too have a range of meanings (e.g., parallel vertical lines may indicate rain falling, headbands, paths, teeth, or other items).

Another set of graphics (animal footprints, circles, and lines) is used in conversations about journeys and places. "The circle signifies a locale and the line a path or movement from place to place"; these signs may be used by men or women, but "men apply them more widely, giving them a featured place in their storytelling and ancestral designs" (1986:119). In general, circles have female, domestic, and enclosed meanings, while lines represent males, paths, and movement. Combined forms may be used by men to represent ancestors and are drawn on the body or on ceremonial boards.

Munn's close analysis of these signs and their relationships to kinship groups, myths, and dreams brought out the psychological significance of this graphic tradition. She pointed out the connections of signs with a person's identity, fertility, and territory. Designs and songs are "complementary channels of communication; each is a repository of narrative meaning, and the production of one may evoke the other" (1986:148). The Walbiri's sense of self is closely related to specific ancestors and locations portrayed in stories and ceremonies; these are differentiated by gender:

> Women's stories are focused in the rhythms of family life: the activities of sleeping and eating that are localized in the camp, the separation of men and women for hunting and foraging activities and their reunification at night within the camp. . . . In men's narratives, on the other hand, the site-path patterns forms a "language" for the macrotemporal rhythms of nomadic movement from place to place. . . . The circular "camp" connotes the vital activities of eating, sleeping (dreaming), and sexuality of the family camp; similarly, the track line expresses movement toward and away from the camp, with its connotations of following game and food. . . . In addition, men's narratives bind events to an objective geographical space through the listing of named places. (Munn 1986:214; compare Basso 1988 on the use of place names in Western Apache storytelling.)

Thus we see that signs, songs, and stories come together in Walbiri life to define and express the essence of gender, personhood, and social unity.

Among the Suyá, a Gê-speaking people of the Amazon basin, song holds a position of great importance to the understanding of personhood and emotional expression. As described by Anthony Seeger (1987), "Singing enabled individuals to create and express certain aspects of self, it established and sustained a feeling of euphoria . . . and it related the present to the powerful and transformative past" (p. 128). While Seeger admitted that long periods of ceremonial singing and dance "probably altered perception," he insisted that this was experienced by Suyá "as social beings, not as purely physiological entities"

(p. 129). Indeed, different types of songs furnished a key to their ethnopsychology.

The Suyá concept of person, we are told, involved three district parts: the physical body, a social identity (derived from naming practices), and a unique spirit, essential to life. According to Seeger:

> One or more song genres were associated with each aspect of the person. Invocations and weeping were associated with the physical body and close relatives. Invocations acted on the body itself. Women usually wept for close kinsmen. Unison songs were usually associated with one or another name-based plaza group, and many solo performances were determined by name-set membership. The shout songs were as individualized as the spirit. Each person had his own for each ceremony, of a style more or less appropriate to his age. (1987:129)

Thus, in the Mouse Ceremony, when men become mice for fifteen hours, enact mythical events including the origin of corn, distribute food, and again become men, individual and community identity are reasserted. "Shouting new songs, leaping, dancing, stamping, and singing the Mouse Songs, they participated in a creative act that far transcended the sounds alone, but was a part of many aspects of their lives and . . . their society" (1987:140).

My own research on music in the Mexican city of Mérida (Yucatan) revealed a series of genres that were associated with age and social class, but that also defined a continuum of psychological attitudes (from nostalgic to romantic to ironic). Like Walbiri signs or Suyá songs, these genres may be used to assert personal and group identity. The people of Mérida have access to a wide range of live and recorded music; individually, however,

> they may identify most strongly with the persistent *cumbia* beat . . . but they still have the option of listening to ballads in nostalgic *trova* or romantic "pop" styles, or of hearing Euroamerican rock with its messages of love, sex, and aggression. To understand how individuals and groups use these forms to discover, construct, or express their own feelings and identities is the next challenge that faces students of urban music. (Bock 1992:53; Kaemmer 1993:148)

STYLE AND PSYCHOLOGY

More than thirty years ago, George Devereux and Weston LaBarre surveyed the work by anthropologists and psychologists on the relationship of art to personality (in Kaplan 1961). It is not my intention to bring this survey up-to-date, but rather to discuss whether our approach to the issue has changed since then.

For Devereux, genuine art always involves the tension between individual affect and cultural convention; if either is missing, you may have expressiveness or craftsmanship, but not art. Culture contributes a *style* that selects both form and appropriate content, and that inevitably distorts the feelings that motivate it: "In brief, art is stylized (distorted) communication, recognizable as art by artist and connoisseur alike'' (Devereux 1961:367). This approach to art calls for interpretation of the (unconscious) messages that are communicated by the work. According to Devereux, aesthetic style provides an ''alibi'' that allows the superego to consider painful or upsetting truths: ''In brief, art can function as a social safety valve precisely because, like wit, it is a compromise and is, moreover, repudiable as to intent and content. It permits the artist to say—and the consumer to hear (or to see)—the forbidden'' (1961:369).

LaBarre's contribution to the two-part essay began with a discussion of children's drawings and projective tests, going on to praise Anthony Wallace's (1950) attempt to infer personality characteristics of ancient Mayan men from three hieroglyphic codices. He then summarized a large number of studies of topics including symbols, myths, folktales, drawings, films, music, rituals, and literature (LaBarre 1961:390:403). Although most of these studies are psychoanalytic, LaBarre pointed out that ''awareness of the value of mythology in studying psychological and ethnographic problems was early evident in the mainstream of American anthropology'' (p. 391).

Common to almost all of these early studies is the notion that the analyst should be able to discover personality traits or dynamics by examining cultural products and performances. A drawing, a dance, or a ritual drama are all treated as materials to be interpreted from the outside, using techniques derived from therapeutic practice. The analyst often makes use of historical or secondhand data, feeling no need to check his or her interpretations with the people described; rather, verification comes from consistency of pattern.

If there has been a major change in the use of evidence from the arts in psychological anthropology, it has been in a shift to a more internal view of the creative process, questioning folk artists and their audiences about their perceptions and motivations and allowing psychological characteristics to emerge from close study of the forms themselves. Thus in the works of Nancy Munn and Anthony Seeger discussed earlier, while the explicit goal is not psychological, we nevertheless learn a great deal about Walbiri and Suyá personality and ethnopsychology. The ''evidence'' is very rich, and the interpretation (e.g., of gender differences or ethnic identity) is tied to artistic practice in each society. (See also the articles in Anderson and Field 1993.)

Of course, not all recent studies strive for such an inside view; but those that do so are less likely than the earlier approach to explain aesthetic diversity by alleged psychological constants or to infer psychopathology from stylized cultural products. A few more examples should help to demonstrate these points.

Raymond Firth (with Mervyn McLean) recently published a study of the songs of a Polynesian society that he has known for over fifty years. The goal of *Tikopia Songs* is to present as faithfully as possible the distinctive musical tradition of an isolated people—their songs of pleasure and of sadness—expressing social relations of affection, conflict, and loss. Although the book has no psychological pretensions, the author is clearly correct to claim that

> Tikopia songs, whether ancient or modern, offer important clues to the understanding of Tikopia ways of thought and patterns of emotional expression. The verbal imagery is often vivid, allusive, metaphorical, revealing attitudes between the sexes, kinship bonds, occasions of joy or sorrow, [and] conceptions of the environment. (Firth 1990:294)

Other careful studies of music that have significant psychosocial implications include Steven Feld's (1982) book on Kaluli aesthetics and John M. Chernoff's (1979) exploration of West African drumming. For instance, in the former we read that "there is no term for singing in unison and indeed Kaluli never . . . sing together, starting and stopping at precise or discrete times. Rather, the important factor is the continuity of flow in the overlapping. . . . The parts are layered, not linear" (Feld 1982:177).

The contrast between this aesthetic and the unison songs of the Suyá or the dirges of Tikopia is striking. It implies cultural and perhaps psychological differences, with the Kaluli style showing similarity to the overlapping, well-blended choral singing of central Africa. Alan Lomax called this style "cohesive" and demonstrated that it correlated cross-culturally with a host of social and economic features, including childhood training for "compliance' rather than "assertion." Lomax concluded that "the kind of training children experience does seem to affect the way the people in the culture sing together. (Lomax et al. 1968:191). If so, song style may be used as one index of personality, but with care not to overgeneralize or to lose sight of individual differences. (On child training and drawing, see Barry, Bacon, and Child 1957 and Alland 1983.)

INFERENCES FROM TEXTS

Oral and written texts are, of course, commonly used to infer the psychological characteristics of their speakers or writers. (For an extreme case, see Doody 1991.) Using their favorite theories, psychologists have analyzed the character and motivation of figures in ancient myths and more recent literary work, as well as their authors and audiences. Anthropologists too have played this game (see the chapter by Robin Fox in this volume), but many have been concerned with exotic texts or with the artful products of personally known informants.

For example, Janet Hoskins (1985) has studied the "changing poetics of personal experience" as documented in the life histories of her Indonesian informant, Maru Daku. A man of "lively intelligence" (who had previously served as an informant for Rodney Needham), Maru Daku was quite willing to describe and interpret local customs for Hoskins; but due to his exposure to Protestant Christianity and to other anthropologists, she at first avoided him. (I had a similar relationship with "Pedro Martinez" during my fieldwork in Tepoztlán; cf. Lewis 1964.) Eventually, they became close, and he began to display his great verbal facility, spontaneously breaking into parallel couplets of formal orations and juicy anecdotes about local affairs. In many ways, he was a typical "marginal man," torn between East and West, between Christianity and the traditions of his ancestors:

> During the course of my work with him, he outlined his life history to me on three different occasions, each time in a totally different way. The first time, shortly after we met, he spoke of his years in government service and his involvement with the outside world. The second time he spoke of his family: his four marriages (one of which ended in divorce) and a scandalous extramarital liaison with a woman of the same matriclan. . . . The third time, impressing me with still another dimension of his life, he told me his ritual history, beginning with his training as a bearer of traditional knowledge and progressing through his participation in his father's feasts and finally his sponsorship of ceremonies in his own name. In each of these accounts, he was outlining one of the anchors of his social world [i.e., government, family, and religion]. (Hoskins 1985:153–54)

The article concluded with a long text in formal style, composed by Maru Daku as a summation of his complex life and a farewell to the ethnographer. In this he modified a traditional genre, the lament narrative, to serve his personal purposes, revealing conflicts and justifying his actions:

> Maru Daku constructed his lament around choices: the choice to work with me, the choice to ignore the jealousy of his fellows, the choice to defy his own illness and exhaustion to finish our translations before I left. . . .
>
> Thus the creation of a version of the self, a life history cast in traditional couplets, is also the creation of new possibilities for Sumbanese poetic expression. It is fitting that such possibilities should have been created by a man who was also instrumental in opening up parts of his own culture to the outside world and translating them into the national language. (Hoskins 1985:166–67)

For an extended discussion of language, poetry, and the self, see Paul Friedrich (1986); on alternative life histories, see also Angrosino (1989). Bock (1993) analyzed a poem by Shakespeare, revealing a specific psychic conflict that will be discussed later. Examples of "exotic texts" that have been examined in part for their psychological implications range from Theodor Reik's (1970) psychoanalytic treatment of ancient myth and scripture to Dennis Tedlock's (1985) ethnographic contextualization of the Quiché Maya Popol Vuh. A recent example based on a familiar text is the discussion of Genesis by Dan W. Forsyth (1991).

Focusing on a dozen stories in Genesis of "conflict between brothers" from Cain and Abel (murder) to Joseph and his brothers (reconciliation), Forsyth argued that sibling rivalry is a persistent theme in the first book of the Bible. Furthermore, with few exceptions, it is the younger brother who triumphs. Forsyth suggested that these "brother stories" convey two (hidden) messages. The first has to do with a historical shift from hierarchy and primogeniture to a more egalitarian and individualistic social order; the second message depicts "the dangers and opportunities of human life as the individual moves from early childhood dependency, through oedipal sexuality and aggression, to the independence, cooperation, and productivity of mature adulthood'' (Forsyth 1991: 462).

The sequence of sibling rivalries is claimed to show increasing autonomy (of the younger brother), diminishing physical coercion, increasing secularization, and increased ''tenderness and respect'' between father and son, culminating (by a sudden mythical shift) in Christian redemption through sacrifice. Taken together, these stories of conflict between brothers ''portray the breakdown of an ascribed hierarchical social order through the anomalous triumph of traditionally subordinate agents,'' leading to a messianic order in which mercy and justice prevail—a resolution that ''may account . . . for the widespread appeal of Genesis'' (1991:502).

Forsyth's argument involves the same kind of selection of cases and abstraction from concrete detail as is found in Claude Lévi-Strauss's structural analysis of myth. When Lévi-Strauss (1963:215) finished with the Oedipus myth, it was shown to have an underlying structure based on binary oppositions between overrating versus underrating of blood relations and between affirmation versus denial of the autochthonous origin of mankind. Similarly abstract conclusions were reached in his detailed studies of kinship systems, food preparation, Amerindian myths, music, and literature, for the goal of Lévi-Strauss was to penetrate the cultural contents to reach an understanding of the human mind.

In this project, he often proposed questions that would not occur to most anthropologists; for example, what is the connection between a certain species of bird, the craft of pottery, and the emotion of jealousy (Lévi-Strauss 1988)? Starting with a Jívaro myth, he pursued these topics throughout the Americas, showing the complex transformations that reduce to an underlying structure that is also realized in other realms of social life (1988:67, 175). It is only at this fundamental structural level that we can glimpse the binary basis of human thought and the processes that he believed are founded in the organization of the brain. Thus Lévi-Strauss can certainly be claimed as a psychological anthropologist, even though he marched to a different drummer.

Psychological interpretations of literature take many forms. It is no longer popular to analyze the neuroses of fictional characters, though many fascinating essays have been written about the reasons for Hamlet's ''delay'' or Leopold Bloom's fantasies. Most recent studies focus on the cultural context of literary works or the psychological dynamics of authors and their audiences. In one well-known study, Stephen Greenblatt (1980) examined sixteenth-century English prose, paintings, poems, and plays. He noted that ''there appears to be an increased self-consciousness about the fashioning of human identity as a manipulable, artful process'' and concluded that ''the Renaissance figures we have considered'' (More, Tyndale, Wyatt, Spenser, Marlowe, and Shakespeare) understood that ''to abandon self-fashioning . . . is to die'' (Greenblatt 1980:2, 257).

Shakespeare's works have been the subject of numerous psychological interpretations, including studies of the personality of the author and his creative use of language as well as attempts to understand Elizabethan culture through the dynamics of his plays (e.g., Schwartz and Kahn 1980). My own work has included all these types of studies. For example, examination of Shakespeare's color vocabulary and the frequency of different basic terms lends support to Berlin and Kay's theory of color-term evolution: "Elizabethan English was a Stage VII language in which 'orange' was just becoming a basic term whereas 'pink' was not yet a color term" (Bock 1990:165). In the same article, studies of silence, body parts, and the "self" as represented in Shakespeare's plays were summarized.

In another paper, one of Shakespeare's poems was analyzed from the point of view of early object-relations theory. "The Phoenix and Turtle" is a peculiar poem of only sixty-seven lines in which the "chaste" love of the turtledove for the mythological phoenix is commemorated. First published in 1601, it was part of a collection in which the two birds frequently represented Elizabeth and Essex; however, I argued that Shakespeare took this occasion "to write about the paradox of ideal love out of the depths of his personal experience" (Bock 1993:55). Thus in the seventh stanza, we read:

So they loved as love in twain
Had the essence but in one,
Two distincts, division none;
Number there in love was slain.

I read this as a statement of the paradoxical dual unity that exists between mother and child during the early months of infancy, the "symbiotic phase" from which "all subsequent human relations form" (Mahler, Pine, and Bergman 1975:48). My argument was that the poet had unusual access to these pregenital experiences and that he expressed them in several obscure passages in this poem and in *Hamlet*, which was written at about the same time. Investigation of bird symbolism added some force to this interpretation, especially with regard to the filial piety of the phoenix and its association with the sun god Hyperion (cf. *Hamlet* I, ii, 140 and III, iv, 56, where the Prince likens his own father to Hyperion).

In the final stanza, we are invited to join in mourning for the Truth and Beauty represented by the phoenix and turtle at their funeral pyre:

To this urn let those repair,
That are either true or fair,
For these dead birds, sigh a prayer.

To the extent that we are moved by this strange poem, it is because we have all experienced the symbiosis of early infancy and mourn its loss. "We move back from the dream, or the memory, or the memory of the dream, into nostalgia for a dual unity that will never again be ours'' (Bock 1993:53).

Anthropological studies of other arts such as cave paintings, dance, pottery, weaving, and ritual performances all have implications for psychology, though these have seldom been spelled out or tested with data from the individuals involved. Tests in which inferences from cultural products or performances are treated as hypotheses about group or individual differences in perception, motivation, or cognition can, obviously, only be done with living (and willing) subjects. Such experiments are difficult to formulate and to carry through; yet they are essential if we are to place much faith in the conclusions of more speculative works. For example, Clyde Kluckhohn's studies of Navajo weaving and ritual sandpaintings led to a hypothesis about ''avoidance of closure'' in this society that was later validated by psychological methods, including projective tests. Such validations are all too rare. (See Carroll 1992; Kaplan and Lawless 1965; Wallace 1950.)

CONCLUSIONS

Perhaps the most interesting recent development in our field has been the turning of psychological attention to the behavior and writings of anthropologists themselves. We have long had anecdotal material on the anal-compulsive behavior of archaeologists, the self-hatred of ethnologists, and the obsessiveness of linguists. Serious studies of these ''character types'' are still lacking, but critical anthropologists such as Marcus and Fischer (1986) and James Clifford (1988) have analyzed ethnographies and museum exhibits as texts that reveal much about the political setting of the work and the personal motivations of the participants.

In a similar work, Clifford Geertz (1988) has discussed the writings of four well-known ethnographers, relating them to the various literary genres that they exemplify. Thus he described the ''recondite,'' ''radical,'' and ''oblique'' style of Lévi-Strauss, contrasting it with the ''assured, direct, and architectonic'' style of Evans-Pritchard, the authoritative ''self-revelation'' of Malinowski, or the ''self-reflexive'' style of Benedict, ''in which distant oddities were made to question domestic assumptions'' (1988:21–23).

Geertz was concerned with the present dilemma of ethnography in a changing world, and he might deny any psychologizing intent; yet he wrote (in his own involuted style) of the ''*suffisance* of Lévi-Strauss, the assuredness of Evans-Pritchard, the brashness of Malinowski, and the imperturbability of Benedict'' (1988:130). These sound a great deal like characterizations of personalities.

The final example of critical self-analysis will be drawn from Renato Rosaldo's (1989) book *Culture and Truth.* In his chapter on ''Imperialist Nostalgia,'' Rosaldo accused certain ethnographers (and perhaps the entire profession) of mourning for traditional ways of life that they have, directly or indirectly, destroyed or transformed:

> Imperialist nostalgia revolves around a paradox: A person kills somebody, and then mourns the victim. In more attentuated form, someone deliberately alters a form of life, and then regrets that things have not remained as they were prior to the intervention. (Rosaldo 1989:69–70).

Although anthropologists usually try to distance themselves from missionaries, government officials, and other agents of colonialism, Rosaldo compared the writings of an American police lieutenant in the Philippines with those of an ethnographer to show how they shared the psychology of nostalgia and how, at least for the policeman, "this attitude absolved him of guilt and responsibility" (1989:79). Also, Rosaldo admitted his own nostalgia as well as his "complicity" in destruction: "We all bore witness, and we participated, as relatively minor players, in the transformations taking place before our eyes" (1989:87); see the even stronger statement in the version of this chapter first published in *Representations* 26:107–22).

We have now reviewed many of the kinds of "evidence from the arts" that have been used by anthropologists to formulate notions about the psychology of different peoples. Walbiri designs, Suyá and Tikopia songs, Sumbanese poetry, biblical narratives, and Shakespearean texts have all been explored to see what they might reveal about the experience of their makers. Yet we have not answered, and probably cannot answer, the master question in all these studies: To what extent do consistencies of pattern within or between art forms and media indicate commonalities of personality?

To do this work at all, we must assume some relationship between art and psychology. As Lévi-Strauss said of language and culture, "There cannot be no relation at all, and there cannot be 100 percent correlation" (1963:79). But when two such different individuals as Picasso and Braque can be credited with the invention of the cubist style, we must surely be cautious in reading personality traits from examples of "expressive culture." Indeed, it is important that students of the arts avoid the "uniformity assumption" (see the chapter "Social Structure and Personality" in part I) and recognize the considerable variability within any social grouping. It is as tempting to generalize about the assertive individualism and "self-fashioning" of the Renaissance as about Navajo "avoidance of closure," forgetting that we are talking about hundreds of thousands of individuals on the basis of highly selective samples.

Yet many of us feel convinced that the arts can move us closer to an understanding of alien ways of perceiving and thinking than almost any other kind of material. As noted earlier, there is a need for validation studies, and we must always remember the distinction between a normative pattern and the diverse motives it may conceal. But with imagination and care, evidence from the arts can and should be used to help us understand the relationship between individual and sociocultural phenomena.

REFERENCES

Alland, A., Jr. 1983. *Playing with Form*. New York: Columbia University Press.

Anderson, R. L., and K. L. Field, eds. 1993. *Art in Small-Scale Societies*. Englewood Cliffs, NJ: Prentice-Hall.

Angrosino, M. 1989. The Two Lives of Rebecca Levenstone. *Journal of Anthropological Research* 45:315–26.

Barry, H., III, M. Bacon, and I. Child. 1957. Relationships between Child Training and the Pictorial Arts. *Journal of Abnormal and Social Psychology* 54:380–83.

Basso, K. 1988. "Speaking with Names": Language and Landscape among the Western Apache. *Cultural Anthropology* 3:99–130.

Bock, P. K. 1990. Elizabethan Ethnosemantics. *Shakespeare Jahrbuch* 990:157–66.

———. 1992. Music in Mérida, Yucatan. *Latin American Music Review* 13:33–55.

———. 1993. "Neither Two Nor One": Dual Unity in The Phoenix and Turtle. Pp. 39–56 in B. J. Sokol, ed., *The Undiscover'd Country*. London: Free Association Books.

Brown, D. E. 1991. *Human Universals*. New York: McGraw-Hill.

Carroll, M. P. 1992. Folklore and Psychoanalysis. *Ethos*. 20:289–303.

Chernoff, J. M. 1979. *African Rhythm and African Sensibility. Aesthetics and Social Action in African Musical Idioms*. Chicago: University of Chicago Press.

Clifford, J. 1988. *The Predicament of Culture: Twentieth-Century Ethnography, Literature, and Art*. Cambridge: MA: Harvard University Press.

Devereux, G. 1961. Art and Mythology (Part I). Pp. 361–86 in B. Kaplan, ed., *Studying Personality Cross-Culturally*. New York: Harper and Row.

Dissanayake, E. 1988. *What Is Art For?* Seattle: University of Washington Press.

Doody, R. S. 1991. Aphasia as Postmodern (Anthropological) Discourse. *Journal of Anthropological Research* 47:285–303.

Feld, S. 1982. *Sound and Sentiment. Birds, Weeping, Poetics, and Song in Kaluli Expression*. Philadelphia: University of Pennsylvania Press.

Firth, R., with M. McLean. 1990. *Tikopia Songs*. New York: Cambridge University Press.

Forsyth, D. W. 1991. Sibling Rivalry, Aesthetic Sensibility, and Social Structure in Genesis. *Ethos* 19:453–510.

Friedrich, P. 1986. *The Language Parallax*. Austin: University of Texas Press.

Geertz, C. 1988. *Works and Lives*. Stanford: CA: Stanford University Press.

Greenblatt, W. 1980. *Renaissance Self-Fashioning*. Chicago: University of Chicago Press.

Hoskins, J. A. 1985. A Life History from Both Sides. *Journal of Anthropological Research* 41:147–69.

Kaemmer, J. E. 1993. *Music in Human Life*. Austin: University of Texas Press.

Kaplan, B., ed. 1961. *Studying Personality Cross-Culturally*. New York: Harper and Row.

Kaplan, B., and R. Lawless. 1965. Culture and Visual Imagery. Pp. 295–311 in M. Spiro, ed., *Context and Meaning in Cultural Anthropology*. New York: Free Press.

LaBarre, W. 1961. Art and Mythology (Part II). Pp. 387–403 in B. Kaplan, ed., *Studying Personality Cross-Culturally*. New York: Harper and Row.

Lévi-Strauss, C. 1963. *Structural Anthropology*. New York: Basic Books.

———. 1988. *The Jealous Potter*. Chicago: University of Chicago Press.

Lewis, O. 1964. *Pedro Martinez*. New York: Random House.

Lomax, A., et al. 1968. *Folk Song Style and Culture*. Washington, DC: American Association for the Advancement of Science. Publication No. 88.

Mahler, M., F. Pine, and A. Bergman. 1975. *The Psychological Birth of the Human Infant*. New York: Basic Books.

Marcus, G., and M. Fischer. 1986. *Anthropology as Cultural Critique: An Experimental Moment in the Human Sciences*. Chicago: University of Chicago Press.

Munn, N. D. 1986. *Walbiri Iconography*. Chicago: University of Chicago Press.

Reik, T. 1970. *Myth and Guilt*. New York: Grosset's Universal Library.

Rosaldo, R. 1989. *Culture and Truth: The Remaking of Social Analysis*. Boston: Beacon Press.

Schwartz, M., and C. Kahn, eds. 1980. *Representing Shakespeare*. Baltimore: Johns Hopkins University Press.

Seeger, A. 1987. *Why Suyá Sing*. New York: Cambridge University Press.

Tedlock, D. 1985. *Popol Vuh*. New York: Simon and Schuster.

Turnbull, C. 1972. *The Mountain People*. Garden City, NY: Simon and Schuster.

Wallace, A.F.C. 1950. A Possible Technique for Recognizing Psychological Characteristics of the Ancient Maya from an Analysis of Their Art. *American Imago* 7:239–58.

CHAPTER FOURTEEN

FIELD OBSERVATIONS OF BEHAVIOR AS A CROSS-CULTURAL METHOD

Ruth H. Munroe and Robert L. Munroe

The systematic observation of behavior constitutes one method among many available to the psychological anthropologist.[1] Behavioral observation has numerous facets, but all the uses and techniques associated with it contain a common element, namely, the potential for quantification. One concomitant of expressing cross-cultural data in quantitative form is that we are thereby aided in achieving both a rigorous formulation and a standard analysis of research questions. Another, very different concomitant is that numerical data necessarily impose severe constraints on our attempts to ''embody'' conceptual variables (cf. Ellsworth 1977). This means that in order to interpret any study properly or even to delineate its ''specified given conditions'' (Homans 1967:25), we must have available a fund of ethnographic knowledge. As Nerlove and colleagues stated the matter, ''Natural indicators . . . must be considered against a *cultural* background'' (Nerlove et al. 1974:268; emphasis added). Thus field-based observational studies have their greatest value when they combine quantification with traditional ethnographic inquiry and when they are, at the same time, organized directly around a specific research question.

Besides featuring quantitative data, the great majority of systematic observational studies have focused on naturally occurring rather than elicited behavior (cf. Bochner 1986). There are occasional exceptions, such as Ainsworth's (1967) informal study of Baganda infants' responses to strangers in the home, Dixon et al.'s (1984) comparison of Gusii and American mother-child interaction around a set teaching task, and Ellis and Gauvain's (1992) comparison of Navajo and Euro-American children's collaborative interactions. But the naturalistic emphasis is characteristic of anthropological research in general, and we will focus on this standard approach in the present chapter.

We shall first discuss the main content areas for which behavior observations have been employed, and include for illustrative flavor some of the major findings. We shall then describe some of the methods to which the research has given rise. In the concluding section, we shall set forth an assessment of behavioral observations plus an indication of questions that might be pursued if this approach is to make an optimal contribution to psychological anthropology. We begin by surveying the content areas of family life, socialization, and child life.

AREAS OF INVESTIGATION

Family Life

In early observational research on family life, results were presented in a form that was essentially raw data. For studies carried out in the Ecuadorian Sierra (Quinn 1966), Tepoztlan (Lewis 1951), and Zuni (Roberts 1956), the corpus of material in each case was made up of static verbal descriptions of ordinary activities, for example, "Josefa gets a load of straw," "Fa68 walks outside," "Mother rises, makes fire and coffee." Although these data sets have still not been systematically quantified and analyzed, the Whitings illustrated their rich comparative potential, pointing out possibilities that ranged from family members' time budgets and economic activities to apparent relationships between household type and the division of labor (Whiting and Whiting 1973). Additionally, since one of the Zuni families studied by Roberts (1956) was observed both at home and at its sheep camp, analysis might yet be made of behavior-setting differences in family life within Zuni culture. Clearly, however, more could eventually be done with these three pioneering contributions despite obvious limitations imposed by their small samples (N = 1 household except in Zuni), lack of consistent focus (except in Ecuador), and relatively low level of detail, especially in Tepoztlán).

Much of the recent observational literature on family life has been supplied by time-allocation research. Spurred by Allen Johnson's (1975) systematic estimates of time use among the Machiguenga, numerous researchers have collected comparable data in various parts of the world. (For an early attempt, see Erasmus 1955). Under Johnson's editorship at UCLA, a broad set of comparative data on time allocation has now been made available in archival form. The series, published by the Human Relations Area Files, is a nine-volume collection of time-allocation observations together with background cultural information. Each volume contains, on diskette, coded data gathered within a given sample community. For most volumes, the technique of observation allowed information to be collected simultaneously for all family members. In published form, these data are presented both in their original format, as coded by the field investigator, and in a standardized form developed by Johnson and his associates. The standardized format more readily allows cross-cultural comparisons, while retention of the original format allows intensive single-culture reanalyses and also greater ease of recoding the data for new purposes.

Accompanying each diskette is a standard set of supporting information, including a census of the individuals observed, methods of data collection and coding rules, and background cultural data (this last comprised of checklists like those in the *Ethnographic Atlas* [Murdock 1967] plus brief discussions of environmental factors, economic organization, social structure, and other information). Societies currently included in the series are the Machiguenga (Baksh 1990; Johnson and Johnson 1987) and Shipibo (Behrens 1988) of the Peruvian Amazon, the Mekranoti of the Brazilian Amazon (Werner 1992), the Yukpa of Venezuela (Paolisso and Sackett 1988), the Efe Pygmies of Zaire (Bailey and Peacock 1988), the Logoli of Kenya (R. L. Munroe and R. H. Munroe 1989), the Black Carib (Garifuna) of Belize (R. L. Munroe and R. H. Munroe 1990a), and the Samoans of American Samoa (R. L. Munroe and R. H. Munroe 1990b). Intracultural hypotheses about household and family (as well as individuals) can already be tested with this data set, and the standardized data format will render cross-cultural testing feasible and efficient as additional cases are added to the sample (cf. Johnson and Behrens 1989).

Socialization

Although the main focus of the Six Cultures Project (B. Whiting 1963; Whiting and Whiting 1975) was children (more information on this project will be given later in this chapter), continuing analyses of the data and the addition of observations from new samples have made it possible also to study maternal behavior. For a sample of a dozen societies investigated in this way by Whiting and Edwards (1988), the mother's behavior was powerfully predicted by age of the child, with older children receiving less nurturance, lower compliance to their requests, and an increase in training pressures (often pressure toward task assignments). Mothers also directed much more training pressure toward girls than boys, while attempting to exert greater dominance and control over boys. In addition, Whiting and Edwards (1988) categorized maternal behavior into three primary types: *training* (in the sub-Saharan African societies), *control* (typically in the non-African subsistence societies), and *sociability* (in the U.S. subsample).

The care and training of infants has been the subject of several observational studies. Whiting and Edwards (1988) speculated about the physical features and behavior of infants that might elicit the universal responsiveness and nurturance with which infant status was associated in their data. Among Efe foragers in Zaire, this constant care is delivered not by the mother alone but by multiple caretakers who rarely put the baby down; some of these caretakers breast-feed other women's infants when necessary. Tronick, Morelli, and Ivey (1992) argued that Efe children develop close emotional ties to many caretakers, and that the finding poses problems for attachment theory, which assumes that a single primary relationship serves as a model for those formed later. Chisholm (1983), however, found less intense interaction between Navajo than Anglo mothers and infants and related this difference to the greater opportunities for nonmaternal interactions experienced by the Navajo infants.

In a different set of studies, the frequency of infant holding proved to be positively related to household density in three of five societies (Borgerhoff Mulder and Milton 1985; R. H. Munroe and R. L. Munroe 1971, 1984; Seymour 1976). In a setting-specific study, Kilbride and Kilbride (1990) observed Baganda infants in the home (over an eight-month period) and found a relationship between specific maternal behaviors and infant sensorimotor skills; for example, lifting of the infant to the shoulder was associated with early performance of visual behaviors.

In the observational research on socialization, much more attention has been paid to mothers than to fathers, probably because mothers figure so prominently in the child-rearing process (cf. Hames 1988). Recent comparative analysis, however, has shown significant cultural variation in fathers' involvement in the lives of their children (Hewlett 1991). The main finding is that fathers are much more likely to be present and to care for children in foraging societies than in farming groups (R. L. Munroe and R. H. Munroe 1992; West and Konner 1976; Whiting and Whiting 1975; Winn, Tronick, and Morelli 1990). The Aka Pygmies of the Western Congo Basin represent the extreme of this tendency among foragers: fathers are within arm's reach of their infants 47 percent of the time over a twenty-four-hour day and, in the forest-camp setting, are within view of the babies a remarkable 88 percent of the time. In other societies, the range of father presence is from 3 to 30 percent of the time (Hewlett 1991).

As an instance of intracultural variation in father involvement, Flinn (1992) found that Trinidadian stepfathers were less likely to interact with stepoffspring and were likelier to be agonistic when they did so than were genetic fathers with their own offspring. The results are consistent with Daly and Wilson's (1980) hypothesis that male parental investment will be preferentially distributed to genetic offspring.

Despite this variability, Mackey (1983), basing his inferences on observations in public places in eighteen societies, concluded that men everywhere associate with children to a significant degree. Nevertheless, these public settings revealed that "men-only" groups surrounding children were much less frequent than "women-only" groups, and that such groups of men were very much underrepresented in the company of infants (as compared with men's presence in the company of older children; cf. also Flinn's [1988] findings on Trinidadian men's attempts to control their daughters' mating relationships).

Only in recent years has observational research been undertaken on the role of siblings in socialization. Findings indicate that older children act as both caregivers and companions, engaging toddlers in ways that facilitate mature responses and guide their participation into culturally meaningful activities (Edwards and

Whiting in press; Leiderman and Leiderman 1974; Sigman et al. 1988; Weisner 1989a, 1989b; Weisner, Gallimore, and Jordan 1988; Zukow 1989). For East Africa, Weisner (1989b) and Edwards and Whiting (1993) have identified a pattern of older sibling behavior that is laced with counterpoised intentions—nurturant and sociable on the one hand, but dominant/aggressive on the other. Edwards and Whiting saw this behavior as presenting the toddler with cognitive challenges that are not posed by the East African mother's caregiving style.

Finally, occasional research has been directed to the role of grandparents in their own offspring's reproductive success (Turke 1989) and their grandchildren's labor contributions (Munroe, Munroe, and Shimmin 1984).

Child Life

Activities. The time devoted by children to work-and play-related activities has been a subject of major interest to investigators. One consistent finding is that in agrarian societies, children's labor—chores, food-related tasks, subsistence work, and child care—tends to increase in a near-linear fashion from postinfancy up to the age of seven or so, and sometimes beyond (Dasen 1988; Erchak 1980; Harkness and Super 1983; Loucky 1088; Munroe, Munroe, and Shimmin 1984; Seymour 1988; Whiting and Whiting 1975). Time devoted to play activities displays a corresponding decrease with age of child. For girls, the upward trend in labor often continues through late childhood and into adolescence. In both hunter-gatherer and urban-industrial societies, however, the level of work evidently stays low throughout childhood. But this generalization about similarities in childhood experiences at the higher and lower ends of cultural complexity is based on a relatively small number of cases and should be supplemented with further research (Draper 1976; R. H. Munroe et al. 1983).

One of the few studies to categorize children's activities in a complex way was a rural Guatemalan investigation by Nerlove et al. (1974). In an attempt to tap natural indicators of cognitive functioning among five- to eight-year-olds, the authors defined a class of "self-managed sequences" that could be manifested in tasks, in rule-based games, or in imaginary play or construction. The frequency of these sequences of behavior in daily life was positively related to children's performance on tests of analytic ability.

A specific aspect of children's activities is the distance typically traveled from home base. On the assumption that distance can be used as an index of environmental experience, two East African studies investigated this phenomenon by observing three- to eight-year-old children during daily activities and calculating their average distance from home. Greater free-time distance from home was a predictor of superior performance on tests of spatial ability (R. L. Munroe and R. H. Munroe 1971; Nerlove, Munroe, and Munroe 1971). Yet a four-year follow-up study with one of these samples found that directed rather than free-time distance from home was now associated with spatial performance, and for boys only (Munroe, Munroe, and Brasher 1985). The overall results indicate that naturally occurring transactions with the physical environment may play a role in spatial learning, but in highly complex ways.

Social Behavior. The Six Cultures Project (in Africa, India, Mexico, Okinawa, the Philippines, and the United States), which marks the most intensive cross-cultural study of children's social behavior ever undertaken, identified approximately 20,000 acts for 134 sample children (Whiting 1963; Whiting and Whiting 1975). Based on analysis of this massive data set, the Whitings arrived at a category system of twelve social acts that represented "a step . . . toward a general taxonomy of social behavior" (Whiting and Whiting 1975:64). The twelve "act types," dealing with sociobehavioral areas like dominance, aggression, nurturance, and prosocial action, were subsequently applied with a high degree of success to a completely different sample of societies. In an observational study of children in American Samoa, Belize (Black Carib), Kenya (Logoli), and Napal (Newars), 85 percent of all social acts proved codable into the category system of the Six Cultures Project (Munroe, Munroe, and Shimmin 1984). Furthermore, there were parallel regularities in social behavior in the two studies. Aggression was higher among boys than girls, and nurturance (offer of help and support) was manifested more frequently by children who were regularly put to baby-sitting chores. The four-culture study also confirmed a Six Cultures finding that the general pattern of social behavior was influenced by engagement in tasks. Children who frequently are involved in task assignments apparently transfer their work style to social situations. "The picture is one of businesslike, efficient, purposeful behavior: Working children engage in a pattern of interaction that itself seems worklike" (e.g., making responsible suggestions, scolding others) (Munroe, Munroe, and Shimmin 1984:375).

Another way in which task assignment apparently can influence social behavior was discovered in a study of the Kenyan Luo. Using the Six Cultures categories, Ember (1973) found that boys given "feminine" work (child care, housework, and so on) displayed social tendencies intermediate between girls and boys. It appeared, in other words, that "boys who were subject to the socialization pressures of tasks usually assigned to girls were more like girls in their social behavior than boys not assigned such tasks" (Ember 1981:558).

Observational research indicates that age and sex segregation both increase as the child develops. Participation in children's groups begins after the toddler stage and grows steadily through childhood. Although the child continues to be in the frequent company of adults, especially of females, its interaction is increasingly directed to peers (Draper 1975; R. H. Munroe and R. L. Munroe 1981; Rogoff 1981, 1990; Wenger 1983; Whiting and Edwards 1988). This gravitation to peer groups becomes sex linked as well during middle childhood when the child disproportionately seeks out and interacts with others of the same gender (Blurton-Jones and Konner 1973; R. H. Munroe and R. L. Munroe 1981; Omark, Omark, and Edelman 1975; Wenger 983; Whiting and Edwards 1988).

Children's social interests have been investigated at a microlevel by recording their attentiveness to others. Guilmet (1979) reported that Navajo children were twice as likely to watch teachers as were Caucasians in the same class. R. L. Munroe and R. H. Munroe (1992) found that within and across four cultures, father-absent boys gazed at the males of their social environment more frequently than did father-present boys. For girls, however, father absence had no such affect.

TYPES OF BEHAVIORAL OBSERVATION

The methods employed for behavioral observation vary greatly, and nearly all investigators would agree with Borgerhoff Mulder and Caro's (1985:332) stipulation that "different goals . . . necessitate the use of different techniques." Their insightful review and others by Whiting and Whiting (1973), Gross (1984), Baksh (1989–90), Bernard and Killworth (1993), Scaglion (1986), and Hawkes et al. (1987) covered problems of sampling, data collection, reliability, coding systems, analysis, interpretation, and replication in observational research. We shall not attempt to resolve these complex issues, but instead confine ourselves to clarifying one central aspect of technique, the collection and recording of data.[2] The observation protocol, as both the "source" and the repository of data, represents a critical element in the technical process of observation, yet remains underspecified in the literature. We shall discuss and give examples of several types of data-recording techniques, focusing on those most commonly used to address the content areas previously considered.

Spot Observations as Used in the Study of Family Life

The spot observation, which consists of "the observer's recording the pertinent features of a subject's activity as soon as he or she is first observed" (Borgerhoff Mulder and Caro 1985:324), yields behavioral records that have been likened to "mental snapshots" (R. H. Munroe and R. L. Munroe 1975; also cf. Gross 1984; Rogoff 1978). These spot checks are particularly good at reducing the problem of human "reactance" (Bochner 1986:167) to being observed, though they do not altogether eliminate the problem (Borgerhoff Mulder and Caro 1985). They have proven particularly useful for the construction of time budgets and are the primary technique in Johnson's comparative time-allocation project, discussed earlier. The specific example of a standard form for gathering spot observations (table 14.1 in the Appendix to this chapter) was used to sample the behavior of children over periods of several months within each of four different societies (R. L. Munroe and R. H. Munroe 1989, 1990a, 1990b; R. L. Munroe et al. in press). The form can easily be adapted for different research interests and for use with individuals of any age.

This particular form facilitates the recording of information pertinent to family life, for example, the individual's location, activity, and the identity of coparticipants and associates of the observed individual, as well as the activity and location of the parents of the observed individual. Additional items on the form ask about whether the observed individual is caretaking a younger child, and whether or not he or she is engaged in voluntary activity.[3] The "snapshot" is supplemented by information from participants after the initial data are recorded. Obviously, meaningful interpretation of data of this sort will depend upon the anthropologist's knowledge of the culture, and we reiterate the point made in the introduction that systematic observation is best carried out in conjunction with ethnographic inquiry.

The individual's activity is to be described in narrative form and subsequently categorized according to a code. Of course, a preconstructed code could be used at the time of observation. Such a procedure would have its own strengths (saving of time, increased reliability) and limitations (loss of contextual data through restricted focus). An example of such a code is given in the following subsection.

Precoded Observational Categories as Used in a Study of Socialization

Hewlett's (1991) research on Aka Pygmy fathers made use of several types of observational formats. One of these is shown in table 14.2 (see the Appendix to this chapter), which lists items coded for each of the sample fathers every fifteen minutes throughout an entire day (6 A.M. to 6 P.M.). The information is similar to that described earlier for table 14.1, but Hewlett, in keeping with the project's focus on paternal infant care, tailored his protocol to include several items on infants. Codes were included, for instance, that described the infant's activity and location and the availability of the father (and the mother) to the infant.

Note that the range of responses was drawn from knowledge of the culture and designed to fit the research question. The code then served as a checklist for the observer. This arrangement allowed Hewlett to include more items than was possible for the protocol represented in table 14.1. Data accuracy for this code and others like it depends heavily upon the observer's detailed knowledge of the code.

Several Types of Observations Used in the Study of Child Life

In the Six Cultures Project, the study of children's social behavior was based on five-minute observational protocols written in narrative form by observers especially trained to record main activity, primarily social. Although this technique does not lend itself well to achieving interobserver reliability, it typically produces rich information that can be mined, then analyzed anew. An example appears in table 14.3 (see the Appendix to this chapter).

As discussed earlier, the Whitings (1975) extracted from their protocols a category system of twelve social acts that were successfully applied to a subsequent project (Munroe, Munroe, and Shimmin 1984). The latter research did not use running narratives but rather an event-sampling approach in which the observer waited for the individual to perform any type of verbal or nonverbal social interaction. The single episode, including the response to the individual (if any), constituted the entire observation. For the purposes of this type of observation, the individual's first social act after the observer arrived was taken as the beginning of an episode. An observer located the child and immediately recorded details of the setting. While doing so, the observer watched for any social behavior on the part of the individual. This behavior could be a clear social initiation, for example, "Let's play marbles," or what would normally be considered a response, for example, "Yeah." The observer watched the immediate effect and filled in the requisite information. The reason for this definition of initiation was the difficulty of actually pinpointing the beginning of a behavioral episode; by using this definition, the observer did not need to do so.

The form allowed the observer to note the details of the individual's behavior, including the nature of the "opening" instigation by the child, the target of the child's behavior, the distance of the target, and the response of the target. The initiating social event was recorded in narrative form (see table 14.4 in the Appendix to this chapter). A corpus of such events was built up by observing each child approximately thirty-five times over a series of occasions. Although the episodic character of this type of data gathering was very different from the running-record protocols of the Whitings, the two projects evidenced strong overlap in proportions of social acts[4] and in a series of parallel findings, as earlier noted. These results demonstrate that stable relationships and robust categories can override variation in the technical aspects of methods.

The final type of observation was developed to ascertain the child's selective attention to others in the social environment (Slaby and Frey 1975). The observation form was structured so that the observer first recorded the personnel present (by relationship, sex, and age) in the vicinity of the child, then focused on the child's direction of gaze. After watching for a ten-second interval as to whom in the environment the child had attended, the observer recorded this information during the next fifty seconds of each minute. The sequence was then repeated ten times in order to complete one observational protocol. (See figure 14.1 in the Appendix to this chapter, in which a completed protocol is presented.)

While the previously discussed techniques were designed to capture "molar-level" behavior of individuals, in the "attention" observations the interest was the microlevel variable of direction of children's eye gaze. The purpose of this particular observation was to obtain an index of children's relative attentiveness to same-sex versus opposite-sex individuals (controlling for the degree to which such individuals were represented in the child's environment during the periods of observation).

The various observation types described briefly in this section offer advantages of several sorts. They can be easily taught—all but Hewlett's have been used by trained local observers as well as by social scientists—and the protocols shown in table 14.1, table 14.4, and figure 14.1 have yielded interobserver and interrater reliability averaging above 80 percent agreement. The advantages of the observations derive in large part from the fact that the techniques rely upon low-interference constructs, that is, "direct accessibility of the stimuli to the sense receptors" (Campbell 1961:340), and not upon intangible or abstract attributes. All of the types capitalize on measuring recurrent features of cultural life rather than attempting to ferret out unique or highly unusual events. Nevertheless, the examples given here are meant to be illustrative and helpful in research planning, not determinate. They can be modified as needed or perhaps used as a stimulus for devising quite different techniques. Highly innovative approaches should also be considered when available techniques seem inadequate or inappropriate for addressing a problem. Methodology ought always to follow from the research question itself.

ASSESSMENT AND DIRECTIONS FOR THE FUTURE

As we have seen, behavioral observation lends itself not only to quantification and hypothesis testing, but also to cross-cultural comparisons. Not surprisingly, the most successful comparisons have been those projects marked by continuity of research. Johnson's edited series on time allocation (Johnson and Behrens 1989; Johnson and Johnson 1987) continues to add cases, and the enlarged sample will eventually allow comparative investigations at several levels, for example, across individuals, within subcultures (or villages) of a single culture, within regions, and on a worldwide basis. Enhancing the value of the cases in Johnson's series is the inclusion of contextual material that amounts to a microethnography accompanying each data set. As to the Six Cultures Project, the original sample (Whiting 1963) has now been doubled with the addition of comparable data from six others (Whiting and Edwards 1988), and the systematicity of the approach will allow interested scholars to add their own groups.

These methodological contributions inevitably have their limitations. Spot observation, with its snapshotlike quality, does not provide a way to register the duration or the ordering of activities (Baksh 1989–90); therefore, some type of continuous observation might be valuable as a complement in future studies for the Johnson series. In the Six Cultures follow-up, some of the outcomes were projected from an inadequate sample size; for example, a separate category of maternal style ("sociability") was posited on the basis of its appearance solely among U.S. mothers (Whiting and Edwards 1988). New samples, especially from modern and modernizing societies, are needed to determine the viability of such a category.

Other studies discussed in this chapter indicate two directions that future research might take. The first is a more fine-grained observational approach. For example, investigations of children have linked cognitive skills with everyday experiences such as the distance traveled from home or the carrying out of self-managed sequences (R. L. Munroe and R. H. Munroe 1971; Nerlove, Munroe, and Munroe 1971; Nerlove et al. 1974). Although these relationships are plausible, they are not self-evidently valid. Observational techniques designed to provide clues to the mental processes being tested are needed (cf. Gauvain 1993). Relevant to spatial ability, for example, might be the manipulation of tools (Munroe, Munroe, and Brasher 1985), or the general activity level (not just distance traveled away from home), measurement of which would be facilitated by an actometer, an instrument that records movement (Eaton 1983). With respect to self-managed sequences and their relationship to analytical abilities, visual records (such as those on film and tape) may prove vital to understanding (cf. Ellis and Gauvain 1992; Gauvain and DeMent 1991; O. R. Johnson 1980). Records of this type can be difficult to collect in field settings (Gross 1984), but they are particularly useful for precise measurement of actions that are swift or complex, or of behavior that changes rapidly in type or sequence (Hutt and Hutt 1970). Ultimately, the detailed knowledge needed to understand the contribution of experiential factors to cognitive performance may be provided by similar observational techniques finely tuned to the problem at hand.

The second direction that research might usefully follow is to integrate observational approaches with other sources of data. Some of this has already been done, as in certain aspects of the Six Cultures Project (Minturn and Lambert 1964) and in Chisholm's (1983) exemplary study of Navajo infancy, but its broader implementation is desirable. For example, the high level of paternal infant care found among foragers is quite different from the usual pattern in agricultural and industrial societies and runs counter to the paternal "deprivation" (Biller 1976) frequently found in the latter cases. Numerous studies (reviewed in Biller 1976 and Stevenson and Black 1988) indicate the significance of the absent father for the psychological development of males, but we have no evidence regarding possible effects of the paternal "saturation" typical for male infants in foraging societies. Psychological data, especially indices of sexual identity from Hewlett's (1991) young Pygmy boys, could tell us something about the possible implications of having the father present for 88 percent of the day, as in the Aka forest-camp settings. Likewise, test information could significantly supplement Ember's (1973) finding that a more feminine social-behavioral style was associated with female task assignments for boys. Formal interviews with parents about stereotypical roles and expected behaviors would also provide meaningful data.

These recommendations are not meant to criticize the cited research for failing to do more than it did, or to say that every conceivable item of relevant data should be collected. They suggest, however, that any investigation can raise the value of its contribution by sharpening its tools of measurement or broadening its research design to include pertinent correlative measures (cf. Weisner 1976). We can do no better than to point out the wisdom of Campbell and Fiske's

(1959) advocacy of employing more than one method and more than one trait in validating the measurement process (Overman 1988). Within this framework, we believe, the systematic observation of behavior has a very important role to play in the future of psychological anthropology.

APPENDIX

Table 14.1
Form for Recording Spot Observations

NAME ______________ NO. ______________ OBSERVER ______________

DATE ______________ TIME ______________

1. CHILD'S LOCATION/DISTANCE:
   HOUSE--INSIDE ________
   OUTSIDE--OWN PORCH/YARD ________ ft. from closest door of house
   OTHER (where?) ______________ ft. from closest door of house

2. WHAT IS CHILD DOING--GENERAL ACTIVITY? ______________________________

   ____

3. WHAT IS CHILD DOING--SPECIFIC ACTIVITY? ______________________________

   ____

4. WHAT IS CHILD HOLDING? FOOD ______________ OTHER ______________

5. WHO IS PARTICIPATING IN SAME GENERAL ACTIVITY AS CHILD/WHAT IS APPROX. DISTANCE FROM CHILD (list nearest person to child first, then next nearest, etc.)?

name/sex	ident.	ad/ch	dist.	name/sex	ident.	ad/ch	dist.
______	____	____	____	______	____	____	____
______	____	____	____	______	____	____	____
______	____	____	____	______	____	____	____

6. WHO ELSE IS WITHIN 10 FEET OF CHILD OR IN SAME ROOM AS CHILD/WHAT IS APPROX. DISTANCE FROM CHILD (list nearest person to child first, then next nearest, etc.)?

name/sex	ident.	ad/ch	dist.	name/sex	ident.	ad/ch	dist.
______	____	____	____	______	____	____	____
______	____	____	____	______	____	____	____
______	____	____	____	______	____	____	____

7. WHERE IS MOTHER? ______________ DISTANCE (from child) ______________

   ACTIVITY ______________________________

8. WHERE IS FATHER? ______________ DISTANCE (from child) ______________

   ACTIVITY ______________________________

9. WHO IS CLOSEST ADULT? ______________ IDENT. ______________ DIST. ______________

10. IS CHILD A CARETAKER FOR A YOUNGER CHILD: YES ______ NO ______

    WHO IS YOUNGER CHILD? ______________ DIST. OF YNG. CHILD FROM CARETAKER ________

11. ASK: WAS CHILD DIRECTED TO DO WHAT HE/SHE IS DOING? YES ______ NO ______

    BY WHOM? ______________________________

Procedural Notes on Table 14.1

The use of observation forms greatly facilitates the collection of data by reminding observers of all details sought. If it is not possible to reproduce large numbers of forms, the investigator might keep a master list of all questions, number these, and, while observing, enter the information by number on blank paper.

As observations are undertaken, certain definitions will necessarily be established. For example, is a long-time visitor to be considered a household member? What defines "working together"? All such decisions should be noted and consistently followed.

All observers should be trained together, or new observers should be trained along with some experienced observers, so that an acceptable level of agreement can be established before observers collect usable data. During training and for all checks on observer agreement (reliability), the "photographic" nature of these observations requires that one member of a pair of observers indicate the moment for the observation; otherwise, a changing scene might appear to indicate low agreement when, in fact, one observer simply "snapped" the scene at a slightly later time than the other. After training, it is necessary for one person (usually the main investigator) to peruse all observations on a daily basis, both to ensure that all data are entered and to clarify any ambiguous information that might later pose coding problems.

Typically, the investigator will set up observation schedules yielding data relevant to the research question. That is, a project focusing on the social companions of adolescents would ascertain the socializing hours for this group and, for each sample member, conduct equal numbers of observations that span these socializing hours.

We wanted information on the child's whereabouts, both specific place and distance from home, making it necessary to measure and map the communities under study. Using the map, observers estimated distance from home. For distances within the child's yard, observers were trained to make estimates. Other distance entries on the form are estimates between the child and other persons. Observers were trained in these "people-to-people" distance estimates using the closest point between two persons as the entered estimate. A zero (0) entry was used to indicate touching. The separate entries for general and specific activity were added to this form after a number of trials without them. The general activity refers to anything that helps explain the child's presence at a certain place and with certain people, and/or the handling of certain material objects. For example, a child noted as being in a maize field with her mother, father, and siblings could be there to work along with them even though, at the moment of observation, the child was leaning on a hoe and gazing upward. In this instance, the initial entry under specific activity would indicate the "leaning," while the general activity would be described as weeding if, after questioning the adults, it was determined that the child was in the field to assist in cultivation.

This particular spot-observation form is designed primarily for the collection of immediately available (i.e., visible) data in relatively small communities where observers know the names of people or can learn them quickly. On the form, however, are some items that may require questioning of the observed child or of others close by. For example, an observer might need to obtain some information about the activity, the whereabouts of parents, or the names of some of the people present. This information is to be obtained after the initial information is recorded and then used to explicate or fill in the observation, not to change the original information about the individual's specific activity, whereabouts, or companions.

Table 14.2
Pre-coded Items Noted Every Fifteen Minutes During Father Focal Observations

(1) Setting
1 = forest camp
.
.
.
12 = village center
.
.

(2) Position of father
1 = sleep
2 = lie
.
.
.
11 = run

(3) Primary activity
1 = eating
2 = food preparation
3 = child care (holding, etc.)
4 = manufacture
5 = hunting
.
.

(4) Items carried
0 = nothing
1 = net
2 = spear
3 = axe
4 = basket
5 = digging stick
6 = infant
.
.
.

(5) Vocalization
0 = none
1 = talking with/to someone
2 = singing
.
.
.

(6) Identification of person speaking to/with
1 = wife
2 = focal infant
.
.
.

(7) Touching
1 = wife
2 = focal infant
.
.
.

(8) Proximity
list all people within one meter

(9) Nearest neighbor (other than holding)
list ID. number of closest person within ten meters

(10) General activity with infant
1 = transporting
2 = playing
3 = nursing
4 = watching infant to help mother
5 = no interaction, infant nearby
6 = feeding
7 = no interaction, infant held
8 = other care
9 = talking with
.
.
.

(11) Position of mother (same codes as 2 above)/ Items carried (same as 4 above)

(12) General activity
A) Of mother
B) With infant

(13) Location of infant
1 = in family hut

(14) Activity of infant
1 = nursing

Table 14.2 (*continued*)

	2 = near (approx. 1 m) family hut		2 = idle
	.		3 = sleeping
	.		4 = eating
	.		5 = visiting
	7 = just outside camp in forest or village fields		.
			.
			.
(15)	Infant held by	(16)	Infant being touched by/within proximity of: (list all within 1 m)
	1 = mother		
	2 = father		
	3 = other (list ID. no.)		
(17)	Availability of mother and father (use 2 codes)		
	1 = within visual range		
	2 = within hearing range		
	3 = out of area/not available		

Source: Adapted from *Intimate Fathers* (pp. 53–57) by Barry S. Hewlett. 1991. Ann Arbor: The University of Michigan Press. Copyright 1991 by The University of Michigan Press. Adapted by permission.

Table 14.3
Protocol: Five-Minute Behavior Observation

NYANSONGO (village in western Kenya, Bantu-speaking Gusii)

Child observed:	Ogoi, 4-year-old boy
Date:	1 February 1957 *Time*: 1:45
Place:	A pasture
Present:	Lawrence, Ogoi's 6-year-old brother
	Aloyse, 6-year-old boy
	Peter, 8-year-old boy
	Manyara, 11-year-old boy

Peter, Aloyse, Lawrence, and Manyara are sitting together. Ogoi is standing on the edge of the group, holding Manyara's slingshot. He comes over to the group and sits down with them. Manyara grabs the slingshot from Ogoi, who makes no protest at all. Manyara is snapping the rubber of the slingshot against Aloyse's foot, with the latter's permission. Everyone, including Ogoi, is intently watching and laughing when Aloyse gets hit. Then Manyara stops. Aloyse spits on Ogoi. Ogoi angrily whines, "Don't spit on me like that." Lawrence tells Aloyse, "You wipe that off him." Aloyse ignores him.

Lawrence says to Ogoi, "Go get the cows." Ogoi does. Peter and Aloyse go to retrieve their own cows. Ogoi is higher up on the hill but runs down to where Lawrence and Manyara, who have moved with the other boys, are. Ogoi sits down with them. Lawrence asks him, "What's in your mouth?" Ogoi opens his mouth to show. Peter, who has just come over, says, "Open your mouth and let's see." Ogoi smiles and opens his mouth. They all tell him to stick out his tongue. He does and all peer in. Suddenly there is fighting between Peter and Manyara. Ogoi just sits and watches it for a long time. Lawrence playfully grabs at Ogoi's foot. He laughs. Lawrence pushes Ogoi over on his back. Ogoi smiles. Lawrence, looking into Ogoi's mouth, says, "Oh look! Here's a tooth that's going to come out!'' Ogoi is still smiling as Lawrence pushes him around on the ground some more. Lawrence and Ogoi then go and join the group which is now shouting across to the next hill that their cows have gone into the maize field. They continue shouting for about five minutes.

Source: From *Children of Six Cultures: A Psycho-Cultural Analysis* (pp. 204–5), by Beatrice B. Whiting and John W. M. Whiting, 1975, Cambridge, MA: Harvard University Press. Copyright 1975 by the President and Fellows of Harvard College. Reprinted by permission.

Table 14.4
Form for Recording Social Interaction

NAME ______________________ NO. __________ OBSERVER ______________

DATE ____________

1. PERSONS PRESENT:

infant male (to 2 yrs.)	IM	______
infant female (to 2 yrs.)	IF	______
young male child (3-8)	YM	______
young female child (3-8)	YF	______
old male child (9-16)	OM	______
old female child (9-16)	OF	______
adult male	AM	______
adult female	AF	______
father	FA	______
mother	MO	______

2 TIME OBSERVATION BEGINS ______

3. TIME OBSERVATION ENDS ______ OR ______ min. ______ sec. later

4. PERSON TO WHOM INSTIGATION DIRECTED (BY CATEGORIES ABOVE) ____________

5. DISTANCE OF PERSON TO WHOM INSTIGATION DIRECTED (FROM CHILD) ____________

6. DESCRIBE INSTIGATION: ____

____

____

____

7. IMMEDIATE (10 second) RESPONSE OF PERSON TO WHOM INSTIGATION IS DIRECTED:

complies	______
refuses	______
acknowledges	______
ignores	______
other (specify)	______

____

---

8. EVENTUAL OUTCOME (two minutes after end time):

successful	______
unsuccessful	______
can't tell	______

ACTIVITY: ____________
PLACE: ____________

Procedural Notes on Table 14.4

As noted in the text, this form is intended for recording data on social interaction. A single sequence is defined as beginning with any social activity on the part of the observed individual and ending when the consequences of that sequence are completed, that is, when the action can be judged with respect to success or failure (if appropriate).

The persons present are recorded initially only by the number of people in each age/sex category, not by name. If there are personnel changes prior to any social interaction, the observer can modify the information. (The age/sex categories of persons present were designed for our particular purposes. These may be dropped or changed to meet the requirements of other studies.)

The social behavior should be described as completely as possible to allow for coding—for example: ''says 'yes' when asked by her mother if her younger brother is with her.'' Inferences should be supplied in parentheses—for example: ''touched YF [young female] on the forearm'' might be supplemented with ''(so the YF would look at the taro that S [the individual being observed] was holding).'' If there is doubt concerning either the response of the other or the eventual outcome, it is best to encourage observers to record the details so that a judgment can be made by the investigator when reviewing the daily observations. Our observers were instructed to obtain no more than three observations in succession, thus avoiding skewing of general results by any unusual activities or styles of interaction.

Figure 14.1
Completed Form for Recording Direction of Gaze

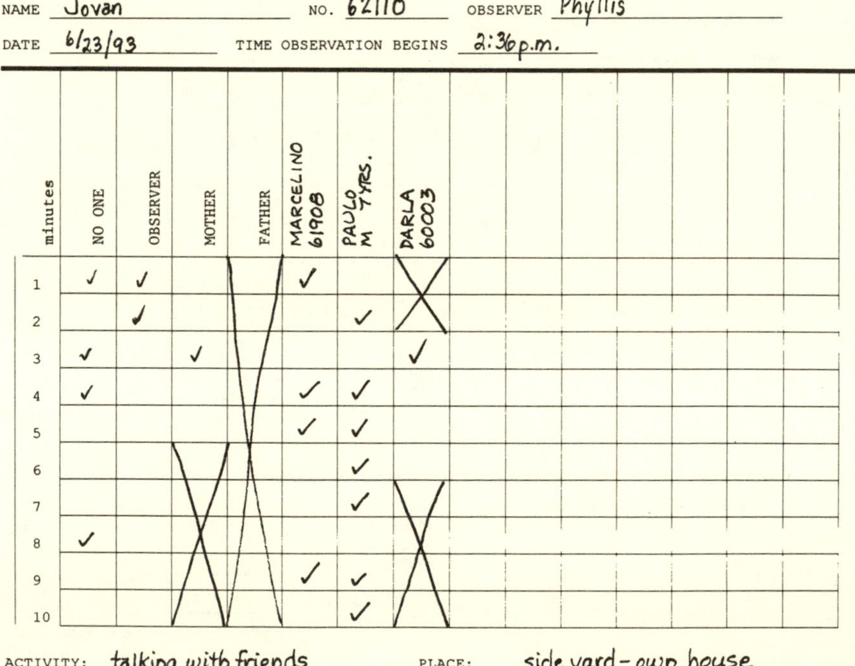

NAME Jovan NO. 62110 OBSERVER Phyllis

DATE 6/23/93 TIME OBSERVATION BEGINS 2:36p.m.

minutes	NO ONE	OBSERVER	MOTHER	FATHER	MARCELINO 61908	PAULO M 7YRS.	DARLA 60003
1	✓	✓		X	✓		X
2		✓		X		✓	X
3	✓		✓	X			✓
4	✓			X	✓	✓	
5				X	✓	✓	
6			X	X		✓	
7			X	X		✓	X
8	✓		X	X			X
9			X	X	✓	✓	X
10			X	X		✓	X

ACTIVITY: talking with friends PLACE: side yard - own house

Procedural Notes on Figure 14.1

In figure 14.1, the blank form is filled in with handwritten entries to illustrate a completed protocol. After noting the persons present by name, identification numbers (if known), or age and sex, the observer begins the ten-minute sequence by observing for ten seconds and recording, on the first line, for fifty seconds. The completed observation form represents ten minutes of elapsed time (one line for each minute) but only one hundred seconds (one minutes, forty seconds) of observed time.

Observers were instructed to complete this form only if the child was in the presence of at least two other persons. The minutes are marked in the left-hand column, followed by preset categories of *no one* (for use if the child gazes into the distance, at an object, or anything except another person at any time during the first ten seconds of the particular minute); the *observer* (for use if the child's gaze is directed at the observer); the *mother* (if present); and the *father* (if present). The additional columns, with persons noted, are similarly employed. Persons who are initially present but leave during the ten minutes are marked out with an X (as with the mother in the illustration). Persons who arrive after the ten-minute period begins are marked as absent in those periods prior to their arrival (as with Darla, a child female ID #600003, who was present only during minutes three to six).

NOTES

The authors are indebted to Mary Gauvain of the University of California, Riverside, for helpful suggestions, and to Sandra Hamilton of Pitzer College for technical assistance in the preparation of this manuscript.

1. This chapter, in confining itself to psychological anthropology—that is, to cross-cultural research centered around psychocultural issues—will not attempt to match the generally broader treatments of behavioral observation to be found in Weick (1985) on social psychology, and in Bochner (1986) and Longabaugh (1980) on cross-cultural psychology. Neither will primatological approaches be covered (Altmann 1974; see also the chapter by William McGrew and Linda Marchant in this volume). Specialized topics such as ecology and optimal foraging (e.g., Smith 1983, 1987) will be considered only insofar as they touch on questions of interest to psychological anthropology.

2. We assume human observers as the instruments of data gathering, rather than the use of film, videotape, tape recorder, or electronic beeper. These alternative methods, while particularly promising for certain questions, pose special challenges in most field settings.

3. For purposes of reliability in data gathering, we recommend the use of the spot observation for a single individual (as the form indicates). Such a procedure is termed "focal sampling," as opposed to simultaneous observation of a number of individuals, termed "scan sampling" (Borgerhoff Mulder and Caro 1985).

4. The Spearman correlation coefficient between the ranked frequencies of the twelve social acts in the Six Cultures Project and those in the authors' four-culture study was .65 ($p < .05$).

REFERENCES

Ainsworth, M.D.S. 1967. *Infancy in Uganda*. Baltimore: Johns Hopkins Press.

Altmann, J. 1974. Observational Study of Behavior: Sampling Methods. *Behaviour* 49:227–67.

Bailey, R. C., and N. R. Peacock. 1988. *Time Allocation of Efe Pygmy Men and Women of the Ituri Forest, Zaire*. Cross-Cultural Studies in Time Allocation, vol. 3. New Haven, CT: HRAF Press.

Baksh, M. 1989–90. The Spot Observations Technique in Time Allocation Research. *Cultural Anthropology Methods Newsletter* 1(2):1–3; 2(2):6–7; 2(3):4–5, 11.

———. 1990. *Time Allocation among the Machiguenga of Camana.* Cross-Cultural Studies in Time Allocation, vol. 7. New Haven, CT: HRAF Press.

Behrens, C. A. 1988. *Time Allocation among the Shipibo of Nuevo Eden.* Cross-Cultural Studies in Time Allocation, vol. 4. New Haven, CT: HRAF Press.

Bernard, H. R., and P. D. Killworth. 1993. Sampling in Time Allocation Research. *Ethnology* 32: 207–15.

Biller, Henry B. 1976. The Father and Personality Development: Paternal Deprivation and Sex-Role Development. Pp. 89–156 in Michael E. Lamb, ed., *The Role of the Father in Child Development.* New York: Wiley.

Blurton Jones, N. G., and M. J. Konner. 1973. Sex Differences in Behavior of London and Bushman Children. Pp. 690–750 in R. P. Michael and J. H. Crook, eds., *Comparative Ecology and Behaviour of Primates.* London: Academic Press.

Bochner, S. 1986. Observational Methods. Pp. 165–201 in W. J. Lonner and J. W. Berry, eds., *Field Methods in Cross-Cultural Research.* Beverly Hills, CA: Sage.

Borgerhoff Mulder, M., and T. M. Caro. 1985. The Use of Quantitative Observational Techniques in Anthropology. *Current Anthropology* 26:323–35.

Borgerhoff Mulder, M., and M. Milton. 1985. Factors Affecting Infant Care in the Kipsigis. *Journal of Anthropological Research* 41:231–62.

Campbell, D. T. 1961. The Mutual Methodological Relevance of Anthropology and Psychology. Pp. 333–52 in F.L.K. Hsu, ed., *Psychological Anthropology.* Homewood, IL: Dorsey.

Campbell, D. T., and D. W. Fiske. 1959. Convergent and Discriminant Validation by the Multitrait-Multimethod Matrix. *Psychological Bulletin* 56:81–105.

Chisholm, J. S. 1983. *Navajo Infancy: An Ethological Study of Child Development.* New York: Aldine.

Daly, M., and M. I. Wilson. 1980. Discriminative Parental Solicitude: A Biological Perspective. *Journal of Marriage and the Family* 42:277–88.

Dasen, P. R. 1988. Développement psychologique et activités quotidiennes chez des enfants africains. *Enfance* 41:3–23.

Dixon, S. D., R. A. LeVine, A. Richman, and T. B. Brazelton. 1984. Mother-Child Interaction around a Teaching Task: An African-American Comparison. *Child Development* 55:1252–64.

Draper, P. 1975. Cultural Pressures on Sex Differences. *American Ethnologist* 2:602–16.

———. 1976. Social and Economic Constraints of Child Life among the !Kung. Pp. 199–217 in R. B. Lee and I. DeVore, eds., *Kalahari Hunter-Gatherers.* Cambridge, MA: Harvard University Press.

Eaton, W. O. 1983. Measuring Activity Level with Actometers: Reliability, Validity, and Arm Length. *Child Development* 54:720–26.

Edwards, C. P., and B. B. Whiting. 1993. "Mother, Older Sibling, and Me": The Overlapping Roles of Caregivers and Companions in the Social World of 2–3 Year-Olds in Ngeca, Kenya. Pp. 305–28 in K. B. MacDonald, ed., *Parent-Child: Descriptions and Implications.* Albany: State University of New York Press.

Ellis, S., and M. Gauvain. 1992. Social and Cultural Influences on Children's Collaborative Interactions. Pp. 155–80 in L. T. Winegar and J. Valsiner, eds., *Children's Development within Social Context,* vol. 2. Hillsdale, NJ: Erlbaum.

Ellsworth, P. C. 1977. From Abstract Ideas to Concrete Instances. *American Psychologist* 32:604–15.

Ember, C. R. 1973. Feminine Task Assignment and the Social Behavior of Boys. *Ethos* 1:424–39.

———. 1981. A Cross-Cultural Perspective on Sex Differences. Pp. 531–80 in R. H. Munroe, R. L. Munroe, and B. B. Whiting, eds., *Handbook of Cross-Cultural Human Development.* New York: Garland.

Erasmus, C. 1955. Work Patterns in a Mayo Village. *American Anthropologist* 57:322–33.

Erchak, G. M. 1980. The Acquisition of Cultural Rules by Kpelle Children. *Ethos* 8:40–48.

Flinn, M. V. 1988. Parent-Offspring Interactions in a Caribbean Village: Daughter Guarding. Pp. 189–200 in L. Betzig, M. Borgerhoff Mulder, and P. Turke, eds., *Human Reproductive Behaviour*. Cambridge, Eng.: Cambridge University Press.

———. 1992. Paternal Care in a Caribbean Village. Pp. 57–84 in B. S. Hewlett, ed., *Father-Child Relations: Cultural and Biosocial Contexts*. New York: Aldine de Gruyter.

Gauvain, M. 1993. The Development of Spatial Thinking in Everyday Activity. *Developmental Review* 13:92–121.

Gauvain, M., and T. DeMent. 1991. The Role of Shared Social History in Parent-Child Cognitive Activity. *Quarterly Newsletter of the Laboratory of Comparative Human Cognition* 13:58–66.

Gross, D. R. 1984. Time Allocation: A Tool for the Study of Behavior. *Annual Review of Anthropology* 13:519–58.

Guilmet, G. M. 1979. Navajo and Caucasian Children's Verbal and Nonverbal-Visual Behavior in the Urban Classroom. *Anthropology and Education Quarterly* 9:196–215.

Hames, R. B. 1988. The Allocation of Parental Care among the Ye'kwana. Pp. 237–51 in L. Betzig, M. Borgerhoff Mulder, and P. Turke, eds., *Human Reproductive Behaviour*. Cambridge, Eng.: Cambridge University Press.

Harkness, S., and C. M. Super. 1983. The Cultural Construction of Child Development. *Ethos* 11: 221–31.

Hawkes, K., H. Kaplan, K. Hill, and M. Hurtado. 1987. A Problem of Bias in Scan Sampling. *Journal of Anthropological Research* 43:239–46.

Hewlett, B. S. 1991. *Intimate Fathers*. Ann Arbor: University of Michigan Press.

Homans, G. C. 1967. *The Nature of Social Science*. New York: Harcourt, Brace and World.

Hutt, S. J., and C. Hutt. 1970. *Direct Observation and Measurement of Behavior*. Springfield, IL: Charles C. Thomas.

Johnson, A. 1975. Time Allocation in a Machiguenga Community. *Ethnology* 14:301–10.

Johnson, A., and C. Behrens. 1989. Time Allocation Research and Aspects of Method in Cross-Cultural Comparison. *Journal of Quantitative Anthropology* 1:313–34.

Johnson, A., and O. R. Johnson. 1987. *Time Allocation among the Machiguenga of Shimaa*. Cross-Cultural Studies in Time Allocation, vol. 1. New Haven, CT: HRAF Press.

Johnson, O. R. 1980. The Social Context of Intimacy and Avoidance: A Videotape Study of Machiguenga Meals. *Ethology* 19:353–66.

Kilbride, J. E., and P. L. Kilbride. 1990. Sociocultural Factors and Perinatal Development of Baganda Infants: The Precocity Issue. *Pre- and Peri-Natal Psychology Journal* 4:281–300.

Leiderman, P. H., and G. F. Leiderman. 1974. Affective and Cognitive Consequences of Polymatric Infant Care in the East African Highlands. Pp. 81–110 in A. D. Pick, ed., *Minnesota Symposia on Child Psychology*, vol. 8. Minneapolis: University of Minnesota Press.

Lewis, O. 1951. *Life in a Mexican Village*. Urbana: University of Illinois Press.

Longabaugh, R. 1980. The Systematic Observation of Behavior in Naturalistic Settings. Pp. 57–126 in H. C. Triandis and J. W. Berry, eds., *Handbook of Cross-Cultural Psychology*, vol. 2. Boston: Allyn and Bacon.

Loucky, J. P. 1988. Children's Work and Family Survival in Highland Guatemala. Ph.D. diss., University of California at Los Angeles.

Mackey, W. C. 1983. A Preliminary Test for the Validation of the Adult-Male Child Bond as a Species-Characteristic Trait. *American Anthropologist* 85:391–402.

Minturn, L., and W. W. Lambert. 1964. *Mothers of Six Cultures: Antecedents of Child Rearing*. New York: Wiley.

Munroe, R. H., and R. L. Munroe. 1971. Household Density and Infant Care in an East African Society. *Journal of Social Psychology* 83:3–13.

———. 1975. Infant Care and Childhood Cognitive Performance in East Africa. Paper presented at the biennial meeting of the Society for Research in Child Development, Denver.

———. 1981. Development of Sex Differences in Four Cultures: A Preliminary Report. Paper presented at the annual meeting of the Society for Cross-Cultural Research, Syracuse, NY.

———. 1984. Household Density and Holding of Infants in Samoa and Nepal. *Journal of Social Psychology* 122:135–36.

Munroe, R. H., R. L. Munroe, C. Michelson, A. Koel, R. Bolton, and C. Bolton. 1983. Time Allocation in Four Societies. *Ethnology* 22:355–70.

Munroe, R. H., R. L. Munroe, and H. S. Shimmin. 1984. Children's Work in Four Cultures: Determinants and Consequences. *American Anthropologist* 86:369–79.

Munroe, R. L., and R. H. Munroe. 1971. Effect of Environmental Experience on Spatial Ability in an East African Society. *Journal of Social Psychology* 83:15–22.

———. 1991. *Logoli Time Allocation* rev. ed. Cross-Cultural Studies in Time Allocation, vol. 5. New Haven, CT: HRAF Press.

———. 1990a. *Black Carib Time Allocation.* Cross-Cultural Studies in Time Allocation, vol. 6. New Haven, CT: HRAF Press.

———. 1990b. *Samoan Time Allocation.* Cross-Cultural Studies in Time Allocation, vol. 8. New Haven, CT: HRAF Press.

———. 1992. Fathers in Children's Environments: A Four-Culture Study. Pp. 213–29 in B. S. Hewlett, ed., *Father-Child Relations: Cultural and Biosocial Contexts.* New York: Aldine de Gruyter.

Munroe, R. L., R. H. Munroe, and A. Brasher. 1985. Precursors of Spatial Ability: A Longitudinal Study in East Africa. *Journal of Social Psychology* 125:23–33.

Munroe, R. L., R. H. Munroe, J. A. Shwayder, and G. Arias. In Press. *Newar Time Allocation.* New Haven, Conn.: HRAF Press.

Murdock, G. P. 1967. *Ethnographic Atlas.* Pittsburgh: University of Pittsburgh Press.

Nerlove, S. B., R. H. Munroe, and R. L. Munroe. 1971. Effect on Environmental Experience on Spatial Ability: A Replication. *Journal of Social Psychology* 84:3–10.

Nerlove, S. B., J. M. Roberts, R. E. Klein, C. Yarbrough, and J. P. Habicht. 1974. Natural Indicators of Cognitive Development: An Observational Study of Rural Guatemalan Children. *Ethos* 2:265–95.

Omark, D. R., M. Omark, and M. Edelman. 1975. Formation of Dominance Hierarchies in Young Children. Pp. 289–315 in T. R. Williams, ed., *Psychological Anthropology.* The Hague: Mouton.

Overman, E. S. 1988. Measurement, Pp. 27–30. in E. S. Overman, ed., *Methodology and Epistemology for Social Science: Selected Papers, Donald T. Campbell.* Chicago: University of Chicago Press.

Paolisso, M. J., and R. D. Sackett. 1988. *Time Allocation among the Yukpa of Yurmutu.* Cross-Cultural Studies in Time Allocation, vol. 2. New Haven, CT: HRAF Press.

Quinn, N. 1966. A Day in the Life of a Woman in Capilla Loma.

Roberts, J. M. 1956. *Zuni Daily Life.* New Haven, CT: HRAF Press.

Rogoff, B. 1978. Spot Observation: An Introduction and Examination. *Quarterly Newsletter of the Institute for Comparative Human Development* 2:21–26.

———. 1981. Adults and Peers as Agents of Socialization: A Highland Guatemalan Profile. *Ethos* 9:18–36.

———. 1990. *Apprenticeship in Thinking: Cognitive Developments in Social Context.* New York: Oxford University Press.

Scaglion, R. 1986. The Importance of Nighttime Observations in Time Allocation Studies. *American Ethnologist* 13:537–45.

Seymour, S. 1976. Household Size and Infant Indulgence in an Indian Town. Paper presented at the annual meeting of the American Anthropological Association, Washington, DC.

———. 1988. Expressions of Responsibility among Indian Children: Some Precursors of Adult Status and Sex Roles. *Ethos* 16:355–70.

Sigman, M., C. Neumann, E. Carter, D. J. Cattle, S. D'Souza, and N. Bwibo. 1988. Home Interactions and the Development of Embu Toddlers in Kenya. *Child Development* 59:1251–61.

Slaby, R. G., and K. S. Frey. 1975. Development of Gender Constancy and Selective Attention to Same-Sex Models. *Child Development* 46P:849–56.

Smith, E. A. 1983. Anthropological Applications of Optimal Foraging Theory: A Critical Review. *Current Anthropology* 24:625–51.

———. 1987. Optimization Theory in Anthropology: Applications and Critiques. Pp. 201–49 in J. Dupré, ed., *The Latest on the Best: Essays on Evolution and Optimality.* Cambridge, MA: MIT Press.

Stevenson, Michael R., and Kathryn N. Black. 1988. Paternal Absence and Sex- Role Development: A Meta-Analysis. *Child Development* 59:793–814.

Tronick, E. Z., G. A. Morelli, and P. K. Ivey. 1992. The Efe Forager Infant and Toddler's Pattern of Social Relationships: Multiple and Simultaneous. *Developmental Psychology* 28:568–77.

Turke, P. W. 1988. Helpers at the Nest: Childcare Networks on Ifaluk. Pp. 173–88 in L. Betzig, M. Borgerhoff Mulder, and P. Turke, eds., *Human Reproductive Behaviour*. Cambridge, Eng.: Cambridge University Press.

Weick, K. E. 1985. Systematic Observational Methods. Pp 567–634 in G. Lindzey and E. Aronson, eds., *The Handbook of Social Psychology*, 3rd ed., vol. 1. New York: Random House.

Weisner, T. S. 1976. Urban-Rural Differences in African Children's Performance on Cognitive and Memory Tasks. *Ethos* 4:223–50.

———. 1989a. Comparing Sibling Relationships across Cultures. Pp. 11–25 in P. G. Zukow, ed., *Sibling Interaction across Cultures.* New York: Springer-Verlag.

———. 1989b. Cultural and Universal Aspects of Social Support for Children: Evidence from the Abaluyia of Kenya. Pp. 70–90 in D. Belle, ed., *Children's Social Networks and Social Supports*. New York: Wiley.

Weisner, T. S., R. Gallimore, and C. Jordan. 1988. Unpackaging Cultural Effects on Classroom Learning: Native Hawaiian Peer Assistance and Child-Generated Activity. *Anthropology and Education Quarterly* 19:327–53.

Wenger, M. 1983. Gender Role Socialization in East Africa: Social Interactions between 2-to-3 Year Olds and Older Children, A Social Ecological Perspective. Ph.D. diss., Harvard University.

Werner, D. 1992. *Mekranoti Time Allocation.* Cross-Cultural Studies in Time Allocation, vol. 9. New Haven, CT: HRAF Press.

West, M. M., and M. J. Konner. 1976. The Role of the Father: An Anthropological Perspective. Pp. 185–217 in M. E. Lamb, ed., *The Role of the Father in Child Development.* New York: Wiley.

Whiting, B. B., ed. 1963. *Six Cultures: Studies of Child Rearing*. New York: Wiley.

Whiting, B. B., and C. P. Edwards. 1988. *Children of Different Worlds.* Cambridge, MA: Harvard University Press.

Whiting, B. B., and J.W.M. Whiting. 1973. Methods for Observing and Recording Behavior. P. 282–315 in R. Naroll and R. Cohen, eds., *A Handbook of Method in Cultural Anthropology*. New York: Columbia University Press.

———. 1975. *Children of Six Cultures: A Psycho-Cultural Analysis.* Cambridge, MA: Harvard University Press.

Winn, S., E. Z. Tronick, and G. A. Morelli. 1990. The Infant in the Group: A Look at Efe Caretaking Patterns. Pp. 87–109 in J. K. Nugent, B. M. Lester, and T. B. Brazelton, eds., *The Cultural Context of Infancy*, vol. 1 Norwood, NJ: Ablex.

Zukow, P. G. 1989. Siblings as Effective Socializing Agents: Evidence from Central Mexico. Pp. 79–105 in P. G. Zukow, ed., *Sibling Interaction across Cultures*. New York: Springer-Verlag.

CHAPTER FIFTEEN

THE EVIDENCE FROM DREAMS

Barbara Tedlock

The questions we ask and the ways we approach our findings, together with the models we use to organize and understand our research, are important aspects of dream research. We examine dreams differently when we ask ourselves, "What caused the dream and what are its manifest contents?" than when we ask, "What does the dream mean, what problems and processes are reflected in the dream?" or "For what purpose is this particular dream being communicated?"

Anthropologists have studied dreams and the culture of dreaming for a variety of reasons. Dream narratives have been examined by researchers in order to learn how members of various cultures classify or categorize and use their dreams (Siegel 1978; Kilborne 1987; Price-Williams and Degarrod 1989). By focusing on the social act of dream narration, other researchers have revealed both the tactical use of dreams in social interaction (Kiernan 1985) and cultural influences on dream content (Dittmann and Moore 1957; Schneider and Sharp 1969). Yet other anthropologists have chosen not to focus their attention on the dream narrative or social context, but rather use dreams in order to investigate human personality (Maccoby and Foster 1970); to test psychological theories of development; motivation, and values (O'Nell 1965; Shweder and LeVine 1975); or to investigate the psychocultural lag between current dreams and the subject or event dreamed about (Lee 1958; Anderson 1971; Johnson 1978).

In the early days of anthropology, scholars described dreams as the ultimate source of religious beliefs concerning the supernatural and the nature of the human soul (Tylor 1871; Frazer 1890; Wundt 1906). However, after the publication of *The Interpretation of Dreams* (Freud 1900), much of the scholarly world lost interest in the social and religious contexts of dreaming. Instead, they followed Freud in separating the nature of the dream experience, or the "manifest dream," from the real meaning of these experiences, which was labeled the "latent dream." According to the psychoanalytic methodology Freud developed, the manifest content of a dream ought to be investigated with the help of the dreamer's associations to the visible elements in the dream report. These associations should then be traced to the hidden or latent thoughts of the dreamer, which were hypothesized as consisting of a combination of wishes and conflicts. In Freudian theory, the manifest content—though often distorted, disguised, or presented in metaphorical form—and the latent content were linked to a distinction between two modes of thought: primary and secondary process. Primary-process thought appears as symbolic imagery and is often described as nonlogical, while secondary-process thought is described as predominantly verbal and logical.

Among anthropologists the response to Freud's work has been mixed. While a number of individuals utilized Freudian concepts and methodologies, others remained skeptical and tested the key hypotheses, and yet others ignored the approach altogether. Individuals who closely followed Freud's psychoanalytic theories and methods have argued that similar latent contents—including sibling rivalry, incestuous attachments, anxiety arising from maternal separation, and fear of castration—are revealed in dream reports gathered in vastly different cultures (Lincoln 1935; Du Bois 1944; Kardiner 1945; Róheim 1946, 1947, 1949, 1950; Devereaux 1951; Kluckhohn and Morgan 1951; Honigmann 1961). A few ethnographers have described various Native American cultures as having independently invented quasi-psychoanalytic techniques of dream interpretation (Toffelmier and Luomala 1936; Wallace 1958; Opler 1959; Bruce 1975; Laughlin 1976).

A number of researchers have employed one or more of the following Freudian methodologies: (1) asking for associations to each dream episode as it is related; (2) focusing on a striking dream element that seems to contain the key to the meaning of the dream; (3) asking for the previous day's residue connected with the dream; and (4) allowing the client to take the initiative. Géza Róheim (1947, 1949) used all of these psychoanalytic methods in his cross-cultural dream research; Cora Du Bois (1944) obtained only a few Alorese dreams with associations; while Dorothy Eggan (1949, 1952, 1961, 1965, 1966) did not press her Hopi consultants for the previous day's residue or free associations, but allowed them to take the initiative in dream telling and free association. Eggan's method of collecting dreams might be described as passive and at a distance in that she allowed her subjects to report whatever dreams they wished (recent or old), and she did not look for associational material. Róheim, on the other hand, was keen to obtain associations to each episode of a dream followed by the telling of a freely chosen story, personal anecdote, or song. Perhaps because he focused on the infantile wish in interpreting dreams, rather than on current conflicts, Róheim argued that in order to understand a dream, an analyst need only be familiar with the simple factual knowledge required to follow the manifest narrative content of the dream. Waud Kracke (1979) disagreed, noting that in order to understand what an individual's dreams reveal about his or her personality, it is necessary to learn the language of dreaming within that individual's culture. Most anthropologists who use the psychoanalytic approach to dream analysis have preferred to combine it with an ethnographic approach to the local culture of dreaming in order to probe both the psychological significance of a dream to a dreamer and its cultural significance. Visionary or prophetic dreams, for example, often transform the psyche of the dreamer; they may simultaneously inaugurate charismatic religious movements and trigger anticolonialist revolts (Mooney 1896; Wallace 1958, 1959, 1972; Fabian 1966; Lanternari 1975; Stephen 1979; Dentan 1986; Huber 1990).

Freud's hypothesis concerning "type dreams," which states that the same manifest content—for example, flying, climbing, or the loss of a tooth—reveals identical latent meanings across cultures, has been tested by anthropologists. Charles Seligman (1921, 1923, 1924) published a request for British colonial officials and missionaries to send him records of native dreams, arguing that if type dreams of the Freudian sort were found frequently in this data base, then the human unconscious was qualitatively so alike worldwide that it was constituted as a common "store" on which fantasy might draw. His store metaphor points to the objectifying notion of dream symbolism as a simple trait that might be measured or weighed by colonial officials and ignores the importance of communicative context, both within these cultures and in the negotiation of reality between colonial administrators and indigenous peoples. This lack of sensitivity to the context and manner in which one's research is conducted can also be seen in the work of Jackson Lincoln (1935), who ignored the influence of social setting on his own collection of Navajo dreams: transactions that took place in Arizona at the Black Mountain Trading Post. After collecting a number of Navajo dreams, together with others that he culled mostly from North American Indian ethnographies, Lincoln separated his dream corpus into unsought or spontaneous dreams occurring in sleep, which he labeled "individual dreams," and sought or induced and tribally important "culture-pattern dreams." These analytical categories, however, failed to correspond with the classificatory schemes of the societies he examined (B. Tedlock 1987a).

While Seligman and Lincoln found that similar sorts of dreams occurred worldwide, the Freudian premise that universal type dreams should mean the same thing everywhere they occurred was not empirically tested until Benjamin Kilborne (1978, 1981) asked a group of Moroccan dream interpreters to explain the meaning of a set of dreams he selected from Freud's publications. Using the ethnopsychiatric approach to dream research, pioneered by George Devereux (1961, 1978, 1980), Kilborne collected traditional Moroccan analyses of fifteen dreams taken from *The Interpretation of Dreams.* Thus in a woman's dream of a deep pit in a vineyard, caused by a tree being torn out, which Freud (1915: 191) had discussed as a classic example of a female castration dream, Kilborne discovered that Moroccan dream interpreters either focused primarily on the pit, leaving out the tree, or else focused on the tree, leaving out the pit. In the first instance, the pit was described as representing an "obstacle" or a "trap" for the dreamer, while in the second case, the tree represented a "good person" who died. Kilborne noted that while Freudian explanations of dream symbolism draw on the notion of universal latent content and on defense mechanisms, Moroccan explanations depend upon the dreamer's social position and on the projection of what is bad upon enemies. He concluded that while type dreams may occur widely, they do not mean the same thing in all corners of the world. While Freud treated dream reports as analyzable, discrete structures requiring secondary associations before they could be adequately interpreted, Moroccans did not make an analyzable entity of either the dream or of the context of interpretation.

It may well be, as Vincent Crapanzano (1981) has argued, that a focus on the dream report and its extractable contents is an expression of Western culture and thus is culture-bound. In turning his anthropological gaze on Western thought, Crapanzano noted that the encounter between psychoanalyst and client is limited by a particular epistemological configuration in which priority is given to the referential or indexical function of language and to the dream text as an objectification, or reduction to, that function. He noted that this epistemological configuration is rooted in the culture of alphabetic literacy and warned anthropologists who study dreams to be wary of its limitations.

While most anthropologists who have applied methodologies borrowed from psychology have chosen the Freudian path, some have followed Carl Jung instead (Layard 1944; Bührmann 1978; Petchkovsky 1984; Martin 1986; Petchkovsky and Cawte 1986). Jungians differ from Freudians in a number of ways. Perhaps the sharpest disagreement centers on Freud's hypothesis that the "manifest" dream is simply a disguise of the "latent" dream that embodies an infantile erotic wish (Steele 1982). Jungians argue that images in dreams reflect the structure of psychological complexes in the personal unconscious that rest upon archetypal cores in the psyche and are subject to the individuating force of the self (J. Hall 1983; Meier 1987). The key problem many anthropologists have with both orthodox Freudian and Jungian analyses is that within these systems dream symbols have been hypothesized as having stable "translations" and universal significance. In Freud's case, symbols have stable meanings, or translations, cross-culturally because they are rooted in physiology, while in Jung's case, it is because they exist in the collective unconscious. (See the chapter by Robin Fox in this volume.)

Due to the strong influence of cultural relativism within anthropology, however, both of these views are generally perceived as unacceptable. As a result, many ethnographers sidestepped universalizing theories, turning instead to an examination of the manifest level of dream interpretation. When they shifted their attention from the latent to the manifest content of dreams, some anthropologists began using the method of content analysis developed by Calvin Hall and his colleagues (C. Hall 1951, 1953; Hall and Van de Castle 1966). While this statistical methodology seemed to require the construction of a random sample of dream reports, George Foster (1973) argued that dream research cannot be carried out like survey research with answers to set questions from every fifth house because most people are reluctant to share their dreams. He suggested collecting dreams only from one's closest friends and then applying content analysis to these dreams on either an elemental or a thematic level. Analyzing dreams on the elemental level requires the researcher to code and tally entities such as settings, objects, characters, emotions, and social interactions. Each element recorded is considered to indicate the presence of either a character trait or a trend of social structure. This type of research, however, implies an inappropriate model for understanding dreaming, which, like other mental processes, is not merely an association of components but a set of patterned sequences. The radical decontextualization necessary to carry out this method loses the story line, so that all that remains is a list of elements and a set of numbers without any associations between the elements. As a result, meaning is lost in favor of quantification.

In content analysis at the thematic level, a set of dream narratives is collected and recurrent themes or motifs are coded and presented in numbers or percentages. Here analysts attempt to get at meaning by laying bare the structural or functional patterns revealing typical motifs. This method is most often used to indicate psychological issues the dreamer is struggling with (Eggan 1949; LeVine 1982; Bilu and Abramovitch 1985), but it has also been used to discuss religion and worldview (Foster 1973; Charsley 1973; Curley 1983; Kiernan 1985; Petchkovsky and Cawte 1986). Since one is able to examine the associations of elements and action sequences, this method alleviates some of the problems with the elemental level of content analysis. The main problem with this method is that it places a greater emphasis on Western dream theory than it does on the dream theory of the culture under analysis. Once again this is a problem of decontextualization, since the idea that dreams primarily deal with psychological issues is not shared by all cultures. Radically different ideas about what a dream is affect the nature of dream narratives worldwide.

Psychologists of both psychoanalytic and cognitive bents have read anthropology in order to compare the dreams of "preliterate," "tribal," "traditional," or "peasant" peoples with their own findings concerning the dreams of "literate," "urban," "modern," or "industrial" peoples. This dichotomy, however, denies people living in other cultures contemporaneity with ourselves. Instead of using typological time to create and set off an object of study such as "tribal dreaming," cultural anthropologists have become interested in intersubjective time in which all of the participants involved are "coeval," that is, share the same time (Fabian 1983). This focus on communicative processes among contemporaries demands that coevalness not only be created and maintained in the field, but also that it be carried over during the write-up process. Robert Dentan (1986:335), while discussing the principle of contraries in which dreams are said to indicate the opposite of what they seem, noted that practitioners of this type of dream interpretation include such widely separated peoples as Ashanti, Malays, Maori, Semai, Zulu, Polish-American schoolgirls, and psychoanalysts. In other words, Westerners share this principle of dream interpretation with people living in faraway, exotic places.

This underlying sameness in human cognition is also stressed within structuralism (Lévi-Strauss 1963). A structural approach to dreaming demonstrates that dreams, like myths, constitute a set of systematic transformations of a single structure consisting of a set of oppositions representing a dilemma or conflict facing a dreamer (Kuper 1979, 1983, 1986; Kuper and Stone 1982). Philippe Descola (1989), in her research among Jivaroan people in South America, found that the individual unconscious and the collective unconscious are related less by contiguity or universal archetypes than by use of encoding devices for the diversity of reality within elementary systems of relationships. She noted that like structuralists, indigenous dream interpreters emphasize the logical operations through which symbols are connected and suggested that we need a comparative grammar of dreams that might elucidate how various cultures choose and combine a set of rules, or codes, for dream interpretation.

The turn away from treating "non-Western dreams" as totally other, that is, as fully knowable objects to be gathered, analyzed, tabulated, and compared with "Western dreams," toward paying attention to the problematics of dream communication and interpretation worldwide has occurred within anthropology for several reasons. First, cultural anthropologists came to distrust survey research in which "data" are gathered for the purpose of testing Western theories concerning universals in human psychology. Thus cross-cultural content analysis in which statistical assertions about dream patterns within particular ethnic groups or genders were the goal have been critiqued by anthropologists (B. Tedlock 1987a; Dentan 1988a). There are several reasons for this, including the fact that sample surveys aggregate respondents who are deeply distrustful of the researcher with those who are not, as if suspicion made no difference whatsoever in the validity of their replies (Scheff 1986). Further, a comparative focus on the extractable contents, underlying structure, or cognitive grammar of a dream report not only omits important phenomena such as pacing, tones of voice, gestures, and audience responses that accompany dream-narrative performances, but is also an expression of the culture of alphabetic literacy and is thus culture-bound (Crapanzano 1981; B. Tedlock 1987a). Another reason for the abandonment of content analysis by anthropologists is their formal training in linguistics, which encourages them to reject the basic assumption of aggregate statistical research, namely, that meaning resides within single words rather than within their contexts (Dentan 1988a). Furthermore, dream symbols taken in isolation can be misleading if the researcher has not spent sufficient time observing and interacting within the culture in order to make sense of local knowledge and produce a "thick description" of that culture (Geertz 1973; Dentan 1988b). Rather than interpreting the language of dream narratives in semanticoreferential, context-independent terms, it is more appropriate to utilize context-dependent, or pragmatic, meaning.

Because of these considerations, anthropologists no longer set out to elicit dream reports as ethnographic objects to be used primarily as raw data for comparative hypotheses. Instead, since the attitudes toward and beliefs about dreams held by a people reveal important aspects of their worldview, constructing a detailed ethnography of dreaming has become an important research goal. Ethnographers tape-record and transcribe verbatim dream narratives along with dreamers' interpretations (Pentony 1961; Fabian 1966; Crapanzano 1975; Graham 1990). The method of ethnographic semantics, in which direct and formal questioning is used, may also be applied in order to ascertain how members of a particular linguistic group categorize their dreams (Keeler 1987; Dentan 1988a; Hollan 1989). The goals of this methodology are to produce a taxonomic system of types of dreams—good, bad, or true, false (Foster 1973; Reid 1978; Ewing 1990)—and to reveal native dream theory and techniques of dream interpretation (B. Tedlock 1981; Basso 1987; Kracke 1987).

This combination of linguistic and ethnographic methodologies, applied within different domains, particularly suits contemporary cultural anthropology, which requires researchers to enter the field for extended periods of time with broad sets of research interests (for example, the religion and worldview of a particular society, the performance of healing, or the construction of self and personhood). By living in the community, ethnographers learn the local language as well as how to interact appropriately, and they are present for various formal and informal social dramas. Sooner or later they are present when a dream is narrated within a family, or to a practicing shaman or other dream interpreter. If this event attracts their attention, they make notes about it in their field journals, and they may later record other such occurrences on audiotape or videotape. Once they have translated their texts, they may ask the narrator, who may or may not be the dreamer, questions about the meaning, significance, and use of the dream account.

This shift in research strategy from eliciting dozens of fixed objects (dreams) to studying naturally occurring situations (dream sharing, representation, and interpretation) is part of a larger movement within anthropology in which there has been a rapidly growing interest in analyses focused on practice, interaction, dialogue, experience, and performance, together with the individual agents, actors, persons, selves, and subjects of all this activity (Bourdieu 1978; D. Tedlock 1979; Ortner 1984). A number of recent ethnographic works display this shift from a narrow focus on the dream as an object to interest in the context surrounding the personal experience and cultural uses of dreaming (Roseman 1986; Degarrod 1989; Desjarlais 1990; Poirier 1990).

Robert Desjarlais (1990), during his fieldwork in Nepal with the Yolmo Sherpa, noted a large degree of agreement among individuals concerning the meaning of dream imagery and found an implicit dictionary of dream symbolism upon which individuals relied most frequently in times of physical or spiritual distress. In this dream-interpretation system, the experience of dreaming is believed to have a close, even causal, connection with the future life of the dreamer. This principle is found in many cultures (Bruce 1975, 1979; Laughlin 1976; Herdt 1977; Kilborne 1978; Kracke 1979; Dentan 1983; Basso 1987; B. Tedlock 1987b; Degarrod 1989; Hollan 1989; McDowell 1989). However, such interpretations are often provisional: not all people in a given society place their faith in them, and in some societies only certain individuals are believed to be able to experience prophetic or precognitive dreams (Devereux 1956; Meggitt 1962; Charsley 1973; Jackson 1978; Dentan 1983; Merrill 1987). Cultural anthropologists who have undertaken substantial fieldwork within American society have found that middle-class dreamers also admit to having experienced dreams of the prophetic or precognitive sort in which they obtain information about future events (Collins 1977; Hillman 1988; Dombeck 1989). The Western conception of dreams as predictors of misfortune or success, together with the anecdotal literature on "psychic dreams," indicates that this form of dream interpretation is far from rare in Western societies (Stevens 1949; Ullman, Krippner, and Vaughan 1973; Persinger 1988; Persinger and Krippner 1989; Tolaas 1990; Partman 1991).

Labeling certain dream experiences "prophetic" or "precognitive," however, does not explain how these and other dream experiences are used within a society. In order to learn about the use of dreaming, researchers cannot simply gather examples of different types of dreams by administering a questionnaire, but must interact intensively with local populations for long periods of time. Thus, while Desjarlais (1990, 1991) discovered an implicit "dictionary" of dream symbolism among the Sherpa early in his fieldwork, it took him some time as an apprentice shaman to learn the precise way in which these dream symbols served as symptoms and signifiers both shaping and reflecting distress. Marina Roseman (1986), through her active participation as a singer within an all-female chorus in Temiar society, learned the manner in which local dream sharing through song connects the musical and medical domains of knowledge and practice. In this Malaysian society, spirit guides teach songs to dreamers by singing them phrase by phrase, and dreamers learn songs during their dreams by repeating the songs phrase by phrase. This dream-teaching relationship is echoed in public performance when a male medium sings a song phrase that is then repeated by a female chorus. In time, Roseman grasped the fact that dream songs varied by the spirit-guide source, creating formal musical genres with characteristic textual content and vocabulary, melodic and rhythmic patterns, dance movements, and trance behavior. These genres vary not only individually, but also regionally and historically. During her fieldwork, Roseman (1990) taped hundreds of dream-song performances, together with intricate dream narratives and interpretations.

Like Roseman and Desjarlais, Lydia Degarrod recorded the majority of her dream materials within a natural setting rather than by arranging formal interviews. During her research among the Mapuche Indians of Chile, she gathered dream accounts and interpretations of these narratives from members of two families who were coping with serious stress caused by witchcraft and illness (Degarrod 1990). Through dream sharing and interpreting, the afflicted members of the families were able to express their anxieties and externalize their illness, and other family members were able to directly participate in the healing of their loved ones. Degarrod hypothesized that these types of family interventions were possible due to the general belief that dreams facilitate communication with supernatural beings and due to the nature of the communal dream-sharing and interpreting system, which allowed for the combination of elements from different individuals' dreams to be related through intertextual and contextual analysis.

During her research among Australian aboriginal people, Sylvie Poirier (1990) found that dreaming was closely intertwined with religious and other cultural beliefs. In Western Australia, dreams represent the privileged space-time of increased receptivity between individuals, the environment, and the ancestral world. Through studying local epistemology, she found that not only was the interpretation of dreams open to multiple readings depending on context, but that dream experience was a primary step in the social construction of the person.

By studying dream sharing and the transmission of dream theories in their full social contexts as communicative events, including the natural dialogical interactions that take place within these events, anthropologists have realized that both the researcher and those who are researched are engaged in the creation of a social reality that implicates both of them. Although ethnographers have long subscribed to the method of participant observation, it still comes as a shock when they discover how important their participation is in helping to create what they are studying. Gilbert Herdt (1987) reported his surprise at discovering the therapeutic dimension of his role in New Guinea as a sympathetic listener to his key consultant, who shared with him erotic dreams that the consultant could not communicate to anyone within his own society. Likewise, the importance to anthropology of the psychodynamic process of transference, or the bringing of past experiences into a current situation with the result that the present is unconsciously experienced as though it were the past (Freud 1914; Bird 1972; Loewald 1986), has only recently been fully realized and described for anthropology. Waud Kracke, during his fieldwork with the Kagwahiv Indians of Brazil, kept a diary containing his personal reactions, dreams, and associations. In an article discussing these field responses, Kracke (1987) not only analyzed his personal transference of his own family relationships to certain key Kagwahiv individuals, but also his cultural transference of American values to Kagwahiv behavior patterns. Other cultural anthropologists have not only recorded their dreams and associations in their field diaries, but have also told their dreams to members of the society in which they were working for the purpose of having them interpreted (Lincoln 1935:31–35; Toffelmier and Luomala 1936:217; Marriott 1952:76–87; Devereux 1961:170–71; Bruce 1975; Jackson 1978; Reid 1978; B. Tedlock 1981; Stephen 1989; Fernandez 1991; Seremetakis 1991:231–36; Shaw 1992).

Some anthropologists who have paid close attention to their dreams while they were in the field have found that this has helped them to integrate their unconscious with a conscious sense of personal continuity in this totally new, even threatening, situation (B. Tedlock 1991). Laura Nader (1970) reported that during her research among Zapotec Indians in Mexico, the amount of her nocturnal dreaming, as well as her ability to remember dreams, multiplied several times over her usual behavior, and that her dreams dealt almost exclusively with her experiences as a child and young adult back home in the United States. It was as though her dreams were reminding her not to lose her American self completely, not to become totally possessed by Zapotec "otherness." Her dreams reassured her that she was indeed still the same person she had been as a child; that there was a continuity within her self, in spite of strong feelings to the contrary.

Juxtapositions of earlier with recent life events in the dreams of fieldworkers is a common experience. A study by Barbara Anderson (1971) of fifteen American academics living in India reported a major change in dream content, moving from an initial retreat to earlier life events toward the establishment of a "secondary identity" that allowed dreams with mixed, but clearly distinct American and Indian elements. In the first month of fieldwork, she and her fellow academics reported dreaming of people from their childhood—old neighbors and school friends—whom they had not thought about in years. During the second month, current family members entered their dream life, shyly and from a great distance; for example, one man's wife talked with him from a doorway. It was not until a good deal later that their dream worlds included a wider spectrum of personages and backdrops with Indian settings in which their spouses, siblings, and children mingled together with Indians. She suggested that these dreams were the resolution of the serious identity crisis that accompanies mixed cultural affiliation.

That this might indeed be the case is revealed in several other ethnographers' narratives. Karla Poewe, a Canadian anthropologist of German extraction who published her memoir of fieldwork experiences in West Africa under the pseudonym Manda Cesara (1982), reported a dream in which she found herself in a position where she and a group of other people had to make a decision between fascism and freedom. Many people found themselves standing in line to join the will of the government, while she chose to swim free of the crowd, singing, "I want freedom." An official approached her and took her to the front of a line of people into a place off to one side. There she had to wait again, and while she was waiting, she saw a child who had also chosen freedom. The child was playing with a cuddly animal that disappeared in the bushes. She did not want to lose the child, but it looked around furtively, then slid through the shrubbery to freedom. As she continued waiting, a gorgeously dressed woman came by and stood before the mirror, saying how absurd it was to emphasize dress. The dreamer moved away from the crowd with the realization that freedom lay beyond the shrubs and awoke. Later, as she established her second cultural identity, her dreams, like those Barbara Anderson reported, changed to include mixed but clearly distinct American and African elements. Similarly, Nadia Seremetakis (1991) kept a dream diary during her ethnographic fieldwork in Inner Mani and shared her dreams with the women she was researching. She reported that her dreaming helped to enculturate her into the autonomous emotive power of women's symbolic practice and that she experienced an erasure of most of the voluntaristic ethos that characterizes scientific inquiry.

Remembered dream images can also serve as a mirror reflecting back to the cultural anthropologist a secure sense of identity. Not all others are equally suitable to serve as "mirrors," however. For some people, it seems to be only in the eyes of their own countrymen, or even themselves, that they can find a mirror. Bronislaw Malinowski reported in his posthumously published field diary: "Today . . . I had a strange dream; homo-sex., with my own double as a partner. Strangely auto-erotic feelings: the impression that I'd like to have a mouth just like mine to kiss, a neck that curves just like mine, a forehead just like mine (seen from the side)" (Malinowski 1967:12). Typically, mirror or double images in dreams represent an attempt to restore, retrieve, or bolster a threatened sense of self through the mechanisms of "projection" and "identification" (Devereux 1978:224). Malinowski's field diaries shocked many people because this self-proclaimed father of participant observation exposed his remarkable lack of participation in, and even respect for, the culture he described. The total absence of Trobriand features in his self-reported dreams is particularly disturbing. In the diaries, which cover two separate one-year periods (1914–15 and 1917–18), he mentioned and briefly reported twenty dreams (Malinowski 1967:12–13, 66, 70, 71, 73, 78, 80, 82, 116, 149, 159, 191, 202, 203, 204, 207, 208, 255, 290, 295). The settings of these dreams were usually in Poland, and the people who appeared most frequently were his mother and boyhood friends, including a girlfriend he expressed guilt about having abandoned. While two of the dreams included colonial officers, none were set within Trobriand culture, nor did they include a single indigenous person. Apparently, Malinowski did not successfully establish a secondary identity in the field that would have allowed for dreams with mixed, but clearly distinct, Polish and Trobriand elements.

In *Sex and Repression in Savage Society*, a book with the express purpose of critiquing the Oedipus complex and dream-interpretation theories of Sigmund Freud, Malinowski claimed that unlike other non-Western peoples, the Trobrianders "dream little, have little interest in their dreams, seldom relate them spontaneously, do not regard the ordinary dream as having any prophetic or other importance, and have no code of symbolic explanation whatsoever" (Malinowski 1927:92). However, a bit further on there is a five-page discussion of the premonitory dreams of fishermen and kula traders, the use of dreams by ritual specialists to initiate novices and to advise their community, dreams in which women's dead kinsmen inform them of their pregnancy, and the sending of dreams by magical means to cause others to fall in love with one. It appears that Malinowski's exaggerated claim of a lack of Trobriand interest in dreams originated from his anxiety to establish Trobrianders as exempt from repression. If this were indeed the case, it would weaken the supposed universality of Freud's Oedipus complex. However, Malinowski began with the faulty premise that in Freudian theory the main cause of dreams is unsatisfied sexual appetite. He then reasoned that the absence of erotic repression among Trobrianders accounts for the noticeable lack of sexual material in their dreams, which in turn explains their lack of concern with dreams in general. But this scarcity of eroticism in the manifest content of dreams may bear the opposite interpretation. If anything, freedom from repression should be indicated by the presence of sexual elements, since wishes that appear undistorted at the manifest level must not have been subject to a remarkable amount of censorship. Thus the absence of sexual elements suggests disguise, which presupposes repression.

Anthropologists no longer set out to elicit dream reports as though they were ethnographic objects that might be arranged, manipulated, and quantified like items of material culture. Rather than making typological or statistical comparisons between the dreams found in so-called Western versus non-Western societies, cultural anthropologists have turned their attention to studying dream theories and interpretation systems as complex psychodynamic communicative events. By studying dream sharing and the transmission of dream theories in their full social contexts, anthropologists have realized that the researcher and the subject of research create a joint social reality that links them in important ways.

Fieldworkers who are currently participating within native contexts and learning the local cultural use of dream experiences are also paying close attention to their own dreams. This has helped them to become aware of the unconscious responses of their informants to them (LeVine 1981) and also of their own unconscious responses to the people they are attempting to understand and describe. In time, perhaps, cultural anthropologists, like psychoanalysts, will develop the necessary skill and training to listen to emotional dream communications of others as well as to their own feelings (Kracke 1978). Rosalind Cartwright and other dream-laboratory researchers have suggested that dreams play an important part in mastering new affective experiences and assimilating them into one's self-schemata (Cartwright 1977; Palombo 1978). This particular form of self-mastery would seem to be an important undertaking, not only for psychoanalysts but also for anthropologists who use participant observation as their key research methodology.

REFERENCES

Anderson, B. G. 1971. Adaptive Aspects of Culture Shock. *American Anthropologist* 73:1121–25.

Basso, E. B. 1987. The Implications of a Progressive Theory of Dreaming. Pp. 86–104 in B. Tedlock, ed., *Dreaming: Anthropological and Psychological Interpretations*. Cambridge, Eng.: Cambridge University Press.

Bilu, Y., and H. Abramovitch. 1985. In Search of the Saddiq: Visitational Dreams among Moroccan Jews in Israel. *Psychiatry* 48:83–92.

Bird, B. 1972. Notes on the Transference: Universal Phenomenon and Hardest Part of Analysis. *Journal of the American Psychoanalytic Association* 20:267–301.

Bourdieu, P. 1977. *Outline of a Theory of Practice*. Trans. R. Nice. Cambridge, Eng.: Cambridge University Press.

Bruce, R. D. 1975. *Lacandon Dream Symbolism: Vol. 1. Dream Symbolism and Interpretation*. Mexico: Ediciones Euroamericanas.

———. 1979. *Lacandon Dream Symbolism: Vol. 2. Dictionary, Index, and Classifications of Dream Symbols*. Mexico: Ediciones Euroamericanas.

Bührmann, M. V. 1978. Tentative Views on Dream Therapy by Xhosa Diviners. *Journal of Analytical Psychology* 23:105–21.

Cartwright, R. D. 1977. *Night Life: Explorations in Dreaming*. Englewood Cliffs, NJ: Prentice-Hall.

Cesara, M. (pseudonym of Karla Poewe). 1982. *Reflections of a Woman Anthropologist: No Hiding Place*. New York: Academic Press.

Charsley, S. R. 1973. Dreams in an Independent African Church. *Africa* 43(3):244–57.

Collins, K. M. 1977. Secret Desires in Social Contexts: An Anthropological Approach to Dreams. M.A. thesis in anthropology, University of Illinois at Chicago.

Crapanzano, V. 1975. Saints, Jnun, and Dreams: An Essay in Moroccan Ethnopsychology. *Psychiatry* 38:145–59.

———. 1981. Text, Transference, and Indexicality. *Ethos* 9:122–48.

Curley, R. T. 1983. Dreams of Power: Social Process in a West African Religious Movement. *Africa* 53(3):20–37.

Degarrod, L. N. 1989. Dream Interpretation among the Mapuche Indians of Chile. Ph.D. diss. in anthropology, University of California at Los Angeles.

———. 1990. Coping with Stress: Dream Interpretation in the Mapuche Family. *Psychiatric Journal of the University of Ottawa* 15(2):111–16.

Dentan, R. K. 1983. *A Dream of Senoi*. Special Studies Series, Council on International Studies, State University of New York. Amherst: State University of New York at Buffalo.

———. 1986. Ethnographic Considerations in the Cross-Cultural Study of Dreaming. Pp. 317–58 in J. Gackenbach, ed., *Sleep and Dreams*. New York: Garland.

———. 1988a. Butterflies and Bug Hunters: Reality and Dreams, Dreams and Reality. *Psychiatric Journal of the University of Ottawa* 13(2):51–59.

———. 1988b. Lucidity, Sex, and Horror in Senoi Dreamwork. Pp. 37–63 in J. Gackenbach and S. LaBerge, eds., *Conscious Mind, Sleeping Brain*. New York: Plenum Press.

Descola, P. 1989. Head-Shrinkers versus Shrinks: Jivaroan Dream Analysis. *Man* 24:439–50.

Desjarlais, R. 1990. Samsara's Sadness: Sherpa Shamanism and the "Calling of Lost Souls." Ph.D. diss. in anthropology, University of California at Los Angeles.

———. 1991. Dreams, Divination, and Yolmo Ways of Knowing. *Dreaming* 1:211–24.

Devereux, G. 1951. *Reality and Dream: Psychotherapy of a Plains Indian*. New York: International Universities Press.

———. 1956. Mohave Dreams of Omen and Power. *Tomorrow* 4(3):17–24.

———. 1961. *Mohave Ethnopsychiatry and Suicide: The Psychiatric Knowledge and the Psychic Disturbances of an Indian Tribe*. Bureau of American Ethology, Bulletin 175. Washington, DC: United States Government Printing Office.

———. 1978. *Ethnopsychoanalysis: Psychoanalysis and Anthropology as Complementary Frames of Reference*. Berkeley: University of California Press.

———. 1980. *Basic Problems of Ethnopsychiatry*. Chicago: University of Chicago Press.

Dittmann, A. T., and H. C. Moore. 1957. Disturbance in Dreams as Related to Peyotism among the Navaho. *American Anthropologist* 59:642–49.

Dombeck, M.-T. B. 1989. Dreams and Professional Personhood: The Contexts of Dream Telling and Dream Interpretation among American Psychotherapists. Ph.D. diss. in anthropology, University of Rochester.

Du Bois, C. 1944. *The People of Alor*. Minneapolis: University of Minnesota Press.

Eggan, D. 1949. The Significance of Dreams for Anthropological Research. *American Anthropologist* 51:177–98.

———. 1952. The Manifest Content of Dreams: A Challenge to Social Science. *American Anthropologist* 54:469:85.

———. 1961. Dream Analysis. Pp. 551–77 in B. Kaplan, ed., *Studying Personality Cross-Culturally*. New York: Harper and Row.

———. 1965. The Personal Use of Myth in Dreams. Pp. 107–21 in T. A. Sebeok, ed., *Myth: A Symposium*. Bloomington: Indiana University Press.

———. 1966. Hopi Dreams in Cultural Perspective. Pp. 237–66 in G. E. von Grunebaum and R. Caillois, eds., *The Dream and Human Societies*. Berkeley: University of California Press.

Ewing, K. P. 1990. The Dream of Spiritual Initiation and the Organization of Self Representations among Pakistani Sufis. *American Ethnologist* 17:56–74.

Fabian, J. 1966. Dream and Charisma: "Theories of Dreams" in the Jamaa-Movement (Congo). *Anthropos* 61:544–60.

———. 1983. *Time and the Other: How Anthropology Makes Its Object*. New York: Columbia University Press.

Fernandez, J. W. 1991. Afterword. Pp. 213–21 in P. M. Peek, ed., *African Divination Systems: Ways of Knowing*. Bloomington: Indiana University Press.

Foster, G. M. 1973. Dreams, Character, and Cognitive Orientation in Tzintzuntzan. *Ethos* 1:106–21.

Frazer, J. G. 1890 [1955]. *The Golden Bough: A Study in Magic and Religion*. 3rd ed., 13 vols. New York: St. Martin's Press.

Freud, S. 1900 [1965]. *The Interpretation of Dreams*. New York: Avon.

———. 1914. Remembering, Repeating, and Working Through. *Standard Edition*, vol. 12:145–56. London: Hogarth.

———. 1915. *Introductory Lectures. Standard Edition*, vol. 15. London: Hogarth.

Geertz, C. 1973. *The Interpretation of Cultures*. New York: Basic Books.

Graham, L. 1990. The Always Living: Discourse and the Male Lifecycle of the Xavante Indians of Central Brazil. Ph.D. diss. in anthropology, University of Texas at Austin.

Hall, C. S. 1951. What People Dream About. *Scientific American* 184(5):60–63.

———. 1953. *The Meaning of Dreams*. New York: Harper and Row.

Hall, C. S., and R. L. Van de Castle. 1966. *The Content Analysis of Dreams*. New York: Appleton-Century-Crofts.

Hall, J. A. 1983. *Jungian Dream Interpretation: A Handbook of Theory and Practice*. Toronto: Inner City Books.

Herdt, G. H. 1977. The Shaman's "Calling" among the Sambia of New Guinea. *Journal de la Société des Océanistes* 33:153–67.

———. 1987. Selfhood and Discourse in Sambia Dream Sharing. Pp. 55–85 in B. Tedlock, ed., *Dreaming: Anthropological and Psychological Interpretations*. Cambridge, Eng.: Cambridge University Press.

Hillman, D. J. 1988. Dream Work and Field Work: Linking Cultural Anthropology and the Current Dream Work Movement. Pp. 117–41 in M. Ullman and C. Limmer, eds., *The Variety of Dream Experience*. New York: Continuum.

Hollan, D. 1989. The Personal Use of Dream Beliefs in the Toraja Highlands. *Ethos* 17:166–86.

Honigmann, J. J. 1961. The Interpretation of Dreams in Anthropological Field Work: A Case Study. Pp. 579–85 in B. Kaplan, ed., *Studying Personality Cross-Culturally*. New York: Harper and Row.

Huber, B. R. 1990. The Recruitment of Nahua Curers: Role Conflict and Gender. *Ethnology* 29: 159–76.

Jackson, M. 1978. An Approach to Kuranko Divination. *Human Relations* 31:117–38.

Johnson, K. E. 1978. Modernity and Dream Content: A Ugandan Example. *Ethos* 6:212–20.

Kardiner, A. 1945. *Psychological Frontiers of Society*. New York: Columbia University Press.

Keeler, W. 1987. *Javanese Shadow Plays, Javanese Selves*. Princeton: Princeton University Press.

Kiernan, J. P. 1985. The Social Stuff of Revelation: Pattern and Purpose in Zionist Dreams and Visions. *Africa* 55(3):304–18.

Kilborne, B. 1978. *Interprétations du rêve au Maroc*. Paris: La Pensée Sauvage.

———. 1981. The Handling of Dream Symbolism: Aspects of Dream Interpretation in Morocco. *Psychoanalytic Study of Society* 9:1–14.

———. 1987. On Classifying Dreams. Pp. 171–93 in B. Tedlock, ed., *Dreaming: Anthropological and Psychological Interpretations*. Cambridge, Eng.: Cambridge University Press.

Kluckhohn, C., and W. Morgan. 1951. Some Notes on Navaho Dreams. Pp. 120–31 in G. B. Wilbur and W. Muensterburger, eds., *Psychoanalysis and Culture: Essays in Honor of Géza Róheim*. New York: Wiley.

Kracke, W. 1978. A Psychoanalyst in the Field: Erikson's Contributions to Anthropology. Pp. 147–88 in *Childhood and Selfhood: Essays on Tradition, Religion, and Modernity in the Psychology of Erik H. Erikson*. Lewisburg, PA: Bucknell University Press.

———. 1979. Dreaming in Kagwahiv: Dream Beliefs and Their Psychic Uses in an Amazonian Culture. *Psychoanalytic Study of Society* 8:119–71.

———. 1987. Encounter with Other Cultures: Psychological and Epistemological Aspects. *Ethos* 15:58–81.

Kuper, A. 1979. A Structural Approach to Dreams. *Man* 14:645–62.

———. 1983. The Structure of Dream Sequences. *Culture, Medicine, and Psychiatry* 7:153–75.

———. 1986. Structural Anthropology and the Psychology of Dreams. *Journal of Mind and Behavior* 7:333–44.

Kuper, A., and A. A. Stone. 1982. The Dream of Irma's Injection: A Structural Analysis. *American Journal of Psychiatry* 139:1225–34.

Lanternari, V. 1975. Dreams as Charismatic Significants: Their Bearing on the Rise of New Religious Movements. Pp. 221–35 in T. R. Williams, ed., *Psychological Anthropology*. The Hague: Mouton.

Laughlin, R. M. 1976. *Of Wonders Wild and New: Dreams from Zinacantan*. Smithsonian Contributions to Anthropology, no. 22. Washington, DC: Smithsonian Institution Press.

Layard, J. 1944 [1988]. *The Lady and the Hare: A Study in the Healing Power of Dreams*. Boston: Shambhala.

Lee, S. G. 1958. Social Influences in Zulu Dreaming. *Journal of Social Psychology* 47:265–83.

LeVine, R. 1981. Dreams of the Informant about the Researcher: Some Difficulties Inherent in the Research Relationship. *Ethos* 9:276–93.

———. 1982. The Dreams of Young Gusii Women: A Content Analysis. *Ethnology* 21:63–77.

Lévi-Strauss, C. 1963. *Structural Anthropology*. New York: Basic Books.

Lincoln, J. S. 1935. *The Dream in Primitive Cultures*. Baltimore: Williams and Wilkins.

Loewald, H. 1986. Transference-Countertransference. *Journal of the American Psychoanalytic Association* 34:275–88.

Maccoby, M., and G. M. Foster. 1970. Methods of Studying Mexican Peasant Personality: Rorschach, TAT, and Dreams. *Anthropological Quarterly* 43:225–42.

Malinowski, B. 1927. *Sex and Repression in Savage Society*. New York: E. P. Dutton.

———. 1967. *A Diary in the Strict Sense of the Term*. Stanford, CA: Stanford University Press.

Marriott, A. 1952. *Greener Fields*. Garden City, NY; Doubleday.

Martin, B. 1986. Bear Symbolism in Dreams: Clinical, Anthropological, and Mythological Perspectives. *Association for the Study of Dreams Newsletter* 3(1):10–11.

McDowell, J. H. 1989. *Sayings of the Ancestors: The Spiritual Life of the Sibundoy Indians*. Lexington: University Press of Kentucky.

Meggitt, M. J. 1962. Dream Interpretation among the Mae Enga of New Guinea. *Southwestern Journal of Anthropology* 18:216–20.

Meier, C. A. 1987. *The Meaning and Significance of Dreams*. Boston: Sigo Press.

Merrill, M. 1987. The Rarámuri Stereotype of Dreams. Pp. 194–219 in B. Tedlock, ed., *Dreaming:*

Anthropological and Psychological Interpretations. Cambridge, Eng.: Cambridge University Press.

Mooney, J. 1896. *The Ghost-Dance Religion and the Sioux Outbreak of 1890*. Fourteenth Annual Report of the Bureau of American Ethnology. Washington, DC: Smithsonian.

Nader, L. 1970. Research in Mexico. Pp. 97–166 in P. Golde, ed., *Women in the Field: Anthropological Experiences*. Chicago: Aldine.

O'Nell, C. W. 1965. A Cross-Cultural Study of Hunger and Thirst Motivation Manifested in Dreams. *Human Development* 8:181–93.

Opler, M. K. 1959. Dream Analysis in Ute Indian Therapy. Pp. 97–117 in M. K. Opler, ed., *Culture and Mental Health: Cross-Cultural Studies*. New York: Macmillan.

Ortner, S. B. 1984. Theory in Anthropology since the Sixties. *Comparative Studies in Society and History* 26(1):126–66.

Palombo, S. R. 1978. *Dreaming and Memory: A New Information-Processing Model*. New York: Basic Books.

Parman, S. 1991. *Dream and Culture: An Anthropological Study of the Western Intellectual Tradition*. New York: Praeger.

Pentony, B. 1961. Dreams and Dream Beliefs in North Western Australia. *Oceania* 32:144–49.

Persinger, M. A. 1988. Psi Phenomena and Temporal Lobe Activity. Pp. 121–56 in L. A. Henkel and R. E. Berger, eds., *Research in Parapsychology*. Metuchen, NJ: Scarecrow.

Persinger, M. A., and S. Krippner. 1989. Dream ESP Experiments and Geomagnetic Activity. *Journal of the American Society for Psychical Research* 83:101–16.

Petchkovsky, L. 1984. A Jungian Commentary on the "Ordinary" Dreams of the Yolngu. *Australian and New Zealand Journal of Psychiatry* 18:245–49.

Petchkovsky, L., and J. Cawte. 1986. The Dreams of the Yolngu Aborigines of Australia. *Journal of Analytical Psychology* 31:357–75.

Poirier, S. 1990. Les Jardins du nomade: Territoire, rêve, et transformation chez les groupes aborigènes du désert occidental australien. Ph.D. thesis, Département d'anthropologie, Université Laval.

Price-Williams, D., and L. N. Degarrod. 1989. Communication, Context, and the Use of Dreams in Amerindian Societies. *Journal of Latin American Lore* 15(2):195–209.

Reid, H. 1978. Dreams and Their Interpretation among the Hupdu Maku Indians of Brazil. *Cambridge Anthropology* 4(3):1–28.

Róheim, G. 1946. The Oedipus Complex and Infantile Sexuality. *Psychoanalytic Quarterly* 15:503–8.

———. 1947. Dream Analysis and Field Work in Anthropology. *Psychoanalysis and the Social Sciences* 1:87–130.

———. 1949. Technique of Dream Analysis and Field Work in Anthropology. *Psychoanalytic Quarterly* 18:471–79.

———. 1950. *Psychoanalysis and Anthropology: Culture, Personality, and the Unconscious*. New York: International Universities Press.

Roseman, M. 1986. Sound in Ceremony: Power and Performance in Temiar Curing Rituals. Ph.D. diss. in anthropology, Cornell University.

———. 1990. *Healing Sounds: Music and Medicine in Temiar Ceremonial Life*. Berkeley: University of California Press.

Scheff, T. J. 1986. Towards Resolving the Controversy over "Thick Description." *Current Anthropology* 27:408–10.

Schneider, D. M., and L. Sharp. 1969. *The Dream Life of a Primitive People: The Dreams of the Yir Yoront of Australia*. Anthropological Studies, no. 1. Washington, DC: American Anthropological Association.

Seligman, C. G. 1921. Note on Dreams. *Sudan Notes and Records* 4:145–61.

———. 1923. Type Dreams: A Request. *Folklore* 34:376–78.

———. 1924. Anthropology and Psychology: A Study of Some Points of Contact. *Journal of the Royal Anthropological Institute* 54:13–46.

Seremetakis, C. N. 1991. *The Last Word: Women, Death, and Divination in Inner Mani.* Chicago: University of Chicago Press.

Shaw, R. 1992. Dreaming as Accomplishment: Power, the Individual, and Temne Divination. Pp. 1–23 in M. C. Jedrej and R. Shaw, eds., *Dreaming, Religion, and Society in Africa.* Leiden: E. J. Brill.

Shweder, R. A., and R. A. LeVine. 1975. Dream Concepts of Hausa Children: A Critique of the "Doctrine of Invariant Sequence" in Cognitive Development. *Ethos* 3:209–30.

Siegel, J. 1978. Curing Rites, Dreams, and Domestic Politics in a Sumatran Society. *Glyph* 3:18–31.

Steele, R. S. 1982. *Freud and Jung: Conflicts of Interpretation.* London: Routledge and Kegan Paul.

Stephen, M. 1979. Dreams of Change: The Innovative Role of Altered States of Consciousness in Traditional Melanesian Religion. *Oceania* 50:3–22.

———. 1989. Dreaming and the Hidden Self: Mekeo Definitions of Consciousness. Pp. 160–86 in G. Herdt and M. Stephen, eds., *The Religious Imagination in New Guinea.* New Brunswick, NJ: Rutgers University Press.

Stevens, W. O. 1949. *The Mystery of Dreams.* New York: Dodd, Mead.

Tedlock. B. 1981. Quiché Maya Dream Interpretation. *Ethos* 9:313–30.

———. 1987a. Dreaming and Dream Research. Pp. 1–30 in B. Tedlock, ed., *Dreaming: Anthropological and Psychological Interpretations.* Cambridge, Eng.: Cambridge University Press.

———. 1987b. Zuni and Quiché Dream Sharing and Interpreting. Pp. 105–31 in B. Tedlock, ed., *Dreaming: Anthropological and Psychological Interpretations.* Cambridge, Eng.: Cambridge University Press.

———. 1991. The New Anthropology of Dreaming. *Dreaming* 1:161–78.

Tedlock, D. 1979. The Analogical Tradition and the Emergence of a Dialogical Anthropology. *Journal of Anthropological Research* 35:387–400.

Toffelmier, G., and K. Luomala. 1936. Dreams and Dream Interpretation of the Digueño Indians of Southern California. *Psychoanalytic Quarterly* 5:195–225.

Tolaas, J. 1990. The Puzzle of Psychic Dreams. Pp. 261–70 in S. Krippner, ed., *Dreamtime and Dreamwork.* Los Angeles: Jeremy P. Tarcher.

Tyler, E. B. 1871 [1891]. *Primitive Culture.* 2 vols. London: John Murray.

Ullman, M., S. Krippner, and A. Vaughn. 1973. *Dream Telepathy.* New York: Macmillan.

Wallace, A.F.C. 1958. Dreams and Wishes of the Soul: A Type of Psychoanalytic Theory among the Seventeenth Century Iroquois. *American Anthropologist* 60:234–48.

———. 1959. Cultural Determinants of Response to Hallucinatory Experience. *AMA Archives of General Psychiatry* 1:74–85.

———. 1972. *The Death and Rebirth of the Iroquois.* New York: Vintage Books.

Wundt, W. 1906. *Völkerpsychologie.* Leipzig: W. Engelmann.

CHAPTER SIXTEEN

TRANCE AND MEDITATION

Erika Bourguignon

Trance is a psychiatric and psychological term that has had significant use in psychological anthropology as well as in the history and anthropology of religion. The word *trance* appears in English as far back as the writings of Chaucer, where it had several different meanings. In contemporary psychiatry, it has been defined as a dissociative state involving "a disturbance or alteration in the normal (ordinary) integrative functions of identity, memory or consciousness" (Task Force on DSM-IV 1991:K:4) and as an "altered state of consciousness with markedly diminished or selective focused or impairment" (p. K:4). While trance is treated in these definitions as a pathological state, both the official classification of psychiatric disorders of the American Psychiatric Association (*DSM-III-R*) (1987) and various cross-cultural psychiatrists (e.g., Field 1960; Pfeiffer 1971) note that when trance or dissociation occurs in a religiously or culturally sanctioned context, it need not be a sign of pathology.

Such terms as *trance*, *altered* (or *alternate*) *state of consciousness*, and *dissociative state* have also been used, often interchangeably, by students of religious behavior, including anthropologists and historians. (*Ecstasy* and *enthusiasm*, whether as nouns or adjectives, as well as *mystic states*, also appear in these contexts.) These terms "refer to a category of psychobiological states and behavior amenable to objective observation and study" (Bourguignon 1973: 5); however, "The cultural meaning supplied for these states and the institutional framework within which they operate vary from society to society" (p. 3). *Meditation* refers to certain methods used to induce a variety of trance states.

Human behavior, including trance, is always located in a cultural context, and it is this context that gives behavior its meaning and structures it in accordance with certain expectations. The French ethnomusicologist G. Rouget (1985:3) similarly defined trance as a "state of consciousness composed of two components, one psycho-physiological, the other cultural.'' Or, as Ward (1989:17) noted, ''Although ASC's [altered states of consciousness] are also characterized by observable psychological, physiological, and behavioral correlates, their definition is ultimately based upon subjective experience.'' The emphases in these formulations vary somewhat, and there is some disagreement among these authors. For example, Rouget (1985) strongly stated that subjective experiences, which Ward stressed, are unknowable by the student of the phenomena in question.

It must be emphasized that only for analytic purposes is it possible to separate psychobiological from sociocultural and personal elements in a given sequence of trance behaviors. In experiential and phenomenological terms, for the person who experiences the trance and for the group that is in some way affected by it, no such separation is possible or meaningful.

The psychiatric definition of trance fits this phenomenon into the domain of pathology. However, both normal and pathological individuals may exhibit trance behavior. It may appear spontaneously in response to various physical and/or psychological stresses; as such, it may be a pathological response or one that involves the individual's marshaling of defenses. It may even be part of an endogenous healing process (R. H. Prince 1980). On the other hand, trance may be intentionally induced or systematically taught (Simons, Ervin, and Prince 1988).

Physiological and psychological factors leading to trance range from fevers to temporal-lobe seizures (epilepsy), sudden fright, prolonged fear, or intense pain. Trance may also be intentionally induced by various methods, including the ingestion of psychoactive substances, meditation, sensory deprivation, austerities, hypnosis, or participation in rituals involving sensory overload, including drumming, dancing, hyperventilation, and crowding (Ludwig 1966). When trance appears spontaneously, it is often considered an indication of pathology. However, trance may also appear in normals as well as in persons suffering from various types of psychopathology. These may include hysteria (a term now rarely used in psychiatry), multiple personality disorder, fugue states (a type of dissociative reaction), and epilepsy. Trance, in some forms, is often interpreted in religious terms. Here, too, when trance occurs spontaneously, a negative evaluation may be placed on it.

TRANCE AND POSSESSION

From the perspective of psychological anthropology, the study of trance includes several dimensions: What is the cultural context in which trance occurs? What is (or are) the cultural meaning(s) of trance? Who are the trancers? What is their (expected) behavior? What initiates or induces trance? These initial questions lead to many others that may be pursued. For example, if trance is considered undesirable, what is the community response? Trance, or dissociation, appears to be a universal human capacity; it is seen in some form in all human societies. It has its roots in mammalian biology (Wedenoja 1990; Bourguignon 1991).

Human societies have utilized this capacity in a number of different ways consistent with the worldview of the specific groups. Virtually all preindustrial societies have institutionalized one or more forms of trance in a religious context (Bourguignon 1973). Many examples of such religious traditions can also be seen in modern, culturally diverse nation-states. Spiritualism and Pentecostalism, both of which utilize trance states, each in its own ways, are the most rapidly growing religious movements in both Latin America and sub-Saharan Africa, often building on older religious traditions (Crapanzano and Garrison 1977; Glazier 1980; Stoll 1991). The same is also true for new or revitalized religions in many parts of Africa and Asia (McFarland 1967; Stoller 1989; Jordan 1990). At the same time, interest among anthropologists in the phenomenon of trance in its cultural context has greatly increased in the recent past (Crapanzano 1973, 1980; Harner 1973; Kendall 1985; Locke and Kelly 1985; Lewis 1986, 1989). This is also true of historians (Walker 1981; J. C. Brown 1986; Garrett 1987), students of literature (Hutchison 1986), psychiatrists (Sargant 1957, 1974; Jilek 1974, 1982), and psychologists (Hilgard 1977; Katz 1982; Krippner 1989; Ward 1989).

Given the great diversity in the contexts and manifestations of trance behavior in religious settings, various classifications have been proposed. These relate to the student's research aims and research tradition as well as the regional and ethnographic foci of the study. Bourguignon (1973) distinguished between trance and possession trance. The latter includes dissociative states that are interpreted, in the societies in which they occur, as due to the "possession" or takeover of the individual by a spirit or other alien entity. The former are all the various sorts of trance that are given different interpretations. While trance (without possession) is a broad and varied category, it typically involves visions (hallucinations). These are traditionally believed to be the experiences of the (or a) soul of the trancer. In native North America, this experience is typically related to the tradition of the vision quest, in which a young person (generally an adolescent boy) seeks the aid of a guardian spirit. In the Arctic, in parts of Asia and South America, and in some other areas, this trance state is more likely to be interpreted as due to the temporary absence of the soul and its journey, its encounters and struggles with spirit beings, and so on. Thus this category includes the religious forms generally referred to as "magical flight" and "shamanism" (Eliade 1964).

Neither trance nor possession trance constitutes a unitary phenomenon, nor does this terminology define or specify in detail the great range of reported religious behaviors and experiences. However, it serves as a first ordering device of the vast diversity of sometimes overlapping subtypes. It has made it possible to classify not only the behaviors, beliefs, and experiences of individuals and groups, but also the societies in which they are typically to be found.

A somewhat different classification was proposed by Rouget (1985), based on his interest in the relationship between trance and music. He noted that "ecstasy" (literally, "standing outside one's self") is associated with solitude, silence, immobility, sensory deprivation, and hallucinations (or visions). This state is followed by recollection. There is no music. Violent onset of the trance is absent. The mystic states and visions of Christian saints and Muslim Sufis and the state of *samadhi* in Yoga meditators represent examples of ecstasy in this sense. For Rouget, "trance" is the opposite of ecstasy. It occurs in the company of others, and there is a violent onset ("crisis"), sensory overload, and amnesia after the event. Music plays an important role in these ritual occasions. Rouget further distinguished two forms of trance: "shamanism" on the one hand and "possession" on the other. In the former he included shamanistic trance, "communial" trance (as in Pentecostal churches), and emotional trance; in the latter he included only the phenomenon of "possession" (that is, the acting out of another personality) when this state is induced intentionally in a ritual setting. These types of trance, then, are distinguished with reference to the associated belief system as well as by various behavioral manifestations, and, importantly for Rouget, their relationship to music. Subjective experience, he argued, is not accessible to the researcher. Shamanism is characterized by the shaman's spirit journey (also called "magical flight") and the observation that he produces his own music, usually drumming and singing. In possession trance ceremonies, music is made by others and, to a considerable extent, controls the behavior of the possessed person.

Because of his concern for the presence of music, Rouget excluded ecstasy from his study and combined shamanism and possession in his concept of trance. However, it must be noted that like the visions of Rouget's ecstatic, the shaman's spirit journey is a subjective experience, and both the shaman and the ecstatic remember the event afterwards and report on it to others. Only possession trance is followed by amnesia. Also, Rouget omitted from his discussion types of possession belief that interpret spontaneous trances (those that are not intentionally induced). Nor was he concerned with those types of possession that are not expressed in trance at all but that serve as explanations for illness or the acquisition of powers.

In contrast to authors who distinguish between visionary trance and possession trance, some others (Peters and Price-Williams 1980; Lewis 1981, 1989, 1986) rejected such distinctions. They preferred to stress the common features shared by these forms of religious behavior. Lewis (1981:33), for example, considered Western mediums, through whom spirits of the dead speak, to be shamans, writing: "They have spirit familiars at their command. . . . They are thus 'masters of spirits' and so shamans." Moreover, he considered religious phenomena to be fluid and therefore opposed any classifications, which, he feared, promote "confusion and distortion." This fear of classification is related to a rejection on his part of systematic comparative studies and the testing of hypotheses. Peters and Price-Williams (1980), on the other hand, did seek to test hypotheses. They asked whether shamans are pathological individuals, a claim that has often been made. They defined a shaman as a ritual specialist "who enter[s] into a controlled ASC [altered state of consciousness] on behalf of his community" (Peters and Price-Williams 1980:399). They argued that what matters is that these ritual specialists, whether they engage in magical flight or spirit possession, remain in control of their trance, entering and leaving it at will. In contrast to Rouget, they emphasized the experiential aspect of the altered state. In this respect they found high agreement among the ritual specialists in their sample societies. Thus, because these specialists retain control over their trance states, Peters and Price-Williams argued that they are nonpathological individuals. In Tibet and Nepal (Reinhard 1976; Peters 1981), mixed types appear: ritual specialists first experience spirit possession and later magical flight.

When one is dealing with large quantities of data for comparative purposes, classification represents a first necessary step. Such ordering of the data makes it possible to go beyond the presentation of ethnographic descriptions to the formulation and testing of hypotheses about relationships among various aspects of behavior, belief, and experience, as well as relationships between them and their larger sociocultural contexts. While ethnographers have focused on the manifestations of trance in the context of specific cultures and societies, comparativists have sought to identify relevant features of societies in which these behaviors occur. The distinction between trance and possession trance has made it possible to discover such relationships between religious and societal phenomena. Various studies (Bourguignon 1973; Bourguignon and Evascu 1977; Winkelman 1986; Shaara and Strathern 1992) have found a relationship between trance type and societal complexity. Thus small-scale societies, which lack political complexity (typically with economies based on hunting and gathering), are most likely to have a form of visionary trance. Larger, more politically complex societies (typically dependent on some form of agriculture) are more likely to have possession trance. Visionary trance is often induced by means of psychoactive substances or austerities, but this is rarely the case for possession trance. The former is also more frequently practiced by men and the latter by women. This has made Lewis (1989) see in possession trance a response by socially downtrodden individuals, and to look at it as an expression of opposition between the sexes. There is also some indication of a relationship between societal flexibility or rigidity and the type of trance that is institutionalized (Greenbaum 1973; Shaara and Strathern 1992).

There is also a strong geographic association of visionary trance with native North America, where it occurs in the form of the vision quest, the Native American church, and shamanism among Inuit. Possession trance is very widespread and typically associated with sub-Saharan Africa and also Southeast Asia (Bourguignon and Evascu 1977). In many African traditions, such as the Bori cult of the Hausa in West Africa and the Zar cult of East Africa, attempts are made to meet the spirit's demands and to turn it into an ally (Boddy 1989; Lewis 1989). Possession religions also appear among many African-American peoples. Examples are Cuban Santeria, Haitian Vodou, Shango in Trinidad, and

Brazilian religions such as Xango, Candomble, Umbanda, and, in a much more Europeanized version, Kardecismo, which is a form of Spiritualism. In large nation-states, as in Brazil or the contemporary United States, where there is much social and cultural differentiation, various types of trance- and possession trance–based religions may coexist. They flourish alongside of the more formally acknowledged religious institutions ("mainline denominations"), where such practices are generally absent. Yet even among the latter, glossolalia ("speaking in tongues") and other "gifts of the Spirit" involving altered states of consciousness appear, as among Catholic charismatics (Csordas 1990). Examples of possession trance may be found in religious groupings as diverse as Pentecostal churches (Horwatt 1988), Spiritualism, and New Age religions (Hughes 1991; Danforth 1989). Trance is found in various meditation-based disciplines such as transcendental meditation (TM) and other Hindu- and Buddhist-derived practices in the United States, including Yoga.

When, where, and how trance occurs and how trancers behave and are treated varies with cultural beliefs and practices. Simons, Ervin, and Prince (1988) have shown how trance is taught and learned in the Thaipusam ritual among Indians in Singapore. It is expressed most dramatically in anesthesia for what are normally very painful practices such as piercing the face with large needles and other metal objects. These authors hypothesized that endorphins, chemicals produced in the brain in response to stress, are responsible for these remarkable performances.

When possession trance appears spontaneously, it may be considered undesirable. Jewish, Christian, Moslem, and Hindu orthodoxies include means of exorcising possessing spirits. These practices were largely in abeyance in the West for many years, but they have made a return since the early 1970s (Goodman 1981). A genuine Catholic exorcism was shown in the United States on national television in 1991. Exorcism often involves a ritual specialist who interrogates the spirit in the possessed person as to its identity, the reason for its presence, and perhaps its wishes. In Christianity, authority for this practice is taken from New Testament accounts of Jesus driving out demons.

Trance phenomena, interpreted in various religious contexts and in a number of different ways, have a long history in the West. Trance interpreted as demonic spirit possession requiring exorcism appears in numerous accounts, both Christian and Jewish (Trachtenberg 1961; Oesterreich 1966). This theme becomes particularly frequent in connection with the witchcraft prosecutions in colonial America, including those of Salem, Massachusetts (Starkey 1949, 1973; Hansen 1969; Spanos 1983).

Quite a different type of trance and with a different set of interpretations, behavior patterns, and social consequences is found in various movements of prophecy and religious innovation. The historian Clarke Garrett (1987) has described trance phenomena among French descendants of the persecuted Huguenots in France during the seventh century. These movements of trance prophecy spread to Holland and England and ultimately led to the founding of the Quaker movement and that of the Shakers, which had its most successful development in the United States.

During the eighteenth and nineteenth centuries, when belief in spirit possession had declined in the traditional Western religions, trance appeared in two other contexts. The first was hypnosis, initially called "animal magnetism" and Mesmerism; the second was Spiritualism (or in France and Latin America, Spiritism), which involved mediums who contacted the dead. Both hypnosis and Spiritualism were phrased in terms of science rather than religion. In the context of an interest in Spiritualism and the work of the Society for Psychic Research, William James and Morton Prince discovered the first cases of what they named multiple personalities (M. Prince 1975; Kenny 1986). At the same time, there was considerable interest, starting with the French psychiatrist J. M. Charcot and his students (including Sigmund Freud), in the phenomenon of hysteria or hysterical neurosis. Charcot and Janet were much impressed by the similarities in the behavior of their hysterical patients and what they were able to discover about cases of demonic possession in earlier centuries, particularly the famous case of the possessed nuns of Loudun (Huxley 1952; Certeau 1970). Charcot's student Janet coined the term *dissociation* in reference to hysteria. Under certain conditions of stress, trance states may acquire epidemic proportions. Such epidemics of trance have appeared in the form of the "dancing mania" linked to a religious sect in Germany and the Low Countries in the late Middle Ages (Hecker [1888] 1970). More recent trance epidemics have been repeatedly reported from various places. For example, outbreaks have occurred among young women factory workers and students in Malaysia (Ong 1987).

It is interesting to note that trance induced by psychological means can mimic the whole range of phenomena found in pathological or drug-induced states. These include not only hallucinations, amnesia and anesthesia, and feats of great strength and fearlessness, but also phenomena like depersonalization and derealization that in other contexts are frightening and considered to be indicators of severe pathologies (Castillo 1990).

Current psychiatric classifications have largely eliminated the concepts of hysteria or hysterical neurosis, and the dramatic symptoms of hysteria that Charcot presented to his students and audiences are not in evidence today. Conversion phenomena, such as psychogenic paralyses, and dissociative and fugue states, which used to be criteria of a diagnosis of hysteria, are still seen; however, they are now classified under separate headings. Trance states may be due to temporal-lobe seizures (epilepsy) or may mimic such states. Jilek and Schwartz are among those scholars who have suggested that when these states are part of expected behavior in a religious context, they resemble pathology rather than represent it. They are said to be "pathomorphic" (Jilek 1974) or "pathomimetic" (Schwartz 1976). Winkelman (1986) has carried out a comparative study that shows signs of temporal-lobe involvement in possession trancers but not in visionary trancers. However, his interpretation is based on descriptions of behavior, not on specific diagnostic studies of individuals. The question remains why certain societies either provide special opportunities for individuals with these characteristics or, alternatively, choose pathological forms of behavior as models for religious behavior, that is, for making contact with nonhuman persons or with the dead.

As noted earlier, cultural techniques can produce states that resemble those resulting from the use of psychoactive drugs or from various pathologies. What is feared and fear-producing can also be valued and intentionally induced. That is, trance can be valued as a positive experience for the individual and also for the community. Responses to stress, whether personal or collective, can be turned into coping strategies: being saved or feeling renewed or reborn. Particular suffering can be reinterpreted as evidence of salvation or election. These are also important themes in Judaism and Christianity. Crisis cults (La Barre 1971), revitalization movements (Wallace 1970), or millenarian movements (Lanternari 1963) all have their beginnings in charismatic leaders, many of whom have experienced (or claim to have experienced) revelations and personal transformations. Examples of such leaders may been seen in the founder of the Shakers, Mother Ann Lee (Garrett 1987), and in the Seneca Indian prophet, Handsome Lake (Wallace 1970).

Trance, in whatever form, may be considered an expression of distress (personal or social) that may be turned into personal as well as social healing. While it has been argued that culturally sanctioned trance states or possession trance states are pathomimetic rather than pathological, the existence of such culturally patterned forms of trance indicates points of stress in the social fabric. Thus the vision quest and the search for a guardian spirit point to the insecurities and perils of the hunter's and warrior's life. The magical flight and the shaman's struggle with spirits deal largely with matters of illness and healing; African women's possession trance religions address their specific needs; and so on. K. M. Brown (1991) showed how vodou, both in Brooklyn and Haiti, addresses the problems of those who serve the spirits of that religion.

FORMS OF MEDITATION

It can be argued that the desire to find solutions to problems and to experience the state that produces creative resolutions, insight, or what is experienced as salvation, contact with the world of the spirits, or detachment from the problems and suffering of living has led individuals and communities to invent or discover techniques that lead to altered states of consciousness or trance. In some few creative individuals—prophets, cultural innovators, artists—such states have at times appeared spontaneously. It is their experiences and perhaps achievements that trance-induction techniques are designed to recapture and make available to those willing to submit to them.

Meditation is such a technique. Samuel (1990) spoke of it as a "technology of consciousness." In greater detail, we may say that the term refers to a class of techniques and practices with deep roots in religious traditions that aspire to mystic states. These states may either be seen as ends in themselves or as steps to a higher goal. The techniques of meditation, then, aim at achieving a complex of spiritual and physical results; they include a variety of bodily as well as mental or spiritual exercises and are informed by a variety of systems of belief. While systems of meditation vary greatly, there is generally an emphasis on a narrow focusing of attention that is aided by prescribed practices. They may also be accompanied by various austerities, such as fasting, isolation, or long hours of immobility.

Forms of meditation are historically associated with traditions of mysticism. Examples of such mystical traditions may be found in Judaism (e.g., Kabbalah), monastic Catholicism, Islam (Sufis), Hinduism (Yoga), and various branches of Buddhism (North Asian forms such as Lamaism in Tibet, Zen in Japan, or Teravada Buddhism in Southeast Asia). In some respects, the vision quest of the Plains Indians of native North America is similar to the meditation practices of these mystic traditions. The quest includes isolation, fasting, and other austerities as well as mental concentration in the form of singing of specific songs focusing on the hoped-for guardian spirit (Lame Deer and Erdoes 1972). There is also an important difference here: the vision quest is a one-time, initiatory undertaking, whereas meditation is ideally a lifelong practice.

In the pragmatic culture of the United States, as William James (1902) pointed out at the turn of the century, meditation has often been stripped of its mystical and transcendant aims. Rather, it has been applied to practical, generally health-fostering, aims. This is typified by the widespread practice of adapted forms of Hatha Yoga and by transcendental meditation (TM). James noted the development of what he called "the Religion of Healthy Mindedness," which gave rise to a "mind-cure" movement. Mary Baker Eddy and the Christian Science church were part of this trend or movement. One of the streams contributing to this development was derived from Hinduism. James noted the existence of a "Gospel of Relaxation" and of the "Don't Worry Movement" (James 1987:109). He attributed some of their success to the fact that all make use of suggestion. "Mind-cure," he wrote (James 1987:109), "has made what in our protestant countries is an unprecedented use of the sub-conscious life. . . . [I]ts founders have added systematic exercise in passive relaxation, concentration and meditation, and have even evoked something like hypnotic practice." He went on to say, "It has been left to mind-curers to reintroduce methodical meditation into our religious life" (James 1987:367). It is interesting to see how these lines, written before 1902, describe many aspects of the current situation.

In the Catholic tradition, meditation to achieve ecstasy or "mystic union" with God is termed *orison* or mental prayer and contemplation. It is exemplified by the teachings and experience of famous mystics such as Teresa of Avila, John of the Cross, and Ignatius of Loyola. The latter's *Manual of Spiritual Exercises* teaches the practice of meditation, conceived of as the systematic elevation of the soul to God. The focusing of attention, which is a key part of the many techniques of meditation, requires a narrow field of contemplation. In

Catholicism, the focus may be on the crucifixion or the wounds of Christ. In his book *Major Trends in Jewish Mysticism*, Gershom Scholem (1961) described the techniques of meditation of the thirteenth-century Kabbalist Abraham Abulafia. These involved meditating on the letters of the Hebrew Alphabet. Scholem saw a connection between Abulafia's system and "that ancient spiritual technique which has found its classical expression in the practices of the Indian mystics, who follow the system know as *Yoga*" (Scholem 1961:139). In particular, Scholem here emphasized similarities not only in teachings regarding breathing and body postures during meditation, but also with reference to the doctrine of ecstatic visions. However, he did not offer any suggestions as to what the "connection" between Yoga, or its predecessors, and Jewish mysticism might be. This raises the larger question of whether the various mystical traditions can be traced to a common origin or whether the techniques of meditation, leading to mystical experience, have been discovered or invented many times. The truth may be both. That is, some historical connections or evidence of diffusion from a common source may indeed be documented, while others remain obscure. The argument for independent invention is strengthened by precontact Native American examples of practices similar to Old World meditation.

An interesting point made by Scholem is that for Kabbalists, the ultimate aim of meditation is for a man to encounter himself in mystical ecstasy. He cited a passage in which a Kabbalist reported literally seeing himself. This is reminiscent of the "depersonalization" phenomenon reported by Castillo (1990), referred to earlier, for yogis and transcendental meditators. Thus, regardless of the specific traditions, it seems that some of the psychological outcomes of meditation and their underlying mechanisms may be constant.

Spiro (1982) has described meditation in the context of Theravada Buddhism and in its actual practice on the village level in Burma. Here the aim is the abolition of suffering for the individual through release from rebirth, accomplished first through the abolition of desire. A crucial step in achieving release is meditation. This is of two types, tranquility meditation and, only later, insight meditation. Tranquility is achieved by concentration, focusing the mind on a limited class of objects and clearing the mind of all others. This system is highly structured, and specific exercises are prescribed. An example is the ten meditations on the human corpse. Such meditations are practiced for many hours over a course of several years. Only a minority of Burmese villagers, or Buddhists in general, can undergo such rigorous practices and such isolation from the requirements of practical life. In spite of many important similarities among them, teachings concerning meditation vary widely, both in the specific means employed and in the aims sought. For example, comparing Buddhist and Hindu meditation, Spiro (1982:51 n. 21) wrote that "*jhana* [trance] and supernatural powers, which in Buddhism are to be left behind in order to proceed to nirvana, are the very goals sought in Hindu meditation."

An example of meditation practices to develop such powers comes from the writings of the French scholar Alexandra David-Neel. Speaking of meditation among Tibetan lamas, she noted that meditation "includes a large number of practices which combine mental concentration with various breathing gymnastics and aim at different results, either spiritual or physical" (1953:407). She described an exercise that "consists in displacing one's consciousness in one's own body. . . . One attains by means of these strange drills, psychic states entirely different from those habitual to us. They cause us to pass beyond the fictitious limits which we assign to the *self*. . . . [W]e grow to realize that the *self* is compound, impermanent; and that the self, as *self*, does not exist" (1953: 439).

In addition to accounts of spiritual and psychological transformation by mystics, Tibetan lamas and Hindu yogis, in particular, have claimed extraordinary physical feats. David-Neel reported witnessing young lamas, emerging from a lengthy course of meditation, proving their mastery by drying their wet robes in winter in the snow at night by increasing their body heat. Others have claimed to be able to reduce their heart rate, their breathing rate, and other physiological functions not usually under voluntary control. In the past, these claims have generally been met in the West by skepticism and even by accusations of fraud.

Interest in meditation and other trance-inducing techniques (notably an interest in psychoactive drugs) was revived in the West in the 1960s. Meditation, as it is now practiced in the United States and in Europe, is primarily of two kinds: the austere form of Zen Buddhism and the less demanding, more accessible forms of transcendental meditation and Yoga. With the spread of interest in meditation in the West at a time of innovations in technology and experimental techniques (electroencephalogram, biofeedback, operant conditioning), a number of psychologists have undertaken to test various claims and to reproduce these performances in the laboratory under controlled conditions. There exists a sizable literature on this topic, and only a few instances can be cited here. Spiegelberg (1962) and Deikman (1966) have described the phenomenon variously referred to as "derealization" or "deautomatization," which may occur as a result of prolonged contemplation of an object. (It also appears spontaneously in pathological subjects.) The object of contemplation appears to lose its "real" nature, becoming "animate" and acquiring other, out-of-the-ordinary attributes. Castillo (1990) has reported this phenomenon as occurring outside the laboratory among TM meditators. Wallace and Benson (1972) also worked with TM adepts, investigating physiological changes during meditation. They found that their subjects' consumption of oxygen and elimination of carbon dioxide decreased significantly, as did their respiratory rate and the volume of air they breathed. Blood lactate declined rapidly, and electrical resistance of the skin increased. In the EEG, the slow alpha waves increased in intensity. Studies of Zen meditators have shown comparable results, as have studies of Western subjects using biofeedback. The important point here is that mental practice (meditation) modified the physiological state in unexpected ways. Practiced meditators, however, did not require biofeedback to achieve these results.

The reduction in blood lactate levels and increased electrical skin resistance give evidence of increased relaxation, which is beneficial to persons suffering from anxiety. These results are the opposite of what one would find in situations of threat, when the organism marshals its energies for flight or fight. These results are also quite different from what is found in hypnotized subjects, suggesting that the state of the meditator is not one of autohypnosis, as has often been claimed. Benson et al. (1982) tested three Tibetan yogis and found that they were able, by means of meditation techniques, to increase the temperature in their fingers and toes by 8.3°C (15° F). These meditation techniques have been described in the writings of the Dalai Lama (Mullin 1985).

This body of research has produced some interesting results but also raises important questions. The work of the psychophysiologists has been circumscribed in a number of ways and for a number of reasons. To begin with, it focuses on the verification of claims that appeared to contradict the received wisdom of Western science. The results have strongly supported an approach that rejects the mind/body dichotomy. Mental processes are found to have testable physical consequences (Fischer 1971). Moreover, Emerson has shown, on the basis of a review of the experimental literature, that belief systems appear to influence neurophysiology: "The results of different studies seem to indicate that the religion of the meditator determines to a great extent the way in which his EEG pattern as well as his metabolism will change during the course of meditation" (1972:25).

Because of the methods employed in psychophysiology, the emphasis has been on laboratory studies, where controlled conditions and equipment are available. Only subjects accessible to a laboratory have been examined: Western meditators, particularly TM practitioners, and a few Asian specialists willing to cooperate and able to perform under difficult conditions, including the distractions of being observed and wired to equipment. That is, the sample has been limited to highly proficient meditators. What to meditators is a spiritual undertaking is a psychophysiological experiment in the laboratory.

The explanatory schemes that account for the phenomena observed for Hindus and Buddhists are meaningless to Western scientists, who have no explanations for their observations. As the neurologist Gerald Edelman (1989:212) said with reference to dreams: "Great care must be exercised in relating physiological states to the content of conscious states in language-bearing animals." On the whole, however, we know more of the physiological processes of meditators than of possession trancers, whose transformations occur in the context of much physical activity and cannot, realistically, be taken into the laboratory. Neher (1962) claimed that in the laboratory, drum rhythms typical of possession trance ceremonies produced significant physiological changes in a small sample of subjects. Rouget (1985:172–76) examined and vigorously rejected this research or its relevance to a study of a possible relationship between music and trance. The study by Simons, Ervin, and Price (1988) of the Thaipusam ritual has already been mentioned. It is a good example of the fact that what is possible in the laboratory cannot necessarily be done in the setting of an actual ritual: the experimenters were not allowed to draw blood from the subjects they observed because this would have destroyed the religious purposes of the ritual.

CONCLUSIONS

Anthropological interest in trance has shifted over the years, and the amount of research on the topic has varied over time as intellectual trends have concentrated on one topic or another. Early studies were primarily interested in trance in connection with matters of religion: Worship, divination, and so on. Much of the literature of the past twenty-five years has stressed concern with psychopathology and healing. From an interest in the possible psychopathology of trance healers (shamans), the focus shifted to the healing functions of the religious specialists, to trance religions as healing centers and ''support groups'' for patients, and to trance itself as a cathartic or therapeutic process (Kiev 1964; Sargant 1957). Recently, there has been a shift to text and discourse analysis.

The study of trance is particularly appropriate for anthropological research, since ideally it represents a focus to which all fields can contribute. It is also a complex interdisciplinary topic. There is a psychobiological dimension, including evolutionary aspects (Edelman 1989); a developmental perspective, as well as pathology, prophylaxis, and therapy, might profitably be pursued by psychological anthropologists. There is also the matter of learning, which clearly plays an important role in the culturally stylized forms of trance that have been observed. Room exists for ethnography and comparative research, for archaeology and linguistics, for folklore, ethnomusicology, and study of dance, for visual anthropology, and for other anthropological concerns as well. There is also room for interdisciplinary research, building on the contribution of neurophysiologists, psychologists and psychiatrists, nutritionists and biochemists, musicologists, students of theater, and art historians. This list is far from exhaustive.

A number of promising integrative models have been proposed (e.g., Raybeck, Shoobe, and Grauberger 1989) that bring together information from various disciplines. When testing in the field becomes a reality, our understanding will be enhanced a bit further. Yet we may be sure that new questions will then arise, for the evidence from trance can be used to support various positions in psychological anthropology. It gives strength to arguments in favor of a basic common human nature and to the observation that culture utilizes the human body and its potentials, including variations in consciousness, as a ground for building meanings. The process is circular, for these meanings are then turned into the structures that reproduce trance states in their specific social and cultural contexts. We learn of these meaning systems by utilizing a phenomenological approach in our research. Such a phenomenological, relativistic approach not only can coexist but indeed is interdependent with a univeralist approach, leading to an understanding of both the unity and the diversity of human nature (see the Introduction to this volume).

REFERENCES

American Psychiatric Association, 1987. *Diagnostic and Statistical Manual of Mental Disorders*. 3rd ed. rev. (*DSM-III-R*). Washington: DC: American Psychiatric Association.

Benson, et al. 1981. Body Temperature Changes during the Practice of Gtum-Mo-Yoga. *Nature* 295:234–36.

Boddy, J. 1989. *Wombs and Alien Spirits: Women, Men, and the Zar Cult in Northern Sudan*. Madison: University of Wisconsin Press.

Bourguignon, E. 1973. Introduction: A Framework for the Comparative Study of Altered States of Consciousness. Pp. 3–35 in E. Bourguignon, ed., *Religion, Altered States of Consciousness, and Social Change*. Columbus: Ohio State University Press.

———. 1991. A. Irving Hallowell, the Foundations of Psychological Anthropology, and Altered States of Consciousness. *Psychoanalytic Study of Society* 6: 17–41.

Bourguignon, E., and T. L. Evascu. 1977. Altered States of Consciousness in a General Evolutionary Perspective: A Holocultural Analysis. *Behavior Science Research* 12(3):197–216.

Brown, J. C. 1986. *Immodest Acts: The Life of a Lesbian Nun in Renaissance Italy*. New York: Oxford University Press.

Brown, K. M. 1991. *Mama Lola: A Vodou Priestess in Brooklyn*. Berkeley: University of California Press.

Castillo, R. J. 1990. Depersonalization and Meditation. *Psychiatry* 53:158–68.

Certeau, M. de 1970. *La Possession de Loudun*. Paris: Juilliard.

Crapanzano, V. 1973. *The Hamadsha: A Study in Moroccan Ethnopsychiatry*. Berkeley: University of California Press.

———. 1980. *Tuhami: Portrait of a Moroccan*. Chicago: University of Chicago Press.

Crapanzano, V., and V. Garrison. 1977. *Case Studies in Spirit Possession*. New York: John Wiley and Sons.

Csordas, T. J. 1990. Embodiment as a Paradigm for Anthropology. *Ethos* 18:5–47.

Danforth, L. M. 1989. *Firewalking and Religious Healing: The Anastenaria of Greece and the American Firewalking Movement*. Princeton: Princeton University Press.

David-Neel, A. 1932. *Magic and Mystery in Tibet*. New York: Crown. (Selection reprinted in M. Mead and N. Calas, eds. *Primitive Heritage*. New York: Random House, 1953.)

Deikman, A. 1966. Deautomatization and the Mystical Experience. *Psychiatry* 29:324–38.

Edelman, G. M. 1989. *The Remembered Present: A Biological Theory of Consciousness*. New York: Basic Books.

Eliade, M. 1964. *Shamanism: Archaic Techniques of Ecstasy*. Trans. W. Trask. New York: Pantheon Books.

Emerson, V. F. 1972. Can Belief Systems Influence Neurophysiology? Some Implications of Research on Meditation. *Newsletter-Review, the R. M. Bucke Memorial Society* 5:20–31.

Field, M. 1960. *Search for Security: An Ethno-Psychiatric Study of Rural Ghana*. Evanston: Northwestern University Press.

Fischer, R. 1971. A Cartography of Ecstatic and Meditative States. *Science* 174:897–904.

Furst, P. T. 1976. *Hallucinogens and Culture*. San Francisco: Chandler and Sharp.

Garrett, C. 1987. *Spirit Possession and Popular Religion: From the Camisards to the Shakers*. Baltimore: Johns Hopkins University Press.

Glazier, S. D., ed. 1980. *Perspectives on Pentecostalism*. Washington, DC: University Press of America.

Goodman, F. D. 1981. *The Exorcism of Anneliese Michel*. Garden City, NY: Doubleday.

Greenbaum, L. 1973. Societal Correlates of Possession Trance in Sub-Saharan Africa. In E. Bourguignon, ed., *Religion, Altered States of Consciousness, and Social Change*. Columbus: Ohio State University Press.

Hansen, C. 1969. *Witchcraft in Salem*. London: Hutchinson.

Harner, M. J. 1973. The Role of Hallucinogenic Plants in European Witchcraft. In M. J. Harner, ed., *Hallucinogens and Shamanism*. London: Oxford University Press.

Hecker, J.F.C. 1970 [1888]. *The Dancing Mania of the Middle Ages*. New York: B. Franklin.

Hilgard, E. R. 1977. *Divided Consciousness: Multiple Controls in Human Thought and Action*. New York: Wiley.

Horwatt, K. 1988. The Shamanistic Complex in the Pentecostal Church. *Ethos* 16:128–45.

Hughes, D. J. 1991. Blending with Another: An Analysis of Trance Channeling in the United States. *Ethos* 19:161–84.

Hutchinson, G. B. 1986. *The Ecstatic Whitman: Literary Shamanism and the Crisis of the Union*. Columbus: Ohio State University Press.

Huxley, A. 1952. *The Devils of Loudun*. New York: Harper.

James, W. 1987 [1902]. *Varieties of Religious Experience*. Reprinted in *Writings, 1902–1910*. New York: Library of America.

Jilek, W. G. 1974. *Salish Indian Mental Health and Culture Change: Psychohygienic and Therapeutic Aspects of the Guardian Spirit Ceremonial*. Toronto: Holt, Rinehart and Winston.

———. 1982. Altered States of Consciousness in North American Indian Ceremonials. *Ethos* 10: 326–43.

Jordan, D. K. 1990. Eufunction, Dysfunction, and Oracles: Literary Miracle Making in Taiwan. Pp. 98–115 in D. K. Jordan and M. J. Swartz, eds., *Personality and the Cultural Construction of Society*. Tuscaloosa: University of Alabama Press.

Katz, R. 1982. *Boiling Energy: Community Healing among the Kalahari Kung*. Cambridge, MA: Harvard University Press.

Kendall, L. 1985. *Shamans, Housewives, and Other Restless Spirits*. Honolulu: University of Hawaii Press.

Kenny, M. G. 1986. *The Passion of Ansel Bourne: Multiple Personality in American Culture*. Washington, DC: Smithsonian Institution Press.

Kiev, A., ed. 1964. *Magic, Faith, and Healing*. New York: Free Press.

Krippner, S. 1989. A Call to Heal: Entry Patterns in Brazilian Mediumship. Pp. 186–206 in C. Ward, ed., *Altered States of Consciousness and Mental Health: A Cross-Cultural Perspective*. Newbury Park, CA: Sage.

La Barre, W. 1971. Materials for a History of Crisis Cults: A Bibliographic Essay. *Current Anthropology* 12:3–44.

Lambek, M. 1981. *Human Spirits: A Cultural Account of Trance in Mayotte*. Cambridge, Eng.: Cambridge University Press.

Lame Deer, J., and R. Erdoes. 1972. *Lame Deer, Seeker of Visions*. New York: Simon and Schuster.

Lanternari, V. 1963. *The Religions of the Oppressed: A Study of Modern Messianic Cults*. New York: Knopf.

Lewis, I. M. 1981. What Is a Shaman? *Folk* 23:25–35.

———. 1986. *Religion in Context: Cults and Charisma*. Cambridge, Eng.: Cambridge University Press.

———. 1989 [1971]. *Ecstatic Religion*. 2nd ed. London: Routledge.

Locke, R., and E. Kelly. 1985. *A Preliminary Model for the Cross-Cultural Analysis of Altered States of Consciousness. Ethos* 13:3–55.

Ludwig, A. 1966. Altered States of Consciousness. In Trance and Possession States. *Archives of General Psychiatry* 15:225–34.

MacFarlane, A. 1991 [1971]. *Witchcraft in Tudor and Stuart England*. Prospect Heights, IL: Waveland Press.

Mullin, G. H., ed. 1985. *Selected Works of the Dalai Lama II*. Ithaca, NY: Snow Lion.

Neher, A. 1962. A Physiological Explanation of Unusual Behavior in Ceremonies Involving Drums. *Human Biology* 4:151–60.

Oesterreich, T. K. 1966 [1921]. *Possession, Demoniacal and Other*. New York: University Books.

Ong, A. 1987. *Spirits of Resistance and Capitalist Work Discipline: Factory Women in Malaysia.* Albany: State University of New York Press.

Peters, L. 1981. *Ecstasy and Healing in Nepal.* Malibu, CA: Undena Publications.

Peters, L., and D. Price-Williams. 1980. Toward an Experiential Analysis of Shamanism. *American Ethnologist* 7:397–418.

Pfeiffer, W. M. 1971. *Transkulturelle Psychiatrie: Ergebnisse und Probleme.* Stuttgart: Georg Thieme Verlag.

Prince, M. 1975. *Psychotherapy and Multiple Personality: Selected Essays.* Ed. N. G. Hale. Cambridge, MA: Harvard University Press.

Prince, R. H. 1980. Variations in Psychotherapeutic Procedures. Pp. 291–349 in H. C. Triandis and J. G. Draguns, eds., *Handbook of Cross-Cultural Psychology*: Vol. 6: *Psychopathology.* Boston: Allyn and Bacon.

Raybeck, D., J. Shoobe, and J. Grauberger. 1989. Women, Stress, and Participation in Possession Cults: A Reexamination of the Calcium Deficiency Hypothesis. *Medical Anthropology Quarterly* 3:139–61.

Reinhard, J. 1976. Shamanism and Spirit Possession: The Definition Problem. Pp. 12–23 in J. T. Hitchcock and R. L. Jones, eds., *Spirit Possession in the Nepal Himalayas.* New Delhi: Vikas Publishing House.

Rouget, G. 1985. *Music and Trance: A Theory of the Relations between Music and Possession.* Chicago: University of Chicago Press.

Samuel, G. 1990. *Mind, Body, and Culture: Anthropology and the Biological Interface.* Cambridge, Eng.: Cambridge University Press.

Sargant, W. 1957. *Battle for the Mind.* London: Heinemann.

———. 1974. *The Mind Possessed.* Philadelphia: Lippincott.

Scholem, G. G. 1961. *Major Trends in Jewish Mysticism.* New York: Schocken Books.

Schwartz, T. 1976. The Cargo Cult: A Melanesian Type–Response to Change. Pp. 157–206 in G. A. DeVos, ed., *Responses to Change: Society, Culture, and Personality.* New York: Van Nostrand.

Shaara, L., and A. Strathern. 1992. A Preliminary Analysis of the Relationship between Altered States of Consciousness, Healing, and Social Structure. *American Anthropologist* 94:145–60.

Simons, R., F. R. Ervin, and R. Prince. 1988. The Psychobiology of Trance/I: Training for Thaipusam. *Transcultural Psychiatric Research Review* 25:249–66.

Spanos, N. P. 1983. Ergotism and the Salem Witch Panic: A Critical Analysis and an Alternative Conceptualization. *Journal of the History of the Behavioral Sciences* 19:358–69.

Spiegelberg, F. 1962. *Spiritual Practices of India.* New York: Citadel Press.

Spiro, M. E. 1982. *Buddhism and Society: A Great Tradition and Its Burmese Vicissitudes.* 2nd exp. ed. Berkeley: University of California Press.

Starkey, M. 1949. *The Devil in Massachusetts.* New York: Knopf.

———. 1973. *The Visionary Girls.* Boston: Beacon Press.

Stoll, D. 1991. *Is Latin America Turning Protestant? The Politics of Evangelical Growth.* Berkeley: University of California Press.

Stoller, P. 1989. *Fusion of the Worlds: An Ethnography of Possession among the Songhay of Niger.* Chicago: University of Chicago Press.

Task Force on DSM-IV. 1991. *DSM-IV Options Book: Work in Progress 9/1/91.* Washington, DC: American Psychiatric Association.

Trachtenberg, J. 1961. *Jewish Magic and Superstition: A Study in Folk Religion.* Cleveland: World Publishing Company: Philadelphia: Jewish Publication Society of America.

Walker, D. P. 1981. *Unclean Spirits: Possession and Exorcism in France and England in the Late Sixteenth and Early Seventeenth Centuries.* Philadelphia: University of Pennsylvania Press.

Wallace, A.F.C. 1970. *The Death and Rebirth of the Seneca.* New York: Knopf.

Wallace, R. K., and H. Benson. 1972. The Physiology of Meditation. *Scientific American* 226:85–90.

Ward, C. 1989. Introduction. Pp. 8–35 in C. Ward, ed., *Altered States of Consciousness and Mental Health: A Cross-Cultural Perspective*. Newbury Park, CA: Sage.

Wedenoja, W. 1990. Ritual Trance and Catharsis: A Psychobiological and Evolutionary Perspective. Pp. 275–307 in D. K. Jordan and M. J. Swartz, eds., *Personality and the Cultural Construction of Society*. Tuscaloosa: University of Alabama Press.

Winkelman, M. 1986. Trance States: A Theoretical Model and Cross-Cultural Analysis. *Ethos* 14: 174–203.

CHAPTER SEVENTEEN

HALLUCINOGENS, MANAGED STATES OF CONSCIOUSNESS, AND ADOLESCENTS: CROSS-CULTURAL PERSPECTIVES

Charles S. Grob and Marlene Dobkin de Rios

This chapter examines the traditional role of hallucinogenic plants administered by adults to adolescents either individually or in groups in three distinct areas of the world—among the Australian aborigines of the central desert region, among the Chumash Indians of California, and among the Shangana-Tsonga youth of Mozambique. Our intent is to understand the way in which hallucinogenic drugs have played a major role in the transformation of adolescent boys and girls into fully participating members of adult society. This contrasts with contemporary patterns of adolescent drug abuse in Euro-American societies where "abuse" rather than "use" patterns prevail in the face of dysfunctional family life, dysphoria, and self-medication.[1]

Numerous anthropologists have argued that legal constraints on drug use in Euro-American society contrast with ritualistic use of such plant drugs in traditional tribal societies of the world. The difference will help us to understand the role of "managed altered states of consciousness" administered by tribal elders to adolescents, both male and female, as a culturally accepted didactic device to prepare youth for new adult roles. Furthermore, the pattern of plant-drug use by youths in tribal societies suggests the possibility of nondrug, integrative rituals at adolescence to respond to the societal problems of alienation, economic disfranchisement, social-status ambiguity, and meaninglessness in industrial societies.

As Shedler and Block (1990) suggested, contemporary psychological studies of adolescent drug use decontextualize such abuse from societal breakdown, meaninglessness, and social stress. Cultural variables such as those previously

[1]Adapted with permission from *Journal of Drug Issues* 22(1):121–38, 1992.

mentioned create a set of problems for Western youth that may not be coded into the survey research instruments that are used to discern adolescent drug abuse patterns. In contrast, the cultural anthropologist investigating plant-drug use patterns in non-Western societies examines the total social and cultural context of meaning in which drug use occurs, especially where such use is usually sanctioned by adult members of the community (Dobkin de Rios 1984a, 1984b). We will show how cultural contexts of meanings associated with hallucinogenic drugs in traditional societies and with the management of adolescent consciousness states by tribal elders contrast dramatically with American drug use patterns and concepts of the self in Western societies. We conclude with an examination of some potential options to rectify the patterns of self-destructive drug abuse in contemporary American society.

AMERICAN ADOLESCENT DRUG ABUSE

Before examining American adolescent drug abuse issues, it is important to understand the ahistoric tendency in Western psychological science. Philip Cushman (1990) argued that there is an implicit presumption or bias in favor of self-contained individualism as an unquestioned value. He held that the current Western concept of self is that of the bounded, masterful self, an unchangeable transhistorical entity. While Cushman demonstrated that cultural conceptualizations and configurations of the self are formed by the economics and politics of respective eras, his analysis of contemporary American society as it impacts the self is important for our discussion of adolescent drug abuse. In his article "Why the Self is Empty," Cushman maintained that since World War II, the configuration of an empty self has emerged in the U.S. middle classes, empty in part because of the loss of family, community, and tradition. The self has to be filled up by consuming goods, calories, experiences, romantic partners, and empathic therapists in attempts to combat the growing alienation and fragmentation of its era (1990:600). The results of the changes in the self have led to a sense of meaninglessness in the West. Inner emptiness can be expressed in many ways, including low self-esteem, values confusion, eating disorders, and drug abuse (which Cushman argued is the compulsion to fill the emptiness with chemically induced emotional experiences) as well as the absence of personal meaning and the hunger for spiritual guidance. What Geertz (1973) has described as the web of meaning—the tools of traditional cultures, such as stories, songs, beliefs, rituals, ceremonial objects, costumes, and potions—no longer plays an important role in Western society. Compelled to fill up the empty self, aggressively consuming in order to be soothed and integrated, the individual must take in and merge with a drug or an ideology to avoid fragmenting into feelings of worthlessness and confusion. Maladaptive attempts have resulted in such lifestyles as that of the adolescent drug subculture.

It is commonly recognized that psychotropic substance abuse among American adolescents has reached epidemic proportions over the last two to three decades. In spite of increasing attention given to this phenomenon by the media and the government, as well as health and educational authorities and services, widespread misuse and abuse of drugs and alcohol by the young have persisted virtually unabated. Experimentation with unsanctioned intoxicants has become so widespread that it is now statistically normative for adolescents to engage in some degree of illegal drug taking.

This phenomenon can be easily observed by examining the precipitous rise in the use of marijuana, the most commonly utilized illegal substance, among successive cohorts of graduating American high-school seniors. For the cohort born in 1945 and graduating from high school in 1963, there was a 2 percent lifetime prevalence of marijuana use by the age of eighteen. This figure increased to 19 percent for the class of 1968 (born in 1950), 48 percent for the class of 1973 (born in 1955), and 60 percent for the class of 1978 (born in 1960). Although more recent epidemiological surveys indicate a modest decline of adolescent marijuana use during the 1980s (lifetime prevalence dropped to 54 percent for the class of 1985), the United States nevertheless continues to have a more severe and pervasive substance abuse problem than any other industrialized nation. The most recent statistics reveal that over 60 percent of high-school seniors have used an illicit substance at some time in their lives (Johnston 1985). Furthermore, the implications of earlier experimentation with psychotropic drugs are serious. In the late 1960s, the mean age of first use of an illegal substance was nineteen to twenty; by the late 1970s, it was fifteen. A consequence of this trend has been the increasing tendency for rapid progression to more dangerous patterns of multiple drug abuse (Clayton and Ritter 1985).

Although most educational and media attention has been directed toward adolescent use and abuse of illicit psychotropic substances, alcohol and cigarette use has remained at alarmingly high levels. The lifetime prevalence by the senior year of high school of alcohol use is 92 percent, and of cigarette use, 69 percent. The thirty-day prevalence of alcohol use among high-school seniors is 66 percent, with 5 percent daily drinkers and 37 percent admitting to binge drinking of five or more consecutive alcoholic drinks in the two-week period prior to being surveyed. Thirty percent of high-school seniors admit to smoking cigarettes on an intermittent basis, with 20 percent smoking daily (Johnston 1985). Over the course of the life span, either alcohol or cigarettes alone will eventually cause significantly greater morbidity and mortality than all the illicit substances combined; thus the degree to which their use is sanctioned and even encouraged by prevailing societal attitudes at the expense of acknowledging and understanding ''safer'' psychotropic substances and traditions of use is alarming and even damaging to the health and longevity of younger generations.

The strongest predictor of substance abuse is having a peer group whose activities are centered around the acquisition and use of psychotropic substances (Cushman 1990). Many of the factors known to be associated with substance abuse, including poor academic performance, rebelliousness, and delinquency, as well as low self-esteem and depression, precede rather than follow the initiation of substance abuse (Kandel 1982).

Adolescence is often a period of considerable stress and insecurity. "Mind-altering" substances are frequently used to escape from the painful and discordant processes of adolescence. Yet this attraction is deceptive; the habitual flight into drug-induced euphoria inevitably culminates in the failure to acquire the developmental skills necessary for future psychological health. Furthermore, the chronic and compulsive utilization of powerful mood-altering substances has a significant dulling effect upon cortical tone, thus impairing the attainment of optimal cognitive function and impeding the path of developmental growth (Baumrind and Moselle 1985). Developmental fixation and regression are among the serious risks of chronic substance abuse in contemporary adolescence. The adverse developmental consequences of substance abuse in adolescence include persistent identity diffusion, lack of clarity about goals, creation of a false sense of autonomy, impaired capacity for deferred gratification, and a fixation of the negative identity characteristics of early adolescence.

As the extent and duration of substance abuse and dependence increase, the afflicted adolescent will experience greater alienation and estrangement from the mainstream of cultural life. Intensified degrees of loneliness and isolation, along with pronounced feelings of hopelessness and helplessness, perpetuate the need for further drug-induced refuge and escape. As the process intensifies and the individual fails to respond to efforts aimed at internal control, self-esteem progressively deteriorates. The concurrent and cumulative effects of impaired developmental maturation, deteriorating psychosocial functioning, and declining self-esteem will place the adolescent at greater risk for dangerous and potentially lethal behavior, including explicit suicidal acts. Intervention must identify those at greatest risk for progression from casual use to chronic dependence (Grob 1986). Preexisting clinical depression is known to be a critical predictive factor in the transition from being free of drug use to drug experimentation and to later dependence on marijuana. Furthermore, persistent depression in habitual adolescent users will predict the development of polysubstance abuse (Paton, Kessler, and Kandel 1977). Early identification and treatment of those depressed adolescents who are at risk for the initiation and evolution of serious drug abuse behaviors is critical. This analysis of contemporary American adolescent drug abuse contrasts dramatically with the data to follow concerning three tribal societies of Australia, North America, and Africa.

THE AUSTRALIAN ABORIGINES OF THE CENTRAL DESERT REGION

Extensive data are available on adolescent initiation rites among Australian aborigines at the time of European contact and before Westernization (see Eliade 1965, 1973; Durkheim 1915; Berndt 1964; Basedow 1925; Spencer and Gillen 1899; Horne and Aiston 1924). However, little has been done to examine the role of the hallucinogenic plant pituri (*Duboisia hopwoodii*) in the genital operations that mark the transition to manhood among aboriginal adolescents (Dobkin de Rios 1984a). Scopolamine and hyoscyamine alkaloids of the plant, which give rise to hallucinations and illusions, were also highly valued among these hunting and foraging peoples for their ability to quiet hunger and quench thirst (see also Johnson and Clelland 1933).

Aborigines lacked fixed settlements and had relatively few material goods. Their small nomadic social units were permeated by religious awe and reverence for their environment. Initiation rites at puberty had the important function of creating a cohesive cohort of males who would suffer intergenerational hazing and harassment and undergo plant hallucinogenic inductions that were integrated into death and rebirth symbology. As a cohort member, the youth would be reborn as a new individual, put aside things of childhood, and now be able to marry, procreate, and contribute to the economic surety of his group.

The pituri plant had enormous economic value to the aborigines. Pituri roads existed with extensive trade networks that extended from northern to southern desert areas, which permitted aborigines to trade the plant. Most of the aboriginal weaving and written communications systems, including nets, dilly bags, and marker sticks, were used to carry the pituri plant or identify the trader in hostile territory. The pituri roads crossed rivers and high mountain ranges where natives would trade the plant over hundreds of miles. The plant was used as a token of friendship toward strangers and as a stimulant and social comforter to foster feelings of amity. It was also employed to trap emus, parrots, and kangaroos in water holes. Elders who acted as seers to obtain power and riches would ingest the plant. Interestingly, it was used as payment to elders who circumcised and subincised youth; also, Johnston and Clelland (1933) documented that the plant was taken by youths during genital operations such as circumcision and subincision. By the 1950s, pituri use had disappeared, pushed out by Lutheran appropriation of the plant harvest (Hart 1983, personal communication). This had the effect of bringing tribal members to mission settlements. Commercial smoking tobacco was also introduced into Australia at the time of European contact and quickly became popular among aborigines, despite the availability of thirteen different wild species of native tobacco that had been chewed as a wad.

Commentaries by Durkheim based on the fieldwork reports of a variety of early scholars described pubertal rites of initiation and the sacred role that human blood played in the cult. Among the Arunta, one tribal group of the central desert region, after subincision took place, the blood was collected. The youth's mother drank the blood from the circumcision, and the youth licked blood from the knife, after which the blood was buried. Intergenerational conflict was expressed in scarification of the initiates, blanket tossing of these youth, their placement on a bed of leaves atop hot coals, and beatings on the scalp to "promote hair growth." The rites of circumcision and subincision, which have been of interest to the psychoanalytically oriented scholar, were believed to confer power on the genital organs. Explanations of this custom range from Bettelheim's psychoanalytic approach (1954) to that of Cawte (1964), who suggested that the goal of such operations was to create a totemic likeness to the bifid penis of the kangaroo, a mammal of great importance to aboriginal life. The painful mutilation of an organ was believed to give a sacred character to it, and through the experiences of pain, an individual was said to gain great power and strength. Aborigines symbolized this suffering as the sign that certain ties attaching the youth to his everyday, secular environment were broken.

Eliade (1965) described Bora rites in eastern aboriginal society where young men were removed from the women's area, isolated in the bush, given religious instruction and floggings, and circumcised and subincised. The boys remained in the bush for one year and were subjected to many austerities, including sleep deprivation and fasting. They were kept in darkness and silence. The symbolism of death and rebirth—the death of childhood and the rebirth of the individual into a new adult status—was prominent here. The initiates did not report negative experiences such as fear and anxiety, but rather revelations that allowed them to view the world and themselves as sacred. No doubt the use of pituri in these genital operations in highly septic environments provided an amnesiac experience, much as the alkaloid, scopolamine, played a popular role in obstetrics in the 1940s and 1950s, when "twilight sleep" was the predominant childbirth anesthesia.

In order to separate men from their mothers, male blood was used through the initiation rites as a symbol of strength and fertility. Van Gennep's (1983) stages of transition in initiation rituals—separation, liminality, and reintegration—can be utilized to describe the rites among aborigines in which the hallucinogenic plant pituri traditionally played an important role, particularly in the third and fourth stages:

1. Segregation of novices into special isolated camps
2. Education about sacred matters received from elders
3. Bodily operations such as circumcision and subincision
4. Disclosure of meanings of ritual objects presented to novices in secret ceremonies
5. Final cleaning of all traces of the sacred world and the ceremonial return to ordinary life

The symbolic concept of death and rebirth as the outcome of hallucinogenic plant-drug use is widely found among traditional societies of the world (see Dobkin de Rios 1984a). It was so profound in aboriginal societies that mothers behaved as if their sons were dead and mourned them accordingly. The elder who performed the circumcision was believed to be a designate of a supernatural being. Five or six weeks after the circumcision, subincision was performed, and this custom of cutting the male urethra was believed to be done to rid the body of the mother's female blood. After a series of ordeals, the young man was thought to be a changed person, ready to fully participate in adult society.

THE CHUMASH OF CALIFORNIA

Numbered among the tribelets of California that subsisted on acorn gathering, fishing, and hunting, the Chumash Indians of the Santa Barbara region combined the vision quest at adolescence of many North American Indian groups with a powerful hallucinogenic substance, *Datura meteloides*, commonly known as jimsonweed or *toloache*. The datura plant probably diffused northward as the result of Aztec trade and was incorporated into a common pubertal custom of austerities to mark the passage of the youth into adulthood.

The plant was taken in the form of a decoction, with the leaves, stems, and even the roots pounded and soaked in water. As with other hallucinogens, the drug's visions were believed able to confer knowledge of the future or to make supernatural beings visible to the imbiber. Paranormal events such as clairvoyance were said to result from the drug's ingestion, and people were believed to be able to see things hidden from ordinary view or events at a distance or in the future (Driver 1969:114).

Much of the data here draws on ethnographic work of Harrington between 1912 and 1922 (1942) and the cultural analysis of Chumash narrative texts that prominently feature datura tales (see Blackburn 1974). Gayton (1928) wrote that a common feature of the drug's use at puberty was through group administration. Like other vision quests undertaken by North American Indian tribal peoples, the drug helped the individual to obtain a supernatural helper or guardian spirit. In the southern part of California among the Gabrielino and Luiseno youths, datura was used in a puberty ritual integrated into a larger ceremonial complex called the Chingichnich cult, where initiates undertook ordeals and learned esoteric lore. Driver (1969) argued that the cult was named after the highest-ranking god in the area. The central theme of the cult was to obtain contact with the supernatural through the medium of the hallucinogenic plant. After the plant was crushed in a sacred mortar reserved for this purpose, each initiate drank from the mortar directly. Occasional mortality occurred. The visions were principally of animals who taught the initiate a song or dance. As in other vision quests recorded across the continent, the animal became a lifelong guardian spirit or helper of the boy and was thought to be essential to his success as a hunter or shaman or for any other activity that he engaged in. The ceremony was guided by an individual sponsor who instructed the boy in the religious lore of the tribelet and taught him various sacred songs and dances (1969:350). (On the vision quest, see the chapter by Bourguignon in this volume.)

Datura was used by Gabrielino and Luiseno men only once in their life, attesting to the general concern among North American Indians who utilized datura regarding their ability to control the effects of the plant. In other areas of California, datura drinking rituals were held every spring, and individuals could choose to imbibe as often as they liked. Tribal groups further east, including the Mohave, Yuma, and Desert Cahuilla, had no well-developed datura ceremony, but individuals took the plant whenever they wished.

Most data are available on the Chumash (Applegate 1975), who drank datura after the onset of puberty on an individual basis and not as part of group activity. Throughout North America, individual puberty initiations existed so that a youth could obtain a tutelary spirit as the result of his personal quest. By means of a personal religious experience that elsewhere consisted mainly of withdrawal into solitude and a break with the community of the living, the novice had a personal experience through dreams and visions that were provoked by a course of ascetic practices. The vision quest included fasting for four days after purification by purges, dietary prohibitions, and ascetic exercises (e.g., steam baths in icy water). Among the California and Northwest Coast tribal groups, however, we see a change with the introduction of the Mexican toloache plant, datura. Among the Chumash, both men and women took datura individually any time after the onset of puberty, although there was no formal initiation rite. This was done in the village rather than in an isolated spot. A guardian spirit was believed to come to a person who was under the effects of datura. At a later time, the youth might take the plant again to strengthen his/her bond with the dream helper. The plant was used for specific culturally determined goals such as communicating with spirits of the dead or divining the future—all of which were individual rather than collective goals. This contrasted with the mountain Cahuilla Indians of southern California, for example, where there was a group initiation with datura when enough boys reached an age suitable for the ceremonies. In all cases, it was believed that the drug permitted the individual access to supernatural power and engendered strength, courage, and success in later life. Women could obtain courage from drinking the plant potion, particularly in childbirth and to obtain immunity from danger.

Like other traditional societies that used plant hallucinogens, the Chumash recognized the need for purification, abstinence from sex, and a moderate diet consisting of thin, unsalted acorn gruel and abstinence from salt, sweets, meat, and fat. Chumash youth were expected to be reverent, concentrated, and careful not to offend the datura spirit by talking too freely about their experiences. Applegate (1975) argued that datura was incorporated into an already-existing vision-seeking complex among the California tribes such as the Chumash. Other extreme practices found elsewhere in North America like self-torture, mutilation, or solitary vigils at a remote spot were missing from the Chumash pattern.

A religious specialist, called the *toloachero* or datura giver, prepared and administered the drink. Often, five old men who assembled to administer the potion questioned the youth afterwards. The datura giver received payment for his services. The drug was considered to be dangerous, and it required great skill to prepare a dose sufficient to provide the response of a spirit helper, but that would not be toxic or lethal. The spirit of datura was propitiated in an attempt to ensure that the individual ingesting the substance would not sicken and die.

The first Chumash datura experience was seen to be the most carefully controlled. When elders thought that the adolescents were strong enough to stand the treatment, they were given the plant. This probably took place a few years after puberty but before they were sexually experienced. The five datura givers assembled together in the youth's house and administered the potion to him. He was told to pay attention to his dreams, and when he awoke he was sung to and instructed to see beyond surface appearances, "to see the other world beyond this world" (Applegate 1975). It was important that the youth receive an animal spirit helper such as a hawk or coyote to offer him lifelong protection and guidance. After the intoxication ended, the datura givers asked the youth what he had seen in his visions and, in turn, interpreted them for him. The elders "moralized," and in the youth's hypersuggestible state, they were able to inculcate culturally important moral systems and values. Other cultural uses of the plant included that of medicine, and it was part of the quest for shamanistic power should the individual wish to become a knower of spirits, to acquire spirit helpers, or to harm his enemies.

THE SHANGANA-TSONGA OF MOZAMBIQUE

T. F. Johnston (1972, 1976, 1977) published a series of articles of the Shangana-Tsonga of Mozambique and the then northern Transvaal based on fieldwork carried out between 1968 and 1970. These people are a Bantu-speaking group numbering about 1.2 million in Mozambique and 700,000 in northern Transvaal. They are a patrilineal society who worship spirits of their ancestors. They grow maize, squash, groundnuts, and sugar cane and keep a few goats and cattle. They live in an unfertile and arid environment where horticultural subsistence is hazardous, and due to the migrant labor situation, all of the arduous horticultural tasks are performed by women. In this rural traditional society, infertility and infant mortality are very high, and malnutrition and diseases such as syphilis are prevalent. Generally it is not determined whether a husband or wife is the infertile partner. Swiss doctors have estimated infertility in Tsonga women to be about 30 percent and infant mortality during the first year of life as 35 percent. Tsonga brides who prove childless are in great trouble, not only because cattle that have been paid for them as bridewealth would have to be returned, but because the cattle have often been used to bring the girl's brother a wife, thus involving a chain reaction. Therefore, a barren woman may expect a lifetime of disgrace and working for others.

A fertility school for nubile adolescent girls is mandatory and takes place periodically after the May harvest when the hallucinogenic plant *Datura fatuosa* is given to induce visions of a fertility god. Rituals emphasize the newly acquired adulthood status of initiates and the possibility of motherhood. A chief's primary wife officiates at the ceremony and inserts porcupinelike straws between the legs of initiates representing the regrowth of pubic hair that is shaved off before the rites. A tree that yields a white sap likened to semen is climbed; as the young woman clings to it with her legs wrapped around the trunk, it is said that she is learning about sexual intercourse. The officiant attempts to combat the possibility of sterility from witchcraft by mixing human fat or powdered bone (probably dug up from a cemetery) with the datura plant as an antidote. Music plays an important role in the girl's initiation rite, evoking stereotypic visionary patterns linked to the presence of the fertility god. Novices are expected to see bluish green color patterns under the effects of the plant. Johnston's sample of twelve women reported seeing green snakes, worms, whirlpools, and river banks. These blue-green snakes are found under the eaves of Tsonga huts and are believed to be ancestral gods. The main goal of the rituals is for the girls to hear the voice of the fertility god, stimulated largely by the suggestions of the officiant, who is knowledgeable about Tsonga ritualistic lore. Johnston argued that the officiant psychologically manipulates the group of novices to ensure group conformity during the rituals. The plant diminishes the girls' critical faculties and causes decreased reality testing and increased hypersuggestibility. The author suggested that the dissolution of self-boundaries under the plant's influence evokes primary-process thinking where external suggestions assume a concrete reality and a supramotivational state ensues. The officiant "becomes the silent inner voice. Manipulating the novices with powerful music, she leads them into the various consecutive mimes and dances . . . it is she who suggests the music-color association, the hearing of voices and the fertility vision" (1977:229). The ritual situations display the tripartite sequence of separation, liminality, and reincorporation of the novices, leading to socially recognized Tsonga identity. Thus the focus of the hallucinogenic experience by adolescent females at puberty is to establish a group social identity that takes precedence over that of individual identity. All of the rites marshal biochemical, psychophysiological, musical, and cultural mechanisms and are directed toward a group status-defining goal. Johnston argued that the African sociomusical behavior in the context of adolescent drug use is pragmatic and problem solving and represents "a culture's adaptive response to ecological and environmental pressures" and that "their particular mode of manifestation is determined by deep-rooted historical and psychological factors" (1977:234).

Datura ingestion during Tsonga puberty-school rituals is intended to obtain fertility and to protect women against barrenness by witchcraft. The novices are led firmly and authoritatively through a series of preparatory stages into the hallucinogenic rite. They are psychologically attuned to this rite by the women coaching them to achieve specific social goals. They see and hear what is expected of them at the appropriate time and place while they are under the influence of the datura plant. When the rituals are terminated, Tsonga girls are viewed as mature women of their group who can now fulfill the role demanded of them in their society. Once they emerge from the special datura rituals, they are eligible for marriage and thus bring cattle to their fathers. The rituals teach and reinforce the social role of women to please the husband, bear his children, keep the home, and till the soil. Intergenerational activity includes the officiant deflowering each girl with a long, twisted antelope horn, which is a symbol of authority.

DISCUSSION

Some important similarities recur in the data presented here on the Australian aborigine, the Chumash, and the Shangana-Tsonga. In all cases, we find that hallucinogenic plants were used to create states of consciousness, particularly hypersuggestible ones, in order to enculturate the adolescents with a fast-paced experience necessary for their survival and functioning as adult members of the community. These states were induced to heighten learning and to create a bonding among members of the cohort group, when appropriate, so that individual psychic needs would be subsumed to the needs of the social group. This was done to ensure survival. Cohort identity might be fostered in Australia by the austerities and painful changes that accompanied genital mutilation; the sleeplessness and beatings constituted a sort of aboriginal "boot camp" where one would identify with one's cohorts, upon whom survival might depend. The use of hallucinogens that created an amnesiac state, which heightened a death and rebirth experience, served cultural goals of "whipping into shape" the youth who died in his/her role as a child in order to be reborn as a fully participating adult member of society who can procreate and produce.

A key feature of such rituals for adolescents at puberty was the hypersuggestibility caused by the drug plants (see Ludwig 1969). In the altered state of consciousness managed by adult tutors, the religious and secular values and the emotional patterns appropriate to the culture would be modeled for the youths by their elders. This was done in a short-term learning milieu created during the altered state. While we would not expect to find homogeneity in outcomes of all youths subject to such rituals, it is certainly one way that a culture has available to it to inculcate conformity patterns in youth people that might contribute to group survival and harmony. Fernandez (1982), in fact, stated that in another African group, the Fang of Gabon, youths are given more and more of the plant hallucinogen *Iboga* until they have the culturally desired vision. Some young people have been reported to die from excessive dosages if they do not measure up to adult expectations of their ability to experience the preternatural.

A recent article by Simon (1990) focusing on a mechanism for social selection and successful altruism argued that human docility and bounded rationality are implicated in the evolution of altruistic behavior. Simon argued that since docility—receptivity to social influence—contributes greatly to fitness in the human species, it will be positively selected. We can argue here that the use of plant hallucinogens to create docility states in adolescents for the purpose of maturity preparation in a powerful psychotechnology implicitly utilized in tribal societies such as the ones under discussion.

THE FUNCTION OF DRUG INITIATORY RITUALS AT PUBERTY

Zoja (1989) examined the critical role of initiation rites in traditional societies and the degree to which they have become stultified, meaningless, and pathologized in contemporary society. In tribal settings, initiation of the individual provides personal regeneration and radical change and is essential to the process of growth and maturity and the acquisition of meaning. According to Zoja, all people possess an innate, archetypal need for initiation, but modern life denies us awareness of this need for renewal. Drugs often become a desperate, albeit futile, substitute for initiation among Western youth.

Psychotropic drugs have played an important role in the lives of men and women throughout recorded history. The incorporation of these plants in group or individual initiation rites in tribal societies is widespread. Such drugs are believed to be of sacred origin and have been treated with awe and reverence. In tribal societies, plant hallucinogens were in limited supply and were protected from abuse and profanation by deviants insofar as they remained under adult control and administration. One particular recurrent theme found among such societies where plant hallucinogens are used that is important in our discussion is that of release into initiatory death followed by the emergence into initiatory rebirth (see Dobkin de Rios 1984a). The child/adolescent undergoes sharp changes in the acquisition of a new identity, one that is richly imbued with meaning and that merits societal respect.

Western societies lack initiatory and transitional rites and traditions. Instead, the synthetic and manufactured drugs that are available are recognized to have become a major problem with which contemporary society must contend. The sacred and reverent utilization of psychoactive substances among tribal peoples has become a profaned and pathological phenomenon now defined as drug abuse.

In the tribal societies discussed in this chapter, pubertal initiation rites were typically collective and shared experiences (although the lack of economic resources among the Chumash made group rituals difficult, so that individual plant-drug ingestion in the village was the case). Hallucinogenic plant use was thoroughly embedded in the social milieu and was of utmost importance. The goal was to facilitate individual growth and development, allowing society to benefit from the sacred experiences of its youth. Culturally expected visions were provoked by shamanic manipulation of set and setting to provide revelation, blessings, healing, and ontological security for those using the sacramental plants. Ethical principles that emphasized cohort identity and identification and procreative and vocational success were deeply in the sacramental use of these psychoactive substances. Lying and licentiousness were repudiated. With the advent of state-level societies, the visions and ethics integral to the sacred traditional use of these plants may have been sacrificed as altered states were appropriated by state-level hierarchic functionaries (Dobkin de Rios and Smith

1977). In their place we find the mindless destruction of lives and values due to contemporary drug abuse.

Traditional societies commonly incorporated extensive preparatory and purification exercises preceding the actual psychoactive substance–facilitated initiation rite. The long period of time spent in preparation and the reverence with which the process was approached served as limiting factors for its use. As long as the pre–state-level society remained free from external destructive forces such as warfare, conquest, and other actions by state-level civilizations, such initiation rites continued to be regarded as sacred experiences. Psychoactive substances in tribal societies were not abused, but were perceived as sacraments facilitating controlled entry into valuable states of consciousness in which "visions" essential for the continued existence of the society could be accessed. In state-level and stratified societies, such rites of passage played an insignificant role. Plant-drug use took on esoteric ritual significance in ancient Greek Eleusinian mysteries (Wasson et al. 1978). As Harner argued (1973), medieval European society found a particular role for the hallucinogenic plants in witchcraft and alchemy.

Contemporary Western society, on the other hand, has developed a destructive, nonsacred use of drugs. The respect and reverence with which psychoactive sacraments have been utilized in tribal society have been abandoned. Drug initiation has become drug addiction. The sacred visions that served a socially enriching function have been lost. Repetitive, compulsive, and habitual drug use, emerging from both individual and societal pathology, has led to ever-increasing dangers to drug users and to society at large.

PUBLIC POLICY IMPLICATIONS

Shedler and Block (1990) have identified important implications in public policy from their research on drug use and abuse among American youth. They suggested that drug education may be addressed more successfully by encouraging sensitive and empathic parenting, building childhood self-esteem, fostering sounder interpersonal relations, and promoting involvement and commitment to meaningful life goals. They concluded that there are serious inadequacies with the conventional wisdom that no level of drug use is considered safe, and that it is dangerous to suggest otherwise. They also found that occasional experimentation with marijuana is not personally or socially destructive (Shedler and Block 1990:628). These ideas are reinforced by the data on traditional non-Western societies that have been presented in this chapter.

Adolescents who are in drug treatment do not represent the general population of adolescents but a specially constituted subpopulation. Thus for some adolescents, experimentation with drugs is highly destructive because drugs easily become part of a broader pathological syndrome. The cross-cultural data, too, show that drug experimentation does not have to be psychologically catastrophic. This is especially true when a cultural context of meaning gives pattern and structure to the drug experience. The reporting of stereotypic visionary patterns that serve as vehicles to reinforce cultural goals demonstrates this phenomenon (see Dobkin de Rios 1984a).

Why is drug abuse for young people in particular such a disconcerting and frightening problem? Contemporary society no longer possesses viable, preestablished paths to initiation. The tribal process of initiation culminates as rebirth into a new life, endowed with special qualities and new meaning. The coming of age in non–state-level tribal societies was a solemn rite of passage in which the initiates were consecrated into adulthood. In the absence of such initiation, we are left with widespread alienation and despair. Perhaps we must view the process of drug addiction in contemporary life as a spiritual quest—a search by the individual for transcendent experience, for meaning, and for personal identity. In this approach, we may be better equipped to address the tragedy of contemporary drug abuse and to rediscover a path to lead us from the alienation and malaise of industrial societies into a symbolic initiation and rebirth experience. (See the chapter by Simon Ottenberg in Part II.)

REFERENCES

Applegate, R. B. 1975. The Datura Cult among the Chumash. *Journal of California Anthropology* 2(1):7–17.

Basedow, H. 1925. *The Australian Aboriginal.* Adelaide: Preece and Sons.

Baumrind, D., and K. A. Moselle. 1985. A Developmental Perspective on Adolescent Drug Abuse. *Advances in Alcohol and Substance Abuse* 4:41–45.

Berndt, C. 1964. The Role of Native Doctors in Aboriginal Australia. In A. Kiev, ed., *Magic, Faith and Healing.* Glencoe, IL: Free Press.

Bettelheim, B. 1954. *Symbolic Wounds: Puberty Rites and the Envious Male.* Glencoe, IL: Free Press.

Blackburn, T. 1974. Chumash Oral Traditions: A Cultural Analysis. Ph.D. diss., UCLA.

Cawte, J. E. 1964. Australian Ethnopsychiatry in the Field: A Sampling in N. Kimberley. *Medical Journal of Australia* 1:467–72.

Clayton, R. R., and C. Ritter. 1985. The Epidemiology of Alcohol and Drug Abuse among Adolescents. *Advances in Alcohol and Substance Abuse* 4:69–79.

Cushman, P. 1990. Why the Self is Empty: Toward a Historically Situated Psychology. *American Psychologist* 45:599–611.

Dobkin de Rios, M. 1984a. *Hallucinogens: Cross-Cultural Perspectives.* Albuquerque: University of New Mexico Press. (reprinted 1992 Garden City Park, NY: Avery Publishing Group).

———. 1984b. *Visionary Vine: Hallucinogenic Healing in the Peruvian Amazon.* Prospect Heights, IL: Waveland Press.

Dobkin de Rios, M., and D. E. Smith. 1977. Drug Use and Abuse in Cross-Cultural Perspective. *Human Organization* 36(1):15–21.

Driver, H. 1969. *Indians of North America.* 2nd ed., rev. Chicago: University of Chicago Press.

Durkheim, E. 1915. *The Elementary Forms of the Religious Life.* Trans. Joseph Ward Swain. Glencoe, IL: Free Press.

Eliade, M. 1965. *Rites and Symbols of Initiation: Mysteries of Birth and Rebirth.* New York: Harper and Row.

———. 1973. *Australian Religions: An Introduction.* Ithaca, NY: Cornell University Press.

Fernandez, J. W. 1982. *Bwiti. An Ethnography of the Religious Imagination in Africa.* Princeton, NJ: Princeton University Press.

Gayton, A. H. 1928. The Narcotic Plant Datura in Aboriginal American Culture. Ph.D. diss., University of California, Berkeley.

Geertz, C. 1973. *The Interpretation of Cultures*. New York: Basic Books.

Grob, C. 1986. Substance Abuse: What Turns Casual Use into Chronic Dependence? *Contemporary Pediatrics* 3:26–41.

Harner, M. 1973. Hallucinogens and Witchcraft. In M. J. Harner, ed., *Hallucinogens and Shamanism*. London: Oxford University Press.

Harrington, J. P. 1942. Culture Element Distributions XIX: Central California Coast. *University of California Anthropological Records* 7.

Horne, G., and G. Aiston. 1924. *Savage Life in Central Australia*. London: Macmillan.

Johnston, L. D. 1985. *Highlights from Student Drug Use in America*. Ann Arbor: University of Michigan Press; Rockville, MD: National Institute of Drug Abuse.

Johnston, T. F. 1972. *Datura fatuosa*: Its Use in Tsonga Girls' Initiation. *Economic Botany* 26:340–351.

———. 1976. Power and Prestige through Music in Tsongaland. *Human Relations* 27:235–46.

———. 1977. Auditory Driving, Hallucinogens, and Music-Color Synesthesia in Tsonga Ritual. In B. M. du Toit, ed., *Drugs, Rituals, and Altered States of Consciousness*. Amsterdam: Balkema Press.

Johnston, T. H., and J. B. Clelland. 1933. The History of the Aborigine Narcotic, Pituri. *Oceania* 4:201–89.

Kandel, D. B. 1982. Epidemiological and Psychosocial Perspectives on Adolescent Drug Use. *Journal of the American Academy of Child Psychiatry* 21:328–37.

Ludwig, A. 1969. Altered States of Consciousness. In C. Tart, ed., *Altered States of Consciousness*. New York: Wiley.

Paton, S., R. Kessler, and D. Kandel. 1977. Depressive Mood and Adolescent Illicit Drug Abuse: A Longitudinal Analysis. *Journal of Genetic Psychology* 131:267.

Shedler, J., and J. Block. 1990. Adolescent Drug Use and Psychological Health. *American Psychologist* 45:612–30.

Simon, H. 1990. A Mechanism for Social Selection and Successful Altruism. *Science* 250 (December 21):1665–68.

Spencer, B., and F. J. Gillen. 1899. *The Native Tribes of Central Australia*. London: Macmillan.

van Gennep, A. 1984. *Rites of Passage*. New York: Columbia University Press.

Wasson, G., A. Hoffman, C. A. Rueck, and R. Rueck. 1978. *The Road to Eleusis: Unveiling the Secret of the Mysteries*. New York: Harcourt Brace Jovanovich.

Zoja, L. 1989. *Drugs, Addiction, and Initiation: The Modern Search for Ritual*. New York: Sigo Press.

CHAPTER EIGHTEEN

SELF AND PERSON

Thomas J. Csordas

For the constructs of "self" and "person," as much as or more than any other constructs in anthropology, theory conditions the nature of what we take to be evidence. The theoretical complexity surrounding these notions is evident in the existence of a cluster of common English terms with overlapping or near-synonymous meanings: self, spirit, soul, psyche, ego, agent, character, personality, subjectivity, subject, inner man, person, mind, consciousness, identity, individual, and mental substance, along with a series of technical philosophical terms such as monad, transcendental unity of apperception, *Dasein, pour-soi, être-au-monde*, and transcendental ego (Zaner 1981:112; Whittaker 1992:198–201). Different disciplines use terminology that reflects the way they construe the subject matter. Social psychology tends toward an analytic isolation of aspects of self, as in self-concept, self-image, self-awareness, self-esteem, and self-identity (Gecas 1982). Clinical psychology tends to formulate self-processes such as growth, actualization, integration, fragmentation, and alienation. Legal studies are generally less concerned with the self than with the person (including the corporation as a fictive person)—an entity that has clearly articulated rights and responsibilities within civic and political life. Philosophy has a long tradition of dealing with other issues related to self (Zaner 1981:112; Taylor 1989), as well as with the ethical and ontological status of persons (James 1983:342–71; Rorty 1976).

Within the large set of related terms just listed, the notions of self and person are the most central to contemporary anthropological discourse. Limiting our analysis to these two concepts does not completely resolve the terminological complexity, however. There are several reasons for this. First, the place of each in relation to the larger set has changed over time in theoretical discourse. For example, in American anthropology from the 1930s through the 1950s, the concept of self was subordinated to that of personality in the work of the Culture and Personality school. During the 1960s and 1970s, the concept of self became more explicit, yet tended to be subordinated to that of identity (e.g., Postal 1965; Robbins 1974; Singer 1984). Thus one could examine "identity processes" such as formation, confirmation, management, change, dissolution, diffusion, or conflict (Robbins 1973:1208–16). This interest in personal identity became in turn an important component of anthropological studies of ethnic identity (DeVos and Romanucci-Ross 1975; Singer 1984), which have more recently begun to incorporate the language of self on the collective level (Dominguez 1989; Ohnuki-Tierney 1987, 1990). By the 1980s the concept of self had come fully into its own (Whittaker 1992), partly supplanting that of identity. As part of the same intellectual movement, the notion of person reemerged (Shweder and Sullivan 1990), and both came into a new discursive relation with concepts of emotion, experience, and meaning.

Second, even at present there are various ways of construing these terms in relation to one another. The self is sometimes implicitly or explicitly regarded as a kind of entity, and sometimes as a kind of cultural and psychological process (Marsella 1985:290–94; Johnson 1985:97, 105). The person may be regarded as a social fact independent from any notion of self, or as the sociocultural objectification of experiential processes designated by the term itself. In short, the way analytic concepts are grouped is critical to the way ethnographic evidence is construed. For example, two of the most influential articles in the current discussion are Fogelson's (1982) treatment of "person, self, and identity" and Harris's (1989) treatment of "individual, self, and person." The substitution of "individual" for "identity" in these titles reflects not only a change in discourse over the course of a decade, but the inclination of Fogelson toward the psychocultural perspective of American anthropology, and of Harris toward the sociological approach of British anthropology. That is, seen through the conceptual lens of identity, the relation between self and person emphasizes issues of both culture and subjectivity. On the other hand, seen through the conceptual lens of the individual, self and person are placed in the context of both social relationships and the biological nature of the individual human organism.

Third, it is methodologically critical whether an author chooses to treat the topic from the perspective of what has been called cultural psychology (Stigler, Shweder, and Herdt 1990; also the chapter by J. Miller in this book) or from that of ethnopsychology (White and Kirkpatrick 1985). In brief, the former approach concentrates on psychological processes in cultural context, treating self and person as analytic domains or fundamental categories. The latter concentrates on indigenous psychological theories, asking about the presence, nature, and cultural consequences of notions of self and person as formulated by members of the societies being analyzed. Both perspectives may be relevant in any particular study. Analysis is especially complex in cultural settings where the existence of indigenous concepts does not necessarily imply their relevance throughout a population, as is the case for concepts of self and nonself in Hindu and Buddhist societies (Bharati 1985; Spiro 1982).

In this chapter, I will not trace the development of concepts of self and person within anthropology (see Hallowell 1955; Fogelson 1982; Johnson 1985; Marcus and Fischer 1986: chap. 3; and Whittaker 1992 for such treatments). Neither will I attempt a comprehensive review of literature on self and person (see Chang 1988). Instead, I will first briefly summarize four classic sources in psychology, sociology, and anthropology that have definitively shaped discussions of self and person in contemporary anthropology: works by James, Mead, Hallowell, and Mauss. I will then describe a series of conceptual models that are prominent ways of construing ethnographic evidence in anthropological accounts: self as entity, self as semiosis, self as bodily orientation, self and emotion, the psychodynamic self, and social person.

FOUR CLASSIC POSITIONS

The chapter on "The Consciousness of Self" in William James's classic 1890 text, *The Principles of Psychology*, is both a careful theoretical analysis and a document of ethnographic and historical value for understanding the ethnopsychology of a certain segment of American society. James's definition was that "a man's Self is the sum total of all that he *can* call his, not only his body and psychic powers, but his clothes and his house, his wife and children, his ancestors and friends, his reputation and works, his lands and horses, and yacht and bank-account" (1981:291). This self has four components, including the material self, the social self, the spiritual self, and pure ego. It is characterized by certain kinds of self-feelings or emotions and by typical actions of self-seeking and self-preservation (1981:292).

James was much concerned with the commonsense unity among these various aspects of selves, that is, with the intuition of an entity in relation to which "the self's constituents stick together as they do for thought" (1981:337). In an important footnote, he suggested that "the sense of my bodily existence, however obscurely recognized as such, *may* then be the absolute original of my conscious selfhood, the fundamental perception that *I am*. All appropriations *may* be made *to* it, *by* a thought not at the moment immediately cognized by itself" (1981: 341n). James also distinguished between the "Me" and the "I," referring to the difference between self as an existential unity and as the power of reflection. This distinction between the "empirical self" and the "judging thought" (1981: 371) parallels the phenomenological one between preobjective and objective (Csordas 1990). Interestingly, James carried out his discussion of the relation between the Me and the I in the context of empirical evidence about "mutations of the self" in cases of alterations of memory, multiple personality, and mediumship or possession (1981:373–400).

For James, the nucleus of the self was bodily existence. For the sociologist George Herbert Mead, it was language, and in the chapter on self in his classic

Mind, Self, and Society, he stated that "we can distinguish very definitively between the self and the body" (1934:136). Whereas James distinguished between the "sciousness" of self and the reflective consciousness of judging thought, Mead distinguished between mere consciousness and rational self-consciousness (1934:138). He asserted that "the self, as that which can be an object to itself, is essentially a social structure, and it arises in social experience" (1934:140). The self originates in symbolic social activity such as language, play, and games. Through the "conversation of gestures" that takes place in these forms of social communication, unity of self is achieved by assimilating the attitude of the community or "generalized other" (1934:154). In this process, "social or group attitudes are brought within the individual's direct field of experience, and are included as elements in the structure or constitution of the self" (1934:158). In other words, "What goes to make up the organized self is the organization of attitudes which are common to the group" (1934:162). Mead argued that James's grounding of the self in "self-feeling" neglects the social origin of the self, and further that the essence of this social self is not affective but cognitive. The final consequence of the social (in contrast to the individual) theory of the self, as Mead himself noted, is that "the individual enters as such into his own experience only as an object, not as a subject" (1934:225).

The most influential contribution to this debate by an American anthropologist was a series of papers by A. Irving Hallowell (1955). Hallowell adopted a protophenomenological stance, defining self in terms of self-awareness. While for Hallowell self-awareness is a characteristic of individuals, it is constituted in and thoroughly conditioned by sociocultural context, with the result that the distinction between subjectivity and objectivity itself becomes blurred (1955: 81–86). To emphasize this point, he specified that the context of human life is a "culturally constituted behavioral environment," a concept borrowed from Gestalt psychology that "takes account of the properties and adaptational needs of the organism in interaction with the external world as constituting the actual behavioral field in terms of which the activities of the animal are more thoroughly intelligible" (1955:86). Within this environment, the constituting role of culture is to provide basic *orientations* that serve as conditions for self-awareness. There are five basic types of orientation: that of self to others, that of self to a diversified world of objects whose attributes are culturally constituted and symbolically mediated through language, that of self within discrete spatial and temporal frames of reference, that of self toward objects within the behavioral environment with reference to motivations for the satisfaction of its needs, and that of self to values, ideals, and standards that define the normative or moral framework of life (1955:89–110).

Hallowell supported his position with evidence drawn from autobiographical and experiential accounts by Ojibwa informants. He observed that the Ojibwa behavioral environment did not stress ontological distinction between humans and supernatural beings, but differentiated between human and nonhuman selves with respect to how they ranked in order of power (1955:181). Humans must orient to these other selves as persons, with the implication that the category of "person" can include entities other than human beings, and hence that our accustomed concept of person reflects our own cultural subjectivity and is not an objective category that can legitimately be used in analysis of other cultures (1976:359). A small corpus of work directly inspired by Hallowell has examined issues including indigenous concepts of self, orientational self-processes, spirit possession, and the nature of persons as features of the behavioral environment (Bourguignon 1965; Black 1977a, 1977b; Hay 1973, 1977; A. S. Straus 1977; T. Smith 1989; Csordas 1990, 1993).

On the European side, the most important anthropological contribution was the single brief 1938 essay by Marcel Mauss, "A Category of the Human Mind." Like Hallowell, Mauss sidestepped the consequences of rigid dichotomy between individual and social theories by asserting that he was treating a fundamental category of the human spirit (*l'esprit humain*). While fundamental, however, it is not immutable, and his strategy was to trace its historical development.

For Mauss the person and the self represented different stages of this development. The most rudimentary stage is that of the character or role (*personnage*), evidence for which Mauss found in the societies of American Indians and aboriginal Australians. In these societies, he argued, there are a fixed number of personages represented by names or masks, into which various individuals succeed (1985:4). A transitional state was that of the *persona*, still a kind of fixed identity transmitted by the family in cultures such as ancient India, China, and Rome. According to Mauss, only in Rome did the persona evolve into the true moral person (*personne*) with the decisive creation of citizenship in the revolt of the plebs and the adoption of forenames, surnames, and pseudonyms. The Christians later "made a metaphysical entity of the 'moral person' (*personne morale*), after they became aware of its religious power" (1985:19). The final stage, achieved under the influence of sectarian movements in the seventeenth and eighteenth centuries, is transformation of the person (*personne*) into the self (*moi*), where "the 'self' (*moi*) equals consciousness, and is its primordial category" (1985:21). A group of scholars recently combined their diverse expertise to examine the implications of Mauss's argument and fruitfully subjected his use of ethnographic evidence, his historical method, and his use of philosophical categories to critical scrutiny (Carrithers, Collins, and Lukes 1985).

MODELS OF EVIDENCE FOR SELF AND PERSON

Self as Entity

The question whether the self is a kind of entity is as old in Western thought as the debate about the nature of the soul or of "mental substance." Shweder and Sullivan's (1990) critique of notions of the person as a central processing mechanism or as a vessel for autonomous mental states implied that these positions presuppose an entity grounded in Western cultural traditions. This contrasts with a semiotic definition of person that, they argued, is more valid cross-culturally. In empirical research, the idea that an entified self is a distinctly Western notion often serves as a foil against which cross-cultural evidence for various types of nonentified self is marshaled. Perhaps the best-known formulation of this position is by Geertz, who made no strict distinction between a culture's concept of person and the psychological self that goes along with that person:

> The Western conception of the person as a bounded, unique, more or less integrated motivational and cognitive universe, a dynamic center of awareness, emotion, judgment, and action organized into a distinctive whole and set contrastively both against other such wholes and against its social and natural background, is, however incorrigible it may seem to us, a rather peculiar idea within the context of the world's cultures. (1984: 59; see Johnson 1985; Murray 1993; and Spiro 1993 for analysis and debate of this statement.)

By and large, this line of discussion has focused less on defining or disavowing the essence or core of self than on the existence and nature of boundaries between self and society. Comparison between India and the West has played a significant role in formulating this issue. The problem of entity is central to Marriott's (1976a) formulation of a contrast between the integrated Western "individual" and the Indian "dividual" that is relatively discontinuous across contexts and is permeated by the substance of those contexts. Dumont (1970) contrasted the discrete individual of Western civilization and the person subordinated to social hierarchy in Hindu civilization. More recently, Shweder and Bourne (1982) conducted a comparison of Indians (Oriya) and Westerners (American) from which they concluded that within the holistic Indian worldview the person-society relationship is formulated as socioeconomic and organic, while the corresponding Western relationship is egocentric and contractual. The autonomous, bounded individual is conceivable for Indians, but such an individual can exist only outside of society in the form of the ascetic world-renouncer (1982:128–31).

Beyond the Indian subcontinent, Shore (1982) showed that Samoan personhood is shifting and flexible, embedded in a web of relationship so that rather than being conceivable as a rounded, integrated entity with a consistent essence, each self is like a multifaceted gem, with each facet defined by a relationship. Kondo (1990) described the self in Japan as multiple, gendered, and crafted in contexts of power. Variations on the theme of an unbounded self are evident in the early work of Leenhardt (1975) on the New Caledonian cosmocentric person, and of Stairs (1992) on the ecocentric self of the Inuit. (See also the related notions from cross-cultural psychology of allocentric and idiocentric person in Triandis et al. 1988).

The sociocentric-egocentric contrast has been exceedingly productive, but it can easily be misconstrued to denote a strict distinction between East and West in matters of person and self, thereby falling prey to what Said (1978) has called the dichotomizing fallacy of "Orientalism." Gaines (1982:181–86) identified a similar distinction between the entified "referential" self of North European cultures and the contextually defined "indexical" self of Mediterranean or Latin European cultures.

In her analysis of emotional overinvolvement in the families of Latino and Anglo-American schizophrenic patients, Jenkins (1991:412) argued that—from the standpoint of emotion (in contrast, for example, with a jural standpoint)—kin relations presuppose some form of interpersonal boundary. Furthermore, the consequences of traumatic events and the universal existence of an incest taboo both suggest that at least minimal boundedness is present in any culture. Among the Tshidi of southern Africa, Comaroff (1986:127–29) identified bounded selfhood as the product of socialization, "for only a stable and contained persona could engage in give-and-take with its immediate context." At the same time, "Personhood was not confined in space and time to a corporeal cocoon; it permeated the world through its material and spiritual extensions."

Roseman, who studied ritual healing among indisputably sociocentric Temiar of Malaysia, nevertheless emphasized that for them, "the cultural subscript of sociocentric interdependence . . . is the continual reinstatement of an independent, bounded self. It is all too easy to typify the sociocentric self as a static state, to envision an idyllic scene of interconnected entities where separation and alienation are not an issue." At the same time, egocentric selves in societies such as the United States exist "in tension with a cultural subscript that values interdependence" (1991:47). Likewise, Hollan (1992) found autonomous aspects of the experiential self among the ostensibly sociocentric Toraja of Indonesia, as well as relational aspects of self in the United States independent of differences in overt cultural models. Rosenberger (1989) suggested that in Japanese society, the self is constituted in a dialectic relation between the sociocentric and egocentric. McHugh (1989) argued that among the Gurung of Nepal, while great value is placed on integration in a social network, the person is conceived as a discrete entity with needs and impulses that may contradict demands for social cohesion. Finally, in India itself, Mines (1988) used life-history data to argue against the position that the demands of hierarchy rule out individuation and personal autonomy, showing how personal goals, rebellion against hierarchy, and individual responsibility are important themes of adult life.

Self as Language and Semiosis

We have already examined George Herbert Mead's definition of the self in terms of language and communication processes. Mead's influence is strongest in the sociological field of symbolic interactionism. One of the few anthropologists to explicitly elaborate a Meadian concept of self is Kapferer (1979, 1983).

In his interpretation of exorcistic healing rituals in Sri Lanka, Kapferer emphasized specialized forms of communication characteristic of cultural performances. He showed how performance negates and then reconstitutes the social self, reinserting it in its rightful place in the cosmic hierarchy, superior to the demons by which the patient had been terrorized.

There are several reasons for the relative backgrounding of G. H. Mead's influence in anthropology. M. B. Smith (1985) argued that recent developmental studies show that some aspects of selfhood do not depend on language. The recent prominence of metaphor theory and the notion of metaphor as constitutive of self has also in part supplanted the Meadian formulation. Another reason is that the more empirically explicit work of Erving Goffman has had greater resonance for anthropologists concerned with the self. Bock (1988) summarized the influence of Goffman's analyses of communication, presentation, role, and behavior on psychological anthropology and argued for their enduring relevance to the discipline. The rise of sociolinguistics and the ethnography of communication have also given the discipline its own theoretical discourse about the role of language in constituting the self (Hymes 1961).

Following Boas (1988:87), there have been occasional ethnographic observations on the psychological implications of particular pronominal usages. For example, Chang discussed the "honorific humble system" in Korean, in which verb forms indicate the status relations between speakers so strongly that personal pronouns become superfluous, and concluded that "on the overt level there is no individual" (1988:192). However, the theoretical inspiration for placing pronominal usage in a larger semiotic field has come less from Boas or Mead than from Charles Sanders Peirce. The leading anthropological proponent of Peircean semiotics has been Milton Singer (1984, 1989). Singer has persistently pursued the anthropological implications of Peirce's definition of man as a symbol (1984:55), his definition of the self as a "loosely compacted person . . . made of the sympathetic feelings through which social and cultural consciousness are communicated," and his dictum that "my language is the sum total of my self" (1984:70–71). Singer has elaborated these ideas in terms of the inner dialogue of I-Me and outer dialogue of I-You, the relations among the pronominal cluster I-It-Thou as a semiotic structure, the relation between personal and social identity, and the contrast between identity in the United States and in India. T. Straus (1989) has similarly elaborated the Peircean notion of pronominal usage in a study of the northern Cheyenne self, arguing that the role of second-person pronouns is evidence for a description of Cheyenne culture as more intimately "tuistical" (in Peirce's locution) than the ego-focused cultures of Europe.

Daniel (1984) developed Peirce's semiotic as a method of cultural interpretation in his treatment of the person in Tamil Nadu, India. Working with Peirce's distinction among symbol, icon, and index, he first analyzed the cultural semiotic of the village context, progressively narrowing his focus to the household and then to the sexual and emotional life of persons. Daniel emphasized the importance to interpretation, and by implication to the cultural constitution of persons, of dialogue in the play of signs and the interaction among people. Crapanzano (1992) has also elaborated the importance of dialogue as well as other linguistic modes, including textuality and indexicality, in the anthropological construction of self. Crapanzano emphasized the life history, for example, in his portrait of Tuhami, a Moroccan tilemaker (Crapanzano 1980). He developed an approach that, mediated by the work of Lacan, links semiotic processes to psychological processes first outlined in the work of Freud. Both Daniel and Crapanzano are part of a movement in anthropology that simultaneously acknowledges the methodological importance of linguistic processes like dialogue in the relation between anthropologist and informant, and the empirical importance of those processes in the self-constituting social interactions among participants in the cultural milieus with which they are concerned. The post-Meadian theme of a dialogic self has also found currency in the interdisciplinary discourse of hermeneutics and the interpretive method (Taylor 1991).

Another linguistic modality that has become prominent in anthropological studies of self and person is narrative. This trend is due in part to the work of scholars such as the philosopher Paul Ricoeur (1991) and the psychologist Jerome Bruner (1990); see also Polkinghorne (1991). White (1991) has emphasized the importance of narrative in the construction of person, self, and identity on the island of Santa Isabel in the Solomon Islands. Focusing on the treatment of issues that come before Muslim courts, Rosen (1989) examined the role of ideas of person and narrative style in articulating the notion of responsibility in Arab Islamic life. From a developmental perspective, the narrative construction of self in childhood has been addressed by Nelson (1989) and by Miller et al. (1990). Good (1992) and Garro (1992) have examined the narrative reconstruction of the self among patients afflicted with chronic pain. Finally, recent collections by Abu-Lughod and Lutz (1991) and by Watson-Gegeo and White (1990) have elaborated the notion of discourse, particularly with respect to political aspects of emotion and conflict relevant to the enactment of self and the construction of person concepts.

In sum, following the insights of Mead, Boas, and Peirce, the approach to the self through language and semiosis ranges from the specific analysis of pronominal usage to a semiotic anthropology that places the self at the interpretive center of culture and to broad notions of dialogue, narrative, and discourse as modalities of self-construction.

Self as Orientation

We noted earlier that Hallowell defined self not only abstractly in terms of self-awareness, but concretely in terms of its modes of orientation. This theme has until recently been less explicitly developed among anthropologists than that of the repertoire of persons within behavioral environments. The anthropologically oriented philosopher Charles Taylor (1985), in his cultural history of the self in Western society, placed a great deal of emphasis on orientation in moral space as an interpretive theme. Anthropologists who emphasize orientation are more or less explicitly phenomenological in their methods and more or less explicit at identifying the body and bodily experience as the "orientational locus of self" (Csordas 1993; cf. Zaner 1980).

In his classic work on the person in New Caledonia, Leenhardt reported a conversation in which his interlocutor pointed out that his people had "always acted in accord with the spirit. What [Europeans] brought us is the body" (1979: 164). In the indigenous worldview, the person was diffused with other persons and things in a unitary sociomythic domain. The idea of a circumscribed human body was the principle of objectification and individuation of the person and brought about discrimination between the body and the mythic world. Similarly, Lienhardt reported that the Dinka language "compels its speakers to integrate the moral and physical attributes of persons together with the physical matrix of the human body"; the importance of this bodily matrix is evident in their use of their word for "body" where we would use "self" (1985:150–51).

Stromberg suggested that self-processes such as religious conviction and commitment are characterized by strong relationships between symbols and "affect-laden aspects of the self" (1985:58). He borrowed from Dilthey (1958) the term *impression point* to denote the experience in which the link between symbol and self is forged; it is "a physical experience of the symbol, an embodiment that establishes for the believer the possibility of the commitment relationship" (Stromberg 1985:59). Csordas (1993) used the domain of religious experience to formulate working definitions of self intended to be applicable across cultures: self is neither substance nor entity, but an indeterminate capacity to engage or become oriented in the world, and it is characterized by effort and reflexivity. Self-processes are orientational processes in which aspects of the world are thematized, with the result that the self is objectified, most often as a "person" having a cultural identity or set of identities (see Whiting 1990).

Frank (1979) offered a phenomenological variant of the life-history method to demonstrate orientational self-processes. In her life history of a woman born without limbs, she showed how this woman's sense of embodiment was complete and culturally typical, including capacities for motility and sexuality (Frank 1986). Frank thus demonstrated how the bodily synthesis that grounds our sense of self as orientation in the world is not determined by anatomical completeness but is a function of experience prior to the analytic distinction between physical and social. Roseman's (1991) description of the self in relation to others among the Temiar of Malaysia vividly shows the role of the senses as orientational self-processes. For the Temiar, the olfactory mode is evident in the interpersonal sensitivity to odor, the visual in the sensitivity to where one's shadow falls, the tactile in the etiquette of handling and exchanging objects, and the auditory in the notion that voice, sound, and music are manifestations of the souls of plants, animals, humans, and other natural objects.

Self and Emotion

Psychological anthropologists have since the mid-1970s turned systematic attention to the study of the relation between culture and emotion (Lutz and White 1986; Lutz 1988; Schieffelin 1976, 1983; the chapter by Janis Jenkins in this volume; for related developments in psychology, see Markus and Kitayama 1991). The concerns of this group are coterminous with those of anthropologists interested in the problems of person and self when they both address the topic of ''self and emotion'' (Levy and Rosaldo 1983; White and Kirkpatrick 1985; J. Smith 1981; Ito 1987). Rosaldo, a leader in this field, organized a group of scholars that carried the anthropological study of shame beyond the conventional figuration of ''shame versus guilt'' as ''external versus internal'' forms of social control to a richer understanding of the self in morally motivated situations (Levy and Rosaldo 1983). In other work, Rosaldo (1980, 1984) showed how the development of the self among the Ilongot of the Philippines is understood as a maturational movement from a youthful condition dominated by *liget* (anger or passion) to one dominated by *beya* (knowledge). The Ilongot case led her toward a theory of self that problematized the distinction between thought and feeling, and to the suggestion that emotions should be considered as ''embodied thoughts'' (Rosaldo 1984).

As the distinction between thought and feeling is critical to understanding the relation between self and emotion, so is the distinction between public and private. Geertz (1973) approached the problem of person in Bali with a definition of culture as public, insofar as culture patterns subsist in observable clusters of symbols. For Balinese, the moral order and aesthetic order are coterminous, embodied in an elaborate system of etiquette that does not entirely deny involvement and feeling but does not culturally emphasize or symbolically elaborate them. The most salient emotion is thus a kind of social shame/guilt (*lek*) that Geertz argued is best glossed as ''stage fright,'' and social relations typically exhibit an affective style characterized by lack of climax. Geertz's argument was challenged by Wikan (1987), who argued for the salience of the private domain of emotion. She suggested that it is not stage fright but the fear of sorcery that can result in illness and mental confusion that accounts for the necessity felt by Balinese to maintain an outward veneer of composure and invulnerability. Wikan's portrait of concern for ''true feelings'' along with rightness and virtue lends a substantially different cast to the Balinese self than does Geertz's account.

The distinction between internal and external definitions of emotion in relation to self leads us to ask if there is a bodily core to emotion, as James held (see the earlier summary of James's analysis of the self), or if instead emotion is essentially symbolic or cultural. Those who make this distinction are likely to denote the bodily component of affect as ''feeling'' and the symbolic component as ''emotion'' (see the chapter by Janis Jenkins in this volume). In his discussion of emotion categories among the Pintupi of Australia, Myers (1986) objected to the terms *self* and *person* because of their psychological and hence internal connotations, preferring to discuss the "cultural subject." This allowed him to extend the notion of subjectivity beyond the bounds of individual consciousness, on the premise that "if the structures of subjectivity . . . are a product of human action, they reflect the conditions of that action as much as individual intention" (1986:105). Emotions then become forms of judgment, interpretation, or evaluation of the relationships between individuals and their circumstances. Myers described a constellation of emotion categories centered around the value of relatedness (*walytja*), including happiness (*pukurlpa*), compassion (*ngaltu*), grief (*yalurrpa*), pining (*watjilpa*), and shame/respect (*kunta*). This discussion is continuous with those of the preceding section of this chapter in that emotions are held to orient Pintupi within their social world.

The Psychodynamic Self

Psychodynamic and psychoanalytic approaches have long been part of psychological anthropology. With the movement toward interpretive method in anthropology as a whole, psychoanalytic work has increasingly dealt with concepts such as person, self, and emotion (Paul 1980; Kracke and Herdt 1987). Ewing suggested that contemporary anthropological, particularly ethnopsychological, works are often successful in describing the "organizing principles of indigenous theories of the self, but have had difficulty in capturing the ambiguity and creativity of ongoing social processes" (1987:16). In a comparison of an interaction between psychotherapist and patient and an interaction between ethnographer and informant, she demonstrated how psychoanalytic method can make such processes accessible to interpretation.

Ewing (1990) has offered a psychoanalytic approach to the problem of entity and boundedness discussed earlier. Basing her definition of self on the notion of self-representation, she argued that in any culture there are indeterminately constituted "shifting selves" characterized by inconsistency and strategic or rhetorical possibilities for multiple self-representations. Ewing believed that psychodynamic processes such as condensation, displacement, transference, and identification are semiotic processes that organize the play of self-representations to create the illusory sense of wholeness and continuity that is a phenomenological hallmark of "self."

Most current psychoanalytic approaches to self and person are explicitly concerned with the relation between cultural meaning and personal experience, and many ethnographies are explicitly "person centered" (LeVine 1982). Herdt concentrated on initiation rituals among the Sambia of New Guinea, showing both that they are transitional processes in a social sense and that ritual objects such as sacred flutes are "transitional objects" in the psychoanalytic sense introduced by Winnicott (Herdt 1987), and examining how ritual mutilation of initiates is psychosexually connected to male gender identity, authority, and relations between men and women (Herdt 1990). Kracke (1978, 1987) used psychodynamic interviews and dream accounts from the Kagwahiv Indians of Brazil to show how childhood psychological and interpersonal dynamics are reiterated in adult relationships, particularly those between leaders and followers of the small Kagwahiv social grouping of several nuclear families. In his ethnography of Tahiti, Levy (1973) adopted a loosely psychodynamic approach to people's "experience as Tahitians." Levy organized his description of Tahitian persons into categories of body, soul, and interpersonal relationships. Though he offered no definition of self, Levy equated self with identity, focusing on Tahitian self-perception as a Meadian or Jamesian "I."

In his study of religious ascetics in Sri Lanka, Obeyesekere introduced the notion of *personal symbols*, "cultural symbols whose primary significance and meaning lie in the personal life and experience of individuals" (1981:44). For example, in Sri Lanka the matted hair of the ascetic is an optional personal symbol, while the shaved head of the Buddhist monk is a cultural requisite of his status. The personal symbol is unlike other cultural symbols in that it becomes invested with self-constituting experiential significance and is created anew by each individual (1981:45–46). Poole (1987) used the notion of personal symbol in an analysis of the psychological makeup of a young boy among the Bimin-Kuskusmin of Papua New Guinea. During the period leading up to an important initiation rite, the boy was diagnosed as being possessed by a culturally significant bird. By elaborating the cultural images of possession into a series of personal symbols, the boy expressed the psychological ambivalence of his Oedipal circumstances.

The Social Person

Mauss (1985) argued that the social category of the person has undergone historical development in Western civilization, one of those stages being the *personne morale* defined in terms of his or her place and status in society. Radcliffe-Brown (1922), with his concept of "social personality," turned this historical category into a theoretical one. Fortes (1987), who adopted Radcliffe-Brown's notion, presumed it to be a direct adaptation from Mauss. In Fortes's formulation, "It is the society that creates, defines, indeed imposes the distinctive signs and indices that characterize, and the moral and jural capacities and qualities that constitute the *personne morale* as we find it in that society" (1987: 249). Thus for the Tallensi, crocodiles as animals are not considered to be persons, but certain crocodiles who inhabit sacred pools identified with human ancestors are considered to be persons. In this theoretical perspective, personhood is not an innate characteristic of an individual but a social status to be attained, whereas the self is a psychological attribute of an individual that is quite distinct and may or may not figure into the argument. This distinction between personhood and self or soul is also present in some forms of Hinduism where the self, soul, ego, or *atman* is continuous from birth to birth through successive reincarnations, while its successive embodiments may only qualify as persons if they are born as human beings, and then not always (Carter 1982: 126).

It is also the case that not all human beings have the social status of persons in their societies. For example, while both a fetus and a baby are biological entities, whether and at what point they are defined as "persons" vary across cultures. Among the northern Cheyenne, children are not participants in the moral community because they lack knowledge or responsibility for their actions and are therefore considered only "potential" persons (Fogelson 1982; A. S. Straus 1977). Among the Mande peoples of Africa, a newborn is not yet a member of the worldly family, remaining unnamed till eight days after birth. The shape of the placenta is examined to determine whether the newborn is in fact not a human person but a *saa* or spirit child (R. Whittemore, personal communication). For the Tallensi, "It is not until an infant is weaned and has a following sibling (*nyeer*) that it can be said to be on the road to full personhood," a status that is in fact "only attained by degrees over the whole course of life" (Fortes 1987:261). Lugbara refer only to a mature adult male as a person, specifically because he is localized in genealogical space and time and with respect to moral obligations and authority, while an infant is regarded as a thing (Middleton 1971:495). In Maharashtra, India, one does not become fully a person until after marriage, and a small child is regarded as not really a person at all. If one dies before the appearance of its first teeth, it is buried, not cremated, and death pollution is not observed (Carter 1982:129). Among the poorest of Brazil, children are often neither baptized nor named till they are toddlers, and the infant that dies is considered neither a human child nor yet a blessed angel. Instead, "The infant's humanness, its personhood, and its claims on the mother's attention and affections grow over time, slowly, tentatively, and anxiously" (Scheper-Hughes 1990:560). The current North American debate about abortion is in part about whether the person begins at conception, at birth, or some other time.

Adult notions about the components or constituent parts that make up a person vary markedly across cultures, with these constituent parts often referred to by ethnographers as various kinds of "souls." The Cherokee recognize four such souls; the death of a person is not complete until all four souls have departed the body, and it takes each a different period of time to depart (Fogelson 1982: 90). Integral to the Balinese self are four "spiritual siblings," each associated with a part of the body, a mantra, texts, temples, dances, and topographical features (Connor 1986:28). The Temiar of Malaysia have an animating head soul associated with language and expression; a heart soul that is the locus of thought, feeling, and awareness; a distinctive "odor" soul that is the composite of the person's labors in obtaining food; and a body soul or "shadow-form" (Roseman 1991:24–45). The Dogon have, in addition to their body, two gendered and intelligent body souls, two irrational body souls, four sexual souls, two souls located in the clavicles that symbolize nourishment, and a vital force or energy that circulates through the body along with the blood (Dieterlen 1971:

206). The Lugbara individual is composed of a body, a soul localized in the stomach or liver that endows its owner with social responsibility in lineage matters, an *adro* or element of spirit and divinity, a *tali* that gives an individual the power to influence others, breath, which is a sign of life that vanishes at death, and a shadow that is also thought to vanish at death (Middleton 1971: 493–94). Charismatic Christians in North America conceptualize the person as a composite of body, mind, and spirit (Csordas 1993), and Western scientific theories also frequently distinguish different aspects and dimensions of the self (James 1981; Mead 1934; Bailey 1983). It is likely that such multiple souls or components represent or objectify various aspects of connectedness to the social environment.

CONCLUSION

The notions of self and person constitute a rich field for research in psychological anthropology. I have attempted to demonstrate the importance of this field by organizing its literature into categories that serve to define it for anthropologists: entity, semiosis, orientation, emotion, psychodynamics, and social person. Given the inevitable oversimplification of any such scheme, it goes without saying that many of the sources cited had to be mentioned in more than one of these categories. Moreover, within and beyond these categories, we could become yet more specific, defining self and person in relation to topics such as agency, awareness, autonomy, adjustment, appetite, aspiration, actualization, or affliction. Some of these concerns are already more or less well addressed in the literature; others have not yet received adequate attention; still others might be dismissed as of little value for cross-cultural research. Perhaps the greatest challenge is to insist on cross-culturally valid definitions of the constructs of self and person in the face of the rhetorical pull of commonsense meanings that are powerfully motivated in the everyday discourse of our own culturally constituted behavioral environment. Yet there is little doubt that these issues remain critical to our understanding of culture and the meaning of being human.

REFERENCES

Bailey, F. G. 1983. *The Tactical Uses of Passion: An Essay of Power, Reason, and Reality*. Ithaca, NY: Cornell University Press.

Bharati, A. 1985. The Self in Hindu Thought and Action. Pp. 185–230 in A. Marsella, G. DeVos, and F. Hsu, eds., *Culture and Self: Asian and Western Perspectives*. London: Tavistock Publications.

Black, M. B. 1977a. Ojibwa Power Belief System. Pp. 141–51 in R. D. Fogelson and R. N. Adams, eds., *The Anthropology of Power*. New York: Academic Press.

———. 1977b. Ojibwa Taxonomy and Precept Ambiguity. *Ethos* 5:90–118.

Boas, F. 1988. The Limitations of the Comparative Method of Anthropology. Pp. 85–93 in P. Bohannan and M. Glazer, eds., *High Points in Anthropology*. 2nd ed. New York: Alfred A. Knopf.

Bock, P. K. 1988. The Importance of Erving Goffman to Psychological Anthropology. *Ethos* 16:3–20.

Bourguignon, E. 1965. The Self, the Behavioral Environment, and the Theory of Spirit Possession. In M. E. Spiro, ed., *Context and Meaning in Cultural Anthropology*. New York: Free Press.

Bruner, J. 1990. *Acts of Meaning*. Cambridge, MA: Harvard University Press.

Carrithers, M., S. Collins, and S. Lukes, eds. 1985. *The Category of the Person: Anthropology, Philosophy, History*. Cambridge, Eng.: Cambridge University Press.

Carter, A. T. 1982. Hierarchy and the Concept of the Person in Western India. Pp. 118–41 in A. Ostor, L. Fruzzetti, and S. Barnett, eds., *Concepts of Person: Kinship, Caste, and Marriage in India*. Cambridge, MA: Harvard University Press.

Chang, S. C. 1988. The Nature of the Self: A Transcultural View. *Transcultural Psychiatric Research Review* 25:169–203.

Comaroff, J. 1985. *Body of Power, Spirit of Resistance: The Culture and History of a South African People*. Chicago: University of Chicago Press.

Connor, L. 1986. Balinese Healing. Pp. 21–38 in L. Connor, P. Asch, and T. Asch, *Jero Tapakan: Balinese Healer*. Cambridge, Eng.: Cambridge University Press.

Crapanzano, V. 1980. *Tuhami: Portrait of a Moroccan*. Chicago: University of Chicago Press.

———. 1992. *Hermes' Dilemma and Hamlet's Desire: On the Epistemology of Interpretation*. Cambridge, MA: Harvard University Press.

Csordas, T. J. 1990. Embodiment as a Paradigm for Anthropology. *Ethos* 18:5–47.

———. 1993. *The Sacred Self: A Cultural Phenomenology of Charismatic Healing*. Berkeley: University of California Press.

Daniel, E. V. 1984. *Fluid Signs: Being a Person the Tamil Way*. Berkeley: University of California Press.

DeVos, G., and L. Romanucci-Ross. 1975. *Ethnic Identity: Cultural Continuities and Change*. Chicago: University of Chicago Press.

Dieterlen, G. 1971. L'Image du Corps et les Compsantes de la Personne chez les Dogon. In G. Dieterlen, ed., La Notion de Personne en Afrique Noir. Special issue of *Colloques Internationaux du C.N.R.S.* 544:205–29.

Dilthey, W. 1958. *Gesammelte Schriften*. Stuttgart: B. G. Teubner Verlagsgesellschaft; Goettingen: Vandenhoeck und Ruprecht.

Dominguez, V. 1989. *People as Subject, People as Object: Selfhood and Peoplehood in Contemporary Israel*. Madison: University of Wisconsin Press.

Dumont, L. 1970. *Homo Hierarchicus*. Trans. M. Sainsbury. Chicago: University of Chicago Press.

Ewing, K. P. 1987. Clinical Psychoanalysis as an Ethnographic Tool. *Ethos* 15:16–39.

———. 1990. The Illusion of Wholeness: Culture, Self, and the Experience of Inconsistency. *Ethos* 18:251–78.

Fogelson, R. D. 1982. Person, Self, and Identity: Some Anthropological Retrospects, Circumspects, and Prospects. Pp. 67–109 in B. Lee, ed., *Psychosocial Theories of the Self*. New York: Plenum Press.

Fortes, M. 1987. The Concept of the Person. Pp. 247–86 in M. Fortes, *Religion, Morality, and the Person: Essays on Tallensi Religion*. Cambridge, Eng.: Cambridge University Press.

Frank. G. 1979. Finding the Common Denominator: A Phenomenological Critique of Life History Method. *Ethos* 7:68–94.

———. 1986. On Embodiment: A Case Study of Congenital Limb Deficiency in American Culture. *Culture, Medicine, and Psychiatry* 10:189–219.

Gaines, A. 1982. Cultural Definitions, the Person, and Behavior in American Psychiatry. Pp. 167–92 in A. Marsella and G. White, eds., *Cultural Conceptions of Mental Health and Therapy*. Boston: Reidel.

Garro, L. 1992. Chronic Illness and the Construction of Narratives. Pp. 100–37 in M.-J. D. Good, P. Brodwin, B. J. Good, and A. Kleinman, eds., *Pain as Human Experience: An Anthropological Perspective*. Berkeley: University of California Press.

Gecas, V. 1982. The Self-Concept. *Annual Review of Sociology* 8:1–33.

Geertz, C. 1973. Person, Time, and Conduct in Bali. Pp. 360–411 in C. Geertz, *The Interpretation of Cultures*. New York: Basic Books.

———. 1983. "From the Native's Point of View": On the Nature of Anthropological Understanding. Pp. 55–70 in C. Geertz, *Local Knowledge*. New York: Basic Books.

Good, B. 1992. A Body in Pain: The Making of a World of Chronic Pain. Pp. 29–48 in M.-J. D. Good, P. Brodwin, B. J. Good, and A. Kleinman, eds., *Pain as Human Experience: An Anthropological Perspective*. Berkeley: University of California Press.

Hallowell, A. I. 1955. *The Self in Its Behavioral Environment*. In A. I. Hallowell, *Culture and Experience*. Philadelphia: University of Pennsylvania Press.

———. 1976 [1960]. Ojibwa Ontology, Behavior, and World View. Pp. 357–90 in A. I. Hallowell, *Contributions to Anthropology*. Chicago: University of Chicago Press.

Harris, G. G. 1989. Concepts of Individual, Self, and Person in Description and Analysis. *American Anthropologist* 91:599–612.

Hay, T. 1973. A Technique of Formalizing and Testing Models of Behavior: Two Models of Ojibwa Restraint. *American Anthropologist* 75:708–30.

———. 1977. The Development of Some Aspects of the Ojibwa Self and Its Behavioral Environment. *Ethos* 5:71–89.

Herdt, G. 1987. Transitional Objects in Sambia Initiation. *Ethos* 15:40–57.

———. 1990. Sambia Nosebleeding Rites and Male Proximity to Women. Pp. 366–400 in J. Stigler, R. Shweder, and G. Herdt, eds., *Cultural Psychology: Essays on Comparative Human Development*. Cambridge, Eng.: Cambridge University Press.

Hollan, D. 1992. Cross-Cultural Differences in the Self. *Journal of Anthropological Research* 48: 283–300.

Hymes, D. 1961. Linguistic Aspects of Cross-Cultural Personality Study. Pp. 313–59 in B. Kaplan, ed., *Studying Personality Cross-Culturally*. New York: Harper and Row.

Ito, K. 1987. Emotions, Proper Behavior (*Hana Pono*) and Hawaiian Concepts of Self, Person, and Individual. Pp. 45–71 in A. B. Robillard and A. J. Marsella, eds., *Contemporary Issues in Mental Health Research in the Pacific Islands*. Honolulu: Social Science Research Institute, University of Hawaii.

James, W. 1981. *The Principles of Psychology*. Cambridge, MA: Harvard University Press.

Jenkins, J. H. 1991. Expressed Emotion and Schizophrenia. *Ethos* 19:387–431.

Johnson, F. 1985. The Western Conception of Self. Pp. 91–138 in A. Marsella, G. DeVos, and F. Hsu, eds., *Culture and Self: Asian and Western Perspectives*. London: Tavistock Publications.

Kapferer, B. 1979. Mind, Self, and Other in Demonic Illness: The Negation and Reconstruction of Self. *American Ethnologist* 6:110–33.

———. 1983. *A Celebration of Demons: Exorcism and the Aesthetics of Healing in Sri Lanka*. Bloomington: Indiana University Press.

Kondo, D. 1990. *Crafting Selves: Power, Gender, and Discourses of Identity in a Japanese Workplace*. Chicago: University of Chicago Press.

Kracke, W. 1978. *Force and Persuasion: Leadership in an Amazonian Society*. Chicago: University of Chicago Press.

———. 1987. Encounter with Other Cultures: Psychological and Epistemological Aspects. *Ethos* 15:58–81.

Kracke, W., and G. Herdt, eds. 1987. Interpretation in Psychoanalytic Anthropology [special issue]. *Ethos* 15:3–143.

Leenhardt, M. 1979. *Do Kamo: Person and Myth in the Melanesian World*. Trans. B. M. Gulati. Chicago: University of Chicago Press.

LeVine, R. 1982. *Culture, Behavior, and Personality*. 2nd ed. Chicago: Aldine.

Levy, R. 1973. *Tahitians*. Chicago: University of Chicago Press.

Levy, R., and M. Rosaldo, eds. 1983. Self and Emotion [Special Issue]. *Ethos* 11.

Lienhardt, G. 1985. Self: Public, Private: Some African Representations. Pp. 141–55 in M. Carrithers, S. Collins, and S. Lukes, eds., *The Category of the Person: Anthropology, Philosophy, History*. Cambridge, Eng.: Cambridge University Press.

Lutz, C. A. 1988. *Unnatural Emotions: Everyday Sentiments on a Micronesian Atoll and Their Challenge to Western Theory*. Chicago: University of Chicago Press.

Lutz, C. A., and L. Abu-Lughod, eds. 1991. *Language and the Politics of Emotion*. Cambridge, Eng.: Cambridge University Press.

Lutz, C. A., and G. White. 1986. The Anthropology of Emotions. *Annual Review of Anthropology* 15:405–36.

Marcus, G., and M.M.J. Fischer. 1986. *Anthropology as Cultural Critique: An Experimental Moment in the Human Species*. Chicago: University of Chicago Press.

Markus, H., and S. Kitayama. 1991. Culture and the Self: Implications for Cognition, Emotion, and Motivation. *Psychological Review* 98:224–53.

Marriott, M. 1976a. Hindu Transactions: Diversity without Dualism. Pp. 109–42 in B. Kapferer, ed., *Transaction and Meaning: Directions in the Anthropology of Exchange and Symbolic Behavior*. Philadelphia: Institute for the Study of Human Issues.

———. 1976b. Interpreting Indian Society: A Monistic Alternative to Dumont's Dualism. *Journal of Asian Studies* 36:189–95.

Marsella, A. 1985. Culture, Self, and Mental Disorder. Pp. 281–307 in A. Marsella, G. DeVos, and F. Hsu, eds., *Culture and Self: Asian and Western Perspectives*. London: Tavistock Publications.

Mauss, M. 1985 [1938]. A Category of the Human Mind: The Notion of Person; the Notion of Self. Pp. 1–25 in M. Carrithers, S. Collins, and S. Lukes, eds., *The Category of the Person: Anthropology, Philosophy, History*. Cambridge, Eng.: Cambridge University Press.

McHugh, E. 1989. Concepts of the Person among the Gurungs of Nepal. *American Ethnologist* 16: 775–86.

Mead, G. H. 1934. *Mind, Self, and Society*. Ed. C. W. Morris. Chicago: University of Chicago Press.

Middleton, J. 1971. The Concept of the Person among the Lugbara. In G. Dieterlen, ed., *La notion de personne en Afrique noir. Colloques Internationaux du C.N.R.S.* no. 544:491–506.

Miller, P. J., R. Potts, H. Fung, L. Hoogstra, and J. Mintz. 1990. Narrative Practices and the Social Construction of Self in Childhood. *American Ethnologist* 17:292–311.

Mines, M. 1988. Conceptualizing the Person: Hierarchical Society and Individual Autonomy in India. *American Anthropologist* 90:568–79.

Murray, D. W. 1993. What Is the Western Concept of the Self? On Forgetting David Hume. *Ethos* 21:3–23.

Myers, F. R. 1986. *Pintupi Country, Pintupi Self: Sentiment, Place, and Politics among Western Desert Aborigines*. Washington, D.C.: Smithsonian Institution Press.

Nelson, K., ed. 1989. *Narratives from the Crib*. Cambridge, MA: Harvard University Press.

Obeyesekere, G. 1981. *Medusa's Hair: An Essay on Personal Symbols and Religious Experience*. Chicago: University of Chicago Press.

Ohnuki-Tierney, E. 1987. *The Monkey as Mirror: Symbolic Transformations in Japanese History and Ritual*. Princeton: Princeton University Press.

———. 1990. The Ambivalent Self of Contemporary Japanese Cultural Anthropology 5:197–216.

Paul, R. A. 1980. Symbolic Interpretation in Psychoanalysis and Anthropology. *Ethos* 8:286–94.

Polkinghorne, D. E. 1991. Narrative and Self-Concept. *Journal of Narrative and Life History* 1: 135–53.

Poole, F. 1987. Personal Experience and Cultural Representation in Children's "Personal Symbols" among Bimin-Kuskusmin. *Ethos* 15:104–35.

Postal, S. 1965. Body Image and Identity. *American Anthropologist* 67:455–62.

Radcliffe-Brown, A. R. 1922. *The Andaman Islanders*. Cambridge, Eng.: Cambridge University Press.

Ricoeur, P. 1991. Narrative Identity. *Philosophy Today* 35:73–81.

Robbins, R. H. 1974. Identity, Culture, and Behavior. Pp. 1199–1222 in J. J. Honigmann, ed., *Handbook of Social and Cultural Anthropology*. New York: Rand McNally.

Rorty, A., ed. 1976. *The Identities of Persons*. Berkeley: University of California Press.

Rosaldo, M. Z. 1980. *Knowledge and Passion: Ilongot Notions of Self and Social Life*. Cambridge, Eng.: Cambridge University Press.

———. 1984. Toward an Anthropology of Self and Feeling. Pp. 137–57 in R. Shweder and R. LeVine, eds., *Culture Theory: Essays on Mind, Self, and Emotion*. Cambridge, Eng.: Cambridge University Press.

Roseman, M. 1991. *Healing Sounds from the Malaysian Rainforest: Temiar Music and Medicine*. Berkeley: University of California Press.

Rosen, L. 1989. Responsibility and Compensatory Justice in Arab Culture and Law. Pp. 101–20 in B. Lee and G. Urban, eds., *Signs, Self, and Society*. Berlin: Mouton de Gruyter.

Rosenberger, N. R. 1989. Dialectic Balance in the Polar Model of the Self: The Japan Case. *Ethos* 17:88–113.

Said, E. 1978. *Orientalism*. New York: Random House.

Scheper-Hughes, N. 1990. Mother Love and Child Death in Northeast Brazil. Pp. 542–65 in J. Stigler, R. Shweder, and G. Herdt, eds., *Cultural Psychology: Essays on Comparative Human Development*. Cambridge, Eng.: Cambridge University Press.

Schieffelin, E. 1976. *The Sorrow of the Lonely and the Burning of the Dancers*. New York: St. Martin's Press.

———. 1983. Anger and Shame in the Tropical Forest: On Affect as a Cultural System in Papua New Guinea. *Ethos* 11:181–91.

Shore, B. 1982. *Sala-ilua*: A Samoan Mystery. New York: Columbia University Press.

Shweder, R., and E. J. Bourne. 1982. Does the Concept of the Person Vary Cross-Culturally? Pp. 97–137 in A. J. Marsella and G. M. White, eds., *Cultural Conceptions of Mental Health and Therapy*. Boston: Reidel.

Shweder, R., and M. A. Sullivan. 1990. The Semiotic Subject of Cultural Psychology. Pp. 399–416 in L. Pervin, ed., *Handbook of Personality: Theory and Research*. New York: Guilford Press.

Singer, M. 1984. *Man's Glassy Essence: Explorations in Semiotic Anthropology*. Bloomington: Indiana University Press.

———. 1989. Pronouns, Persons, and the Semiotic Self. In B. Lee and G. Urban, eds., *Signs, Self, and Society*. Berlin: Mouton de Gruyter.

Smith, J. 1981. Self and Experience in Maori Culture. Pp. 145–60 in P. Heelas and A. Lock, eds., *Indigenous Psychologies: The Anthropology of the Self*. London: Academic Press.

Smith, M. B. 1985. The Metaphorical Basis of Selfhood. Pp. 56–88 in A. Marsella, G. DeVos, and F. Hsu, eds., *Culture and Self: Asian and Western Perspectives*. London: Tavistock Publications.

Smith, T. 1989. Ojibwe Persons: Toward a Phenomenology of an American Indian Lifeworld. *Journal of Phenomenological Psychology* 20:130–44.

Spiro, M. E. 1982. *Buddhism and Society: A Great Tradition and Its Burmese Vicissitudes*. 2nd exp. ed. Berkeley: University of California Press.

———. 1993. Is the Western Concept of the Self "Peculiar" within the Context of the World Cultures? *Ethos* 21:107–53.

Stairs, A. 1992. Self-Image, World-Image: Speculations on Identity from Experiences with Inuit. *Ethos* 20:116–26.

Stigler, J. W., R. A. Shweder, and G. Herdt, eds. 1990. *Cultural Psychology: Essays on Comparative Human Development*. Cambridge, Eng.: Cambridge University Press.

Straus, A. S. 1977. Northern Cheyenne Ethnopsychology. *Ethos* 5:326–57.

Straus, T. 1989. The Self in Northern Cheyenne Language and Culture. Pp. 53–68 in B. Lee and G. Urban, eds., *Signs, Self, and Society*. Berlin: Mouton de Gruyter.

Stromberg, P. 1985. The Impression Point: Synthesis of Symbol and Self. *Ethos* 13:56–74.

Taylor, C. 1989. *Sources of the Self: The Making of the Modern Identity*. Cambridge, MA: Harvard University Press.

———. 1991. The Dialogical Self. Pp. 304–14 in D. R. Hiley, J. Bohman, and R. Shusterman, eds., *The Interpretive Turn: Philosophy, Science, Culture*. Ithaca, NY: Cornell University Press.

Triandis, H. C., R. Bontempo, M. Villareal, M. Asai, and N. Lucca. 1988. Individualism and Collectivism: Cross-Cultural Perspectives on Self-Ingroup Relations. *Journal of Personality and Social Psychology* 54:323–38.

Watson-Gegeo, K. A., and G. White, eds. 1990. *Disentangling: Conflict Discourse in Pacific Societies*. Stanford, Calif.: Stanford University Press.

White, G. 1991. *Identity through History: Living Stories in a Solomon Islands Society*. Cambridge, Eng.: Cambridge University Press.

White, G. M., and J. Kirkpatrick. 1985. *Person, Self, and Experience: Exploring Pacific Ethnopsychologies*. Berkeley: University of California Press.

Whiting, J.W.M. 1990. Adolescent Rituals and Identity Conflicts. Pp. 357–65 in J. Stigler, R. Shweder, and G. Herdt, eds., *Cultural Psychology: Essays on Comparative Human Development*. Cambridge, Eng.: Cambridge University Press.

Whittaker, E. 1992. The Birth of the Anthropological Self and Its Career. *Ethos* 20:191–219.

Wikan, U. 1987. Public Grace and Private Fears: Gaiety, Offense, and Sorcery in Northern Bali. *Ethos* 15:337–65.

Zaner, R. M. 1981. *The Content of Self: A Phenomenological Inquiry Using Medicine as a Clue*. Athens, OH: Ohio University Press.

CHAPTER NINETEEN

INITIATIONS

Simon Ottenberg

Unfortunately, there is little agreement as to what is meant by *initiation.* La Fontaine (1985) distinguished puberty rites for individuals from collective rituals, which she designated ''initiations''; other scholars are more inclusive (e.g., Schlegel and Barry 1979). Some scholars limit their concern to rites at the age of puberty. Initiations of adults into secret societies and other groupings, such as Freemasonry and Chinese secret societies, are not discussed here. These have rarely been considered in the context of adolescent rites, though La Fontaine (1985) placed them together. I shall examine four types of initiation studies: ethnographies of single cultures or subcultures; regional analyses; cross-cultural studies (usually based on ethnographic data from the Human Relations Area Files); and general syntheses that draw on a variety of sources.

The ethnographic studies have been largely gender linked, with men studying male initiations, women, female ones. More field studies of initiation have probably been done by males than females, so that we have a larger body of lengthy data on male rites. Field studies in depth have mainly been those where a number of boys or a number of girls are initiated at once. In these cases, initiation often has a double aspect of entree into a special society and into the larger social world of the community. Such rites seem particularly to attract the Western scholar by their dramatic, symbolic, and aesthetic aspects and by their ''exotic'' qualities, including aggressive and unusual behaviors toward the initiands. Initiations of individuals attract less scholarly attention and have been less fully reported.

Many explanations of the causes, functions, meanings, and effects of initiations have been suggested. Psychological and psychoanalytical theories compete with physiological, general maturational, social, symbolic, gender, and religious ones. No agreement is likely in the future. Most initiations, due to their symbolic, multifunctional nature, are capable of being interpreted by a number of different scholarly approaches. Theories can roughly be divided into intrapsychic ones that focus on the needs and the effects of the rites on the initiand and social studies that are concerned with societal needs and the effects of initiations on the community; partisanship of each view has sometimes been intense and dogmatic. Indeed, the psychology of those studying initiation is probably as important as that of those being studied.

With some notable exceptions, field studies have limited themselves to the initiation itself, that is, to the "novices" entering initiation and leaving with a certain experience and wisdom, rather than also paying attention to pre- and postinitiation experiences. But initiands come to initiation with a certain background and skills, and maturation does not end with initiation but continues (see the discussion of child development in the chapter by Barbara Rogoff and Gilda Morelli in part II). Initiation is only one aspect of development and may not even be the most crucial one. Field studies that link the pre- and postinitiation periods with initiation will throw a stronger light on these rites. Ottenberg (1989) indicated that in one Igbo group, Afikpo, boys enter initiation with well-developed skills in music, masquerading, performance, and organizational activity, and with some ritual ability. Certain aspects of the initiation replicate rites the boys have experienced earlier. Barry and Schlegel (1980) suggested that social solidarity and sex differentiation, which are often strongly emphasized in initiation ceremonies, are present and are important factors in early childhood socialization, while Granzberg (1972, 1973) correlated early socialization practices with the effects of initiation. Much less is known of the other participants, especially the feelings and reactions of parents and siblings.

Regional studies are few. The most outstanding have been overviews of south central Africa (Richards 1956:app. A), Africa in general (Riesman 1986:85–88), Western North America (Driver 1941), and Melanesia (Allen 1967; Herdt 1982a). They frequently lead to questions of diffusion and history (Loeb 1929: 286–87).

Cross-cultural studies of initiations have created and tested important hypotheses, psychological and social; but problems of sample size, accuracy of the initial data, and interpretation of particular results lessen the strength of the conclusions. The problem is compounded by the fact that initiations are generally multifunctional. The few general studies of initiation that exist do not employ cross-cultural statistical techniques. La Fontaine (1985), Reik (1962), and Lincoln (1981) focused on a particular argument or viewpoint, drawing examples from their own work and that of others.

CHARACTERISTICS OF ADOLESCENT INITIATIONS

How common are initiations? There are no good statistics. Schlegel and Barry defined an adolescent initiation ceremony as "some social recognition, in ceremonial form, of the transition from childhood into the next stage" (1979:199).

In their cross-cultural sample of over 180 societies, a considerable number of societies in the sample lacked any initiations at all. Thirty societies held initiations only for girls, 17 societies only for boys, and 46 for both sexes. Despite the prevalence of studies of male initiations, initiations are more common for females. Of the girls' initiations, 87 percent were for individual girls, while for boys, 47 percent were for individuals, 43 percent for large groups. Thus, despite a common image in anthropology, many boys' initiations do not take place in substantial groups.

There is a worldwide trend toward the decreasing importance of traditional initiation rituals—ending, shortening, or secularizing them. Also, children are initiated at a younger age, when they are less able to comprehend the nature of the experience, thus changing the impact of rites that formerly occurred at puberty. This trend directs students of initiation to rely on historical data and the older ethnographic literature or to attempt analyses comparing traditional rites and contemporary social movements, as in Gesch's (1985) study of a New Guinea cargo cult.

The multifunctionality of initiations makes analyses difficult, and functional interpretations are notoriously difficult of proof. Even a people's stated reasons for performance may be deceptive. Suggested functions include status change to adulthood, recognition of sexual maturity, incorporation into the larger society, creating a sense of ethnic identity and/or of social solidarity, a working through of Oedipal or of early childhood experience, preparing for adult gender roles and identifying with the proper gender, channeling assertive aggressive and sexual tendencies of the young into socially acceptable adult roles, maintaining gerontocratic control of the younger generation, inculcating the basic cultural values of the society into the maturing individuals, and teaching new skills and attitudes. There is much confusion in the literature between the causes of initiation and their effects. Brain (1977:198) attempted to list major causes and the effects of initiation separately for each gender and argued that "structural-functionalist explanations are satisfying to explain the effects of the rites; the causes of them are only to be sought in unconscious psychological processes of thought," an interesting viewpoint, which, however, seems to deny the existence of psychological effects.

One function of initiations rarely mentioned by scholars is that in many societies, the death rate for children is so high that initiation has a celebratory quality. The community rejoices at the likelihood that the initiates will live to adulthood and reproduce. Why this is so seldom discussed is not clear, except that those who study initiations may be primarily looking forward to the future and not to the past life of the individual.

Physiological changes at adolescence are extremely important since, while they are expected, they are not controllable. What can be controlled are the new behaviors that are their consequence. Many rites mark the change from children's aggressive and largely nonsexual competitions to sexual, political, and economic competition, as well as competition over mates and fertility. Particularly for males, initiations mark the movement out of a family-oriented situation into the larger society. This is true to a lesser extent for girls, where movement is from one family situation as a child to another as a wife. In many societies, girls are more likely than boys to marry soon after initiation; thus initiation has differing meanings for each gender on this score alone.

Initiations inevitably emphasize gender distinctions. Because menstruation, virginity, and clitoridectomy may be involved in female initiations, and circumcision in males, the rites tend to stress differing physiological and sexual processes for each gender. Attention is frequently also called to the physical body of the initiand through scarification, tattooing, chipping teeth, and cutting the hair or otherwise changing its style. Beatings or floggings, genital excision, and divestment of clothes or wearing special dress and body markings transform the initiand's body from a biological organism into a cultural being. Changes in dress and appearance after the rite so that the new initiates can be publicly recognized are not rare. These rites may alter the initiand's sense of his or her body.

Where a number of persons of one sex are initiated together, emotional and social bonding may occur that lasts for a lifetime and that involves social cooperation and respect. This bonding may act to subdue frictions among persons of the same sex and age at a later time. Yet strong peer groups may also exist before initiation, and these groups can encourage reluctant individuals to be initiated to keep up with their age mates.

Some initiations involve tests of strength, of verbal skill or silence, of personal skills, or of the ability to stand physical pain. The ability to react to these tests positively is seen as a sign of growing maturity, yet individuals seem nearly always to be initiated, no matter how poorly they react. The tests may be administered under the control of older persons by those initiated not long before, the testers giving with a certain glee and sense of their own power what they recently received. Alternatively, the tests may be administered by older persons symbolically representing parents or other adult kin. Morinis (1985:171) suggested that the pain inflicted in initiations heightens personal awareness, exaggerating the opposition between self and society in the initiands' minds and moving them toward the development of adult consciousness.

Secrecy may be involved in the initiation rites; people who have not been through the initiation are not supposed to know about certain aspects of the rites. Yet, as Pernet (1982) indicated, women often know men's secrets. The secrets may be apparently trivial (special words or terms; the sound of a flute or bull roarer), or they may represent a complex opening stage to the understanding of the philosophy and cosmology of the group. La Fontaine (1977:424) wrote that "what is significant is not *what* is secret but that there *are* secrets, the possession of which separates the initiates from others" (see also Bellman 1984). Yet secret objects may be invested with complex multiple meanings, like the flute and its music among the Sambia of New Guinea (Herdt 1981). Cultural secrets are a test of the ability of the individual knowing them to control himself or herself;

they are tests of maturity. Secrets give the holders a measure of social control over others who do not know them, but initiation may be only the first entry into a number of levels of secrecy. Psychologically, initiation secrets link the private and secret thoughts of children with adult social secrets, reaffirming that there are secret aspects to adult life (Ottenberg 1989).

Initiation rites are often associated with multiple aesthetic forms, some of which may be new to the initiands: instrumental music, singing, dancing, speech making, masquerading and special dress, and places specially prepared for the event. These forms may create strong emotional impressions and assist in stimulating a variety of conscious and unconscious thoughts and wishes. They help make pleasurable that which must be done in the society, and complement the tests for the initiands. These aesthetic objects are, as a rule, rich in symbolism and may stimulate unconscious material among the initiands and the other participants. While the initiation rites appear to be primarily for the initiands, they also affect the other participants and witnesses.

Initiation must be ego satisfying for the initiand and, for some, a bit frightening. This is likely the first time when so much special attention has been paid by so many persons to the boy or girl undergoing initiation.

The rites range from those with little or no involvement with religious and magical forces to deep entanglement in which the passage to adulthood associates the initiand with one or more of the major spiritual forces of the society, investing the person with spiritual qualities. The rites may also expose the initiand to the culture's core values and to those of his or her gender and social status. These values may not be explained directly to the individual. Many scholars feel that initiation is not primarily a learning situation, although some direct learning of cultural rules and values and guides to sexual behavior and to taboos may occur. Yet Precourt (1975), in a cross-cultural study of thirty-seven societies, found that there was substantial learning in the ritual and secular areas, but that these two forms of learning operated largely independently of one another.

THEORIES AND DATA

The starting points for initiation studies are the sociological theory of van Gennep and the psychoanalytic approach of Freud. Van Gennep (1960) distinguished between social and physical puberty and the rites associated with them (see also Gluckman 1962). He pointed out that some of what have been called puberty rites are really social rites, as they occur before or after physiological puberty. But van Gennep's main contribution has been the idea that any change of social status is marked by rites, and that these involve separation followed by a period of transition or marginality and then reincorporation into society. This tripartite scheme provides the basis of analysis of initiations by many scholars. It also links initiations to other rites, although all three elements do not always occur together. Precourt (1975:242–43) indicated that of societies he sampled with initiations, seventeen had some form of these three stages.

La Fontaine (1977:434) has criticized van Gennep's emphasis on the change of status in initiations, charging that "initiation rituals are concerned with the transfer and vindication of traditional knowledge and not primarily with the change of status in the individuals who pass through the knowledge" and that "the elders' claim to authority legitimized by their greater knowledge . . . also supports this position." Crapanzano (1981) pointed out that Moroccan boys' circumcision rites occur individually before puberty. He called this early circumcision a "rite of return," since the boy goes back to being a boy afterwards in everyday behavior. This is symbolized toward the end of the rite when, after circumcision, he is carried on his mother's bare back with his bleeding penis pressing against her. Clearly, then, the issue of circumcision and/or initiation before puberty and its relationship to adolescent maturation needs consideration. Are those initiated at an early age or even at adolescence really men and women, or still boys and girls? In fact, even if the rites occur at adolescence, the initiates are often in an ambiguous status for some years.[1]

Victor Turner (1962, 1964, 1967, 1969, 1974) developed detailed symbolic analyses of Ndembu initiations. Focusing on the second period of van Gennep's scheme, which he called the *liminal* period, Turner argued that this is a time of great cultural creativity. In the liminal state, many things and much behavior appear reversed or jumbled in contrast to the everyday order. The apparent change from the everyday social structure may be an illusion, since seniors are generally in charge of the initiations; but since it markedly differs from everyday structures, this "antistructure" reiterates the importance of the former.

In the liminal state, regardless of their status in everyday life, the bond of initiands to one another is very intense. Turner called this the *communitas*. The bonds "are anti-structural in the sense that they are undifferentiated, equalitarian, direct, extant, non-rational, existential, I-thou . . . relationships" (1974:274). Although phrased in social terms, this also refers to a psychological state different from most bonding in everyday life. Turner indicated that liminality, antistructure, and *communitas* are general phenomena occurring in a wide variety of situations in every society, from holidays to rituals to pilgrimages to political movements and natural disasters. There is a basic human need for relief from the tensions and boredom of the everyday social order, which we can translate as a deep human psychological need, and which frequently plays a central role in initiations.

Freud (1952:153 n. 1; 1967:156) saw circumcision as a symbolic substitute for castration: a subjection to and acceptance by the boy of the father's will. Knocking out of teeth and the cutting of hair are equivalent symbolic elements. Reik (1962) also drew on the idea of a worldwide Oedipus complex, using initiation data to argue that circumcision is a symbolic punishment by the father for the son's incestuous wishes toward his mother. The beatings and sufferings of the son in initiation, his symbolic death and rebirth, are punishment for his aggressive and murderous wishes toward his father. The rites are performed to prevent mother-son incest and the murder of the father.

The psychoanalyst/anthropologist Róheim drew more richly from ethnographic data than most early psychoanalytic interpreters. In one paper (1929), he argued that initiation rites involve death and rebirth, an idea that Eliade (1958) later took up in a different framework. According to Róheim, a hero dies, is reborn, and is identified with a musical instrument: the hero is a spirit, the instrument a phallus. Castration in males finds its equivalent in females: "An attack upon the genital organ [that] evokes similar unconscious attitudes in the female as the idea of castration does in the case of the male" (1929:189). Female head hair cutting at puberty is associated with coitus. In a later paper on childbirth and initiations, Róheim (1942) discussed anxiety at both events, employing van Gennep's tripartite scheme but overlaying it with psychoanalytic interpretations. Using his own Australian materials, he argued that initiations involve anxiety about separation from the mother as well as castration anxieties: circumcision is a symbolic separation from the mother. Food taboos during and after the rites symbolize oral separation from the mother as feeder. The boy acquires various objects during or at the end of the rites that symbolize his penis, including a bull roarer employed in love magic. Thus Róheim attempted to integrate ethnographic details of aboriginal initiations with classical Freudian theory.

In an oft-cited work based on his therapy with severely disturbed children, Bettelheim (1962) was critical of the Oedipal theory, arguing that "we must go back in childhood beyond the age of the Oedipal situation" (1962:19). For him the rites have less to do with castration anxieties than with the duality of the sexes. Wanting to shift emphasis from the id to a more positive ego-oriented psychology, he claimed that others have "overlooked the more hidden fascination with pregnancy and birth" (1962:22) to focus on castration. Initiation rites for males express boys' envy of the vagina and a desire to possess it while keeping their own organs. Male initiations rites are a pretense at birth, which is why they are kept secret. Bettelheim's ideas of male envy of female sexual organs and males' desire to bear children were partly drawn from Mead's (1949) comparisons of the sexes. Some of the children Bettelheim worked with developed spontaneous initiation rituals.[2]

In a pioneer cross-cultural study with a sample of fifty-five societies, Whiting, Kluckhohn, and Anthony (1958) tested some psychoanalytic ideas, assuming that "boys tend to be initiated at puberty in those societies in which they are personally hostile towards their fathers and dependent on their mothers" (1958: 361). The rites prevent open revolt against the father, break the strong mother attachment, and create a shared identity with adult males. The son's envy of the father may be weak or strong depending on relationships in the Oedipal triangle in various cultures. The authors suggested that if infant and mother share the same bed for at least a year with the exclusion of the father, with a postpartum sex taboo, severe initiation rites will occur. This correlation proved statistically significant for sleeping arrangements and postpartum taboo, and for both together.

Kitahara (1974), who tested Freud's theory of circumcision as symbolic castration with a sample of 111 societies, confirmed Whiting, Kluckhohn, and Anthony's approach with regard to the importance of sleeping arrangements. Kitahara found that if the father sleeps away or in the same house as the mother but in a different bed, the result is a weaker Oedipal situation. If the father sleeps in the same home as mother and son but the latter two do not sleep together, there is less likely to be circumcision than in the other cases.

Smith's (1970) little-known study is critical of the Whiting, Kluckhohn, and Anthony work for its vague functionalism, its confusion about causes, and its circularity. Using the same data, Smith found that the close mother-infant sleeping arrangements, the absent father, and a postpartum sex taboo all produce aggressive behavior on the father's part toward his offspring. These variables are associated with initiation rites for both sexes and the development of a warlike ethos in society.

John Whiting developed another position involving status envy. Burton and Whiting (1961) examined the statuses a person wishes he could occupy but from which he is barred. In societies where the child and mother engaged in a rather exclusive relationship, the mother was the envied one, and the initiation rites served "psychologically to brainwash the primary feminine identity and to establish firmly the secondary male identity" (1961:90). The authors did not consider integrating the two theories, that is, that status envy and the Oedipus complex are different aspects of the same phenomenon. Whiting (1964) also noted that genital mutilations at initiation occurred largely in Africa and the insular Pacific. The long postpartum sex taboo in these regions is influenced by protein deficiency, breast feeding being the healthiest solution. Thus he arrived at an ecological explanation for sociological arrangements that have psychological implications, providing a possible cause of initiations. (For a critical view of this approach, see Bock 1967.)

In a more recent study, Whiting and colleagues (Munroe, Munroe, and Whiting 1981) took yet another tack. Using a sample of sixty-four societies, they hypothesized that male initiations are associated with patrilocal residence and exclusive mother-infant sleeping arrangements. They argued that in male-dominated societies, the child first envies his mother as the one controlling resources and comes to realize that it is his father who has the power and resources. "The function of the rites . . . is to solve the intrapsychic conflict by supporting the secondary desire to be a man through excision of the prepuce—a symbol of the boys' infantile desire to be a woman" (1981:615).

The authors then related their study of the couvade by hypothesizing that "given close mother-infant contact which produces an initial feminine identity, this will tend to be ritually rejected by circumcision rites in societies with corporate patrilineages and tend to be ritually expressed by the practice of couvade when corporate patrilineages are absent" (1981:627). This was significant in a sample of ninety-six societies, only two of which had both practices, suggesting that in some way they act as alternatives to each other. The work points the way to more sophisticated cross-cultural studies by employing a larger sample than many earlier ones, dealing with multiple variables, and, as the authors stated, employing both sociogenic and psychogenic theory rather than one alone.

Stephens (1962) tested aspects of the Oedipus complex cross-culturally, arguing for the link of polygyny, long mother-infant intimate relationship, and the postpartum sex taboo. The latter sets up alternating periods of sex activity and continence for the mother. During times of continence, the mother is more sexually interested in her children and more sexually arousing to them (1962:192). Focusing on a boy's attraction for the mother, Stephens argued for a strong correlation between the postpartum sex taboo and a change of residence at adolescence (1962:78–79), but he did not follow this up by asking whether those societies that do this thus have no initiation or less severe ones than other societies. While he was concerned that the long postpartum sex taboo is linked to boys' sexual attraction to their mothers, he was not convinced that it leads to father-son rivalry, partly based on his analysis of folktale materials (1962: 158–59).

Norbeck, Walker, and Cohen (1962) drew more from an American cultural anthropological tradition skeptical of cross-cultural statistical procedures and of psychodynamic interpretations of cultural materials. They were particularly critical of Whiting, Kluckhohn, and Anthony's correlation of long mother-infant son ties and the absent father with initiation or avoidance at puberty, claiming that the study misinterpreted some ethnographic data, that there have been serious problems with definitions and interpretations in cross-cultural studies, and that the data used are often thin. They criticized the taking of cultural materials out of context, the selection of the ritual elements to be tested, the statistical techniques employed, and the authors' failure to distinguish between physical and social puberty rites. They clearly preferred explanations that require intensive examinations of individual cultures over the cross-cultural method (1962: 480).

Thus, Norbeck, Walker, and Cohen raised doubts that psychological interpretations of stress, anxiety, envy, and other emotional states can be inferred unless they are explicitly expressed in the cultures. This is an unresolved issue today, although more sophisticated attention now is being paid to the emotional context of cultural behavior (Briggs 1970; Howes 1991; Lutz 1988). Further, they raised questions about the relative value of detailed studies of initiation in specific cultures as against cross-cultural studies of these rites. The better the descriptions of the individual cases, the more accurate are the cross-cultural studies; but cross-cultural studies raise issues to be investigated in individual studies. The two approaches are complementary.

In a cross-cultural study involving initiation for both sexes, Yehudi Cohen (1964) attempted to link childhood maturation, incest taboos, and legal systems. He distinguished two stages of puberty, the first at the ages of eight to ten (the latency period), in which biochemical changes occur. This period is confusing to the child, who cannot understand what is happening to him physiologically. The second stage is less confusing, as the child can observe physical changes occurring to him. Cohen argued that "more societies will take formal and explicit steps in connection with the first stage of puberty than the second stage, and whatever steps are taken in connection with the first stage will be more drastic than those taken in connection with the second stage" (1964:50). The "drastic" steps of the first period are extrusion of the child from his living quarters, most importantly by making him sleep away from his original home, and the implementation of brother-sister incest taboos. The first stage of puberty extrusion is not a functional equivalent of initiation, for the latter is also likely to occur. Cohen also argued (1964:101) that "fewer societies would take formal, explicit and institutionalized steps" in the second stage than in the first and that what steps are taken "will be less drastic." He suggested that scholars have overemphasized the trauma of initiation, for he saw the second stage as shared, which cushions its shock and produces a strong bond among the initiands. Considering the suffering that occurs in some boys' initiations, Cohen's interpretation of what is drastic and what is not is interesting but perhaps faulty.

In another cross-cultural study of initiation for both sexes, Young (1965) was also critical of psychological interpretations, preferring sociological ones. He drew from Goffman's (1959) interactionist approach to regard initiation as a dramatization: "The communication strategy typically employed by solidarity groups in order to maintain their highly organized, but all the more vulnerable definition of the situation" (Young 1965:3). Employing a cumulative step scale of degree of dramatic recognition for each sex, he concluded that "male initiation rites are generally more elaborate or intense than those for females" (1965: 16). Young argued that the high level of dramatization in collective male rites creates strong male identity in boys and a high level of male solidarity. The "dramatizations of status change in a group are most elaborate when the solidarity of the group is great" (1965:41). For males, the size of the society providing the most dramatic rites is in the middle range, where there is limited role specialization; in more complex societies, role specialization is more important than initiation, while in small-scale societies there seems little need for dramatic rites (1965:30).

Some of Young's findings on the correlation between type of society and initiation are not inconsistent with the work of Schlegel and Barry (1980), who related adolescent initiations to the economy and social organization. One hypothesis that proved significant is that in societies at the simplest subsistence levels, girls' initiations predominate; in societies of the middle range, both sexes will have rites to about the same extent; while in complex societies, initiations tend to be absent. Precourt (1975:242) also suggested that public initiations tend to be associated with tribal (e.g., egalitarian) societies, while secret societies and their initiations are found in chiefdoms.

Granzberg (1972) used psychological tests on both initiated and uninitiated Hopi boys of the same school age two months before initiation, right after initiation, and two months later. The tests showed a significant decrease in aggressiveness and increase in dependency for the initiated boys, thereby confirming Whiting, Kluckhohn, and Anthony (1958). Granzberg also believed that his results supported Young's (1965) symbolic interactionist analysis since the changed behavior suggests an increase in social solidarity. Initiation reduced disruptive childhood behavior.

Granzberg (1973) then carried out a cross-cultural study of a sample of thirty-two societies that, like the Hopi, have preinitiation socialization patterns of indulgence followed by compliance training (according to Barry, Child, and Bacon 1963), presumably producing aggressive and impulsive behavior. Some 73 percent of the societies showed initiation rites with masking and/or disciplinary whipping. Only 24 percent without indulgence/compliance training had these rites. The study is of interest since it focuses on the *quality* of social interactions during socialization. A parent can have close contact with a child over a long period of time and yet be hostile to it, resentful of it, strict, or indulgent, so that length of mother-child contact or "father absence" may not be the crucial factor in regard to initiation.

In a survey of Melanesian societies from a social anthropological viewpoint, Allen (1967) explained the extensive variations in initiation rites in terms of social structure. He found that the greatest division of the sexes in Melanesia occurs where patrilineal descent, patri-virilocal residence, and exogamy occur and the descent group forms a local community. Thus males who are members of the same descent group are involved in the same initiations. Allen argued that almost the same extent of division of the sexes occurs in Melanesian matrilineal societies with matri-uxorial residence and exogamy. Thus he equated extreme gender division with certain combinations of descent, marital residence, and presence of exogamy. The more these features exist, the more likely it is that compulsory initiation will occur for all males.

Paige and Paige (1981) were also explicitly critical of all psychological theories of initiation. Examining the reproductive rituals of birth, puberty, and menstruation, they argued that in preindustrial societies, "the issue of kinship loyalties, particularly of loyalties of new or potential members of the society, may be subject to transfer, renegotiation, or dissolution" (1981:43). This is done through ritual because of difficulties (never fully explained) of doing so politically or legally. Initiation is a political form whose strength depends on the strength of consanguinal corporate kin groups, what the authors called "fraternal interest groups." Circumcision is viewed as a mechanism used by the strong fraternal interest group to reduce its potential fission. Menarcheal ceremonies are more likely to occur in societies where fraternal interest groups are weak or absent. These ideas tested positively with a sample of 108 societies.

REGIONAL STUDIES

A remarkable series of studies of male initiations has been done in New Guinea in the past forty years. Many of the earlier ones (K. Read 1952, 1965; Allen 1967; Berndt 1962; Langness 1967; Newman 1965; Shaw 1990; Strathern 1970; Tuzin 1976, 1980, 1982; Watson 1964) emphasized social and general anthropological concerns, such as male social solidarity, warrior status, and gender distinctions. (We have already discussed Allen's work.) However, there has been a shift in recent years to more intensive symbolic analyses, in which the work of Victor Turner has had some influence (Barth 1975; Schieffelin 1976), and again to studies that blend cultural symbolism with social and psychological analysis, often of a psychoanalytic kind (Herdt 1981, 1982a, 1982b, 1982c, 1984, 1987a, 1987b; Koch 1974; Poole 1981, 1982; R. Lidz and T. Lidz 1977; T. Lidz and R. Lidz 1989).

The interest in psychoanalytic interpretations of initiation rites, which seemed to decline after an initial period of cross-cultural testing and of considerable criticism, has revived in numerous field studies (see also Ottenberg's 1989 Nigerian study). In keeping with changes in the field of psychoanalysis itself, the newer psychogenic view places less emphasis on the Oedipus complex and more on the pre-Oedipal period (Stoller and Herdt 1982, 1985; R. Lidz and T. Lidz 1977). The complex and dramatic New Guinea male initiation rites cannot be fully explained by cultural and social analysis alone; much of the behavior associated with flutes, the forced nose and penis bleeding, and the homoerotic activities seem to call for psychodynamic interpretation.

In the Eastern Highlands, where many of the studies have been carried out, each gender is seen as being quite different in physical and psychological nature; there is a distancing of men from women, the latter being seen as dangerous (Keesing 1982:6–13; Strathern 1970; Allen 1967). Heterosexual relationships are often brief and restricted, viewed by men as potentially dangerous for them, and there is considerable gender antagonism. Emphasis on male warriorhood occurs, and men spend a good deal of time away from females in club houses. Male nose or penis bleeding in emulation of menstruation is not rare, and ritual homosexuality is found in the rites of some societies; homoerotic behavior may occur at other times (Herdt 1984). Male secret societies are common, with elaborate collective initiations that involve physical attacks on the initiands.

The flute plays important symbolic roles in these rites and in other secret-society activities. Male rites imitate female reproductive powers, and there is a covert theme of male envy of the female's natural reproductive abilities. Boys become men through ritual processes; girls turn into women through natural ones. The initiation of males involves secrecy from females, and initiation is often a gradual process of revelation over time (see Herdt 1981). Though recognizing that some of its features occur elsewhere, Keesing (1982:11) felt that the New Guinea initiation "pattern is a genus distinct from other initiation systems and male cults elsewhere in the tribal world.'' Female rites, often at menarche, are very much simpler and are performed individually.

The best-known psychogenic interpretation of New Guinea initiations, also richly employing cultural symbolism, is Herdt's work on the Sambia (1981, 1982a, 1982b, 1982c, 1984, 1987a, 1987b). The Sambia mother breast-feeds the child for several years, with postpartum sex taboos lasting for at least a year. Because of male fear of female pollution, the father generally stays away from his wife; thus the children have little contact with him but much interaction with the mother and with playmates. This creates a feminine identity in children of both sexes, which is consistent with a girl's identity. Though there is some activity at a girl's menarche, girls have no elaborate initiation and few serious problems in maturation. But for the boys there is the need for ''masculinization'' (Herdt 1984) to produce men who will be fierce warriors in the endemic local fighting that used to occur there. Mothers do not generally oppose this process by trying to hold their sons to themselves.

Among the Sambia, masculinization occurs in six stages, each lasting a short time. The first three collaborative rituals involve homosexual activities only. The last three are individual rites, the first two of which involve bisexual relationships for the males, and the third only heterosexual ones. The first stage is for males ages seven to ten, the second ages ten to thirteen, the third the years fourteen to sixteen, the fourth for older unmarried males, the fifth for men married but not yet cohabiting with the spouse, and the last at twenty to thirty years, when cohabitation occurs (Herdt 1981:55, table 4). Boys have an unrelated older male as initiation guide and from the first stage are frequently required to perform fellatio with the bachelors who have finished the third stage. Semen is equated by the Sambia with the mother's milk and breast. This action, which continues through the third stage, is believed necessary to produce warrior males out of effeminate boys and to remove the mother's influence. Males have no natural maleness and sexuality as females have a natural physiology; males must produce and maintain their gender identity through these oral sex acts. Thus, paradoxically, homoerotic behavior is employed to create masculine men who will be heterosexual in later life.

Herdt (1982c) discussed the complex symbolism of forced nose bleeding. R. Lidz and T. Lidz (1977), two psychiatrists who carried out clinical work in New Guinea, had suggested that men's practice of nose, tongue, and penis bleeding shows envy of women's natural capacities and is not a symbolic castration of boys by their fathers. The initiation rites do not counter the boy's incestuous wishes but allow men to relate to women sexually.

Herdt discussed the use of flutes and their music in the rites. Though kept secret from women, flutes represent a female spirit and are said to be erotically arousing, symbolizing the phallus, breast feeding, fellatio, and other matters. Herdt (1982b:83) felt, not only for the Sambia but for New Guinea, ''that pre-Oedipal development seems as basic and pervasive as the status-envy and post-Oedipal conflict factors postulated by Whiting and his colleagues.'' Herdt also used Winnicott's (1971) concept of the *transitional object* of infancy to interpret initiations. He suggested (1987a) that the flutes, the initiand's guide, and the first bachelor with whom the initiand performs fellatio are transitional objects, serving to move the boy from his mother's influence to the world of males.

The research in New Guinea shows that detailed studies of initiation from both a psychoanalytic and a cultural symbolic framework are possible, studies that avoid the rigidities of earlier psychoanalytic analyses and that move beyond the issues raised in the early cross-cultural studies. The changes are due to more intensive and sensitive field research and developments in psychoanalysis. Even those who are working in the New Guinea initiation field today who do not employ a psychoanalytic approach—and there are a goodly number—now focus not only on the initiand but on the total set of actors in the rites and the symbolism that applies to them as well.

FEMALE INITIATION RITES

An important feature of female initiation in contrast to rites for males is the menarche, a specifically timed indicator of potential fertility, as well as more general breast and genital development. Female rites may occur before, at, or not long after first menstruation and are often related to it, if rites occur at all. A male's first ejaculation or change of voice does not seem to be accorded the same interest by persons in the culture or by anthropologists (but see M. Read (1959:110–11). First menstruation often demands attention, as it and the blood are often subject to both rules and taboos that the girl and others must follow (La Fontaine 1972:164; Buckley and Gottlieb 1988). In a sixty-two-society cross-cultural study composed mostly of hunting, gathering, and fishing societies, Kitahara (1984) emphasized the menstrual aspect and female physiology in girls' puberty rites. Stephens (1962:chap. 5) suggested that elaborate menstrual taboos are partly caused by the intensity of castration anxiety in the population at large. Although he did not follow up this point, it suggests that female initiations may have to deal with this anxiety, particularly if clitoridectomy is performed.

Rites for girls frequently symbolize the fact that women bear children, and failure to bear offspring is often attributed to women. For example, Schlegel and Barry (1980:708) rated fertility as the primary focus of girls' rites. For boys the focus is responsibility, while fertility and sexuality are second. The reasons that female adolescent initiations are more common than those of males on a worldwide basis (Schlegel and Barry 1979) may relate precisely to the fertility issue: the concern that women have children, that their children do not die, and that mothers do not die in childbirth. In food-collecting societies where female fertility is not maximized, "women are highly valued both for their productive and procreative activities. In the cold language of economics, each reproductive woman becomes a scarce and valued resource" (Schlegel and Barry 1980:711). Perhaps this explains the emphasis on female rites in food-collecting societies.

Attitudes toward women may vary in agricultural communities, where females are not quite such a precious commodity.

Girls frequently marry shortly after their puberty rites, while the influence of the initiation is still upon them. In fact, in some societies, such as the Nyakyusa (Wilson 1957:86–127), one rite suffices for both events. But males often marry at an older age, when they are socially more mature and more distanced from the puberty rites, which by then are more emotionally resolved and settled within them.

A detailed study of female initiation rites is Richards's oft-cited social anthropological analysis of Bemba girls' rites in the then Northern Rhodesia (1956). After earlier individual ceremonies to mark the menarche, the initiation rite involves groups of girls, with some participation of fathers and the future husbands. The study emphasized social structures and roles and the meanings of social symbols and values in the *chisungu* ceremonies. Richards explained their relationships to agricultural and chieftaincy rites, but she was surprised by the fact that the rites do not seem to express the matrilineality found among the Bemba. While many studies limit themselves to initiation alone, Richards viewed initiation in a field of mostly adult rituals, making her study richer by this extension.

Each Bemba initiand has a surrogate mother who remains as the girl's advisor through her marriage and for years afterwards, though we are not informed whether the presence of this new figure markedly changes the relationship of the girl to her true mother. Of further interest is the presence of material objects—particularly pottery emblems produced by women at the initiation representing domestic items, animals or birds, or fertility symbols, or having historical reference—employed in teaching the girls, partly through songs associated with them. The use of such objects suggests Winnicott's (1971) transitional objects of infancy (see also Herdt 1987a), here being employed to facilitate a growing personal identity at adolescence.

Richards indicated that a Bemba girl has little understanding of what is done during her initiation, but in future years she may assist in other initiations and acquire more knowledge, and if she is interested, she may ask questions and gain greater insight. The initial initiation is largely experiential, and it is only at future rites that the cognitive level becomes significant. This suggests that since a series of such experiences leads to maturity rather than the first rite, anthropologists might pay more attention to this longer process for both males and females. Initiation is but one step in a succession of initiation rites adding to the maturity of the person.

Following Radcliffe-Brown (1922), Richards struggled with how a social anthropologist handles the emotional aspects of rites. She occasionally referred to the unconscious, but her analysis of emotions was largely confined to describing the observed emotional states of those in the rites and their social meanings. Richards's survey (1956:170–86) of similar girls' initiation ceremonies in largely matrilineal south central Africa suggests a link between descent and the rites.

Another useful early African social anthropological study is that of Wilson (1957:86–127) on the Nyakyusa of Malawi and Tanzania. The rite is individually done, with the girl in only partial seclusion for three months at the mother's home; her mother, age mates, and future husband are much involved. The event acts "to protect the physical and mental health of the girl and to ensure her fertility" (1957:103). Puberty and marriage ceremonies are united, the first flowing into the second. Father-daughter contact during the rite is forbidden until such time as he presents her a gift, suggesting (but not to Wilson) that there is an unconscious emotional link between the two at a time when the future husband can sleep with her and sexually play with but not penetrate her. From betrothal at the age of eight or so a similar taboo exists on her future husband's father, perhaps transferring unconscious wishes toward her father to him; but since he lives in a different community from the son, this is not a serious problem.[3]

This work excels in presenting Nyakyusa interpretations of the girls' rite and their symbolic references, but Wilson eschewed almost all interpretation. "Our business is to lay bare the symbolic pattern of the Nyakyusa tradition without reference to the Western tradition" (1957:7). An approach that presses the anthropologist to obtain the maximum interpretive material from those studied is desirable, and presenting the discussion without confusing emic and etic interpretations is a useful goal. However, I feel that Wilson's work cries out for psychological interpretation.

Gough (1955) analyzed girls' initiations in two Nayar and two Tiyyar castes in India. She stated that "it was not possible to explain sociologically why certain persons should take part in the rites, rather than other persons, why certain material objects should be used, and indeed, why it should be necessary to perform this ceremony at all" (1955:45). She opted for classical psychoanalytic explanations focusing on the unconscious motivations of caste members.

Held roughly every ten to twelve years, this four-day collective rite for girls of premenarche age, some quite young, involves the whole community, including the girl's lineage. Its central aspect is the tying of an ornament around the girl's neck with a white thread by a ritual bridegroom, often a prominent and sometimes a religious elder. The girl then spends three days in seclusion in symbolic marriage with the ritual bridegroom; here a ritual defloration occurs. This "bridegroom" is not likely to become her husband at a later date. The end of the rite symbolizes their "divorce." Before the rite, the girls are secluded for three days in an act that resembles what they go through at the menarche. Gough felt that the initiation symbolizes the value of having plenty of husbands in polyandrous and polygamous societies.

Gough's psychoanalytic interpretations drew on concepts of Ernest Jones, Melanie Klein, and Sigmund Freud. She viewed the rites as an expression of the girls' incestuous wishes for the male parent image and at the same time as expressing fear of incestuous sexual attack. She asked, "Why is it deemed necessary for a girl to 'menstruate' and be deflowered (both symbolically) before she has attained puberty and is likely to enter into real sexual relations? The first part of my hypothesis is that this rite issues out of the marked horror of incest in these castes, which makes it necessary for the natal kinsmen of a woman to renounce the rights to her mature sexuality before she is in fact mature" (1955:64).

Gough supported her views with the analysis of key ritual symbols, suggesting that the Oedipus complex is present in these largely matrilineal societies, with some transfer of incestuous wishes of females from the father to the mother's brother (1955:66–68). She also adduced a general male fear of deflowering women and argued that virgins are unconsciously associated with the mother as forbidden sexual objects.

Gough's interpretations have been attacked by Yalman. While he accepted her use of historical data, he accused her of abandoning social structural explanations and overlooking an important association between concepts of the purity of women and the purity of castes. Where marriage ties are diffuse and marriage alliances are not well worked out, as in this region, rites are "called for to render her caste position at least ritually secure" (Yalman 1963:46). Leach (1970), dissatisfied with both Gough and Yalman, said that they were operating on an intuitive level of symbolic analysis, giving meanings to single symbols alone, incorrectly attributing the same meaning to a symbolic throughout the culture. His analysis requires dealing with a system of symbols in binary opposition, using a structural approach in the style of Lévi-Strauss. He suggested how to do this but offered no full analysis. As in other initiation studies, the interpretation of these rites seems to depend upon the theoretical orientation of the researcher.

Among recent studies, Jean Comaroff's (1985:114–18) brief analysis of *bojale* females' initiation in the Tshidi Chiefdom of the Tswana in southern Africa is rich in interpretation, as is the larger section on the male rites. She clearly felt that the two rites should be seen together. "For just as male rites projected man as a skillful human being, the creator of a domain which transcended the female periphery, *bojale* complemented this with an image of woman as incompletely socialized, capable of producing value but not of transforming it into enduring social form" (1985:114). The collective ritual of already-menstruating girls, now largely defunct, occurred at the poor margins of town and involved placing the glowing end of an ignited stick in a cut in the girl's right thigh, the piercing of her hymen, and flogging, as well as learning various arts of womanhood for about a month in the absence of males. At one point, it involved all the town's females. This rite opened the girls to sexual access and marriage, with a taming of their sexuality, whereas the male rites encouraged greater assertiveness. This quieting aspect is likely to be widespread in female initiation rituals. Men at Afikpo in Nigeria and in Limba country in Sierra Leone expressed the idea that women's sexuality was erratic and had to be controlled (personal researches).

Yet Comaroff also felt that there were contrary elements in the Tswana girls' rites: ''Provocative song and dance, intrusive noise and explicit accusation'' expressed ''female resistance to established gender relations'' (1985:117). This underlying emotional resentment against perceived gender inferiority needs careful examination in other girls' initiation studies.

The social anthropologist La Fontaine (1972, 1977, 1985) stressed the importance of viewing female maturation in Bugisu on the Kenya-Uganda border in terms of three interrelated *rites de passage* (first menstruation; marriage; and birth of the first child) rather than through the analysis of the first rite alone. She showed (1972:177) how symbolic statements at each of these rites are repeated at one or both of the others. Thus she presented a broad, if nonpsychological, view of the setting of girls' rites of maturity.

In Bugisu the ritually pure girl becomes polluted upon her menarche. She must observe taboos and is secluded until her period ends, when she goes to greet kin in and out of her community and is fed a ceremonial meal by her mother's brother, who performs a sacrifice for her. According to La Fontaine (1972:165–67), this later rite is a recognition of the girl's mother's procreative power as well as that of the girl. She further linked this rite to marriage and first birth by employing a nature-culture dichotomy where the menarche is closest to nature. Defloration of the bride represents the domination of the cultural, symbolizing men's control over women and over their reproductive capacities (1972:179–82). Whether one agrees with this particular interpretation or not, coping with the maturation process clearly requires special attention in many societies. Still another detailed text describing individual girls' initiations among the Ashanti of Ghana (Sarpong 1977) is of interest, though lacking in conceptualization. Tests of endurance are absent; there is no incision and little formal instruction. The event in this matrilineal society lasts only six or seven days.

Frisbee (1967) described a four-day individual Navajo girl's puberty in considerable detail. Like Wilson (1957), she provided a great deal of information on what Navajo give as the reason for the rite and their conceptions of its meanings. She also placed the initiation in the context of other rites and myths. There was virtually no theoretical analysis, but Frisbee offered a detailed study of the music, the song texts, and the physical process of ''molding'' the girl during the rite.

A study by Farrar of Mescalero Apache girls' rites emphasized their functions in stressing cultural values. She wrote, ''The physical event of puberty forms a nucleus around which many attributes—believed to be essential for describing and defining what constitutes Mescalero Apache ethnicity—coalesce'' (1980: 146). Unfortunately, she did not further discuss ethnicity, though Mescalero Apache culture is today embedded in a multicultural situation, suggesting that an increasing function of initiations, for boys as well as girls, is to implant a strong sense of ethnic identity in the adolescent. Ethnic identity issues have not been totally absent in earlier studies, but today they seem more significant as intercultural communication has increased (Keesing 1982:16–17).

In her chapter on "Marriage, Maternity, and the Initiation of Girls" (1985: 162–80), La Fontaine rightly rejected an older idea in anthropology that female rites are imitative of male rites (Loeb 1929:250). She agreed with Comaroff (1985) that both rites should be considered together. La Fontaine distinguished between girls' puberty rites and initiation (1985:14). The former are largely family affairs, done individually for each girl in association with the menarche; the latter are larger social affairs, with collective initiation and more numerous participants, that incorporate the girls more fully into the whole society. Thus she suggested that the reason so little has been written on girls' initiations is that "such rites are relatively uncommon" because "organized groups of women are rarely found as the building blocks of social structure" (1985:162–63).

Like Brown (1963a), Schlegel and Barry (1980), in their cross-cultural studies, placed puberty rites and initiation together as initiations; they stated that in their sample "a slight majority have them for one sex only, with more than twice as many societies holding ceremonies for girls only as compared to ceremonies for boys only" (1980:698). Young (1965:19) also found that girls' initiations are generally done individually. The matter of definition is extremely important in cross-cultural studies. La Fontaine's conception of girls' initiations, if tested, would probably yield considerably different results than those of Brown or of Schlegel and Barry.

Brown defined girls' initiations as consisting of "one or more prescribed ceremonial events, mandatory for all girls of a given society and celebrated between their eighth and twentieth years. The rite may be a cultural elaboration of menarche, but it should not include betrothal or marriage customs" (1963b: 838). Using a cross-cultural sample of seventy-five societies, she tested the hypothesis that female initiation occurs in societies where a girl continues to reside at her mother's home after marriage. The results were statistically significant. Brown explained the ritual as necessary for the initiate and others around her to mark her status change, since she spends her life with the same persons. Conflict over sex identity, another issue for Brown (1963b:842–47), was seen as a consequence of close mother-daughter sleeping arrangements fostering close identity; since the girl moves as an adult into a strong male world, a painful initiation is desirable to mark her gender, indicated by a genital operation and tatooing. Her final hypothesis was that only when females have important roles in the subsistence economy will female initiation be practiced, to ensure that they fulfill their future role. It tested significantly positive.

Driver (1969) was critical of Brown's statistical methods and of what he considered to be the small size of her sample, as he was of all of the earlier cross-cultural approaches. He believed that she had no right to claim that matrilocality is the cause of girls' puberty rites, since the cause, in his calculation, only occurs in nineteen of forty-two of her cases. His attempts to reformulate her data to a significant level failed. (However, Schlegel and Barry [1980:703], using a different sample of fifty-six societies, later confirmed her findings).

Driver also doubted that a high level of female economic participation in a society can be a cause of puberty rites. To this Brown (1970) replied that she was writing of correlation and not cause, that her sample was the best she could attain at the time, and that Driver failed to address the question of why girls' rites exist in North America to a considerable extent but are not painful. Driver (1971) responded that judging by Brown's text, she was writing of causal relationships and that more current cross-cultural work recognized the need for larger samples. This is now generally recognized to be true.

Driver (1941) had earlier carried out distributional study of girls' initiations among Indians in Western North America, finding them to be widespread. Coming from an American historical anthropological tradition, he postulated, on the basis of cultural element distribution, that certain traits in the Indian girls' rites are historically older. This is one of the few initiation studies to present much historical depth, although other analyses indicate recent changes and declines in these rites.

Driver's work raises the question of the role of diffusion in initiation studies (see Bock 1967). Initiation rites for both sexes appear clustered in certain geographic areas, such as West Africa and Melanesia. Can diffusion rather than psychogenic factors account for their spread? Or is a model that incorporates both history and cause necessary. In the Limba Chiefdom of Bafodea in Sierra Leone, my own research shows that compulsory women's secret societies with accompanying girls' initiation and clitoridectomy spread from the south about one hundred years ago. Did the existing social and psychological conditions make people there "ready" for this change? If so, since the culture has been very slow-changing, why did the initiations not exist before? The issue is particularly important regarding psychological explanations of initiation, which seem to be at a distant pole from historical ones. Can they be reconciled?

In a cross-cultural sample of sixty-two societies, Kitahara (1984:133) disagreed with Brown's matrilocal residence hypothesis since girls' rites are much more widespread than matrilocal/ambilocal societies, and since they occur so frequently at the time of genital maturation. He preferred a physiological focus, pointing out that girls' rites are frequently individually done, without the participation of the larger community. "We may speculate that such rites are conducted in order to let the young girl realize the seriousness of her existence brought about by her genital maturation" (1984:135). Kitahara (1984:136–41) found that girls' puberty rites are more likely to occur in societies with extensive menstrual taboos; when these rites are present, they are more likely to occur at the point of puberty, done individually for each girl and by women alone. However, Buckley and Gottlieb's (1988) study of menstruation cautioned against too stereotyped a view of menstrual taboos, distinguishing menstrual taboos from rules. This critique probably applies to Kitahara's work.

Since a surprising fifty-eight out of sixty-two societies in Kitahara's sample were food collectors, Kitahara stated that in these societies, pregnancy affects women's work abilities, and that many children pose a problem to feed and to move. Thus attention to a woman's procreation capabilities is vital.

Lincoln (1981) suggested that since females do not move into the overt sociopolitical sphere of the community or larger political groupings to the degree that men do in many cultures, there is less reason for them to leave their residential area for initiation. Initiation space changes for him were symbolic, as they were for Van Gennep (1960). In most *rites de passage*, those changes occurring in initiation may foretell later ones in marriage (Lincoln 1981:100). Arguing that girls' initiation addresses ontological rather than social hierarchical concerns, he noted that for females an *additive* process of new clothes, jewelry, and scarification is found, while for men a *taking away* of clothing, hair, and other items occurs. How true this is on a worldwide basis is uncertain, but his suggestion that the difference is because females lack status to begin with in contrast to men is not convincing, since, in fact, they do not lack status. Yet his argument echoes Teilhet's (1983) study of Polynesian men and women's art, where men's work is produced by cutting away, as in carving, while women's is by building up, as in pottery. Lincoln pointed out (1981:94–96) that Navajo initiation involves beliefs in molding the girl's body. Carrying his ideas further, one could posit basic differences in human psychological processes by gender that influence the structure and symbolism of the rites. Lincoln considered Tiv girls' scarification to be an initiation ritual, while Laura Bohannan (1981:vi), who did research among the Tiv, wrote in the foreword to Lincoln's book that to the Tiv, it is not a ritual. Does one take a people's own conception of initiation into one's analysis or only that of the anthropologists. Presumably both.

In a work on girls' initiation from a Jungian analyst's viewpoint, Shorter (1987) argued that women in Western societies need some sort of ritual to express their womanhood. She examined five female patients who in the course of contact with her created their own initiationlike rites in impromptu ways, which had positive effects for them, "creating a new relationship between spirit and body" (1987:43). "If the individual urge is a natural one and the individual response is an archetypical impulse the initiand feels a powerful nonpersonal pull toward enactment but, at the same time there are innumerable ways of imagining the response" (1987:43–44). This suggests a strong personal need, even in Western society, for female initiation, which echoes Bettelheim's study (1962) *Symbolic Wounds*.

Another Jungian work, a collection of papers on initiation for both sexes (Mahdi, Foster, and Little 1987) contains a chapter by Hine (1987:304–26) suggesting that in Western society, initiationlike rites are desirable not only at adolescence but at various times in life for persons outside of the therapeutic situation. Some of his cases were of informal rites in which parents and other adults take an initiative, suggesting that they feel a need for some rite for their children. Both this and Shorter's work suggest that it would be profitable to look at non-Western societies where there appear to be no adolescent rites for either one or both genders and to see whether similar processes are at work or not (see the chapter by Charles Grob and Marlene Dobkin de Rios in this volume). Hall (1987), a Jungian analyst writing in the same collection, suggested that neuroses may be attempts to avoid initiation into the next higher stage of life. Cases of regression to childhood in Western society are common enough. The question is whether compulsory initiation in non-Western societies helps prevent regression or merely masks it. And what is the situation in societies that lack overt adolescent rites?

CONCLUSIONS

It is increasingly evident that historical, psychological, social, and symbolic interpretations of initiations can exist side by side. While specific scholars may prefer one or two over the others, it is difficult to omit the others and still develop a thorough analysis, whether in a single study in the field or in cross-cultural work. Problems for the future involve how they can be integrated to resolve particular issues, rather than thus standing side by side. More data on and interpretation of individually performed male initiations are needed. The focus of research with a theoretical bent has been almost entirely on the often more dramatic collective initiations. Analyses that integrate male and female initiations within a single culture, where they occur, would enrich our understanding of the rites in particular cultures. Few of these exist today.

Field studies that look at female initiations from a psychogenic viewpoint are also lacking. Scholars seem to believe that because of mother-infant bonding, male gender identity—whether phrased in sex envy, pre-Oedipal, or Oedipal terms—is the crucial issue. It is assumed that female adolescent maturation is generally smooth. Yet this may be an illusion, for the girl's emotional ties to her mother, and in different ways toward her father, still must be broken. Many girls go to marriage shortly after initiation, often in strange quarters, while they are not yet emotionally mature. How do their initiation rites meet these challenges?

Greater emphasis might be placed on linking general theories of aggression in society to initiations. Such theories have been neglected in initiation studies compared to theories of sexuality. In specific cultures, for example, questions about the place of aggressive acts in initiatory events (and outside of the ritual situation) might be studied in psychological, sociological, or cultural terms, or all three.

Cross-cultural studies of possible equivalents to initiation rites would be helpful. Some individual studies suggest that change of residence (Whiting, Kluckhohn, and Anthony 1958; Wilson 1957; Stephens 1962) or the couvade (Munroe, Munroe, and Whiting 1981) may be such a factor. A search for quite informal mechanisms of initiation in societies that lack formal rites might be profitable. The retesting of some of the earlier cross-cultural studies with larger samples, distinguishing between puberty rites and social initiations, would be helpful.

Greater clarity regarding cause, function, effect, and meaning in initiation rites is desirable, for these concepts are sometimes confused or merged. The concept of function particularly needs consideration, since it has largely been abandoned in other areas of anthropology in recent years, yet it is employed quite freely in initition studies.

A better understanding of the psychological role of aesthetic forms in initiation, of the effects of masking and of the dramatization of the rites, would be of value. Scholars who work on the aesthetic forms are rarely concerned with initiation theories, nor do they frame their analyses in ways that would make an integration possible; and those who study initiations are rarely concerned with the analysis of aesthetic components, though they may describe them.

A greater understanding of the skills and experiences that initiands bring to the initiations, and of their lives a few years after the rites when the initiated individuals are not yet fully mature, would allow the scholar to see initiations more from the initiand's perspective and to investigate the gradual working (or nonworking) of the initiations on the individuals. Finally, more sensitive readings of the meanings of initiations and the feelings about them on the part of participants other than the initiands would broaden our understanding of the rites. A search for ethnopsychological explanations of the rites beyond the more obviously expressed ones would also be enlightening.

NOTES

1. Durkheim (1965 [1912]:36–63, 414–33), who wrote about the same time as Van Gennep, seemed unaware of his ideas and argued that initiation involved the transition from the profane world to the sacred. Durkheim basically saw these rites as maintaining the status quo.

2. The early psychoanalytic works on initiations, particularly those by Freud (1952) and Nunberg (1949), suffer from old-fashioned ideas equating preliterates with Western children and the mentally disturbed.

3. Wilson stated (1957:90) that "there is no circumcision or initiation of men other than the coming out ceremony, when a whole generation of men takes over responsibility for the administration and defence of their kingdom." But since men live in age villages, fathers, sons, and grandsons in separate communities within an agnatic and chiefdom structure, physical separation may serve as a functional equivalent to initiation.

REFERENCES

Allen, M. R. 1967. *Male Cults and Secret Initiations in Melanesia.* London: Cambridge University Press.

Barry, H., III, I. L. Child, and M. K. Bacon. 1963. Relation of Child Training to Subsistence Economy. *American Anthropologist* 61:169–99.

Barry, H., III, and A. Schlegel. 1980. Early Childhood Precursors of Adolescent Initiation Ceremonies. *Ethos* 8:132–45.

Barth, F. 1975. *Ritual and Knowledge among the Baktaman of New Guinea.* Oslo: Universitetsforlaget; New Haven: Yale University Press.

Bellman, B. L. 1984. *The Language of Secrecy: Symbols and Metaphors in Poro Ritual.* New Brunswick, NJ: Rutgers University Press.

Berndt, R. M. 1962. *Excess and Restraint: Social Control among a New Guinea Mountain People.* Chicago: University of Chicago Press.

Bettelheim, B. 1962. *Symbolic Wounds: Puberty Rites and the Envious Male.* New, rev. ed. New York: Collier.

Bock, P. K. 1967. Love Magic, Menstrual Taboos, and the Facts of Geography. *American Anthropologist* 69:213–17.

Bohannan, L. 1981. Foreword. Pp. v–vii in Bruce Lincoln, *Emerging from the Chrysalis: Studies in Rituals of Women's Initiation.* Cambridge, MA: Harvard University Press.

Brain, J. L. 1977. Sex, Incest, and Death: Initiation Rites Reconsidered. *Current Anthropology* 18: 191–208.

Briggs, J. L. 1970. *Never in Anger: Portrait of an Eskimo Family.* Cambridge, MA: Harvard University Press.

Brown, J. K. 1963a. Adolescent Initiation Rites among Preliterate Peoples. Pp. 75–85 in Robert E. Grinder, ed., *Studies in Adolescence.* New York: Macmillan.

———. 1963b. A Cross-Cultural Study of Female Initiation Rites. *American Anthropologist* 65: 837–53.

———. 1970. Girls' Puberty Rites: A Reply to Driver. *American Anthropologist* 72:1450–51.

Buckley, T., and A. Gottlieb, eds. 1988. *Blood Magic: The Anthropology of Menstruation.* Berkeley: University of California Press.

Burton, R. V., and J.W.M. Whiting. 1961. The Absent Father and Cross-Sex Identity. *Merrill-Palmer Quarterly of Behavior and Development* 7(2):85–95.

Cohen, Y. A. 1964. *The Transition from Childhood to Adolescence.* Chicago: Aldine.

Comaroff, J. 1985. *Body of Power, Spirit of Resistance: The Culture and History of a South African People.* Chicago: University of Chicago Press.

Crapanzano, V. 1981. Rites of Return: Circumcision in Morocco. *Psychoanalytic Study of Society,* 9:15–36.

Driver, H. E. 1941. Culture Element Distribution XVI. Girl's Puberty Rites in Western North America. *University of California Anthropological Records* 6:2.

———. 1969. Girl's Puberty Rites and Matrilocal Residence. *American Anthropologist* 71:905–8.

———. 1971. Brown and Driver on Girl's Puberty Rites Again. *American Anthropologist* 73:1261–62.

Durkheim, E. 1964 [1915]. *The Elementary Forms of the Religious Life.* New York: Free Press.

Eliade, M. 1958. *Rites and Symbols of Initiation: Mysteries of Birth and Rebirth.* New York: Harper and Row.

Farrer, C. R. 1980. Singing for Life: The Mescalero Apache Girls' Puberty Ceremony. Pp. 125–54 in C. Frisbie, ed., *Southwestern Indian Ritual Drama.* Albuquerque: University of New Mexico Press.

Freud, S. 1952. *Totem and Taboo: Some Points of Agreement between the Mental Lives of Savages and Neurotics.* New York: Norton.

———. 1967. *Moses and Monotheism.* New York: Vintage Books.

Frisbee, C. J. 1967. *Kinaaldá: A Study of the Navajo Girls' Puberty Ceremony.* Middletown, CT: Wesleyan University Press.

Gesch, P. F. 1985. *Initiative and Initiation: A Cargo Cult–Type Movement in the Sepik against Its Background in Traditional Village Religion.* Studia Instituti Anthropos 33. St. Augustin, West Germany: Anthropos-Institut.

Gluckman, M., ed. 1962. *Essays on the Ritual of Social Relations.* Manchester: Manchester University Press.

Goffman, E. 1959. *The Presentation of Self in Everyday Life.* Garden City, NY: Doubleday.

Gough, E. K. 1955. Female Initiation Rites on the Malabar Coast. *Journal of the Royal Anthropological Institute* 85:45–80.

Granzberg, G. 1972. Hope Initiation Rites—A Case Study of the Freudian Theory of Culture. *Journal of Social Psychology* 87:189–95.

———. 1973. The Psychological Integration of Culture: A Cross-Cultural Study of Hopi Type Initiation Rites. *Journal of Social Psychology* 90:3–7.

Hall, J. A. 1987. Personal Transformation: The Inner Image of Initiation. Pp. 326–37 in L. C Mahdi, S. Foster, and M. Little, eds., *Betwixt and Between: Patterns of Masculine and Feminine Initiation*. La Salle, IL: Open Court.

Herdt, G. H. 1981. *Guardians of the Flutes: Idioms of Masculinity*. New York: McGraw-Hill.

———, ed. 1982a. *Rituals of Manhood: Male Initiation in Papua New Guinea*. Berkeley: University of California Press.

———. 1982b. Fetish and Fantasy in Sambia Religion. Pp. 44–98 in G. H. Herdt, ed., *Rituals of Manhood: Male Initiation in Papua New Guinea*. Berkeley: University of California Press.

———. 1982c. Sambia Nose-Bleeding Rites and Proximity to Women. *Ethos* 10:190–231.

———, ed. 1984. *Ritualized Homosexuality in Melanesia*. Berkeley: University of California Press.

———. 1987a. Transitional Objects in Sambia Initiation. *Ethos* 15:40–57.

———. 1987b. *The Sambia: Ritual and Gender in New Guinea*. New York: Holt, Rinehart and Winston.

Hine, V. 1987. Self-Generated Ceremonies of Passage. Pp. 304–26 in L. Mahdi, S. Foster, and M. Little, eds., *Betwixt and Between: Patterns of Masculine and Feminine Initiation*. La Salle, IL: Open Court.

Howes, D., ed. 1991. *The Varieties of Sensory Experience: A Sourcebook in the Anthropology of the Senses*. Toronto: University of Toronto Press.

Keesing, R. M. 1982. Introduction. Pp. 1–43 in G. H. Herdt, ed., *Rituals of Manhood: Male Initiation in Papua New Guinea*. Berkeley: University of California Press.

Kitahara, M. 1974. Living Quarter Arrangements in Polygyny and Circumcision and Segregation of Males at Puberty. *Ethnology* 13:401–13.

———. 1976. A Cross-Cultural Test of the Freudian Theory of Circumcision. *International Journal of Psychoanalytic Psychotherapy* 5:535–46.

———. 1984. Female Physiology and Female Puberty Rites. *Ethos* 12:132–50.

Koch, K.-F. 1974. Sociogenic and Psychogenic Models in Anthropology: The Functions of Jale Initiation. *Man* 9:397–422.

La Fontaine, J. 1972. Ritualization of Woman's Life-Crises in Bugisu. Pp. 159–86 in J. La Fontaine, ed., *The Interpretation of Ritual: Essays in Honour of A. I. Richards*. London: Tavistock Publications.

———. 1977. The Power of Rights. *Man* 12:3–4,421–37.

———. 1985. *Initiation*. New York: Viking Penguin.

Langness, L. L. 1967. Sexual Antagonism in the Bena Bena Highlands. *Oceania* 37:161–77.

Leach, E. 1970. A Critique of Yalman's Interpretation of Sinhalese Girl's Puberty Ceremonial. Pp. 819–28, vol. 2, in J. Pouillon and P. Maranda, *Échanges et Communications: Mélanges offerts à Claude Lévi- Strauss à l'occasion de son 60ème anniversaire*. The Hague: Mouton.

Lidz, R. W., and T. Lidz. 1977. Male Menstruation: A Ritual Alternative to the Oedipal Transition. *International Journal of Psychoanalysis* 58:17–31.

Lidz, T., and R. W. Lidz. 1989. *Oedipus in the Stone Age: A Psychoanalytic Study of Masculinization in Papua New Guinea*. Madison, CT: International Universities Press.

Lincoln, B. 1981. *Emerging from the Chrysalis: Studies in Rituals of Women's Initiation*. Cambridge, MA: Harvard University Press.

Loeb, E. M. 1929. Tribal Initiations and Secret Societies. *University of California Publications in American Archaeology and Ethnology* 25:249–88.

Lutz, C. A. 1988. *Unnatural Emotions: Everyday Sentiments on a Micronesian Atoll and Their Challenge to Western Theory*. Chicago: University of Chicago Press.

Mahdi, L. C., S. Foster, and M. Little, eds. 1987. *Betwixt and Between: Patterns of Masculine and Feminine Initiation*. La Salle, IL: Open Court.

Mead, M. 1949. *Male and Female: A Study of the Sexes in a Changing World.* New York: Morrow.

Morinis, A. 1985. The Ritual Experience: Pain and the Transformation of Consciousness in Ordeals of Initiation. *Ethos* 13:150–74.

Munroe, R. L., R. H. Munroe, and J.W.H. Whiting. 1981. Male Sex-Role Resolutions. Pp. 611–32 in R. H. Munroe, R. L. Munroe, and B. B. Whiting, eds., *Handbook of Cross-Cultural Human Development.* New York: Garland.

Newman, P. L. 1965. *Knowing the Gururumba.* New York: Holt, Rinehart, and Winston.

Norbeck, E., D. E. Walker, and M. Cohen. 1962. The Interpretation of Data: Puberty Rites. *American Anthropologist* 64(3) 1:463–85.

Nunberg, H. 1949. *Problems of Bisexuality as Reflected in Circumcision.* London: Imago.

Ottenberg, S. 1989. *Boyhood Rituals in an African Society: An Interpretation.* Seattle: University of Washington Press.

Paige, K. E., and J. M. Paige. 1981. *The Politics of Reproductive Ritual.* Berkeley: University of California Press.

Pernet, H. 1982. Masks and Women: Toward a Reappraisal. *History of Religions* 22:45–59.

Poole, F.J.P. 1981. Transforming "Natural" Woman: Female Ritual Leaders and Gender Ideology among Bimin-Kuskusmin. Pp. 116–65 in S. B. Ortner and H. Whitehead, eds., *Sexual Meanings: The Cultural Construction of Gender and Sexuality.* Cambridge, Eng.: Cambridge University Press.

———. 1982. The Ritual Forging of Identity: Aspects of Person and Self in Bimin-Kuskusmin Male Initiation. Pp. 100–54 in G. H. Herdt, ed., *Rituals of Manhood: Male Initiations in New Guinea.* Berkeley: University of California Press.

Precourt, W. E. 1975. Initiation Ceremonies and Secret Societies as Educational Institutions. Pp. 231–50 in R. W. Brislin, S. Bochner, and W. J. Lonner, *Cross-Cultural Perspectives on Learning.* New York: Wiley.

Radcliffe-Brown, A. R. 1922. *The Andaman Islanders.* Cambridge, Eng.: Cambridge University Press.

Read, K. E. 1952. The Nama Cult of the Central Highlands of New Guinea. *Oceania* 23:1–25.

———. 1965. *The High Valley.* London: Allen and Unwin.

Read, M. 1959. *Children of Their Fathers: Growing Up among the Ngoni of Nyasaland.* London: Methuen.

Reik, T. 1962. The Puberty Rites of Savages: Some Parallels between the Mental Life of Savages and of Neurotics. Pp. 91–166 in T. Reik, *Ritual: Four Psychoanalytic Studies.* New York: Grove Press.

Richards, A. I. 1956. *Chisungu: A Girls' Initiation Ceremony among the Bemba of Northern Rhodesia.* London: Faber and Faber.

Riesman, P. 1986. The Person and the Life Cycle in African Social Life and Thought. *African Studies Review* 29(2):71–138.

Róheim, G. 1929. Dying Gods and Puberty Ceremonies. *Journal of the Royal Anthropological Institute* 59:181–97.

———. 1942. Transition Rites. *Psychoanalytic Quarterly* 11:336–74.

Sarpong, P. 1977. *Girls' Nubility Rites in Ashanti.* Tema: Ghana Publishing Corporation.

Schieffelin, E. L. 1976. *The Sorrow of the Lonely and the Burning of the Dancers.* New York: St. Martin's Press.

Schlegel, A., and H. Barry III. 1979. Adolescent Initiation Ceremonies: A Cross-Cultural Code. *Ethnology* 18:199–210.

———. 1980. The Evolutionary Significance of Adolescent Initiation Ceremonies. *American Ethnologist* 7:696–715.

———. 1991. *Adolescence: An Anthropological Inquiry.* New York: Free Press.

Shaw, R. D. 1990. *Kandila: Samo Ceremonialism and Interpersonal Relationships.* Ann Arbor: University of Michigan Press.

Shorter, B. 1987. *An Image Darkly Forming: Women and Initiation.* London: Routledge and Kegan Paul.

Smith, S. M. 1970. Initiation Ceremonies: A Test of an Alternative Hypothesis—A Cross-Cultural Study. M.A. thesis, University of Washington.

Stephens, W. N. 1962. *The Oedipus Complex: Cross-Cultural Evidence.* Glencoe, IL: Free Press.

Stoller, R. J., and G. H. Herdt. 1982. The Development of Masculinity: A Cross-Cultural Contribution. *Journal of the American Psychoanalytic Association* 30:29–59.

———. 1985. Theories of Origins of Male Homosexuality: A Cross-Cultural Look. *Archives of General Psychiatry* 42:399–405.

Strathern, A. J. 1970. Male Initiation in the New Guinea Highlands. *Ethnology* 9:373–79.

Turner, V. W. 1962. Three Symbols of Passage in Ndembu Circumcision Ritual: An Interpretation. Pp. 124–73 in M. Gluckman, ed., *Essays on the Ritual of Social Relations.* Manchester: Manchester University Press.

———. 1964. Symbols in Ndembu Ritual. Pp. 20–52 in M. Gluckman, ed., *Closed Systems and Open Minds: The Limits of Naivety in Social Anthropology.* Edinburgh: Oliver and Boyd.

———. 1967. *The Forest of Symbols: Aspects of Ndembu Ritual.* Ithaca, NY: Cornell University Press.

———. 1969. *The Ritual Process: Structure and Anti-Structure.* Chicago: Aldine.

———. 1974. *Dramas, Fields, and Metaphors: Symbolic Action in Human Society.* Ithaca, NY: Cornell University Press.

Tuzin, D. F. 1976. *The Ilahita Arapesh: Dimensions of Unity.* Berkeley: University of California Press.

———. 1980. *The Voice of the Tambaran: Truth and Illusion in Ilahita Arapesh Religion.* Berkeley: University of California Press.

———. 1982. Ritual Violence among the Ilahita Arapesh: The Dynamics of Moral and Religious Uncertainty. Pp. 321–55 in G. H. Herdt, ed., *Rituals of Manhood: Male Initiation in Papua New Guinea.* Berkeley: University of California Press.

Van Gennep, A. 1960 [1909]. *The Rites of Passage.* Chicago: University of Chicago Press.

Watson, J. B., ed. 1964. New Guinea: The Central Highlands. *American Anthropologist* 66:pt. 2.

Whiting, J.W.M. 1964. Effects of Climate on Certain Cultural Practices. Pp. 511–44 in W. H. Goodenough, *Explorations in Cultural Anthropology: Essays in Honor of George Peter Murdock.* New York: McGraw-Hill.

Whiting, J.W.M., R. Kluckhohn, and A. Anthony. 1958. The Function of Male Initiation Ceremonies at Puberty. Pp. 359–70 in E. E. Maccoby, T. Newcomb, and E. Hartley, eds., *Readings in Social Psychology.* 3rd ed. New York: Holt.

Wilson, M. 1957. *Rituals of Kinship among the Nyakyusa.* London: Oxford University Press for the International African Institute.

Winnicott, D. W. 1971. *Playing and Reality.* London: Tavistock Publications.

Yalman, N. 1963. On the Purity of Women in the Castes of Ceylon and Malabar. *Journal of the Royal Anthropological Institute* 93:25–58.

Young, F. W. 1965. *Initiation Ceremonies: A Cross-Cultural Study of Status Dramatization.* Indianapolis: Bobbs-Merrill.

CONCLUSIONS

TOWARD THE TWENTY-FIRST CENTURY

Philip K. Bock

At the end of our journey through more than sixty years of research concerning the relationship of individual to sociocultural phenomena, what conclusions can be reached? We have seen attempts to establish universals of "human nature" alternating with studies of particular cultures or social categories, supplemented by investigations of specific topics such as art, myth, trance, or initiation rites across space and time. If done with care, all of these approaches are valid. They also complement and correct one another as the pendulum of opinion swings from the universal to the particular and back (see the Introduction to this volume; also Wikan 1992).

As we look forward to a new century, it is tempting to predict the future direction of the discipline. Some of my colleagues feel that the universalizing tendency associated with behavioral psychology and sociobiology has run its course, and that anthropological studies of self and emotion require a more humanistic and "agent-centered" approach. According to Erik Erikson (1987: 716), before her death, Ruth Benedict warned against "the biologizing of human behavior, be it in the crude form of racism or the refined projection of 'human nature.' " However, I suspect that the revelations of genetics, behavioral ecology, and biopsychology about the universal constraints on human behavior will continue to hold center stage for some time. Nor is this necessarily a "bad thing," for humanistic anthropologists must do their homework if they hope to really understand and counterbalance these scientific movements. It will not do just to throw up one's hands in horror or to scream "racism!" or "reductionism!"

What we can and should look forward to, I believe, is an era of interactive "mixed models" in which human (and perhaps pongid) intentionality and self-awareness will coexist with physiological mechanism and a broadened conception of the effective environment. Such a synthesis will require us to overcome the dualisms that afflict so much work in psychology and anthropology (Oyama 1985).

Reviewing the contributions to this volume, I find an intriguing mixture of concerns. Steven Piker leads off by discussing the early Culture and Personality movement, starting with Boas and his students and taking us through the liberal infusion of psychoanalysis by Kardiner and his followers to the highly individualized approaches of La Barre, Wallace, and Spiro. Alice Schlegel picks up the story, describing the work of the Whitings and their students in field and library as they formulated dynamic hypotheses and tested them using observational and correlational methods.

My own chapter in part I calls attention to a parallel tradition of research in which features of social structure (such as class, gender, or role) that cut across traditional cultural lines are shown to be associated with significant behavioral regularities. It follows that the often implicit assumption that a ''culture'' corresponds in one-to-one fashion to a single type of ''personality'' needs to be abandoned and a search for regularities both within and between societal groups undertaken.

Ronald Casson reviews the research tradition known as ''cognitive anthropology,'' showing its continuing interplay with anthropological linguistics. Though for ease of exposition his examples are primarily in American English, similar methods of textual and taxonomic analysis are used in other societies and in the formulation of ''cultural models'' that have recently been linked with features of human motivation (D'Andrade and Strauss 1992). This attempt to give ''directive force'' to cognitive structures is promising even though, at times, it recalls the children's story on which its proponents were raised in which ''I think I can'' and ''I thought I could'' are added to an otherwise mechanical tale.

Janis Jenkins presents a valuable overview of recent research on ''evoked emotion'' as a measure of mental disorder in the individual and the group, placing this work in a wider context that should interest all anthropologists who are trying to deal systematically but sensitively with the topic of emotion. As a student and colleague of Arthur Kleinman, Jenkins brings an important perspective to psychological anthropology, suggesting new ways to link ''cultural categories'' with ''personal experience'' (Kleinman 1988).

A similar concern motivated an article by Jerome Barkow (1984) that I published (and later reprinted) in the *Journal of Anthropological Research.* In ''The Distance between Genes and Culture,'' Barkow challenged his fellow advocates of inclusive fitness theories to make explicit ''the psychological assumptions that a sociobiological interpretation of culture traits necessarily entails'' (1984: 367). His chapter in part I similarly encourages the use of neo-Darwinian theory by anthropologists while insisting that the psychological *mechanisms* that link segments of DNA to adaptive (or nonadaptive) behavior be specified and not merely assumed.

Psychologist Joan Miller makes a valiant attempt to explicate the sources and goals of "cultural psychology," an approach that was inventing itself and changing even as she wrote. Despite its focus on "comparative human development" (Stigler, Shweder, and Herdt 1990), this approach still strikes me as highly programmatic, claiming for itself all that is best in past research while struggling for a coherent identity. It is surely the most "postmodern" of contemporary approaches, as revealed in the words of one of its founders:

> Cultural psychology is not psychological anthropology. . . . It is psychological anthropology without the premise of psychic unity. . . . Cultural psychology tries to synthesize, or at least combine, some of the virtues of general psychology, cross-cultural psychology, psychological anthropology, and ethnopsychology while seeking to disencumber itself of their vices. (Shweder 1991:90–91)

It is not Miller's fault if I am still somewhat confused. I had thought my own definition of psychological anthropology as "all anthropological investigations that make systematic use of psychological concepts and methods" (Bock 1988: 1) was broad enough to encompass even cultural psychology; apparently not.

The chapters in part II present an enormous variety of evidence for the mutual relevance of culture and psychic functioning, some of which tends to the universal (chapter 11 on myth; chapter 16 on trance; chapter 19 on initiation) and some to the particular (chapter 10 on discourse; chapter 13 on art; chapter 15 on dreams). Virtually every one of these chapters, however, suggests lines of research that could be profitably pursued into the next century. Some of the topics are relatively narrow (e.g., chapter 8 on primate handedness and chapter 17 on adolescent drug use), yet they deal with important issues using systematic ethological and ethnological comparisons, respectively. Other topics are quite broad (e.g., chapter 9 on human ontogeny and chapter 18 on the concepts of self and person), but they too propose novel ways of thinking about enduring anthropological problems as our science prepares to enter a new century.

Some readers will surely feel that essential topics and methods have been neglected in this handbook. (I regret the absence of planned chapters on human ethology, projective tests, and demography, whose authors withdrew too late to be replaced.) But I have done my best in the time and space allotted to present a useful reference work for the advanced student and professional. The treatment of some areas is necessarily abbreviated, but I believe that the comprehensive references will lead the reader to most of the important sources available at the time of writing. The responsibility for any "blind spots" is mine.

I must confess to a personal impatience with the use of the term "model" in contemporary anthropology. This useful concept, borrowed from the natural sciences, has now been watered down to the point where it often seems to be a synonym for "idea" or even "notion." In my more cynical moods, I have been known to define an anthropological model as "a diagram with arrows" (in which the terms are unmeasurable and the significance of the arrows undefined).

A cultural model, then, is "a diagram with arrows and with words in CAPITAL LETTERS." (For a helpful treatment, see Kaplan 1964:part VII.)

A final word of caution: like any academic field, psychological anthropology is subject to intellectual and political influences from the "wider culture." It has its share of trendy topics, stylish forms, and short-lived stars. It also has somewhat inbred elites who may, for a time, monopolize institutions and journals, disparaging forerunners and claiming original truths. Happily, none of the contributors to this volume has indulged in that kind of supremacist rhetoric. Whatever our unconscious Oedipal tendencies, we respect and honor the "ancestors," trying to learn from them while correcting their errors without the need for character assassination. This attitude is, I think, the healthiest for the future of psychological anthropology (cf. Schwartz, White, and Lutz 1992). For we still have almost everything to learn about the relationship of the individuals to their societies.

REFERENCES

Barkow, J. 1984. The Distance between Genes and Culture. *Journal of Anthropological Research* 40:367–79. (Reprinted in P. K. Bock, ed., Approaches to Culture and Society: Selected Articles, 1945–85. *Journal of Anthropological Research* 42:373–85.)

Bock, P. K. 1988. *Rethinking Psychological Anthropology: Continuity and Change in the Study of Human Action*. New York: W. H. Freeman.

D'Andrade, R. G., and C. Strauss, eds. 1992. *Human Motives and Cultural Models*. Cambridge, Eng.: Cambridge University Press.

Erikson, E. H. 1987. *A Way of Looking at Things*. New York: Norton.

Kaplan, A. 1964. *The Conduct of Inquiry*. San Francisco: Chandler.

Kleinman, A. 1988. *Rethinking Psychiatry: From Cultural Category to Personal Experience*. New York: Free Press.

Oyama, S. 1985. *The Ontogeny of Information: Developmental Systems and Evolution*. Cambridge, Eng.: Cambridge University Press.

Schwartz, T., G. M. White, and C. Lutz, eds. 1992. *New Directions in Psychological Anthropology*. Cambridge, Eng.: Cambridge University Press.

Shweder, R. A. 1991. *Thinking through Cultures: Expeditions in Cultural Psychology*. Cambridge, MA: Harvard University Press.

Stigler, J. W., R. A. Shweder, and G. Herdt. 1990. *Cultural Psychology: Essays on Comparative Human Development*. Cambridge, Eng.: Cambridge University Press.

Wikan, U. 1992. Beyond the Words: The Power of Resonance. *American Ethnologist* 19:460–82.

SELECTED BIBLIOGRAPHY

Adorno, T. W., E. Frenkel-Brunswik, D. J. Levinson, and R. N. Sanford. 1950. *The Authoritarian Personality*. New York: Harper and Row.

Agar, M. 1974. Talking about Doing: Lexicon and Event. *Language in Society* 3:83–89.

Andersen, E. S. 1978. Lexical Universals of Body-Part Terminology. Pp. 335–68 in J. H. Greenberg, C. A. Ferguson, and E. A. Moravcsik, eds., *Universals of Human Language*, vol. 3: *Word Structure*. Stanford, CA: Stanford University Press.

Annett, M. 1985. *Left, Right, Hand, and Brain: The Right Shift Theory*. London: Lawrence Erlbaum Associates.

Barash, D. P. 1982. *Sociology and Behavior*. 2nd ed. New York: Elsevier.

Barkow, J. H. 1973. Darwinian Psychological Anthropology: A Biosocial Approach. *Current Anthropology* 14:373–88.

———. 1984. The Distance between Genes and Culture. *Journal of Anthropological Research* 40: 367–79.

Barnouw, V. 1985. *Culture and Personality*. 4th ed. Homewood, IL: Dorsey Press.

Barth, F. 1975. *Ritual and Knowledge among the Baktaman of New Guinea*. Oslo: Universitetsforlaget; New Haven: Yale University Press.

Bateson, G., and M. Mead. 1942. *Balinese Character: A Photographic Analysis*. New York: New York Academy of Sciences.

Beeman, W. O. 1985. Dimensions of Dysphoria: The View from Linguistic Anthropology. In A. Kleinman and B. Good, eds., *Culture and Depression: Studies in the Anthropology and Cross-Cultural Psychiatry of Affect and Disorder*. Berkeley: University of California Press.

Bellah, R., R. Madsen, W. M. Sullivan, A. Swindler, and S. M. Tipton. 1985. *Habits of the Heart: Individualism and Commitment in American Life*. Berkeley: University of California Press.

Benedict, R. 1932. Configurations of Culture in North America. *American Anthropologist* 34:1–27.

———. 1934. *Patterns of Culture*. Boston: Houghton Mifflin.

Berlin, B. 1992. *Ethnobiological Classification: Principles of Categorization of Plants and Animals in Traditional Societies*. Princeton: Princeton University Press.

Berlin, B. and P. Kay. 1969. *Basic Color Terms: Their Universality and Evolution*. Berkeley: University of California Press.

Bersoff, D. M., and J. G. Miller. 1993. Culture, Context, and the Development of Moral Accountability Judgments. *Developmental Psychology* 29:664–76.

Besnier, N. 1990. Language and Affect. *Annual Review of Anthropology* 19:419–51.

Betzig, L., M. Borgerhoff Mulder, and P. Turke, eds. 1988. *Human Reproductive Behavior*. New York: Cambridge University Press.

Boas, F. 1939. *The Mind of Primitive Man*. New York: Macmillan.

Bock, P. K. 1979. *Modern Cultural Anthropology*. 3rd ed. New York: Knopf.

———. 1980. *Continuities in Psychological Anthropology: A Historical Introduction*. San Francisco: W. H. Freeman.

———. 1986. *The Formal Content of Ethnography*. Dallas: International Museum of Cultures.

———. 1988. *Rethinking Psychological Anthropology: Continuity and Change in the Study of Human Action*. New York: W. H. Freeman.

Boesch, E. E. 1991. *Symbolic Action Theory and Cultural Psychology*. Berlin: Springer-Verlag.

Bond, M. H., ed. 1986. *The Psychology of the Chinese People*. New York: Oxford University Press.

Bornstein, M. H. 1980. Cross-Cultural Developmental Psychology. Pp. 231–81 in M. H. Bornstein, ed., *Comparative Methods in Psychology*. Hillsdale, NJ: Erlbaum.

Bourguignon, E. 1991. A. Irving Hallowell, The Foundations of Psychological Anthropology, and Altered States of Consciousness. *Psychoanalytic Study of Society* 16:17–41.

Bronfenbrenner, U., F. Kessel, W. Kessen, and S. White. 1986. Toward a Critical Social History of Developmental Psychology: A Propaedeutic Discussion. *American Psychologist* 41:1218–30.

Brown, C. H. 1986. The Growth of Ethnobiological Nomenclature. *Current Anthropology* 27:1–19.

Brown, G., and T. Harris. 1978. *Social Origins of Depression: A Study of Psychiatric Disorder in Women*. New York: Free Press.

Brown, J. K. 1963. A Cross-Cultural Study of Female Initiation Rites. *American Anthropologist* 65: 837–853.

Brown, K. M. 1991. *Mama Lola: A Vodou Priestess in Brooklyn*. Berkeley: University of California Press.

Bruner, J. S. 1986. *Actual Minds, Possible Worlds*. Cambridge, MA: Harvard University Press.

Campbell, D. T. 1961. The Mutual Methodological Relevance of Anthropology and Psychology. Pp. 333–52 in F.L.K. Hsu, ed., *Psychological Anthropology*. Homewood, IL: Dorsey.

Canguilhem, G. 1989. *The Normal and the Pathological*. New York: Zone Books.

Carrithers, M., S. Collins, and S. Lukes, eds. 1985. *The Category of the Person: Anthropology, Philosophy, History*. Cambridge, Eng.: Cambridge University Press.

Casson, R. W., ed. 1981. *Language, Culture, and Cognition: Anthropological Perspectives*. New York: Macmillan.

Cheney, D. L., and R. M. Seyfarth. 1990. *How Monkeys See the World*. Chicago: University of Chicago Press.

Clifford, J. 1988. *The Predicament of Culture: Twentieth-Century Ethnography, Literature, and Art*. Cambridge, MA: Harvard University Press.

Clifford, J., and G. Marcus, eds. 1986. *Writing Culture: The Poetics and Politics of Ethnography*. Berkeley: University of California Press.

Cohen, A. 1992. Prognosis for Schizophrenia in the Third World: A Reevaluation of Cross-Cultural Research. *Culture, Medicine, and Psychiatry* 16:53–75.

Cohen, Y. A. 1964. *The Transition from Childhood to Adolescence*. Chicago: Aldine.

Cole, M. 1988. Cross-Cultural Research in the Sociohistorical Tradition. *Human Development* 31: 137–57.

———. 1990. Cultural Psychology: A Once and Future Discipline? Pp. 279–335 in R. A. Dienstbier and J. Berman, eds., *Nebraska Symposium on Motivation*. Lincoln: University of Nebraska Press.

Corin, E. 1990. Facts and Meaning in Psychiatry: An Anthropological Approach to the Lifeworld of Schizophrenics. *Culture, Medicine, and Psychiatry* 14:153–88.

Cosmides, L., and J. Tooby. 1987. From Evolution to Behavior: Evolutionary Psychology as the Missing Link. Pp. 277–306 in J. Dupré, ed., *The Latest on the Best: Essays on Evolution and Optimality*. Cambridge, MA: MIT Press.

Crapanzano, V. 1992. *Hermes' Dilemma and Hamlet's Desire: On the Epistemology of Interpretation*. Cambridge, MA: Harvard University Press.

Cronk, L. 1991. Human Behavioral Ecology. *Annual Review of Anthropology* 20:25–54.

Csordas, T. J. 1993. *The Sacred Self: A Cultural Phenomenology of Charismatic Healing*. Berkeley: University of California Press.

D'Andrade, R., and C. Strauss, eds. 1992. *Human Motives and Cultural Models*. Cambridge, Eng.: Cambridge University Press.

Darnell, R. 1990. *Edward Sapir: Linguist, Anthropologist, Humanist*. Berkeley: University of California Press.

Dawkins, R. 1989. *The Selfish Gene*. 2nd ed. New York: Oxford University Press.

Desjarlais, R. 1992. *Body and Emotion: The Aesthetics of Illness and Healing in the Nepal Himalayas*. Philadelphia: University of Pennsylvania Press.

Devereux, G. 1978. The Works of George Devereux. In G. D. Spindler, ed., *The Making of Psychological Anthropology*. Berkeley: University of California Press.

Dougherty, J.W.D., ed. 1985. *Directions in Cognitive Anthropology*. Urbana: University of Illinois Press.

Drew, P., and A. J. Wootton, eds. 1988. *Erving Goffman: Exploring the Interaction Order*. Cambridge, Eng.: Polity Press.

Durkheim, E. 1915. *The Elementary Forms of the Religious Life*. Trans. J. W. Swain. London: Allen and Unwin.

Edgerton, R. B. 1971. *The Individual in Cultural Adaptation: A Study of Four East African Peoples*. Berkeley: University of California Press.

———. 1985. *Rules, Exceptions, and Social Order*. Berkeley: University of California Press.

———. 1992. *Sick Societies: Challenging the Myth of Primitive Harmony*. New York: Free Press.

Ekman, P. 1972. Universals and Cultural Differences in Facial Expressions of Emotion. Pp. 207–83 in J. K. Cole, ed., *Nebraska Symposium on Motivation*. Lincoln: University of Nebraska Press.

Ellis, S., and M. Gauvain. 1992. Social and Cultural Influences on Children's Collaborative Interactions. Pp. 155–80 in L. T. Winegar and J. Valsiner, eds., *Children's Development within Social Context*, vol. 2. Hillsdale, NJ: Erlbaum.

Ember, M. 1983. On the Origin and Extension of the Incest Taboo. Pp. 65–108 in M. Ember and C. R. Ember, eds., *Marriage, Family, and Kinship: Comparative Studies of Social Organization*. New Haven: HRAF Press.

Erchak, G. M. 1992. *The Anthropology of Self and Behavior*. New Brunswick, NJ: Rutgers University Press.

Erikson, E. H. 1987. *A Way of Looking at Things*. New York: Norton.

Ewing, K. P. 1990. The Dream of Spiritual Initiation and the Organization of Self Representations among Pakistani Sufis. *American Ethnologist* 17:56–74.

Feldman, C. F. 1987. Thought from Language: The Linguistic Construction of Cognitive Representation. Pp. 131–46 in J. Bruner and H. Haste, eds., *Making Sense: The Child's Construction of the World*. London: Methuen.

Fenichel, O. 1945. *The Psychoanalytic Theory of Neurosis*. New York: Norton.

Festinger, L. 1957. *A Theory of Cognitive Dissonance*. Stanford, CA: Stanford University Press.

Flavell, J. H. 1963. *The Developmental Psychology of Jean Piaget*. Princeton: Van Nostrand.

Flinn, M. V. 1992. Paternal Care in a Caribbean Village. Pp. 57–84 in B. S. Hewlett, ed., *Father-Child Relations: Cultural and Biosocial Contexts*. New York: Aldine de Gruyter.

Frake, C. O. 1975. How to Enter a Yakan House. In M. Sanches and B. Blount, eds., *Sociocultural Dimensions of Language Use*. New York: Academic Press.

Freud, S. 1900. *The Interpretation of Dreams*. London and New York: Hogarth. Standard Edition, vols. 4, 5 (1955).

———. 1913. *Totem and Taboo*. London and New York: Hogarth. Standard Edition, vol. 13.

———. 1923. *The Ego and the Id*. London and New York: Hogarth. *Standard Edition*, vol. 19 (1962).

———. 1961. *Civilization and Its Discontents*. New York: Norton.

Gauvain, M. 1993. The Development of Spatial Thinking in Everyday Activity. *Developmental Review* 13:92–121.

Geertz, C. 1973. *The Interpretation of Cultures*. New York: Basic Books.

———. 1988. *Works and Lives*. Stanford, CA: Stanford University Press.

Gergen, K. J. 1989. Realities and Their Relationships. Pp. 51–62 in W. J. Baker, M. E. Hyland, R. van Hezewizk, and S. Terwee, eds., *Recent Trends in Theoretical Psychology*. New York: Springer-Verlag.

Goodnow, J. J. 1976. The Nature of Intelligent Behavior. Questions Raised by Cross-Cultural Studies. Pp. 169–88 in L. B. Resnick, ed., *The Nature of Intelligence*. Hillsdale, NJ: Erlbaum.

Goody, J. 1977. *The Domestication of the Savage Mind*. Cambridge, Eng.: Cambridge University Press.

Gorer, G., and J. Rickman. 1962. *The People of Great Russia*. New York: Norton.

Greenfield, P. M. 1976. Cross-Cultural Research and Piagetian Theory: Paradox and Progress. Pp. 322–45 in K. F. Riegel and J. A. Meacham, eds., *The Developing Individual in a Changing World*, vol. 1. Chicago: Aldine.

Hallowell, A. I. 1955. Culture and Experience. Philadelphia: University of Pennsylvania Press.

Haraway, D. 1991. *Simians, Cyborgs, and Women: The Reinvention of Nature*. New York: Routledge.

Harkness, S. 1992. Human Development in Psychological Anthropology. Pp. 102–22 in T. Schwartz, G. White, and C. Lutz, eds., *New Directions in Psychological Anthropology*. Cambridge, Eng.: Cambridge University Press.

Herdt, G. H., ed. 1984. *Ritualized Homosexuality in Melanesia*. Berkeley: University of California Press.

Hochschild, A. R. 1983. *The Managed Heart: Commercialization of Human Feeling*. Berkeley: University of California Press.

Hopper, K. 1991. Some Old Questions for the New Cross-Cultural Psychiatry. *Medical Anthropology Quarterly* 5:299–330.

Howard, A. 1985. Ethnopsychology and the Prospects for a Cultural Psychology. Pp. 401–20 in G. M. White and J. Kirkpatrick, eds., *Person, Self, and Experience: Exploring Pacific Ethnopsychologies*. Berkeley: University of California Press.

Hsu, F.L.K. 1961. *Clan, Caste, and Club. A Comparative Study of Chinese, Hindu, and American Ways of Life*. Princeton: Van Nostrand.

Hunt, E., and F. Agnoli. 1991. The Whorfian Hypothesis: A Cognitive Psychology Perspective. *Psychological Review* 98:377–89.

Jahoda, G. 1982. *Psychology and Anthropology: A Psychological Perspective*. London and New York: Academic Press.

———. 1992. *Crossroads between Culture and Mind: Continuities and Change in Theories of Human Nature*. London: Harvester Wheatsheaf.

James, W. 1987 [1902]. *Varieties of Religious Experience*. Reprinted in *Writings, 1902–1910*. New York: Library of America.

Jenkins, J. H., and M. Karno. 1992. The Meaning of "Expressed Emotion": Theoretical Issues Raised by Cross-Cultural Research. *American Journal of Psychiatry* 149:9–21.

Johnson, M. 1987. *The Body in the Mind: The Bodily Basis of Meaning, Imagination, and Reason*. Chicago: University of Chicago Press.

Kardiner, A., with R. Linton. 1939. *The Individual and His Society*. New York: Columbia University Press.

Kardiner, A., with R. Linton, C. Du Bois, and J. West. 1945. *The Psychological Frontiers of Society*. New York: Columbia University Press.

Kay, P. 1970. Some Theoretical Implications of Ethnographic Semantics. In Current Directions in Anthropology. *Bulletin of the American Anthropological Association* 3(3)2:19–31.

Kay, P., and W. Kempton. 1984. What Is the Sapir-Whorf Hypothesis? *American Anthropologist* 86:65–79.

Kleinman, A. 1988. *Rethinking Psychiatry: From Cultural Category to Personal Experience.* New York: Free Press.

Kleinman, A., and J. Kleinman. 1991. Suffering and Its Professional Transformation: Toward an Ethnography of Interpersonal Experience. *Culture, Medicine, and Psychiatry* 15:275–301.

La Fontaine, J. 1985. *Initiation.* New York: Viking Penguin.

Lakoff, G., and M. Johnson. 1980. *Metaphors We Live By.* Chicago: University of Chicago Press.

Lamb, M. E. 1993. Nazism, Biological Determinism, Sociobiology, and Evolutionary Theory: Are They Necessarily Synonymous? *International Journal of Comparative Psychology* 6(3):149–57.

Levinson, D., and M. J. Malone. 1980. *Toward Explaining Human Culture: A Critical Review of the Findings of Worldwide Cross-Cultural Research.* New Haven: HRAF Press.

Lévi-Strauss, C. 1963. *Structural Anthropology.* New York: Basic Books.

———. 1966. *The Savage Mind.* Chicago: University of Chicago Press.

Levy, R. 1984. Emotion, Knowing, and Culture. In R. Shweder and R. LeVine, eds., *Culture Theory: Essays on Mind, Self, and Emotion.* Cambridge, Eng.: Cambridge University Press.

Lewis, I. M. 1981. What Is a Shaman? *Folk* 23:25–35.

Lincoln, B. 1989. *Discourse and the Construction of Society.* New York: Oxford University Press.

Ludwig, A. 1969. Altered States of Consciousness. In C. Tart, ed., *Altered States of Consciousness.* New York: Wiley.

Lutz, C. 1988. *Unnatural Emotions: Everyday Sentiments on a Micronesian Atoll and Their Challenge to Western Theory.* Chicago: University of Chicago Press.

Lutz, C., and G. White. 1986. The Anthropology of Emotions. *Annual Review of Anthropology* 15: 405–36.

MacDonald, K. 1986. Civilization and Its Discontents Revisited: Freud as an Evolutionary Biologist. *Journal of Social and Biological Structures* 9:307–18.

Malinowski, B. 1944. *A Scientific Theory of Culture, and Other Essays.* Chapel Hill: University of North Carolina Press.

Manson, W. 1988. *The Psychodynamics of Culture.* Westport, CT: Greenwood Press.

Marchant, L. F., and W. C. McGrew. 1991. Laterality of Function in Apes: A Meta-Analysis of Methods. *Journal of Human Evolution* 21:425–38.

Markus, H., and S. Kitayama. 1991. Culture and Self: Implications for Cognition, Emotion, and Motivation. *Psychological Review* 98:224–53.

———. In press. *Emotion and Culture: Multidisciplinary Perspectives.* Washington, DC: American Psychological Association.

Marsella, A. J., G. DeVos, and F.L.K. Hsu, eds. 1985. *Culture and Self: Asian and Western Perspectives.* New York: Tavistock Publications.

McGrew, W. C. 1992. *Chimpanzee Material Culture: Implications for Human Evolution.* Cambridge, Eng.: Cambridge University Press.

Mead, M. 1928. *Coming of Age in Samoa.* New York: Morrow.

———. 1939. *From the South Seas.* New York: Morrow.

———. 1942. *And Keep Your Powder Dry.* New York: Morrow.

———. 1949. *Male and Female: A Study of the Sexes in a Changing World.* New York: Morrow.

———. 1950. *Sex and Temperament in Three Primitive Societies.* New York: New American Library, Mentor Books.

———. 1953. National Character. In A. L. Kroeber, ed., *Anthropology Today.* Chicago: University of Chicago Press.

Merton, R. K. 1957. *Social Theory and Social Structure.* Glencoe, IL: Free Press.

Miller, B. D., ed. 1993. *Sex and Gender Hierarchies.* Cambridge, Eng.: Cambridge University Press.

Miller, J. G., and D. M. Bersoff. 1992. Culture and Moral Judgment: How Are Conflicts between Justice and Interpersonal Responsibilities Resolved? *Journal of Personality and Social Psychology* 62:541–54.

Munroe, R. L., and R. H. Munroe. 1992. Fathers in Children's Environments: A Four-Culture Study.

Pp. 213–29 in B. S. Hewlett, ed., *Father-Child Relations: Cultural and Biosocial Contexts.* New York: Aldine de Gruyter.

Nesse, R. M. 1987. An Evolutionary Perspective on Panic Disorder and Agoraphobia. *Ethology and Sociobiology* 8:73s–85s.

———. 1989. Evolutionary Explanations of Emotions. *Human Nature* 1:261–89.

Nesse, R. M., and A. T. Lloyd. 1992. The Evolution of Psychodynamic Mechanisms. Pp. 601–26 in J. H. Barkow, L. Cosmides, and J. Tooby, eds., *The Adapted Mind: Evolutionary Psychology and the Generation of Culture.* New York: Oxford University Press.

Nolen-Hoeksema, A. 1990. *Sex Differences in Depression.* Stanford, CA: Stanford University Press.

Ogbu, J. U. 1982. Socialization: A Cultural Ecological Approach. Pp. 253–67 in K. M. Borman, ed., *The Social Life of Children in a Changing Society.* Hillsdale, NJ: Erlbaum.

Oyama, S. 1985. *The Ontogeny of Information: Developmental Systems and Evolution.* Cambridge, Eng.: Cambridge University Press.

Palombo, S. R. 1978. *Dreaming and Memory: A New Information-Processing Model.* New York: Basic Books.

Parman, S. 1991. *Dream and Culture: An Anthropological Study of the Western Intellectual Tradition.* New York: Praeger.

Paul, R. A. 1989. Psychoanalytic Anthropology. *Annual Review of Anthropology* 18:177–244.

Polkinghorne, D. E. 1991. Narrative and Self-Concept. *Journal of Narrative and Life History* 1: 135–53.

Price-Williams, D. R. 1980. Anthropological Approaches to Cognition and Their Relevance to Psychology. Pp. 155–84 in H. C. Triandis and W. Lonner, eds., *Handbook of Cross-Cultural Psychology*, vol. 3. Boston: Allyn and Bacon.

Radin, P., with commentaries by K. Karenyi and C. G. Jung. *The Trickster: A Study in American Indian Mythology.* London: Routledge.

Riesman, D., N. Glazer and R. Denney. 1961. *The Lonely Crowd.* New Haven: Yale University Press.

Rosaldo, M. Z. 1984. Toward an Anthropology of Self and Feeling. Pp. 137–57 in R. A. Shweder and R. A. LeVine, eds., *Culture Theory: Essays on Mind, Self, and Emotion.* Cambridge, Eng.: Cambridge University Press.

Rosaldo, M., and L. Lamphere, eds., 1974. *Woman, Culture, and Society.* Stanford, CA: Stanford University Press.

Rumelhart, D. E. 1980. Schemata: The Building Blocks of Cognition. In R. J. Spiro, B. C. Bruce, and W. F. Brewer, eds., *Theoretical Issues in Reading Comprehension.* Hillsdale, NJ: Erlbaum.

Runyan, W. McK. 1984. *Life Histories and Psychobiography.* New York: Oxford University Press.

Russell, J. 1991. Culture and the Categorization of Emotions. *Psychological Bulletin* 110:426–50.

Sampson, E. E. 1991. *Social Worlds, Personal Lives.* San Diego: Harcourt Brace Jovanovich.

Sapir, E. 1956. *Culture, Language, and Personality: Selected Essays.* Ed. D. Mandelbaum. Berkeley: University of California Press.

Scarr, S., and K. McCartney. 1983. How People Make Their Own Environments: A Theory of Genotype → Environment Effects. *Child Development* 54:424–35.

Scheper-Hughes, N. 1979. *Saints, Scholars, and Schizophrenics: Mental Illness in Rural Ireland.* Berkeley: University of California Press.

———. 1992. *Death Without Weeping.* Berkeley: University of California Press.

Schieffelin, B. B., and E. Ochs, eds. 1986. *Language Socialization across Cultures.* Cambridge, Eng.: Cambridge University Press.

Schlegel, A. 1972. *Male Dominance and Female Autonomy: Domestic Authority in Matrilineal Societies.* New Haven: HRAF Press.

Schlegel, A., and H. Barry III. 1991. *Adolescence: An Anthropological Inquiry.* New York: Free Press.

Schwartz, T., G. M. White, and C. Lutz, eds. 1992. *New Directions in Psychological Anthropology.* Cambridge, Eng.: Cambridge University Press.

Segerstrale, U. 1990. The Sociobiology of Conflict and the Conflict about Sociobiology. Pp. 273–85 in J. van der Dennen and V.S.E. Falger, eds., *Sociobiology and Conflict.* New York: Chapman and Hall.

Seligman, C. G. 1924. Anthropology and Psychology: A Study of Some Points of Contact. *Journal of the Royal Anthropological Institute* 54:13–46.

Shorter, B. 1987. *An Image Darkly Forming: Woman and Initiation.* London: Routledge and Kegan Paul.

Shweder, R. A. 1990. Cultural Psychology—What Is It? Pp. 1–43 in J. W. Stigler, R. A. Shweder, and G. Herdt, eds., *Cultural Psychology: Essays on Comparative Human Development.* Cambridge, Eng.: Cambridge University Press.

Shweder, R. A., and E. J. Bourne. 1984. Does the Concept of the Person Vary Cross-Culturally? Pp. 158–99 in R. A. Shweder and R. A. LeVine, eds., *Culture Theory: Essays on Mind, Self, and Emotion.* Cambridge, Eng.: Cambridge University Press.

Singer, M. 1961. A Survey of Culture and Personality Theory and Research. Pp. 9–90 in B. Kaplan, ed., *Studying Personality Cross-Culturally.* New York: Harper and Row.

Slavin, M. O., and D. Kriegman. 1992. *The Adaptive Design of the Human Psyche.* New York and London: Guilford Press.

Sperber, D. 1985. Anthropology and Psychology: Towards an Epidemiology of Representations. *Man* 20:73–87.

Spindler, G. D., ed. 1978. *The Making of Psychological Anthropology.* Berkeley: University of California Press.

Standen, V., and R. A. Foley. 1989. *Comparative Socioecology: The Behavioural Ecology of Humans and Other Mammals.* Special Publication no. 8 of the British Ecological Society. Oxford: Blackwell Scientific Publications.

Steele, R. S. 1982. *Freud and Jung: Conflicts of Interpretation.* London: Routledge and Kegan Paul.

Stoller, R. J., and G. H. Herdt. 1982. The Development of Masculinity: A Cross-Cultural Contribution. *Journal of the American Psychoanalytic Association* 30:29–59.

Strickland, B. 1992. Women and Depression. *Current Directions in Psychological Science* 1(4): 132–35.

Symons, D. 1989. A Critique of Darwinian Anthropology. *Ethology and Sociobiology* 10:131–44.

Taylor, C. 1989. *Sources of the Self: The Making of the Modern Identity.* Cambridge, MA: Harvard University Press.

Tedlock, B., ed. 1987. *Dreaming: Anthropological and Psychological Interpretations.* Cambridge, Eng.: Cambridge University Press.

Tooby, J., and L. Cosmides. 1990. On the Universality of Human Nature and the Uniqueness of the Individual: The Role of Genetics and Adaptation. *Journal of Personality* 58:17–68.

———. 1992. The Psychological Foundations of Culture. Pp. 19–136 in J. H. Barkow, L. Cosmides, and J. Tooby, eds., *The Adapted Mind: Evolutionary Psychology and the Generation of Culture.* New York: Oxford University Press.

Triandis, H. C., and A. Heron, eds. 1981. *Handbook of Cross-Cultural Psychology*, vol. 4. Boston: Allyn and Bacon.

Turner, V. W. 1969. *The Ritual Process: Structure and Anti-Structure.* Ithaca, NY: Cornell University Press.

———. 1974. *Dramas, Fields, and Metaphors: Symbolic Action in Human Society.* Ithaca, NY: Cornell University Press.

Tyler, S. A., ed. 1969. *Cognitive Anthropology.* New York: Holt, Rinehart and Winston.

Van Gennep, A. 1984. *The Rites of Passage.* New York: Columbia University Press.

Vine, I. 1987. Inclusive Fitness and the Self-System: The Roles of Human Nature and Sociocultural Processes in Intergroup Discrimination. Pp. 60–80 in V. Reynolds, V. Falger, and I. Vine, eds., *The Sociobiology of Ethnocentrism: Evolutionary Dimensions of Xenophobia, Discrimination, Racism, and Nationalism.* Beckenham, Kent: Croom Helm.

Weisz, J., F. M. Rothbaum, and T. C. Blackburn. 1984. Standing Out and Standing In: The Psychology of Control in America and Japan. *American Psychologist* 39:955–69.

White, G. 1992. Ethnopsychology. Pp. 21–46 in T. Schwartz, G. White, and C. Lutz, eds., *New Directions in Psychological Anthropology.* Cambridge, Eng.: Cambridge University Press.

White, G. M., and J. Kirkpatrick, eds. 1985. *Person, Self, and Experience: Exploring Pacific Ethnopsychologies.* Berkeley: University of California Press.

Whiting, B. B., ed. 1963. *Six Cultures: Studies of Child Rearing.* New York: Wiley.

Whiting, B. B., and C. P. Edwards. 1988. *Children of Different Worlds.* Cambridge, MA: Harvard University Press.

Whiting, B. B., and J.W.M. Whiting. 1975. *Children of Six Cultures: A Psycho-Cultural Analysis.* Cambridge, MA: Harvard University Press.

Whiting, J.W.M. 1990. Adolescent Rituals and Identity Conflicts. Pp. 357–65 in J. Stigler, R. Shweder, and G. Herdt, eds., *Cultural Psychology: Essays on Comparative Human Development.* Cambridge, Eng.: Cambridge University Press.

Whiting, J.W.M., and I. L. Child. 1953. *Child Training and Personality: A Cross-Cultural Study.* New Haven: Yale University Press.

Whiting, J.W.M., R. Kluckhohn, and A. Anthony. 1958. The Function of Male Initiation Ceremonies at Puberty. Pp. 359–70 in E. Maccoby, T. Newcomb, and E. Harltey, eds., *Readings in Social Psychology.* 3rd ed. New York: Holt.

Whittaker, E. 1992. The Birth of the Anthropological Self and Its Career. *Ethos* 20:191–219.

Wierzbicka, A. 1986. Human Emotions: Universal or Culture-Specific? *American Anthropologist* 88:584–94.

Winkelman, M. 1986. Trance States: A Theoretical Model and Cross-Cultural Analysis. *Ethos* 14: 174–203.

Winson, J. 1985. *Brain and Psyche: The Biology of the Unconscious.* Garden City, NY: Doubleday.

Witkowski, S., and C. H. Brown. 1977. An Explanation of Color Nomenclature Universals. *American Anthropologist* 79:50–57.

Zoja, L. 1989. *Drugs, Addiction, and Initiation: The Modern Search for Ritual.* Boston: Sigo Press.

INDEX

ABOUT THE EDITOR AND CONTRIBUTORS

JEROME H. BARKOW is Professor of Social Anthropology at Dalhousie University, Halifax, Nova Scotia, where he has taught since 1971. He is the author of the 1989 book *Darwin, Sex, and Status* and coeditor of the 1992 work *The Adapted Mind.* He has conducted research in West Africa, Canada, and the Philippines.

NIKO BESNIER is Associate Professor of Anthropology at Yale University. He has conducted fieldwork in Western Polynesia, principally on Nukulaelae Atoll. His publications focus on emotionality and personhood, gossip and oratory, power and prestige, sex and gender, and literacy.

PHILIP K. BOCK (Editor) is Professor Emeritus of Anthropology at the University of New Mexico, where he taught for over thirty years. His fieldwork was in Canada and Mexico. Besides psychological anthropology, he has published on formal theory, ethnomusicology, and Shakespeare. He edits the *Journal of Anthropological Research.*

ERIKA BOURGUIGNON is Professor Emeritus of Anthropology at the Ohio State University, where she has taught for the past forty-four years. Her research includes fieldwork among Native Americans and in Haiti, as well as holocultural studies. Her work has focused on psychological anthropology, with special emphasis on altered states of consciousness and possession beliefs.

RONALD W. CASSON is Professor of Anthropology at Oberlin College. He has done rural and urban fieldwork in Turkey and has published on cognitive and linguistic anthropology, kinship, and social organization. He edited *Lan-*

guage, Culture, and Cognition. His most recent article is "Russett, Rose, and Raspberry: The Development of English Secondary Color Terms."

THOMAS J. CSORDAS is Associate Professor of Anthropology at Case Western Reserve University. His work in psychological and psychiatric anthropology has concentrated on themes of cultural phenomenology, embodiment, person and self, ritual language, religious movements, and therapeutic process in ritual healing. He has conducted fieldwork among Catholic charismatics and Navajo Indians.

MARLENE DOBKIN DE RIOS is Professor of Anthropology at California State University, Fullerton, and Associate Clinical Professor of Psychiatry and Human Behavior at the University of California, Irvine. She has specialized in cross-cultural aspects of healing, culture, and hallucinogens and is the author of three books and numerous papers based on her work in the Peruvian Amazon.

ROBIN FOX is University Professor of Social Theory at Rutgers, where he founded the Department of Anthropology twenty-eight years ago. His fieldwork was in New Mexico and Western Ireland. He has published twelve books on subjects ranging from kinship and marriage to neonate cognition and the anthropology of law.

CHARLES S. GROB, M.D., is Associate Professor of Psychiatry at Harbor/UCLA Medical Center, Torrance, California. He specializes in adolescent and child psychiatry and has published on the role of hallucinogenic substances in psychiatric practice.

JANIS H. JENKINS is Associate Professor of Anthropology and Psychiatry at Case Western Reserve University in Cleveland, Ohio. She has conducted studies of schizophrenia, depression, and trauma. Her ethnographic work has been with Mexican, Salvadoran, and Puerto Rican populations. She is on the Board of Directors for the Society for Psychological Anthropology and the Editorial Board of *Culture, Medicine, and Psychiatry.*

LINDA F. MARCHANT is Associate Professor of Anthropology at Miami University, Oxford, Ohio. She has studied primate behavior, especially laterality of function in chimpanzees, with recent fieldwork in Gombe National Park, Tanzania. Her most recent publication is "Are Gorillas Right-Handed or Not?" in *Human Evolution* (with William McGrew).

WILLIAM C. MCGREW is Wiepking Distinguished University Professor of Anthropology, Psychology, and Zoology at Miami University, Oxford, Ohio. He has studied the ethology and socioecology of primates, concentrating on wild chimpanzees in Tanzania, Senegal, and Gabon. His most recent book is *Chimpanzee Material Culture* (Cambridge University Press).

JOAN G. MILLER is Associate Professor of Psychology at Yale University, where she has taught for nine years. She has conducted fieldwork among children and adults in Mysore, India, with her research centering on the cultural grounding of interpersonal morality and of everyday social perceptions.

GILDA A. MORELLI is Assistant Professor of Psychology at Boston College. Her fieldwork examines the sociocultural basis of parenting and early social development in a foraging and farming community of a rainforest region in Zaire, focusing recently on cultural variation in children's responsibility for learning their community's mature practices.

ROBERT L. MUNROE is Professor of Anthropology at Pitzer College (of the Claremont Colleges), where he has taught for thirty years. He has conducted fieldwork in Africa, Central and North America, Asia, and the Pacific. His primary research interest is cross-cultural human development.

RUTH H. MUNROE is Professor of Psychology at Pitzer College. She has served as Secretary-General of the International Association for Cross-Cultural Psychology and is currently on the editorial boards of *Cross-Cultural Research*, *Ethos*, and the *Journal of Social Psychology*. Her publications have focused on cross-cultural human development.

SIMON OTTENBERG is Professor Emeritus of Anthropology at the University of Washington. His research in Africa has dealt with political organization, social change, and art. A 1989 book examined *Boyhood Rituals in an African Society* (University of Washington Press), detailing the reactions of the initiates to their experiences.

SUSAN OYAMA, Professor of Psychology at John Jay College, City University of New York, wrote *The Ontogeny of Information* and coauthored (under the pen name John Klama) *Aggression: The Myth of the Beast Within*. Her primary interests are in the role of development in evolution, the nature-nurture dichotomy, and the relationships between the biological and social sciences.

STEVEN PIKER is Professor of Anthropology at Swarthmore College, where he has taught since 1966. His fieldwork in Thailand emphasized religion and socialization. More recently, he has done research on religious conversion in the United States and has chaired the Department of Sociology and Anthropology at Swarthmore.

BARBARA ROGOFF is Professor of Psychology at the University of California,

Santa Cruz. Her fieldwork in Highland Guatemala focuses on children's learning through participation in the activities of their communities. She is the author of *Apprenticeship in Thinking: Cognitive Development in Social Context* (1990) and *Guided Participation in Cultural Activity by Toddlers and Caregivers* (1993).

ALICE SCHLEGEL is Professor of Anthropology at the University of Arizona. Her fieldwork has been with the Hopis of Arizona. Her major publications have dealt with socialization, gender, family, and social organization. Recently, she has done cross-cultural studies of adolescent socialization.

BARBARA TEDLOCK is Professor of Anthropology at the State University of New York at Buffalo. Her fieldwork has been at Zuni Pueblo in the American Southwest and among Highland and Lowland Maya of Guatemala and Belize. Besides psychological anthropology, she has published on linguistics, visual anthropology, ethnomusicology, and ethnoastronomy. She is Editor-in-Chief of the *American Anthropologist.*